JOHN KNOX

Godwin

JASPER RIDLEY

OXFORD UNIVERSITY PRESS
NEW YORK AND OXFORD

LIBRARY OF CONGRESS CATALOGUE CARD NUMBER: 68-55648

PRINTED IN THE UNITED STATES OF AMERICA

CONTENTS

APPENDIXES

LIST OF PLATES

CHAPTER I

The State of Scotland

At the beginning of the sixteenth century, Scotland was a poor, primitive, and far-away country which the civilized nations of Europe regarded with contempt and romantic fascination. It was a part of Christendom, but a remote and backward part. When Scottish scholars went to Paris or Cologne to study, and Scottish clerics visited Rome to participate in the life of the international Church, the Frenchman, German, and Italian gazed at them in wonder. To the European, Scotland was a weird, barbaric land, inhabited in the north by wild Scots and savages, and ending in a great field of stone and ice, where nothing grew; a land of great cold, where it was light all night in summer, but where there were only four hours of daylight in winter; where a strange kind of bird did not lay eggs, but dropped its offspring alive from the branches of the trees; the land where the Devil lived. It was a land of mystery. William Maitland of Lethington complained to Cecil that he lived 'in a corner of the world, separated from the society of men'; and Lord James Stewart, Earl of Moray, the future Regent of Scotland, who, like Lethington, was well acquainted with France and European culture, wrote to the Elector Palatine that in Scotland he was 'almost beyond the limits of the human race'.[1]

It was in this distant kingdom that John Knox was born at the beginning of the reign of James V. There is some doubt as to the date of his birth, but everything indicates that he was born in 1514. For 260 years it was an accepted historical fact that he was born in 1505, but this was due to an error in the biography published in David Buchanan's edition of Knox's *History of the*

[1] See especially Aeneas Silvius, *Aeneas Silvius in Europam*, sig. g. 4, and *Commentarii Rerum Memorabilium*, p. 4; Peter Swave's diary (Feb.–July 1535) (*L.P.* viii. 1178, Hume Brown, *Early Travellers in Scotland*, pp. 25–27, 56–57); Jean de Meun, *Le Roman de la Rose*, xi. 282, verse 10186; Juvénal des Ursins, *Histoire de Charles VI*, p. 155; Lethington to Cecil, 26 Dec. 1561; Moray to Frederick, Elector Palatine, 23 Sept. 1564 (*Sc. Cal.* i. 1053; ii. 84).

Reformation in Scotland in 1644. There is a dispute about the place, as well as the date, of Knox's birth. When Knox was granted citizenship of Geneva in 1558, he gave his place of birth as Haddington in Scotland; but Theodore Beza, who succeeded Calvin as the chief pastor of Geneva, wrote in his *Icones* in 1580 that Knox came from Gifford; and seventeenth-century writers say the same. Some modern authorities have believed that he was born in the village now called Gifford, which is some four miles south of Haddington; but at that time the village was called Bothans, and was not known as Gifford until 1668. It is more likely that Knox was born in Giffordgate, within the town of Haddington.

Giffordgate was the name of a district of Haddington which lies on the east side of the Tyne, on the other side of the river from the main part of the town. In 1785 there was an old tradition in Haddington that a house which was then still standing in Giffordgate, opposite the church across the Tyne, was the house in which Knox was born; and later research among the title deeds of property in Giffordgate has shown that in the sixteenth century someone by the name of Knox owned property in the vicinity of this house. There is, therefore, good reason to believe that the local tradition is right as regards the approximate site of Knox's birthplace, though it is very unlikely that the house which was standing there in 1785, and was pulled down soon afterwards, was the actual house where he was born. At the suggestion of Carlyle, an oak tree was planted in 1881 near the place where the house stood.[1]

Haddington lay a little to the west of the road from Berwick to Edinburgh, in the comparatively fertile countryside of Lothian. It was famous for its ale and its orchards, being one of the very few areas in Scotland that were able to grow fruit. In 1598 an English traveller, Fynes Moryson, called it a 'pleasant village'. Haddington was one of the royal burghs of Scotland: but a Scottish town, with its one main street and little alleys leading off it, looked like a village to an Englishman. Unlike an English

[1] Life of Knox, in 1644 edn. of Knox's *History of the Reformation in Scotland* (London edn., sig. a; Edinburgh edn., unpaginated); Beza, *Icones*, sig. Ee3; 'Registre des Bourgeois' of Geneva, 24 June 1558 (Knox, *Works*, vi. xvii); Spottiswood, *History of the Church of Scotland*, ii. 179; Richardson, 'On the present state of the question "Where was John Knox born?"', and supplementary note by D. Laing (*Proceedings of the Society of Antiquaries of Scotland*, iii. 52–59); Barclay, 'Account of the Parish of Haddington' (*Archaeologica Scotica*, i. 69–70, 121). For a summary of the conflicting statements, see Laing, in *Works*, vi. xvii n.; and see *infra*, App. I.

town it was not surrounded by walls, for Edinburgh and Perth were the only Scottish towns with walls; and in comparison with the great cities of Europe, the population was very small. When Knox was born, Paris, which Francis I of France once described as a province rather than a town, had a population of over 200,000. Ghent, Naples, Lisbon, Prague, Rome, and Rouen were near 100,000; Augsburg, Danzig, and London already exceeded 50,000, and London would be twice as large by the mid century. Edinburgh, the largest town in Scotland, probably had a population of about 15,000. Only five other towns, Dundee, Aberdeen, Perth, Glasgow, and St. Andrews, had more than 2,000; the population of Haddington was probably about 1,500.[1]

The inhabitants of Haddington, like those of other burghs, consisted of merchants and craftsmen, who were freemen of the burgh, and their paid servants and apprentices, who were unfreemen. In every Scottish burgh there was bitter antagonism between the merchants and the craftsmen, which seems to have had no parallel in any other country of Europe. The merchants had gained complete control of the burghs. They had excluded all other citizens from voting in elections for the burgh council, which in most cases consisted of the wealthier merchants, who re-elected themselves every year and filled vacancies in their number by co-option. The craftsmen, who were about as numerous as the merchants and often as rich, resented their exclusion from political power in the burgh. The merchants on the burgh council made regulations for the government of the burgh, excluding unfreemen from selling in the weekly market, and drastically restricting the right of strangers to enter the burgh at all; making regulations for the annual fair, which was held at Haddington for two days at Michaelmas; fixing the prices of goods, and the hours during which they could be sold; punishing brawlers and harlots by enforcing public repentance, by pillory at the market cross, or by whipping, branding, and banishment from the town; appointing

[1] Hume Brown, *Scotland in the time of Queen Mary*, p. 20; Fynes Moryson's *Itinerary*, Pt. i, Bk. iii, Chap. 5 (Hume Brown, *Early Travellers in Scotland*, p. 82). Estimates of the population of Edinburgh in the sixteenth century vary considerably. Hume Brown gives it as high as 30,000 (*Scotland in the time of Queen Mary*, p. 52); Lord Eustace Percy as low as 9,000 (*John Knox*, pp. 221–2). Robert Lamond, in 'The Scottish Craft Guild as a Religious Fraternity' (*S.H.R.* xvi. 194) estimates that there were 3,000 families in Edinburgh in 1560. In 1558 there were 1,453 men in Edinburgh available for military service (*Edinburgh Burgh Records*, iii. 23–25 (5 and 10 June 1558)).

the watch by which citizens, each taking their turn of duty, patrolled the streets at night to prevent the entry of strangers into the town and the breaking of the curfew by the inhabitants. Knox, like all his contemporaries who were afterwards subjected to the discipline of Knox's Church, was brought up in a society in which his private life was governed by regulations from the moment when he was awakened at 6 o'clock by the tolling of the burgh bell to the ringing of the curfew at 9 p.m.

Life for John Knox was hard and simple in Haddington, in the dry, cold climate of the east coast; for there were few comforts in a Scottish town in the early sixteenth century. The houses were small, even the largest consisting only of two or three rooms, with stairs and a forecourt, or booth, protruding in front of the house, where the merchant sat and sold his wares and the craftsman carried on his trade, reducing the width of the street to a few yards. Even the wealthiest merchants only had a few possessions. In their wills they disposed of a few pewter plates, wooden mugs, platters, and spoons, but no glass and very little silver; a few beds, a table, one chair for the father of the house, some stools and trestles, perhaps a pair of sheets, and their garments, their stock-in-trade, and their small but sturdy Scottish horse, and livestock such as pigs, which ran freely in the town. When Aeneas Silvius visited Scotland in 1436, he noted that the king's palaces were less comfortable and luxurious than the house of a moderately wealthy merchant in Nuremberg.[1]

The harshness of life in the tiny Scottish towns was due to the poverty of the country, with its poor soil, its primitive methods of agriculture, and its system of land tenure. The Scottish husbandman did not enjoy the security of tenure of the English copyholder, but usually held his small holding on a short lease of three or five years. The soil was so wet that it was often easier to cultivate the hill-sides, which drained better. The farmer worked his wretched holding with eight oxen and a wooden plough for three

[1] Gross, *The Gild Merchant*, i. 213–25; Grant, *The Social and Economic Development of Scotland before* 1603, p. 427; Croft Dickinson, *Scotland from the earliest times to 1603*, pp. 233–51; Hume Brown, *Scotland in the time of Queen Mary*, pp. 42, 102, 108–10, 142–61, 189–93; Warrack, *Domestic Life in Scotland 1488–1688*, pp. 12–31, 71–72; J. H. Burns, 'The Scotland of John Major' (*Innes Review*, ii. 69–70); Sir J. B. Paul, 'Edinburgh in 1544 and Hertford's Invasion'; Paton, 'Old Edinburgh' (*S.H.R.* viii. 113–19, xxxii. 61–70); Inventory of the goods of James Raddock (*Stirling Burgh Records*, pp. 8, 74–75).

or four years in succession, raising as high a crop as possible of that poor quality barley known as bere, and then allowed the fields to lie fallow for another three or four years. He had to pay his rent to the landlord, and his tithes to the Church, paying in kind as there was not much money in circulation, leaving the bere in the fields until the collectors arrived and removed their due: and if the collectors were late in coming, the whole crop might be ruined. After a snowy winter or a wet spring, there was always a food shortage and the possibility of a famine. Only the sea saved the Scots. Every part of Scotland was within sixty miles of the open sea, where fish at least was plentiful. Fish was by far the most important export which the Scots could exchange abroad for wines from Bordeaux and Norwegian timber, which was badly needed for shipbuilding, though coal and peat could be used for fuel, and houses could be built from stone, mud, and thatch. Scotland, which might have been expected at least to have been rich in forests, was suffering from an acute shortage of timber by the fifteenth century, and though it was not a treeless waste, as it appeared to foreign travellers, the scarcity was sufficiently serious to make unauthorized felling of trees punishable by death.[1]

This poverty at home drove the Scot abroad, where he arrived as an unwelcome immigrant. He made his way into Berwick market, despite all the regulations designed to stop him, and went much further afield, travelling all over northern Europe, riding or walking forty miles a day, which was more than the ordinary Englishman cared to travel. The Scottish pedlar was a familiar figure in Norway, Poland, and East Prussia, where the villagers welcomed the annual visit from their Scotsman; but the merchants of the country resented his presence, and the Scots were hampered by discriminatory legislation, restricted in their movements, and murdered on the highway. Even in France they ran into difficulties with the local merchants, though here they were always welcomed if they wished to join the French army, and a regiment of Scots Guards had been retained by the King of France, under the command of a Scottish nobleman, since the beginning of the fifteenth century.[2]

[1] Croft Dickinson, *Scotland from the earliest times to 1603*, pp. 275–6 n., 373; J. H. Burns, 'The Scotland of John Major' (*Innes Rev.* ii. 65–76); Hume Brown, *Scotland in the time of Queen Mary*, pp. 7–12, 78; *Acts Parl. Scot.* ii. 343 (12 June 1535).

[2] *A.P.C.* 19 June 1546; Scheyvfe to the Council of State (24 Sept. 1550) (*Span. Cal.* x. 180); Hume Brown, *Scotland in the time of Queen Mary*, p. 64; Fischer, *The*

The 'Old Alliance' with France had been the basis of Scottish foreign policy, according to legend since the days of Charlemagne, in fact since 1173. It was directed against the 'ancient enemies of England', the prosperous and powerful Southerns who for more than 400 years had threatened and dominated Scotland. But the alliance was hampered by the geographical position of Scotland, which made it difficult for the Scots to maintain contact with their French allies. The safest and most usual way to travel from Scotland to France was by land through England, a journey that normally took twelve days but could be done in less, and then by sea from Dover to Calais, or from Rye to Dieppe. But this could only be done if the English government granted a safe-conduct to the traveller, for any Scot arriving in England without a safe-conduct was liable to be arrested and held till a ransom was paid. This method of travel was of course closed in war-time. The usual sea route from Leith and the east coast ports, the 'fair way'[1] to France by sea, was dangerous unless the English were friendly; for otherwise the ship was liable to attack off Holy Island, Hull, and Yarmouth, and in the Straits of Dover, and, apart from this, she might be in grave difficulty in the event of rough weather unless she had been granted a safe-conduct to shelter in the English ports. The western road from Dumbarton to Le Havre or Brest meant encountering rougher seas, and the English fleet might be lurking off Anglesey; while the road by the far west, passing the other side of Ireland, meant running the risk of being driven out into mid-Atlantic, and was so dangerous that the Papal Nuncio to Scotland in 1543 preferred to take the risk of travelling secretly through England without a safe-conduct, and face the fury of Henry VIII rather than the Atlantic storms.[2]

At the beginning of the fourteenth century, a brilliant Scottish leader had routed and humiliated the English, and had won freedom and independence for Scotland, at a time when England had a weak and incompetent King, and was divided by civil war. The Scots in 1500 still lived on the memory of Bruce and the victory

Scots in Eastern and Western Prussia, pp. 3, 14, 17–19; D. Baird Smith, 'Le Testament du Gentil Cossoys'; Sinclair, 'The Scottish Trader in Sweden'; Brill, 'A Sixteenth Century complaint against the Scots' (*S.H.R.* xvii. 190–8; xxv. 289–92; xxvii. 187–91).

[1] John Manne to Sadler, 10 May 1545 (*L.P.* xx [i]. 698).

[2] Grimani to Cardinal Farnese, 9 Oct., 27 Nov., and 11 Dec. 1543 (*S.H.R.* xi. 14, 22, 24; *L.P.* xviii [ii]. 435).

of Bannockburn: but Bannockburn and the successful War of Independence was almost the only victory which the Scots could set up against an endless succession of defeats at the hands of the English. Again and again the kings of England had marched their armies out of Berwick, destroying the Merse and Lothian, which by ill luck for the Scots was one of the few comparatively fertile areas of Scotland, and capturing Edinburgh. The Scots could make no effective resistance in the field, and they made no attempt to defend their unwalled towns, but removed the turf roofs of their houses and the stone which formed the walls, and quickly rebuilt the houses after the English had gone. They retaliated by desultory raids over the Border, and more effectively by piracy at sea, attacking the ships of the English merchants and their Burgundian allies, and plundering rich Portuguese vessels on their way to English ports. The Englishman regarded his wars against Scotland as a punitive expedition, for his contempt for the Scot went deeper than his contempt for the French and all other foreigners. The Englishman despised the Frenchman as an over-civilized dandy, 'more glorious in words than deeds';[1] but he despised the Scot as a barbarian, with the contempt of a colonial power for the native, of a powerful, efficient nation for a poor, weak, and backward one. This remained the attitude of the ordinary English officer towards the Scots throughout the whole of Knox's lifetime, whatever the policy of the English government might be, and whatever the religious and ideological issues involved.

John Knox, as an inhabitant of Haddington, must have been particularly conscious in his youth of the malice of the ancient enemies. 'Keeping Haddington, ye win Scotland', Sir Thomas Palmer told the Protector Somerset in 1548;[2] and the neighbourhood of Haddington, only forty miles from the English frontier, on the road from Berwick to Edinburgh along which all invading English armies marched, was the scene of one of the great patriotic legends of Scotland. A hundred and fifty years before Knox was born, King Edward III of England had marched into Haddington, ravaging Lothian in the terrible 'Burned Candlemas' of February 1356. In the nearby village of Whitechurch, the English massacred the children. A few of the children, who had been hidden in an oven by their

[1] Harvel to Russell, 31 May 1545 (*L.P.* xx [i]. 843).
[2] Palmer to Somerset, 30 June 1548 (*Sc. Cal.* i. 269).

mothers, were found by a cruel English soldier, but were saved by the intercession of one of his kindlier comrades, who led the children to the sanctuary of the church. There the same cruel soldier broke in upon them, and the children watched in terror as he kicked the altar and robbed the image of the Virgin Mary, breaking a finger of the statue as he wrenched off a ring. But suddenly a miracle occurred. The image of the Crucified One moved to avenge His despoiled mother, and fell forward on to the head of the soldier, killing him instantly. Further punishment was in store for the impious Southerns, for a gale arose at sea, scattering the English fleet which was cruising off the coast with supplies for their army, and thus forcing English Edward to retreat into his own country.[1]

As a youth Knox, with the other subjects of James V, faced the continual danger of violence from their fellow Scotsmen as well as from the ancient enemies. England was becoming an efficient, centralized state under an absolute monarchy, and was willingly accepting government by a ruthless royal dictator in order to avoid the dangers of lawlessness and civil war. Scotland still lived under feudal anarchy. In the hundred years before Knox was born, every king of Scotland had met his death by violence. Only one had been as old as 15 when he ascended the throne, and none had survived beyond the age of 42. An English observer who reported on the political structure of Scotland about the middle of the sixteenth century was shocked at the weakness of the royal power. 'Order and discipline in their commonwealth', he wrote, 'fadeth loose betwixt both the authorities of Prince and nobility.' The nobles' 'authority over their tenants, clients and vassals is so great, that they regard more their patron or nobleman as their Prince'.[2] Both justice and military organization were feudal. In the countryside justice was administered in the courts of the sheriff, an office which was hereditary in the great noble families; and the only army on which the king could rely to fight the old enemies or to suppress rebellion was an army assembled by proclamation at the market cross of every burgh, calling on all men between 60 and 16 to come 'boden in feir of war' with their own weapons and food

[1] Major, *History of Greater Britain*, pp. 296–7; Boece, *Chronicles of Scotland*, pp. 330–1; Abbot Bower, *Scotichronon*, Bk. xiv, Chap. xiii (Rankin, 'Whitekirk and the Burnt Candlemas' (*S.H.R.* xiii. 135–6)).

[2] 'Brief View of the State of Scotland in the Sixteenth Century' (Pinkerton, *History of Scotland*, p. 503).

for fifteen days. They came with their local lord, and generally fought on whichever side he was fighting.

For enforcement of the law there was only the watch in the town and the hue and cry in the country. The only prisons, apart from the great castles of the king and nobles, were in the tolbooths, the small town hall in every burgh, from which it was comparatively easy to escape, and which could not house more than a few offenders at the same time. The authorities had to rely largely on a system of open arrest, by which the accused man was summoned to attend his trial on pain of being 'put to the horn', a procedure by which a herald, after sounding his horn, proclaimed at the market cross of the burghs that the wanted man was an outlaw, and summoned all men to assist in apprehending him. But horning was not often effective. The malefactor at the horn withdrew among his kin and friends in a district where the authorities dared not enter, and stayed there, perhaps for several years, until some agreement was reached under which he was relaxed from the horn. The solemn contracts, duly drawn up in correct legal form, by which a family promises to forgive the murderer of their kinsman in consideration of a sum of money being paid as compensation,[1] show the state of justice in sixteenth-century Scotland, as do the bands made between powerful lords to support and defend each other against their enemies and 'unfriends', which were often accompanied by a less formal agreement to assist each other in murdering some mutual enemy.

Occasionally a more effective method of law enforcement was adopted in the Highlands and Border country. The king granted a commission of fire and slaughter to one or more of the Lowland earls, authorizing them to exterminate all the adult males of some Highland clan or Border family, with a pardon under the Great Seal of Scotland for any crime which might be committed by anyone who assisted in this lawful enterprise. The women and children were allowed to live and starve, though on one occasion they were deported to a barren shore in Norway. They gained no sympathy from the Lowland Scot, who believed, in the words of

[1] See, e.g., Contract between the Earl of Eglinton and Lord Boyd, 2 May 1530 (*Misc. of Abbotsford Club*, i. 9–12); Contract between Lord Fraser and the Clanranald, 6 July 1572 (J. Edwards, 'A Scottish Bond of Friendship betwixt Lord Lovat and the Captain of Clanranald, 1572' (*S.H.R.* xxiv. 176–8)); Deed of remission and forgiveness granted by the Beatons to John Leslie of Parkhill for the murder of Cardinal Beaton, 3 July 1575 (*H.M.C. 3rd R.* 504).

the Court poet, Montgomerie, that God had made the Highlander out of a lump of horse manure.[1]

At the beginning of the sixteenth century this wild, poor, and despised nation had produced a great king. James IV was one of those leaders of a small nation who by their ability and stature can make the world forget for a decade or two the weakness of their country. He was the ideal Christian king. Modern writers have often pointed out the contrast between his pious devotions, pilgrimages, and penances, and the immorality of his private life: but everything that James did, whether it was attending mass five times a day, making love to the ladies at his brilliant Court, or distinguishing himself in the jousting lists and the hunting field, was what was expected from a king in Christendom in 1500. James made Scotland a force to be reckoned with in international diplomacy. He built a formidable navy, imported great cannon from Flanders, sent a token force to help the King of Denmark suppress a revolt in Sweden, offered to arbitrate in disputes between German princes, and made more or less serious preparations to lead a new Crusade against the Turks; but instead of a Crusade there was a major European war.

In 1513 James invaded England in support of his French ally. But the battle on Branxton Moor, which the Scots, who did not know the district, called Flodden, destroyed the illusion that Scotland was one of the great nations of Christendom, shattered Scottish morale for a generation, and demonstrated the harsh realities of the balance of power which had been obscured by the personality of James IV. The Scottish host of at least 20,000 men was annihilated by an English reserve army—the main English army was engaged in France—which was inferior in numbers and equipment, but greatly superior in discipline and training. James's magnificent Flemish cannon, which had been dragged to the battlefield by 356 oxen and more than 150 soldiers, were wrongly sighted, and fired harmlessly over the heads of the enemy, while the smaller English guns and the well-trained English archers broke up the Scottish formations. The Scots then took off their shoes and charged headlong, led by James himself. Their long

[1] James V's commission to the Earl of Moray to pass upon the Clanchattan and Bagenocht 'for to destroy them aluterlie', 10 Nov. 1528 (*Spalding Club Misc.* ii. 83–84); Act of Judiciary of the Earl of Argyll, 8 July 1550 (*H.M.C. 6th R.* 630); *Reg. of Privy Council of Scotland*, i. 184–7, 248–50 (12 Nov. 1561 and 22 Sept. 1563); Montgomerie, *Poems*, p. 280.

spears, nearly 18 feet in length, should have given them the advantage in hand-to-hand combat against the English foot with their short bills; but the English side-stepped the charging Scots, cut through the wooden shafts of the spears with their bills, and then massacred their disarmed enemies. James IV, the two archbishops, 12 of Scotland's 20 earls and 13 of her 32 lords, and 10,000 men, half the total Scottish army, were killed, leaving an 18-months-old king, and a nobility consisting largely of children. The English lost only 1,500 men.[1]

As a result of Flodden, Scotland became an even more important factor in European politics, but as a pawn, not a power. A struggle arose as to who should be the Regent between Margaret, the Queen Dowager, and John Stewart, Duke of Albany. The Queen Dowager was an English princess, the sister of Henry VIII; the Duke of Albany was a French nobleman who was related in blood to the kings of Scotland, but had lived in France since the age of 2. Their struggle was a struggle for influence between England and France: at Greenwich and Fontainebleau, the regency of Scotland was bargained against a fortress in Italy or a town in Flanders, without any Scotsman being consulted. When Albany installed himself as Regent, Margaret fled to England, to grace her brother's Court with her presence and act as hostess at his hunting lodges; when she returned to Scotland and ousted Albany, Albany returned to his military and diplomatic duties in France. Meanwhile, in the Scotland of Knox's childhood, law and order broke down completely. Great lords were murdered in public by the supporters of their rivals. The tolbooths were stormed while the courts of law were in session by armed bands of the defendant's kinsmen, who were determined to prevent him from being convicted. In April 1520 there was the clash in Edinburgh that became known as 'Cleanse the Causeway'. The Hamiltons set upon the Douglases at the meeting of Parliament: a fight ensued, and eighty-seven men were left dead in the streets before the citizens were able to resume their daily business. The criminal records tell of slaughters, mutilations, blood-shedding, and fire-raising all over the Lowlands; of children struck by angry lairds

[1] See Gladys Dickinson, 'Some Notes on the Scottish Army in the first half of the Sixteenth Century'; note by J. D. Mackie (*S.H.R.* xxviii. 138; xxxviii. 135); R. L. Mackie, *King James IV of Scotland*, pp. 259–76; W. Mackay Mackenzie, *The Secret of Flodden*, pp. 75–93. For the Flodden death-roll, see *The Scottish Antiquary*, xiii. 104–6, 171. There is some confusion as to the exact number of earls and lords who fell.

until they could not rise; of men seized in their homes and incarcerated without authority in neighbouring castles; of cows beaten to death by hostile neighbours.[1]

Men were attacked in the streets, in their dwelling houses, and in their fields. The Earl of Eglinton, after imprisoning a merchant of Irvine, set his men on the merchant's wife, 'cruelly striking her, and pulling out her hair in great quantities'. The laird of Balluny and his wife came with four friends to break up the ditches on the lands of the Countess of Crawfurd, wounding the Countess in the throat. Robert Douglas of Dowchie was attacked on the highway as he was going home at night by Thomas Harrot and all the male and female members of his family, who cut off one of his fingers and left him for dead. In revenge Douglas went at night to his assailants' house, and cut Thomas Harrot in the face and arm; then, seeing that Harrot's wife was pregnant, he gave her 'sundry strokes with foot and hand' to kill the unborn child. This is not the only case in the criminal records of child-slaughter by kicking pregnant women. The courtesy towards ladies, which had been so marked at the Court of James IV, did not go deep in Scottish life. As crime went so often unpunished, the people protected themselves by self-defence and retaliation. The monks of Dunfermline took the precaution of inserting a clause in their leases that their tenant would forfeit his lease if he attacked the monastery, on horse or on foot, except under the king's authority. John Knox grew up in a brutal world.[2]

[1] Pitcairn, *Criminal Trials*, i [i]. 24–25, 136–7, 201, 222, 225, 330, 336, 343, 381, 399; James V's pardon, 22 May 1527 (*Charters relating to the City of Edinburgh 1143–1540*, pp. 205–8).

[2] Pitcairn, i [i]. 74, 180, 411–12, 456; Feu-charter by the Arch-Dean of St. Andrews and the Commendator of Dunfermline, 12 Jan. 1555 (*H.M.C. 3rd R.* 499).

CHAPTER II

Sir John Knox

VERY little is known about John Knox's family and parentage. In the biography published in David Buchanan's edition of Knox's *History of the Reformation in Scotland* in 1644, it is stated that he was born 'of honest parentage. . . . His father was a brother's son of the House of Ranfurly, which is an ancient family of gentlemen in the west.' This shows clearly that Knox's family were not highly placed in the social scale, and were below the rank of gentlemen: if the biographer could have said that Knox came from a noble or gentle family, he would certainly have done so. The best that he could say of Knox's family was that it had some cousins in the west who were gentlemen: obviously the branch of the family that lived at Haddington in the east were lower in status. This is confirmed by Knox's friend and follower, John Davidson, who wrote in his poem about Knox that 'he descended but of lineage small'. Knox's father was almost certainly a freeman of the burgh of Haddington, though we do not know whether he was a merchant or a craftsman. Knox's brother William became a merchant at Prestonpans, and Knox himself, in later life, had more support from the merchants than from the craftsmen in Edinburgh; but this was for political reasons, and had nothing to do with Knox's social origin. Knox's father was called William; he may have been killed at Flodden. Nothing is known about Knox's mother, except that her surname was Sinclair. Knox sometimes used the name Sinclair as an alias when he was engaged in revolutionary activity.[1]

[1] Davidson, 'Ane Breif Commendatioun of Uprichtnes' line 108 (Rogers, 'Three Poets of the Scottish Reformation' (*Trans. R.H.S.* iii. 249)); Life of Knox, in Knox, *History*, 1644 edn. (London edn., sig. a; Edinburgh edn., unpag.); Marginal note by the transcriber of Knox's letters in 1603 (*Works*, iv. 245). For William Knox, see Mary of Lorraine to Edward VI, 24 Feb. 1551/2 (*Sc. Cal.* i. 390). For Knox's role as spokesman for the Edinburgh merchant class, see A. B. Hart, 'Knox as a man of the world' (*American Hist. Rev.* xiii. 259–80); W. Stamford Reid, 'The Middle Class Factor in the Scottish Reformation' (*Church History*, xvi. 137–55).

The name Knox was a common one throughout the Scottish Lowlands. The K in the name was probably pronounced, and not left mute as in the modern pronunciation. In the sixteenth century the spelling of names had not become standardized; writers wrote a name as they pleased and therefore tended to write it phonetically, particularly foreigners, who wrote the name phonetically in the spelling used in their own language. Most Scottish and English contemporaries wrote the name 'Knox', 'Knocks', or 'Knokkes'. Foreign writers usually wrote it 'Cnox', or in Latin 'Knoxus' or 'Cnoxus'. The Spanish ambassador in London on one occasion wrote it 'Quenoques'. But sometimes the K must have been dropped in pronunciation, for some writers, including Lethington, sometimes wrote it 'Nox'. Whatever pronunciation was adopted, it was near enough to the Latin word *nox* (night) and *noceus* (a criminal) to give Knox's opponents the opportunity for a hostile pun. The Catholic writer Nicol Burne says 'Ye might more justly have called him Kmnox *quasi nox, a nocendo*'; and Alexander Baillie writes about 'that black Zwinglian night-spirit wherewith our Knox was inspired'.[1]

As Knox was probably an intelligent child who showed an interest in academic studies at school, it was natural that he should be educated for a career in the Church. Not that it was necessary for a churchman to be educated; for the level of education among priests was lower than anywhere else in Christendom. Throughout Europe, for many centuries, the clergy had been the only section of the population which could read and write, though literacy was now becoming sufficiently widespread to make written political propaganda an important and dangerous factor. In sixteenth-century Scotland many priests could not read or sign their names. Sir David Lindsay in his poems caricatured drunken Sir John Latinless, the priest who did not know any Latin except the words of the mass; but a far more orthodox Catholic, Archibald Hay, in his *Panegyric to the Lord Cardinal David Beaton*, declared that he wondered what the bishops were thinking about when they admitted to the handling of the Lord's holy body men who hardly knew the order of the alphabet. By this time many laymen,

[1] Beza, *Icones*, sig. Ee3; Guzman de Silva to Philip II, 21 Nov. 1564 (*Span Cal. Eliz.* i. 275); Lethington to Mary Queen of Scots, 20 Sept. 1569 (*Sc. Cal.* ii. 1142); Huggarde, *The Displaying of the Protestantes*, p. 118; Nicol Burne, *The Disputation concerning the Controversit Headdis of Religion*, p. 129; Baillie, *A true information of the Unhallowed offspring . . . of our Scottish Calvinian gospel*, p. 18.

particularly the merchants in the towns, could write; and probably the clergy as a class were not much better educated than the population as a whole.[1]

There were surprisingly good facilities for acquiring a rudimentary education in the Scotland of Knox's youth. The merit of the Scottish educational system at this period has been grossly exaggerated, but, considering the poverty of Scotland and its backwardness in every other respect, the provisions for education were remarkably advanced. The Church had established many song schools all over the country, where children were taught the elements of religious knowledge and trained for singing in the church choir. Knox probably went to a song school, or some other 'little school', at the age of 7. At a later age children could go to the grammar schools which existed in most of the burghs, and, in theory at least, were open free of charge to every child in the burgh and the neighbouring countryside. David Buchanan implies that Knox was educated at Haddington Grammar School, and he probably went there at the age of 10. Here the teaching consisted largely of Latin grammar, a subject usually called 'Donat' from the textbook used, the Latin grammar of Donatus, the fourth-century Roman author. But Knox may have been in time to use the new Latin grammar written by John Vaus, the first Scotsman ever to write an educational textbook, which was published in 1522 in Paris, owing to the great difficulties involved in operating a printing press in Scotland.[2]

Beza says that Knox studied under John Major at St. Andrews University, and this is almost certainly correct, though it was generally accepted until recent years that he was educated at Glasgow University and not at St. Andrews. Young men usually proceeded from the grammar school to the university at the age of 15, and Knox probably went to St. Andrews University in about 1529. Major had left for Paris in 1526, and taught for five

[1] Sir David Lindsay, 'Kitteis Confessioun' (Lindsay, *Works*, i. 126); Archibald Hay, *Ad D. Davidem Betoun Card. Panegyricus*, f. xxxi (Hay Fleming, *The Reformation in Scotland*, p. 42); Hay Fleming, 'The Influence of the Reformation on Social and Cultural Life in Scotland' (*S.H.R.* xv. 23); D. Partick's Introduction to *Statutes of the Scottish Church*, pp. lxxx–lxxxv.

[2] Grant, *History of the Burgh Schools of Scotland*, pp. 48–50; Durkan, 'Education in the Century of the Reformation' (*Essays on the Scottish Reformation*, pp. 145–6); Life of Knox, in Knox, *History*, 1644 edn. (London edn., sig. a; Edinburgh edn., unpag.). David Buchanan states that Knox was educated at 'the grammar school in the country', which obviously means the grammar school at Haddington.

years at the Sorbonne, but he returned to St. Andrews in 1531, and taught theology at St. Salvator's College. Knox must have studied Arts at the University for at least two years before proceeding to the study of theology, and then for the three or four years beginning in 1531 or 1532 studied theology under Major at St. Salvator's.[1]

Major, who was himself a native of Haddington, was one of the leading intellectuals of Europe. He had written several important books, including his *History of Greater Britain* in which, considering the matter coolly and free from patriotic prejudice, he had suggested that Scotland would have much to gain from a union with England. When he taught at the Sorbonne, the students had been astounded to discover that Major, a Scot from this distant land of savages, had a deeper understanding of Aristotle and Aquinas than any doctor in the University of Paris. Unlike the ordinary teacher of theology, he did not lecture only on Peter Lombard's *Books of the Sentences*, the leading textbook of scholastic theology, but introduced his students to the text of the Latin Bible, though fundamentally Major was a conservative in his teaching, as well as in his religious opinions. He did nothing to modernize the teaching at St. Andrews; he taught scholastic theology and philosophy, but none of the new studies and modes of thought introduced by the Renaissance.[2]

Scholastic theology, with its logic, its rigidity, its formalized method of abstract discussion, was an excellent intellectual exercise; but it exasperated impatient young men. Melanchthon deplored the fact that Major, who at the Sorbonne was the prince of Paris divines, should indulge in such wagon-loads of trifling, and fill pages with argument as to whether there can be any horsemanship without a horse and whether the sea was salt when God made it. This kind of teaching made no appeal to students in a period of social transformation, and in every university of Europe youth was in revolt against scholastic theology. In Scotland, which prided itself on its education and its three universities—

[1] Beza, *Icones*, sig. Ee3; J. M. Anderson's Preface to *Early Records of the University of St. Andrews*, pp. xxiv, xxx, xxxviii–xli.

[2] For Major, see Ross, 'Some Scottish Catholic Historians'; J. H. Burns, 'New Light on John Major' (*Innes Rev.* i. 5–20; v. 83–97); Cooper, 'The Principals of the University of Glasgow before the Reformation' (*S.H.R.* xi. 252–65); C. M. MacDonald, 'John Major and Humanism' (*S.H.R.* xiii. 149–58); Durkan, 'The Cultural Background in Sixteenth Century Scotland' (*Essays on the Scottish Reformation*, pp. 281–4); Aeneas Mackay's Preface to Major's *Greater Britain*, pp. i–cxv.

one more than England had—the small intellectual *élite* was being trained on a syllabus which had been accepted for generations in every university of Europe, but which was now being rejected by progressive opinion everywhere. In the new University of Aberdeen, which had introduced the study of medicine into the curriculum, and at St. Leonard's college at St. Andrews, some sympathy for the new ideas in teaching was to be found; but the theological college of St. Salvator's remained immune from progress.[1]

According to Beza and David Buchanan, Knox did very well academically at the University. Beza says that Knox began to study with such proficiency that it was thought he would one day become a more subtle sophist than his master John Major himself, but that after reading the works of St. Jerome and St. Augustine, he realized the errors in the conventional teaching. David Buchanan also states that Knox became more proficient than Major in scholastic theology, and says that he was awarded a degree when he was still very young and was ordained before the time ordinarily allowed by the canons.[2] But it is difficult to believe that Knox could ever have rivalled Major as a schoolman, for in most of his writings in later life his approach was very different from that of the schoolmen. He was intelligent enough to understand the subleties of scholastic theology, but temperamentally had no inclination to do so. He probably found university life altogether uncongenial. Restless, bursting with energy, and eager to dominate, he was not the type to settle down to the methodical study of scholastic theology in the quiet of a university town.

Knox must have shown ability at the university in order to persuade the authorities to give him a dispensation to be ordained a priest before he reached the canonical age of 24, as he was not in a position to use any influence to obtain dispensations. James IV had obtained a dispensation to have his illegitimate son appointed as the Archbishop of St. Andrews, the Primate of Scotland, at the age of 11. At the time when Knox was completing his studies under Major, the Pope granted James V a dispensation to allow three of his bastards, all of them under 5 years old, to be appointed

[1] J. D. Mackie, 'Scotland and the Renaissance' (*Proceedings of the Royal Philosophical Society of Glasgow*, lxi. 78–80); Lorimer, *Patrick Hamilton*, pp. 42–43, 52–55.

[2] Beza, *Icones*, sig. Ee3; Life of Knox, in Knox, *History*, 1644 edn. (London edn., sig. a; Edinburgh edn., unpag.).

abbots and priors of five of the richest monasteries in Scotland.[1] Knox's request was more moderate: he asked to be allowed to become a priest at the age of 22 instead of waiting another two years. The dispensation was granted, and Knox was ordained a priest on Easter Eve, Saturday, 15 April 1536, by William Chisholm, Bishop of Dunblane. He had been ordained as a deacon a fortnight earlier, on Saturday, 1 April. Chisholm was probably in Edinburgh at the time, attending Parliament. Knox, who resided at Haddington and St. Andrews in the diocese of St. Andrews, would normally have been ordained by his own Ordinary, the Archbishop, not by the Bishop of Dunblane. Chisholm probably acted as a substitute for Archbishop James Beaton in carrying out the ordinations on this occasion, and ordained Knox and his fellow ordinands in Edinburgh.[2]

After he became a priest, Knox was always referred to in official documents as 'Sir John Knox'. This title was not used by priests who had obtained their degree of Doctor of Divinity, so it is clear that Knox was only awarded a degree of Bachelor of Divinity at St. Andrews. As the priesthood fell into disrepute, the title 'Sir', applied to priests, had begun to arouse ridicule, and priests were often mocked as 'the Pope's knights'.

By becoming a priest Knox had achieved the ambition of every intelligent lad of humble origin. Then the difficulties began. There were far too many priests in Scotland. The estimates of the total population of Scotland in the sixteenth century vary from 500,000 to 800,000. There were more than 3,000 priests, or approximately one for every fifty of the adult male population, which is the equivalent of a quarter of a million clergymen in modern Britain. At the same time, owing to the corruption of the Church, the Scottish people were suffering from a lack of spiritual care. By the sixteenth century the great monasteries that had been established throughout the Lowlands had acquired the livings of most of the parish churches. Of the thousand-odd parishes in Scotland, less than a hundred had a resident parson. In the others the parson was a monastery or a cathedral church, or sometimes a layman to whom the living had been granted. In many cases the monasteries appointed and paid a chaplain to reside in the parish and carry out

[1] See James V to Clement VII, 27 Feb. 1532/3 (*Letters of James V*, p. 235); Clement VII's Dispensation, 30 Aug. 1534 (*H.M.C. 6th R.* 670).

[2] P. J. Shearman, 'Father Alexander McQuhirrie, S.J.' (*Innes Rev.* vi. 42–45).

the spiritual duties of a parish priest; but often they preferred to save the money, for nearly all the monasteries in the kingdom were ruled by a prior who was a layman, a great noble who never intended to take holy orders, but held the priory *in commendam* by dispensation and thrived on the tithes paid by the parishioners to the monastery as their parish priest. While many parish churches were crumbling into ruins through lack of repair, and there were some in which no mass had been celebrated for years, young men like Knox, who had recently been ordained, were unable to obtain a living. All other classes grumbled at the great wealth of the Church, and a bishop or a canon in a cathedral might live very well, enjoying luxuries imported from abroad which few of the nobility were able to enjoy. But the priest without a benefice was lucky if he could earn a meagre living of ten marks a year (£6. 13*s.* 4*d.*) as a paid chaplain in some parish appropriated to a monastery, or as a chantry priest, saying his many daily masses alone in some church, praying for the soul of the deceased founder of the chantry, or carrying out secular duties as the parish clerk; for clerical stipends had not been increased since the thirteenth century. Some took a post as tutor to the children of a noble or country laird. Others broke the canonical regulations and engaged in trade, or acted as notaries, who performed the duties of solicitors.[1]

Nothing is known of Knox's life during the four years after his ordination, but he was obviously unable to obtain a benefice, for by 1540 he was acting as a notary in the neighbourhood of Haddington and calling himself a notary apostolic. Notaries appointed under licence of the Pope were known as notaries apostolic, to distinguish them from the imperial notaries appointed under licence of the Holy Roman Emperor, from the episcopal notaries appointed by the bishop of the diocese, and the royal notaries appointed under the authority of recent Acts of Parliament after examination by their bishop. Since 1503 no one could become a notary without being examined by the bishop of the diocese; but notaries who had been granted a licence by the Pope nearly always described themselves as 'notary apostolic', because this was the traditional form and also enabled them, if necessary, to act in causes before the courts in Rome and elsewhere throughout

[1] D. McKay, 'Parish Life in Scotland 1500–1560' (*Essays on the Scottish Reformation*, pp. 85–90); Bellesheim, *History of the Catholic Church of Scotland*, ii. 312; Croft Dickinson, *Scotland from the earliest times to 1603*, pp. 125–6, 273.

Christendom. Notaries were in theory recruited from clerics in minor orders and ordained priests were not supposed to be appointed as notaries; but this rule was often violated in practice, as it was in Knox's case, for legal fees were high, and notaries could earn much more money than priests and chaplains. Many priests who had been admitted as notaries when in minor orders continued to practise after becoming priests, and Knox probably took the precaution of being admitted as a notary when he was in minor orders, receiving the pen and paper and taking the oath at the traditional ceremony.

For at least three years Knox was a small country lawyer, a member of the class that has provided so many successful politicians and revolutionary leaders in every part of the world since Knox's time. By far the greatest part of a notary's activities was concerned with titles to land, drafting deeds, and registering enfeoffments; but he also sometimes dealt with other matters such as wills, the borrowing and repayment of money, indentures of apprenticeship, processes against ships, marriage contracts, the obtaining of dispensations, and the recording of a client's protest in his Protocol Book. He might occasionally deal with litigious matters, such as divorces and actions for slander in the ecclesiastical courts, though pleading in court was left to advocates and proctors. A notary had no office from which he worked, and no legal textbooks, except his *Formularium* of legal precedents, and perhaps the *Burgh Laws*, the *Regiam Majestatem*, and a manual of canon law in manuscript. He visited his clients in their houses, travelling sometimes over a large area, often risking attack from robbers as he carried large sums of gold to pay over, on behalf of his client, to a creditor at the altar of some local church, where much legal business was conducted. His clients, who were usually illiterate, regarded the notary with great suspicion, for he had many opportunities for fraud and often took advantage of them. The profession proudly claimed a patron saint, St. Yves of Brittany, though the people alleged that he was the only lawyer in all history to be canonized, and sang of

St. Yves of old, a Breton lief,
A lawyer was, yet not a thief,
Which made the people wonder.[1]

[1] See D. Murray, *Legal Practice in Ayr and the West of Scotland in the Fifteenth and*

On 13 December 1540 Knox went to the market cross of Haddington, as notary for his client James Ker of Samuelston, to hear the king's messenger read out an order of the court which had been obtained in judicial proceedings against Ker. James Ker was related to the highest nobles of the land. His sister Nicolas had married Lord Home, and was the mother of the living Lord Home and Elizabeth Home, Lady Hamilton, the divorced wife of James Hamilton, first Earl of Arran, who for many years had been the heir presumptive to the throne of Scotland. Elizabeth's divorce proceedings were continually being examined by lawyers in Scotland and England, for if the divorce was invalid, the Earl of Lennox, and not her stepson, the Earl of Arran, was the heir to the Scottish Crown. James Ker may have been a distant relative of Knox, as the mother of Ker and Lady Home was a Sinclair, like Knox's mother. This is the first of several occasions on which the records show Knox acting in connexion with Ker of Samuelston. On 21 November 1542 a claim for four chalders of bere, which was being heard in the Burgh Court of Haddington, was referred to arbitration, Knox and James Ker being appointed as arbitrators for one of the parties.

Four months later Knox acted in two independent transactions on two consecutive days, both of which took place in Ker's house in the village of Samuelston, near Haddington. The first dealt with the feu-ferme, or hereditary lease, of land at Ley Acres, near the burgh moor of Haddington, which Ker held from his great-niece Janet Home, Lady Hamilton of Samuelston. Elizabeth Home, the former Countess of Arran, held a life rent on the land, which she now proceeded to assign to her uncle James Ker. A document written by Knox, who describes himself as 'minister of the sacred altar in the diocese of St. Andrews, notary by apostolic authority', records that at 4 p.m. on 27 March 1543, in the ninth year of the pontificate 'of our Holy Father in Christ and our lord, Lord Paul III, Pope by divine providence', the parties, Elizabeth Home Lady Hamilton and James Ker, executed this deed in the house of James Ker in Samuelston in the presence of several parties and witnesses, including Lord Herries and Knox himself. At this transaction of legal business, which was also a family reunion,

Sixteenth Centuries, pp. 7–14, 24–27, 82–83, 86–87; Sir J. B. Paul, 'Clerical Life in Scotland in the Sixteenth Century', and 'Social Life in Scotland in the Sixteenth Century' (*S.H.R.* xvii. 177–89, 296–8).

Knox met the great lady who might have been Queen of Scotland, and his first encounter with the great House of Hamilton, with whom he later had so much to do as friend and foe, was as a country solicitor in this village in Lothian.

Next day Knox was one of the witnesses to a legal transaction that took place at Ker's house between a procurator for Lord Home and young William Brounefield. The documents seem to suggest that Knox was William Brounefield's tutor and was residing with Brounefield at James Ker's house in Samuelston.[1] He could easily combine the duties of a private tutor with casual work as a notary, and it was a recognized form of employment by which poor priests augmented their slender income. Knox was perhaps acting as tutor to several boys, including Ker's sons, in the village of Samuelston. This is the last known record of Knox's activities as a notary. In May 1545 a Chancery clerk in St. Andrews by the name of John Knox registered a dispensation for marriage which Cardinal Beaton had granted to an applicant;[2] but this clerk is not likely to have been Knox, as he is not referred to as 'Sir John Knox', and there is no other reason to believe that Knox was a Chancery clerk in St. Andrews.

The only other light which illuminates the obscurity of Knox's early years is the lurid light thrown by the writings of his enemies. The Catholic propagandists who wrote about Knox in the fifty years after his death accused him of having committed adultery with his stepmother in early youth. The accusation was first made, without directly mentioning the stepmother, by Archibald Hamilton in a book published in Paris in 1581, nine years after Knox's death. He stated that as a boy, with precocious lust, Knox defiled his father's bed. Archibald Hamilton was a man from the Western Isles who was brought up as a Protestant in the years immediately after the Reformation, and met Knox when he was studying at St. Andrews University; but he was converted to Catholicism and joined the Scottish Catholic refugees in France, where he wrote violent attacks on the Scottish Protestants. In the same year James Laing, a Scottish Catholic who had become Rector of the Sorbonne, repeated the accusation more specifically

[1] For these transactions of Knox as a notary, see the text of documents printed by Laing, 'Documents connected with Knox as a notary', and T. Thomson, 'Notices of the Kers of Samuelston, etc., in illustration of the previous deeds' (*Proceedings of the Society of Antiquaries of Scotland*, i. 59–68).

[2] W. J. Anderson, 'John Knox as Registrar' (*Innes Rev.* vii. 63).

in his book, also published in Paris, *Concerning the Life and Deaths of the Heretics of our Time*. Laing wrote that Knox had scarcely reached manhood before he violated his stepmother, and that it was the action of his bishop in pursuing him for this crime that turned Knox against the Church and led him to progress from adultery to heresy and high treason. If there was any truth in this story, it is strange that it was never thrown at Knox by his enemies during his lifetime, and that Archibald Hamilton did not mention it in his first book against the Scottish Calvinists, which he wrote in 1577, in which he attacked Knox at considerable length and made other allegations against his morals.[1]

It is easy to trace the origin of this story. The intimate spiritual relationship between Knox and his mother-in-law, Mrs. Bowes, who lived with Knox and her daughter for several years, naturally gave their enemies the opportunity to accuse Knox of committing incestuous adultery with Mrs. Bowes, of having both the mother and the daughter. The tale improved, in time, from incest with the mother-in-law in middle age to incest with a stepmother in adolescence. A new element was introduced in 1563, when Knox was minister of St. Giles's in Edinburgh, by a gossiping woman, who said that Knox had been discovered with a harlot in a *killogy*, or cave; and in 1600 John Hamilton, another Scottish Catholic refugee in exile, who, as well as writing scurrilous pamphlets against the Scottish Protestants, was occasionally employed by Catholic rulers as a paid assassin, wove the three stories of Mrs. Bowes, the stepmother, and the *killogy* into one. He stated that Knox in his youth had violated both a mother and her daughter in a *killogy* when he was a priest at Haddington. The story is no more trustworthy than the story about Calvin having been branded for sodomy and the other allegations of Knox's Catholic critics about the morals of their Protestant opponents.[2]

There remains the question as to whether there is any truth in the accusations of lechery that were so freely levelled against Knox. In view of the tone of religious controversy in sixteenth-

[1] Archibald Hamilton, *Calvinianae Confusionis demonstratio*, p. 253; Laing, *De Vita et Moribus atque Rebus Gestis Haereticorum nostri temporis*, p. 113. Archibald Hamilton makes no reference to the incident in his *De Confusione Calvinianae sectae apud Scotos* in 1577 (see pp. 64–66).

[2] *Edinburgh Burgh Records*, iii. 162, 164 (18 and 25 June 1563); John Hamilton, *A facile traictise, contenand, first, an infallible rule to discern true from false religion*, p. 60. See also Rainald, *Calvino-turcismus*, p. 260; Baillie, *A true information*, pp. 10–11, 14.

century Scotland, no weight at all can be attached to the allegations of Archibald Hamilton, Laing, Nicol Burne, and John Hamilton, that Knox was an unbridled lecher—in Laing's words, 'a lascivious he-goat',[1] who, even when he was an old man, burned with desire for the love of girls. But before rejecting out of hand all suggestions that Knox led an immoral life in his youth, we should remember that Knox, in his twenties, was not yet the Great Reformer of historical legend, but a young priest and solicitor of East Lothian who obviously could not have found a full outlet for his energy in his notarial or tutorial duties; that other great Protestant leaders, such as Beza, led an immoral life in their youth before achieving spiritual contentment; that immorality, either with resident concubines or in irregular attachments, was rife in all ranks of the Scottish clergy in the reign of James V;[2] and that the years 1542–5 were years of war, plague, and chaos in Lothian, when loose standards of morality could be expected to become looser still. In such circumstances it would be surprising if a man with the vitality and emotionalism of Knox, who showed such interest in women in later middle age, should have succeeded in observing chastity until he married at the age of 41; but to assume automatically that he led an immoral life is to take too simplified a view of human nature, and to overlook the possibility of exceptional strength of character, or of some psychological abnormality, in a strange and remarkable man.

We do not know when Knox first developed the profound and sincere religious sensitivity which was an important feature of his character, though it was often obscured by the other side of Knox—the tough political fighter and the master of sarcastic prose; but we know that it originated in his reading of Scripture. When Knox was dying he asked his wife to read aloud the seventeenth chapter of St. John's Gospel, and said: 'Go read where I cast my first anchor.'[3] It was his study of Jerome and Augustine that first disgusted him with scholastic theology; it was events beyond his control, the actions of other people, that first drove him to play an active part in the Protestant movement; but it was the deeply spiritual passages in the seventeenth chapter of St.

[1] Laing, *De Vita et Moribus . . . Haereticorum*, pp. 114–15.

[2] For a contemporary Catholic view of the immorality of the Scottish clergy, see J. C. Barry, 'William Hay of Aberdeen: a Sixteenth Century Scottish Theologian and Canonist' (*Innes Rev.* ii. 82–99).

[3] Bannatyne, *Memorials*, p. 288.

John that first stirred his fundamentally religious nature. The ordinary Scottish priest never read the Bible. Knox would have read it at St. Andrews as one of Major's students, but the first inspiration is not likely to have come to him in the lecture room. It is much more likely to have been in some quiet room or field near Haddington that Knox first cast his anchor in the seventeenth chapter of St. John.

Knox had now reached the age of 30. He was a short man, but broad-shouldered. He had black hair, and his general complexion was swarthy, though the rounded cheeks on his long face were ruddy. His beard, which in later life was a hand and a half long, was thick and black and never acquired more than a few grey hairs. As a young man, he had perhaps not yet acquired the air of authority, the countenance which Sir Peter Young described as 'grave and stern, but not harsh': but already there was the natural dignity which was emphasized by the well-proportioned limbs and the long fingers, and the deep-sunken, dark blue eyes which were always lively and could flash with anger under the bushy eyebrows on his narrow forehead.[1] Both the spiritual and the aggressive side of his character must have been well developed by this time, making him disgusted with the immorality of Scottish life and the betrayal of the flock by the Church, as well as utterly frustrated by the life of a country notary and children's tutor.

This in itself would not necessarily have made Knox a Protestant. Men of a quieter and more reflective temperament, like gentle John Watson, the canon of Aberdeen, dreamed of reforming the corrupt Church by spiritual example:[2] but Knox's nature would lead him to have dreams of a different kind. There is no evidence, except for the assertions of Knox's opponents, that the words 'Root out! Root out!' were always on his lips, and only indirect authority that he ever said: 'Down with those crow nests, else the crows will big in them again;' but on this occasion Burne and Lord Herries did no injustice to Knox.[3] This was what Knox

[1] For this description of Knox's appearance, see Peter Young to Beza, 13 Nov. 1579 (Hume Brown, *John Knox*, ii. 323). No portrait of Knox was painted during his lifetime; the only genuine portrait of Knox was painted by Adrian Vaensoun from memory, seven years after Knox's death, and sent by Young to Beza. See note under frontispiece.

[2] For John Watson, see Father G. Hill, 'The Sermons of John Watson, Canon of Aberdeen' (*Innes Rev.* xv. 3–34).

[3] Nicol Burne, *The Disputation concerning the Controversit Headdis of Religion*, p. 129; Lord Herries, *Historical Memoirs of the Reign of Mary Queen of Scots*, p. 38; Row,

thought, even if he did not utter the words. By 1543 he was probably already dreaming of rooting out the nests in which the corruption, immorality, and hypocrisy were bred; but it was nothing but dreams. The reality was teaching Latin grammar and literature, a little French, and the rudiments of religious instruction to young William Brounefield at Samuelston. Not long after the spring of 1543, Knox left Samuelston and moved seven miles away to Longniddry, a village five miles west of Haddington and barely a mile from the sea. Here he taught two new pupils, the two sons of the laird, Sir Hugh Douglas of Longniddry. Knox became a member of Longniddry's household. He was still there when Wishart came to Lothian, and changed the future course of Knox's life.

History of the Kirk of Scotland, p. 12. See also the report of the Jesuit priests of Scotland to Pope Clement VIII in 1594 (Stevenson-Nau, pp. 105–44).

CHAPTER III

Wishart

HERESY first appeared in Scotland at the beginning of the fifteenth century, when Lollards, fleeing from persecution in England, found their way across the Border. One of them, James Resby, was burned as a heretic at Perth in 1407. In 1433 the Czech Hussite, Paul Crawar, was arrested when studying at St. Andrews University and burned. After this, for many years, the Church had no more trouble from heretics; but Lollard doctrines somehow took root in the south-west, in a few scattered villages in Kyle in Ayrshire, where a group of heretics were rounded up and put on trial in 1494, but released through the personal intervention of James IV.[1] Thirty years later the Church faced a more serious threat, as the fire which Luther had started in Germany in 1517 spread all over Christendom.

Protestantism came to Scotland from the German Hansa towns, entering through the ports of the east coast, through Leith, Dundee, and Montrose. Dundee, the second town of Scotland, a bustling burgh of some 6,000 modern-minded citizens, from which, on an average, a ship sailed twice a week to Dieppe or Bordeaux, to Veere, Bremen, Danzig, or Bergen,[2] became the strongest Protestant centre in Scotland. Within ten years of Luther's act of defiance of 31 October 1517, Protestant propaganda tracts were being smuggled into Dundee, including the English translation of the New Testament which the English Protestant, Tyndale, had published in Germany and embellished with a few marginal notes directed against the Pope and the established Church. Tyndale's Bible had aroused great anxiety among the authorities in England, where Wolsey and the bishops had searched everywhere for the book and had publicly burned every copy they could find. In Scotland, where the government was much weaker and the

[1] For Paul Crawar, see Calderwood, *History of the Kirk of Scotland*, i. 48; George Thomson, *De Antiquitate Christianae religionis apud Scotos* (*S.H.S. Misc.* ii. 126). For the case of the Lollards of Kyle, see Knox, *History*, i. 7–11.

[2] Grant, *The Social and Economic Development of Scotland before 1603*, p. 362.

Church much more corrupted than in England, the round-up of Lutheran literature was much less effective.

When drastic measures were finally taken, the persecution had some peculiarly Scottish features. The first victim to be singled out was not some merchant or artisan, or a priest who had strayed from the orthodox teaching, but Patrick Hamilton, a young man of 24, who was a member of one of the noblest houses in Scotland. The Hamiltons were at feud with the Douglases, whose chief, the Earl of Angus, was at this time the ruler of Scotland. Like other influential lairds, Patrick Hamilton held an abbey *in commendam*, though he was not in holy orders; but he had chosen a way of life which was very different from that of the ordinary noble or gentleman. After studying at St. Andrews University, he wrote a book which was condemned as heretical, and fled to Germany. He returned, and took up residence at Kincavil near Linlithgow, where he proceeded to propagate his opinions among his kinsmen and tenants. James Beaton, the Archbishop of St. Andrews, was naturally alarmed to hear that a local laird, especially one who was related to the Hamiltons, was using his influence to contaminate the people in the neighbourhood of the royal palace of Linlithgow; but he dared not send men to arrest him in his own country. He therefore lured Patrick Hamilton to St. Andrews, and there had him seized, tried, and burned.

By burning heretics the Scots were staking a claim to be regarded as a civilized nation. This land where crime went unpunished, where the king's authority could not be enforced, where the Church had so degenerated that it had virtually ceased to function over large areas of the country, had at least shown itself capable of dealing with the crime of heresy as it was dealt with throughout Christendom. The University of Louvain was favourably impressed and wrote a letter to the University of St. Andrews, congratulating them on the burning of Patrick Hamilton. But in one respect the proceedings against Patrick Hamilton had been extraordinary: they had been rushed through with great speed. In other countries the accused heretic was arrested, or summoned to appear before the authorities; often he came of his own free will, not under guard. He was imprisoned for several weeks, sometimes for months, and repeatedly questioned and required to dispute with eminent theologians, both before and after his public trial and excommunication, before he was eventually burned on the appointed day. In Patrick Hamilton's case, his trial, condemnation, and execution were rushed through within twelve hours on a grim Leap Year's Day in 1528. The execution was the slowest part of the business, for it was one of those terrible occasions when the fire burned slowly. Patrick Hamilton took six hours to die. The gunpowder that had been placed among the faggots, in the hope that it would shorten his sufferings, exploded, but only blew off one hand and the left side of his face, and he remained alive and conscious in the fire. The Prior of the Black Friars in St. Andrews, who had preached the sermon, approached the burning man and urged him to repent before he died. An English martyr would have replied with a quiet refusal, and died repeating some Scriptural text. Patrick Hamilton roared defiance at the Prior, declared that he was an emissary of Satan, and warned him that he would indict him before the judgement seat of Jesus Christ. This, at least, is Knox's account. Another eminent Protestant, Alexander Aless, who was present at Patrick Hamilton's execution, says that 'the martyr never gave one sign of impatience or anger, nor ever called to Heaven for vengeance upon his persecutors'. Aless was a Scot, but when he wrote this passage he had lived for many years in England and Germany. Knox's account of Patrick Hamilton's last words, if they do not show the difference between a Scottish and an English martyr, show the difference between Aless and Knox.[1]

In his *History*, Knox described the effect of Patrick Hamilton's death in a famous passage: 'When these cruel wolves had, as they supposed, clean devoured the prey, they find themselves in worse case than they were before; for then within St. Andrews, yea, almost within the whole realm (who heard of that fact), there was none found who began not to inquire: Wherefore was Master Patrick Hamilton burned?' And when they examined the heresies of which he was accused, 'many began to call in doubt that which before they held for a certain verity'.[2]

From the beginning of his personal reign, James V was eager to demonstrate his hatred of Protestantism, denouncing 'pullulent heresies' which had been brought into Scotland with foreign

[1] Lorimer, *Patrick Hamilton*, pp. 104–6, 125–6, 151, 154; the doctors of Louvain to Archbishop Beaton and the doctors of Scotland, 21 Apr. 1528 (printed in Lorimer, op. cit., pp. 238–9); Knox, *History*, i. 12–14; Pitscottie, *The Historie and Cronicles of Scotland*, i. 308–12; Foxe, *Acts and Monuments*, iv. 558–63.

[2] Knox, *History*, i. 15.

merchandise, and telling the Pope of his determination 'to banish the foul Lutheran sect' from his realm. His opposition to the 'Lutheran madness' became more marked when his uncle, Henry VIII of England, abolished the Papal authority in England.[1] Henry proposed an alliance to James, advising him to break with Rome and enrich himself by seizing the Scottish monasteries, as Henry had done in England; but James preferred to stick to the Old Alliance with France and become the Pope's champion in the British Isles. He relied chiefly on the advice of David Beaton, the nephew of Archbishop James Beaton, an able and worldly young diplomat, who soon rose to become Abbot of Arbroath and Bishop of Mirepoix in France. James then persuaded the Pope to appoint Beaton as Cardinal Legate as a reward for the energy with which he persecuted heretics, and finally appointed him to succeed his uncle as Archbishop of St. Andrews. In the seven years that followed the overthrow of Papal supremacy in England in 1533, nine heretics were burned in Scotland, and many more fled to England as refugees. Here they discovered that Henry VIII was not as Protestant as they had hoped. Nearly all of them fell foul of the authorities, and after Henry promulgated the Act of the Six Articles in 1539 and intensified his persecution of Protestants, most of them fled to Lutheran Germany, a safer land of refuge. But the ordinary Scot in Scotland thought that Henry VIII was a Protestant, and from the first, Protestantism in Scotland became associated with England and the ancient enemies, and orthodoxy in religion with Scottish patriotism.

In 1541 Henry VIII again tried to win over James, and travelled north to meet him at York. At the last moment James refused to come; Beaton and the bishops had persuaded him not to go, for they feared that he would be won over to a pro-English, anti-Papal policy. Every Scottish Protestant historian in the sixteenth century, and Knox above all, attributed all the miseries of Scotland in the next thirty years to the fact that the meeting in York did not take place, and blamed the bishops for this; and the reports of the English spies at the time prove that Knox was right in holding the bishops responsible.[2] The result was war with England, and an

[1] See, especially, James V to Clement VII, 27 Oct. 1529; James V to Ferdinand King of the Romans, 1 July 1534; James V's Instructions to George Hay, 31 July 1540; James V to Paul III, 12 Apr. 1541 (*Letters of James V*, pp. 161, 271, 405, 424).

[2] Knox, *History*, i. 30–32, 35–40; Gilby, *Admonition to England and Scotland* (in *Works*, iv. 559); Buchanan, *History of Scotland*, ii. 176–7; Pitscottie, i. 341–4; Marillac

ignominious defeat at Solway Moss, where the Scots, though outnumbering the English, fled in panic, with their general leading the way at full gallop. A few days later, James V died in despair, at the age of 30, leaving his daughter Mary Queen of Scots to succeed to the most insecure throne in Europe when she was 6 days old.

At the death of James V, James Hamilton, Earl of Arran, seized power. He became Regent for the baby Queen, with the title of Governor of Scotland, and opened negotiations with Henry VIII. Henry proposed a marriage between Mary Queen of Scots and his son, Prince Edward, insisting that Mary should be sent to the English Court. Arran agreed, and adopted a strongly pro-English policy. If Arran wished to be pro-English, the obvious thing to do was to support Protestantism in Scotland. Suddenly, in the spring of 1543, the position of the Scottish Protestants changed overnight, without any action on their part: from being a persecuted sect, they became protégés of the Governor of Scotland. Beaton was imprisoned. An Act of Parliament was passed, making it legal to read the Bible in English; and Arran gave out that anyone who prevented the reading of the Bible should be punished by death. Scottish Protestant priests and friars, who had been living in England in fear of arrest and burning under the Act of the Six Articles, returned to Scotland and preached Protestant doctrines under Arran's protection. One of them, Thomas Gwilliam, the former Prior of the Black Friars monastery at Inverness, became Arran's chaplain, as did John Rough, a Protestant monk. Gwilliam and Rough preached throughout Lothian, Fife, and Angus. They were acclaimed in Dundee, but had no success in Edinburgh; when Rough preached in St. Giles's cathedral and in the abbey of Holyroodhouse, only the presence of Arran and the Earl of Angus prevented the congregation from tearing him in pieces.[1]

One of the audience who heard Gwilliam when he preached in Lothian was John Knox. It was Gwilliam who first converted Knox to Protestantism, though Gwilliam was too moderate for Knox's liking. Knox afterwards wrote that Gwilliam was of solid judgement, a fluent speaker, and reasonably learned by the stan-

to Francis I, 12 Oct. 1541 (Kaulek, *Correspondance Politique de M.M. de Castillon et de Marillac*, p. 347); Rutland, etc., to Norfolk, 22 Sept. 1542 (*Hamilton Papers*, i. 217).

[1] *Acts Parl. Scot.* ii. 415, c. 12; Suffolk, Tunstall, Parr, and Sadler to the Council, 13 Feb. 1542/3; Lisle to Suffolk, 15 Feb. 1542/3; Sadler to Henry VIII, 20 Mar. 1543 (*Ham. Pap.* i. 418, 426, 486).

dards of 1543, and that 'his doctrine was wholesome, without great vehemency against superstition'. He found Rough, 'albeit not so learned, yet more simple, and more vehement against all impiety'.[1]

Henry VIII did not rely only on the Scottish Protestants. The powerful Douglas family had been English agents since their head, the Earl of Angus, had married Henry's sister, the widow of James IV. Angus and his brother Sir George Douglas, whose sister had been burned for high treason by James V, had lived in England for fourteen years. Many of the Scottish Border robbers raided and burned the lands of their fellow-countrymen as directed by the English government, in return for English protection and asylum in England in the event of danger. The Lord of the Isles was in English pay, and ready to ravage Argyllshire when Henry commanded. But the rising Protestant movement in Scotland was another force which Henry could utilize for his own ends; and ultimately these ideological traitors proved to be the only ones on whom Henry could rely, as none of the others remained loyal to England throughout. They were also the only English agents in Scotland who were not continually demanding increased payment in hard cash for their services, though they were ready to accept English money and rewards. When, soon after the death of James V, Sir Ralph Sadler was sent to Edinburgh as the English ambassador, one of his main objects was to encourage the growth of Protestantism in Scotland.

The English generals, at their northern headquarters at Darlington, urged Henry to send printed copies of the English Bible to Scotland.[2] This put Henry in a dilemma. He had always considered that the Bible in the vernacular was a subversive influence; for in England, as elsewhere, it had led to endless theological argument not only between priests and scholars but between merchants, artisans, and husbandmen, which was intolerable to a despotic ruler who expected his subjects to be obedient and to show complete uniformity in religion. The people began to quote biblical texts against the established doctrines of the Church and, instead of accepting the latest royal proclamation as the final authority on matters of religious doctrine, found it in the words of the Bible, as interpreted by themselves or by some Protestant preacher.

[1] Calderwood, i. 155–6; Knox, *History*, i. 42.

[2] *Reg. P.C.S.* i. 4 (20 June 1545); Promise by Commissioners of Donald, Lord of the Isles (4 Sept. 1545) (*State Papers of Henry VIII*, v. 504–6).

Carlyle thought that this portrait, which was painted for Lord Somerville about 1760 from an earlier engraving, was the genuine picture of Knox; but it is obviously a portrait of a seventeenth-century personage (see Drummond, 'Notes upon some Scottish Historical Portraits—John Knox and George Buchanan' (*Proceedings of the Society of Antiquaries of Scotland*, xi. 237–64); but see also Borgeaud, 'Le "vrai portrait" de John Knox' (*Bulletin de la Société de l'Histoire du Protestantisme français*, lxxxiv. 11–36)). Apart from the seventeenth-century costume, the features differ in almost every particular from Sir Peter Young's description of Knox (see supra, p. 25)

Henry was eager to send English Bibles to Scotland in order to subvert the nation, but his hatred and fear of Protestant extremism made him reluctant to encourage heresy anywhere. He decided to send the Bibles, but warned Arran of the dangers of Bible-reading and urged him to prohibit anyone in Scotland from arguing as to the meaning of biblical texts. At the same time, in May 1543, he directed his Parliament, in his own realm, to pass an Act which forbade any man below the rank of gentleman and any woman even to read the Bible, on pain of death by hanging. He told Arran that he intended shortly to issue a new formulary of faith—which soon became known as the King's Book—and that as soon as this was available, he would send it to Scotland. It would then no longer be necessary for the Scots to read the Bible. But Scottish Protestantism was not to be confined within the limits imposed by the King's Book.[1]

On 31 August 1543 a crowd in Dundee attacked the friaries, destroying the images and looting the valuables. Individual acts of destruction of images had been a common form of Protestant protest, in England and Scotland and elsewhere: but a violent mass demonstration of this kind was something new in Britain. Within a few days, the monasteries in Angus and Fife had been stormed. Arran sent a company to do the same in Edinburgh, but here there was still strong popular support for the established Church, and the whole town, both men and women, assembled at the ringing of the common bell to protect the friaries and drive off the attackers. The indignant people believed that the attack had been organized by the English ambassador, Sadler, and the fury of the people rose against England and the Governor. Sadler reported that it was universally rumoured that Arran was a heretic and a good Englishman who had sold the realm to Henry. Sir George Douglas warned his English paymasters that if Henry marched against Scotland, 'there is not so little a boy but he will throw stones against it, the wives will come out with their distaffs, and the commons universally will rather die in it, yea, and many noblemen and all the clergy fully against it'. Copies of the English Bible were burnt in the streets of Edinburgh. Suddenly, after several months of quarrels and intrigues, Arran joined with Beaton and

[1] Suffolk, Tunstall, Parr, and Sadler to the Council, 27 Feb. 1543; Henry VIII to Sadler, 4 Apr. 1543 (*Ham. Pap.* i. 445, 499); *Statutes of the Realm*, 34 & 35 Hen. VIII, c. 1.

the Queen Dowager, Mary of Lorraine, and reversed his policy and defied Henry. He repudiated the marriage contract between Mary and Prince Edward, and expelled Sadler. Angus and Sir George Douglas were arrested, but pardoned and rewarded for their former treason with a pension of £1,000 each, in return for their agreeing to fight for their country and cease being English spies. Arran abandoned his pro-Protestant policy, and Protestants were once more persecuted.[1]

In the spring of 1544 Knox and the inhabitants of East Lothian experienced war as it was waged by the old enemies against the almost defenceless Scots. Henry VIII sent an army to Leith under the command of Edward Seymour, Earl of Hertford, the future Protector Somerset, with instructions to burn Edinburgh. Hertford told Henry that on military grounds it would be much more useful to fortify Leith than to burn Edinburgh: but Henry's aim was to terrorize the population and shatter Scottish morale. Arran and Cardinal Beaton assembled an army, but withdrew, leaving Edinburgh defenceless; and Hertford burned every house in Edinburgh, including the abbey and palace of Holyroodhouse, leaving nothing standing except the castle and St. Giles's Cathedral. Then the army marched home to Berwick by land, destroying everything on the way. 'We left neither pile, village, town nor house in our way homewards unburned', an English soldier wrote. On 17 May they reached Haddington, and the same soldier recorded: 'We burned a fair town of the Earl Bothwell's called Haddington, with a great nunnery and a house of friars.' The people of Haddington were more fortunate than their neighbours at Dunbar, where the English postponed setting fire to the town in order to trap the inhabitants. 'Having watched all night for our coming and perceiving our army to dislodge and depart,' wrote the English soldier, 'they thought themselves safe of us, were newly gone to their beds; and in their first sleeps closed in with fire; men, women and children were suffocated and burned.'[2]

[1] Sadler to Suffolk and Tunstall, 4 and 5 Sept. 1543; Sadler to Suffolk, Parr, and Tunstall, 9 June 1543; Sadler to Henry VIII, 20 Mar. 1542/3 (*Ham. Pap.* i. 477; ii. 15, 20–21; *Sadler Pap.* i. 216); La Brosse's Report (24 Nov. 1543) (*Two Missions of Jacques de la Brosse*, p. 20); Grimani to (Cardinal Farnese), 30 Nov. 1543 (*S.H.R.* xi. 21); the Agreement of Greenside, 13 Jan. 1543/4 (*State Pap.* v. 355–7); *Reg. of Privy Seal of Scotland*, iii. 987, 988 (7 Dec. 1544); Sir George Douglas to Mary of Lorraine, 28 Sept. (1544) (*Scottish Correspondence of Mary of Lorraine*, p. 108).

[2] The Council to Hertford, 10 and 17 Apr. 1544; Hertford, Lisle, and Sadler to Henry VIII, 6, 9, 15, and 18 May 1544 (*Ham. Pap.* ii. 325–6, 338–41, 361–9, 371–5,

These atrocities were being committed by the ancient enemies in the name of Protestantism. Every action of the English leaders was calculated to make the Scottish people associate the doctrines of Luther with the dreaded red cross of St. George which the English wore on their white uniforms. Whenever Hertford burned a town or village, he left a leaflet fixed to the church door telling the people that they had their cardinal to thank for this, as Beaton was responsible for carrying on the war. The English commanders knew how to hit the Scots where it hurt most. The Scots could rebuild their wretched houses quite easily, and had come to accept the burning of their homes by the English as one of the facts of life: but by burning every boat on the east coast of Scotland the English could deprive the Scots of their fish. As the Scots did not submit, the terror raids were resumed in the autumn in the Border areas. The English waited until the autumn, after the Scots had gathered in their crops, so that they could burn the barns where the bere was stored. Between November 1544 and September 1545 the English army raided Scotland two or three nights every week, determined to 'keep the Scots waking', and to burn and starve them into submission. Only the Scottish rain saved the Scots; occasionally it was so wet that the English could not burn a Scottish town.[1]

This policy of terrorism was not unsuccessful. It broke the will to resist of large sections of the Scottish people, as they saw their houses and their winter store of food burnt night after night, without any attempt by their leaders either to organize resistance or to negotiate for peace. In the attack on Jedburgh, the Scots lost 160 men killed, and the English lost 6. At Skraysburgh the figures were even more ominous: 3 Scots were killed and 38 taken prisoner without any Englishman being killed or even wounded. The Scots became convinced that every one of their leaders was in English pay: it was said that every decision taken at meetings

379–80); Hertford to Henry VIII, 12 Apr. 1544 (*State Pap.* v. 371–3); *The late expedicion in Scotlande made by the Kynges Hyhnes Armye*, pp. 9–10 (in Dalyell, *Fragments of Scottish History*).

[1] Paget to Hertford, 11 Mar. 1543/4; List of English raids in Scotland, 2 July–17 Nov. 1544, 8–23 Sept. 1545, and 12 June 1544–4 July 1546 (Haynes, *A Collection of State Papers*, pp. 22, 43, 52–54; *L.P.* xxi [i]. 1279); Wharton to Suffolk, 8 Dec. 1543; Hertford to Henry VIII, 21 Mar. 1544; Shrewsbury, Tunstall, and Sadler to Queen Katherine Parr and the Council, 17 and 23 Aug. 1544 (*Ham. Pap.* ii. 213, 311, 446–8); Chapuys to Mary of Hungary, 31 May 1544 (*Span. Cal.* vii. 113; *L.P.* xix [i]. 603); Hertford, Sadler, Bowes, etc., to Henry VIII, 18 Sept. 1545 (*State Pap.* v. 523).

of the Scottish Privy Council was known in Berwick within twenty-four hours, and three days later the news had been carried to the King of England in London. More and more Scots were prepared to take 'assurance' from England. These collaborators, known as 'assured Scots', took an oath to Henry VIII as overlord of Scotland, promised to spread the Word of God—that is to say, Protestant doctrines—in their district, and undertook to burn the lands of any Scot when ordered to do so by Henry; in return they were protected by the English from the vengeance of patriotic Scots, and except when unfortunate mistakes were made, their property was not destroyed in the English raids. Most of the gentlemen in the Merse and Lothian 'assured'. The surest sign of defeatism was that the people directed their hate, not against the old enemies, but against their own leaders. When Edinburgh was burning, the English generals heard the women of the town, watching the destruction of their homes from the hill outside the town, cursing Beaton and blaming him for their sufferings, crying out 'Woe worth the Cardinal!'[1]

The Scottish Protestant movement thrived on the defeatist mood. The devastation wrought by the English did not destroy the trust of the Scottish Protestants in Henry VIII as a liberator, despite the fact that they would have had a much bigger chance of being burnt as heretics by Henry in England than by Beaton and Arran in Scotland. John Elder, a Scottish Protestant, wrote to Henry, telling him that he had just cause to invade Scotland, and urged him to suppress the Scottish bishops, priests, and monks, to 'hunt, drive and smoke the foresaid Papistical foxes . . . out of their caves'. When Knox wrote his *History* in 1566, and described these events of twenty years before, he wrote approvingly of King Harry and interpreted every event from the English point of view.[2]

It was in December 1545 that Knox took the first step on the road which led him to his historical destiny. The instrument of

[1] List of English raids in Scotland (June 1544); Draft Articles of Contract between Henry VIII's Commissioners and Lennox (June 1544) (*L.P.* xix [i]. 762(2), 779(6)); *The Complaynt of Scotlande*, p. 109; Henry VIII's Instructions to Wharton and Bowes, (15 Apr. 1544) (*State Pap.* v. 386–7); Maitland, *Narrative of the Principal Acts of the Regency*, p. 2; Hertford, Lisle, and Sadler to Henry VIII, 9 May 1544 (*Ham. Pap.* ii. 369); Somerset to Luttrell, 21 Jan. 1547/8 (*Scottish Correspondence of Mary of Lorraine*, p. 215).

[2] John Elder to Henry VIII (1543?) (*Bannatyne Misc.* i. 17); Knox, *History*, i. 30–58.

the change was George Wishart. Wishart was almost exactly the same age as Knox, but had led a far more eventful life. He came from a gentleman's family in Montrose. After studying at St. Andrews and Louvain, he fled to England to escape prosecution for heresy; but there he ran into further trouble. As a result of a sermon which he preached at Bristol, he was denounced as a heretic and examined by Cromwell and Cranmer and a commission of bishops on a charge of heresy. He recanted and carried his faggot, and thus, like so many English martyrs, began his career with a recantation under Henry VIII before suffering martyrdom under a more wholeheartedly Papist ruler. When he returned to Scotland with the other refugees in 1543, he began preaching at his home town of Montrose, and then went to Dundee and Kyle, the two great Protestant centres in Scotland, taking possession of the parish churches and preaching from the pulpit to packed congregations or, if his entry to the church was barred by the authorities, addressing enormous crowds at open-air rallies in the fields nearby. The reformers in Scotland succeeded in doing what the English reformers never attempted: they built up an organized Protestant party, supported by at least one great nobleman, the Earl of Cassillis, and several lairds who were influential in their localities, by the merchants of Dundee, and by the little fishing ports of Ayrshire, and keeping in close organizational contact with members of the party in other parts of Scotland. The gentle, peace-loving Wishart, who hated bloodshed, was their mouthpiece; behind him were the tougher men, the lairds who organized the movement, who were always ready to use violence if Wishart had not restrained them, and were secretly in touch with the old enemies. Several of them were receiving English money, and had told Henry VIII that they were ready to assassinate Cardinal Beaton.[1]

[1] For Wishart, see Durkan, 'George Wishart: his early life' (*S.H.R.* xxxii. 98–99); Rogers, 'Memoir of George Wishart, the Scottish Martyr' (*Trans. R.H.S.* iv. 260–363); Ricart, *The Maire of Bristowe is Kalendar*, p. 55; Jeffries, Mayor of Bristol, to Cromwell, 9 June 1539 (*L.P.* xiv [i]. 1095); Knox, *History*, i. 60–65; Foxe, v. 625–36. Rogers (op. cit., p. 305) and Andrew Lang (*John Knox and the Reformation*, p. 20) believed that this passage in Foxe's book was written by Knox; but this appears unlikely, on stylistic grounds. For the plan to assassinate Beaton, in which a man named Wishart was involved, see Hertford, Tunstall, Holgate, and Sadler to Henry VIII, 17 Apr. 1544; the Council to Hertford, 26 Apr. 1544 and 30 May 1545; Hertford, Tunstall, and Sadler to Paget, 12 July 1545; Sadler to Brunstane, 12 July 1545 (*State Pap.* v. 377–8, 449–50, 470–2 and n.; Haynes, p. 32); but on grounds of character, it seems unlikely that the Wishart involved in this plot was George

Knox first met Wishart at a time when things were going badly for the Protestant party. Beaton had struck back and had hanged and drowned five Protestants in 1544 for insulting the Virgin and images of saints and for eating goose on a fast day, though he had been unable to arrest Wishart in Dundee or Kyle, and his two attempts to have him murdered had failed. The English, over-confident after their easy victories, had allowed themselves to be trapped and defeated by the Scots on Ancrum Moor; a small detachment of French troops had landed at Dumbarton to revive Scottish morale; while the Emperor Charles V's separate peace with France had thrown the English on to the defensive and forced them to concentrate all their efforts on preventing a French invasion of England. These events had dampened the Anglophile and Protestant enthusiasm of many of the Scottish nobles. By the autumn of 1545 the Protestant leaders had told Wishart to discontinue his public preaching and move about from place to place to avoid capture; but he decided to visit Lothian, where he had not yet preached, and rouse the people there, as he had done in Dundee and Kyle. When he arrived at Leith, he found that his most powerful supporters had deserted him: Cassillis and the lairds of Ayrshire failed to meet him as they had arranged. The lairds of Lothian, including Sir Hugh Douglas of Longniddry, whose sons were being taught by Knox, remained loyal. In the second week of December 1545 Knox went with Longniddry and the other members of his household to meet Wishart at Leith. The lairds of Brunstane and Ormiston also came with their servants, as did a number of other lairds.[1]

Although it was at the command of his employer that Knox came to Leith and first played an active part in the Protestant movement, he obviously complied willingly with Longniddry's instructions, for he had been a Protestant supporter since he had heard Gwilliam preach two years before. He acquired a great admiration for Wishart. In his *History* he described him as 'that blessed martyr of God, Master George Wishart, a man of such graces as before him were never heard within this realm, yea, and are rare to be found yet in any man, notwithstanding this great light of God that since his days has shined unto us'. Like all his

Wishart. As to this, see Rogers, op. cit., pp. 307–15. For the contrary view, see e.g., Durkan, in *Innes Rev.* i. 158–61.

[1] Knox, *History*, i. 55, 63–65, 67.

companions, he was deeply impressed by the tall young preacher, with his close-cropped hair and long black beard, his gentleness of manner, his abstemious way of life, his neat but sombre dress, and his surprising habit of washing himself in a bath-tub every night.[1]

The lairds tried to persuade Wishart to lie low and not preach; but he refused. 'I lurk as a man that were ashamed,' he said, 'and durst not show himself before men'; and he told them that he would dare to preach if they would dare to hear, though he prophesied that he would soon be captured and burnt. The lairds then decided to stay with Wishart, with all their household servants, to give him as much protection as possible against his enemies, and also against the local inhabitants, because the Scots regarded strangers with great suspicion. The people were under a legal duty to drive away any trespasser or wolf, and anyone entering a town or village where he was not known was liable to be driven off, or ducked in the local pond. Nothing like this would happen to Wishart if he was escorted by the local lairds and their men. For the next five weeks Longniddry's boys did not receive much tuition, for Knox, with the other members of Longniddry's household, was in constant attendance on Wishart. Brunstane and Ormiston and their men were also always there, though the other lairds took it in turns to join the group.[2]

On the first Sunday, 13 December, Wishart preached in Leith. Directly the sermon was over, the lairds persuaded Wishart to leave the town, because Arran and Beaton were expected to arrive in Edinburgh from Linlithgow in a few days' time, and they were sure that Wishart would not be safe in Leith. They decided that Wishart should stay with them in their own houses, moving from one to the other to avoid the likelihood of arrest. Wishart usually slept at either Longniddry, Ormiston, or Brunstane, but sometimes at the houses of other lairds. As they moved around the windswept countryside of East Lothian near the sea during the short winter days, the group carried arms. Knox sometimes carried a two-handed sword in Wishart's party. The two-handed sword was the traditional weapon of the Scots: even nobles fought with it in battle. As Knox was a priest, it was

[1] Ibid. 60; Foxe, v. 626.

[2] Knox, *History*, i. 65–66; *Reg. of P.C.S.* i. xxii–xxiii (5 Feb. 1497/8); Hume Brown, *Scotland in the time of Queen Mary*, p. 65.

improper, according to the canon law, for him to carry arms; but in Scotland nearly all the priests carried arms, having at least a whinger for self-protection. This was the least of the offences which Knox was committing by joining the group escorting Wishart.[1]

There is something symbolic in the first appearance on the page of history of the leading figures of the Reformation. Calvin first appears at his writing-desk, already writing a learned tome at the age of 23. Cranmer is first seen burrowing in the Bible to find scriptural texts to justify his king in divorcing his wife and marrying his mistress. Luther's first appearance was more vigorous, nailing his theses to the door of the church in Wittenberg, striking at the old Church with every blow of the hammer. But Knox is the only one who enters carrying a two-handed sword. It is also symbolical that Knox does not enter alone, but with a group, as a member of an organized body, somewhat loose and vague in its doctrine, but efficient in its organization, and ruthless and resolute. It was through armed organization that Knox was to fulfil his mission.

On the second Sunday, 20 December, Wishart preached in the church at Inveresk, near Musselburgh, to a large congregation which included Sir George Douglas, the Earl of Angus's brother. After the sermon he openly declared his support for Wishart, and offered to ensure his personal safety. But Douglas could not be trusted; he had several times betrayed both the English and Scottish governments, to both of whom he had sworn allegiance, and he was not there when, within a month of his reassuring words, Wishart needed the protection which he had promised. On the next two Sundays Wishart preached at Tranent, again to a large congregation.[2] In no other country in Christendom in 1545 could a band of some thirty to fifty heretics, carrying arms, have marched openly around the country, within fifteen miles of the capital city, entering churches without authority and preaching to large crowds for four successive weeks, without any interference from the government.

[1] Knox, *History*, i. 66, 69. For priests carrying arms, see Synodal Statutes of St. Andrews (fourteenth century) (*Statutes of the Scottish Church*, p. 70); and see D. McKay, 'Parish Life in Scotland' (*Essays on the Scottish Reformation*, pp. 96–97); and John Major, *In Quantum*, Dist. xv, q. xx, f. cxx C (cited in J. H. Burns, 'The Scotland of John Major' (*Innes Rev*. ii. 74)).

[2] Knox, *History*, i. 66–67.

The churchgoers of Inveresk and Tranent who listened to the itinerant preacher who had occupied their church with his followers must have found the proceedings strange. Instead of the usual Latin service of the mass, they heard a lengthy and fiery sermon. Wishart sometimes celebrated communion, but it was the sermon, a thing almost unknown in the established Church, which was the essential feature of the Protestant proceedings. Wishart usually preached for at least an hour, and sometimes more. He probably did not hold very precise theological doctrines. During his exile from Scotland he had been for a short time with the Lutherans in Germany, but he had also translated the Helvetic Confession of the Zwinglians of Basel.[1] He denounced ceremonies, prayers to the saints, and veneration of images in his sermons, and advocated the marriage of the clergy, but concentrated chiefly on general denunciations of the sins of society and the Church, with much citing of Scripture, and a warning of evils and punishments to come.

Another strange feature of Wishart's services was the singing of songs by his congregation. Music formed an important feature of the Catholic service of the mass, but that was the peculiar Church music, the later Medieval Church polyphony with its complicated parts, which was very different from the songs of the Scottish people and could only be sung by trained singers. The Protestants substituted singing by the people in simple tunes and in popular music. When Wishart preached in Lothian, the congregation heard, perhaps for the first time, *The Good and Godly Ballads* sung by the men who escorted Wishart and anyone else in the audience who knew the words, for they all knew the tunes. *The Good and Godly Ballads* had been written and printed by the Wedderburn brothers in Dundee about a year before. Some of the songs were metrical versions of the Psalms; others were translations of German Lutheran hymns; and others were new versions of popular songs, which were slightly adapted to give them a religious meaning instead of the coarse ditties of the original version, and were sung to the same tune.[2]

[1] Leslie, *History of Scotland*, ii. 290: Wishart's translation of the Helvetic Confession of February 1536 was printed under the title *The Confession of the Faith of the Switzerlands*, probably in London in 1548, and reprinted in 1844 (*Wodrow Misc.* i. 7–23).

[2] See M. Patrick, *Four Centuries of Scottish Psalmody*, pp. xv, 3, 5–6. For the Wedderburns, and the history of *The Good and Godly Ballads*, see A. F. Mitchell's Introduction to the Scottish Text Society's edition of *The Good and Godly Ballads*, pp. xvi–xl.

On Sunday, 10 January the group for the first time entered the town of Haddington.[1] Here they met with a set-back: unlike all the other places where Wishart had preached in Lothian, the attendance at the morning service was disappointing. At the afternoon service it was worse, for there were only about a hundred people in the great church, which was one of the largest in Scotland. Wishart had expected that he would draw bigger crowds in Haddington than anywhere else in Lothian, with people coming from the town and the surrounding countryside; for he knew that an audience of several thousands sometimes assembled in Haddington church to watch a morality play. He was sure that Patrick Hepburn, Earl of Bothwell, forewarned of their coming, had advised the citizens of his town of Haddington to stay away from the church on pain of his displeasure. Next day, on the Monday, Wishart preached again in the church at Haddington, but the attendance was equally poor. The party slept the night at Lethington, where old Sir Richard Maitland, the laird of Lethington, received them with his usual courtesy, though he was not one of their supporters. He was a charming and cultured gentleman, a good poet, who held aloof from personal feuds and religious strife, and concentrated on maintaining his personal integrity amid increasingly deteriorating moral standards, refusing to take assurance from England, though he held lands within a few miles of the frontier,[2] and lamenting the barbarities of the civil wars which he witnessed during the last thirty years of his ninety years of life. Knox wrote that Wishart 'lay in Lethington, the laird whereof was ever civil, albeit not persuaded in religion'.[3] As this is the only known occasion on which Knox wrote a friendly word about a Papist, he was obviously not immune to old Lethington's charm.

Wishart returned to Haddington next day, to deliver his fourth sermon in three days in the parish church. Just before his sermon he received a letter from his supporters among the Ayrshire lairds, who again refused to travel to Lothian to meet him. This threw Wishart into one of his fits of depression, and he told Knox that he wearied of the world, as he perceived that men began to weary

[1] For Wishart's experiences at Haddington and Lethington, and his arrest at Ormiston, see Knox, *History*, i. 67–71.

[2] Maitland, *Narrative of the Principal Acts of the Regency*, p. 2.

[3] Knox, *History*, i. 67.

of God. The attendance at the church was as bad as ever. In his sermon Wishart condemned the low attendance and prophesied that disaster and strife would overtake the town. Knox and the Protestants, who expected their leaders to have the gift of prophecy, afterwards interpreted Wishart's utterances as prophesying the battles of 1548 and 1549, when Haddington was in the front line of the war between England and France; but probably many pessimistic persons in the district in 1546 were prophesying that strangers would possess Haddington and that the inhabitants would be chased from their own habitations, for this had occurred at Haddington and many other towns in southern Scotland during the previous two years. Wishart also prophesied, as he had done in all his other sermons in Lothian, that he would soon be captured and burnt. This had also been foreseen by many others, including the lairds who were now hastily abandoning Wishart.

The next to go was Douglas of Longniddry. After the sermon he said goodbye to Wishart and withdrew with his household. Ormiston, Brunstane, and Sandilands of Calder, with their servants, continued to stay with Wishart. It is not clear why Longniddry left Wishart at this stage. Knox, in his account, does not criticize him for doing so, but suggests that Wishart took a fond and last farewell of all his followers, having decided to go alone to his death. In that case, it is not clear why the other lairds remained with Wishart. Perhaps Longniddry, after a month of constant attendance on Wishart, had in any case decided that he must leave him for the time being, and was fortunate to get out with a few hours to spare.

Knox did not wish to leave Wishart. In his *History* he described their last parting outside the town of Haddington on a bitterly cold afternoon on Tuesday, 12 January 1546, referring to himself, as he does throughout the book, in the third person. He urged Wishart to let him stay, but Wishart said: '" Nay, return to your bairns, and God bless you. One is sufficient for a sacrifice." And so he caused a two-handed sword (which commonly was carried with the said Master George [Wishart]) be taken from the said John Knox, who, albeit unwillingly, obeyed, and returned with Hugh Douglas of Longniddry.'[1] Knox must have left Wishart with mixed feelings. He was not the type of man who was eager to be a martyr: this prospect did not appeal to his aggressive

[1] Ibid. 69.

personality. Eager for living, and longing to strike a blow another day, he would unconsciously have welcomed an excuse to avoid martyrdom. But he had been deeply impressed by Wishart, and did not wish to leave the little group with whom he had spent these five stirring weeks after thirty years of pointless existence. He therefore offered to leave his employer, and risk all, to stay with Wishart and defend him to the end with a two-handed sword. When Wishart told him that a sacrifice was not required of him and ordered him to return to Longniddry, he did not persist. With the rest of Douglas's household, he walked back to Longniddry, leading his horse by the bridle, for it was unsafe to undertake the five mile journey on horseback because of the heavy frost.

Wishart and the rest of the party went to Ormiston for the night. At midnight, Bothwell surrounded the house. The three lairds and their servants could have put up a determined resistance, but Bothwell told them that Beaton and his soldiers were at Elphinstone Tower, less than a mile away, and Wishart agreed to surrender after Bothwell had given his word that he would not hand them over to Beaton. Bothwell broke his promise, and took them to Beaton at Elphinstone. Brunstane escaped into the woods before they reached Elphinstone, and gained the shelter of Angus's castle at Tantallon. Wishart, Ormiston, and Calder were imprisoned in Edinburgh Castle. Calder gained his freedom by making over his man-rents to Beaton. Ormiston escaped over the Castle wall in broad daylight. Wishart was taken to St. Andrews, condemned as a heretic, and strangled and burnt.

Longniddry's decision to leave Wishart saved Knox's life. The lairds' servants who were at Ormiston when Wishart was seized were apparently allowed to go free; but Knox would not have escaped so easily. Being a priest, his offence would have been considered much more serious. He would have been taken to St. Andrews with Wishart and charged with heresy. Only a recantation could have saved him; and Knox would not have recanted if he had been together with Wishart. If Knox had stayed with Wishart some nine hours longer, he would have been burnt as a heretic in 1546.

CHAPTER IV

The Castle of St. Andrews

THE Protestants at first hoped that Wishart's life would be spared. They thought that Arran would hold him as a hostage. This would serve a double purpose: Arran could threaten to burn Wishart if the Protestants caused further trouble, and to release him if the Catholics displeased him in any way. Knox said that 'the godly' expected Arran to do this, and were surprised at the 'foolishness of the Governor' in not doing so. 'But where God is left,' wrote Knox, 'what can counsel or judgement avail?'[1] This comment is revealing of the attitude of the Scottish Protestants: God's punishment of Arran took the form of depriving him of the ability to think of this clever idea. It would not have occurred to anyone in England that martyrdom might be avoided in this way.

But English and Scottish Protestants reacted very differently to persecution. In England Gardiner, Bonner, Cranmer, and the other bishops who had sentenced many Protestant martyrs to the fire were in no danger of assassination; but in Scotland Beaton was to meet with a bloody retribution for his merciless enforcement of the law. Knox writes that 'men of great birth, estimation and honour, at open tables avowed, that the blood of the said Master George should be revenged, or else they should cast life for life. Amongst whom John Leslie, brother to the Earl of Rothes, was the chief; for he, in all companies, spared not to say, "That same whinger (showing forth his dagger) and that same hand, should be priests to the Cardinal".'[2]

On 29 May 1546 a party of sixteen young gentlemen, led by John Leslie's brother Norman, and including William Kirkcaldy of Grange, the son of the former Lord Treasurer of Scotland, broke into St. Andrews Castle, after killing the sentry at the gate, and stabbed Beaton to death in the presence of his terrified page. After insulting his corpse and urinating in the dead man's mouth,

[1] Knox, *History*, i. 72. [2] Ibid. 74.

they hung the body over the castle wall for the inhabitants of St. Andrews to see. They then proceeded to hold the castle against Arran and the government. They were able to take advantage of all the fortification work which Beaton had been carrying out during the previous three years, and they found that the castle was equipped with cannon. They also found Arran's son in the castle. He had been living there with Beaton, officially to receive tuition and guidance from the cardinal, but in fact as Beaton's hostage to ensure the friendship of Arran. He now remained in the castle as the hostage of Beaton's murderers.[1]

The murder of a cardinal was a horrible crime by all the canons of the Church, and as Beaton was Chancellor of Scotland and the leader of national resistance in time of war, it was also a flagrant challenge to the authority of the State. The coolness with which his murder was received shows the state of affairs that had been reached in Scotland and Christendom. It caused much less indignation among contemporaries than among historians three hundred years later. Knox wrote that Beaton's death 'was dolorous to the priests, dolorous to the Governor, most dolorous to the Queen Dowager', as Beaton had been 'the comfort to all gentlewomen, and especially to wanton widows'—this being a reference to Mary of Lorraine, who was widely believed to have been Beaton's mistress. The Parliament of Scotland condemned the 'cruel and treasonable slaughter' of the cardinal, but the Protestants rejoiced that within three months of Wishart's execution his butcher had been struck down by the vengeance of God.[2]

Abroad, the murder of Beaton was treated with complete cynicism. Henry VIII, who had tacitly encouraged the murderers without getting directly involved, did not hide his delight, and his ally Charles V, the temporal head of Christendom and the leading champion in Europe of the Catholic Church, was almost

[1] For the murder of Beaton, see Knox, *History*, i. 76–78; *Diurnal of Occurrents*, p. 42; Pitscottie, ii. 83–84; Leslie, *History*, ii. 290–2; Lord Herries, p. 16; (David Maitland) to Wharton, 30 May 1546 (*State Pap.* v. 561 n.). The number of the murderers of Beaton differs in all these accounts, ranging from 18 (*Diurnal of Occurrents*) to 9 (Leslie). The most reliable authority on this point is perhaps Knox, who gives the number as 16; for though Knox is often inaccurate, he knew all the murderers personally. The Scottish Parliament attainted 34 persons as being guilty of Beaton's murder (*Acts Parl. Scot.* ii. 479 (14 Aug. 1546)); but these cannot all have been present at the actual killing. For Beaton's fortifications at St. Andrews, see *Rentale Sancti Andree*, pp. 176, 194–5, 199, 222–4; Knox, *History*, i. 59.

[2] Knox, *History*, i. 79; *Acts Parl. Scot.* ii. 479 (14 Aug. 1546).

as unashamed in his pleasure at the blow that the French had suffered through Beaton's death. The English ambassador, Thirlby, the Bishop of Westminster, wrote from Charles's Court at Ratisbon to Paget, the Secretary of State: 'I had almost forgotten to tell my gladness of your tidings of the Cardinal of Scotland. It is half a wonder here that you dare be so bold as to kill a cardinal.' When Charles's daughter, Mary of Hungary, the Regent of the Netherlands, who was as devout a Catholic as her father, was informed of the murder by the English ambassador in Brussels, she commented casually that the English 'were despatched of a great enemy'. The French government accepted it unemotionally as a diplomatic defeat, while even the Pope's denunciation of the crime seems to be lacking in heat and little more than a formal protest.[1]

Knox has often been denounced by his critics for his attitude to the death of Beaton. He has been held morally responsible for the killing because of his subsequent association with the murderers and the joy and gusto with which he described the murder in his *History*.

> How miserably lay David Beaton, careful Cardinal! And so they departed, without *Requiem aeternam* and *Requiescat in pace* sung for his soul. Now, because the weather was hot (for it was in May, as we have heard), and his funeral could not suddenly be prepared, it was thought best, to keep him from stinking, to give him great salt enough, a cope of lead, and a nook in the bottom of the Sea Tower (a place where many of God's children had been imprisoned before) to await what exequies his brethren the bishops would prepare for him. These things we write merrily.

His more sober comment on the murder was: 'These are the works of God, whereby He would admonish the tyrants of this earth, that in the end He will be revenged of their cruelty, what strength so ever they made in the contrary.' This was probably Knox's opinion at the time, when he was twenty years younger and a less embittered man than he was in 1566 when he wrote his *History*; but at least in 1546 he did not think that murder was a matter to be taken lightly. Two years later Knox told Kirkcaldy of Grange and his companions that they would only be justified in

[1] Thirlby to Paget, 15 June 1546 (*State Pap.* xi. 219); Carne to Paget, 10 June 1546; St. Mauris to Prince Philip of Spain, 4 July 1546 (*L.P.* xxi [i]. 1038, 1214; *Span. Cal.* viii. 289).

escaping from prison in France if they could do so without killing an innocent soldier who was guarding them as his duty required; and he must have carefully considered how far the murderers of the cardinal were justified by the tenets laid down in Scripture and by Protestant doctrines. Knox, unlike Henry VIII's bishops and Mary of Hungary, would have been deeply concerned with the moral aspect of Beaton's murder.[1]

The murder was not an isolated act, but incidental to an attempted *coup d'état*. Both politically and morally it should be compared, not to a murder in twentieth-century Britain, but to the assassination of the ruler of a state in the Middle East in the course of a revolution organized by a band of officers. The death of Beaton was less important than the fact that the murderers held the castle of St. Andrews, 'a castle', as Arran told the Pope, 'scarcely four hours' sail from England'.[2] Arran and Mary of Lorraine denounced Norman Leslie and his comrades not for murder but for high treason. The situation was particularly serious for the Scottish government because six days after Beaton's death the French commissioners at Camp near Calais at last agreed to the English peace terms, after many months of negotiations in which Scotland was one of the main points at issue, though no Scottish representative was allowed to take part. Francis I in effect abandoned the Scots to the mercy of Henry VIII, and made a separate peace with England.

In this very critical situation Arran and his government were almost inactive; he was perhaps restrained by the knowledge that Norman Leslie held his son as a hostage in the castle. It was not until the end of August that Arran had assembled an army and marched to St. Andrews. He then waited before the castle for nearly three months while he unsuccessfully tried to lay a mine, and quarrelled with the Lords of the Council as to who should pay for the operation. At the end of November operations began, the Governor and the Castilians, as the defenders of the castle were called, exchanging artillery fire for a few hours every day for a fortnight. Henry VIII sent a ship to St. Andrews with supplies for revictualling the castle; but just before Christmas the Castilians agreed to accept the armistice which Arran offered them. Arran

[1] Knox, *History*, i. 78–79, 109.

[2] Arran to Paul III and the Cardinals, 1 Sept. 1546 (Theiner, *Vetera monumenta Hibernorum et Scotorum historiam illustrantia*, p. 618; *L.P.* xxi [ii]. 6).

agreed to pardon them and restore them to all their lands and offices which had been forfeited; the Castilians agreed not to deliver the castle to Henry VIII, but refused to surrender it to Arran until they had received absolution from the Pope for the murder of the cardinal. Until the absolution arrived from Rome, the Castilians would continue to hold the castle, with full liberty to come and go from the castle and to revictual it by land or sea. The Castilians then wrote to Henry VIII and urged him to try, by secret means, to influence the Pope to refuse to grant absolution, so that they could continue to hold the castle. French diplomacy, on the other hand, exerted its influence to persuade the Pope to grant the absolution as quickly as possible.[1] The little castle of St. Andrews was an English bridge-head in Scotland, less than 60 yards in diameter, but of vital importance in international politics.

Meanwhile John Knox, after the five weeks with Wishart, had gone back to the humdrum daily life of a boys' tutor, and was once again a passive spectator of great events. While Wishart was burnt and Beaton murdered, Knox taught the rudiments of Latin, French, and divinity to his pupils. In addition to Longniddry's two sons he now had a third pupil, Alexander Cockburn, the eldest son of the laird of Ormiston, who had met Knox when they were escorting Wishart. But the officials of the diocese of St. Andrews had heard of Knox's association with Wishart. They knew that there was a heretical priest at Longniddry in the diocese. They did not make any determined effort to catch Knox, for the Scottish Church always persecuted spasmodically and incompetently, and Beaton's murder disrupted the administration of the diocese of St. Andrews for several months; but Knox took the precaution of moving from place to place, which was usually an effective method in Scotland of avoiding arrest. By residing in turn at the houses of the various Protestant lairds in the district, he reduced the chances of being captured in any surprise raid which the diocesan officers or Bothwell's men might make in

[1] Arran to Paul III and the Cardinals, 1 Sept. 1546; Stewart of Cardonald to Bishop, 11 Jan. 1547; Dandino to Cardinal Farnese, 20 Jan. 1547 (Theiner, p. 618; *L.P.* xxi [ii]. 6, 695, 727); *Reg. P.C.S.* i. 26, 38, 55–58 (11 June, 21 Aug., (Nov.), and 19 Dec. 1546); *Acts Parl. Scot.* ii. 471–80 (14 and 16 Aug. 1546); Selve to Francis I, 10 and 28 Nov. 1546; Selve to Annebaut, 10 Dec. 1546 (*Correspondance de Selve*, pp. 54, 66–67, 74); Balnavis's report to Henry VIII (Dec. 1546); Lord Eure to Henry VIII, 25 Dec. 1546, enclosing spies' reports (*State Pap.* v. 579–84). For complaints about Arran's inactivity at St. Andrews, see Methven to Mary of Lorraine, 31 Dec. (1547) (*Scottish Correspondence of Mary of Lorraine*, pp. 208–9).

Longniddry, Brunstane, or Ormiston. The hunt for Knox was intensified after John Hamilton, Bishop of Dunkeld, the illegitimate brother of the Governor of Scotland, began acting as Archbishop of St. Andrews after Beaton's death; but no serious attempt was made to arrest him. Knox's brother William had also become a Protestant. As a merchant at Prestonpans he travelled through Scotland, and was able to perform a useful service to the movement by carrying messages from Protestants in the east to those in Kyle.[1]

Knox began to think seriously of leaving Scotland. He had no desire to be a martyr, and the constant fear of arrest and the strain of moving from place to place was becoming unbearable. In England many Protestants thought it wrong to emigrate to avoid arrest, but Scots had fewer compunctions about disobeying the government, and for twenty years Protestants had been leaving the country to escape persecution. Knox did not wish to go to England, as so many other emigrants had done, because he believed that though the Pope's name had been suppressed there, his laws and corruptions remained in full vigour. He had no illusions about King Harry, though he supported him to the full in every action which he took against the Scottish Papist government. He knew that this tyrant who persecuted Protestants so cruelly in his own realm was more responsible than anyone else for the development of Protestantism in Scotland, which rose and fell as the red cross of England advanced and retreated; but he had learned, perhaps from Wishart, that the religion in England was not the religion in which he believed. Knox was never a sycophantic admirer of England, though he realized the beneficial influence of England in Scottish politics. The Earl of Angus, during his pro-English periods, took off his hat whenever the name of Henry VIII was mentioned, and said: 'The King my master, God save His Grace!' Sir George Douglas declared that he prayed to God to recompense Henry for his great goodness. John Elder, the Protestant from Caithness, wrote that all honest stomachs in Scotland ought to love Henry.[2] Many other Scottish Protestants were deceived about Henry's religion

[1] Knox, *History*, i. 81–82; Glencairn to Bishop and Colquhon, 11 Apr. 1547 (*Sc. Cal.* i. 12).

[2] Lisle to Suffolk, 15 Feb. 1543; Sir George Douglas to Henry VIII, 20 June 1544 (*Ham. Pap.* i. 426; ii. 414); Elder to Henry VIII (1543?) (*Bannatyne Misc.* i. 1).

and régime, and thought of him as an untarnished Protestant champion. But Knox was always a realist in politics. He knew that Henry VIII was no Protestant, though his armies might liberate the Scottish Protestants as the hosts of the pagan Cyrus had liberated the Jews in Babylon.

As Knox did not wish to go to England, the alternative was Germany, where he would have had the opportunity, like other Scottish refugees, of studying at the Protestant universities of Wittenberg and Marburg. Some Scottish Protestants had taken refuge in Denmark, but most of them had gone to Germany, as Protestantism had come to Scotland from Germany, and in Scotland, as in England, was always called 'Lutheranism'. The possibility of going to Switzerland had probably not occurred to Knox. He must have been fully aware of the existence of Swiss Protestantism, especially as Wishart had translated the Helvetic Confession; but he was probably only vaguely conscious of the doctrinal controversy between Luther and the Zwinglians. The Scottish Protestants were organized as a political party, working to destroy the established Church with the aid of English armies; and theological controversies about the Real Presence, which had split the Protestants of Germany and Switzerland into bitterly hostile factions, could not assist the struggle in Scotland. The Scottish Protestant movement was political and pragmatic from the beginning, and was never troubled with arguments about the Real Presence. This was perhaps the reason why the Scottish Protestants never split on questions of doctrine. Their denunciations of the Pope as Antichrist, of the 'blasphemous mass', and of the doctrine of justification by works, and their prophecies of the ultimate triumph of the elect, could all be advocated without going beyond Lutheranism. Later, after Knox had been in Geneva, the doctrines of the Scottish Protestant Church could develop, logically and painlessly, into Calvinism.

It was again Sir Hugh Douglas of Longniddry who changed the course of Knox's career. On 19 March 1547 the Church authorities presented a petition to the Privy Council urging them to take sterner action against heretics who were propagating the pestilential heresies of Luther, and particularly those sacramentaries who attacked the Sacrament of the Altar. Arran and the Privy Council issued an order on the same day, directing the churchmen to give Arran a list of the names of all heretics who held opinions against the Sacrament of the Altar, or who taught heresy. The drive against the Protestants was instigated by John Hamilton, acting as Archbishop of St. Andrews; but while the persecution was launched throughout the diocese of St. Andrews, in the Archbishop's cathedral town a band of Protestant rebels, who had been declared traitors by Parliament, were holding the Archbishop's castle, and coming and going from it as they pleased into the town and beyond, happily awaiting their pardon, which they themselves were trying to delay for as long as possible in order to have an excuse for continuing to hold the castle. Arran was honouring the truce terms, making no attempt to molest the holders of the castle, and restoring Norman Leslie to his hereditary judicial office of Sheriff of Fife, which had been forfeited after his attainder in Parliament and given to a Hamilton. The government seemed determined to show the Protestants that the only way in which they could avoid persecution was to slaughter a cardinal and seize a castle.[1]

Longniddry and Ormiston suggested that Knox and his pupils should go to St. Andrews Castle. Many other Protestants were coming to the castle. Since the truce in December, the sixteen men who had murdered Beaton had been joined by over 120 supporters, including Sir James Kirkcaldy of Grange, a former Lord High Treasurer of Scotland, whose son William was one of the murderers of Beaton, Sir Henry Balnavis of Halhill, a former Secretary of State, and Rough, who had become the preacher to the Castilians. Longniddry and Ormiston did not go to St. Andrews, but they may have thought that it was the safest place for their boys, and for Knox, if the new drive against heretics reached the Lothian villages. Immediately after Easter, in the middle of April 1547, Knox went to St. Andrews Castle with Longniddry's two sons and young Ormiston.

Knox had not been in the castle for more than a few days before he attracted the attention of the ablest Protestant leader in Scotland. On arriving at the castle Knox continued teaching his pupils St. John's Gospel, just as he had been doing at Longniddry. He taught them in the castle chapel, at a fixed hour every day. One day Balnavis and Rough came into the chapel while Knox was teaching the boys; they listened to what he was saying, and were

[1] *Reg. P.C.S.* i. 61–64 (19 Mar. 1546/7); *Acts of the Lords of Council in Public Affairs 1501–1554*, p. 562.

impressed by his doctrine. Balnavis was the most important Protestant politician in the country. He had become a Lutheran while completing his studies at the University of Cologne, but he kept his conversion secret, and on returning to Scotland he was appointed by James V to be a judge of the newly formed Court of Session before he had reached the age of 30. When Arran became Regent, he chose Balnavis as his Secretary of State, and Balnavis had been chiefly responsible for the implementation of Arran's pro-Protestant policy of 1543. After Arran's change of policy, Balnavis was dismissed from office and imprisoned, but was later released. He joined the murderers of Beaton in August 1546, just before the siege of the castle began, and became their chief political adviser. He knew that they could only survive if England helped them, so he left the castle with John Leslie during the siege to go to London, rowing out through the winter sea to an English ship, while Arran's men were driven off by the fire of the English soldiers on the deck. A politician who could take a risk like this was not afraid to pursue his treason to its logical conclusion. In London Balnavis negotiated an agreement with Henry VIII, by which the Castilians agreed to hold the castle for Henry, to send Arran's son to England, and to deliver their 4-year-old Queen into Henry's hands. In return Henry promised to revictual and aid the Castilians, and to help them to further the Protestant religion.[1]

At Easter 1547 Balnavis, who had returned to St. Andrews during the truce, was on the point of leaving on a second visit to England. Before he left, he and Rough invited Knox to preach in the parish church. The Castilians had reached an agreement with the orthodox clergy of St. Andrews under which both Rough and the Catholic preachers could preach there. The chief preacher for the orthodox clergy was John Winram, the Sub-Prior of the priory of St. Andrews, who was acting head of the priory, as the Prior was Lord James Stewart, the 16-year-old bastard of James V, who was not in holy orders. Winram was also Vicar-General of the diocese of St. Andrews during the vacancy in the archiepiscopal see. He and a number of friars engaged in a verbal contest

[1] Knox, *History*, i. 81–82; Selve to Francis I, 28 Nov. 1546; Selve to Annebaut, 29 Nov. 1546 (*Correspondance de Selve*, pp. 67–68; *L.P.* xxi [ii]. 455, 461); Articles touching the Castle of St. Andrews (Feb. 1547) (*Sc. Cal.* i. 2); and see the draft of these articles by William Kirkcaldy of Grange (autumn 1546) (*L.P.* xxi [ii]. 123(2) and Errata).

with Rough. Thus at the time when the Privy Council, at the request of the Church, had ordered a persecution of heretics throughout the realm, the Catholic clergy and the heretics shared the same pulpit in the metropolitan seat. It was an extraordinary arrangement, but no more extraordinary than the whole situation that existed in St. Andrews during the truce. The orthodox clergy realized that in the last resort the cannon on the castle walls would be the final authority.

Knox refused the invitation to preach. He wrote in his *History* that 'he utterly refused, alleging "That he would not run where God had not called him"; meaning that he would do nothing without a lawful vocation'. But he agreed to write out arguments for Rough to use in his debates with John Annand, the Principal of St. Leonard's College, whom Knox calls a 'rotten Papist'.[1] As Knox's arguments were more effective than those that Rough had thought out for himself, Balnavis and Rough were more determined than ever that Knox should preach. They discussed the matter with Sir David Lindsay of the Mount, who had been herald and Court poet to James V. Lindsay had not joined the Castilians. His services to Protestantism did not go beyond mocking the clergy and the orthodox doctrines of the Church in his plays and poems: he had not the slightest intention of committing high treason for the cause. But he was living in St. Andrews, and was quite willing to have friendly intercourse with the Castilians during the truce. It is not clear why he was consulted about Knox's preaching; perhaps he had been asked to arrange the selection of preachers in the parish church as a kind of neutral arbiter between the clergy and the Castilians. They decided that Rough, as the chief preacher in the castle, should publicly summon the reluctant Knox, in the name of the whole congregation, to fulfil the duty of preaching.

'Upon a certain day', wrote Knox in his *History*, 'a sermon [was] had of the election of ministers: what power the congregation (how small that ever it was, passing the number of two or three) had above any man, in whom they supposed and espied the gifts of God to be, and how dangerous it was to refuse, and not to hear the voice of such as desire to be instructed.'[2] Rough then turned to Knox, and called on him to preach and not to refuse the burden. He asked the congregation to show that they had instructed him

[1] Knox, *History*, i. 82–83. [2] Ibid.

to call upon Knox, and the congregation called out that this was so. At this Knox burst into tears, and withdrew to his room. He remained in a state of deep depression and anxiety until the day of his first sermon came. Everyone could see how gloomy he was, for he never smiled, avoided company as much as possible, and spent all his time by himself.

Knox's reluctance to preach is easy to understand. He had never preached a sermon before. Even if he had had a benefice, he would probably never have delivered a proper sermon, and as an unbeneficed priest he naturally had had no opportunity to preach within the framework of the orthodox Church. The prospect of preaching a sermon for the first time, in the parish church of St. Andrews in the face of a partly hostile audience, was enough to daunt many a novice, particularly a man of a nervous and tempestuous character like Knox. But there was something more than stage fright here. If Knox became one of the Protestant preachers, he would be taking on the mantle of Gwilliam, Rough, and Wishart. He would not merely be escorting a prophet and protecting him with a two-handed sword, but would be taking on the function of a prophet himself. This was a great responsibility for any sincere and conscientious man. The fact that he had been ordained a priest by a Church which he now despised was obviously irrelevant to this problem: he had to convince himself that he had been chosen by God for the task.

In later years Knox was often accused of being a false prophet, of arrogantly claiming to be divinely ordained, and presumptuously putting himself forward as a man of God. For this reason Knox was anxious to emphasize, in his *History* in 1566, that he had not rushed to assume the office of prophet, but had been chosen by the congregation at St. Andrews and forced, very unwillingly, to accept it. In the nature of things, accusations of being a 'self-appointed leader' are often thrown at revolutionaries who assume the leadership of their movement without having been appointed to it by the lawful authority of an established government; and this applied particularly in the case of Knox, who asserted so confidently that he was God's messenger, and like Elijah and John the Baptist had been extraordinarily called by God himself. But Knox never claimed to have power independently of his followers: he always considered himself as the servant, under God, of the congregation. He took on his mission as a preacher and Protestant leader, with all its responsibilities and dangers, because he had been appointed to the post, not by himself or by the Bishop of Dunblane who ordained him in 1536, but by the Protestant party in the Castle of St. Andrews, assembled as the congregation in church.

He seems to have taken the final plunge on the spur of the moment. Annand was preaching, replying to Rough, in the parish church, and Knox was present in the congregation. Annand asserted that he relied, against the arguments that Knox had written for Rough, on the unchallengeable authority of the Church, the spouse of Jesus Christ. Knox then called out from the audience that the Church of Rome was not the spouse of Christ, but a harlot, and offered to maintain, in a disputation with Annand, that the Roman Church had degenerated further from its old purity in the days of the Apostles than had the Church of the Jews from the ordinance of Moses when they consented to the death of Christ. Annand refused to dispute with Knox, but the congregation demanded that Knox should justify his assertion in a sermon; for though they could not all read his writings, they could all hear him preach.

It was now impossible for Knox to refuse to preach, and on the next Sunday he preached in the parish church. He gives a summary of this first sermon in his *History*. Taking a text from the seventh chapter of Daniel, he declared that the Church of Rome was Antichrist. He referred to the private lives of some of the popes, asserted that man is justified by faith only, and not by works of man's invention like pilgrimages and pardons, and attacked the fasting laws of the Church, the prohibition of the marriage of the clergy, and the mass. These were the usual Protestant doctrines. When attacking the Pope as Antichrist, he emphasized that 'Antichrist was not to be restrained to the person of one man only', but referred to all the Pope's followers. Knox was clearly thinking in terms of party against party, of Catholics against Protestants, which was the basis of all his theology.

Knox's old teacher John Major was present in the audience, along with many leading figures of the University, Winram the Sub-Prior, and many canons and friars. Knox, who before he began to preach had had to summon all his courage to force himself to go into the pulpit, at the end of the sermon threw out a direct challenge to these eminent theologians. He invited any member of the audience who disputed the accuracy of anything that he had quoted from Scripture, doctor, or history, to come to him, and he would prove that his quotation was correct. Knox's sermons impressed his listeners; both supporters and opponents realized that he was a man to be reckoned with. Some said: 'Others sned [lopped] the branches of the Papistry, but he strikes at the root, to destroy the whole.' Others said: 'Master George Wishart spake never so plainly, and yet he was burnt; even so will he be.'[1]

After a few weeks John Hamilton decided that he could not continue to ignore the heresy that was being preached in the parish church in his archiepiscopal seat; but he obviously realized that there was nothing that he could do to prevent it. He wrote to Winram and reprimanded him for tolerating the heresy, but he did not directly order him to take action against the heretics. Winram, for his part, took half-hearted action, which would enable him to say that he had started proceedings against the heretics, without arousing the antagonism of the powerful rebels in the castle. He summoned Rough and Knox to attend a meeting with himself and several friars in St. Leonard's yards, and presented them with articles containing a list of the heretical doctrines which they had been preaching in St. Andrews.[2] This was the accepted form at a trial for heresy; but Winram assured Rough and Knox that he was not sitting there as a judge, but wished merely to argue with them about these doctrines. Rough and Knox had been asserting that no man could be head of the Church, that the Pope was Antichrist, that nothing could be added by man to religion as laid down in the New Testament, that the mass was abominable idolatry and a profanation of the Lord's Supper, that there was no Purgatory, and that praying for the dead was vain, and praying to the saints idolatrous. They also asserted that the bishops were not bishops unless they preached themselves and not by substitutes, and that the tithes, by God's law, did not necessarily belong to the churchmen. The doctrine about the tithes associated the Protestant movement with the widespread opposition to paying over the tithes to the Church.

Knox told Winram and the friars that these doctrines were true, and called on Winram, whom he had heard was not unsympathetic to Protestantism, to admit this; but Winram invited Knox to

[1] Knox, *History*, i. 83–86.

[2] For the articles and the ensuing disputation, see ibid. 87–92.

dispute on the articles, and they discussed the lawfulness of the ceremonies of the Church. The disputation was conducted with great courtesy on both sides. Winram was a skilful theologian, and scored one debating point over Knox; for when Knox stated that anything which was not permitted in Scripture was sinful, Winram asked whether it was sinful for a man to ask for a drink, though this was not authorized in Scripture, forcing Knox to explain that he had been referring only to religious ceremonies, not to such things as eating and drinking. But Knox held his own with Winram, and completely demolished his next opponent, a Franciscan friar named Arbuckle. Arbuckle soon made a great blunder. He said that the Apostles had not received the Holy Ghost when they wrote their Epistles, but received Him later when they ordained the ceremonies. 'Few would have thought that so learned a man would have given so foolish an answer', wrote Knox in his *History*, 'and yet it is even as true as he wore a grey cowl.' Winram was forced to point out that Arbuckle was quite wrong on this point. There were many friars in Scotland whose learning and ability in argument were no higher than Arbuckle's.

Winram soon found a more effective way of checking the Protestant preachers than by disputations such as this. He arranged for every learned man in the priory and University to preach in the parish church on Sundays, so that there was no vacant Sunday on which Knox and Rough could preach. Apparently Winram succeeded in tricking the Castilians into accepting this new arrangement by ensuring that the University and abbey men who preached made no criticism of Protestant doctrines; it was enough for Winram that they stopped Knox and Rough from preaching. But Knox preached in the parish church on weekdays. He exposed the trick by which he had been prevented from preaching on Sundays, and commented on the sudden urge to preach which had seized the theologians of the University and priory. Knox said that he hoped that they would show the same zeal in preaching at times and places when there was more need to find preachers than there was now in St. Andrews, and warned his congregation that if these preachers should at any time attack the doctrines which he had taught them, they were not to accept what the preachers said until they had heard his reply.

The sermons of Knox and Rough in the parish church converted many of the citizens of St. Andrews, who came to the castle to join the Castilians at the communion service in the chapel. Knox says that the communion was administered in the same purity as it was later administered in Scotland after the Reformation.[1] It cannot have been precisely the same service that was used in Scotland after 1560, as this had not yet been drafted; it was probably a form of service that Wishart and Rough and other Scottish Protestant ministers had developed for themselves, being based in all essentials on the Protestant services at Strasbourg.

The men who held St. Andrews Castle for the Protestant cause, and attended the Protestant administration of the Lord's Supper in all its purity, were not saintly individuals. They were violent young lairds and sons of lairds, who had murdered a cardinal in circumstances of great brutality, in some cases for a private grudge as well as for religious and political motives. This savage act, and their successful holding of the castle for a year against the Governor of Scotland, had not tamed them or lessened their energy and arrogance. During the truce they rode out into the countryside of Fife and terrorized the neighbourhood. The chronicler Pitscottie was a good Protestant, but he could not forget what he had seen and heard as a young adolescent in Fife in 1547, and thirty years later he recorded in his *History of Scotland* how the Castilians burned and killed, and 'used their bodies in lechery with fair women, serving their appetite as they thought good'. He states that Knox strongly censured them for their conduct and warned them that God would punish them, but it made no difference to their behaviour. According to Spottiswood, Rough was so disgusted with them that he left the castle in May or June, after he had been with them for nearly a year; but this is not what Rough told Lennox and Lord Wharton when he asked for asylum in England, for he said that he had left the castle for a short time, and was unable to return when the second siege began. Knox remained in the castle. His life at St. Andrews gave him opportunities for preaching, for self-expression, for gaining converts in the town, for helping the Protestant cause, and perhaps even for persuading the gentlemen to reform their conduct, for he did not hesitate to reprimand them for their way of living, and for their pride.[2]

[1] Knox, *History*, i. 93.

[2] Pitscottie, ii. 86–87; Buchanan, *History*, ii. 214; Spottiswood, i. 171; Lennox and Wharton to Somerset, 29 Sept. 1547 (*Sc. Cal.* i. 48).

The Castilians had become arrogant and over-confident, and were convinced that they were safe in the castle. The Scottish feudal armies were notoriously incompetent in the art of capturing castles, and the Castilians knew the old popular saying: 'Scots take no walls.' Arran's failure to take the castle for over a year had strengthened their sense of security. When the Pope's absolution for the murder of Beaton arrived, they showed no inclination to surrender the castle as they were bound to do under the terms of the truce.[1] They were relying on help from England. Henry VIII had died soon after the truce was signed, but the Duke of Somerset, who was Protector for the young King of England, Edward VI, continued Henry's policy and had ratified the agreement with Balnavis, who had again returned to the castle.

But the importance of St. Andrews was more clearly realized in Edinburgh, Poissy, and Augsburg than it was in London. Somerset was dilatory in taking action. He was somewhat displeased with the Castilians, who had made the truce without the consent of the English government, and had refused to send Arran's son to England, and he felt that he could subdue the Scots without their assistance. He therefore made his preparations to assemble a great army in the north to invade Scotland by land, and was not eager to alter his general strategy to help his agents in the Castle of St. Andrews, whom he considered useful only as a diversion. Nor had he realized that the new King of France, Henry II, was prepared to take far more risks than his father had done, and attached much more importance to Scotland. Somerset had been receiving reports from his spies, for the previous five months, of French preparations to send a fleet to Scotland, and he had ceased to take them seriously.[2]

At the end of June 1547 some twenty French galleys sailed out of Rouen under the command of Leon Strozzi, the Prior of Capua. Strozzi still bore the title of Prior of Capua, though he had never been in holy orders. He and his brother Peter Strozzi had been driven out of Florence by the Medici, and had entered the service

[1] See Arran's Instructions to Paniter (May 1547) (*H.M.C. 5th* R. 651); Cardonald to Wharton, 2 Apr. 1547 (*Sc. Cal.* i. 10).

[2] Van der Delft to Charles V, 25 Aug. 1547 (*Span. Cal.* ix. 140); Lord Cobham to Paget, 7 and 10 Feb. 1546/7; Grey to Somerset, 10 Feb. 1546/7; Padilla to Wallop, 11 Feb. 1546/7; Carne to Paget, 7 Mar. 1546/7; Sir E. Wotton to Somerset, 13 Mar. 1546/7: and Patrick's report (*Cal. For. Pap. Edw. VI*, No. 25 and Calais Papers Nos. 15, 22, 23, 24(1), 67 and 67(1)).

of the King of France, where Peter had become Henry II's leading general, and Leon one of his chief admirals. With a good wind behind them, and in calm and sunny weather, the galleys made good progress towards St. Andrews. Knox says that they arrived before the castle on 29 June, but this is incorrect. He was probably exactly a week out, for on 5 July Strozzi forced his way into Tynemouth harbour, without permission, to collect fresh water, and could have been off St. Andrews by next day. Strozzi had moved so quickly that he had taken both his friends and foes by surprise. By the time that Odet de Selve, the French ambassador in London, had heard that Strozzi had sailed through the Straits of Dover, and Somerset was protesting to Selve about the incident at Tynemouth, the French were bombarding St. Andrews Castle from the sea.[1]

As it was essential for the French to act quickly before the English fleet came to the rescue, it was worth while for Strozzi to try the effect of a sudden bombardment; but he was unsuccessful. The Castilians fired back at the ships. The French did no damage to the castle, though they knocked down a few houses in the town with their gun-fire: but the cannon in the castle hit one of the galleys, and killed several of Strozzi's men. Strozzi then withdrew his fleet to Dundee, and sent word to Arran that he had arrived and intended to take the castle. Arran, who had no idea that Henry II was sending a fleet for this purpose, was with his army at Langholm, near Dumfries on the Western Marches, ready to resist the threatened English invasion. When he heard of Strozzi's arrival, he marched with his army to St. Andrews. He had plenty of time, for Somerset had ordered the English forces to muster at Newcastle on 24 August.[2]

The Castilians were naturally jubilant after their first skirmish with the French navy. They expected to see the English fleet arrive at any moment, though they boasted that even if the English

[1] Knox, *History*, i. 94; and see the reports of the French and the Emperor's ambassadors (*Span. Cal.* ix. 122, 124–5, 129–31, 506, 509, 511; *Correspondance de Selve*, pp. 161–4, 166, 168–9). Andrew Lang (in *John Knox and the Reformation*, p. 27) ignores the reports of the incident at Tynemouth, which places the date of Strozzi's arrival at St. Andrews a little earlier than Lang suggests; for Selve, writing on Thursday 14 July, states that Strozzi was at Tynemouth 'last Tuesday', which must mean 5, not 12, July. See also Lord Eure to Somerset, 13 July 1547 (*Cal. State Pap. Dom., Edw. VI, etc.*, vi. 327).

[2] Knox, *History*, i. 95; Pitscottie, ii. 88–89; Somerset to Warwick (Aug. 1547) (*Sc. Cal.* i. 28); Selve to Henry II, 2 Aug. 1547 (*Correspondance de Selve*, p. 176).

did not come, it would not matter, as they would be able to hold the castle alone against the powers of Scotland, France, and England if necessary. Knox was not so confident. He tells of how, when the Castilians were celebrating their victory, 'he lamented, and ever said "They saw not what he saw". When they bragged of the force and thickness of their walls, he said "They should be but egg-shells". When they vaunted "England will rescue us," he said "Ye shall not see them; but ye shall be delivered in your enemy's hands, and shall be carried to a strange country".'[1] This shows that Knox, if not a prophet, was at least too level-headed and realistic to be deceived by typical soldiers' morale-boosting talk. On 24 July the French galleys reappeared, and Arran arrived with his army in St. Andrews. He invested the castle on the land side, and summoned the Castilians to surrender. They refused. Arran's men dug trenches around the castle, and waited.

Strozzi had realized that as there was no time to starve the defenders into submission, the capture of the castle by assault must be planned as a serious military operation. He decided to take the cannon from his galleys and haul them up to the roof of the abbey church and the roof of St. Salvator's College, from where they could fire right into the castle. This meant dragging the cannon along streets in the town that were within range of the Castilians' cannon; but by an elaborate system of ropes and pulleys, Strozzi succeeded in doing this at night, and placing big guns on the abbey church and on St. Salvator's. His feat won the admiration of an Italian engineer whom Somerset had sent to aid the Castilians with his expert advice. He warned his boasting colleagues that they now had to do with an enemy who understood the art of war. The admiration of the Castilians' military experts for Strozzi was not reciprocated, for the Prior of Capua told Arran that if the Castilians had had any military experience, they would long ago have knocked down the top of the abbey church and the college with their cannon, to prevent the besiegers placing cannon on them.

At 4 o'clock on the morning of 30 July, the French opened fire. After six hours' bombardment, the whole of the south wall of the castle had been shattered, the east blockhouse had been completely shot away, and several of the defenders lay dead in the castle close. At 10 a.m. the fine weather broke at last, and there was a violent

[1] Knox, *History*, i. 95–96.

downpour of rain which halted the bombardment; but the castle was no longer defensible. The breach in the walls had made it possible to take the castle by storm, and Strozzi was making his preparations for this, offering to free the galley slaves in his ships who volunteered to take part in the assault, when the Castilians sent young William Kirkcaldy of Grange to ask Strozzi for terms. Some of the defenders were in favour of risking all in a wild and desperate sortie, but it was decided to wait until Kirkcaldy returned with Strozzi's conditions.[1]

If any terms were agreed in writing, the writing has not survived, and there is a dispute as to what was agreed. Knox says that Strozzi offered, in the name of the King of France, to spare the lives of the Castilians and transport them to France, where they would be free to enter the King's service or, if they did not wish to do so, to go to any country except Scotland. The Catholic writers say that Strozzi offered to spare their lives, but would make no other promises. The first report that reached the French Court was that Strozzi had won St. Andrews Castle on terms; but within a fortnight of the surrender the English ambassador in France had heard what was presumably the official French version —that Strozzi had refused the Castilians' capitulation terms and had insisted upon their unconditional surrender. Strozzi had no need to offer generous terms, in view of the hopeless position of the defenders. By the laws of war he would have been entitled to refuse them quarter, as they had chosen to 'abide the cannon', and put them all to the sword: but it was not unusual for a commander to save the lives of his men by offering the defenders their lives and freedom before ordering the final assault, and Strozzi may have overlooked the fact that his King and the politicians did not consider the Castilians as enemy soldiers, but rebels. This is the most likely explanation, and would explain why the St. Andrews prisoners were not made to row on the journey back to France, but were only condemned to be galley slaves after they reached Rouen. The Castilians decided to surrender to Strozzi, but not to Arran or to any Scotsman, for they claimed that the Scottish government had betrayed them by violating the terms of the truce made in December. The advantages of surrendering to Strozzi were obvious. If they surrendered to the French navy, it was

[1] Pitscottie, ii. 89–90; Knox, *History*, i. 96; St. Mauris to Charles V, 15 Aug. 1547 (*Span. Cal.* ix. 514–15).

easier to claim that they were prisoners of war, and not traitors and murderers.[1]

Whatever the surrender terms may have been, it is clear that Strozzi himself did not violate them. He did not hand his prisoners over to Arran, but took them to the French galleys. Longniddry's decision to send his boys and their tutor to the castle had led Knox to an unforeseen destination. Knox was taken to the galleys with about 120 other prisoners. It was lucky for him that he was put on the ship, for he would probably have suffered a worse fate if he had fallen into Arran's hands. His sermons had made him a notorious figure in St. Andrews during the previous two months, and the people had been saying that he would be burned, like Wishart. It was an obvious move for Arran and his brother, the Archbishop, to put the two heretical preachers of the castle on trial for heresy now that the castle had fallen; but Rough, who had left the castle before, found his way to Carlisle,[2] and Knox was on a French galley. Perhaps it was at the special request of Balnavis and the Castilian leaders, who insisted that Knox was one of them, that he, too, was taken to the ships.

They waited off St. Andrews for a week, while Strozzi destroyed some more of the castle to make it useless as a fortress in case the English arrived at St. Andrews, and removed all Beaton's valuables, which were said to be worth £100,000. Then the galleys sailed away to France. Strozzi was anxious to avoid the English fleet, especially as France was not officially at war with England. He passed by the east coast of England and through the Straits of Dover without encountering the English. Somerset had been much too slow. Towards the end of July he heard about Strozzi's first repulse at St. Andrews, and decided that it would be worth while, after all, to send a fleet to help the Castilians, or at least to attack the French galleys as they sailed away, for Somerset had no great hopes that the castle would hold. It was only on 1 August, two days after the castle surrendered, that he ordered Lord Clinton, the Lord Admiral, to prepare for the expedition, and the fleet did not reach

[1] Knox, *History*, i. 96; Leslie, *History*, ii. 295; St. Mauris to Prince Philip of Spain, 15 Aug. 1547; St. Mauris to Charles V, 15 Aug. 1547 (*Span. Cal.* ix. 132, 515); Selve to Henry II, 5 Aug. 1547 (*Correspondance de Selve*, p. 178). St. Mauris wrote to Prince Philip: 'I understand, Sire, that the castle was surrendered conditionally, on terms'; but on the same day, he wrote to Charles V that the English ambassador had told him that Strozzi had insisted on unconditional surrender.

[2] Lennox and Wharton to Somerset, 29 Sept. 1547 (*Sc. Cal.* i. 48).

This is usually said to be a portrait of Tyndale; but it may be the only genuine likeness of Knox—the picture by Vaensoun, which Peter Young sent to Beza on 13 November 1579. If this is the Vaensoun portrait, it did not arrive in time to be published in Beza's *Icones* in 1580; but it was published in the French translation of *Icones*—*Les vrais pourtraits des hommes illustres*—in 1581. In 1620 it was published in *Chalcographia Britannica*, where, for the first time, it was said to be a picture of Tyndale; and afterwards the portrait of Tyndale at Magdalen College, Oxford, was painted from this picture. Cf. Borgeaud, 'Le "vrai portrait" de John Knox' (*Bulletin de la Société de l'Histoire du Protestantisme français*, lxxxiv. 11–36); Carruthers, 'On the Genuine and Spurious Portraits of Knox' (*The United Free Church Magazine*, May 1906, pp. 16–21)

the neighbourhood of St. Andrews until 20 September. The English then seized the fort of Broughty Crag, near Dundee, which they held and fortified, establishing very friendly relations with the Protestant burgh. By this time Somerset in person had invaded Scotland. At Pinkie, near Musselburgh, his army of 16,000 men met 25,000 Scots, and inflicted upon them as great a defeat as they had suffered at Flodden. The Scots lost 7,000 killed, and the English lost a few hundred.[1]

But Pinkie was six weeks too late to help Knox and the Castilians. After defying the power of the Governor of Scotland for fourteen months, the Castilians had surrendered to the Prior of Capua and the French navy after a five-day siege and six hours' bombardment; while the Scottish people cheerfully took note of the fact in a popular song:

> Priests content you now; priests content you now;
> For Norman and his company has filled the galleys fow [full].[2]

[1] *Diurnal of Occurrents*, p. 44; Pitscottie, ii. 90–91; Knox, *History*, i. 98; van der Delft to Charles V, 24 and 27 July 1547 (*Span. Cal.* ix. 127, 129); Selve to Henry II, 22 July and 2 Aug. 1547; Selve to Montmorency, 23 July 1547 (*Correspondance de Selve*, pp. 168, 170–1, 176); Somerset's Instructions to Clinton, 1 Aug. 1547; Clinton, Sir A. Dudley, etc., to Somerset, 24 Sept. 1547; Sir A. Dudley to Somerset, 8 Oct. 1547; Dundee Burgh Council to Sir A. Dudley, 27 Oct. 1547 (*Sc. Cal.* i. 30, 46, 56, 71). For Pinkie, see Knox, *History*, i. 98–101, where Knox shows more sympathy for the sufferings of the Scots than might have been expected; and Pitscottie and the other chroniclers. See also Sir James Fergusson, *The White Hind and other Discoveries*, pp. 15–32.

[2] Knox, *History*, i. 97.

CHAPTER V

The Galleys

THE French galleys reached France before the middle of August, without any mishap, despite the fact that, to the joy of Knox and the prisoners, they ran aground on the sand at one point. They touched first at Fécamp, and then sailed up the Seine to Rouen. The prisoners of St. Andrews were still expecting to be set free when they arrived in France, as they believed that Strozzi had promised to do this under the terms of surrender of the castle; but they were disillusioned when they reached Rouen. The principal gentlemen among them, including Balnavis, Norman and John Leslie, the laird of Grange, and his son William Kirkcaldy, were taken off the ships and imprisoned in various castles in Rouen, Brest, Cherbourg, and Mont-Saint-Michel. The rank and file, including Knox, were to be used as galley slaves. For the time being they were kept in the galleys in which they had sailed from Scotland, lying at anchor in the Seine at Rouen. Knox writes that they were 'miserably entreated'.[1]

The galleys were an important class of ship in the French navy. They were between 100 and 150 feet long, and about 30 feet wide and 6 feet high, and could not sail in rough seas as safely as larger ships. They were usually used in the Mediterranean, but they could sail to Scotland in summer by the eastern road. When the wind was insufficient, they were propelled by twenty-five oars, each 40 to 50 feet long, passing through the oar-holes at the side of the ship, with six men rowing to each oar. When the galley was in action against an enemy, the number of rowers was reduced to four per oar, to give more room for the soldiers to move about in the ship.[2]

As no one was prepared to row in the galleys voluntarily, the work was done by forced labour, and the rowers were known as

[1] Knox, *History*, i. 96–97.

[2] Jal, *Archéologie Navale*, i. 279–301, 307, 317 (comparing the measurements of galleys given by Picherone della Mirandola in the sixteenth century, Crescentio in 1607, Hobier in 1622, and Marteilhe in 1701); Marteilhe, *Memoirs of a Protestant condemned to the galleys of France*, i. 130–4.

forsairs, or slaves. The practice of using prisoners for work in the galleys was taken over by the Italian states from the Turks. Turkish prisoners of war, vagrants, and convicted criminals were used. The French had started using convict labour in the galleys in 1532, and ten years later, during the war between France and the Emperor, both sides were using prisoners of war, though this was considered to be a violation of the laws of war.[1] In 1548 each French galley contained 150 *forsairs*, as well as a small crew of free French sailors. The *forsairs* were under the command of the *comite* who was responsible to the captain for the rowing of the ship; under the *comite* were the *sous-comites*, who supervised the *forsairs*' work in their section of the ship. The maintenance of order and the punishment of serious offences was in the hands of the *argousin*. Although the chief duty of the *forsairs* was to row when required, they also performed many other tasks, such as repairing the sails, threading the ropes, preparing and distributing the food to the *forsairs* at their bench, guarding the store-room, and acting as batmen to the captain and *comite*.

Conditions in the French galleys were very harsh. They were sufficiently terrible for a life sentence in the galleys to be considered the heaviest punishment after capital punishment, and the alternative for convicts whose death sentence was commuted. The *forsairs* were chained to their bench, day and night, by a chain fastened to their legs, except when it was necessary to release them for some special reason. They were better dressed than many of Henry II's subjects, for once a year they were issued with a uniform, consisting of a loose-hanging woollen brown robe, such as all French sailors wore, a vest, two shirts and two pairs of canvas breeches, and a red cap. They were not given any shoes, presumably to make their escape more difficult, but whenever they were taken on shore they were issued with a pair of shoes, which they had to hand in when they returned to the galley. Their diet consisted of ship's biscuit and water, with vegetable soup three times a week. Henry II gave orders that they were to receive as large a quantity of ship's biscuit as was necessary, but in some galleys it was sometimes as low as three ounces per day. Wine was given only to those who were permitted to work on land.[2]

[1] Harvel to Henry VIII, 24 Sept. 1542; Hertford to Paget, 13 Apr. 1546; Carne and Rede to Petre, 16 May 1546 (*L.P.* xvii. 840; xxi [i]. 594, 846).

[2] Henry II's order, 15 Mar. 1547/8; Pantero-Pantera, *Armata Navale* (Jal, i. 304, 307–8 n., 313–16).

It is difficult to know exactly how terrible were the conditions of work in the galleys in Knox's time. The famous account by the Huguenot, Marteilhe, of his sufferings in the galleys of Louis XIV refers to a period more than 150 years later, and in some respects things seem to have been a little better in 1547 than in 1702. Marteilhe's account of being forced to row sometimes for ten, twelve, or twenty hours at a stretch cannot have been general; the usual rule was to make the *forsairs* row in shifts, with only one-third of them rowing at any given time, except when in action against the enemy, or in some other emergency. But there is no doubt that galley slaves worked long hours at exhausting toil, driven on by the fear of the whip of the *sous-comite* on their naked bodies. Captain Pantero-Pantera's manual advises *comites* to be severe and incorruptible. The whip was certainly used on shirkers, and a cruel *comite* or *sous-comite* would flog without any justification. The prospect of the galleys terrorized the French criminal classes, demanded all the fortitude of religious martyrs, and roused the determination of the Englishman to defend his country from French invasion. In 1559 John Aylmer tried to rouse the patriotism of his English readers by warning them that if their country was conquered by the pocky Frenchman and the scurvy Scot, 'thy son and thou shall be made galley slaves. . . . Thy son's inheritance shall be chains in the galley, wherewith he shall be fettered, a whip upon his bare skin if he row not to the death, and an horse loaf and water for his daily diet.'[1]

The galleys were the labour camps of the sixteenth century. But Knox was the type of man who survives a labour camp. He was physically in his prime at the age of 33, and obviously robust. He had the strength of body and will to work at his oar, bending forward over the bodies of the men in front, and back as the men behind went back, for hour after hour, weakening, almost breaking down, but surviving. He was intelligent enough to avoid the worst brutalities of the *comite* and *sous-comites*; he was not the cringing type who invites ill-treatment, but neither would he deliberately have courted martyrdom by provoking the officers. Not being stupid, slow-witted, or incompetent, he would not have exasperated them, and they probably regarded him with some sympathy as a hard-working and useful member of the crew.

[1] Marteilhe, i. 137; Jal, i. 306, 307–8 n.; Aylmer, *An Harborrowe for Faithfull and Trewe Subiectes*, sig. P2.

Above all, he had the will to live, and was sustained by his faith, and the utter conviction that he was in the right and his persecutors in the wrong.

How much ill-treatment Knox suffered depended largely on the personality of the individual *sous-comite* who patrolled, whip in hand, that portion of the galley containing the bench to which Knox was chained. But directives from higher authority may have influenced the prisoners' treatment to some extent. The fate of Knox and his colleagues was a subject of international interest and diplomatic representations. Knox says that the Pope wrote to Henry II urging him to show severity to the murderers of Cardinal Beaton; but Knox is obviously not a reliable authority on this point. In fact, the murderers of the Cardinal came off best, for it was the chief murderers who, because of their rank and political importance, were confined in the fortresses and avoided the galleys. Knox also says that 'from Scotland was sent a famous clerk (laugh not, reader) Master John Hamilton of Milburn', sent by Arran to Henry II and the Cardinal of Lorraine, who was the brother of the Queen Dowager of Scotland, to urge that the Castilians should be 'sharply handled'.[1]

On the other hand, from the very beginning Somerset interested himself in the fate of the prisoners in the galleys. Here the Scottish prisoners were helped by the fact that England and France were not openly at war, but in what would today be called a state of cold war; their soldiers fought each other in Scotland, and they attacked each other's ships, but Selve and Wotton remained as ambassadors in London and Paris. It was also fortunate for the Scots that some English subjects, who had been sent as military experts to St. Andrews Castle, had been put in the galleys along with the other Castilians, which gave Somerset good grounds for intervening. Within three weeks of the fall of St. Andrews Castle, Somerset proposed to Selve that the captured Englishmen and five of the leading Scottish Castilians should be exchanged for Scottish prisoners held in England. Selve refused; he told Somerset that he was sure that his King intended to treat the prisoners of St. Andrews as criminals, and not as prisoners of war. Somerset said that there was no possible justification for this in the case of the English subjects, and immediately restricted the freedom granted to Scottish prisoners in England as a reprisal for

[1] Knox, *History*, i. 97.

the holding of English prisoners of war in the French galleys. Somerset raised the matter several times with Selve in the next few months; whenever Selve protested about the seizure of French merchant ships by the English, Somerset countered with protests at the detention of Englishmen in the galleys.[1]

After spending a few months at Rouen, the galleys set off on a journey, with Knox for the first time rowing as a galley slave. They sailed down the Seine and round the coast of Brittany to Nantes, where the galleys were to stay for the winter. Here the prisoners were released from their exhausting labour until next spring; but during the winter of 1547–8 they had other troubles. The galley slaves were expected to attend mass, which was sometimes celebrated in the galley, and sometimes on shore; but the Scottish prisoners decided from the first to put up an organized resistance against going to mass. Norman Leslie and the laird of Grange, who were imprisoned at Cherbourg, refused to go to mass; William Kirkcaldy of Grange and other prisoners in Mont-Saint-Michel said that they would go to mass on condition that they could stab the priest, but not otherwise. The lower-class prisoners in the galleys were no less resolute. Knox says that although they were threatened with torments if they refused to go to mass, the authorities 'could never make the poorest of that company to give reverence to that idol'. When the French crew sang the *Salve Regina* on Saturday nights, the Scots demonstratively put on their caps or hoods, or, if they did not have any headgear available, found some means to cover their heads. They were fortunate not to be severely punished for this behaviour; but religious persecution in France at this time was somewhat spasmodic. It is surprising that the priests who were present took no action when the Scottish *forsairs* put on their caps, or when they refused to attend mass; but no doubt the naval officers were not so interested. Slackness at the oar would be mercilessly punished by the lash, but refusal to attend mass worried them less, and it was not easy to overcome the resistance of so many men.[2]

[1] Selve to Montmorency, 17 and 23 Aug. 1547, and 1 July 1548; Selve to Henry II, 29 Aug. and 21 Nov. 1547, 21 and 26 Jan. 1547/8, and 30 Sept. 1548 (*Correspondance de Selve*, pp. 185, 191, 193, 239, 273, 275, 394, 452); and see the Abbot of Dryburgh to Warwick, 15 Dec. 1547 (*Sc. Cal.* i. 101). For Scottish complaints of English ill-treatment of prisoners of war, see Alexander Gordon to Huntly, 18 Jan. (1548) (*Scottish Correspondence of Mary of Lorraine*, pp. 213–14).

[2] Knox, *History*, i. 97, 107–8. For the spasmodic nature of the religious persecution

There is a well-known passage in Knox's *History* which deals with an incident that occurred soon after the galleys arrived at Nantes. He describes how, when the *Salve* was sung, 'a glorious painted lady was brought in to be kissed, and amongst others was presented to one of the Scottishmen then chained'. This Scotsman was probably Knox himself, for in his *History* he often refers to himself anonymously in this way. Knox

> gently said 'Trouble me not; such an idol is accursed; and therefore I will not touch it.' The Patron and the Arguesyn, with two officers, having the chief charge of all such matters, said 'Thou shalt handle it'; and so they violently thrust it to his face, and put it betwix his hands; who, seeing the extremity, took the idol, and advisedly looking about, he cast it in the river, and said 'Let our Lady now save herself; she is light enough; let her learn to swim.' After that was no Scottishman urged with that idolatry.

Both the defiance and the caution were typical of Knox. He threw the statue into the Loire after accepting it under duress, and taking the precaution of first looking round to make sure that no one saw him throw it into the river.[1]

By March 1548 preparations had begun for sending a great fleet from France to Scotland. In Rouen, Le Havre, Dieppe, and Nantes, and as far away as Marseilles, the ships and galleys were got ready, the sailors' leave was stopped, and soldiers from the eastern frontier and all over France were sent to the ports of Normandy and Brittany to be ready for embarkation. The English thought of sending saboteurs to set fire to the ships in the French ports, and if this had been done it might have ended Knox's career at an early stage; but fortunately for the prisoners in the galleys, they did not carry out their plan. At the beginning of June the greatest French fleet that had ever put to sea, consisting of 145 sail, with great ships as well as 26 galleys, and carrying 7,000 soldiers, mustered off Boulogne and sailed to Scotland under the command of Durand de Villegaignon, that great sea captain, part philosopher and part swindler, who later played an important part in the colonization of Brazil. Knox and his colleagues from St. Andrews Castle were separated and distributed among the other

in France, as compared with Portugal, see George Buchanan's First Defence before the Lisbon Inquisition (1550) (Aitken, *The Trial of George Buchanan before the Lisbon Inquisition*, pp. 13, 15).

[1] Knox, *History*, i. 108.

slaves throughout Villegaignon's galleys. As France was still at peace with England, the fleet was supposed to have been loaned to her Scottish allies, and as soon as they left the French ports they ran up the Scottish red lion at their mastheads. They passed through the Straits of Dover and reached the Firth of Forth by the middle of June. Despite the state of peace, French troops were in action against the English at Haddington. When Somerset left Scotland after his great victory at Pinkie, he left a garrison, which was largely composed of Spanish and Italian mercenaries, in occupation of Haddington, and in the summer of 1548 Arran, with the help of French soldiers under Marshal d'Essé, laid siege to the town. Villegaignon's ships were sent to Scotland carrying French soldiers and German mercenaries as reinforcements for d'Essé, with instructions to cruise off the coast of Lothian with victuals and supplies for the besieging army at Haddington, and to drive off any English ships which attempted to help the besieged garrison.[1]

Knox now rowed as a galley slave in his enemies' ship off the coast where he had spent his childhood and his early years of manhood, while his native town was a battle-ground for English, French, Spanish, Italian, and German soldiers, and the key to the international politics of Western Europe. He cannot have been able to see much of the land which he knew so well, for a *forsair* chained to his bench could not easily look over the side of the galley, nearly 6 feet high. His sympathies were entirely with the English, against his own country and the side for which he was forced to labour as a slave: but the Scottish people as a whole had turned firmly against the ancient enemies and their Protestant supporters. Somerset's proclamation, in which he offered friendship to the Scots, and a union of Scots and English on equal terms in a kingdom to be known as Great Britain, had fallen on deaf ears, and the English commanders often failed to differentiate between friendly 'assured Scots' who favoured the Word of God, and their Papist leaders. Longniddry and Ormiston, who were supplying the English generals with information and advice, had their lands

[1] See the reports of Wotton and the English spies, and of St. Mauris and Selve (*Cal. For. Pap. Edw. VI*, Nos. 73, 84, and Calais Papers Nos. 138, 138(1), 148, 148(1), 151, 151(1), 155, 155(1), 158, 158(1), 160, 160(1); *Span. Cal.* ix. 549–50, 554–5, 557, 561–2, 565; Teulet, *Papiers d'État relatifs à l'Histoire de l'Écosse*, i. 186; *Correspondance de Selve*, pp. 326, 348, 372, 380, 382); Grey to Somerset, 12 and 18 June 1548; Luttrell to Somerset, 20 June 1548 (*Sc. Cal.* i. 242, 250, 256); Knox, *History*, i. 101–2.

ravaged by the English soldiers; and things reached the point where the English ordered all friendly Scots to wear a red cross sewn on their clothes, back and front, or otherwise they would be treated as enemies. Faced with such an alternative, most Scots chose to be patriotic and, encouraged by the trained French soldiers fighting at their side, wreaked their vengeance on the Southerns who had committed such cruelties in Scotland. English officers who took care to surrender to the French and not to the Scots sometimes found themselves lynched by the Scottish soldiers before the French had time to intervene; and though the French professed to be shocked at the savagery of their native allies, they made no serious attempt to prevent their violations of the laws of war. Jean de Beaugué, a French officer in d'Essé's army, describes in his memoirs how he sold an English prisoner to some Scots in exchange for a horse, and how the Scots, after dragging the prisoner round a large field and torturing him, killed him and cut him up into a thousand pieces, and divided the pieces amongst themselves.[1]

The voyage to Scotland in the summer of 1548 was the hardest part of Knox's captivity. His health broke down completely. The first year in the galleys was always the worst. A wise *comite* did not overwork the *forsairs* sentenced for life during the first year. By breaking them in gently, he found that by the second year they could undertake much heavier work, and were likely to survive for quite a long time. But not all *comites* were wise, and under conditions of warfare the hours of labour tended to be longer, and conditions worse. Apart from death from overwork and disease, which ran riot among exhausted and underfed men in the close quarters of a galley, their English friends could not select their victims when they bombarded or burned a galley, and the Scottish

[1] Jal, i. 298; Somerset's proclamation (Sept. 1547) (*Warrender Pap.*, i. 17); John Mardeley's poem, 6 Sept. 1547 (*H.M.C.*, *Cecil*, i. 213); 'Somerset's Epistle or Exhortation' (Jan. 1547/8) (*The Complaynt of Scotlande*, pp. 239, 241–2); Ormiston and Longniddry to Warwick, 9 Nov. (1547); Grey to Somerset, 5 Jan. 1547/8; Wyndham to Somerset, 11 Mar. 1547/8; Thomas Wharton and Thomas Grey to Grey, 23 Feb. 1547/8; Somerset's Instructions to Brende, (Feb.) and 21 May 1548; Grey to Angus (June 1548) (*Sc. Cal.* i. 81, 120, 174, 177, 233, 236 enclosure, 342); Beaugué, *Histoire de la Guerre d'Écosse*, pp. 51, 103–4; Somerset to Luttrell, 21 Jan. 1547/8; Clinton to Luttrell, 16 Aug. (1548) (*Scottish Correspondence of Mary of Lorraine*, pp. 215–16, 265–6); Selve to Henry II, 14 Jan. 1548, enclosing memorandum of proposals made to Huntly (*Correspondance de Selve*, p. 269). And see Pollard, 'The Protector Somerset and Scotland' (*E.H.R.* xiii. 464–72).

Protestants, chained to their bench, ran a greater risk of being killed in action than the French on board. There was also the danger of shipwreck. In July one of the largest of the French warships, the *Cardinal*, sank in good weather in the mouth of the Forth, thanks entirely to the negligence of the crew. The galley slaves rejoiced: 'God would show', wrote Knox, 'that the country of Scotland can bear no Cardinals.' Then the English ships came up and attacked the French galleys, which made off with the English in pursuit. When the English captured a galley, they released the galley slaves; but the French fought off their pursuers, and set one of the English ships on fire, and escaped to Inchcolm, where they landed and took refuge in a fort on the island.[1]

In July, Villegaignon took a few of his ships on a secret mission round the north of Scotland to Dumbarton, where they received the 5-year-old Mary Queen of Scots on board, and carried her safely past Cornwall to France. The rest of the fleet remained off the east coast, where they engaged in an action at Broughty, bombarding the English garrison from the sea without much effect. At Leith they revictualled, and were honoured with a visit from the Queen Dowager, Mary of Lorraine. Some English soldiers from the garrison at Broughty, who had been taken prisoner by the Scots, were handed over to the French and put on board the galleys to work as galley slaves. This led to new protests from Somerset to Selve, and Lord Grey, the commander of the English forces in Scotland, informed Mary of Lorraine that as the English had no galleys, and could not retaliate by putting their prisoners into the galleys, he would hang his prisoners if the Scots and French persisted in this violation of the laws of war.[2]

Although the prisoners of St. Andrews had been split up, some of them were in the same galley with Knox. James Balfour was placed near him, and the two men could talk and fortify each other in their ordeal. Knox's spirit was unbroken, and his religious faith and determination to survive somehow kept him alive.

[1] Pantero-Pantera, *Armata Navale* (Jal, i. 304); Knox, *History*, i. 104; Grey to Somerset, 7 Aug. 1548; Clinton to Shrewsbury and Grey, 10 Aug. 1548 (*Sc. Cal.* i. 310, 313); and see Moir Bryce, 'Mary Stuart's voyage to France in 1548' (*E.H.R.* xxii. 43–50). For the risk of plague in galleys, see Roeulx's note, in Chapuys to Granvelle, 25 June 1545 (*Span. Cal.* viii. 79; *L.P.* xx [i]. 1036).

[2] Knox, *History*, i. 104; Beaugué, p. 30; Grey to Somerset, 3 and 7 Aug. 1548; Clinton to Shrewsbury and Grey, 10 Aug. 1548 (*Sc. Cal.* i. 307, 310, 313); Selve to Montmorency, 1 July 1548 (*Correspondance de Selve*, pp. 394–5).

Sometimes Balfour would ask Knox whether he thought that they would ever get out of the galleys. Knox always told him that he knew that God would deliver them from this bondage, and he never wavered in this belief. While they were lying between Dundee and St. Andrews, Knox became dangerously ill; everyone thought that the end was near. James Balfour asked him to turn his eyes towards the land and say whether he could recognize it. Knox saw the steeple of the parish church of St. Andrews, which was visible for many miles out to sea. He murmured to Balfour that he knew it well, for he saw the steeple of the church where he had preached his first sermon, and that he knew that he would not die until he had preached and glorified the name of God again in the same place.[1]

Knox did not die. The regulations provided for reasonable medical care for the *forsairs*, who were allowed to have extra rations, and even fresh meat, if the barber-surgeon recommended it, and he recovered his strength, though he was very ill for some time. He remained in the Forth till September, when Villegaignon sent most of the galleys back to France, but kept a certain number in Scotland for the winter. Knox was separated from Balfour, who remained in the Forth, while Knox, on another ship, returned to France. It was late in the year to undertake the journey, for the voyage to Scotland was not considered to be safe for galleys after the middle of August. As the seas on the western road were now too rough for galleys, they had to risk an encounter with the English fleet off England. There was the further difficulty that not only were they unable to take shelter, in the event of bad weather, in the English ports, but Charles V and Mary of Hungary had refused a French request for permission for the ships to enter the ports of the Netherlands on their journey, though isolated ships would be allowed to shelter if they were driven in by a storm. But the fleet returned safely to France, with the loss of only one vessel, which was captured by the English in the Straits of Dover.[2]

Knox spent a second winter in the galleys in France, this time being stationed at Rouen. While he was there he succeeded in

[1] Knox, *History*, i. 108–9.

[2] Henry II's order, 15 Mar. 1547/8 (Jal, p. 308 n.); Knox, *History*, i. 104, 111; Thirlby and Petre to Henry VIII, 18 June 1545 (*State Pap*. x. 470); Mary of Hungary to St. Mauris, 3 and 8 May 1548; News sent from Poissy by St. Mauris, 27 Dec. 1548 (*Span. Cal*. ix. 325, 565–8). For the difficulties of navigating galleys in Scottish waters, see Soranzo's report (1 or 2 May 1551) (*Ven. Cal*. v. 703, p. 353).

getting in touch with Balnavis, who had been imprisoned in the old castle of Rouen. Balnavis wrote a book on Justification, and sent the manuscript to Knox in the galleys, asking him to read it and approve it. Knox states that the manuscript 'was sent to me in Rouen, lying in irons, and sore troubled by corporal infirmity, in a galley named *Notre Dame*'. He was still in very bad health after his breakdown during the previous summer, but he decided to write a summary of Balnavis's book 'to the more instruction of the simple' among the prisoners of St. Andrews. The authorities must have known what he was doing, for he could not have written his summary of the book, chained to his bench in the galley, without the knowledge of the *comite* and the *argousin*. The *forsairs* had plenty of leisure-time during the winter months. Most of them spent it doing small handicraft work, making mats, baskets, and other small objects which they were allowed to sell to the public on the dockside, using the money thus obtained to buy food to supplement their meagre ration of ship's biscuit. If Knox, having somehow obtained writing materials, chose to spend his time writing a theological treatise instead of making something which he could sell for money, the officers of the galley no doubt thought that he was mad, but did not care, so long as he rowed well during the summer months.[1]

Knox wrote a summary, chapter by chapter, of Balnavis's book, as well as a short epistle to his fellow prisoners.[2] It is the earliest of Knox's writings which has survived. We obviously cannot form a fair judgement of Knox's views in 1548 from this summary, for he was making a précis of the work of another, not expressing his own opinions; but it is interesting to observe what parts of Balnavis's original manuscript Knox included, and what parts he omitted, in his summary. There is nothing in Balnavis's book which goes beyond the accepted Lutheran teaching, and indeed nothing that could not have been accepted by Henry VIII's bishops. He advocated the Lutheran doctrine of justification by faith alone. On the question of obedience to the government—or, to use sixteenth-century language, to the prince and magistrates—Balnavis was strictly orthodox.

[1] Knox, 'Epistle to the Congregation of the Castle of St. Andrews' (*Works*, iii. 8–9); Pantero-Pantera, *Armata Navale* (Jal, i. 314).

[2] Balnavis's treatise is printed in *Works*, iii. 439–542, and Knox's summary at pp. 10–28.

In his summary Knox followed Balnavis's arrangement, and reproduced his basic ideas; but he rewrote Balnavis's text, and thus, by his additions and omissions, altered the emphasis on a number of points. Knox omitted Balnavis's section on the Trinity and many of his references to the New Testament, as well as a eulogistic mention of 'the glorious Virgin Mary'; but most of Balnavis's references to Abraham, Jacob, and Rebecca are retained, and in Knox's summary the emphasis on the Book of Genesis is more marked. Knox reproduced Balnavis's traditional doctrine of the duty of obedience to the prince and magistrates, but, unlike Balnavis, he expressly stated that this did not apply if rulers ordered the subject to commit sin. This qualification was in theory accepted by everyone, but Knox, like Luther, clearly expressed it, while Balnavis, like Henry VIII's bishops in their formularies of faith, made no mention of it. Knox wrote that it was the command of God that princes should be obeyed. 'The life of princes should be pure and clean, as a mirror to their subjects; and should admit into their kingdoms no worshipping of God, except that which is commanded in the Scriptures. . . . The office of the subject is, to obey his prince, and rulers placed by him; giving unto them honour, custom and tribute, not requiring the cause why they receive the same; for that pertaineth not to the vocation of a subject.'[1] The opinion of Knox and Balnavis on the duty of obedience to the prince hardly seems to be reconcilable with their practice in the Castle of St. Andrews; but their action in resisting the Governor of Scotland could be justified on the grounds that they were acting as loyal subjects of the King of England, the lawful overlord of Scotland.

Both Balnavis and Knox put forward the doctrine, which was emphasized by all sixteenth-century theologians, of the duty of obedience of servants, wives, and children to masters, husbands, and fathers. Balnavis put greater emphasis on the duty of obedience than Knox. Balnavis addressed servants: 'Pretend not to be equal with your lord or master, because ye are both of one Christian religion, but serve him the better.' Knox merely stated that while it was the duty of the lord to pay the promised reward to

[1] Cf. Knox's summary, and Balnavis's treatise (*Works*, iii. 16–17, 26–27, 455, 540); and cf. the Lutheran Confession of Augsburg (Jenkyns, *The Remains of Thomas Cranmer*, iv. 273–92 n.) with Henry VIII's *Bishops' Book* and *King's Book* (Lloyd, *Formularies of Faith put forth by authority during the reign of Henry VIII*, pp. 152–5, 315–18).

his servants, the duty of the servant was to work faithfully, and labour to the profit and utility of his lord, without fraud or simulation, as he would serve Jesus Christ. 'And thou, woman,' wrote Balnavis, 'exercise thee in nourishing and upbringing of thy children; in ruling all things within thy house as thou hast commandment of thy husband; take care upon his direction, as thy head, and transgress not his commandment, for that is the will of God.' Knox, who has gone down in history with a reputation as an anti-feminist, is less extreme on this point than Balnavis, and states far more clearly the mutual obligations of husband and wife. 'The office of the husband is, to love and defend his wife, giving to her only his body. The office of the wife is likewise, to love and obey her husband, usurping no dominion over him. And the office of them both is, to instruct their children in God's law.'[1]

Knox added a composition of his own to his summary of Balnavis's book. It was a message of encouragement addressed to all his fellow prisoners, and in every line Knox shows his sense of solidarity with the group, his determination to fight and crush the enemy, and his conviction that God would give the Protestants the ultimate victory. Every move that Satan makes to damage the small flock of Jesus Christ is turned, by God's grace, to the profit of the congregation. Satan made Joseph go into Egypt, but the result was the achievement of Moses; he made the Jews worship idols, but this led to Daniel's journey to Babylon, where he converted Darius to the true religion; he made the Jewish priests, 'who then were esteemed the true Church of God', to persecute the Apostles, but the banishment of the Apostles caused God's Word to be spread in foreign lands. 'And now we have not the Castle of St. Andrews to be our defence, as some of our enemies falsely accused us, saying, if we wanted our walls we would not speak so boldly'; but they knew that victory was sure. The ungodly, in the day of anguish and trouble, shall despair, and curse the Lord God into their hearts. They shall be numbered to the sword, and in the slaughter shall they fall. Their vestments of spider's webs shall not abide the force of the Lord's wind. This fate shall befall them because they hold the wrong opinions, because they call light darkness, and darkness light.[2] The threatenings

[1] *Works*, iii. 27, 537, 541.

[2] Knox, *Epistle to the Congregation of the Castle of St. Andrews* (*Works*, iii. 5–11; for passages cited, see pp. 7, 9, 11).

of Isaiah were never more terrible than when paraphrased by John Knox in the galleys.

During this second winter in the galleys, Knox was able to get into contact with some of the other gentlemen in the prisons. Like Balnavis, the prisoners at Mont-Saint-Michel asked Knox for spiritual guidance on an important moral and religious issue. Young William Kirkcaldy of Grange, Peter Carmichael, and Robert and William Leslie, wished to try to escape from prison; but they had doubts as to whether this was morally justifiable. These young Protestant gentlemen were ruthless political fighters, but they were men of principle, and did not wish to do something which was wrong and against the laws of God. The slaughter of Beaton had been justified, for there they had acted as the instrument of God's vengeance on the murderer of Wishart and the other martyrs. The defence of St. Andrews Castle had been lawful, for they were defending themselves against a treacherous attack by Arran, whom they did not recognize as the lawful ruler of Scotland. In refusing to go to mass in France, they were putting God's commandment before the orders of the King of France, and were rightly refusing to obey an order to sin. But were they justified in deceiving their warders, disobeying the lawful authority of the King of France in France, and avoiding martyrdom by flight, in order to gain their own personal freedom? Kirkcaldy managed to consult his father, the laird of Grange, who was in prison at Cherbourg. Grange advised his son not to try to escape, because he feared that it would result in worse treatment for the rest of the Scottish prisoners. The French authorities had not yet introduced the rule, which was enforced in the next century under Louis XIV, that if a prisoner escaped from the galleys, the five other slaves at his bench, and the twelve on the adjoining benches, were to be flogged, in order to induce the slaves to do all they could to prevent an escape;[1] but the remaining prisoners could expect a tightening of the conditions of their captivity, if not actual reprisals, if any of their colleagues escaped. Several of the other Scottish prisoners expressed the same opinion. Young Kirkcaldy and the lairds at Mont-Saint-Michel then asked Knox's advice.

Knox wrote back secretly and told Kirkcaldy and his colleagues that they were justified in trying to escape, but only provided that they could do this without killing anyone.[2] Many other men

[1] Marteilhe, i. 265. [2] Knox, *History*, i. 109.

imprisoned for their religious or political beliefs have faced this identical problem, and have examined their conscience to decide whether they were entitled to kill an innocent prison warder in order to escape. Knox told the prisoners of Mont-Saint-Michel that under no circumstances must they break God's commandment in order to regain their freedom. At this stage in his life, Knox took very seriously the commandment 'Thou shalt not kill'. Everyone accepted that it was not to be interpreted as an absolute prohibition on the taking of human life. There were recognized circumstances in which it was lawful to kill—in obedience to the government when enforcing law and order and punishing criminals, and in war, fighting for a just cause. To these obvious cases, Knox and the Scottish Protestants had added another which was not generally accepted—the killing of a wicked ruler like Beaton. But murdering a prison warder in order to make escape possible, or safer, did not come within any exception. Knox's answer may have come as a surprise to Kirkcaldy, for he had not hesitated to kill the innocent porter at the castle of St. Andrews, who had tried to prevent him from entering to kill Beaton.[1] But Kirkcaldy had not consulted Knox before this operation.

Knox urged Kirkcaldy and his comrades to reject the laird of Grange's advice and go ahead with their escape without thinking of the consequences for the other prisoners. 'Such fear', wrote Knox, 'proceeded not from God's Spirit, but only from a blind love of the self';[2] a good enterprise should never be stopped for fear of consequences that were entirely in the hands of God. Ill though he was, Knox was still uncowed. He would not advise a policy of cowardice, and he did not hesitate to sacrifice himself and his fellow prisoners for the sake of letting Kirkcaldy and his friends strike a blow at the enemy.

In the galleys at Rouen during the winter months, whatever the persecutions which had to be endured from the naval officers or from priests who wished to force them to hear mass, there was at least a respite from the labour of rowing, and the *forsairs* could recover their strength for the new journeys next spring. But when the dreaded spring came, it brought sudden freedom to Knox. There had been several proposals during the previous eighteen months for an exchange of prisoners between the French and the English, and a limited agreement on this question was now reached

[1] Knox, *History*, i. 76. [2] Ibid. 109.

through the mediation of the King of Denmark. The French refused to release the leading Protestant gentlemen in the fortresses, but agreed to free many of the lesser prisoners in the galleys. James Balfour and all the other Castilians who were in the galleys that had remained in Scotland were released before the end of the winter; and some of the prisoners in the galleys in France were freed a little later. Knox was set free at the end of February or the beginning of March 1549 with his colleague, Alexander Clark, and allowed to go to England. We do not know why Knox was chosen as one of those to be released; perhaps, as his health had broken down, the ship's captain or the *comite* thought that he would not be of much use at the oar and could profitably be exchanged for a sturdy French prisoner in England.[1]

In his letter to William Kirkcaldy and his comrades, Knox had prophesied that though the Castilians had all been taken prisoner together, they would regain their liberty at different times and in different ways. Kirkcaldy, Carmichael, and the Leslies escaped on the evening of 6 January 1549, while all the guards at Mont-Saint-Michel were celebrating Twelfth Night with the usual heavy drinking. They overcame the guards and tied them up and locked them in, but did not kill any of them. They bribed a French boy to act as guide and lead them to the coast; but he made off with their money and told the authorities, and the four Scotsmen wandered through the countryside, avoiding the search for them and dividing into two parties to facilitate their escape. The two Leslies hid in Rouen. Kirkcaldy and Carmichael reached Le Conquet disguised as beggars, and took employment as sailors on a French merchant ship. After more than three months, they were landed at a port in the west of England. Some weeks after Knox had been released and had arrived in England, he received a visit from Kirkcaldy and Carmichael, and heard from them about all their adventures and their deliverance.[2]

The other prisoners of St. Andrews had to wait a little longer for their freedom. In July 1550 Mary of Lorraine and the Cardinal of Lorraine persuaded Henry II to release the gentlemen in the

[1] Ibid. 110–11; the Abbot of Dryburgh to Warwick, 15 Dec. 1547 (*Sc. Cal.* i. 101); Borthwick to Somerset, 7 Jan. 1548/9 (*Cal. For. Pap. Edw. VI*, No. 115).

[2] Knox, *History*, i. 109–10; Mary of Lorraine's Instructions to de Visque and Fourquevaux (1549) (Gladys Dickinson, *Mission de Beccarie de Pavie, Baron de Fourquevaux, en Écosse, 1549*, p. 28); and see E. Dupont, 'Les Prisonniers Écossais du Mont St. Michel au Seizième Siècle' (*S.H.R.* iii. 506–7).

castles and allow them to return to Scotland, where they were pardoned and restored to their lands and offices. The Queen Dowager had quarrelled with Arran, and was building up a party in Scotland against him; and she now began her policy of making concessions to the Protestants in order to weaken Arran, a policy which was to have such disastrous results for her family and the Catholic Church. The Cardinal of Lorraine hoped that the murderers of Cardinal Beaton would help further the fortunes of the Guise family. The men of humble birth who had been with Knox in the galleys were of no use in a faction struggle for power in Scotland, and they remained at the oar for a third weary summer; but during the winter of 1550–1 they were all set free. Of all the prisoners of St. Andrews who had been sent to the galleys, not one had died under the strain; the only one, out of the whole company of 120, who died in captivity was John Melville, who died a natural death in the castle of Brest.[1]

But Knox had suffered for his faith in the galleys. The sixteenth century, like the twentieth century, was an age of propaganda, and stories about the sufferings of martyrs and prisoners played an important part in the propaganda. Martyrs like Anne Askew, Hooper, and others wrote simple and moving accounts of their sufferings in prison, of the tortures to which they were subjected, and the mockery and insults which they endured.[2] Bale and John Foxe published these stories, and roused the pity and indignation of their Protestant readers. Knox might have written an account of the sufferings of a galley slave which, nearly two hundred years before Marteilhe, would have stirred the anger of Protestant Europe at the treatment of Protestants in the French galleys. He did not do so. In the whole of Knox's writings, there are only a few short references to the 'torments of the galleys';[3] and in his *History* there is nothing about torments. The references are to resistance, to caps kept on during religious ceremonies, to the throwing of the statue of the Virgin into the river, to threats by the prisoners to 'stick' the

[1] Knox, *History*, i. 111; St. Mauris to Charles V, 9 Mar. 1549 (*Span. Cal.* ix. 347–8); Instructions to Commissioners for the exchange of prisoners, 19 May 1549 (*Sc. Cal.* i. 347); Mason to the Council, 14 June, 20 July, and 14 Sept. 1550; the Council to Mason, 11 July 1550 (Tytler, *England under Edward VI and Mary*, i. 295–6; *Cal. For. Pap. Edw. VI*, Nos. 217, 221, 224, 238). See also Holcroft to Somerset, 27 Sept. 1549 (Stevenson, *Illustrations*, p. 49).

[2] Foxe, v. 538–49; vi. 647–8.

[3] Knox to Mrs. Bowes (1553) (Letter XXI); Knox to Anne Locke, 31 Dec. 1559 (Knox, *Works*, iii. 387; vi. 104).

priest at mass. It is not an account of the sufferings of a martyr in a lonely prison cell, but of mass resistance by prisoners of war. As with some modern reminiscences of prisoners of war, the reader is almost sorry for the guards. Knox makes no attempt to arouse the reader's pity for himself.

Knox may have been lucky enough to have had a relatively mild *sous-comite*, to have been allowed his rest after a reasonable shift, and never to have felt the whip on his bare shoulders as he pulled his oar; but there must have been, at least, many insults and humiliations which had to be borne, many instances of bullying and taunting, and the raucous bawling of orders in the international language of the sea, with the dreaded shout of '*Arranque! Arranque!*'[1] to make the galley slaves row faster. Not even for the sake of Protestant propaganda was Knox prepared to let the world know about them. He saw himself as trampling on his enemy, not writhing under his enemy's foot, and if there were moments in the galleys when he was trampled on, he was eager to forget them and to tell no one else. Many Protestants gloried in their sufferings, and seemed almost to be seeking martyrdom. Knox did not want martyrdom; he wanted victory.

[1] Jal, i. 309 n.

CHAPTER VI

Berwick and Newcastle

When Knox landed in England in March 1549, he found himself in the predicament that always faces a man whose political sympathies lead him to take refuge with the national enemies of his country. The English 'Southerns', who had committed such terrible ravages in Scotland in recent years, and were at this very moment fighting desperately in the ruins of Knox's native town of Haddington, were for Knox the liberators whose power was his only worldly protection. He had waited in vain for them at St. Andrews, scanning the horizon day after day in the hope of sighting their ships; but when all seemed lost, they had extended their strong arm to pluck him from the French galleys, and had received him in England as an honoured guest. But government policy could not eradicate the deep-seated hatred of the Scots felt by every Englishman, which had never been stronger than at the present time. The English commanders reported that they had never seen men so universally angry with their enemies as their soldiers were with the Scots. Their contempt for Scottish backwardness and poverty was unbounded. As for the friendly 'assured' Scots like Knox, the ordinary English attitude was that though bad Scots were good Englishmen, they must always remember that one could never trust a Scot.[1]

Nor did the fact that Knox had come to England as a refugee for religion endear him to large sections of the English people. By 1549 Protestant refugees were coming to England in large numbers from France and Flanders, until there were some 5,000 foreign refugees in London, out of a total population in the city of about 80,000. The English hatred of foreigners was proverbial, and the refugees were very unpopular, being blamed by the people

[1] Norfolk to the Council, 2 and 6 Sept. 1542; Sadler to Henry VIII, 26 Nov. 1543; Suffolk and Tunstall to the Council, 6 Dec. 1543 (*Ham. Pap.* i. 172, 184; ii. 116, 129); Otwell Johnson to John Johnson, 16 May 1545 (*L.P.* xx [i]. 747).

for the rising prices and the food shortages. It was said on all sides that England had become a harbour for all infidelity.[1]

The government showed every consideration to Knox. Within a few weeks of his arrival in England, on 7 April 1549, the Privy Council gave orders that Knox was to be paid £5 by way of reward. At this time, when the average wage of an unskilled labourer was 7*d.* per day, and wine imported from Bordeaux cost just over 6*d.* per gallon, £5 was the equivalent of about £150 today; and the phrase 'by way of reward' was used to indicate that the payment was made in gratitude for services, or as a tribute to past achievements.[2] Apart from this initial gift, Knox was given a permanent post. He was appointed as preacher at Berwick. He travelled north, and thus arrived, by way of the French galleys, at the frontier town, less than three miles from Scotland and a day's ride from Lothian and the village of Longniddry, which he had left only two years before when he made his fateful journey to the Castle of St. Andrews.

Even in peace time Berwick was never an easy parish for a priest to administer. Its peace time population was about 3,500, of which more than one-third were soldiers or workmen connected with the garrison and fortifications. The men in the town outnumbered the women by nearly four to one. Berwick was the headquarters of the Lord Warden of the Eastern Marches. Under him the government of Berwick was divided between the Marshal of Berwick, in command of the garrison, and the Mayor, who governed the civilians subject to any overriding orders from the Lord Warden. There was general dissatisfaction among the garrison. The officers resented being stationed at Berwick, disliking the cold, windy climate, and the other ranks were discontented because their pay was nearly always in arrears. The shortage of funds in Berwick was responsible for the failure to repair the great wooden bridge over the Tweed, which was over two hundred years old and had been officially reported unsafe more than

[1] Ochino to Musculus, 23 Dec. 1548 (*Original Letters relative to the English Reformation*, p. 336); Newsletter from Rome, 23 May 1551; Chamberlain to the Council, 7 June 1551 (*Cal. For. Pap. Edw. VI*, Nos. 370 (1), 374; Tytler, *England under Edward VI and Mary*, i. 380); Scheyvfe's advices (Jan.), 21 Apr. and 14 Sept. 1551 (*Span. Cal.* x. 218, 278–9, 368).

[2] *A.P.C.* 7 Apr. 1549. For the price and wage levels in 1549, see Thorold Rogers, *History of Agriculture and Prices*, iii. 632; iv. 523, 652; and at Berwick in particular, in Accounts of the Earl of Rutland's steward, June 1549 (*H.M.C., Rutland*, iv. 351).

thirty years before, and the failure to proceed with the plan to build a new parish church. The church where Knox preached was much too small for the large congregation of soldiers and civilians who huddled together there in such close proximity that it greatly increased the danger of plague.[1] The streets were so full of garbage and filth that it was difficult to walk through the town.

Knox's position as a Scot was in some ways easier in Berwick than elsewhere. The people of Berwick were more friendly to the Scots than were Englishmen in other parts of England. Many of the citizens were themselves of Scottish origin. A large part of the population consisted of illegal Scottish immigrants, who had crossed the frontier and entered the first town which they reached in the wealthier southern country. They came chiefly to get English currency, for the English pound sterling exchanged in Scotland for £5 14*s*. in Scottish pounds. From time to time the Marshal of Berwick ordered them to be expelled; but the Mayor and the civil authorities were lax in enforcing the order. The Scots in Berwick were subjected to many restrictions by the military authorities, who in 1549 were expecting a Scottish invasion and were very conscious of the danger from Scottish spies; any Scottish-born person who tried to enlist as a soldier or join the watch, or who approached the walls at night, was to be put to death as a traitor.[2] Knox, having been sent to Berwick as a preacher by the Privy Council, with his record of service to the King of England's friends at St. Andrews and his sufferings in the French galleys, was in a privileged position; and though the records have not survived, he was almost certainly granted either letters of naturalization, or at least the lower status of denizenship, which exempted him from most of the restrictions imposed on aliens. He learned to speak English as fluently as Scots, the English dialect which was spoken by the Lowland Scots, and for the rest

[1] See the Register of the inhabitants of Berwick (June 1565) (*Cal. For. Pap. Eliz.* vii. 1232); Bedford to Cecil, 3 Aug. 1566 (Stevenson's *Illustrations*, p. 163); Rutland to the Council, 14 and 24 Oct. 1549; the Council to Rutland, 21 Oct. 1549 (*H.M.C., Rutland*, iv. 193, 198–9); Sir W. Eure and Shelley to Suffolk, 10 Dec. 1543 (*Ham. Pap.* ii. 219–20); Articles of the Captain of Berwick (1552?) (*Cal. State Pap. Dom., Edw. VI, etc.*, vi. 421). See Brende to Cecil, 3 May 1559 (*Cal. For. Pap. Eliz.* i. 600); and see L. O. Henderson, 'The Old Tweed Border Bridge' (*S.H.R.* xxxiii. 22–26).

[2] Book of Statutes and Ordinances of Berwick (24 May 1542) (*L.P.* xvii. 343); Articles exhibited by the Captain of Berwick against the Mayor and freemen (1549); Rutland to the Council, 14 and 21 Oct. 1549 (*H.M.C., 12th R.* iv. 53–54; *Rutland*. iv. 194, 196–7); Scheyvfe to the Council of State (24 Sept. 1550) (*Span. Cal.* x. 180).

of his life, even after he returned to Scotland, he preferred to write and speak in English rather than in Scots.

The turbulent conditions in Berwick had become much worse in war-time. In addition to the usual peace-time garrison, 200 foot and 100 horse were stationed in the town. These were all Englishmen; there were no foreign mercenaries in Berwick, though there were Germans at Alnwick, Italians at Morpeth, Irish at Bamborough, and Spaniards at various places. Just over half the total forces in Northumberland were foreign mercenaries, and they caused much trouble in the district; they were in arrears with their pay, and vented their anger on the people, looting, raping, and killing. In the autumn of 1549 the Italian mercenaries at Morpeth mutinied as they were passing through Berwick, and killed two of the English soldiers of the garrison. Relations were almost as bad between the English troops and the people of Berwick. The English soldiers returning on sick leave from the front line at Haddington could find no house in Berwick that was prepared to give them shelter, but were left to die of want in the streets. John Brende, one of Somerset's secretaries, reported to the Protector after a visit to the north that there was better order among the Tartars than in Berwick, that no man could have anything unstolen, and that food prices were very high. He added that if the situation was to be reformed, the man in the pulpit at Berwick would have to be a stern disciplinarian as well as a stirring preacher.[1]

The authorities may have thought that Knox filled the requirements which Brende had listed as necessary for a preacher in Berwick. He had acquired some experience of the duties of a preacher in an unruly garrison town at St. Andrews in 1547, when he had castigated the profligacy of the defenders of the castle. It was also perhaps considered suitable to appoint a Scotsman as a preacher in Berwick, in view of the large numbers of Scots in the town.

In England Knox encountered a very different political and religious system from that which he had known in Scotland. The English Reformation had been carried out from above, by royal

[1] List of Garrisons in towns of Northumberland, 24 May and (Oct.) 1549; Dacre to Rutland, 14 Oct. 1549; Rutland to the Council, 14 and 24 Oct., and 11 Nov. 1549 (*H.M.C., 12th R.* iv. 36–37, 44, 46, 49; *Rutland*, iv. 193–4, 199–200); Brende to Somerset, 14 Nov. 1548 (cited in Lorimer, *John Knox and the Church of England*, p. 18).

decree; it was based on the principle that it was for the king, and the king alone, to make religious innovation, and to prescribe the religious doctrine that his people had to believe. Since the death of Henry VIII, England had been ruled by Somerset, and the religious policy was directed by Thomas Cranmer, the Archbishop of Canterbury. During the reign of Henry VIII, religious policy had largely depended on whether Cranmer or Stephen Gardiner, Bishop of Winchester, had, for the time being, won the King's ear and persuaded him to adopt a Protestant or a Catholic policy. Now, under Edward VI, Cranmer was firmly in control, and nothing held him back except his timidity and moderation. He and Somerset had abolished the heresy statutes and the Act of the Six Articles, and had suspended the burning of heretics, though under a novel interpretation of the common law they still burned an occasional Anabaptist. They had introduced the administration of the communion in two kinds, directing that the wine, as well as the bread, was to be given to the congregation. Images had been removed, and prayers to the saints and the doctrine of justification by works had been condemned in the Book of Homilies which Cranmer had issued. A few weeks before Knox arrived in England, they made the greatest advance of all. The Act of Uniformity enacted that after Whitsun 1549 the old Latin church service should be replaced by the English service in the first Book of Common Prayer which Cranmer had drafted; and another statute permitted priests to marry.[1]

Gardiner had opposed all these measures. As early as the summer of 1547 he feared that Cranmer's meagre reforms were the thin end of the wedge, and the beginning of a process which would lead to revolution and the subversion of authoritarianism in Church and State. 'You see religion so beset', he wrote to Cranmer, 'that once the door is open, you cannot withstand the attack of those bursting in.'[2] Cranmer and Somerset sent Gardiner to the Fleet prison in London for disobeying the royal authority and refusing to support the new religious policy; but they had every intention of resisting the attack from the extremists to which

[1] *Statutes of the Realm*, 1 Edw. VI, c. 1, 12; 2 & 3 Edw. VI, c. 1, 21; Cranmer to Bonner, 24 Feb. 1547/8 (Wilkins, *Concilia*, iv. 22–23); 'The Homily of Salvation', 'The Homily of Faith', and 'The Homily of Good Works' (in Cranmer, *Works*, ii. 128–49). For the legality of burning heretics at common law without statutory authority, see Holdsworth, *History of English Law*, i. 616–17.

[2] Gardiner to Cranmer (July 1547) (Muller, *Letters of Stephen Gardiner*, p. 334).

they had opened the door. They opened the door a little wider when they persuaded the French to free John Knox from the galleys, and allowed him to come to England.

The authoritarian principle of the State and Church of England did not give much scope for preachers, and no one in England was permitted to preach as Wishart, Rough, and Knox had preached in Scotland. In addition to the ordinary restrictions, by which no one was permitted to preach without a licence from the bishop of the diocese, and unlicensed preachers were immediately arrested, from time to time all licences were revoked, and preaching was only permitted under a special licence from Cranmer. Occasionally all preaching was forbidden, and the preachers were ordered to read out passages from the official formularies of faith without making any comment on them. This had occurred in September 1548 when the preachers were ordered not to preach any sermons at all, but to read out the Homilies that Cranmer had issued in 1547. Any preacher who disobeyed these orders, or who made any criticism of the government's religious policy, was summoned before the Privy Council and imprisoned.[1]

The duties that Knox was expected to perform, as a preacher at Berwick, had been clearly laid down in a letter which Somerset had written to all licensed preachers in the summer of 1548. It was to expound the policy of the government, and to go as far as, and no further, than the government had gone.

> It is not a preacher's part [wrote Somerset] to bring that into contempt and hatred which the prince doth either allow, or is content to suffer. . . . Why should a private man, or a preacher, take this royal and kingly office upon him; and not rather, as his duty is, obediently follow himself, and teach likewise others to follow and observe, that which is commanded? . . . It is the part of a godly man not to think himself wiser than the King's Majesty and his Council, but patiently to expect and to conform himself.[2]

This was a new experience for Knox. At St. Andrews he had preached under the protection of a revolutionary garrison, denouncing the doctrines of a government and Church which were too weak to stop him. At Berwick he was expected to be the

[1] See, e.g., Henry VIII to Cranmer, 12 July 1536; Proclamations of 6 Feb. and 23 Sept. 1548 (Wilkins, iii. 807–8; iv. 21, 30); Hooper to Bullinger, 27 Dec. 1549 and 5 Feb. 1550 (*Orig. Letters*, pp. 71–72, 76).

[2] Somerset to the preachers, 13 May 1548 (Wilkins, iv. 27).

mouthpiece of an authoritarian government that was far more friendly to him but with whose doctrines he did not entirely agree, and which would not tolerate any deviation from its narrow directives. Knox adapted himself brilliantly to this unfamiliar situation; during his four years in England, he became a consummate politician.

At Berwick Knox's diocesan bishop was Cuthbert Tunstall, Bishop of Durham. Tunstall was 75 years old. In his youth he had been one of the leading humanist intellectuals in Europe, and an intimate friend of Sir Thomas More and Erasmus. For more than thirty years he had served Henry VIII as a diplomat and administrator, negotiating with the French, the Scots, and the Emperor, sitting on the Council of the North, and directing the defence of the realm against the Scots and the military preparations for the invasions of Scotland. Twenty-five years before, as Bishop of London, he had been in charge of the first drive against Lutheran books and the first English Bibles; and throughout his twenty years as Bishop of Durham he had played a leading part in the doctrinal struggles among the bishops, as the ally of Gardiner and a foremost member of the Catholic faction. Under Edward VI, he had opposed the Act of Uniformity and all the Protestant reforms that Cranmer had introduced. But Knox would get no sympathy from Cranmer and the leaders of the Protestant faction if he resisted Tunstall's authority in his diocese. Somerset and Cranmer expected every priest to obey his bishop, just as they expected every bishop to obey the Protector and the Privy Council, and would uphold Tunstall's authority in his diocese.

Knox was fortunate in taking up his position at Berwick at a time when the English Reformation was about to move in a more radical direction. Within a few months of Knox's arrival in England, disturbances broke out all over the south, including a formidable revolt in Devonshire directed against the English services of the Book of Common Prayer; but they were all suppressed by the government's German mercenaries. In October Somerset, who was disliked by the nobles and the landlords for being too sympathetic to the agrarian rebels, was overthrown by a *coup d'état* organized by John Dudley, Earl of Warwick, and the majority of the Lords of the Council. For some weeks it was widely believed that Warwick intended to revert to a Catholic policy;[1] but

[1] See Hooper to Bullinger, 7 Nov. and 27 Dec. 1549; Dryander to Bullinger,

by the end of 1549 he had shown that he had, on the contrary, decided to be a more extreme Protestant than Somerset. Warwick was completely opportunist in religious matters, but he was prepared to press the Reformation further than Cranmer really wished to go, and to gain the support of the Protestant radicals as well as of the landlord class; his real object was to consolidate his power and amass an enormous fortune for himself and his friends. For the rest of Edward's reign the English Reformation was to be identified with the radical Zwinglian religious doctrine, with enclosures, oppression of the people by the landlords, the looting of Church property by influential courtiers, and general corruption and moral decadence.

The Zwinglian doctrine of the Lord's Supper was only gradually introduced into the doctrine of the Church of England. The denial of the Real Presence of Christ in the bread and wine in the Sacrament of the Altar had been the most vital issue in the religious controversies of the previous twenty years. Throughout Catholic Europe, and under Henry VIII, heretics who denied the Real Presence, or 'sacramentaries' as their opponents named them, were burned without mercy. On this point Luther was as firm as Henry VIII and the Pope, and he had split with Zwingli, and denounced the Zwinglians with great passion, because of their denial of the Real Presence. Cranmer, who had originally believed in the Real Presence, had been converted by Nicholas Ridley to a contrary opinion, and, after much hesitation, had openly repudiated the Real Presence in the House of Lords in December 1548, along with other Protestant bishops. When, in the autumn of 1549, all preaching licences were revoked, and for the first time even bishops were forbidden to preach in their dioceses without a licence from Cranmer, every preacher who applied for a new licence was required to subscribe to some articles that Cranmer had drafted. These articles included a denial of the Real Presence, and a declaration that Christ's Presence in the bread and wine was spiritual.[1]

Knox was therefore free at Berwick to preach against the Real Presence, and he repeatedly attacked the mass in his sermons. It is not clear what exactly were the opinions on the sacrament which

3 Dec. 1549, Stumphius to Bullinger, 28 Feb. 1550 (*Orig. Letters*, pp. 69–71, 353, 464–5); van der Delft to Charles V, 17 Oct. 1549 (*Span. Cal.* ix. 462).

[1] Hooper to Bullinger, 27 Dec. 1549 and 5 Feb. 1550 (*Orig. Letters*, pp. 71–72, 76).

Knox held at this time. The leading Protestant theologians who denied the Real Presence differed amongst themselves as to the precise nature of the Presence; but there is no indication as to whether Knox, during his residence in England, was closer to the doctrine of Bucer, of Peter Martyr and Cranmer, of Calvin, or of Bullinger and the Zwinglians of Zürich. Knox never formulated his opinions on the nature of the Presence with any clarity. He could use as bitter invective as any extremist pamphleteer in vilifying and ridiculing the mass and the adoration of the Host; but he always celebrated the Lord's Supper with great reverence. It was not in his nature to enter into subtle analysis of this deep theological question. It was only during his four years in England that he was directly concerned with the issue. He was probably content during this time to attack the doctrine of the Real Presence as idolatry, and the conception of the mass as a sacrifice, without worrying over any differences between the doctrines of Bucer, Cranmer, or the extremists; afterwards, when he went to Geneva, he naturally accepted the *Consensus Tigurinus*, the Agreement of Zürich which Calvin and Bullinger had reached in 1549. Knox's mission was not to define the nature of the Presence, but to overthrow the blasphemous mass.

In the spring of 1550 a new figure began to dominate the English Reformation. John Hooper became the mouthpiece of forces who were determined to press the Reformation further than Cranmer was willing to go. In March 1550 Hooper preached the Lenten sermons to the King, and made three demands. He called for the abolition of altars, vestments, and kneeling at the Lord's Supper. Altars were used for a sacrifice, and should be replaced by the communion tables of the Lord's Supper; vestments were Papistical, and were the garb of the priesthood of the Aaronites, who had been condemned in Scripture; and kneeling at communion implied adoration of the Host and a belief in the Real Presence. Hooper demanded that the congregation should sit to receive communion. The government accepted his demand for the abolition of altars, because of the influence of Ridley, the Bishop of London, who was one of Cranmer's closest collaborators; but Cranmer and Ridley refused to agree to Hooper's other two demands. When Hooper, thanks to Warwick's influence, was appointed Bishop of Gloucester, Cranmer and Ridley insisted that he should wear vestments at his consecration.

Hooper refused. In this controversy Hooper stood for the individual's right of conscientious objection, while the bishops, led by Ridley, insisted on the duty of obedience and submission by the individual to authority. Eventually the Privy Council sent Hooper to the Fleet. After three weeks in prison he submitted, and agreed to be consecrated in vestments. He was then released, and took his place with Cranmer and Ridley as a respected and obedient member of the bench of bishops.[1]

Knox in the north reacted differently from Hooper. He made no open criticism of vestments or kneeling at communion, and did not make any individual stand in resistance to authority. Instead he put his doctrines into practice without being technically guilty of any breach of the law. The rubrics of the communion service in the Book of Common Prayer, which by the Act of Uniformity of 1549 was the only communion service that could lawfully be celebrated, gave directions as to the actions and gestures of the priest and congregation, as well as stating every word that was to be spoken during the service. It had aroused the strong opposition of the Catholic clergy by its abolition of the words referring to sacrifices and the prohibition of the elevation of the Host; but it was also criticized by many Protestant theologians, like Bucer and Calvin, for retaining many of the old Popish superstitions. Knox made no public criticism of the Prayer Book, and carried out its directives when he celebrated communion in Berwick. But the Book of Common Prayer said nothing about the posture in which the congregation should receive communion. For centuries the communion had been received kneeling, and no one in England had questioned this until Hooper's sermon in March 1550; the Prayer Book was silent on this point because it had never occurred to Cranmer and the divines who drafted it that anyone would receive communion in any other way. Knox told his congregation in Berwick to receive the communion sitting. He was not disobeying any rubric of the Prayer Book by doing so.

Knox does not appear to have referred, in any of his sermons at this stage, to the question of sitting at communion. Having violated the spirit, without contravening the letter, of the Book of

[1] Hooper's 4th Sermon on Jonah, 5 Mar. 1550 (Hooper, *Works*, i. 488). For the vestments controversy, see Jasper Ridley, *Nicholas Ridley*, pp. 222–31; Jasper Ridley, *Thomas Cranmer*, pp. 308–10, 313–14, and the authorities there cited.

Common Prayer in his practice in Berwick, he was not eager to draw the attention of the authorities to what he had done, and force a head-on clash on an issue in which Tunstall and the Privy Council would be united against him. Instead his confrontation with Tunstall came on an issue in which Knox, and not the Bishop, had the support of the Council. In his sermons he concentrated on attacking the mass, arguing that the whole concept of the mass as a sacrifice was idolatrous. This was a thing which Cranmer had not yet dared to do, though he already believed it as strongly as Hooper and Knox. His communion service in the Book of Common Prayer had abolished the words which referred to sacrifice in the canon, and had forbidden the elevation of the Host, in order to abolish the traditional conception of the mass. But he and his colleagues had not told the people what they were doing, either in the Prayer Book or anywhere else; and the communion service was officially named, in the Book of Common Prayer, 'the Holy Communion, commonly called the Mass'.[1]

Tunstall believed firmly in the Real Presence. Times had changed since the days when he had played a leading part in introducing the Act of the Six Articles in Parliament, and it was no longer possible for him to have a preacher arrested and burnt for denying the Real Presence. He had, on the contrary, been ordered to enforce in his diocese the English service of the Book of Common Prayer, against which he had voted in Parliament, and to suppress the old Latin mass, and he had obeyed. But he had not been ordered to deny the truth of the Real Presence, or to permit his clergy to do so. He therefore summoned Knox to appear before the Council of the North and defend his doctrine that the mass was idolatry. The Council of the North exercised the power of the Privy Council north of the Trent; it was composed of the great northern peers and royal officials, and Tunstall, like former bishops of Durham, was a leading member. The Council of the North normally sat in York, but held one session each year in Hull, Durham, and Newcastle. Knox was summoned to appear before the Council of the North in Newcastle, and on 4 April 1550 he defended his doctrine in a speech before the Councillors and a number of other persons, including some eminent theologians, who had been invited to attend. Tunstall was present. Knox preserved a written copy of the text of his speech, which he

[1] *Liturgies of Edward VI*, p. 76.

later published under the title *A Vindication of the Doctrine that the Sacrifice of the Mass is Idolatry*.[1]

Knox's speech is revealing of his character and his approach to religious controversy. He defended his doctrine in a very different way from that in which Cranmer and Ridley and the English Protestant theologians upheld the Zwinglian doctrine in their subtle disputations; but it was equally far removed from the demagogy of the popular preachers. Knox was argumentative rather than denunciatory, but polemical rather than learned, and based his arguments on broad principles, not on patristic texts. His choice of words was significant. He made no reference to the Sacrament of the Altar, or to the Real Presence, but spoke throughout against 'the mass'. The mass was the name of the service, which every layman knew; the Sacrament of the Altar was the sacrament that took place during the service, and the Real Presence was the reason why the mass was celebrated. In talking about the mass, rather than the Sacrament of the Altar or the Real Presence, Knox used the popular and not the theologians' phraseology, and attacked the practice rather than the theory.

Knox addressed his distinguished audience with due respect, and said that if he could not prove that his doctrine was true by Scripture, he would recant it as a wicked doctrine and confess that he was most worthy of grievous punishment. In order to prove that the sacrifice of the mass was idolatrous, he put forward a proposition which could be used to carry the Reformation much further than Cranmer and the government had so far gone: that no ceremony could be justified if it was not found in Scripture, for God did not permit man to add anything to what He had prescribed in the Bible. This was the basis of all Knox's doctrine, which he had put forward in his disputation with Winram at St. Andrews. At St. Andrews he had expressly asserted the absolute authority of Scripture over the authority of the Church of Rome; but at Newcastle he did not expressly assert the absolute authority of Scripture over the authority of the King and the Privy Council. He left it to his audience to draw this conclusion for themselves. At Newcastle he was not preaching under the shadow of the cannon of a revolutionary garrison. Knox was well aware of the

[1] It was originally printed, together with Knox's *Letter to the Queen Regent*, in 1556. It is reprinted in *Works*, iii. 33–70; for the passages cited below, see pp. 36–37, 50–51, 62–63, 66, 68, 70.

difference between the position of Winram and Tunstall, and between the power of Arran and of Warwick.

To prove his argument Knox unhesitatingly chose a violent passage from Scripture, and applied it with an awful and fearless logic which was characteristic of him. He referred to Saul's disobedience to God's command to exterminate the population of Amalek.

Disobedience to God's voice is not only when man doth wickedly contrary to the precepts of God, but also when of good zeal, or good intent, as we commonly speak, man doth anything to the honour or service of God not commanded by the express word of God, as in this matter plainly may be espied. For Saul transgressed not wickedly in murder, adultery or like external sins, but saved one aged and impotent King (which thing who would not call a good deed of mercy?) and permitted the people, as said is, to save certain bestial to be offered unto the Lord; thinking that God should therewith stand content and appeased, because he and the people did it of good intent. But both these called Samuel idolatry.

He also used the story of Amalek to threaten, with a flash of ferocity, the Catholics and conservatives in his audience.

Advert, ye that presently persecute the people of God, albeit your pains be deferred, yet are they already prepared of God; this people of Amalek were not, immediately after the violence done against Israel, punished; but long after, they were commanded to be destroyed by Saul, man, woman, infant, suckling, oxen, cattle, camels and asses; and finally all that lived in that land.

Then Knox turned to the words of the canon in the mass, arguing, in the spirit of all the canonists turned theologians who disputed on the Real Presence in England, that the words of the canon are *Hoc est enim corpus meum*, while the words of Scripture are *Hoc est corpus meum*. But when Knox asserted that Christ was sacrificed only once, on the cross, and that if the Papists believed that they were sacrificing Christ again in the mass they must believe that they were shedding His blood anew, he presented this familiar Protestant argument in his own typical style.

If in your mass ye offer Jesus Christ for sin, then necessarily in your mass must ye needs kill Jesus Christ. . . . And so, Papists, if ye offer Christ in sacrifice for sin, ye shed His blood and thus newly slay Him. Advert to what fine [end] your own desire shall bring you, even to be slayers of Jesus Christ. Ye will say, ye never pretended such abomination.

I dispute not what ye intended; but I only saw what absurdity doth follow upon your own doctrine. . . . But now will I relieve you of this anguish; dolorous it were daily to commit manslaughter, and oftentimes to crucify the King of glory. Be not afraid; ye do it not; for Jesus Christ may suffer no more, shed His blood no more, nor die no more. For that He hath died, He so died for sin, and that once; and now He liveth, and death may not prevail against Him. And so do ye not slay Christ, for no power ye have to do the same. Only ye have deceived the people, causing them believe that ye offered Jesus Christ in sacrifice for sin in your mass; which is frivole and false, for Jesus Christ may not be offered because He may not die.

Knox took the opportunity to refer to the three issues that Hooper had raised in his Lenten sermon before the King exactly a month earlier—altars, vestments, and kneeling to receive communion. We do not know whether Knox had heard of Hooper's sermon at Whitehall when he spoke before the Council of the North. In any case, he was again cautious. He did not, like Hooper, openly argue that altars, vestments, and kneeling at communion should be abolished; he merely pointed out that at the Last Supper Christ received the communion sitting at a table with His disciples, and did not wear vestments, and that there was no authority in the Bible for adopting any other practice.

Knox ended by launching a counter-attack against the preacher who had preached before the Council of the North at the sermon on the previous Sunday, which Knox had attended. This criticism of a preacher who had been chosen to preach on an important occasion, and who had supported the doctrine of the Real Presence, must have greatly displeased Tunstall. But Tunstall knew that if he took any action against Knox, the Privy Council in London might hear of it, and this would probably lead to an order from the Privy Council not only vindicating Knox's opinion about the Real Presence, but prohibiting the old orthodox doctrine from being advocated by Tunstall's supporters. So Tunstall took no action. Knox returned to Berwick, and nothing further was heard of the incident.

Soon afterwards Knox no longer had any need to fear Tunstall. In the autumn of 1550 Tunstall was accused of having been involved in the conspiracy against the government in Yorkshire in the previous year. It was almost certainly a frame-up inspired by Warwick, who had plans to get rid of Tunstall and seize a large part of the revenues of the see of Durham during the vacancy in the see. Tunstall was summoned to London, where he was placed under house arrest at his London residence; after remaining there for a year, he was sent to the Tower. A bill to deprive him of his bishopric passed the House of Lords only against the strong opposition of Cranmer, and was thrown out in the House of Commons; but he was eventually deprived in October 1552 by a Royal Commission. He remained in prison during the rest of Edward's reign, and spent his time in writing a book in defence of the Real Presence.[1]

Knox showed a similar caution in dealing with the immorality and corruption which was rampant in Berwick and throughout the realm. The Protestant and Catholic theologians adopted exactly the same attitude towards immorality. Both agreed that it was the duty of the State to prevent and punish immorality, and neither questioned the right of the government and clergy to interfere in every detail of the private life and recreations of the people. They both supported the laws that prohibited adultery and fornication, swearing, dicing and card-playing, and wearing of ostentatious or frivolous clothes; they were both equally incapable of enforcing these laws against the powerful and wealthy classes of society; and they both denounced the other for their inability to do what they could not do themselves. Before the Reformation the Protestants had been loud in their denunciations of the immorality of the clergy, the rapacity of the monks as landlords, and the failure of the leaders of the Church to root out the corruption; now every Papist pulpit in Europe rang with invectives against the sexual licence and corruption which was tolerated in heretic England.[2]

As might have been expected, the Reformation had made matters worse in England. It had been introduced by the King and the nobility, and had weakened all the traditional beliefs without engendering any revolutionary enthusiasm among the people for some new ideal. Respect for the old order had broken down, and the use of excommunication by the bishops and their courts had been so savagely attacked by the reformers that ex-

[1] Scheyvfe to Mary of Hungary, 17 Aug. 1550 (*Span. Cal.* x. 166); *House of Lords Journal*, 31 Mar. 1552. Tunstall's book is his *De Veritate Corporis et Sanguinis Domini nostri Jesu Christi in Eucharistia*.

[2] See van der Delft to Charles V, 14 Jan. 1550 (*Span. Cal.* x. 6).

communication had fallen into disuse. The easy-going laxity of pre-Reformation days had been replaced by open cynicism. Cranmer's chaplain, Thomas Becon, complained that 'men which can prattle of the Gospel very finely', and who could dispute about justification by faith, did not lead a virtuous life or make any attempt to restrain their licentiousness or covetousness: all their religion lay in language and dispute. James Haddon, who was chaplain to the Duke of Suffolk, the father of Lady Jane Grey, was distressed that while this great Protestant nobleman prohibited his servants from playing cards, he himself played cards and gambled with his wife. Another Protestant, Traheron, wrote that 'religion is indeed prospering, but the wickedness of those who profess the Gospel is wonderfully on the increase'. At Berwick the soldiers of the garrison were forbidden to play cards—except during twenty days at Christmas—in accordance with the general rule, under pain of three days' imprisonment and the forfeiture of their winnings, which were to be used for paying for the repair of Berwick bridge. But the Earl of Rutland, the Lord Warden of the Eastern Marches, played cards every night with the officers of his household, and, while the bridge was still dangerous, and work had not yet started on the new church for Knox and his congregation, Rutland's gambling debts were paid from the funds which would otherwise have been available for the bridge and the church.[1]

The honest Protestants were disgusted with the situation, and their preachers denounced the greed and oppression of the landlords and the selfishness and wickedness of all classes. But they were impeded, in their denunciation of vice, by the knowledge that they all depended on the worst offenders, not only for their own livelihood and preferment, but for the continuation and extension of Protestantism in England. If they denounced Warwick, Pembroke, Suffolk, and Northampton, these peers might jettison the Protestants and reinstate the old Catholic religion, as they had nearly done in October 1549. So the Protestant preachers acted on the principle of not mentioning names. They condemned vice and covetousness in all classes of society, and sometimes went so far as to say that covetousness was prevalent among the

[1] Becon, *Jewel of Joy* (Becon, *Works*, ii. 415–16); Haddon to Bullinger (Aug. 1552); Traheron to Bullinger, 12 June 1550 (*Orig. Letters*, pp. 282, 324); Book of Statutes and Ordinances of Berwick (24 May 1542) (*L.P.* xvii. 343); Proceedings against men who played cards (June 1549); Accounts of Rutland's steward, July–Nov. 1549 (*H.M.C.*, *12th* R. iv. 40; *Rutland*, iv. 361–2).

nobility and the ruling classes; but they did not say that Warwick was covetous, that Pembroke oppressed his tenants, and that Suffolk and Rutland gambled in defiance of the law which they themselves enforced against others.

Knox adopted the same principle at Berwick. He later blamed himself for the restraint which he had shown, and for his failure to denounce openly the great offenders; but it would have been difficult for him to have done anything more. Being an alien and a member of a hated and despised nation, who had been liberated from the French galleys and granted political asylum by the English government, his position was even more difficult than that of the English preachers. An earlier Scottish refugee, Alexander Aless, had discovered fifteen years before how deeply the English ecclesiastical authorities resented any criticism of their conduct by a Scotsman.[1] In the circumstances, it is surprising that Knox went as far as he did.

Knox's sermons in Berwick had their effect across the frontier. The Scottish Protestant movement had not recovered from the heavy blows which it had suffered in 1547, when all the leaders had been caught in St. Andrews Castle. Some of these leaders, like Knox, Rough, and Kirkcaldy of Grange, were now in England. Others like Norman Leslie, released from imprisonment and the galleys, had entered the French army, and were rendering brave and honourable service to the King of France against the Emperor. Those who had returned to Scotland under the amnesty had reconciled themselves to the government. In 1550 another Protestant martyr, Adam Wallace, who had succeeded Knox as tutor to Ormiston's children, was condemned as a heretic by Archbishop Hamilton, Winram, and other judges because he had read the Bible. He was hanged and burnt in Edinburgh. But though Protestantism appeared to be crushed, under the surface Scotland was seething with religious discontent. In 1551 the German Protestant, John of Ulm, who had come to England as a refugee, accompanied his employer, the future Duke of Suffolk, to Scotland after the end of the war, and on returning to England wrote to the Swiss Protestant Gualter an encouraging account of the strength of Protestantism in Scotland:

> In the leaders of that nation I can see little else than cruelty and ignorance, for they resist and oppose the truth in every possible way. As for

[1] Aless, *Of the auctorite of the word of God agaynst the bisshop of London*, unpag.

the common people, however, it is generally thought that more of them are rightly persuaded as to true religion than here among us in England. This seems to be a strange state of things, that among the English the ruling powers are virtuous and godly, but the people have for a long time been most contumacious; while in Scotland, on the contrary, the rulers are most ferocious, but the nation at large is virtuous, and exceedingly well disposed towards our most holy religion.[1]

The Protestants in Scotland, steadfast though dispirited, heard the voice of Scottish Protestantism speaking loudly in Berwick. Many of them crossed the Border to hear Knox preach, and decided to leave their homes and remain in Berwick as members of his congregation. It was, in one sense, an admission of defeat, as it showed that they had temporarily abandoned hope of any success in Scotland; but it strengthened Knox's position in England, and preserved the organizational nucleus of the movement. If Arran and Mary of Lorraine had been as cruel and ferocious as John of Ulm thought them, they would have taken some action about the presence of Knox and his Scottish congregation less than three miles from the Scottish frontier. Henry VIII, Elizabeth I, and Charles V would have made strong diplomatic representations against the harbouring of their rebels, and would probably have arranged to have Knox kidnapped and murdered, or carried across the Border to be tried and executed as a traitor. But with the mild and lazy rulers of Scotland, Knox ran no risk of suffering the fate of Brancetour, Rincón, and Story.[2] The presence of Knox and his congregation in Berwick caused more anxiety to the English than the Scottish government, for it was an additional cause of illegal immigration from Scotland.[3]

By the summer of 1551 Knox was preaching regularly in Newcastle, though he still preached and celebrated the communion with his congregation in Berwick. The two towns were 60 miles

[1] John of Ulm to Gualter, 29 May 1551 (an unsatisfactory English translation is in *Orig. Letters*, p. 434). For the proceedings against Wallace, see Knox, *History*, i. 114–16; Foxe, v. 636–41; Calderwood, i. 262–71.

[2] For the attempts of Henry VIII's agents to kidnap the English refugee, Brancetour, in Paris in 1540, see Wyatt to Henry VIII, 7 Jan. (1540) (*State Pap*. viii. 219–29). Rincón, a Spanish refugee sent as the French envoy to the Turks, was murdered by Charles V's agents in 1541. The English Catholic refugee, Story, was kidnapped from Antwerp in 1570 by Elizabeth I's agents, and subsequently executed.

[3] Northumberland to Cecil, 28 Oct. 1552 (Haynes, p. 136); Northumberland to Cecil and Petre, 23 Nov. 1552 (Tytler, *England under Edward VI and Mary*, p. 142); Scheyvfe to the Council of State (24 Sept. 1550?) (*Span. Cal.* x. 180).

apart, but were joined by one of the few good roads in England. A determined horseman could cover the distance, even without post-horses, in one long day's ride, though travellers usually took two days over the journey. Knox may have preached in other places in Northumberland, but he did not travel widely throughout the wild country, and the task of bringing religion to the people of the country districts was left to Bernard Gilpin in the next decade. Knox was not by nature a missionary; he preferred to stay in the livelier and more political atmosphere of the towns, and to deal, if indirectly, with the controversial religious issues of the day, rather than to preach elementary doctrine to new converts in the backwoods. He did not have a benefice in Newcastle, but preached in the parish church of St. Nicholas, where William Purye was vicar.[1]

From the point of view of the authorities, Knox's preaching in Newcastle had an unfortunate result. Many of the Scots in Berwick followed Knox to Newcastle, and others, who had not yet come to England, came from Scotland to join Knox's congregation. The government had almost resigned themselves to the fact that Berwick was full of Scots, but were displeased to see the growth of another Scottish colony at Newcastle. It is remarkable that this influx of Scots into Newcastle, though it annoyed the authorities, does not seem to have led to any outburst of anti-Scottish hatred among the English population of the town. The Scots must have behaved themselves very well. Despite all the national prejudice against them, there seem to have been no complaints of a growth of lawlessness and crime in Newcastle, or any other allegations of misconduct against the Scots. It is a tribute to their discipline, and to the guidance of Knox. These Scots in Berwick and Newcastle, who had been born and bred in the most backward and lawless country of Western Europe, maintained a standard of morality in their private lives which was rare in the England of Edward VI. Their conduct was very different from that of the Castilians at St. Andrews; but the members of Knox's congregation at Berwick and Newcastle were the idealists of the Protestant movement. They were humble men and women who had no political ambitions or desire to enrich themselves, but were inspired by a sincere

[1] There is no evidence for the belief expressed by Lorimer (in *John Knox and the Church of England*, pp. 47–48) that it was Knox who converted Holy Island to Protestantism, or that Knox was an evangelist to all the country around Berwick.

devotion to their cause, and united under the guidance of a determined but cautious leader.

In August 1551 the sweating sickness reached Newcastle. The mild winter and early spring of 1550–1 led to the heaviest outbreak for over thirty years; it reached its peak in London in July, and then spread to the north in the autumn. Knox delivered some of his strongest sermons at Berwick and Newcastle against the immorality of the country while the sweat was raging in Newcastle. Like all his contemporaries, Knox considered that plagues and diseases were sent by God either as a punishment for sin or as a trial. The preachers in Augsburg and Paris interpreted the sweating sickness in England as a sign of God's indignation with Protestant heresy: to the Protestant preachers in England, it was a punishment for the vices and immorality of the nobles and other classes.[1]

A few weeks later Knox took a greater risk. In October 1551 Somerset and several of his friends were arrested on a charge of high treason. The country was shocked. Everyone believed that Somerset was innocent, but no one dared to say so openly; for Warwick, who was now created Duke of Northumberland, pressed the charges relentlessly. William Cecil, who had been Somerset's secretary and was now Secretary of State under Northumberland, played the chief part in prosecuting Somerset and his party. The courtiers and the English ambassadors abroad, as usual on such occasions, wrote to Northumberland, vilifying Somerset and praising Northumberland for his zeal in suppressing the conspiracy. Cranmer made his usual half-hearted intervention for the fallen man, but was cowed into submission. Hooper, who had been Somerset's chaplain but had conceived a ridiculous admiration for Northumberland, said nothing. The only man who publicly denounced the arrest of Somerset was Knox.

Almost as soon as the news reached Newcastle, Knox preached in the town on All Saints' Day. He was guarded in his words, and did not mention Northumberland by name; but the meaning of his sermon was sufficiently clear to alarm Sir Robert Bradling, a former Mayor of Newcastle, who was in the congregation. Knox said that the Papists had deliberately instigated the rift between

[1] Knox, *Letter to the Faithful in London, Newcastle and Berwick* (*Works*, iii. 167); Wotton to Cecil, 10 Aug. 1551 (Haynes, p. 116); Pickering to the Council, 17 Jan. 1552/3 (*Cal. For. Pap. Edw. VI*, No. 608).

the two chief pillars of Protestant England in the hopes that if one of them destroyed the other, they would be able to destroy the survivor. If one of them put his innocent friend to death, he himself would soon be ruined.[1]

In January 1552 Somerset was beheaded, to the indignation of the people. Northumberland's government was more unpopular than any since the beginning of the century; the number of arrests, and sentences of mutilation for sedition, which had dropped sharply under Somerset's government, now rose to a higher level than it had ever reached under Henry VIII. In the summer of 1552 Northumberland visited the north. He had a plan for appropriating for himself and his friends a large part of the revenues of the see of Durham during the vacancy in the see, before appointing Ridley to succeed Tunstall as bishop, with Ridley's chaplain Grindal as bishop of a new see to be created at Newcastle.[2]

When Northumberland arrived in Newcastle at the end of June, Knox, who was now the most famous preacher in the diocese, preached a number of sermons before the Duke. Northumberland visited various places in the district, including Berwick, and Knox accompanied him as his official preacher. Knox states that he spoke with great vehemence in these sermons before Northumberland about the punishments that would fall on England if the sin, vice, and misconduct of the rulers continued.[3] It would be interesting to know what Knox said in these sermons, and still more interesting to know what he said in his private conversations with Northumberland; for when Northumberland returned to the south at the end of August, Knox travelled with him. Northumberland had invited Knox to come to Court and preach before the King.

Northumberland's decision to favour Knox was in line with his general policy. Against Somerset, who had had the support of Cranmer and the Protestant moderates, Northumberland had based himself on the Protestant extremists. This placed him in an excellent position to appropriate the episcopal revenues for himself on the pretext of abating the pomp and pride of the bishops, and won the support of the Protestant radicals, who hailed him as

[1] Knox, *Letter to the Faithful in London, Newcastle and Berwick;* Knox, *Admonition to England* (*Works*, iii. 167, 277–8).

[2] Ridley to Gates and Cecil, 18 Nov. 1552 (Ridley, *Works*, p. 336); Scheyvfe's advices, 20 Nov. 1552 (*Span. Cal.* x. 591); Strype, *Life of Grindal*, pp. 10–12.

[3] Knox, *Letter to the Faithful in London, Newcastle and Berwick* (*Works*, iii. 167–8).

a saviour. John of Ulm described him, along with Suffolk, as one of the two most shining lights of the Church of England; and Hooper called him 'that faithful and intrepid soldier of Christ'.[1] Northumberland had made the extremist Hooper a bishop. When Hooper defied the authority of Church and State over vestments, Northumberland allowed Cranmer and Ridley to discipline him; now Hooper caused no more trouble, and still admired Northumberland. Northumberland obviously thought that Knox would react to his promotion in the same way as Hooper.

In the summer of 1552 Northumberland had more need than ever before of the support of the extremists. His relations with Cranmer had become very strained. Cranmer was opposed to the deprivation of Catholic bishops like Tunstall by irregular process when they had not been guilty of disobedience to the royal authority, and to the looting of Church property by Northumberland.[2] Northumberland brought Knox to Court to use him against Cranmer. Here he made a miscalculation, for though Northumberland was an able political intriguer, he was the sort of politician who believed that all men had their price, and was not well acquainted with men of the type of Knox.

Knox now moved to the centre of English political life after three years in Northumberland. These had been very happy years for Knox, and for the rest of his life he always longed to return to Northumberland. His health during this time had not been good, perhaps because he was still suffering from the effects of his life in the galleys; but he had been able to engage in what he calls 'bodily exercise', by which he means outdoor sports—probably bowls, archery, and perhaps hunting. He had met, during these years, the young girl whom he was later to marry, Marjory Bowes, and her mother Elizabeth Bowes. Now, as Protestant rule in England was nearing its end, he moved to higher spheres.

[1] John of Ulm to Bullinger, 25 Mar. 1550; Hooper to Bullinger, 27 Mar. 1550 (*Orig. Letters*, pp. 82, 399).

[2] Scheyvfe's advices, 20 Nov. 1552; Scheyvfe to Granvelle, 20 Nov. 1552 (*Span. Cal.* x. 591, 593); Ridley, *A Piteous Lamentation of the Estate of the Church of England* (Ridley, *Works*, p. 59); *House of Lords Journal*, 31 Mar. 1552.

CHAPTER VII

London

NORTHUMBERLAND rejoined the Court at Salisbury on 29 August, and travelled with Edward VI by Wilton, Winchester, Basing, and Reading to Windsor and Hampton Court. Knox probably travelled with him, and preached before the King on his progress; at any rate, we know that at the end of September he preached before Edward at Windsor, and in October at Hampton Court.[1] His sermon at Windsor threw English politics into a ferment. It was caused by the coming into force of the Second Book of Common Prayer.

The Prayer Book of 1549 had been criticized from the beginning by Protestant theologians as well as by Catholic reactionaries and the conservative populace, and the German Protestant, Bucer, at Cambridge, had subjected it to a detailed criticism in his *Censura*. As a result of this Protestant criticism, a new Prayer Book was drafted, and was given force of law by the second Act of Uniformity in March 1552. The Act prescribed that the Second Book of Common Prayer was to come into force on All Saints' Day, when it was to replace the service in the first Book of Common Prayer as the only form of service which was permitted by law to be celebrated in England. The second Prayer Book was much more Protestant than the first; it suppressed nearly all the old ceremonies of which Bucer had complained, and many vestments were abolished; and the communion service, which was no longer called the mass, contained words which were hardly compatible with belief in the Real Presence. Amid all these welcome advances, there was one set-back for the Protestant extremists. The

[1] *A.P.C.* 29 Aug. and 8, 9, 14, 18, and 30 Sept. 1552; Scheyvfe to Mary of Hungary, 10 Sept. 1552 (*Span. Cal.* x. 562, where 'Shrewsbury' is obviously an error for 'Salisbury'); 'King Edward's Journal', 24, 26, and 28 Aug., and 2, 5, 7, 10, 12, 15, and 28 Sept. 1552 (Burnet, *History of the Reformation of the Church of England*, v. 83–85); Knox, *Letter to the Faithful in London, Newcastle and Berwick* (*Works*, iii. 168). The sermons at Windsor to which Knox there refers can have been preached only between 15 and 28 Sept. 1552, and those at Hampton Court between 28 Sept. and 10 Oct. 1552 ('King Edward's Journal' (Burnet, v. 84–85, 88)).

new communion service, unlike the communion service in the first Book of Common Prayer, contained a rubric expressly ordering that the communicants should receive the communion on their knees.[1]

The practice of sitting to receive communion had been adopted not only by Knox and his congregation at Berwick, but also by the Polish refugee, John à Lasco, and his congregation of foreign Protestants in London. The issue had also been discussed in the commission which was drafting the Code of Ecclesiastical Law. On this commission the radicals had actually been successful, for the draft code which was approved by the commissioners directed that the communion was to be received sitting; but the Code of Ecclesiastical Law was never given force of law. The Second Book of Common Prayer contained a contrary direction, thanks to the efforts of Cranmer, Ridley, and Peter Martyr. It marked the victory, on this issue at least, of the moderates over the extremists.[2]

When Knox preached at Windsor at the end of September 1552, the Second Book of Common Prayer was due to come into force in about five weeks' time. Knox declared that the provision in the new Prayer Book that ordered that the communion should be received kneeling was sinful and idolatrous, as it implied adoration and worship of a piece of bread, whereas God alone should be worshipped. There was no longer anything to be gained by keeping silent on this matter, and Knox decided to make a last effort to prevent the order about kneeling from coming into force. The fact that he was a hated Scot, a refugee, and a country preacher newly arrived at Court, did not deter him from criticizing a practice that had been adopted for centuries, had been affirmed by the Primate and his colleagues, and had already been given force of law as from 1 November by Act of Parliament.

Knox's sermon had a great effect at Court. The Flemish Protestant refugee Utenhove wrote to Bullinger in Zürich that it had given rise to disputes among the bishops. 'This good man,' he wrote, 'a Scotsman by nationality, has so wrought upon the minds of many persons that we may hope some good to the

[1] For Bucer's *Censura*, see Bucer, *Scripta Anglicana*, pp. 456–503; for the Second Book of Common Prayer, see *Liturgies of Edward VI*, pp. 187–355; the rubric ordering kneeling is on p. 279. See also *Statutes of the Realm*, 5 & 6 Edw. VI, c. 1.

[2] À Lasco, *Forma ac ratio tota Ecclesiastici Ministerii, in peregrinorum . . . instituta Londini in Anglia* (*Joannis a Lasco Opera*, ii. 114–22); Cardwell, *Reformation of Ecclesiastical Laws*, p. 31; Cranmer to the Council, 7 Oct. 1552 (Lorimer, *John Knox and the Church of England*, p. 103).

Church will at length arise from it'; and the Emperor's ambassador reported that Northumberland had 'brought hither a new Scottish apostle, who has already begun to pick holes in the new and universal reformation' which had been introduced by the Second Book of Common Prayer. There was an influential party, which included Hooper and John à Lasco, who agreed with Knox; the King was sympathetic to the Protestant extremists, and easily alarmed at the suggestion that dregs of Popery still remained in the new Prayer Book; while Northumberland was eager to do anything to annoy and weaken Cranmer. On 27 September the Privy Council gave orders to the printers to suspend the distribution of the prayer books until the matter was decided. They also ordered Cranmer to justify the rubric which ordered kneeling at communion. On 7 October Cranmer wrote to the Council and told them that he had discussed the question with Ridley and Peter Martyr, who agreed that to kneel at communion did not imply adoration of the Host, but was merely a gesture of reverence for the sacrament of the Lord's Supper. The Privy Council was still not satisfied, and Cranmer was ordered to postpone his departure for his diocese and attend a meeting of the Council a few days later to discuss the matter. It was eventually decided on 27 October, five days before the new Prayer Book was to come into force, to retain the direction as to kneeling, but to insert an additional passage in the Prayer Book, stating that the fact that the communicants received the sacrament on their knees did not imply any adoration of the elements, as Christ was not really present, corporally, in the bread and wine; this was impossible, because Christ was in Heaven on the right hand of God the Father, and could not be in two places at the same time.[1]

With only five days to go before the Prayer Book came into force, the new rubric presented a problem for the printers. They printed it on loose sheets, and stuck it in at the appropriate page in the Prayer Book; in the hurry, mistakes were made, and in some

[1] Utenhove to Bullinger, 12 Oct. 1552 (*Orig. Letters*, p. 592, an unsatisfactory translation, in which 'conciniatoris ducis Northumbriae' is translated as 'chaplain [not 'preacher'] to the Duke of Northumberland'); Scheyvfe to Granvelle, 20 Nov. 1552 (*Span. Cal.* x. 593); *A.P.C.* 27 Sept. and 8, 11, and 27 Oct. 1552; Cranmer to the Council, 7 Oct. 1552; Cecil's memorandum, 20 Oct. 1552 (Lorimer, *John Knox and the Church of England*, pp. 103–6). For the black rubric, see Second Book of Common Prayer (*Liturgies of Edward VI*, p. 283). Knox's sermon was almost certainly delivered at Windsor about the end of September; see *A.P.C.* 27 Sept. 1552, and the movements of the King and Court, from 'King Edward's Journal' and *A.P.C.*

copies the extra page was stuck in at the wrong place, at the beginning or at the end of the pages dealing with the communion service.[1] The new rubric, which shocked the many Catholics in the country, became known as the 'black rubric'. The black rubric was probably drafted by Cranmer; it bears the mark of his style and method of argument. It was certainly not drafted by Knox, though this was widely believed at the time. Knox did not believe that the statement in the rubric was true; he believed that kneeling to receive communion did imply belief in the Real Presence, and the black rubric stated precisely the opposite.

The publication of the black rubric was therefore not a compromise, but a victory for Cranmer; yet in another sense it was a victory for Knox. The black rubric would never have been issued if it had not been for Knox's sermon at Windsor, and although the Second Book of Common Prayer had eliminated the words in the communion service that suggested that Christ was present in substance in the bread and wine, there was nothing which expressly repudiated the Real Presence until the black rubric was added. It was therefore thanks to Knox that, for the first time, the Prayer Book contained an unequivocal denial of the Real Presence. The Catholics considered that Knox was responsible. Eighteen months later, when the triumphant Catholic party, under Queen Mary, staged their great disputation at Oxford with their captives Cranmer, Ridley, and Latimer, the bullying prolocutor, Weston, who presided at the disputation, taunted Latimer with the fact that when England was Protestant, 'a runagate Scot [Scottish refugee] did take away the adoration or worshipping of Christ in the sacrament, by whose procurement that heresy was put into the last communion book; so much prevailed that one man's authority at that time'. Although it has often been suggested that the 'runagate Scot' to whom Weston referred was Aless, not Knox, there is no doubt that Knox was meant. Aless, who had left England fifteen years earlier, in 1539, had never publicly attacked the mass during his stay in England; had he done so, under Henry VIII, he would probably have ended his days at Smithfield. Nor had Aless's authority ever 'prevailed' to any great extent in England. Weston was certainly referring to Knox's activities eighteen months before, in 1552, when Knox had been responsible for a rubric which, in Catholic

[1] See, e.g., the three copies of the first edition of the Second Book of Common Prayer in the British Museum, where the black rubric is inserted at different places.

eyes, did undoubtedly 'take away the adoration or worshipping of Christ in the Sacrament'.[1]

But in October 1552 the decision of the Privy Council put Knox in a difficult position. After 1 November his congregation at Berwick would be guilty of disobeying a rubric in the Book of Common Prayer if they continued to sit to receive communion, and might even be accused by the authorities of participating in a religious service other than that prescribed in the Act of Uniformity. Knox wrote to his friends in Berwick and instructed them, in future, to receive the communion on their knees. His very long letter can only be described as an elaborate attempt at face-saving.

He took a long time in getting to the point, beginning with references to examples in Scripture of the triumph of the ungodly over the godly, of Cain over Abel, and of Esau over Jacob. He then summarized, under eight heads, the cardinal points of the doctrine which he had taught in Berwick. There was nothing in this doctrine which would not have been accepted by Cranmer and the Church of England at the time—justification by faith; prayers only to God, without mediation of the saints; that baptism and the Lord's Supper were the only two sacraments; that Christ was only sacrificed once, upon the cross; the duty of performing good works; and the duty of obedience to the magistrates, which Knox, after three and a half years in England, stressed as strongly as Cranmer could have wished.

> Remembering always, beloved brethren, that due obedience be given to magistrates, rulers and princes, without tumult, grudge or sedition; for how wicked that ever themselves be in life, as how ungodly that ever their precepts or commandments be, ye must obey them for conscience sake; except in chief points of religion; and then ought ye rather to obey God nor man; not to pretend to defend God's truth or religion (ye being subjects) by violence or sword, but patiently suffering what God shall please be laid upon you for constant confession of your faith and belief.

Two years later, Knox was to revise his opinion drastically on this subject.

It was only at the end of this long letter, after a lengthy declaration of his willingness to suffer death for God's truth and his lack of interest in his corporal, as opposed to his spiritual, welfare, that Knox at last came to the point.

[1] Latimer's disputation, 18 Apr. 1554 (Foxe, vi. 510).

I signify unto you that as I neither repent nor recant that my former doctrine, so do I (for divers causes long to rehearse) much prefer sitting at the Lord's table either to kneeling, standing or going, at the action of that mystical supper. But because I am but one, having in my contrair magistrates, common order, and judgements of many learned, I am not minded, for maintenance of that one thing, to gainstand the magistrates, in all other and chief points of religion agreeing with Christ and with His true doctrine, nor yet to break nor trouble common order.

He therefore advised them to submit to the magistrates and receive the communion on their knees; but he wrote that he had only agreed to do this on three conditions, all of which had been granted to him. The first was the insertion of the black rubric; the second, that the authorities admitted that kneeling was not necessary for receiving communion, but was only a ceremony thought godly by man, and not by Christ Himself; the third, that the authorities did not condemn what he had done in Berwick, but recognized that he had attempted to follow what Christ Himself had done. 'These things granted unto me, I neither will gainstand godly magistrates, neither break common order, nor yet contend with my superiors or fellow preachers, but with patience will I bear that one thing; daily thirsting and calling unto God for reformation of that and others.'

Knox told the congregation of Berwick that they had done nothing wrong in sitting at communion, for hitherto there was no law which forbade this, except the statute of the Roman Antichrist. But now that the upper powers had ordered them to kneel, they would not be damned, or judged as shrinking from Christ, if they obeyed, provided that they stated openly that they did so unwillingly, and only in obedience to the magistrates. He ended by again assuring them that it was not fear of death or corporal punishment that had led him to advise them to obey the magistrates. 'Less offence it is to bear this one thing (with dolour of your hearts, daily calling unto God for reformation of the same), than to provoke the magistrates to displeasure, seeing that in principals we all agree. This for your order, which ye shall not order nor change till ye be especially commanded by such as hath authority.'[1]

[1] Knox, 'Epistle to the Congregation of Berwick', printed in Lorimer, *John Knox and the Church of England*, pp. 251–65. It is not included in Knox's *Works*. For the passages cited, see pp. 259, 261–3.

If the situation in England had been the same as that which had existed a few years earlier, Knox would never have got away with an evasive submission such as this. Under Henry VIII a document of this kind would have been regarded as an utterly inadequate recantation which aggravated Knox's earlier offence, and as a hidden act of defiance. Knox would have been summoned before the Privy Council and ordered to make a cringing confession of guilt in the pulpit at Berwick, under threat of being burnt; and from what we know of Knox's character there is every reason to believe that he would have done as he was required. But Cranmer was far more tolerant than his old master, and was prepared to make submission as easy as possible for Knox. If Knox's letter to the congregation of Berwick had been published, the authorities might have taken further action; but it was a private letter, and was allowed to remain private, except perhaps in the town of Berwick. Cranmer did, however, place Knox in a certain difficulty by the wording of his Articles of Religion, and hardly had the dispute about the rubric been settled when the issue of kneeling was again raised by Knox in connexion with the Articles.

For some time there had been a need for a new formulary of faith, as the doctrine of the Church of England had radically changed since the Bishops' Book and the King's Book of Henry VIII's reign. Cranmer had therefore drafted articles, which were eventually issued as the Articles of Religion of 1553. In the reign of Elizabeth these Articles were reissued, in an amended form, as the Thirty-nine Articles of 1562, which are still today the official statement of the beliefs of the Church of England. Knox played an important part in drafting the Articles. Cranmer, after working on the Articles for nearly three years and submitting them to an informal assembly of the bishops, finally completed his draft in September 1552, and sent the Articles to the Privy Council. On 21 October the Council ordered that the Articles were to be examined by Harley, Bill, Horne, Grindal, Perne, and Knox. Harley, Bill, Grindal, and Perne were royal chaplains, and it has often been assumed that the task of examining the Articles was entrusted to the royal chaplains, and that consequently Knox was a royal chaplain; but in fact the minutes of the Privy Council make it clear that while four of the six divines who examined the Articles were royal chaplains, Knox and Horne were not. It was natural that Knox should have been selected for this duty, as Northumberland would have relished the prospect of his criticizing Cranmer's draft.[1]

Cranmer had drafted forty-five articles. The thirty-eighth article stated that the Second Book of Common Prayer was holy, godly, and provable by God's Scriptures in every rite and ceremony, and in no point repugnant thereto, both as regards the common prayers and ministration of the sacraments as well as in the Ordinal. Knox and some of his colleagues presented a memorandum to the Privy Council objecting to the thirty-eighth article. They argued that it was incorrect to state that the ceremonies in the Prayer Book were all provable by God's Scriptures, because the Prayer Book contained a rubric which directed that the communion should be received kneeling, and there was nothing in the Bible which justified this rubric. It has been suggested that Knox did not write this document, because it is unlike his usual style, and the closely reasoned, textual arguments resemble those used by Becon, Hutchinson, and John à Lasco. But Knox was quite capable of realizing that a memorandum to the Privy Council should be written in a rather cooler style than that which he ordinarily used; and there are from time to time some rhetorical questions and other flashes of fire reminiscent of Knox. The authors of the memorandum argued that if the communion was received kneeling, this would encourage the Papists; for 'albeit we cry never so loud that in that action no adoration ought to be given to no creature, yet whisper they, yea, and plainly do they speak: "Cry what they list", saith the Papists, "yet are the Gospellers compelled to do the self same thing that we whom they call idolators do in every gesture and behaviour".'[2]

Not all the six preachers agreed with Knox on this question,[3] but he persuaded them to amend Cranmer's draft by substituting a more modified approval of the Second Book of Common Prayer,

[1] *A.P.C.* 2 May and 21 Oct. 1552; Cranmer to Cecil, 19 Sept. 1552 (Cranmer, *Works*, ii. 439–40). As to whether Knox was a royal chaplain, see Dixon, *History of the Church of England*, iii. 325–7 n., 478–9 n.; Gairdner, *Lollardy and the Reformation*, iii. 340–1.

[2] The text of the memorandum is printed in Lorimer, *John Knox and the Church of England*, pp. 267–74; the passage cited is at p. 269; and see Lorimer's opinion as to its authorship.

[3] This seems clear, because the authors of the memorandum wrote that the Articles had been submitted 'to certain learned preachers, and among whom we most unworthy were accounted', thus showing that at least two, but not all, of the six preachers drafted the memorandum.

though the amended thirty-eighth article still approved of the Prayer Book far more strongly than Knox could have wished. Whereas Cranmer's draft had stated that the Prayer Book and Ordinal were 'by God's Scripture provable in every rite and ceremony', the new draft submitted by Knox and his colleagues stated that the ceremonies in the Prayer Book and Ordinal were 'in nothing repugnant to the wholesome liberty of the Gospel . . . but very well agree with it, and in many things highly advance the same; and therefore they are to be received and approved by all faithful members of the Church of England'. As Knox believed that it was sinful to adopt any ceremony invented by man that was not prescribed in Scripture, he could not have believed that kneeling to receive communion was 'in nothing repugnant to the wholesome liberty of the Gospel'; but he knew when it was necessary to compromise, and he signed the amended draft of the Forty-five Articles together with his five colleagues.

They sent the document to the Privy Council before 20 November 1552, when the Council sent the amended draft back to Cranmer for his comments. Cranmer was obviously not prepared to accept the amendments to Article 38, because when the Articles were eventually published in May 1553, Article 38, which had become Article 35 in the final document, approved of the Prayer Book more warmly than Knox and his colleagues had done, though it did not contain the statement, which was in Cranmer's original draft, that the ceremonies in the Prayer Book were all provable by Scripture. There were also disagreements about Article 26 of the final draft, which dealt with the nature of a sacrament. The Forty-five Articles of Knox and his five colleagues expressed the Zwinglian view that God confers grace independently of the sacraments, though the sacraments are a sign of grace: the final Forty-two Articles laid down the higher view that grace was conferred through the two sacraments, which were not merely a sign, but a channel, of grace. This change was probably due to Cranmer.[1]

[1] *A.P.C.* 20 Nov. 1552; Cranmer to Cecil, 24 Nov. 1552 (Cranmer, *Works*, ii. 441). Cranmer's original draft of the Forty-five Articles has not survived; the draft as amended by Knox and his colleagues was published by Hardwick, *History of the Articles of Religion*, pp. 279–88. The text of the Forty-two Articles, as eventually issued in 1553, in English and Latin, is in *Liturgies of Edward VI*, pp. 526–37, 572–82. For the differences between these documents, and the controversy about the Articles, see Lorimer, *John Knox and the Church of England*, pp. 108–28; Gairdner, *Lollardy and the Reformation*, iii. 357–61; Dixon, iii. 480–4 and n.

In October 1552 Lord James Stewart, the Prior of St. Andrews, passed through London on his way from France to Scotland. Lord James, the illegitimate son of James V, who had been Prior of St. Andrews by Papal dispensation since the age of 7, had fought gallantly in the war against England in 1548–9, and was still a Catholic; but while he was in London, he and Knox met for the first time. The Catholic writers thirty years later magnified this meeting into one of the great cloak-and-dagger stories of the sixteenth century. Nicol Burne stated that Lord James and Knox met secretly in London, and plotted to make a revolution in Scotland in order to overthrow the Catholic Church and put Lord James in power in the place of his half-sister, Queen Mary. This plan was carried out between 1559 and 1567, when Lord James, who had become Earl of Moray and leader of the Protestant party, was made Regent for the infant James VI after Mary's forced abdication. Nicol Burne gives the impression that every move in the Protestant political strategy, every advance, every retreat, every ruse and pretended concession, from Knox's sermon at Perth to Mary's imprisonment in Lochleven, were all carefully planned, up to fifteen years in advance, at a secret meeting between Knox and Lord James in St. Paul's Cathedral in October 1552. Absurd though this story is, we know from Knox that the meeting took place in London, and it is remarkable that as early as October 1552 the Catholic nobleman of the royal Scottish house should have met the notorious Protestant refugee who was disturbing even Protestant England with his heresies. Knox makes it clear that Lord James was still a Catholic at this time, but he was perhaps beginning to turn.[1]

In the autumn of 1552 Knox's prospects lay in England, not in Scotland. Northumberland intended to handle Knox as he had handled Hooper, pursuing the well-known tactic of taming an extremist by promoting him to high office. At the height of the furore over the Prayer Book and kneeling at communion, less than two months after Knox's arrival from the north, Northumberland decided to appoint him Bishop of Rochester. The bishopric of Rochester had become the starting-point for a career

[1] Nicol Burne, *Disputation concerning the Controversit Headdis of Religion*, p. 156; Knox, *History*, ii. 78. Croft Dickinson (ibid. 78 n.) suggests that the meeting took place either in July or December 1552; but Knox was not in London in July, and Lord James passed through London on his return from France in October, not December; see Scheyvfe to Mary of Hungary, 29 Oct. 1552 (*Span. Cal.* x. 582).

on the episcopal bench. During the previous three years, the office had been held by Ridley, Ponet, and Scory; as the Catholic bishops were deprived of their sees for disobedience, the Protestant bishops moved up to greater sees, leaving Rochester vacant for a new Protestant appointee.

On 27 October, at the same meeting at which the Privy Council settled the controversy over the Prayer Book and gave orders for the printing of the black rubric, the Council awarded Knox a cash payment of £40, which was more than the annual stipend of most parish priests. Next day Northumberland wrote to Cecil, the Secretary of State, who was his closest political collaborator:

> I would to God it might please the King's Majesty to appoint Mr. Knox to the office of Rochester bishopric; which for three purposes should do very well. The first, he would not only be a whetstone, to quicken and sharp the Bishop of Canterbury, whereof he hath need; but also he would be a great confounder of the Anabaptists lately sprung up in Kent. Secondly, he should not continue the ministration in the north, contrary to this set forth here. Thirdly, the family of the Scots, now inhabiting in Newcastle chiefly for his fellowship, would not continue there, wherein many resorts unto them out of Scotland, which is not requisite. Herein I pray you desire my Lord Chamberlain and Mr. Vice-Chamberlain to help towards this good act, both for God's service and the King's.

Northumberland never made a show of his power, and handled his colleagues in the Council with tact; but his influence was supreme, and this letter was enough to make Cecil, and the Chamberlain and Vice-Chamberlain, Lord Darcy and Sir John Gates, take the necessary measures to appoint Knox to the bishopric of Rochester.[1]

Knox was confronted with the greatest test of character which he faced in his life. He stood in danger of corruption, and he knew it. His *Epistle to the Congregation of Berwick*, in which he told them to agree to kneel to receive communion, shows that he was acutely aware of this.[2] Knox protested too much in this letter, harping continually on his readiness to suffer death for his faith and the disinterestedness of his motives in instructing them to submit. He

[1] *A.P.C.* 27 Oct. 1552; Northumberland to Cecil, 28 Oct. 1552 (Tytler, *England under Edward VI and Mary*, p. 142).

[2] Knox, 'Epistle to the Congregation of Berwick' (Lorimer, *John Knox and the Church of England*, pp. 251–65).

was trying to convince himself, to appease the gnawing feeling of guilt that he was allowing himself to be corrupted by Northumberland, who had compelled him to tell his congregation at Berwick to kneel to receive communion, while he himself was rewarded for his compliance with £40 and the bishopric of Rochester.

Knox refused the bishopric. After his death the Presbyterian and Puritan writers believed that he did so because he condemned the whole principle of episcopacy; but there is no reason to believe that Knox, during his years in England, was opposed to episcopacy, and this was not his motive in declining Northumberland's offer. He refused the bishopric because he was confronted with the choice between the bench of bishops and his congregation in the north, and he chose his congregation in the north. As Bishop of Rochester, Knox could have done a great deal to suppress immorality and Popery and restore ecclesiastical discipline in his diocese, as Hooper had done in the diocese of Worcester and Gloucester; he would have been a most forceful and formidable bishop. He could also have used his influence with greater effect than hitherto in the doctrinal disputes about the Prayer Book, the Articles of Religion, the Code of Ecclesiastical Law, and any other issue which might arise for discussion in the House of Lords and Convocation, or in the less formal and more secret meetings of the bishops which had largely taken the place of the formal sessions of Convocation. But as a bishop in the south, Knox would have become separated from his congregation in the north not only in a physical sense, but politically and in religion. They would have known nothing about his activities, as a member of the opposition minority in the synods, in pressing for a more radical reformation; they would only have heard of his subscribing the formularies that Cranmer and the majority had carried, and enforcing the orders of the Privy Council in his diocese, and suppressing the extremist sects. It might have demoralized all his followers in the north; the congregation might have disintegrated, and slipped back to Scotland to compromise with the Scottish government and the Church of Rome.

If Knox had become Bishop of Rochester, he would have become separated not only from his congregation in Berwick and Newcastle, but from Scottish Protestantism. This was a step which he would not contemplate. He made this clear in a private letter to his closest friend, his future mother-in-law Mrs. Bowes, in January 1554. 'What moved me to refuse, and that with displeasure of all men (even of those that best loved me), those high promotions that were offered by him whom God hath taken from us for our offences [Edward VI]? Assuredly, the foresight of trouble to come. How oft have I said unto you, that the time would not be long that England would give me bread.'[1] Knox was one of those refugees who never resign themselves to a permanent exile, but think always of returning, as victors, to their native country from which they have fled as traitors. Few Scotsmen have been less nationalistic, in the narrow sense, and more cosmopolitan than Knox; but though he had learned to adapt himself well to English politics, his roots were in the revolutionary Protestantism of Scotland, not in the authoritarian Protestantism of England. He was not prepared to sever those roots for the sake of a mitre.

Cecil was particularly eager that Knox should accept the bishopric. At the beginning of December, he sent Knox to visit Northumberland at the Duke's house in Chelsea, which was then a fashionable residential village on the river, some five miles from London. The only information as to what transpired at the interview is in Northumberland's letter to Cecil of 7 December.

> Mr. Knox's being here to speak with me [he wrote] saying that he was so willed by you, I do return him again, because I love not to have to do with men which be neither grateful nor pleasable. I assure you I mind to have no more to do with him, but to wish him well. . . . And for my own part, if I should have passed more upon the speech of the people than upon the service of my master, or gone about to seek favour of them without respect to His Highness' surety, I needed not to have had so much obloquy of some kind of men; but the living God, that knoweth the hearts of all men, shall be my judge at the last day with what zeal, faith and truth I serve my master.

It is clear that Knox had told Northumberland that he did not wish to be a bishop, but wished to return to his congregation in the north; and Northumberland's letter suggests that he also criticized him for his vices and covetousness. But he cannot have been too outspoken, because though Northumberland was annoyed at Knox's attitude, he continued to show him a certain degree of favour. Two days after Northumberland's letter, the

[1] Knox, *Exposition of the Sixth Psalm of David*, written to Mrs. Bowes on 6 Jan. 1554 (*Works*, iii. 122).

Privy Council gave Knox a letter of recommendation to Lord Wharton, who was Northumberland's deputy as Lord Warden of the Eastern, Middle, and Western Marches.[1]

Knox left for the north immediately, and on Christmas Day he preached a sermon at Newcastle which was the most daring he had yet preached. He passed beyond generalizations and unspecified attacks on corruption and vice, and warned against the influential forces that were working for the restoration of Popery. He had obviously learned at Court about the worrying state of the King's health, though this was kept strictly secret from the public, and he realized that the Catholic Mary might soon come to the throne. Mary, alone of all the King's subjects, had been permitted to defy the Act of Uniformity with impunity. Thanks to the diplomatic pressure and the threats of Charles V, she had been allowed to have the Catholic mass celebrated in her house for two years after the first Act of Uniformity came into force, and though the Council eventually prohibited her mass and arrested her chaplains, she continued to have her mass in secret, with the unofficial connivance of the Council. Mary defied the Council, insulted the high officers of State who visited her, and mocked the mildness of the Protestant government and its weakness towards the Catholics. 'The pain of your laws', she told the Lord Chancellor, 'is but imprisonment for a short time', and this would not deter her chaplains from celebrating mass in her house. After Mary came to the throne, she told the Emperor's ambassador that during her brother's reign she had always had mass celebrated in secret in her household, and that Edward and all the Privy Council were well aware of this. During the last year of Edward's reign, she was invited to Court, and treated with every mark of honour by the Council. Northumberland was obviously trying to ingratiate himself with the princess who might become Queen at any moment.[2]

The threat of a restoration of Henrician Catholicism, if not full Popery and allegiance to Rome, when Mary became Queen, must have been obvious to Cranmer and all the Protestant bishops who knew the state of Edward's health; but none of them gave any

[1] Northumberland to Cecil, 7 Dec. 1552 (Tytler, *England under Edward VI and Mary*, ii. 148); *A.P.C.* 9 Dec. 1552.

[2] Knox, *Admonition to England* (*Works*, iii. 297); *A.P.C.* 29 Aug. 1551; Renard, Scheyvfe, etc., to Charles V, 2 Aug. 1553 (Gachard, *Voyages des Souverains des Pays-Bas*, iv. 89; *Span. Cal.* xi. 131).

public sign, by action or word, that they were conscious of the danger. They would have considered it a violation of the sacred principle of Christian obedience to the Prince if they had warned against the dangers that might arise under a future sovereign; for to warn of possible dangers under a future Papist Queen was by implication to advise that some action should be taken to prevent those dangers from occurring. It is significant that the only preacher in England who gave this warning was the Scottish immigrant, John Knox, though his personal position was much weaker than that of Cranmer and the bishops.

In his sermon on Christmas Day, Knox couched his warning in a form which, on the surface, could not be said to be seditious, but was a strong defence of the King and the existing régime in Church and State. He said that whoever in his heart was an enemy to Christ's Gospel and doctrine, as it was now preached in England, was also an enemy to God and a secret traitor to the Crown and commonwealth of England; these men were thirsting for the King's death, which their iniquity would procure, and they did not care who might reign over them, provided that they might set up idolatry again. This was a clear warning against secret Papists in high places, though again Knox was too wise to mention names; it would have been as rash to have named Mary as the enemy to Christ's Gospel as to have named Northumberland and his friends in the denunciations of covetous nobles. As it was, the Mayor of Newcastle denounced Knox for his sermon, and Lord Wharton reported the matter to the Privy Council. 'Against me were written articles', Knox wrote, 'and I compelled to answer, as unto an action of treason.'

Lord Wharton and the Earl of Westmorland, who was in the north, were inclined to treat the accusation seriously; but Knox appealed to Northumberland for assistance, and Northumberland again came to Knox's aid. He wrote to Cecil on 9 January that he had received a letter from 'poor Knox, by the which you may perceive what perplexity the poor soul remaineth in at this present'. He explained that he did not wish Knox to remain for long in the north, but intended to use him in different parts of the country, and told Cecil to make it clear to Lord Wharton that Knox was in favour at Court, 'with commandment that no man shall be so hardy to vex him, or trouble him for setting forth the King's Majesty's most godly proceedings'. As for the Mayor of Newcastle, he was to be reprimanded for his 'greedy accusation' against Knox, and for 'his malicious stomach towards the King's proceedings'. Northumberland obviously still hoped to make use of Knox. If the possibility of excluding Mary from the throne in favour of Lady Jane Grey had already arisen in his mind, he may have considered that sermons such as Knox had preached in Newcastle might be useful in certain circumstances.[1]

The Privy Council were determined to keep Knox away from his congregation at Newcastle and Berwick. They decided to appoint him to a benefice in London, and not to give him the opportunity of refusing it, as he had refused the bishopric of Rochester. On 2 February 1553 the Council ordered Cranmer to appoint Knox as Vicar of All Hallows Church in Bread Street in London.[2] The benefice had been held by Thomas Sampson, another Protestant radical, who later became the leader of the Puritan resistance to Elizabeth's government on the question of vestments; it was now vacant on Sampson's appointment as Dean of Chichester. Cranmer had the right of presentation to the benefice, but as the Council had ordered him to appoint Knox, he naturally obeyed without question. This put Knox in a difficulty; if he refused to accept the benefice, after the order of the Privy Council, he would be guilty of an act of disobedience for which he might be punished by imprisonment; but he did not wish to accept a benefice in London. The Bishop of London was Nicholas Ridley. Every irregularity in the services in the church in Bread Street would be immediately reported to Ridley and sternly dealt with; for Ridley would ensure that Knox complied with every order of authority and did not deviate by an inch from religious orthodoxy. Knox decided to enlist the assistance of Northumberland. He somehow persuaded Northumberland to agree that he ought to be allowed to refuse the benefice. He probably convinced him that it would interfere with his activities as a preacher, which Northumberland still believed he could utilize to his own advantage.

Knox refused to accept the benefice of All Hallows, and was chosen as one of the preachers to deliver the Lenten sermons at

[1] Knox, *Admonition to England* (*Works*, iii. 297 and n.); Northumberland to Cecil, 9 Jan. 1552/3 (Tytler, *England under Edward VI and Mary*, ii. 158–60); and see also Knox to Mrs. Bowes, Letter VIII (*Works*, iii. 357), which was probably written soon after Christmas 1552; see *infra*, App. IV.

[2] *A.P.C.* 2 Feb. 1552/3.

Court. The other preachers selected were Edmund Grindal, John Bradford, Thomas Lever, and James Haddon. The King was now seriously ill with tuberculosis; during the Lent of February and March 1553 he was too ill to leave his palace of Whitehall. Here, in the palace overlooking the river, Knox and his fellow preachers delivered their sermons to this precocious, brilliant boy of 15 and his assembled courtiers. The preachers made the strongest attack that had yet been made on the vices and corruptions of the men in power, and their sermons angered their audience even more than Latimer's sermons at Court in 1548. This time it was not only one preacher, but a concentrated attack, week after week, by all the Lenten preachers. Knox says that Haddon 'most learnedly opened the causes of the bypast plagues', and that Lever spoke about the poverty of the people and of new plagues which would soon fall upon the country. Grindal attacked the officers of the King's household who railed against the preachers. Bradford 'spared not the proudest', and described how Somerset, during the year before his arrest in 1551, had become so cold in hearing God's Word that he visited the masons who were building his sumptuous house instead of attending sermons. 'God punished him, and that suddenly', said Bradford to the courtiers, 'and shall he spare you, that be double more wicked?' This common line adopted by the preachers suggests that they had agreed among themselves to denounce the increasing corruption and greed of Northumberland and his friends, which reached a new peak during the spring of 1553 with the seizure of every ornament and candlestick that could be found in the churches. If the action of the Lenten preachers was organized, this was probably due to the fact that they included among their number a product of Scottish Protestantism.[1]

Knox himself, in his sermon, which was the last that he preached before Edward VI, dealt with more political issues, with the danger of secret Papists in office. He said that the most godly princes often had officers and chief councillors who were most ungodly, conjured enemies to God's true religion and traitors to their princes. He explained that there were two reasons why godly princes permitted wicked men to have authority under them. Some of them were kept in office because they were such experienced administrators that it seemed impossible to govern the

[1] Knox, *Letter to the faithful in London, Newcastle and Berwick* (*Works*, iii. 175–7).

country without them; while others concealed their hatred for their King and for God's true religion so well that no one suspected it, and waited for a suitable opportunity to show themselves. Knox, with a political perception almost unique among sixteenth-century preachers, put his finger on the greatest problem that confronts a new régime in every era. Most of the councillors of Edward VI fitted into one or other of these two categories, if not into both; but Knox was particularly suspicious of William Paulet, the Lord High Treasurer, an able civil servant who was kept in office by Henry VIII, Edward VI, Mary, and Elizabeth, and survived every change in policy and religion, rising in turn to be Lord St. John, Earl of Wiltshire, and Marquis of Winchester. He is said to have attributed his successful career to the fact that he came of the willow, and not of the oak. Knox made an unmistakable allusion to Paulet in the sermon. He said that Shebna was Hezekiah's Controller, his Secretary, and ultimately his Treasurer. If David and Hezekiah were deceived by Achitophel and Shebna, he asked, 'What wonder is it then, that a young and innocent King be deceived by crafty, covetous, wicked and ungodly Councillors? I am greatly afraid that Achitophel be Councillor, that Judas bear the purse, and that Sobna be scribe, Controller and Treasurer'.[1]

This account of Knox's sermon was written a year later by Knox himself in very different circumstances, and it is possible that in fact he was not as strong and outspoken as he afterwards made out; but he and his fellow-preachers said enough to arouse the indignation of the courtiers. The whole Council informed the preachers that they would hear no more of their sermons, and called them 'undiscreet fellows' and 'prating knaves'; but Knox and his colleagues completed their Lenten sermons at Court without modifying their criticism.[2]

The preachers, on the other hand, won the admiration of Nicholas Ridley. Ridley was obviously referring to these Lenten sermons when he praised the preaching of Lever, Bradford, and Knox in his *Piteous Lamentation of the Miserable Estate of the Church of Christ in England*, which he wrote two years later while awaiting death in prison at Oxford. He picked out these three preachers,

[1] Knox, *Admonition to England* (*Works*, iii. 280–2).

[2] Knox, *Letter to the faithful in London, Newcastle and Berwick* (*Works*, iii. 177 and n.).

along with Latimer, as the most outspoken critics of the vices of the nobles and members of the government.

> As for Latimer, Lever, Bradford and Knox, their tongues were so sharp, they ripped in so deep in their galled backs, to have purged them, no doubt, of that filthy matter that was festered in their hearts, of insatiable covetousness, of filthy carnality and voluptuousness, of intolerable ambition and pride, of ungodly loathsomeness to hear poor men's causes, and to hear God's Word, that these men, of all other, these magistrates then could never abide.

Ridley's tribute to Knox is striking, for doctrinally they were far apart. Ridley was one of the most authoritarian of the Protestant bishops. It was Ridley who was chiefly responsible for the Council's action against Hooper on the question of vestments, and for the petty persecutions inflicted on à Lasco's congregation of foreign Protestant refugees in London. If Knox had become Vicar of All Hallows in Bread Street, in Ridley's diocese, a clash between them would have been inevitable. But in personality the two men had something in common, with their courage, their vigour, their sense of discipline, and their determination to reduce their opponents to obedience. Even on issues when Ridley was most critical of Knox's attitude, he paid tribute to his wit and learning; and it is clear from the writings of both Ridley and Knox that they had a mutual respect for each other.[1]

The preachers had gone too far for Northumberland. Before the end of Lent, he condemned their sermons in a debate in the House of Lords. He said that the bishops should prevent the preaching of sermons such as those which had recently been delivered by certain preachers, because these sermons, which had criticized the seizure of the Church goods, were scandalous and tended to sedition and commotion; the bishops should ensure that such things did not recur, and that the preachers cease, in their sermons, to attack the prince and his ministers, for otherwise the bishops themselves would suffer along with the preachers. Northumberland's outburst seems to have alarmed Cranmer, for he made a typically mild and defensive reply. According to the Emperor's ambassador, Scheyvfe, 'he excused himself, affirming that he had not heard anything about it, and that if there was any

[1] Ridley, *Piteous Lamentation*; Ridley to Grindal (1555) (Ridley, *Works*, pp. 59, 533–4).

truth in it, it had only been done in order to check and note these vices and abuses'. Northumberland replied that there were quite enough other vices in the country for the preachers to criticize.[1]

Knox was summoned before the Privy Council. The only report that we have of this incident was written nearly a hundred years later, and published in David Buchanan's *Life of Knox* in the 1644 edition of Knox's *History*, and by the Scottish Protestant historian Calderwood; but David Buchanan states that he obtained his information from a letter written by Knox himself on 14 April 1553. The story must be wrong in some details, but there is no reason to doubt that it is substantially accurate. Cranmer was there, with Paulet the Lord Treasurer, Cecil and Petre the Secretaries, and other Lords of the Council; but Northumberland was apparently not present at the meeting. The Council did not raise the question of his Lenten sermons, but dealt with older offences. He was asked why he had refused to accept the benefice in London, and whether it was because he believed that a Christian could not lawfully hold office in the Church of England as it was now constituted. Knox extricated himself from his predicament with his usual tact. He explained that he was fully prepared to take office in the Church of England, though he was aware of his inadequacies, and he had refused the benefice only because he believed that he would be able to serve in London less usefully than elsewhere. Then he told them that Northumberland had ordered him to refuse the benefice. This must have come as a bombshell to Cranmer and the Councillors, and made it very difficult for them to proceed in the absence of Northumberland. The Councillors then changed the subject, and asked Knox why he had refused to kneel at communion. He was ultimately dismissed with an assurance that the Council bore no ill will against him, but esteemed him; but he was apparently asked to give another assurance, in writing, that he was prepared to receive the communion on his knees, and doubtless did so.[2]

The Council did not know what to do with Knox. They did not force him to take the benefice in London, but they did not wish him to return to his congregation in the north, or to preach any

[1] Scheyvfe's advices, 10 Apr. 1553 (Gairdner, *Lollardy and the Reformation*, iii. 400–1; *Span. Cal.* xi. 32–34).

[2] Life of Knox, in Knox's *History*, 1644 Edinburgh edn., unpag.; Calderwood, i. 280–1. See *infra*, App. III.

more sermons at Court. Eventually they decided to send him to preach in Buckinghamshire. On 2 June the Council sent a letter to the local magnates and the justices of the peace in Buckinghamshire, recommending Knox as a preacher.[1] He was preaching in Buckinghamshire when Edward VI died five weeks later.

While Knox was in London during the winter of 1552–3, he had an encounter with one of the free-thinking extremists who were always described as Anabaptists by all Catholics and Protestants. Since the death of Henry VIII, there had been a growth in the number of strange sects in London and the south-eastern counties, which were the most Protestant parts of England and the district where the refugees from Flanders were most numerous. Two Anabaptists, Joan Bocher and the Dutch refugee, George van Paris, had been burnt as heretics by Northumberland's government; and now Henry Hart's Freewillers, and the Family of Love, a sect which had been founded by the Dutchman, Henry Niclaes, were active in Essex and Kent, along with other extremist groups and individuals. These groups not only denied infant baptism, but held far more fantastic and unorthodox opinions. They were tiny, insignificant sects, libertarian in outlook, and against all religious discipline; many of them were pacifist and opposed to the authority of the State. They were religious Anarchists, the cranks of the sixteenth century. Knox was utterly opposed to these Anabaptists; apart from the fact that he disagreed with their opinions, men of this type must have been psychologically repulsive to him. Like Hooper, who temperamentally had more in common with the Anabaptists, Knox denounced them mercilessly.

Six years later, when Knox wrote his book on predestination, which was a long polemic against Anabaptists, he described his meeting with this Anabaptist, 'at London the winter before the death of King Edward'. The Anabaptist approached Knox and asked to see him privately. He made Knox promise not to reveal their conversation to anyone, because 'the matters that he had to communicate with me were so weighty, and of such importance, as since the days of the Apostles the like was never opened unto man'. He gave Knox a book, which he said had been written by God, 'even as well as was any of the Evangelists', and asked for Knox's opinion of the book. Knox consulted a merchant named

[1] *A.P.C.* 2 June 1553.

Henry Farrour, whom he describes as 'a faithful brother', and began to read the book in the presence of Farrour and the Anabaptist. The book asserted that the world, and the wicked creatures in it, were created not by God but by the Devil, and that this was why the Devil was called 'the Prince of the World'. Knox

gently said: 'Can any reasonable man will me to believe things directly fighting against God's verity and plain word revealed?' 'Tush', said he, 'for your written word, we have as good and as sure a word and verity that teacheth us this doctrine, as ye have for you and your opinion.' And then I did more sharply answer, saying 'Ye deserve the death as a blasphemous person and denier of God if ye prefer any word to that which the Holy Ghost hath uttered in His plain Scriptures.' At which words he took pepper in nose, and snatching his book forth of my hand, departed after he had thus spoken: 'I will go to the end of the world; but I will have my book confirmed and subscribed with better learned men than you be.' In me, I confess, there was great negligence, that neither did retain his book, neither yet did present him to the magistrate.[1]

The remarkable thing about this story is that Knox did not denounce the Anabaptist, even though his friend, the merchant Farrour, knew what had happened and might have reported Knox for his failure to do so. The mild and placid Cranmer would have reported the Anabaptist to the authorities and had him burnt. So would the cool Protestant intellectual John Taylor, Bishop of Lincoln, who fifteen years earlier had denounced John Lambert to Cranmer, and sent him to a frightful death in the fire, for having shown him a private document in which he criticized the Real Presence; so would the radical John à Lasco, who had told the authorities about the heresies of the Anabaptist, George van Paris, in his congregation of foreign Protestants in London; and so perhaps would almost every man at the Court. Knox did not denounce the Anabaptist, not because he had any sympathy for him, but because it was not in his nature to do so. He preferred to castigate in the pulpit rather than to inform in secret, to denounce Anabaptism rather than to report an Anabaptist, to attack great lords rather than to secure the arrest and burning of an extremist crank. When he wrote his book six years later, he blamed himself for his failure to denounce the Anabaptist; but even then he did

[1] Knox, *On Predestination* (*Works*, v. 420–1)

not mention the man's name, which could still have led to his arrest and execution in Elizabeth's England. Cranmer was described by his secretary, Ralph Morice, as always bearing a good face and countenance unto the Papists, pardoning their offences, and, on the other side, being somewhat over-severe against the Protestants. No one could say this of Knox. If Knox pardoned an offence, it was the offence of this Anabaptist, and if he was over-severe, it was against the powerful supporters of the Church of Rome.[1]

During his four years in England, Knox had established himself as one of the leaders of the non-Anabaptist left wing of the Protestants. Only Hooper could equal him in stature among the radicals. We do not know whether Knox and Hooper ever met. They might easily have met when Hooper came to London from his diocese of Worcester in February 1553 to preach at Court and attend the session of Parliament; but there is no record of what the two men thought of each other. Hooper does not refer to Knox in any of his surviving works, and the only reference to Hooper in Knox's writings is in an attempt to use Hooper's constancy as a martyr, and his opposition to vestments, as a weapon in Knox's struggle with the supporters of the Book of Common Prayer at Frankfort.[2] Doctrinally, Hooper and Knox were very close, but they represented different attitudes of mind, and were the founders of different traditions. Hooper has been called the father of Nonconformity. He stands at the head of a long line which leads through the seventeenth-century Quaker and the Victorian free-thinker, through George Fox and Holyoake, to the conscientious objector of modern times. Knox was not a man of this type. He is not the father of Nonconformity and individual resistance, but of the revolutionary tradition. He is closer to the Russian Bolsheviks than to Hooper's spiritual descendants.

In every situation, Hooper and Knox reacted differently. Hooper admired Northumberland, and was completely deceived by him; Knox never trusted Northumberland, but made use of him for his own ends. Hooper proclaimed his beliefs, without

[1] See Foxe, v. 227–8; Latin edn., p. 202; Morice, 'A declaration concernyng . . . that most Reverent Father in God, Thomas Cranmer' (in Nichols, *Narratives of the Days of the Reformation*, p. 246).

[2] *The Troubles at Frankfort*, p. 39; the English Congregation's Supplication to the Senate of Frankfort (22 Mar. 1555); Knox's memorandum on events at Frankfort (*The Troubles at Frankfort*, p. 42; *Works*, iv. 33, 36–37, 44).

considering the political consequences; Knox never compromised his principles, but never went further than appeared to be tactically advisable. Hooper defied the law, and suffered imprisonment for his doctrines; Knox stayed just within the law, and avoided imprisonment. Hooper submitted, accepted a bishopric, and as a result ceased to be a cause of trouble to the authorities; Knox refused a bishopric, and remained a serious cause of trouble, but one with which it was very difficult to deal. Most important of all, Hooper resisted throughout as an individual; Knox was the spokesman for his congregation of Scots in the north, and resisted in England, as he had done in the French galleys, with the group. In the end, when Popery returned, Hooper refused to flee, and offered himself for martyrdom. Knox fled, and afterwards led a successful revolution. Hooper died at the stake; Knox lived to send his enemies to the gallows.

CHAPTER VIII

Mrs. Bowes and Marjory

WHILE he was living in Berwick between 1549 and 1551, Knox met Mrs. Elizabeth Bowes, the wife of Richard Bowes, and their daughter Marjory, who became his wife. The Bowes family had become one of the most influential in the north. By origin they were merely country gentlemen, and no equals of the great semi-feudal noble families, such as the Percies, the Nevilles, and the Dacres, which still existed in Northumberland and Cumberland; but they had risen through loyal service to the Crown in war and peace, and through profitable marriages had acquired large estates in Northumberland, Durham, and the North Riding of Yorkshire. Richard Bowes's eldest brother, Sir Ralph Bowes, had been knighted at Flodden; and a second brother, Sir Robert Bowes, the most successful member of the family, was Warden of the Eastern and Middle Marches and a member of the Council of the North.

Richard Bowes lived at Dalden, near Seaham in Durham, and, after performing the usual duties of a country gentleman and a justice of the peace for many years, had been appointed Captain of Norham Castle, the largest of the English fortresses on the frontier. His wife Elizabeth was the daughter and co-heiress of Sir Roger Aske, of Aske Hall near Richmond in Yorkshire. When Knox first met her, she had been married for nearly thirty years, and had had fifteen children. Marjory was the fifth of her ten daughters.[1]

Norham was only seven miles from Berwick. From this great castle, standing high on the south bank of the Tweed, Knox could gaze on a wide expanse of his native Scotland, less than a hundred yards across the water but completely inaccessible to him. It was

[1] For the history of the Bowes family, see *History of Northumberland*, i. 177, 192 n.; xi. 325 n.; xii. 215; xiii. 325; Hutchinson, *The History and Antiquities of the County Palatine of Durham*, iii. 253–4. Richard Bowes was appointed Captain of Norham at some date between September 1544 and May 1546 (see *L.P.* xxi[i]. 1279, pp. 625, 630). See also Laing's Preface to *Works*, vi. xxxiii.

here that he began that intimate relationship which reached its full development in smaller and humbler houses in Geneva and Edinburgh.

History has been more interested in Knox's relationship with his mother-in-law than with his wife. As Mrs. Bowes afterwards lived with Knox and her daughter, and continued to live with Knox after Marjory's death, she was naturally accused by the Catholics of being Knox's mistress. All Catholics were convinced that Protestant priests, particularly those who married, were lusting libertines, and that Protestant women were harlots, and the fact that Mrs. Bowes lived under the same roof with Knox was all the ammunition that the Catholic pamphleteers required. They could not miss the opportunity of accusing Knox of having intercourse with both the mother and the daughter, because it was a stock theme of Catholic propaganda that the mother of Anne Boleyn had been the mistress of Henry VIII, and they could cite the further example of Knox and Mrs. Bowes to show that this kind of incestuous adultery was a favourite Protestant vice. The Scottish Catholic *émigré* monk, Alexander Baillie, writing in 1628, added the detail that when Knox was accused of having had the mother and daughter, he gave the same reply that Sir Francis Bryan had given to Henry VIII when Henry had discussed with him the propriety of possessing Anne Boleyn as well as her mother: that to have intercourse with a mother and her daughter was no worse than eating both a hen and her chick.[1] The suggestion that Mrs. Bowes was Knox's mistress is probably as untrue as this anecdote.

Mrs. Bowes's relationship with Knox was a spiritual and ideological one. Within a short time of meeting Knox, she fell under his influence and looked to him as her pastor and guide. It is fashionable today to laugh at Mrs. Bowes, with her spiritual fervour, her constant anxiety that she was a reprobate who would not be saved, her repeated requests to Knox to elucidate some passage in Scripture which puzzled and disturbed her; but Mrs. Bowes was a brave and remarkable woman. Her whole background was conservative; she had been taught to accept the traditional beliefs, both as regards religion and social behaviour. When she was born, in the last years of Henry VII's reign, her family and all the gentry and people of Yorkshire were Papists;

[1] Baillie, *A true information*, pp. 40–41.

there was no Protestant heretic within many miles of Aske Hall. Even after Henry VIII repudiated the Papal supremacy, the north remained sturdily Catholic. Mrs. Bowes's distant relative, Robert Aske, led the great Catholic rising, the Pilgrimage of Grace, in 1536, and was hanged as a traitor; and though the Bowes brothers and the royal officials in the north remained loyal to the King, accepted the dissolution of the great northern monasteries, claimed their share of the monastic lands, and adapted themselves to all the changes in doctrine when the order came from Court, they were at heart as Catholic as their neighbours. Mrs. Bowes, as the wife of the Captain of Norham Castle, was expected to conform to the religious changes, as her husband did, without antagonizing the Catholic gentry of Northumberland, and to take no further interest in religion. Instead, she thought out her religion for herself, and became an enthusiastic Protestant.

Many educated women were doing the same all over the country, often in direct disobedience to their husbands' wishes. Although both Catholic and Protestant doctrine taught the duty of wives to obey their husbands in all things, there was an exception where matters of religion were concerned: religion was the only issue on which an independent-minded woman could justifiably resist the tyrant of the family, conscious that if God was to be obeyed rather than man, He was to be obeyed rather than her husband. The spread of Protestantism among women aroused the special indignation of the Catholics. Catholic propagandists denounced the subversive Protestant agitators who incited wives to disobey their husbands, and children to disobey their fathers; and the government of Henry VIII struck particularly hard at Protestant wives. The Act of Parliament of 1543, which forbade anyone below the rank of gentleman from reading the Bible on pain of death, extended the prohibition to all women, even those of the highest class.[1]

We do not know whether Mrs. Bowes risked hanging by reading the Bible in the last years of Henry's reign; but after 1547 she could do so without fear of punishment, and instead of accepting religious doctrine without question from the chaplain at Norham Castle, she read the Bible herself, trying to interpret it and reconcile apparently conflicting passages. She became an intimate

[1] *Statutes of the Realm*, 34 & 35 Hen. VIII, c. 1. For the Catholic view of Protestant women, see, e.g., Huggarde, *The displaying of the Protestantes*, pp. 74–78.

friend of the Scottish preacher at Berwick, John Knox. In Mary's reign this intrepid woman, at the age of 50, left her husband and her home, and the life of a country gentlewoman, to escape from England illegally, going with Knox and her daughter to Geneva as a refugee, and then returning with them to Scotland to face the drab, harsh life of a backward country in the chaos of revolution. Mrs. Bowes's language and modes of thought appear strange in the twentieth century, but she was the prototype of the modern woman who dares everything and sacrifices all for a cause.

Knox was probably the first person who gave Mrs. Bowes any encouragement. With Knox and his congregation of Scots at Berwick, she at last found a group of people who did not disapprove and ridicule her Protestant zeal, but who took her seriously and encouraged her. She naturally reacted enthusiastically, finding in Knox a man with a mind and outlook like her own. Their relationship became intimate and, on her side at least, emotional. Knox reciprocated her feelings to a considerable extent, though later, after her death, he wrote that he had at times found her something of a trial.[1] Her over-sensitive conscience led her to approach him again and again, asking for an assurance from him that she was one of God's elect and would not be damned. Knox, who as a youth had endured the rigours of lower middle-class life in Scotland, who had suffered in the galleys, and who spent every day preaching and working for the cause, had no doubts that he would be saved; Mrs. Bowes, who had done and suffered nothing for her faith, and had always lived the life of a lady of position, was haunted by her fear that she was damned. In all his sermons Knox tried to instil into his audience a sense of duty, a fear of God, a horror of sin and damnation; but he had to do exactly the opposite with Mrs. Bowes. In his letters to her, he tried to reassure her, to persuade her to worry less, and to convince her that she would undoubtedly be saved. Despite his occasional exasperation, he admired her profound sincerity and felt a real affection for her. All his letters to her show a close affinity, and great understanding and kindness.

There is no real reason to believe that there was anything sexual in his feeling for her, though one passage in his letters is capable of this interpretation. It occurs in a letter written to

[1] Knox, 'Epistle to the faithful Reader', 12 July 1572, in Knox, *Answer to Tyrie* (*Works*, vi. 513–14).

Mrs. Bowes during the reign of Edward VI. Knox had heard from one of the members of his congregation that Mrs. Bowes was alarmed over the fact that Knox had been too reluctant to castigate her for her sins.

> I remember myself so to have done [he wrote] and that is my common consuetude, when anything pierceth or toucheth my heart. Call to your mind what I did standing at the cupboard in Alnwick; in very deed I thought that no creature had been tempted as I was. And when that I heard proceed from your mouth the very same words that he troubles me with, I did wonder, and from my heart lament your sore trouble, knowing in myself the dolour thereof. And no other thing, dear sister, meant I; and therefore think not that I either flatter you, or yet that I conceal anything from you; no, for if I had been so minded, I had not been so plain in other cases.[1]

It would be interesting to know what Knox had done at the cupboard in Alnwick, and what it was that had tempted him so greatly; but though he may be referring to an occasion when he was tempted to make some sexual advance to Mrs. Bowes, this letter, like so many of his other letters to her, is so cryptic, so steeped in allegorical methods of thought, so full of allusions to matters known to them both and left unexplained, that it would be very unwise to deduce anything of the kind. Mrs. Bowes was about nine years older than Knox, and though this in itself may mean little, a woman of 45, who had borne fifteen children, was unlikely, in the sixteenth century, to have retained her sexual attractions. If Knox was ever tempted to commit some sexual impropriety, he is particularly unlikely to have chosen a devoted woman member of his congregation, whose admiration for him was of an intellectual and spiritual nature.

Our knowledge of Knox's family relationships depends largely on his letters to Mrs. Bowes. Mrs. Bowes kept many of the letters which Knox wrote to her—perhaps all of them—and she obviously brought them with her when she came to live with him, and left them behind when she left his household; for in 1572, after the death of Mrs. Bowes, Knox wrote that the letters were in his possession. Unfortunately, the original letters no longer exist; but in 1603 they were copied out in manuscript by a writer who seems to have been a relative or acquaintance of Knox's second

[1] Knox to Mrs. Bowes, 26 Feb. (1552?) (Letter III, *Works*, iii. 350, where it is wrongly dated 1553; see *infra*, App. IV).

wife. It is strange that neither McCrie nor David Laing, who first published the letters in the nineteenth century, nor any of Knox's biographers, have pointed out that there are a number of obvious errors in the dating of the letters, though Lord Eustace Percy realized that at least one of the letters was wrongly dated.[1] These incorrect dates are given in what purports to be the text of the letters themselves. Though the transcriber obviously acted in good faith, he seems sometimes to have incorporated, into the last lines of a letter, the date on which he thought that the letter was written; on other occasions, he obviously made a copying mistake. This naturally raises the suspicion that there may be other errors; but the transcriber cannot have invented the highly spiritual and gentle tone of the letters. The striking difference between the style of the letters and that of Knox's other writings has often been commented on, for the letters reveal a completely different Knox from the writer of the *History of the Reformation in Scotland* and the polemical pamphlets—a softer and kinder Knox than we would otherwise know.

Although no letter in the manuscript of 1603 is dated earlier than 1553, some of the letters were certainly written in 1551. The correspondence doubtless began in this year, when Knox left Berwick and resided much of the time at Newcastle, and could no longer pay his regular visits to Norham Castle. During the next two years he wrote to Mrs. Bowes from Newcastle, Carlisle, and London, reassuring her and answering her requests for the elucidation of some scriptural passage. He tells her that he has no doubt that she will be saved; she must not worry if she is sometimes tempted. 'I am even equally certified of your election in Christ', he writes from Newcastle, 'as that I am that I myself preacheth Christ to be the only Saviour, etc. I have more signs of your election than presently I can commit to write.' From London he writes: 'Despair not, mother, your sins (albeit ye had committed thousands more) are remissable'; and again from London: 'Mother, there is no danger of everlasting death.' When he received an agonized letter from Mrs. Bowes, in which she accused herself of having committed the sins of Sodom and Gomorrah,

[1] Knox, 'Epistle to the faithful Reader', 12 July 1572, in Knox, *Answer to Tyrie* (*Works*, vi. 514); *The Epistles of John Knox* (MS. volume of 1603), in Edinburgh University Library (MS. Laing iii. 345); Laing's notes, in *Works*, iii. 335; Lord Eustace Percy, *John Knox*, pp. 10–11. See *infra*, App. IV.

he thought it was time to administer a rebuke. It was sinful of her to accuse herself of crimes that she had not committed, for it was ungrateful to God who had prevented her from committing them; but he assumed that she had done so because she did not know what the sins of Sodom and Gomorrah were. The sins of Sodom and Gomorrah were pride, 'wherewith I think ye be not greatly troubled', riotous living, idleness, unmercifulness to the poor, and unnatural filthiness. 'In which of this, mother, are ye guilty? . . . Do you think that every stirring and motion of the flesh, or yet every ardent and burning lust, is the sin of Sodom?'[1]

Sometimes Knox gently corrected Mrs. Bowes's theological errors and doubts. She had read that some philosophers believed that the world had always existed and had never had a beginning; Knox explained that the Devil had persuaded them to believe this, but the Word of God would compel even the Devil himself to grant and acknowledge God alone to be the Creator, and the world not to have the beginning of itself. He also interpreted the thirty-fourth chapter of Genesis for Mrs. Bowes. Mrs. Bowes was perturbed by the story of the killing of the Shechemites by the sons of Jacob after Shechem had ravished their sister Dinah, while the Shechemites were still weak from the effect of having been circumcised at the suggestion of the sons of Jacob, as a condition of their permitting the marriage of Dinah to Shechem. Mrs. Bowes wished to know whether the sons of Jacob had acted rightly. Knox explained that they had offended most grievously, for as they were not magistrates they had no right to punish the Shechemites. Moreover, they had made God's name odious to the neighbouring nations by cruelly and deceitfully killing the Shechemites under pretence of religion and of receiving them in league with God. But the Shechemites had also sinned, for they had converted to the true religion for the wrong motive. 'And so the justice of God found them worthy of punishment, and so permitted them, justly on His part, to be afflicted and destroyed by the ungodly.' This conception of God using wicked men to punish other wicked men was to be given great emphasis by Knox and his colleagues in the Geneva Bible of 1560. It had an important practical political application in the sixteenth century.[2]

[1] Knox to Mrs. Bowes (1551 or 1552), (Dec. 1552), 1 Mar. 1552/3 and (1553) (Letters XIV, XVIII [ii], XIX, and XX, *Works*, iii. 369, 379, 381–3).

[2] Knox to Mrs. Bowes (1551 or 1552) (Letters XIII and XXV, *Works*, iii. 366, 396–7).

As well as trying to reassure Mrs. Bowes that her sins were not as grievous as she supposed, Knox sometimes, perhaps partly by way of giving her further reassurance, revealed to her his awareness of his own insufficiencies. He was not an adulterer, he told her, but his heart was inflamed with foul lusts,

and will lust, albeit I lament never so much. Externally, I commit no idolatry; but my wicked heart loveth the self, and cannot be refrained from vain imaginations, yea, not from such as were the fountain of all idolatry. I am no man-killer with my hands; but I help not my needy brother so liberally as I may and ought. I steal not horse, money nor clothes from my neighbour; but that small portion of worldly substance I bestow not so rightly as His holy law requireth. I bear no false witness against my neighbour in judgement, or otherwise before men; but I speak not the truth of God so boldly as it becometh His true messenger to do. And thus in conclusion, there is no vice repugning to God's holy will, expressed in His law, wherewith my heart is not infected.[1]

On another occasion, he wrote to her of how he was sometimes tempted to relax into a mood of self-satisfaction. 'There is a spiritual pride which is not hastily suppressed in God's very elect children', he explained, 'I can write to you by my own experience'. There were moments when he congratulated himself on having suffered great trouble for Christ's truth, when he thanked God for having freed him from the galleys and placed him in an honourable vocation where his labours were not without fruit. 'O mother, this was a subtle serpent who thus could pour in venom, I not perceiving it; but blessed be my God who permitted me not to sleep long in that estate.' For his mood of self-flattery was soon followed by 'a cup of contra poison', which aroused a feeling of bitter self-reproach, a feeling that he was worthy of damnation for his ingratitude towards his God.[2]

The more we read Knox's letters to Mrs. Bowes, the more obvious it becomes not only that there was nothing physical and sexual in their relationship, but that there was nothing strange or abnormal about it. When allowance is made for the language used by Protestants and Puritans in the sixteenth century, the letters disclose a relationship no different from that which has often existed between a religious teacher and his disciple, between a

[1] Knox to Mrs. Bowes, 23 June 1553 (Letter I, *Works*, iii. 338–9).
[2] Knox to Mrs. Bowes (1553) (Letter XXI, *Works*, iii. 386–7).

political leader and a zealous party member, between a prominent intellectual and his fervent admirer, though it is undoubtedly true that the relationship between Knox and Mrs. Bowes, though not sexual, was one which could exist only between a man and a woman.[1] There has probably never been a more truthful account of Knox's attitude to Mrs. Bowes than that which he wrote himself in July 1572, after the death of Mrs. Bowes and four months before his own death, when he published, as an appendix to his *Answer to a Letter of a Jesuit named Tyrie*, a letter that he had written to Mrs. Bowes in 1554. In an explanatory note, he wrote:

Because that God now in His mercy hath put end to the battle of my dear mother Mrs. Elizabeth Bowes, before that He put end to my wretched life, I could not cease but declare to the world what was the cause of our great familiarity and long acquaintance; which was neither flesh nor blood, but a troubled conscience upon her part, which never suffered her to rest but when she was in the company of the faithful, of whom (from the first hearing of the Word at my mouth) she judged me to be one. Now, seeing her battle is ended, and I am upon the point shortly to follow, this I leave to the posterity for discharge of my conscience and to the instruction of her children: that in Scotland, England, France and Germany I have heard the complaints of divers that feared God, but of the like conflict as she sustained, from the time of her first acquaintance, and long before (as her own mouth, ofter than once, confessed to me) till this hour, I have not known. For her temptation was not in the flesh, nor for anything that appertained to flesh (nò, not when she was in greatest desolation) but it was in spirit; for Satan did continually buffet her, that remission of sins in Christ Jesus appertained nothing unto her, by reason of her former idolatry and other iniquities; for the which, notwithstanding any worldly comfort, I have seen her (not for a start, but in long continuance) pour forth tears, and send to God dolorous complaints, ofter than ever I heard man or woman in my life. Her company to me was comfortable (yea, honourable and profitable, for she was to me and mine a mother); but yet it was not without some cross; for besides trouble and fasherie of body sustained for her, my mind was seldom quiet, for doing somewhat for the comfort of her troubled conscience.[2]

[1] This point is made by Marjorie Bowen (George Preedy), in her biography of Knox, though in other respects her interpretation of Knox's character, and of his relationship with Mrs. Bowes, is unsatisfactory; see Marjorie Bowen, *Life of John Knox*, p. 48 (in 1st edn., published *sub nom.* George Preedy, *Life of John Knox*, p. 59).

[2] Knox, 'Epistle to the faithful Reader', 12 July 1572, in Knox, *Answer to Tyrie* (*Works*, vi. 513–14).

We know far less about Knox's relations with Marjory Bowes than we do of his relations with her mother. It is often assumed that Marjory was an unimportant addition to Knox's family, who was presented to him by Mrs. Bowes in order to give him physical pleasure and to be the mother of his children, while Mrs. Bowes and Knox continued their spiritual collaboration. There is no reason at all for believing this, except that twenty-nine letters from Knox to Mrs. Bowes have been preserved, and only one letter from him to Marjory. This does not mean that it was the only letter that he wrote to her. His letters to Marjory may have been more personal and less theological than those that he wrote to her mother. Mrs. Bowes probably kept all the letters that she received from Knox, rereading them regularly whenever she felt doubts and fears as to her salvation; but Marjory may have preferred to destroy his letters rather than run the risk of allowing Knox's intimate confidences to be read by anyone else, as most of the letters that he wrote to her must have been written while she was living in Norham Castle with her father, who strongly disapproved of her betrothal to Knox. Even if Knox's letters to Marjory were preserved, and were afterwards kept by Knox along with his letters to Mrs. Bowes, they may not have been deemed worthy of transcription by the transcriber in 1603. If they were letters of a personal nature, he may have thought them unedifying; for even if there was nothing indelicate in the letters, the Scottish Protestants in 1603 did not wish to know that Knox had ever written anything which was not concerned with God and the Protestant religion.

The only letter that we have from Knox to Marjory is the first he ever wrote to her. It was obviously written some little time after they had first met; for Knox mentions, as if it were a surprising thing, that 'I think this be the first letter that ever I wrote to you'. But it was written before their betrothal, probably in 1551 or 1552, while Knox was living in Newcastle after leaving Berwick. It deals only with theological questions, which is perhaps the reason why the transcriber of 1603 included it in his manuscript. As in so many of his letters to her mother, Knox wrote to elucidate for Marjory the meaning of two texts of scripture which she had asked him to explain; but the tone of the letter is simpler and calmer than those which he wrote to Mrs. Bowes. He seems to have felt that she was a more level-headed young woman than her mother, and to have relied on her to appease the anxieties of Mrs. Bowes; for he wrote to Marjory: 'The Spirit of God shall instruct your heart what is most comfortable to the troubled conscience of your mother.'

The two texts which Marjory had asked him to explain both had a practical application for her. The first was the injunction of John, in the second Epistle, not to fraternize with those who do not accept the doctrine of Christ, not to receive them in the house, or say good day to them, 'for he that biddeth him godspeed is partaker of his evil deeds'. The second was the second chapter of James's Epistle, in which Christians are exhorted not to offer the seat of honour to the wealthy guest wearing a gold ring and gay clothing, while ordering the poor guest who comes in vile raiment to stand, or sit under the footstool. A young lady who was the daughter of the Captain of Norham Castle met many more unbelievers wearing golden rings and gay clothing than poor members of the congregation in vile raiment, and it was inconvenient and disconcerting to be told that she must avoid social intercourse with them; and at dinner in the castle, the guests were undoubtedly seated according to their rank. Knox went as far as he could to help her. The text from John meant that with regard to teachers of false doctrine contrary to the truth of Christ, 'we communicate with them in nothing that may appear to maintain or defend them in their corrupt opinion. For he that bids them godspeed communicates with their sin; that is, he that approves, by keeping them company, or assisting unto them in their proceedings, to favour their doctrine.' As for the passage from James, this meant 'that in Jesus Christ all that unfeignedly profess Him are equal before Him, and that riches nor worldly honours are nothing regarded in His sight'.[1]

We do not know when Knox married Marjory. By 1553 he is referring to her as his wife in his letters to Mrs. Bowes; but he had not yet celebrated a formal marriage with her. When Knox published, in his *Answer to Tyrie* in 1572, the letter that he wrote to Mrs. Bowes in July 1554, he explained in a note the reason why he called her 'mother' in the letter: 'I had made a faithful promise, before witness, to Marjory Bowes her daughter; and so as she took me for son, I heartily embraced her as my mother.'[2] This means that there had been a formal engagement before witnesses,

[1] Knox to Marjory Bowes (1551 or 1552) (Letter XXIV, *Works*, iii. 394–5).

[2] Knox to Mrs. Bowes, 20 July 1554, in Knox, *Answer to Tyrie* (*Works*, vi. 516).

which in English law was known as a precontract. It was a binding engagement, but no longer legally made the parties husband and wife. Although the marriage itself was not celebrated until after Knox and Marjory had been reunited in Scotland in 1555, the precontract must have taken place just before Knox left Northumberland for London for the second time, in January 1553.[1] The story of Knox and Marjory exchanging their vows at a secret ceremony in November 1553, when Knox, on the run from Queen Mary's officers, was on the point of leaving the country, is a pleasant and romantic one; but it seems very unlikely that he managed to see Marjory after Mary's accession to power, and even if he did, he was certainly referring to Marjory as his wife before this time.

Richard Bowes's attitude towards Knox was very different from that of his wife, but it was perhaps not always as hostile as is usually supposed. The traditional picture of Richard Bowes portrays him as the angry father, despising Knox for his humble birth, scornfully refusing his consent for his daughter to marry him, and denying him all access to Marjory. This is a true enough picture of the position in the autumn of 1553, but things may have been very different before the death of Edward VI, when Knox was an influential preacher at Court. The nobles and gentlemen of Tudor England never despised a low-born upstart until after his fall from power, and if Richard Bowes was typical of his class, his attitude to Knox changed together with the changes in the political situation and the changes in Knox's fortunes.

From the start, Richard Bowes was no doubt prejudiced against Knox because he was a Scotsman, and anxious when he realized the extent of Knox's influence over his wife, and he obviously did not wish to have him as a son-in-law. One thing to which Richard Bowes would not have objected is the fact, which has been adversely commented upon by modern writers, that Knox was about twenty years older than Marjory. It was not uncommon in the sixteenth century for men of 40, 50, or even 60, to marry girls of 15 or 16. Knox was now 37 or 38 years of age, and if he had not married a woman some twenty years younger than himself, he could hardly have married at all, unless he married a widow, as nearly every woman married when she was very young, and it was not easy to find a woman over 20 who was still unmarried.

[1] See *infra*, App. IV.

Richard Bowes had other reasons for objecting to the marriage. No north-country gentleman could have favoured the prospect of seeing his daughter marry a low-class Scottish refugee priest, especially as the marriage of priests had only been legalized a year or so before, and the majority of the people of England disapproved of married priests and their wives.

But it was a different matter after Knox arrived at Norham Castle as preacher in Northumberland's retinue, when the Duke inspected the Border fortresses in the summer of 1552. Six months later Knox returned to the north from London as a royal preacher, preceded by the rumour that he was about to be appointed as Bishop of Rochester. We can safely assume that Knox's precontract to Marjory was not a secret and illegal ceremony, but took place with the consent of her father, which was necessary in law, even if this consent was given reluctantly. It must have been during Knox's short visit to Northumberland at Christmas 1552, because Knox's practice of addressing Mrs. Bowes as 'mother', instead of the usual mode of address 'sister' which he used to the other women of his congregation, dates from January 1553.[1]

The precontract was not immediately followed by marriage. Perhaps Richard Bowes adopted delaying tactics with regard to the marriage, for his brother, Sir Robert Bowes, was well aware of the state of King Edward's health. Marjory did not go to London with Knox. After the accession of Mary, when Knox became a hunted fugitive, the situation changed again. Knox thought and spoke of Marjory as his wife, but Richard Bowes did not. He refused to permit the marriage, or even to recognize the validity of a precontract with a priest, and prevented Knox from seeing either Marjory or Mrs. Bowes; and in January 1554 Knox was forced to flee abroad, leaving Marjory and Mrs. Bowes at Norham. We know nothing of the pressures put on Marjory by her father, during the next two years, to forget the unfortunate connexion with Knox and marry some eligible bachelor of the district; but every gentleman wished to marry off his daughters as early as possible, and as her precontract with a priest was considered void in law by Mary's government, Richard Bowes had every reason to wish to bind her in matrimony to a respectable husband as soon as possible, and thus finally to rule out all possibility of further association with Knox. Marjory and her mother

[1] See *infra*, App. IV.

resisted all the pressure, and at some time before the autumn of 1555 they escaped across the frontier and rejoined Knox in Scotland.[1]

Next summer they went with him to Geneva. Here the daughter of the Captain of Norham Castle settled down as a Swiss housewife, and deeply impressed Calvin by her charm and sweetness of temper. She gave birth to two sons, Nathaniel and Eleazer Knox. Sometimes, between her other duties, she acted as Knox's secretary, though not many married women would have been sufficiently literate and well educated to render such assistance to their husbands. When Knox was too ill to write to John Foxe, the martyrologist, at Basel, Marjory wrote the letter for him, adding a few lines of her own in which she thanked Foxe, with a graciousness and style which she must have learned at Norham, for the gifts which he had sent to her mother and herself.[2]

When Knox returned to Scotland to lead a revolution, Marjory followed him, being given special assistance and priority on the journey through the intervention of the English ambassador in Paris. By this time there was a Protestant Queen in England, and Richard Bowes had died, making no mention of his wife or Marjory in his will, but providing that the legacies which he bequeathed to his four unmarried daughters should be forfeited if they married without the consent of their uncles. Marjory lived for a year at St. Andrews and Edinburgh as the minister's wife, while her husband, in his hour of triumph, thundered from the pulpit to enthusiastic congregations, and laid the foundations of a new national Church. In December 1560 she died, perhaps in childbirth, or from one of the many deadly diseases of the sixteenth century. She was probably not much more than 25 at the time of her death.[3]

Knox makes only a few references to Marjory in his books and his surviving letters; but on these occasions he speaks of her in

[1] See *infra*, pp. 224–5, and App. IV.

[2] *Livre des Anglois*, pp. 8, 14–15 (13 Sept. 1556, 23 May 1557, and 29 Nov. 1558); Calvin to Knox, 23 Apr. 1561; Calvin to Goodman, 23 Apr. 1561 (*Calvini Opera*, xviii. 434–6; *Works*, vi. 124–5); Knox to Foxe, 18 May 1558 (*Works*, v. 5–6).

[3] Throckmorton to Elizabeth I, 13 June 1559 (Forbes, *A Full View of the Public Transactions in the reign of Queen Elizabeth*, i. 129–30; *Cal. For. Pap. Eliz.* i. 833); Richard Bowes's will, 11 Aug. 1558 (*Richmondshire Wills* (Surtees Society), p. 116; and see Laing's Preface to *Works*, vi. lxii); Knox, *History*, i. 351.

much warmer terms than he ever uses of Mrs. Bowes. He never left Mrs. Bowes herself in any doubt as to his feelings for Marjory; in his letters he repeatedly assures Mrs. Bowes that he feels more affection for her than for anyone else except his wife. Marjory is 'my own flesh', 'that which of earthly creatures is most dear unto me'; and he described her, in the letter which she wrote for him to John Foxe, as 'my left hand'. He mentions her death very briefly in his *History of the Reformation in Scotland*, that record of great events from which personal matters are almost entirely excluded: 'He was in no small heaviness by reason of the late death of his dear bedfellow, Marjory Bowes.'[1]

[1] Knox to Mrs. Bowes (Oct. or Nov. 1553), 20 Sept. 1553 and (1554) (Letters XV, XVII, and XXIII); Knox to Foxe, 18 May 1558 (*Works*, iii. 370, 376, 392; v. 5); Knox, *History*, i. 351.

CHAPTER IX

The Flight from England

EDWARD VI died on 6 July 1553. A fortnight earlier he had signed his devise of the Crown, by which he excluded his sister Mary from the throne on the grounds of her illegitimacy, and appointed Jane Grey to succeed him. On 10 July Jane was proclaimed Queen in London; but the next nine days saw the only successful revolution in Tudor England. The people of England rose in support of Mary. Within a few days Mary was at the head of an army at Framlingham in Norfolk, and had been joined by several nobles and gentlemen.

The people did not rally to Mary because she was a Catholic. They rose in defence of the right of hereditary succession to the Crown, and against the hated government of Northumberland. Many of Mary's supporters were Protestants who hardly realized that Mary was a Catholic. Northumberland and the Protestant leaders had done nothing during Edward's reign to prepare the people for the exclusion of Mary; for they had treated her in public with all the respect due to her as the King's sister, and had suppressed the news of her secret mass and her disobedience to the Act of Uniformity. The Protestants of Norfolk and Suffolk who rallied to Mary at Framlingham, remembering Northumberland as the man who had suppressed Ket's rebellion four years before, somehow convinced themselves that Mary had issued a proclamation in which she promised to uphold the Protestant religion and not to marry a foreigner. It seems certain that no such proclamation was ever issued, but it was generally believed by the people of Protestant East Anglia, and Mary and her supporters took care not to disillusion them at this stage of the proceedings. It was the same with the Protestant gentry of the West Country. As soon as Sir Peter Carew heard of Edward's death, he proclaimed Mary Queen at Exeter.[1]

[1] Foxe, vi. 387; Knox, *Admonition to England* (*Works*, iii. 295–6); d'Oysel to Henry II, 14 Jan. 1553/4 (*Ambassades de MM. de Noailles en Angleterre*, iii. 15);

The Protestant leaders among the clergy, on the other hand, were well aware of Mary's religious opinions and what her accession to the throne would mean. Their attitude in July 1553 shows their sincerity, their devotion to their principles, and their utter lack of political understanding. Their devotion to the doctrine of Christian obedience prevented them from making any attempt to stop Mary from succeeding to the Crown. Cranmer had been more reluctant than any of the other Councillors of Edward VI to support Northumberland's plan to devise the Crown to Jane. He was only persuaded to sign by Edward himself, when the dying boy commanded him to do so; he then decided that it was his duty to obey a reigning sovereign even in the matter of excluding a future one. After Edward's death, he sat on Jane's Council. Ridley and Edwin Sandys, the Vice-Chancellor of Cambridge University, preached in favour of Jane at the height of the crisis; but no other Protestant preacher raised his voice on Jane's behalf. John Bale, Bishop of Ossory, whose Protestant propaganda pamphlets had earned him the hatred of the Catholics and who had been stigmatized as 'pernicious, seditious, and slanderous' by Gardiner, proclaimed Mary as Queen in his Irish diocese, and passionately defended her right against Jane Grey. Hooper, according to his own statement, gave active support to Mary, although he knew what to expect if she became Queen. When the news reached him, in his diocese of Worcester and Gloucester, that Jane had been proclaimed and that Mary had risen against her, he rode about from place to place, urging the people to support Mary, and directed Sir John Talbot to raise units of cavalry to fight for her.[1]

Knox's conduct was different from that of any of the other Protestant divines. He showed his usual combination of aggression and shrewdness. He did not share the inhibitions of the English Protestants about attacking a royal princess, and was fully aware of what her victory would entail; but he was not in a position where he could speak freely. When Edward VI died, Knox was in Buckinghamshire, having been sent there as a

Froude, *History of England*, v. 193. For the best account of the events of 6–19 July, see Froude, v. 175–210.

[1] Cranmer to Mary I (Dec. 1553) (Cranmer, *Works*, ii. 443–4); Foxe, vi. 389–90; viii. 590–2; Gardiner to Somerset, 21 May 1547 (Foxe, vi. 30); Bale, *Vocacyon of John Bale to the Bishopperycke of Ossorie* (*Harleian Misc.* vi. 450); Hooper, *An Apology against the untrue and slanderous reports* (Hooper, *Works*, ii. 556–7).

preacher by the Council. Northumberland had ordered Sir Edward Hastings to raise an army of 4,000 militia in Buckinghamshire to resist the enemies of Queen Jane. Hastings had always been a Catholic, and had barely troubled to disguise the fact during the reign of Edward VI; but he had nevertheless been appointed by Northumberland to various official positions because of his rank and family connexions. As soon as Hastings had assembled his 4,000 men in Buckinghamshire, he declared his allegiance to Mary, and on Mary's instructions prepared to march on London. Knox therefore found himself caught in rebel territory.[1]

During the critical days between 12 and 19 July, when the issue between Jane and Mary was still undecided, Knox preached before a large congregation at Amersham. The parson of Amersham, Fisher, was a leading Protestant; but Hastings's soldiers were on every side.[2] Knox afterwards wrote an account of his sermon at Amersham, in which he stated that he had preached these words to his audience:

O England, now is God's wrath kindled against thee. Now hath He begun to punish, as He hath threatened a long while by His true prophets and messengers. He hath taken from thee the crown of thy glory and hath left thee without honour as a body without a head. And this appeareth to be only the beginning of sorrows, which appeareth to increase. For I perceive that the heart, the tongue and the hand of one Englishman is bent against another, and division to be in the whole realm, which is an assured sign of desolation to come. O England, England, dost thou not consider that thy commonwealth is like a ship sailing on the sea; if thy mariners and governors shall consume another, shalt thou not suffer shipwreck in short process of time? O England, England, alas, these plagues are poured upon thee, for that thou wouldst not know the most happy time of thy gentle visitation. But wilt thou yet obey the voice of thy God, and submit thyself to His holy words? Truly, if thou wilt, thou shalt find mercy in His sight, and the estate of thy commonwealth shall be preserved. But O England, England, if thou obstinately wilt return into Egypt; that is, if thou contract marriage, confederacy or league with such princes as do maintain and advance idolatry (such as the Emperor, which is no less enemy

[1] *Chronicle of Queen Jane*, p. 8; Mary I to Sir E. Hastings, 9 July 1553 (Strype, *Ecclesiastical Memorials*, iii [ii]. 171–2); Noailles to Henry II, 18 July 1553 (*Ambassades de Noailles*, ii. 74); Burnet, ii. 384.

[2] Knox, *Admonition to England* (*Works*, iii. 307–8). For Fisher, see *A.P.C.* 16 and 22 Aug. 1553; Foxe, vi. 393.

unto Christ than ever was Nero); if for the pleasure and friendship, I say, of such princes, thou return to thine old abominations, before used under the Papistry, then assuredly, O England, thou shalt be plagued and brought to desolation, by the means of those whose favours thou seekest, and by whom thou art procured to fall from Christ and to serve Antichrist.[1]

This sermon is another example of Knox's political sagacity and cunning. The generalizations, the lamentation for the fate of the country divided by civil war, the warning of future evils to come, could be interpreted as condemning either of the combatants, according to how the audience chose to accept it, or Knox decided to explain it afterwards to anyone who called upon him for an explanation. Knox did not challenge Mary's right to the throne, or refer to her at all; he merely warned against Popery and a foreign marriage. Even this was dangerous, because in Buckinghamshire, unlike in Norfolk and Suffolk, many of Mary's followers, including Hastings himself, were Catholics. But it would have been more difficult for them to take proceedings against Knox for saying this than if he had directly attacked their Queen; for Mary had not given any open indication that she intended to overthrow the Protestant religion or marry a foreign prince, and had, indeed, given her Protestant supporters the impression that she did not intend to do either of these things. On the other hand, his warnings about Papistry, and particularly about the danger of a foreign marriage, might have an adverse effect on the morale of Hastings's men, as Edward's devise, which had now been made public, had referred to the likelihood of Mary marrying a foreigner as one of the reasons for excluding her from the crown.

The only individual whom Knox attacked in his sermon was Charles V. This would ordinarily have been a dangerous thing to do, for attacks on foreign rulers were sternly punished in the sixteenth century. When a preacher in France or the Empire attacked Edward VI as a heretic, the English ambassador made an immediate protest, and, except when international relations between England and the state in question were very bad, the offending preacher was punished by his government. The English Privy Council would not ordinarily have tolerated any attack on the Emperor by a preacher in England; but in July 1553 they

[1] Knox, *Admonition to England* (*Works*, iii. 308–9).

were on the verge of an open rupture with Charles. When Mary's revolt broke out, the Council suspected that the Emperor's ambassador, and other envoys whom Charles had just sent to England, had organized it, though in fact they were doing all in their power to persuade Mary to submit to Northumberland, as Charles was certain that Mary's revolt would fail. Knox was obviously sufficiently well informed about the foreign policy of Jane's government to realize that England was on the point of breaking off diplomatic relations with Charles. The Council would not now take any action against Knox if he called the Emperor a Nero, though ten days earlier they would certainly have done so; and only a handful of people in Amersham would realize the enormity of the offence that Knox was committing by attacking a foreign prince. Most of the English Protestant preachers would have been prevented from doing this by their conscience, as well as by fear of punishment. Knox had no hesitation is denouncing the Emperor as soon as it was safe to do so.

During the next few days the situation deteriorated rapidly. The fleet at Yarmouth, which had been sent to prevent Mary from escaping abroad, mutinied and went over to Mary; the sailors threatened to throw their officers into the sea unless they proclaimed her as Queen. Northumberland, who had marched to Cambridge with an army of 6,000 German mercenaries, found that his men were reluctant to fight against the cousin of their Emperor. When Ridley preached against Mary at Paul's Cross, he was howled down by an angry crowd. Reports were coming in from all over the country of the peers and mayors who were proclaiming Mary in the market towns. London was the only place in England where Jane's government was in control. Knox decided to make his way towards London.

He had reached London by 19 July, the day on which the Catholic Church had its greatest triumph during the sixteenth century. As soon as Northumberland had left London with his army, Mary's secret supporters on Jane's Council began to plot. On 19 July the plotters, headed by Paget, Arundel, and Shrewsbury, won over all the members of the Council, and the Mayor and corporation of London, to declare for Mary. As the rumour spread during the morning, the people of London went mad. The streets were suddenly full of people, and when the Mayor and his escort walked to the cross in Cheapside to proclaim Mary as Queen, they could hardly force their way through the wildly cheering crowds. Within an hour, by the spontaneous action of the clergy and churchwardens, the church bells were ringing throughout the city, and bonfires were lighted in the streets. 'The shouts rose higher than the stars,' wrote an Italian visitor, 'and from a distance the earth must have looked like a Mount Etna.' The whole of the night the crowds thronged the streets, cheering and singing, while the fires burned and the bells rang and the fountains ran wine until well into the next day.[1]

The crowds were celebrating the fall of Northumberland and the triumph of their rightful Queen: but Knox knew that it was the greatest defeat that had ever been inflicted on the Protestant cause in Europe. No victory or defeat for the Lutheran princes of Germany in their war against the Emperor was of comparable importance to the fall of Protestant England. The defeat must have been particularly bitter to Knox because the Catholics claimed it as a proof of God's anger against Protestant heretics; and this argument, as Coverdale, the Protestant Bishop of Exeter, sadly noted in a pamphlet a few months later, had much effect on the people. The victory of Mary and the popular upsurge in her favour had been so unexpected that none of the experienced diplomats and political observers had predicted it. Cardinal Pole hailed it as a miracle and proof of the direct intervention of the Holy Ghost in human affairs. Within a few days, the slogan *Vox populi, vox Dei* was appearing on walls and at cross-roads all over London and south-eastern England.[2]

At this terrible time, Knox preached in London and boldly spoke out against the popular hysteria. He was legally entitled to preach, for his preacher's licence had not been revoked, nor had he been dismissed from his office of a royal preacher. He obviously

[1] For the events of 19 July in London, see Renard, Scheyvfe, etc. to Charles V, (19 July 1553); Advices from England, 20 July 1553 (Weiss, *Papiers d'État du Cardinal de Granvelle*, iv. 37–42; *Span. Cal.* xi. 95–6, 108); Wriothesley, *Chronicle*, ii. 88–89; anonymous letter (July 1553) (*Chronicle of Queen Jane*, pp. 11–12); Machyn, *Diary*, p. 37; *Greyfriars Chronicle*, p. 80; 'A London Chronicle 1523–1555' (*Camden Misc.* xii. 27). The passages in Knox's *Letter to the Faithful in London, Newcastle and Berwick*, and in his *First Blast of the Trumpet* (*Works*, iii. 167–8; iv. 393), show that Knox was in London on 19 and 20 July 1553.

[2] Strype, *Eccl. Mem.* iii [i]. 86; Pole to Mary I, 13 Aug. 1553 (*Ven. Cal.* v. 766); Renard, Scheyvfe, etc. to Charles V, 2 Aug. 1553; Renard to Prince Philip of Spain, 5 Sept. 1553 (Gachard, iv. 92; *Span. Cal.* xi. 134, 209).

avoided attacking the Queen, but he spoke out with great forthrightness against the danger of Popery. The Act of Uniformity was still in force, and the old Latin mass was still illegal; but the Catholic clergy in London immediately began to celebrate the mass in their churches, and Mary prohibited the authorities from taking any measures against them. Knox afterwards wrote that he had preached vehement sermons 'spoken in London in more places nor one, when fires of joy and riotous bankettings were at the proclamation of Mary your Queen'. His words are confirmed by the reports of the Emperor's ambassadors. On 27 July they informed Charles V that 'several preachers, certain Scotsmen in particular, have preached scandalous things of late to rouse up the people, going so far as to say that men should see Antichrist come again to life, and Popery in the land'. The ambassadors did not give the names of these Scotsmen. One of them was undoubtedly John Melvin, who was arrested soon afterwards; another was probably Knox.[1]

For three weeks the situation hung fire. On 2 August Mary entered London and released Gardiner and Bonner and the other Catholic bishops from prison; but apart from Northumberland and Ridley and a few of Jane's most active supporters, who were arrested for high treason, the Protestants were left at liberty. During these weeks Knox wrote a treatise on prayer. It was not printed until July 1554, but he probably circulated it among Protestant congregations in London in August 1553, and probably also sent a copy to his old congregation at Berwick. It was not primarily a controversial document, but was chiefly designed to revive the spirits of the Protestants in this hour of trial, though there was nothing in it which referred directly to the present situation. Why should a Christian pray, asked Knox, if God in any case knew what was in his heart? Because Christ commanded us to pray so that our hearts may be inflamed with continual fear, honour, and love of God. Knox stated that God would not always grant our prayers, but he also stressed that it was essential that when we pray, we must be certain that our prayers would be granted; 'for nothing more offendeth God than when we ask,

[1] Knox, *Letter to the Faithful in London, Newcastle and Berwick* (*Works*, iii. 167–8); Renard, Scheyvfe, etc. to Charles V, 27 July 1553 (*Span. Cal.* xi. 120); *A.P.C.* 24 Aug. 1553; Foxe, vi. 393. See also Noailles to Henry II, 4 and 22 Sept. 1553 (*Ambassades de Noailles*, ii. 136, 163–4).

doubting whether He will grant our petitions; for in so doing we doubt if God be true, if He be mighty and good'.[1]

Knox illustrated this by a reference to his personal experience. He himself 'in anguish of mind and vehement tribulation and affliction, called to the Lord when not only the ungodly, but even my faithful brother, yea, and my own self, that is, all natural understanding, judged my cause to be irremediable. And yet in my greatest calamity, and when my pains were most cruel, would His eternal wisdom that my hands should write far contrary to the judgement of carnal reason.' This is a reference to Knox's experience in the galleys, when he was at the point of death off the coast of Fife in the summer of 1548, and the 'faithful brother' to whom he refers must be his comrade James Balfour, who, as we know from Knox's *History*, was at his side when he was dying in the galleys; though by the time that Knox wrote his *History*, Balfour was no longer Knox's 'faithful brother', but 'blasphemous Balfour', the 'principal misguider now of Scotland', who above all others ought to be abhorred.[2]

In his *Confession and Declaration of Prayers*, Knox referred only briefly and cautiously to controversial and dangerous issues. He wrote that all who pray to God without the mediation of Jesus Christ are odious and abominable before God, and from this he deduced, not only that the prayers of Turks and Jews were not pleasing to God, but that prayers to the saints were to be condemned. His language in these passages was remarkably restrained. He was even more cautious when referring to those who prayed to the Virgin Mary to intercede for us with Christ. 'Alas! whosoever is so minded, showeth plainly themselves to know nothing of Jesus Christ rightly', for they believed that Christ would not hear us unless some person acted as a mediator. 'O Lord, open the eyes of such, that they may clearly perceive Thy infinite kindness, gentleness and love toward mankind.' This was the harshest criticism of his opponents that Knox ventured to make in England in the autumn of 1553; but he had said enough to lay him open to a charge of heresy if the persecution of heretics were resumed, and his courage in writing these passages at such a time should not be underestimated.

At the end of his treatise, Knox added a prayer for the use of

[1] Knox, *A Confession and Declaration of Prayers* (*Works*, iii. 83–109; see pp. 86, 89).
[2] *Works*, iii. 90–91; Knox, *History*, i. 97, 112, 219.

the Protestants. Although it was in no way seditious or illegal, it would greatly have displeased the Queen.

Place above us, O Lord, for Thy great mercies' sake, such a head, with such rulers and magistrates, as feareth Thy name, and willeth the glory of Christ Jesus to spread. Take not from us the light of Thy Evangel, and suffer Thou no Papistry to prevail in this realm. Illuminate the heart of our Sovereign Lady Queen Mary with pregnant gifts of Thy Holy Ghost. . . . Repress Thou the pride of those that would rebel; and remove from all hearts the contempt of the Word. . . . Let Thy Gospel be preached with boldness in this realm. . . . O Lord, let us never revolt, nor turn back to idolatry again.[1]

On 12 August Mary issued a proclamation. Her reason for issuing it was that 'contentions be again much revived, through certain false and untrue reports and rumours spread by some light and evil-disposed persons'. She explained that she would continue to be a Catholic, and greatly desired that her subjects would embrace the same faith; but she had no intention of compelling them to do this by force. She ordered her subjects to live together in peace and charity, prohibited anyone from using 'those new-found devilish terms of Papist or heretic, and such like', and forbade anyone to preach without a special licence from the Queen herself. Anyone contravening the proclamation was to be severely punished.[2] This was a serious blow at Knox's activities. Hitherto he had preached as a royal preacher, but as he was one of the 'light and evil-disposed persons' who had been spreading false rumours and causing contention by his references to Papists, and was in any case well known as a heretical preacher, he had no chance of obtaining a new preaching licence from the Queen.

Next day, on Sunday, 13 August, Bonner's chaplain, Dr. Bourn, preached at Paul's Cross before a congregation that included the Mayor and city officers and Bonner himself, who was about to be restored as Bishop of London in Ridley's place. When Bourn referred to the virtues of Bonner and his unjust imprisonment under Edward VI, he was violently heckled by Protestants in the audience, and someone threw a dagger at Bourn, which narrowly missed him. Two leading Protestant divines, Bradford

[1] *Works*, iii. 94–95, 98, 107.

[2] Proclamation of 18 Aug. 1553 (Foxe, vi. 390). The proclamation was dated 18 Aug., though it had first been issued verbally by Mary to the Lord Mayor on 12 Aug. (*A.P.C.* 13 Aug. 1553).

and John Rogers, tried to appease the fury of their supporters, and escorted Bourn to safety; but this foolish Protestant provocation was seized on by the government as an excuse for measures against the leading Protestants.[1]

On 16 August Bradford and Rogers, who had saved Bourn, were summoned before the Council for their pains, and accused of having instigated the riot. Bradford was sent to the Tower, and Rogers placed under house arrest. On the same day orders were given for the arrest of Becon and Fisher, the parson of Amersham. On 24 August the Scot, John Melvin, 'a very seditious preacher', was imprisoned in Newgate by order of the Council. By the first week in September, Hooper and Coverdale were in prison; on 13 and 14 September, Latimer and Cranmer were sent to the Tower. In nearly ever case the procedure was the same. The victim was summoned to appear before the Privy Council on a given date, and complied, coming freely without an escort, although he knew what was in store for him. This was the usual method of dealing with heretical suspects in England, and was all that was required in the case of Protestants who believed in the duty of Christian obedience to the sovereign.[2]

Knox reacted to the situation like a Scotsman. He did not wait to be arrested, but moved throughout the country. He went first to Kent. Kent was a Protestant stronghold; five months later, it was to be the scene of the Wyatt rebellion. But he could not stay there long. Kent was no nearer to London than East Lothian was to Edinburgh, but the English government was not the Scottish government, and its long arm reached easily into Kent. In any case, it was essential to move about from place to place, and Knox had returned to London by the middle of September.[3] He had now to consider what he was going to do. He knew that like all other Protestants in England he would soon be faced with the choice of going to mass, flight, or martyrdom.

Going to mass was the course adopted by the worldly politicians and by large numbers of Protestants of all classes, from Elizabeth, Cecil, Paget, and Paulet down to the local justices of

[1] Foxe, vi. 391–2; Renard, Scheyvfe, etc. to Charles V, 16 Aug. 1553 (Gachard, iv. 97–98; *Span. Cal.* xi. 169–70); *A.P.C.* 13, 14, 15, and 16 Aug. 1553; Terentianus to John of Ulm, 20 Nov. 1553 (Fuessli, *Epistolae ad ecclesiae Helveticae*, pp. 311–12; *Orig. Letters*, pp. 368–9).

[2] *A.P.C.* 16, 24, 29, and 31 Aug., 1, 13, and 14 Sept. 1553; Foxe, vi. 392–4.

[3] Knox to Mrs. Bowes, 20 Sept. 1553 (Letter XVII, *Works*, iii. 374).

the peace and many of the lower classes. For Knox and the sincere Protestants, this course was excluded. They believed that to go to mass was sinful, as it meant worshipping the bread and wine, which was idolatry. To attend mass was the supreme act of betrayal which could not be forgiven. Knox and his friends considered the Protestants who stayed in England under Mary and went to mass in the same light as the members of the anti-Nazi resistance movement regarded those who collaborated with the Germans and joined a Nazi political organization. They did not condemn Protestants who remained in England, obeying the Queen's laws, as God's law required all good subjects to do, and keeping their Protestant beliefs secret, provided that they did not go to mass; but if they were required to go to mass, they must refuse, even if this meant the stake.

The collaborators included men of many different types. Some, like the infamous Lord Chancellor Rich, distinguished themselves by rounding up and burning Protestants with as much relish as they had persecuted Papists under Henry VIII. Most of them went to mass merely in order to be able to live in peace and quiet. A few, like Paget and Cecil, went to mass, remained in office, or at least in Parliament, and were able to use their position to delay and mitigate the persecution of Protestants and to some extent thwart the Queen's plans. If all the secret Protestant sympathizers on Mary's Privy Council had followed the advice of Knox and the Protestant preachers, and had chosen either exile or martyrdom, the Emperor's ambassador would have been a happier man.[1] If Elizabeth had chosen either course, England would not have reverted to Protestantism in 1559, and might still be a Catholic nation today. But the victims of persecution do not easily forgive collaborators, knowing well that for every one who collaborates in order to help the cause, a hundred only pretend afterwards that this was the reason. Knox and his English colleagues stood firm on the principle that they must choose the fire rather than the mass. This rigid adherence to religious principle was not adopted only by unworldly fanatics. In the sixteenth century, as in other ages, men of cool, detached intellectual judgement—Protestants, Catholics, and Unitarians, like Ridley, Thomas More, and Servetus—were prepared to die rather than deny the

[1] Renard to Charles V, 22 Mar., 17 Apr., and 6 May 1554 (*Span. Cal.* xii. 166–7, 219, 238).

truth of their beliefs. Even the Emperor Charles V, who read Machiavelli's *The Prince* as a textbook, and was the cleverest power-politician of his age, advised Mary that, as a last resort, she must choose death rather than attend a Protestant church service at the orders of the ministers of Edward VI.[1]

As Knox would not go to mass, he had to choose between emigration and martyrdom. The Protestants' doctrine on this point was clear. It was fully justifiable for a Protestant to flee abroad in order to escape martyrdom, for Christ had said: 'If they persecute you in one city, flee unto another.' All the Protestant leaders, including Cranmer and Ridley, strongly urged their followers to flee, warning them not to seek martyrdom before the time which God had appointed, and pointing out that to choose the hardships of a life of poverty abroad was itself an act of sacrifice for the cause. But the zealous Protestants were very reluctant to flee; many of them preferred to stay and die as martyrs. Cranmer, though he urged the other Protestants to escape abroad, refused to flee himself, on the grounds that the rank and file would be discouraged if he, their leader, fled, and that he could do more good as a martyr in England than as an exile abroad. Hooper, who had emigrated to avoid the persecution of the last years of Henry VIII, also took the attitude that the leaders, unlike the rank and file, should remain and suffer martyrdom. 'Once I did flee, and take to my feet,' he said, 'but now, because I am called to this place and vocation, I am thoroughly persuaded to tarry, and to live and die with my sheep.' Latimer, who received six hours' warning that the Queen's officers were coming to arrest him, refused to flee, but rode to meet the officers; he said that he went willingly, being called by his prince to make a reckoning of his doctrine. Many other Protestants, who could not justify their refusal to flee on the grounds that they were leaders, chose martyrdom rather than exile.[2]

Knox decided to go abroad. He has been criticized for this by several modern writers, who contrast his unheroic attitude with that of the martyrs. The criticism is quite unjustified. He was acting on the principles that were accepted by all his colleagues:

[1] Charles V to Scheyvfe, 7 and 17 Mar. and 29 June 1551 (*Span. Cal.* x. 239, 248, 316).

[2] See Ridley, *Piteous Lamentation* (Ridley, *Works*, p. 62); Parker, *De Antiquitate Britannica*, p. 400; Foxe, vi. 645; vii. 464.

persecuted in one city, he fled to another. Many of the most eminent Protestants, including bishops like Ponet and Scory, fled abroad, and none of those who chose martyrdom condemned them for this, even if they themselves preferred to choose the harder path. But Knox was in a different position from the English Protestants. As an alien, the choice between flight and martyrdom was not really open to him. Mary had decided to expel all the foreign Protestant refugees from England, thus striking a blow against heresy and ridding the realm of a turbulent minority, and taking a step that was very popular with the English people. Her government granted passports to Peter Martyr and Poullain and all the aliens who wished to go, though they were compelled to leave nearly all their property behind, and took measures to round up and deport all the refugees. Every move in this process was made in consultation with the Emperor's ambassadors, who, at Mary's suggestion, informed their master of the date when the expulsion was to be enforced, so that the heretics could be arrested by the Emperor's officers as soon as they landed in Flanders. None of the Protestant aliens were executed by Mary's government. They were all expelled from the country a year before any English Protestant was burnt.[1]

But Knox was not easy in his conscience. All around him, in London and Kent, he found Protestants who were refusing to leave England, who were asserting their eagerness to testify for their faith and face death in the fire. Many of them, in due course, gave heroic proof of their resolution; others failed when it came to the pinch, and found that their brave refusal to flee had only led them to accept the mass rather than the hardship of exile. Knox, finding so many of his comrades preferring death to flight, was deeply affected, and haunted by the fear of being a coward. Again and again, in his letters to Mrs. Bowes and his other friends, he sought to justify his decision to flee, and to convince them, and himself, that it was not cowardice which had prompted his decision.

Knox had an additional and personal difficulty. If he left England, it would mean abandoning his wife and Mrs. Bowes.

[1] Renard, Scheyvfe, etc. to Charles V, 16 and 27 Aug., (Aug.), and 4 and 9 Sept. 1553; Charles V to Renard, Scheyvfe, etc., 23 Aug. 1553; Granvelle to Renard, 15 Dec. 1553; Renard to Charles V, 29 Dec. 1553, 23 Jan., and 24 Feb. 1554 (Gachard, iv. 100, 103, 111–13, 280, 307; Weiss, iv. 65; Tytler, *England under Edward VI and Mary*, ii. 312; *Span. Cal.* xi. 172, 179, 188, 193–4, 199–200, 217, 438, 472; xii. 39, 126).

Mrs. Bowes would not be able to leave the country legally; she would have to stay with her husband. Things would be almost as difficult in Marjory's case, for though the wife of an alien would normally be allowed to go with him when he left England, the position might be different in the case of the wife of a priest. The prejudice against the marriage of priests was very strong and widespread among laymen of all classes, as well as among the government and the Catholic clergy. These marriages were treated as invalid and contrary to God's law, despite the fact that they had been legalized in England by the Act of Parliament of 1549; for all Catholic governments refused to recognize the validity of the marriage of priests, even if they had been performed in Protestant states where such marriages were legal. Priests' wives were considered as their mistresses. The priests who had married under Edward VI were compelled to separate from their wives or resign their benefices, and none of the Protestant clergy in prison were allowed to see their wives and children—their harlots and bastards, as the authorities called them.[1] An application for a passport by the wife of a foreign priest, in order to be able to leave England with her husband, was not likely to receive favourable consideration, especially if, as in Marjory's case, the marriage had not gone beyond the stage of the precontract.

When Knox returned to London in the middle of September, he found a letter from Mrs. Bowes awaiting him. Richard Bowes had been raising difficulties about Knox and the future of his wife and daughter. Like other government officials, he was preparing to go to mass as soon as the order came from Court, and had no wish to be burdened with a heretical priest as a son-in-law. He no longer recognized the validity of the precontract, in view of the fact that Knox was a priest, and obviously thought that if Knox left the country, his wife and daughter would sever all connexion with him and be free of his subversive influence. It would be unfair to accuse Richard Bowes of being actuated only by selfish

[1] See, e.g., the cases of Rogers, Saunders, and Hooper (Foxe, vi. 602–3, 609–10, 612, 625, 646–7). For the treatment of married priests in general, see Dixon, iv. 143–60; Hilda Grieve, 'The Deprived Married Clergy in Essex, 1553–1561' (*Trans. R.H.S.* 4th ser. xxii. 141–69). Married priests, who had not taken vows of chastity, were given the choice of divorcing their wives and being transferred to another benefice, or of remaining married and losing all office in the Church, without pensions. Monks and nuns who had married after taking vows were in all cases forced to divorce their spouses, and were punished by imprisonment or lesser penances.

motives. Any husband could be expected to wish to extricate his wife from her association with heretics, and every father would hesitate before allowing his daughter to become the wife of a priest. The Catholic pamphleteers and preachers were letting loose a stream of violent propaganda against married priests and their wives. They drew a sordid picture of the Protestant clergy sharing their wives in common and living utterly promiscuous lives; Protestant women were vilified as a bunch of brazen hussies who had rejected all traditional beliefs in order to adopt new revolutionary doctrines with an intemperate zeal. Richard Bowes, like other country gentlemen, had heard of the 'London ladies' who dared to argue theology with their fathers and their husbands, who left home without permission to join a Protestant congregation, who married one priest and, when they tired of him, divorced him and married another priest, or more likely gave their bodies to satisfy the lusts of several Protestant priests at the same time.[1]

Mrs. Bowes seems to have appealed to Knox to come to Northumberland and speak with her husband, in order to persuade him to let Marjory, and probably Mrs. Bowes herself, emigrate with Knox. Knox realized that this would be a dangerous proceeding. In view of the attitude which Richard Bowes was taking, it was more than likely that if Knox presented himself at Norham Castle, Bowes would cause him to be arrested, as Protestant priests who had done far less than Knox were being arrested in London and elsewhere. But Knox could not leave his wife and her mother without making some effort to save them; apart from his wish to be with them, and his duty to adhere to his spouse, if they remained with Richard Bowes at Norham they would soon be faced with the choice of mass or martyrdom. On 20 September, he wrote to Mrs. Bowes:

It becomes me now to jeopard my life for the comfort and deliverance of my own flesh, as that I will do by God's grace; both fear and friendship of all earthly creature laid aside. I have written to your husband, the contents whereof I trust our brother Harry will declare to you and to my wife. If I escape sickness and imprisonment, be sure to see me soon. Yet, mother, depend not upon me too much, for what am I but a wretched sinner? If ye receive any comfort, it comes from above, from God the Father, who shall provide for you abundantly.

[1] Knox to Mrs. Bowes, 20 Sept. 1553 (*Works*, iii. 374); Huggarde, *The Displaying of the Protestantes*, pp. 74–77.

Whatever become of me, remember, mother, the gifts of God are not bound to any one man, but are common to every man (in his measure) that incalls the Lord Jesus.[1]

Soon afterwards Knox's communications with Mrs. Bowes and Marjory were severed. Knox's servant was stopped when he was carrying one of Knox's letters to Mrs. Bowes, and the letter was taken from him. Knox discovered that the letter had been seized, but he heard nothing from Mrs. Bowes or Marjory; and he therefore decided that he must go to the north himself, despite all the risks involved. He reached Newcastle, and established contact with the members of his congregation; but Northumberland was a particularly dangerous place for Knox, as he was well known in the county, and the Captain of Norham had a personal, as well as a political, reason for wishing to throw him into prison. As soon as he reached Newcastle, the news spread that he had arrived, and the Scots of his old congregation insisted that he should go into hiding and change his lodging frequently, though they were afraid that he would be recognized when he moved from one house to another. Knox believed that they exaggerated the danger, and tried to make them understand that there was nothing incriminating in the letter that had been seized from his servant. It contained nothing 'except exhortation to constancy in that truth which God has openly laid before our eyes, which', Knox explained, 'I am not minded to deny whenever such question shall be demanded of me'.

Knox's chief concern was how to get into contact with Marjory and her mother. He decided to remain hidden, so as to draw as little attention as possible to his presence in Northumberland, and meanwhile to see if he could arrange a clandestine meeting with his wife. But he found that this was quite impossible. He managed to send a letter to Mrs. Bowes in which he explained the position. 'I will obey the voices of my brethren, and will give place to the fury and rage of Satan for a time. And so can I not espy how that either of you both I can speak at this time. But if God please preserve me at this time, whereof I am not yet resolved, then shall there lack in me no goodwill that ye may know the place of my residence.' Apart from his other difficulties, he was now short of money. His salary of £40 a year as a royal preacher was due to be

[1] Knox to Mrs. Bowes, 20 Sept. 1553 (*Works*, iii. 376).

paid in October 1553, but in the circumstances he had not, of course, attempted to claim it. Knox's sense of humour, which was one of his most deep-rooted characteristics, was not destroyed in adversity, and he joked about his financial position in his letter to Mrs. Bowes. 'I will not make you privy how rich I am,' he wrote, 'but of London I departed with less money than ten groats' —that is to say, 3*s.* 4*d.*, or about £5 in terms of present value. He said that by not claiming his salary as a royal preacher he had saved the government money, unless the salary had been pocketed by some official. 'Either the Queen's Majesty or some treasurer will be £40 richer by me.'[1]

Knox did not tell Mrs. Bowes the place where he was hiding. This was partly no doubt because he did not wish to mention it in a letter; but he may also have hesitated to trust her with a secret that would endanger his comrades, as well as his own safety, if she unintentionally betrayed it. There could be no doubt as to Mrs. Bowes's sincerity, but she seems to have been the kind of person who is a liability and a danger in an underground political organization—emotional, over-scrupulous, and naïve. Her next step shows her lack of understanding of the situation. She got into contact with Knox, and asked him to approach her brother-in-law, Sir Robert Bowes. We have to deduce what occurred from a few short and obscure sentences in secret letters written from a fugitive on the run to a confederate; but it appears that Mrs. Bowes hoped that Sir Robert would intervene with her husband on their behalf, to persuade him to permit Marjory to complete her marriage and arrange for her, and perhaps Mrs. Bowes herself, to emigrate with Knox.[2] She obviously did not wish to escape from Norham Castle, or to send Marjory to Knox, without her husband's consent, and thus violate the Christian duty of obedience due from a wife and daughter. Knox realized the uselessness and the danger involved in making contact with Sir Robert Bowes; but he decided, at considerable personal risk, to make the attempt.

Sir Robert Bowes had every reason to disapprove of Knox and to refuse to help him. His virtues and prejudices were those of a man of his class. He was a brave soldier, an efficient diplomat, a conscientious administrator, an able lawyer, and a satisfactory Member of Parliament. He showed unusual care for the welfare of

[1] Knox to Mrs. Bowes (Oct. or early Nov. 1553) (*Works*, iii. 370–2).

[2] Knox to Mrs. Bowes, 20 Sept. and (Nov.) 1553 (ibid. 374–8).

the troops under his command, and took steps to see that officers who had done good service were rewarded with a gift of Church lands. His hatred and contempt for the Scots was profound; he interpreted the courage and resilience which the Scots showed when he burned their wretched hovels as a sign of their barbarian insensitivity. As far as religion was concerned, Bowes, like most of his colleagues, had adopted the convenient doctrine that it was his duty to serve and obey his sovereign and conform to whatever religion was required of him. Having risen to be a member of the Council of the North and Warden of the Marches under Henry VIII, under Edward VI he had moved to the south as a member of the Privy Council itself, and had been appointed Master of the Rolls for life in 1552. Then Sir Robert's guiding principle of obedience to the established authority had led him into difficulties; he subscribed Edward's devise of the Crown to Jane Grey, and sat on Jane's Privy Council during her nine days' reign. Mary had pardoned him, along with all the other councillors, but she did not reappoint him to her own Council, and in September 1553 he resigned his office as Master of the Rolls. A few weeks later, the Council sent him to Berwick, with instructions to negotiate about minor Border disputes with the Scottish representatives.[1]

Sir Robert Bowes met Knox on 6 November. The interview was stormy. Even if Bowes could have forgiven Knox for being a Scot and a married priest, he could never forgive him for being a member of the Protestant party which had been responsible for all the changes in religion and upheavals in the State and for the semi-disgrace in which Sir Robert now found himself. He told Knox that he considered that he and Mrs. Bowes were jointly responsible for all the trouble in the Bowes family. Knox had obviously not expected to have much success with Sir Robert, but he was taken aback by his hostile and insulting attitude. He had prophesied in many sermons that the secret Papists in Edward's Council were only awaiting their opportunity to reveal themselves as persecutors of the Protestants; but his theoretical understanding of the character of the leading royal officials had not prepared him

[1] Sir Robert Bowes to the Council, 12, 13, and 27 May 1546; Sir Robert Bowes to Henry VIII, 14 May 1546 (*L.P.* xxi [i]. 804, 827, 940); Appointment and resignation of Sir Robert Bowes as Master of the Rolls, 9 June 1552 and 18 Sept. 1553; Indenture between English and Scottish Commissioners, 4 Dec. 1553 (*Cal. St. Pap. Dom., Edw. VI, etc.*, i. 40; vi. 430–1; *Cal. Pat. Rolls, Ph. & Mary*, i. 209); *A.P.C.* 14 Oct. and 15 and 16 Nov. 1553.

emotionally for the experience of being abused and browbeaten by a man who had been friendly enough a few months before, and to whose family he was linked by marriage.

Knox's account of the interview in his letter to Mrs. Bowes shows how deeply he was wounded by Sir Robert's behaviour. He was sensitive and thin-skinned, and the type of man who resents insult more than injury. He disliked being in the position, not of a preacher or a debater in a theological argument, but of a suppliant for a personal favour. 'I am not a good orator in my own cause', he explained to Mrs. Bowes, and he was glad to change the subject to theological argument, where he spoke with complete confidence, knowing that he spoke as a messenger of God. But Sir Robert would not listen to the doctrinal reasons by which Knox sought to justify his position, presumably on the question of the marriage of priests. 'Away with your rhetorical reasons,' cried Sir Robert, 'for I will not be persuaded with them.' Knox told Mrs. Bowes that Sir Robert's disdainful and spiteful words had so pierced his heart that life had become bitter to him. Sir Robert had become 'not only a despiser but also a taunter of God's messengers (God be merciful unto him). . . . But what he would not be content to hear of me, God shall declare to him a day to his displeasure, unless he repent.'[1]

Sir Robert Bowes did at least allow Knox to depart unmolested; he did not have him arrested forthwith. But the interview had made Knox's position much more dangerous than before, and the Scots of his old congregation became more insistent that he should leave England. It was now obvious that he would not be able to see Marjory or Mrs. Bowes, and he wrote to Mrs. Bowes, explaining that he might have to emigrate soon. But Knox had nearly left it too late to leave the country. Until a few weeks earlier, he could easily have obtained a passport; but most of the foreign Protestant refugees had already left, and as the government's measures against the Protestants in England increased in severity, it became more doubtful if a heretic as notorious as Knox would be allowed to go in peace. Nearly every day a Protestant preacher was arrested on a charge of sedition in some part of the country; at the universities, Protestant students were receiving savage floggings for speaking disrespectfully of the mass. Knox left Northumberland and made his way to the south, almost certainly

[1] Knox to Mrs. Bowes (Nov. 1553) (*Works*, iii. 378).

going to London. Here, while he hid in the houses of Protestants, he wrote his *Exposition of the Sixth Psalm*, and also began to write a longer treatise, his *Godly Letter of Warning or Admonition to the Faithful in London, Newcastle and Berwick*. His *Exposition of the Sixth Psalm* was written specially for Mrs. Bowes, who had asked him to write it two years before. He urged the Protestants to remember the patience of David and Job under their afflictions, and to take comfort from this.[1]

Parliament had just enacted legislation that abolished the church services of the Second Book of Common Prayer, and re-introduced the old Catholic mass of Henry VIII's reign on 21 December. Many of the Protestants were beginning to waver under the pressure of public opinion, official propaganda, and the increasing threat of persecution; and they had been greatly demoralized by the fact that Northumberland had recanted on the scaffold, and had declared himself a Catholic, for his recantation had been given wide publicity by the government. Knox expressed his deep grief at seeing so many Protestants desert the cause, and then immediately sought to justify himself to Mrs. Bowes for having fled from the north. 'The falling back of such men as I hear daily do turn back to that idol again, is to me more dolorous than, I trust, the corporal death shall be, whenever it shall come at God's appointment. Some will ask then, Why did I fly? Assuredly I cannot tell, but of one thing I am sure, the fear of death was not the chief cause of my flying.'[2]

Before Knox had finished writing this treatise, he found that arrangements had been made for him to leave England. On 6 January 1554 he sent Mrs. Bowes the unfinished manuscript of his *Exposition of the Sixth Psalm*, explaining that he would send her the second part and the longer treatise as soon as possible. 'If it come not to you from the south,' he told her, 'I shall provide that it shall come to you by some other means.' Then he opened his heart to her about the sadness which he felt at parting from her, and his anxiety about the fate of his congregation in the north, and of Protestantism in England.

[1] Knox to Mrs. Bowes (Nov. 1553); Knox, *An Exposition upon the Sixth Psalm of David* (*Works*, iii. 119–33, 378–9; and see especially p. 120); Dixon, iv. 36. See also Knox to Mrs. Bowes, 22 Dec. 1551 (*Works*, iii. 355, where it is wrongly dated 1553; see *infra*, App. IV).

[2] *Statutes of the Realm*, 1 Mary st. 2, c. 2; Noailles to Montmorency, 22 Aug. 1553 (*Ambassades de Noailles*, ii. 117–18); Renard, Scheyvfe, etc. to Charles V, 27 Aug. 1553 (*Span. Cal.* xi. 187); Knox, *Exposition of the Sixth Psalm* (*Works*, iii. 120).

I cannot express the pain which I think I might suffer to have the presence of you, and of others that be like troubled, but a few days. But God shall gather us at His good pleasure; if not in this wretched and miserable life, yet in that estate where death may not dissever us. My daily prayer is for the sore afflicted in those quarters. Sometime I have thought that impossible it had been, so to have removed my affection from the realm of Scotland, that any realm or nation could have been equal dear unto me. But God I take to record in my conscience, that the troubles present (and appearing to be) in the realm of England are double more dolorous unto my heart than ever were the troubles of Scotland.[1]

Knox was fully justified in these sentiments. His congregation in Northumberland, and all the Protestants in England, would soon be facing a far more cruel persecution than had ever been inflicted on the Protestants in Scotland; and the accession of Mary had dealt a heavier blow than the fall of St. Andrews Castle to the fortunes of the Protestants in Scotland as well as in England.

Three weeks later, Knox was in Dieppe. We do not know how he left England, but it is unlikely that at this late stage he took the risk of applying for a passport. The usual sea-route from England to Dieppe was from Rye, but if Knox left England illegally he may have made arrangements with Protestant seamen in London to be taken on a ship direct from the Thames, boarding the ship secretly at night at a city wharf or in Deptford, like the Duchess of Suffolk and other escaping *émigrés*; though in Rye, too, there were Protestant fishermen who were ready to help escaping refugees. The voyage was dangerous. Apart from the risk of arrest by the English authorities at his departure, Knox ran the usual risks of crossing the Channel in rough weather at the beginning of January, and the possibility of capture by pirates at sea. There was the further risk of seizure at sea by English or French warships. France was at war with the Emperor, and the French, who bitterly resented the proposed marriage between Mary and the Emperor's son, Philip of Spain, had sent warships to patrol the Channel in the hope of seizing the Emperor's envoys, Count Egmont and his colleagues, who had just arrived in England to act as proxies for Philip at his betrothal to Mary. English warships were also in the Channel to escort Egmont and the envoys safely from Calais. It might have gone badly for Knox if his ship had fallen in with

[1] Knox, ibid. (*Works*, iii. 120, 132–3).

either the English or the French fleet; but he reached Dieppe in safety.[1]

Five years before, Knox had left the bondage of the French galleys for the freedom of England. Now he escaped from England to return to the safety of France. Henry II had not changed his religion, and still persecuted Protestants; but in his anger at Mary's decision to marry Philip and her close alliance with the Emperor, he had decided not to surrender English Protestant refugees to Mary.[2] Knox would certainly be safer in Dieppe than in the Emperor's territories in Flanders. Many of the English refugees risked the longer and more difficult sea journey to the coast of Friesland, making for Emden, in Protestant territory; but Dieppe, which was the chief French port for the trade with Scotland, had a colony of Scottish merchants and seamen who could give Knox shelter. Knox obviously had addresses and contacts in the Rue d'Écosse in Dieppe; perhaps his brother, William Knox, arranged for his journey and for his reception in Dieppe. It was probably the Scottish sympathizers in Dieppe who supplied Knox with money. Knox, like all political refugees, must have faced the problem of how he would obtain enough money to live in exile; but in none of his writings after reaching Dieppe does he complain of shortage of money, though he did not engage in any trade, or earn his living. During the five years after he left England, he travelled over 7,000 miles by land and sea, not on foot in penury, like some of the exiles, but on horseback, and probably in reasonable comfort. He could not have done this if he had been in financial difficulties. During his years of exile, he was maintained by the contributions and hospitality of members of his congregations and their sympathizers in Dieppe, Frankfort, and Geneva.

In Dieppe, Knox completed his *Exposition of the Sixth Psalm* for Mrs. Bowes. Again he emphasized the need for patience in adversity, the chief lesson of the Psalm; but his chief concern was still to excuse himself for having fled and not having stayed to face martyrdom. He was anxious that his congregation in

[1] Egmont, etc. to Mary of Hungary, 24 Dec. 1553; Egmont, etc. to Renard, 25 Dec. 1553; Egmont, etc. to Charles V, 27 Dec. 1553; Renard to Charles V, 18 Jan. 1554 (Gachard, iv. 269–70, 272, 300; Weiss, iv. 176; *Span. Cal.* xi. 458–61; xii. 32). For the date of Knox's departure from England to Dieppe, see *infra*, App. V.

[2] Wotton's remonstrance to the French government (6 Mar. 1553/4) (*Ambassades de Noailles*, iii. 109–18); Wotton to Mary I, 17 Apr. 1554 (*Cal. For. Pap. Mary*, No. 187); Renard to Charles V, 22 Apr. 1554 (*Span. Cal.* xii. 223–4).

Northumberland should not think that this was due to his lack of faith and his uncertainty as to the truth of his doctrines, and he urged them to remain steadfast in the faith, to refuse to bow down to idolatry, and to have no doubts that he himself was unshaken in his belief in Protestant doctrines. He said that he would not recant one sentence of his former doctrine for all the glory, riches, and rest on earth, and would not bow his knee before that most abominable idol for all the threats that earthly tyrants could devise.

> Albeit that I have in the beginning of this battle appeared to play the faint-hearted and feeble soldier (the cause I remit to God), yet my prayer is that I may be restored to the battle again. . . . England and Scotland shall both know that I am ready to suffer more than either poverty or exile, for the profession of that doctrine, and that heavenly religion, whereof it has pleased His merciful providence to make me, amongst others, a simple soldier and witness-bearer unto men. . . . Mother, for a few sermons by me to be made within England, my heart at this hour could be content to suffer more than nature were able to sustain.

He assured Mrs. Bowes that he intended to return to visit her again within a short time. 'Be ye assured, beloved mother, that neither shall it be the fear of death, nor the rage of the Devil, that shall impede or hinder me. . . . No, I assure you that only God's hand shall withhold me. . . . Mother, be not moved with any wind, but stick to Christ Jesus in the day of this His battle. . . . Avoid that abomination, which oft ye have heard by me affirmed to be damnable idolatry.'[1]

Knox has been reproached by later historians for hypocrisy and cowardice in writing these letters from the safety of exile to his mother-in-law and followers in England, calling on them to refuse to go to mass and face the martyrdom from which he himself had fled. If it is disgraceful for a leader to exhort his followers to die bravely for their cause while he himself remains in safety, this is a disgrace which Knox shares with every revolutionary leader who organizes a resistance movement from the safety of exile, and with every general who, from his headquarters, orders his soldiers to attack. Knox's conduct was fully justified, not only by all the principles of military and revolutionary activity throughout

[1] Knox, *Exposition of the Sixth Psalm*, 2nd part (*Works*, iii. 134–56; the passage cited is on pp. 153–5). For the place and date of writing, see *infra*, App. V.

the ages, but by the accepted religious doctrines of the Protestants, which permitted flight, but not recantation. If Mrs. Bowes and Knox's congregation in England wished to avoid martyrdom without betraying their faith, it was open to them to try to flee from England, as Knox himself had done. Knox never discouraged anyone from following his own example and escaping abroad. He only urged them not to recant and submit to idolatry, as it was his duty to do as their minister and leader.

Knox would probably not have been branded as a coward by future generations if it had not been for his own guilty conscience. The passages in his letters in which he repeatedly denies that he is a coward, and reiterates his eagerness to die as a martyr at the earliest possible opportunity, which he was writing only a few weeks after he had fled to avoid martyrdom, are suspicious. No historian accuses Henry VIII or Elizabeth I of cowardice in urging their soldiers and sailors to risk death in battle without incurring the risks themselves, because Henry VIII and Elizabeth did not write self-exculpatory letters to justify their action. They felt no sense of guilt, as they never considered that their own position was in any way comparable to those of their subjects, who had a duty to die to preserve the safety and suit the convenience of their prince. But Knox did not consider his fellow-Protestants as his subjects or inferiors, and could have no easy conscience while he was safe and they were not.

Knox could justify his flight on grounds of practical politics and religious doctrine, but emotionally he could not justify it. Although he was not the type of man who yearns for martyrdom, he shared the feelings of his colleagues in the English Protestant movement. This movement was composed of idealists as well as careerists. Along with the careerists who joined when Protestantism was successful, there were the idealists who had been attracted to the cause when the only prospect for a Protestant was to be burnt alive. The readiness to carry idealism and selflessness to the point of undergoing torture and death for the cause, which has often been mocked as self-righteousness and masochism, but is one of the most lofty and enobling of human instincts, is deep-rooted in Christianity, with its belief in the purifying effect of suffering and its emphasis on Calvary and the ordeals of its early martyrs. There was not much of this spirit left in sixteenth-century Christianity; even the practice of fasting, the formal manifestation of this spirit, had reached the point where countless numbers of priests and laymen applied for, and obtained, a dispensation permitting them to eat meat in Lent on the grounds that fish did not agree with their digestion. But there were a few Christians in the sixteenth century who were the spiritual descendants of Polycarp and Laurence. Some of them suffered martyrdom on behalf of the Catholic religion; but many of them joined the Protestants. They were the priests, the gentlemen, the merchants, the artisans, and the women who offered themselves for the fire. Their admiration for the heroism of their persecuted comrades, and their readiness to face persecution themselves, was the link that bound them together. To flinch was to betray their brothers; only when they had stood firm under the torture could they be sure that they would not fail.

This sense of guilt assailed Knox strongly during the winter of 1553–4. He never experienced it afterwards. A few years later, he was able to justify his flight without any embarrassment at all. In August 1556 he wrote to a Protestant woman in Edinburgh that Christ had said 'Be ye simple as doves and prudent as serpents' because 'He commands unto them the simplicity of the dove, which can defend herself by no other means from the assaults of ravenous fowls, but only by the swiftness of her wings'.[1]

By March 1557 he was able to face up quite frankly to the question of cowardice in a letter which he wrote from Geneva to Janet Henderson in Edinburgh. After urging Janet Henderson to prefer death in the fire rather than submission to idolatry, in view of the eternal reward of life everlasting which is 'promised for the suffering of a moment', he proceeds:

> If any object, I follow not the counsel which I give to others, for my fleeing the country declareth my fear; I answer, I bind no man to my example; and yet, I trust to God that I do not expressedly against the Word, which God uttereth by me. If the love of this life, or the fear of corporal death, caused me to deny the known verity, or to do anything in the eyes of men which might seem for fear to favour idolatry, then woe unto me for ever, for I were nothing but a traitor to Christ and His religion. But if my fear be so measured that it compels me not to commit open iniquity, then do I nothing against my counsel, which is not mine but the express commandment of Christ Jesus, commanding us to forsake ourselves and to follow him.

[1] Knox to a Protestant woman in Edinburgh, 8 Aug. 1556 (*Works*, iv. 223).

And by November 1558, as Mary's persecution in England was drawing to its end, he had reached the stage when he could urge the members of his old congregations in Berwick and Newcastle to choose death rather than idolatry, without making any reference to his own personal position.[1]

This change in Knox's attitude had taken place because he had thought out a new course of action. When he arrived in Dieppe in January 1554 he could see no real alternative to martyrdom. Flight was justifiable, but only if it enabled the fleeing soldier to fight again another day; and though Knox often used the terms 'soldier' and 'battle' in this connexion, he used them in the strictly metaphorical sense in which they had so often been used in the Christian Church. The battle which the soldier is to fight is the battle which the martyr fights at the stake. By fleeing and avoiding martyrdom, Knox had lost the opportunity of fighting in the only battle which the English Protestant fellowship of martyrs could visualize. He was in a mood of despair during the fortnight that he spent in Dieppe. He wrote to Mrs. Bowes that he hoped that he would soon die from natural causes. It would have been the easiest solution to his problem.[2]

But Knox, in his black mood, was groping his way towards the light. The spirit of the times, which led to the unsuccessful Wyatt rebellion a few weeks after Knox left England, had brought to a head the doubts and problems that had arisen in his mind. He was not satisfied merely to urge the Protestants in England to refuse to go to mass even at the cost of death: his keen, pragmatic mind was contemplating a far more drastic solution. He was asking himself questions and providing answers which were so startling that he dared not accept them without encouragement from greater and wiser men than himself. For this reason he left Dieppe on 28 January 1554[3] and travelled to Switzerland; but no one in Switzerland could give him a satisfactory answer to his questions. He provided the answer himself, and it shocked the sixteenth-century world.

[1] Knox to Janet Henderson, 16 Mar. 1557; Knox, *Epistle to the inhabitants of Newcastle and Berwick* (*Works*, iv. 247; v. 475–94, where Laing states that Knox's letter was written on 16 Mar. 1557/8; as to this, see *infra*, App. IV.)

[2] Knox, *Exposition of the Sixth Psalm* (*Works*, iii. 154–5).

[3] See *infra*, App. V.

CHAPTER X

The *Admonition to England*

DURING the spring and summer of 1554, Knox developed the theory that the subjects of a Catholic sovereign were lawfully entitled to overthrow their sovereign by armed revolution. Knox did not owe this doctrine to Calvin; he developed it several years before Calvin was driven, with great reluctance, to endorse it by implication. Bullinger was nearly as hesitant as Calvin in accepting it. When Knox disputed on this question with Lethington at the General Assembly in Edinburgh in 1564, the only authority that he was able to cite in support of his opinion was the *Apology of Magdeburg*, which was issued by the Protestant pastors of the city in 1550 to justify Magdeburg's armed resistance to Charles V. The theory of the justification of revolution is Knox's special contribution to theological and political thought, though his colleague, Christopher Goodman, and to a lesser extent John Ponet, the former Bishop of Winchester, were reaching the same conclusion at about the same time.[1] The situation had reached a point where it was necessary for the future of the Protestant religion and the history of Europe that someone should proclaim this doctrine. As none of the established leaders of the Protestants dared to do it, the task fell to Knox and Goodman.

Knox was not the first man to advocate political revolution as a means of furthering religion. The idea that religion provides a moral justification for revolutionary violence was present, in a vague form, in many of the peasant revolts of the Middle Ages, and was clearly adopted by Žižka and the Taborites in Bohemia at the beginning of the fifteenth century. It was revived in Germany after Luther began his campaign against Rome, and led to the Peasant War of 1525 and the Anabaptist revolt at Münster in 1534. The followers of Thomas Münzer and John of Leyden

[1] Knox, *History*, ii. 121, 219–30; Goodman, *How Superior Powers ought to be obeyed*; Ponet, *A shorte treatise of politike power*.

were inspired by the Book of Revelation to put to the sword all the enemies of God, and to establish, by violence, the kingdom of Heaven on earth. They were suppressed by the Catholic and Protestant princes with great savagery, more than 100,000 peasants being killed in Germany after the revolt of 1525. These events swung all responsible Protestant opinion against the idea of revolution. Luther urged the German Protestant princes to kill the peasants like mad dogs, and applauded while the lords slaughtered and blinded the peasants and roasted the Anabaptist leaders to death. Calvin, with his lawyer's approach and disciplinarian outlook, condemned the rebels. Even Zwingli, who had waged a religious war in order to retain power in Zürich, and who sympathized with the German peasants, dissociated himself from them, and took steps to suppress the attempts of the Swiss Anabaptists to stir up class hatred and social revolution in the Swiss cities.

The idea of violent revolution lingered on among the Anabaptist sects, but it was limited to the 'lunatic fringe' of sixteenth-century politics. It was advocated only by those who were intellectually, as well as socially, outside the bounds of established society. The Anabaptist weavers, tapsters, and peasants were not only incapable of leading a successful revolution and winning and retaining power, but were unable to produce any theologian or intellectual who could provide theoretical justification for their opinions, and any doctrinal or rational arguments to support them; for neither Melchior Hofmann nor Münzer can be considered as serious thinkers. They were Utopian visionaries, not political theorists. The Anabaptists rejected the traditions of European culture, as well as the class structure of European society. Everyone who valued these traditions and accepted this society believed, after the experience of Münster and the Peasant War, that revolution was the supreme wickedness, the most atrocious manifestation of pride, the sin of Lucifer.

Apart from their fear and hatred of Anabaptist revolution, and their desire to dissociate the Protestant movement from it, the Protestant theologians had an additional reason for opposing revolution in countries where the king became a Protestant. In England and Denmark, as well as in the princedoms of northern Germany, the ruler became the leader of the struggle against the Papacy. As early as 1528 it was clear to the Protestants that royal absolutism would be the weapon which would break the Church of Rome. In that year William Tyndale published his *Obedience of a Christian Man*, in which he revived the ideas of Marsiglio of Padua in the fourteenth century, that the king was supreme in his realm, and that everyone, including bishops and the Pope, should obey him. Tyndale argued that it was the duty of all subjects to obey the king in everything, even if he were wicked. God 'in all lands hath put kings, governors and rulers in his own stead, to rule the world through them', wrote Tyndale. 'Whosoever therefore resisteth them, resisteth God, for they are in the room of God; and they that resist shall receive the damnation. . . . Neither may the inferior person avenge himself upon the superior, or violently resist him, for whatsoever wrong it be. . . . And as it is to resist the king, so is it to resist his officer, which is set or sent to execute the king's commandment.' Even if the king 'be the greatest tyrant in the world, yet is he unto thee a great benefit of God, and a thing wherefore thou oughtest to thank God highly'; the king 'may at his lust do right and wrong, and shall give account but to God only'. It is not surprising that Henry VIII, after reading Tyndale's book, declared that 'this book is for me and all Kings to read'; but it is more remarkable that the doctrine enunciated in the book should have become the guiding principle of the Church of England for nearly 200 years.[1]

Tyndale's doctrine was carried to its greatest length in England. Under Henry VIII and Edward VI, the bishops and divines led the way by the fulsome sycophancy with which they spoke of the king and exalted his authority. But elsewhere the doctrine could be inconvenient for the Protestants. In Scotland, they were saved from its consequences only by the ludicrous claim of Henry VIII to the Crown of Scotland; when Knox and his colleagues resisted the Scottish government, and held St. Andrews Castle against the Queen of Scots, they could justify their conduct to the foreign theologians—the Scots themselves were less interested in this aspect of the business—by claiming that they were loyal subjects of Henry VIII, the King of Scots, whereas Arran and Mary of Lorraine were rebels against him. The problem arose again in 1546, when Charles V decided to overthrow Protestantism in Germany by force, and the Lutheran princes rose in arms against

[1] Tyndale, *The Obedience of a Christian Man* (Tyndale, *Works*, i. 174–5, 177–9); Strype, *Eccl. Mem.* i [i]. 172.

him. The Protestants claimed that they were not rebels, but independent princes waging war against a foreign prince; the Catholics asserted that the German princes were not 'princes' in the theological and political meaning of the term in the sixteenth century, that is to say, independent sovereign states, but subjects of the Emperor. Charles V proclaimed that he was fighting the German Lutherans, not on grounds of religion, but as a prince suppressing a revolt by his subjects. He advised Mary to adopt the same argument when executing Protestants in England, and his son Philip II followed his example in dealing with the revolt of the Netherlands. There was an obvious advantage in accusing the Protestants, not of opposing the Church of Rome, an act which many people in Europe no longer regarded as a crime, but of rebelling against their prince, a sin that everyone viewed with horror.

When Mary became Queen of England, the Protestants were hamstrung by the doctrine of Christian obedience. But Knox and Goodman freed them from their predicament. They presented the Protestant movement with the moral justification for adding the weapon of armed revolt to their arsenal, so that they no longer had to reject, on grounds of principle, the only method of struggle that was likely to be effective. Knox dared to advocate a doctrine which during his years in England had been condemned in every sermon in every pulpit in the country, and which since the days of the Peasant War and Münster had been branded as Anabaptism. But his idea of revolution was very different from that of the Anabaptists. Knox did not call for revolution by an undisciplined mob, by peasants with no political experience, no knowledge of the problems of power, and no hope of success. He visualized revolution organized by a class that was capable of victory. In the first place, he looked to the nobility to lead the revolution, which was natural enough, particularly for a Scot. Eventually he substituted the idea of revolution by the Congregation—that is to say, by a body of men organized as a political party, under the leadership of a few nobles, but depending more on the support of the country gentry and the merchants of the towns than on the nobility.

Knox advanced towards this position only by degrees. Under Edward VI, in his letter to his congregation of Berwick in the autumn of 1552 when he directed them to kneel to receive communion, he had laid down the duty of obedience to the king in as unequivocal a manner as Cranmer or any bishop of the Church of England could require. He had instructed his congregation to obey the king and the magistrates 'how ungodly that ever their precepts or commandments be', and 'not to pretend to defend God's truth or religion (ye being subjects) by violence or sword, but patiently suffering what God shall please be laid upon you for constant confession of your faith and belief'. But the pamphlets which he wrote after Mary's accession mark the changes in his attitude. His first treatise, *A Confession and Declaration of Prayers*, was written within a few weeks of Mary's victory, before the mass had been restored, when Protestant congregations could still meet in safety; and though he had criticized prayers to the saints in this treatise, he had naturally said nothing that could be held to be seditious. Even his warning against the danger of a return to Popery had been hidden in the form of a prayer for the Queen; but in the *Letter to the Faithful in London, Newcastle and Berwick* he spoke more openly. The first part of this work was written in December 1553, when Knox was in hiding in London just before he left England, and the pamphlet was finished at Dieppe in January 1554. As it was intended to be published secretly and distributed in England as illegal propaganda, he did not attempt to disguise his real opinions in order to placate the authorities.[1]

The first edition, which was published in May 1554, begins at once on a note of defiance and threat, with the short poem 'The Persecuted Speaketh' on the cover page:

> I fear not for death, nor pass out for bands;
> Only in God I put my whole trust,
> For God will require my blood at your hands,
> And this I know, that once die I must;
> Only for Christ my life if I give;
> Death is no death, but a mean for to live.

This poem became famous in the Protestant movement a year afterwards, when Hooper, on the night before he was burnt,

[1] Knox, 'Epistle to the Congregation of Berwick' (Lorimer, *John Knox and the Church of England*, p. 259); Knox, *A Confession and Declaration of Prayers*; Knox, *Letter to the Faithful in London, Newcastle and Berwick* (*Works*, iii. 83–107, 165–216). The 'large treatise' to which Knox refers in his *Exposition of the Sixth Psalm* (*Works*, iii. 120) was almost certainly his *Letter to the Faithful in London, Newcastle and Berwick*. Knox must have finished it before he left Dieppe for Switzerland on 28 Jan. 1554, as it was printed by the time that he returned to Dieppe in May.

wrote it on the wall with a lump of coal in the New Inn at Gloucester.[1] But the threat that it contains is a threat of divine, not human, vengeance; and the only course of action that Knox, in this pamphlet, advised his old congregation to pursue was to escape from England before God's plagues were poured down upon the land; if they could not escape, they must refuse to bow down to idols. He reminded them that Daniel and the three children denounced idolatry, not secretly but openly; but he promptly explained that he did not demand of them that they should do as much, and go to the idolaters and say: 'Your Gods made neither Heaven nor earth, and therefore shall they perish, and ye with them, for all your worshipping is abominable idolatry.' He only required that they should not go to mass, not only for their own sake, but for that of their children, to whom they must teach the laws of God. All this could have been written by Ridley or any of the other Protestant pamphleteers, though it is noteworthy that Knox included no exhortation to his readers to pray for the Queen and obey her in all matters not directly conflicting with God's law, such as Cranmer included even in his final declaration at the stake. Like other Protestant pamphleteers, Knox saw the present state of England as God's punishment for the sins of the Protestant magnates in Edward's reign.

At the same time, Knox gave a clear directive to his followers that they must not take the law into their own hands and murder Catholics. 'God shows Himself so offended with idolaters that He commands all such to be slain without mercy. But now, shall some demand, what then? Shall we go and slay all idolaters? That were the office, dear brethren, of every civil magistrate within his realm. But of you is required only to avoid participation and company of their abominations, as well in body as in soul; as David and Paul plainly teaches unto you.' There were many idolaters among the Philistines in Gath, and in Corinth when Paul wrote the Epistle, 'yet neither sayeth David that he will slay any man in that place, neither yet gives Paul any such commandment; wherefore it is plain that the slaying of idolaters appertains not to every particular man'.

But in the *Letter to the Faithful in London, Newcastle and Berwick*, Knox formulated an idea which played an important part in his later doctrine.

[1] *Works*, iii. 161; Hooper, *Works*, ii. xxx.

If the messengers of the Lord that shall be sent to execute His wrath and vengeance shall find you among idolaters, your bodies committing like abominations with them, ye have no warrant that ye shall escape the plagues prepared for the wicked. The whole tribe of Benjamin perished with the adulterers, and yet they were not all adulterers in fact. Whole Amalek was commanded to be destroyed, and yet was not one of them living that troubled the Israelites in their passing from Egypt. Pharaoh was not drowned alone . . . neither yet escaped Jonathan when God punished Saul his father. And why? The Apostle gives the answer: 'Because,' says he, 'men knoweth the justice of God, and doing the contrary are worthy of death, not only they that commits iniquity, but also such as consents to the same.' And who can deny but such men as daily does accompany wicked men, and yet never declares themselves offended nor displeased with their wickedness, does consent to their iniquity?

The Holy Ghost directs us not to obey idolaters, 'be they kings or queens, neither yet that we conceal their impiety. . . . For all those that would draw us from God (be they kings or queens) being of the Devil's nature, are enemies unto God.' Here Knox is already hinting at what he states more explicitly in his *Letter to the Commonalty of Scotland* in 1558—that the Flood, the destruction of Sodom and Gomorrah, and all the other examples of collective punishments inflicted by the divine vengeance in the Old Testament, were punishments of the people for their sin in tolerating evil governments instead of overthrowing them. When God punished the people of Egypt, He was not punishing them for the sins of Pharaoh, but for their own sin in failing to make a revolution against Pharaoh.

In the *Letter to the Faithful in London, Newcastle and Berwick*, an occasional phrase, introduced at random and not followed up, shows that already in January 1554 Knox was beginning to formulate ideas that went far beyond his main line of thought at the time. 'Let a thing be here noted', he wrote, after citing a text from the twenty-seventh chapter of Jeremiah, 'that the prophets of God sometimes may teach treason against kings, and yet neither he, nor such as obeys the word spoken in the Lord's name by him, offends God.' But this was going too far, even in a work that was printed and circulated illegally; and Knox, or his printer, cut out this passage from the printed editions. In many passages the printed editions differed slightly in wording from Knox's manuscript, and some of the alterations had the effect of eliminating some of the most outspoken words that Knox had originally inserted.[1]

A few weeks after he had finished writing this pamphlet in Dieppe, Knox was discussing the problem of revolution with Calvin and Bullinger in Switzerland. He left Dieppe on 28 January and went first to Geneva, where he met Calvin. After Calvin had talked with Knox, he gave him a letter of introduction to Bullinger in Zürich, and also recommended that he should visit Viret, the chief pastor of Lausanne. He gave Knox a letter of introduction to Viret, dated 23 February, in which he wrote: 'This brother, a Scot by nationality, seeks the advice of Zürich, and is travelling to you, not unwillingly I hope. They say that under King Edward he laboured energetically for the faith. He is now eager to increase his learning.' It has been suggested that 'the Scot' to whom Calvin and Bullinger refer was not Knox, but Goodman; but apart from the fact that Goodman was an Englishman and not a Scot, he could hardly have been referred to in the terms in which Calvin wrote about the Scot in his letter to Viret, as he had not done anything particularly noteworthy in the reign of Edward VI. There can be no doubt that the Scotsman who visited Calvin and Bullinger was Knox.[2]

Knox asked Calvin four questions, which he later put down in writing and submitted to Bullinger. The questions were unlike the kind that Calvin was usually asked by his disciples. They referred specifically to the position of Englishmen and Scotsmen, and asked for directions as to the course which Protestants in the two kingdoms were expected by the law of God to pursue in four situations which had arisen there in practice during recent years and at the present time. The questions were as follows:

1. Whether the son of a king succeeding by right of birth on the death of the king his father during his childhood, and not able to govern because of his youth, was a lawful magistrate whom it was necessary to obey by divine law? 2. Whether a woman was entitled by divine law to rule and govern, and whether she could transfer her royal power to her husband? 3. Whether it was necessary to obey a magistrate who enforces idolatry and condemns the true religion? And whether men of position who have castles and towns are entitled to defend

[1] Knox, *Letter to the Faithful in London, Newcastle and Berwick* (*Works*, iii. 184, 189–90, 192–4, 202, 208).

[2] Calvin to Viret, 23 Feb. 1554 (*Calvini Op.* xv. 38–39). See *infra*, App. V.

themselves and their followers by armed force against this ungodly violence? 4. To which party ought godly men to adhere if devout men of position resist an idolatrous king by war?[1]

Calvin answered Knox's questions without hesitation. He told him, very firmly, that under no circumstances whatever was it justifiable for subjects to resist an idolatrous ruler by armed force. As far as women rulers were concerned, Calvin said that as it was contrary to the law of nature for women to rule, a woman sovereign was a punishment imposed by God on mankind for our sins. In exceptional cases, a woman ruler might be a great blessing, like Deborah; but whether she was a Deborah or a tyrant, her people must obey her, for it was no more justifiable to resist a tyrannical woman ruler than to resist any other tyrant. Knox made no attempt to argue and gave Calvin the impression that he accepted his answer. Whatever doubts Knox may have had, he was not ready to maintain a new and revolutionary opinion against the famous Protestant theologian at their first acquaintance. He cut the discussion short, and did not ask Calvin to put his opinions into writing.[2]

When Knox reached Zürich, he found that Bullinger was more encouraging than he might have expected. He submitted his questions in writing to Bullinger, and received written replies which Bullinger had presumably drawn up in consultation with his colleagues, for he calls them the 'Answers of Zürich'. To Knox's first question, they answered that an infant king was a lawful ruler, as had been shown by the example of Edward VI in England. Their answer to the second question was more evasive. By the law of nature and of God, a woman should be subject and not rule; but if she succeeded to the throne, it would be dangerous for pious men to resist the civil laws. There were cases in Scripture of nations being ruled by Deborah and other women; if a woman ruler is impious and tyrannical, the godly can comfort themselves by remembering the fate of Athaliah. The Lord overthrows unjust despotisms through those to whom He furnishes the opportunity to do this. As to whether a woman can transfer her royal power to her husband, this question can only be answered by those who are familiar with the laws and customs of the kingdom. The

[1] Bullinger to Calvin, 26 Mar. 1554; Calvin to Bullinger, 29 Apr. 1554 (*Calvini Op.* xv. 90–91, 125; *Works*, iii. 221–6).

[2] Calvin to Bullinger, 29 Apr. 1554 (*Calvini Op.* xv. 125).

answer to the third question was less equivocal. Bullinger stated that it was not necessary to obey a king or ruler who condemns the true religion and enforces idolatry; the godly ought to resist him even at the risk of their lives, as is shown by the history of Daniel and Our Lord's words in the tenth chapter of Matthew. But Bullinger added a warning note. It often happens that wicked wretches incite the godly to join with them by pretending to act from godly motives, which made it difficult for him to say what should be done in any particular case. On the fourth point, Bullinger was of no assistance at all. He said that the question as to which side the godly ought to support when an idolatrous king fought a godly nobility must be decided according to the particular circumstances in each case as it arose by men whose learning and knowledge of Scripture made them capable of giving the answer; but the most important thing was to become reconciled to God by a true repentance, and to remember that He is the true, and only, deliverer.[1]

These answers were perhaps sufficient for Knox's purpose. Bullinger did not reject out of hand the idea that Protestants might resist an idolatrous sovereign by armed force; and Knox, seeing that one of the most eminent Protestant theologians of the age did not recoil in horror at the suggestion, felt free to go further in this direction than Bullinger himself was prepared to go. Knox probably also discussed these questions with Viret in Lausanne, and perhaps also with Farel in Neuchâtel, Sulcerus in Basel, Musculus and Haller in Berne, and the pastors in St. Gall, for he wrote that he had visited all the congregations of Switzerland and had discussed the questions with all their pastors; but he did not raise the matter with Calvin again when he returned to Geneva. He had decided to take up his residence in Geneva, and to devote himself to study there; but first he returned to Dieppe for a few weeks. He told Mrs. Bowes that he had 'returned to Dieppe to learn the estate of England and Scotland'. During all his years of exile on the Continent, he used Dieppe as his communications centre.[2]

He also wished to make arrangements for his illegal pamphlets to be published and circulated in England. These pamphlets, like all the English Protestants' propaganda pamphlets, were published

[1] Bullinger to Calvin, 26 Mar. 1554 (*Calvini Op.* xv. 91–93).

[2] Calvin to Bullinger, 29 Apr. 1554 (ibid. 125); Knox to Mrs. Bowes, 20 July 1554 (*Works*, iii. 347; and in Knox's *Answer to Tyrie*, *Works*, vi. 520).

under fictitious imprints, with false places of publication. Often the place of publication was an imaginary town that everyone knew did not exist; sometimes, with a defiant humour, these violent attacks on Popery were stated to have been printed in Rome, or in the Pope's castle of St. Angelo. These obviously fictitious imprints had the advantage of warning the readers immediately that the publication was illegal, as well as exasperating the authorities. We know nothing as to where these pamphlets were printed, whether it was done secretly in England or in Protestant towns abroad, or how the manuscript or printed copies were smuggled into England. This is a tribute to the efficient underground work of Knox and his supporters in England. We know about the plans, twenty-five years earlier, to send copies of Tyndale's English Bible into England hidden in bales of linen, from the reports of Wolsey's officers who discovered them; but no such details about Knox's pamphlets are given in the State papers of Mary's government. In October 1554 the English authorities rounded up 150 people who were engaged in distributing seditious books which had been printed abroad by English refugees; but apart from this success, which the Piedmontese ambassador attributed to 'divine inspiration rather than any human artifice or device', their letters contain only reports of unsuccessful house to house searches in London, and complaints that seditious pamphlets are circulating everywhere in England but can never be traced.[1]

On 10 May 1554 Knox wrote a letter from Dieppe to the Protestants in England, which was afterwards published, together with his *Exposition of the Sixth Psalm*, under the title *An Epistle to his Afflicted Brethren in England*. He had now a much clearer view of what was to be done, though he did not state it in his letter because he was thinking of the possibility of making a secret voyage to England to discuss the problem with the Protestants there. He still assures them that he is willing to risk his life if it will further the cause, but he does this much more briefly and less hysterically than in the letters which he had written before his visit to Switzerland; he was now certain that he had chosen the right course,

[1] Rinck to Wolsey, 4 Oct. 1528 (*L.P.* iv. 4810); Stroppiana to Granvelle, 6 Oct. 1554 (*Span. Cal.* xiii. 73); Noailles to Montmorency, 26 Oct. 1554; Noailles to Henry II, 28 Nov. and 16 Dec. 1555 (*Ambassades de Noailles*, iii. 352; v. 240, 254); Michiel to the Doge and Senate of Venice, 26 June and 3 Dec. 1555 (*Ven. Cal.* v. 142, 297).

both as regards his personal position and in his advice to his followers.

Ye would know perchance my judgement, by what means shall the tyrants of England and most obstinate and abominable idolaters be punished. To determinate unto them a certain kind of worldly punishment it appertaineth not to me, but hereof I am so sure, as that I am that my God liveth, that beside their perpetual condemnation and torment in Hell, they shall also be plagued in this present life, except they repent. . . . My own estate is this: since 28 January I have travelled through all the congregations of Helvetia, and has reasoned with all the pastors and many other excellently learned men upon such matters as now I cannot commit to writing; gladly would I by tongue or by pen utter the same to God's glory. If I thought that I might have your presence, and the presence of some other assured men, I would jeopard my own life to let men see what may be done with a safe conscience in these dolorous and dangerous days; but seeing that it cannot be done instantly without danger to others than to me, I will abide the time that God shall appoint. But hereof be assured, that all is not lawful nor just that is statute by civil laws, neither yet is everything sin before God which ungodly persons allege to be treason; but this I supersede to more opportunity, if by any means I may, I intend to speak with you or it be long. . . . In great haste, from Dieppe, 10 May 1554, yours whom ye know, John Knox.[1]

Three weeks later, he wrote again to England. In *A Comfortable Epistle sent to the Afflicted Church of Christ, exhorting them to bear His Cross with Patience*, which is dated from Dieppe on 31 May, he again sought to restrain the Protestants in England from resorting to any acts of violence against the Queen and the Catholics, as he had done in his *Letter to the Faithful in London, Newcastle and Berwick*. He was aware of the danger that the example of Ehud, Judith, and Jehu might lead his brethren to attempt to assassinate Mary and other Catholics in England; but though he tried to deter his followers from individual acts of violence, at the same time he went beyond the conventional attitude that only magistrates are entitled to kill idolaters. This was the opinion that he had put forward some years before in his letter to Mrs. Bowes, when he condemned the murder of the Shechemites by the sons of Jacob on these grounds, and he had reasserted it as recently as

[1] Knox, *An Epistle to his afflicted Brethren in England* (*Works*, iii. 231–6. The passages cited are on pp. 234–6).

January 1554 in his *Letter to the Faithful in London, Newcastle and Berwick*. Now he went further.

Beloved brethren, two things ye must avoid. The former, that ye presume not to be revengers of your own cause, but that ye resign over vengeance unto Him who only is able to requite them, according to their malicious minds. Secondly, that ye hate not with any carnal hatred these blind, cruel and malicious tyrants; but that ye learn of Christ to pray for your persecutors, lamenting and bewailing that the Devil should so prevail against them, that headlings they should run body and soul to perpetual perdition. And note well that I say, we may not hate them with a carnal hatred; that is to say, only because they trouble our bodies; for there is a spiritual hatred, which David calleth a perfect hatred, which the Holy Ghost engendereth in the hearts of God's elect, against the rebellious contemners of His holy statutes. And it is when we more lament that God's glory is suppressed, and that Christ's flock is defrauded of their wholesome food, than that our bodies are persecuted. With this hatred was Jeremy inflamed, when he prayed: 'Let me see Thy vengeance taken upon thine enemies, O Lord.' With this hatred may we hate tyrants, and earnestly may we pray for their destruction, be they kings or queens, princes or prelates. And further ye shall note, that the prayers made in the fervency of this hatred are before God so acceptable, that ofttimes he that prayeth obtaineth the self-same thing that the external words of his prayer do mean; as David, Jeremy and other of the prophets saw with their corporal eyes the hot vengeance of God poured forth upon the cruel tyrants of their age; and I am assured that some, which this day do sob and groan under your tyrantful bishops, shall see, upon the pestilent Papists within the realm of England. . . . For so assuredly as God is immutable, so assuredly shall He stir up one Jehu or other to execute His vengeance upon these bloodthirsty tyrants and obstinate idolaters.[1]

This distinction between private and public vengeance was important in Knox's thinking, and was afterwards given great emphasis in the notes of the Geneva Bible of 1560. The Christian must forgive injuries committed against himself, but not injuries against the Protestant religion; he must love his personal enemies, but must hate the enemies of the party.

In July 1554 two more of Knox's pamphlets were published illegally. The first of these was a second, revised edition of his *Letter to the Faithful in London, Newcastle and Berwick*, which was now issued together with his *Confession and Declaration of Prayers*.

[1] Knox, *A comfortable Epistle to the afflicted Church of Christ* (*Works*, iii. 244–5, 247).

In the first edition the imprint had stated that the book was published by Nicholas Dorcastor in Wittenberg on 8 May 1554. The imprint of the second edition claimed that the publication was 'printed in Rome before the Castle of St. Angel at the sign of St. Peter. July 1554'. The dates were presumably correct, even though the places of publication were not. In the same month another of Knox's pamphlets was published, *A Faithful Admonition made by John Knox unto the Professors of God's Truth in England*, printed at 'Kalyhow', a non-existent town, on 20 July 1554. These pamphlets were obviously written a few months earlier than July, but the *Admonition unto the Professors of God's Truth in England* was certainly not completed before Knox's return from Switzerland. Both of them were probably written at Dieppe in May or June 1554.

The *Faithful Admonition unto the Professors of God's Truth in England*—or, to give it the shorter title by which Knox himself referred to it, the *Admonition to England*[1]—was the longest and most important tract which Knox had so far written. He denounced at length the Protestant nobles for their covetousness and insincerity during Edward's reign, and for now submitting to idolatry, quoting at length from his own sermons at that time, but blaming himself for not having denounced Northumberland and the rest more vigorously, and expressly by name. He attacked not only 'bloody Bonner', 'dreaming Durham' [Tunstall], and 'wily Winchester' the 'Devil's Gardener', but also 'that wretched (alas!) and miserable Northumberland', and Shebna the Treasurer, who for some reason he did not trouble directly to identify as Paulet. Paulet was selected as the epitome of the secret Papists on Edward's Privy Council who had plotted and bided their time:

O who was judged to be the soul and life to the Council in every matter of weighty importance? Who but Sobna. Who could best dispatch business, that the rest of the Council might hawk and hunt and take their pleasure? None like unto Sobna. Who was most frank and ready to destroy Somerset and set up Northumberland? Was it not Sobna? Who was most bold to cry 'Bastard, bastard, incestuous bastard Mary shall never reign over us'? And who, I pray you, was most busy to say 'Fear not to subscribe with my Lords of the King's Majesty's most honourable Privy Council. Agree to His Grace's last will and perfect testament, and let never that obstinate woman come to authority. She is an errant Papist; she will subvert the true religion and will

[1] See Knox, *History*, i. 111.

bring in strangers, to the destruction of this commonwealth'? Which of the Council, I say, had these and greater persuasions against Mary, to whom he now crouches and kneeleth? Sobna the Treasurer.

But, as he denounces the careerist nobles, he has nothing but praise for the Protestant bishops who are in prison awaiting martyrdom. He does not allow any recollection of his past opposition to Cranmer and the more conservative bishops to intrude as he praises the book on the Sacrament of 'that Reverend Father in God Thomas Cranmer', and accuses Gardiner of seeking his blood and that of 'good father Hugh Latimer, and of that most learned and discreet man Dr. Ridley, true Bishop of London'. Knox did not wish, at this time, to rake up memories of past splits among the Protestants; he wished to unite the anti-government forces by using every available issue to discredit the Queen's Councillors. This Scotsman who in his own country had not hesitated to sacrifice his nationalism for the sake of his religion, now tried to rouse the powerful emotion of English nationalism, again in the interests of Protestantism. Whoever could have believed that 'glorious Gardiner' and 'treacherous Tunstall' could have handed over the Crown of England to a Spaniard? 'O thou beast! I speak to you, Winchester, more cruel than any tiger. . . . Ashamest thou not, bloody beast, to betray thy native country and the liberties of the same? Fearest thou not to open such a door to all iniquity, that whole England shall be made a common stew to Spaniards?' The noble realm of England had conferred many honours on Gardiner. 'And wilt thou now, O wretched captive, for all these manifold benefits received, be the cause that England shall not be England? Yea, verily, for so wilt thou gratify thy father the Devil and his lieutenant the Pope.'[1]

These attacks on Gardiner and the Catholic bishops were commonplace in all the tracts of the Protestant pamphleteers, who with some justice attributed to Gardiner the chief responsibility for the persecution of Protestants under Henry VIII and Mary; but none of them uttered a word of criticism of the Queen herself, for they recoiled from committing such a violation of the doctrine of Christian obedience. But in the *Admonition to England*, Knox attacked Mary, and shocked many of his Protestant colleagues as deeply as the Catholics. The implications of his words

[1] Knox, *Admonition to England* (*Works*, iii. 277, 279, 283–5, 296–9).

were far-reaching, as his critics recognized. It had occurred to Knox that if in the reign of Edward VI the Protestant government had put Mary to death, she would not now be in a position where she could persecute Protestants, just as Gardiner and the Emperor's ambassador, Renard, were now advising Mary to find some pretext to put Elizabeth to death in order to prevent the restoration of heresy and the persecution of Catholics when she came to the throne.[1] Knox hesitated to say openly that Mary should have been executed in the reign of Edward VI; but his reference to the possibility of such a thing was sufficient for the Catholics and many Protestants to accuse him of demanding that Mary be killed.

But yet peradventure you wonder not a little why God permitteth such bloodthirsty tyrants to molest and grieve His chosen Church. ... The justice of God is such that He will not pour forth His extreme vengeance upon the reprobate unto such time as their iniquity be so manifest that their very flatterers cannot excuse it. . . . If Stephen Gardiner, Cuthbert Tunstall and butcherly Bonner, false Bishops of Winchester, Durham and of London, had for their false doctrine and traitorous acts suffered death, when they justly deserved the same, then would errant Papists have alleged (as I and other have heard them do) that they were men reformable, that they were meet instruments for a commonwealth; that they were not so obstinate and malicious as they were judged; neither that they thirsted for the blood of any man. And of Lady Mary, who hath not heard that she was sober, merciful, and one that loved the commonwealth of England? Had she, I say, and such as now be of her pestilent counsel, been sent to Hell before these days, then should not their iniquity and cruelty so manifestly have appeared to the world. For who could have thought that such cruelty could have entered into the heart of a woman, and into the heart of her that is called a virgin, that she would thirst the blood of innocents, and of such as by just laws and faithful witnesses can never be proved to have offended by themselves? I find that Athaliah, through appetite to reign, murdered the seed of the kings of Judah. And that Herodias' daughter, at the desire of a whorish mother, obtained the head of John the Baptist. But that ever a woman, that suffered herself to be called the most blessed Virgin, caused so much blood to be spilt for establishing of an usurped

[1] For the proposals to execute Elizabeth, see Charles V to Egmont, Renard, etc., 31 Jan. 1554; Charles V's Instructions to Egmont, 18 Feb. 1554; Renard to Prince Philip of Spain, 19 Feb. and 13 Mar. 1554; Egmont and Renard to Charles V, 8 Mar. 1554; Renard to Charles V, 3 Apr. 1554 (Weiss, iv. 198; Gachard, iv. 342, 374–5; *Documentos Ineditos*, iii. 500; Tytler, *England under Edward VI and Mary*, ii. 321–2, 334 n.; *Span. Cal.* xii. 62, 112, 120, 139–40, 150, 200).

authority, I think is rare to be found in Scripture or history. I find that Jezabel, that cursed idolatress, caused the blood of the prophets of God to be shed, and Naboth to be murdered unjustly for his own vineyard; but yet I think she never erected half so many gallows in all Israel as mischievous Mary hath done within London alone. But you Papists will excuse your Mary the Virgin; well, let her be your virgin, and a goddess meet to maintain such idolaters.

These references to 'Mary the Virgin' were provoked by the eulogy of Mary as 'Mary the Virgin' by the Catholic spokesman and writer, John Harpsfield, in his sermon to Convocation in October 1553.[1]

Knox then proceeded to denounce Mary for breaking her promise, made to the men of Norfolk and Suffolk in July 1553, to uphold the Protestant religion and not to marry a foreigner, and declared that 'under an English name she beareth a Spaniard's heart'. In the course of his denunciation of Spain and Mary's treason to her country, Knox quoted from the passage in his sermon at Amersham in July 1553, when he had said that Charles V was worse than Nero. This was a step which he later had cause to regret.

He ended the pamphlet with a prayer.

God, for His great mercies' sake, stir up some Phinehas, Elias or Jehu, that the blood of abominable idolaters may pacify God's wrath, that it consume not the whole multitude.... Delay not Thy vengeance, O Lord, but let death devour them in haste; let the earth swallow them up; and let them go down quick to the hells. For there is no hope of their amendment, the fear and reverence of Thy holy name is quite banished from their hearts.

He told his readers that if they prayed in this manner, God would 'send Jehu to execute His just judgements against idolaters. ... Jezebel herself shall not escape the vengeance and plagues that are prepared for her portion.' This reference to Jehu convinced Knox's critics that he had called for the assassination of Mary. He might have been in a stronger position to rebut the accusation if he had published his warning against murdering idolaters in his *Admonition to England* instead of in his *Letter to the Faithful in London, Newcastle and Berwick*; but this would not have deterred

[1] Knox, *Admonition to England* (*Works*, iii. 293–5). For Harpsfield's sermon, see Strype, *Eccl. Mem.* iii [i]. 61.

his critics from asserting that he had incited the Protestants to murder the Queen.[1]

In a calmer passage, at the beginning of the *Admonition to England*, Knox had stated that he now realized 'how small was my learning, and how weak I was of judgement when Christ Jesus called me to be his steward'. After staying in Dieppe for about three months, he returned to Geneva to study Greek and Hebrew, and to acquire a deeper knowledge of Calvin's theology. But within a few weeks of his arrival at Geneva, he received a letter from the English Protestants at Frankfort-on-Main, inviting him to come to Frankfort to be their minister.[2] The next six months were not to be a period of quiet study for Knox, but of bitter faction fights and the most squalid aspect of refugee politics. Out of these factional quarrels at Frankfort there arose the Church of Scotland; its Prayer Book and its system of organization were born in Frankfort-on-Main.

[1] *Works*, iii. 296, 309, 328–9.

[2] Ibid. 269; Knox, *History*, i. 110. Knox almost certainly learned Greek and Hebrew at Geneva. Davidson, in his poem, says that Knox knew Greek and Hebrew (Davidson, 'Ane Breif Commendatioun of Uprichtnes', line 117, in Rogers, 'Three Poets of the Scottish Reformation' (*Trans. R.H.S.* iii. 249)). It is unlikely that he learned Greek in Scotland, and he could certainly not have learned Hebrew there.

CHAPTER XI

The Troubles at Frankfort

BY the spring of 1554, about 800 English Protestant refugees had left England. Some of the less religious and more adventurous emigrants found refuge .in France; for as Henry II's relations with Mary deteriorated, and it was evident that open war would not be indefinitely postponed, he granted not only asylum but financial support to the Protestant gentlemen, like Thomas Stafford and Peter Carew and their companions, as well as to English pirates and non-political criminals who escaped from England. But Henry II had no use for Protestant clergymen and scholars, or Protestant women zealots, and none of the religious refugees remained in France. Some of them went first to Denmark, but there they found that Christian III was prepared to give asylum only to Lutherans, and he soon expelled the English refugees, accusing them of being Zwinglians, Calvinists, and Anabaptists. By the summer of 1554, nearly all the English religious refugees were concentrated in five towns—in Emden in East Friesland, in Duisburg in Cleves, in the free Imperial cities of Frankfort-on-Main and Strasbourg, and in Zürich. The largest group, consisting of more than half the total number of the refugees, was in Strasbourg.[1]

On 27 June 1554 a group of some 200 English refugees reached Frankfort-on-Main, among them William Whittingham, a 30-year-old Oxford graduate with strong radical opinions in religion. They had been preceded a few weeks earlier by Valérand Poullain and his congregation of French Protestant weavers from Glastonbury.[2] Frankfort, linked by water along the Main and Rhine to both Basel and the Scheldt, was a great trading city, and the centre of postal communications in Western Europe. The great

[1] Maxwell, *John Knox's Genevan Service Book*, p. 10; Foxe, vi. 430; Garnett, *The Marian Exiles*, pp. 30–32.

[2] *The Troubles at Frankfort*, p. 5 (*Works*, iv. 9); Jung, *Die englische Flüchtlings-Gemeinde in Frankfurt-a-M.*, p. 10.

fairs at Easter and in September drew merchants from many countries to Frankfort, and letters between England and Switzerland were often carried by merchants who met at the Frankfort fair. Since the development of printing, it had become the most important centre of the publishing and book trade in Europe.

As a free city of the Empire, Frankfort was virtually an independent state, with full powers of self-government in its internal affairs. It was governed by the two Mayors, or Consuls, and the city council, which, like the councils of most of the other towns of Europe, had become in practice a self-co-opting body controlled by a few powerful merchant families. Frankfort had adopted Protestantism, and like Nuremberg and Strasbourg stood in the midst of Catholic South Germany as a bastion of the Reformation. But the councillors of Frankfort had learned to temper their Protestant zeal with political caution. Frankfort had joined the Protestants of North Germany in 1546 when Charles V made his attempt to crush Lutheranism by force; but at the height of the war it opened its gates to Charles's armies, after Charles's general had decided that the city was impregnable and had abandoned all attempts to capture it. Charles fined the city 80,000 gold florins, and quartered his troops in Frankfort for nearly a year, but in view of its submission he did not abolish its privileges as a free city. Since then it had become a leading principle of the Frankfort city council that they must not offend the Emperor; and when in 1552 the German Protestants again waged war against Charles, and this time were everywhere victorious, Frankfort fought valiantly for the Emperor and held out successfully against the besieging Protestant armies of Maurice of Saxony.

When Poullain arrived from Glastonbury, he and his congregation had been granted the use of a church in Frankfort by the city authorities. He immediately welcomed the English refugees, and offered them the use of his church. The authorities at Frankfort, like the English government in the days of Edward VI, were determined to ensure that the foreign refugees did not advocate or tolerate any heresy, but as long as they were satisfied on this point they did not insist that the church services of the refugees should conform in matters of detail to those of the churches of Frankfort. Poullain had no difficulty in reaching agreement on this point with Johann von Glauburg, a prominent member of the city council who was the head of one of the three most influential families in

Frankfort, and had three times been Consul of the city.[1] Glauburg had been deputed to deal with the question of the refugees' church. Frankfort was a predominantly Lutheran town, but Calvinism was tolerated, and as the order of service which Poullain had drafted for his congregation was almost indistinguishable from Calvinism, Glauburg had no objection to the services that Poullain proposed to celebrate in the church. It was now agreed between Glauburg, Poullain, and Whittingham that the English refugees should share the Church of White Ladies with Poullain. As for doctrine, Glauburg said that he would be satisfied if the services used by the English, and the doctrines taught by them, were broadly the same as those of Poullain's congregation, though he did not insist on absolute similarity in all details.

This arrangement was very satisfactory for Whittingham. He was not satisfied with all the provisions of the Second Book of Common Prayer, and wished to see it replaced, in a Protestant Church of England, by a more radical and Protestant service. When Glauburg stipulated that the English services should conform to those of Poullain, Whittingham seized the opportunity to discard the features to which he objected in the Book of Common Prayer, and to adopt a new service which was nearer to that of the French Calvinists. It was based on the Book of Common Prayer, but certain features were excluded on the grounds that they might be objectionable to Poullain's French congregation and the authorities at Frankfort, or because they were considered inappropriate in the new circumstances in which the English Protestants found themselves. They decided to dispense with all vestments; the responses of the congregation to the minister, and the Litany, were done away with; the people were to repeat the Lord's Prayer with the minister, and were to sing two Psalms in a plain tune, as in the Continental and Scottish Protestant Churches. In the administration of the sacraments, they removed certain practices which they believed to be 'superstitious and superfluous', chief among which was kneeling to receive communion.[2]

The English at Frankfort could now, like the Apostles and the early Christian communities, elect their own pastors and officers, which even Cranmer, and Bonner and the most conservative of the English bishops, had admitted could be done by any Christian

[1] Kriegk, *Deutsches Bürgerthum im Mittelalter*, pp. 490–1.

[2] *The Troubles at Frankfort*, pp. 6–7 (*Works*, iv. 10–11); Jung, pp. 10–11.

congregation if no bishop or priest had been appointed over them by Christian princes and magistrates. They decided to choose two pastors, and four elders to assist them, and to hold a regular weekly meeting of the male members of the congregation to decide all questions of importance. As there was no one among them whom they considered could adequately fill the office of pastor, they wrote to Haddon in Strasbourg, Lever in Zürich, and Knox in Geneva, to ask them if they would be prepared to come to Frankfort to be their pastors. Haddon, Lever, and Knox had all been Lenten preachers at Whitehall in the last year of Edward's reign, and it was probably because of the fame and notoriety that they had achieved by their vigorous sermons on that occasion that the radical Whittingham invited them to Frankfort.[1]

Whittingham and his colleagues also wrote to the English groups in Emden, Düisburg, Strasbourg, and Zürich, and urged the desirability of uniting all the scattered groups of refugees together in one centre at Frankfort. Several of the English refugees at Emden accepted the invitation and went to Frankfort, the most prominent among them being David Whitehead. But the leaders of the refugees at Strasbourg and Zürich were suspicious from the first of the activities of the congregation in Frankfort. The Strasbourg group wrote a friendly reply in which they said that they did not wish to leave Strasbourg, but offered to send them either Ponet, Bale, or Cox to take charge of their congregation as superintendent and pastor. They also suggested that Scory, who was at Emden, would be a suitable pastor, and, without consulting the refugees at Frankfort, Grindal wrote from Strasbourg to Scory inviting him to go to Frankfort. Ponet, Scory, and Bale had been bishops under Edward VI, and Cox had been King's Almoner, an office which was almost equal to a bishopric in status; they were all men of greater eminence than either Haddon, Lever, or Knox. But Whittingham and his friends did not relish this advice of their Strasbourg brethren, and wrote back that they did not need any superintendents to take charge of their affairs, and had already decided whom they wished to have as pastors.[2]

[1] The English at Frankfort to Knox, 24 Sept. 1554; *The Troubles at Frankfort*, pp. 7, 13–14, 19–20 (*Works*, iv. 11–13). For the views of Cranmer and the English bishops, see the Answers to the Seventeen Questions of 1540 (Burnet, iv. 468–71, 475–7; vi. 244, 247).

[2] The English at Frankfort to the English at Strasbourg, Zürich, Duisburg, and Emden, 2 Aug. 1554 (*The Troubles at Frankfort*, pp. 8–13).

There was a minority among the English refugees at Frankfort who did not approve of the service that Whittingham had adopted, and wished to use the service of the Book of Common Prayer. They wrote to the refugees in Zürich and Strasbourg, and told them what Whittingham and his colleagues were doing. The Zürich group wrote to Whittingham that they were only prepared to come to Frankfort on condition that they could use the service of the Book of Common Prayer in its entirety, 'for we are fully determined to admit and use no other';[1] but the refugees at Strasbourg decided to send some of their members to Frankfort to infiltrate the English congregation there, and to ensure that the Book of Common Prayer was adopted in Frankfort. The Book of Common Prayer for which Whittingham's opponents stood was the Second Book of Common Prayer of 1552, the most radical service book that had ever been promulgated in England, and, as it turned out, a more radical one than any that would be used in the Church of England during the next 400 years; but though the differences between the Second Book of Common Prayer and the order of service which Whittingham had drafted were not irreconcilable, they were to give rise to the doctrinal and personal quarrels that are so common among refugee groups, particularly after their cause has suffered a decisive defeat.

The Frankfort group had not received encouraging replies from the three men whom they had invited to be their pastors. Haddon, who had been one of the signatories of the letter from the Strasbourg group, wrote and told them that, for various reasons, he was unable to accept the invitation. Lever had not replied, but he had signed the discouraging letter from Zürich. As for Knox, he was not over-eager to go to Frankfort, for he had decided to pursue a course of study in Geneva; but Calvin strongly urged him to accept the invitation, and Knox agreed to go. He was therefore the only one of the three that had been invited who had given a favourable reply, and on receiving his acceptance the Frankfort group decided to appoint him as their pastor. Soon afterwards they heard from Scory at Emden that he was prepared to come to Frankfort as their pastor, as Grindal had invited him to do; but Whittingham and his colleagues, who had never

1 The English at Zürich to the English at Frankfort, 13 Oct. 1554 (*The Troubles at Frankfort*, pp. 14–16).

intended to invite him to fill the position, informed him that Knox had already been appointed.[1]

Knox arrived at Frankfort towards the end of November 1554. Others had arrived before him. Bale came in the middle of September, despite the fact that the Frankfort group had refused to appoint him as their pastor. Bale had won fame as a Protestant pamphleteer and playwright, particularly by his moving account of the martyrdom of Anne Askew in the last year of Henry VIII's reign; but his passionate hatred of the Catholics had not drawn him towards the left wing of the Protestant movement. He advocated submission to the authority of the king and the magistrates in its most extreme form; in his play *King John* he had proclaimed that it was sinful to criticize a king even when he had been dead for 300 years. Whitehead and the English from Emden had arrived on 24 October, and Whitehead had been elected to be the temporary minister until the arrival of Knox. When Knox reached Frankfort, he was elected minister by the vote of the congregation, and immediately took up his duties in place of Whitehead.[2]

The Order of Service that Whittingham had adopted in Frankfort was much more in accordance with Knox's opinions than the Book of Common Prayer, to which he objected on fundamental questions of principle. Apart from kneeling to receive communion he objected to certain references in the communion service to the blood, which in his opinion indicated a belief in the Real Presence. He also condemned the provisions in the Book of Common Prayer which authorized the baptism of children to take place, in cases of emergency where the child's life was in danger, in private houses at any time, instead of in the usual public baptism service on one Sunday in each month. This was in accordance with the ancient practice in the primitive Church, where christenings only took place twice a year; but it shows that Knox already believed in the doctrine of predestination, and rejected the orthodox Catholic doctrine of the old Church, to which the Church of England still adhered, that a child who died unbaptized could not

[1] *The Troubles at Frankfort*, pp. 13, 16 (*Works*, iv. 12); Knox, *History*, i. 110.

[2] *The Troubles at Frankfort*, pp. 17, 19 (*Works*, iv. 12). See Bale, *The Examinations of Anne Askewe* (Bale, *Works*, pp. 137–246); Bale, *Kynge Johan*, pp. 85–86. Knox must have arrived in Frankfort between 15 Nov. and 3 Dec. 1554, because he did not sign the letter from the English at Frankfort to the English at Zürich on 15 Nov., but signed the letter to the English at Strasbourg on 3 Dec., and all subsequent letters from the English at Frankfort until he left Frankfort in March 1555.

be saved. The rigidity of Knox's opposition to private baptism may almost be said to be an original contribution of his own to sixteenth-century theology, for both Calvin and Poullain were prepared to permit private baptism in extreme cases.[1]

But strongly though he felt on these issues, Knox was wise enough to see that opposition to Whittingham's Order of Service could not be overcome by a majority vote of the Frankfort congregation. Even at Frankfort there was a minority which strongly supported the Prayer Book and opposed the order of service in use in their congregation, and Knox knew that the opinion of the minority at Frankfort was shared by the great majority of the refugees in the other centres. All the most prominent leaders among the refugees were against the Frankfort service. Ponet and Scory took no part in the controversy, but Bale and Cox opposed it; and of the famous Lenten preachers of 1553, Knox was the only one who supported the Frankfort Order, for Bradford was in prison in England awaiting martyrdom at the stake, and Grindal, Lever, and Haddon were all against Knox on the issue of the service at Frankfort. On the other hand, if all the refugees could be brought together in Frankfort, and the matter discussed at length without going too fast, many of the rank and file in the congregations at Strasbourg and Zürich might be won over to support the changes in ritual and doctrine which Knox desired. Knox's aim was to preserve the unity of the refugees, and move them in a united body as far to the left as it was possible to go without disrupting that unity.

Knox had been in Frankfort for less than a fortnight when Grindal and Chambers arrived from Strasbourg with a letter from the Strasbourg group. A meeting of the English congregation was called to hear Grindal read out the letter and address them on behalf of his colleagues at Strasbourg. The letter, which was signed by Haddon, Sandys, Grindal, and thirteen others, including Knox's future collaborator, Christopher Goodman, was friendly in tone, but urged their Frankfort brethren to use in their church, as far as possible, the service of the Book of Common Prayer, as it had been celebrated in its 'former perfection' in England. If they did not do so, it would give the impression that the English refugees abroad were condemning the chief authors of the Book

[1] Ridley to Grindal (1555) (Ridley, *Works*, pp. 533–4). For Knox's doctrines on baptism, see McMillen, *The Worship of the Scottish Reformed Church*, pp. 246–65.

of Common Prayer, who at this very moment in England were preparing to confirm with their blood their belief in that Book. It would also give their enemies the opportunity to allege that their doctrine was imperfect and changeable. Grindal explained that they would not object if they omitted some ceremonies and things to which the authorities in Frankfort objected, provided that the substance of the Book was retained.[1]

Knox and Whittingham, who acted as spokesmen for the congregation, replied that they would admit everything in the Book of Common Prayer that would stand with God's Word and that the laws of Frankfort would permit. On 3 December the leaders of the congregation at Frankfort wrote a conciliatory letter to the congregation at Strasbourg, which was probably drafted by Knox and Whittingham, in which they said that they had agreed in all matters with Grindal and Chambers. They wrote that although they had omitted certain ceremonies that the laws of Frankfort prohibited, they had made as little alteration as possible in the Prayer Book, so that no one could justly accuse them of thinking that the Book was imperfect, or of continually changing their religion. 'Neither do we dissent from them which lie at the ransom of their bloods, for the doctrine whereof they have made a most worthy confession. And yet we think not that any godly man will stand to the death in defence of ceremonies, which (as the Book specifieth) upon just causes may be altered and changed.'[2] This emphasis on their conformity to the directions of the authorities in Frankfort was more likely to impress the conservatives among the English refugees than any other argument. Knox and Whittingham had handled the situation so tactfully that Bale agreed to sign this letter, along with most of the prominent leaders of the English congregation at Frankfort; but Whitehead did not sign it. He became the leader of the minority which opposed the Order of Service that Whittingham had drafted, and supported the Book of Common Prayer.

As soon as Grindal and Chambers had returned to Strasbourg at the beginning of December 1554, the radical majority at Frankfort suggested that they should immediately adopt the Order of

[1] The English at Strasbourg to the English at Frankfort, 23 Nov. 1554; *The Troubles at Frankfort*, pp. 22–24 (*Works*, iv. 15–17).

[2] The English at Frankfort to the English at Strasbourg, 3 Dec. 1554 (*The Troubles at Frankfort*, pp. 24–26 (wrongly paginated 24–25); *Works*, iv. 17–19).

Service which was in force in the churches at Geneva. This Order had been drafted by Calvin when he was the minister at Strasbourg, and had been published in 1539 under the title of *La Forme de Strasbourg*. Knox opposed this proposal. As long as the Frankfort group were asserting that they were using a service which was virtually identical with the service of the Book of Common Prayer, with the exception of a few objectionable features that were omitted to please the magistrates at Frankfort, they could hope to placate the conservative elements among the refugees, and preserve the unity of the exiled Church of England: but if they openly adopted Calvin's *La Forme* instead of the Book of Common Prayer, they would split the Church at once. Knox therefore refused to use the Genevan service at Frankfort until the English groups at Strasbourg, Zürich, and Emden had been consulted and had approved. On the other hand, he told the congregation that his conscience would not permit him to administer the communion according to the Book of Common Prayer, because of the rubric which directed that the communion was to be received kneeling; for though he had been prepared to agree to this under official pressure in England in 1552, he was now determined to move forward, on this point at least, as cautiously as possible. He therefore suggested that, as some of the congregation objected to his manner of administering the communion to a sitting congregation, he should cease to officiate as minister at Frankfort for the time being, and that some other priest should administer the sacraments while he confined himself to preaching. Knox's supporters, however, refused to agree to his proposal, and insisted that he should officiate as minister. Knox therefore continued to do so, using neither the Book of Common Prayer nor Calvin's *La Forme*, but the Order of Service which Whittingham had drafted.[1]

During the winter of 1554–5, the minority at Frankfort were strengthened by the arrival of a number of new residents, including some of the most eminent of the Protestant refugees. Grindal came from Strasbourg with Edwin Sandys, a former Vice-Chancellor of Cambridge University, who later, in Elizabeth's reign, became Archbishop of York. Cranmer's old chaplain, Thomas Becon, who was becoming one of the Protestant pamphleteers

[1] *The Troubles at Frankfort*, pp. 27–28 (*Works*, iv. 20–21); Maxwell, *John Knox's Genevan Service Book*, pp. 5, 12.

most hated and feared by Mary's government, also came from Strasbourg, along with Richard Alvey, a former Canon of Westminster, and Thomas Cottisford, who had suffered persecution for the cause as early as the time of the Six Articles; and from Zürich came Robert Horne, who had been a royal preacher under Edward VI, and together with Knox had been appointed to examine Cranmer's draft of the Articles of Religion in 1552. All these men joined the minority which supported the Book of Common Prayer.

There was no leader of any stature at Frankfort who supported the majority party except for Knox himself, for although there were able and active younger men among his supporters at Frankfort, they were not yet widely known and respected in the Protestant movement. Apart from Whittingham, John Foxe, Anthony Gilby, and William Kethe supported Knox. Foxe had come to Frankfort from Basel, where earlier in the year he had published, in a Latin translation, the first edition of the book which was soon to be known as his *Book of Martyrs*; when he fled from England, he had brought with him the almost completed manuscript of the book as he had originally conceived it, an account of the persecution of the Lollards in the fifteenth century. Gilby had written some vigorous polemical pamphlets against Gardiner and the English Catholics, and had also translated into English some books of Calvin and other foreign theologians; his pamphlet *Letter of a Man banished out of Leicestershire* had been published together with Knox's *Admonition to England*. Kethe was to become the great song-writer of the Puritan movement, the author of the metrical versions of many of the Psalms, which, 'sung to a plain tune', became not only an important part of the Church service of the Church of Scotland and the English Puritans, but also the battle songs of the movement; a few years later, he wrote his most famous song, the metrical version of the 100th Psalm, 'All people that on earth do dwell'. Another of Knox's supporters was Christopher Goodman, who had signed the letter from the Strasbourg group in November in support of the Book of Common Prayer, and had come to Frankfort with the other supporters of the minority. Soon after his arrival at Frankfort, Goodman joined Knox, and later became his closest associate. But in 1554 none of these men, except Knox himself, had the stature of the leading supporters of the Book of Common Prayer.

The supporters of the Book of Common Prayer also invoked the moral authority of the older leaders who were in Mary's prisons and preparing for death in the fire. The argument that to deviate in any way from the Prayer Book would be interpreted as a repudiation of Cranmer and Ridley, who were regarded as the authors of the Book, had great influence among the refugees. Grindal, who had been Ridley's chaplain, actually succeeded in smuggling a letter to Ridley in his prison at Oxford, informing him about the controversy at Frankfort. Ridley was not permitted to write letters in prison, but he was able to communicate with his friends by writing between the lines of books with a piece of lead which he took from his window. He wrote to Grindal and criticized Knox's opposition to private baptism; for he thought that it was better to permit this in an emergency rather than let the infant die unbaptized. 'Alas that our brother Knox could not bear with our Book of Common Prayer', he wrote, 'matters against which although, I grant, a man, as he is, of wit and learning may find to make apparent reasons, but I suppose he cannot be able soundly to disprove by God's Word. . . . Surely Mr. Knox, in my mind, is a man of much good learning, and of an earnest zeal; the Lord grant him to use them only to His glory.'[1]

But the name of Ridley was of greater assistance to the supporters of the Book of Common Prayer in Frankfort than his actual presence would have been; for Ridley considered that the refugees at Frankfort should adopt the local Order of Service instead of the Book of Common Prayer, and dispense with vestments and kneeling. He had adopted the same attitude towards the foreign Protestants in England when he was Bishop of London, insisting that, except in matters forbidden by God's Word, all residents in a country, including aliens, should adopt the Church services prescribed by the authorities.[2]

At the beginning of December 1554 the minority in Frankfort gained a further accession of strength when Lever arrived from Zürich, and offered himself, in response to their earlier invitation, as pastor to the Frankfort congregation. He agreed to use the existing service which Whittingham had drafted for a trial period

[1] Grindal to Ridley, 6 May 1555; Ridley to Grindal (1555) and (1555) (Ridley, *Works*, pp. 386–95, 533–4; the passage cited is at pp. 533–4); Foxe, viii. 35.

[2] Ridley to Grindal (1555) (Ridley, *Works*, pp. 534–5); Micronius to Bullinger, 28–31 Aug. 1550 (*Orig. Letters*, p. 569).

until Easter, on condition that the Order of Service should then be reconsidered. The majority could not refuse to accept Lever as pastor if the unity of the Church was to be preserved, and on these conditions he was elected joint minister along with Knox; but Knox and Whittingham had no doubt that he had come to Frankfort in order to organize opposition to their religious policy, and they determined to intensify their propaganda among the congregation. They also decided to counter the weight of the authority of Cranmer and Ridley and their eminent opponents among the refugees by enlisting the support of the great foreign theologians whose names were known and respected among the English Protestants, and who, as Knox knew, had frequently criticized certain aspects of the Book of Common Prayer.[1]

On 11 December Whittingham and Knox wrote to Calvin, and asked him for advice and moral support against their opponents. The letter, which was drafted by Whittingham, was strongly worded, and criticized the Book of Common Prayer in no uncertain terms. At the end of January 1555 the congregation of Frankfort received a reply from Calvin. Calvin wrote that the Second Book of Common Prayer retained some of the dregs of Popery, and though it had been perfectly proper to use its Order of Service in England in 1552, as it contained nothing that was manifestly impious, now, when they were reorganizing their Church in new circumstances, they should take the opportunity to improve the service by getting rid of these imperfections, as would doubtless have been done by the authorities in England if the true religion had not been overthrown there. Calvin's letter had some effect on the waverers at Frankfort, but as Knox was determined to prevent his supporters from winning a worthless victory by riding roughshod over the minority at Frankfort, he still refused to adopt the service of Calvin's *La Forme*.[2]

The whole question was debated at great length in the meeting of the congregation, and it was eventually decided to draw up an entirely new form of service. The congregation elected a committee of five members who were to draft the new Order of Service; they were Knox, Whittingham, Gilby, Foxe, and Thomas

[1] *The Troubles at Frankfort*, p. 28 (*Works*, iv. 21).

[2] Whittingham and Knox to Calvin, 11 Dec. 1554; Calvin to the English at Frankfort, 18 Jan. 1555 (*Calvini Op.* xv. 393–4; *The Troubles at Frankfort*, pp. 28–36, where Calvin's letter is dated 20 Jan. (*Works*, iv. 22–30)).

Cole. These five men produced an Order of Service which was adopted next year by the congregation of the English refugees in Geneva, and became known as the 'Order of Geneva'. After the revolution of 1560, it was adopted, again without alteration, as the Book of Common Order of the Church of Scotland. It has often been suggested that the origin of the Scottish Church service book can be traced back to an earlier date, to the service which Knox used at Berwick in the reign of Edward VI; but this is very unlikely. At Berwick, Knox was unable to violate the letter, even though he might contravene the spirit, of the First Book of Common Prayer, and though he could, for a time, introduce the practice of sitting at communion, he could not depart from the Order of Service prescribed in the only service permitted in the realm, and introduce the innovations that were put into practice in Frankfort. The service book of the Church of Scotland was composed by Knox and his four English colleagues at Frankfort-on-Main in February 1555; if we wish to go further back to discover the origins of the Order, we should look, not at Knox's services at Berwick, but to the Order of Service that Whittingham and his friends drew up when they first arrived at Frankfort in July 1554.[1]

When the new Order was presented for approval to the congregation at Frankfort, another violent argument broke out. The majority were in favour of it, but Lever and the supporters of the Book of Common Prayer indignantly rejected it, and accused their opponents of wishing to subvert and split the Church by their 'newfangledness'. Again Knox and his supporters made a concession to the minority. They proposed that the congregation should select a new committee to draft another Order of Service which would be more acceptable to their opponents, and this time they saw to it that the minority was represented on the committee. The new committee consisted of Knox, Whittingham, Lever, and Thomas Parry, a former Chancellor of the diocese of Salisbury, and their terms of reference were to 'devise some order, if it might be, to end all strife and contention'. The committee agreed on a new order of service, which was to be used as a temporary measure until 30 April. They stated that it was based on the Book

[1] *The Troubles at Frankfort*, pp. 36–37 (*Works*, iv. 30). For Knox's service at Berwick, see Knox, 'The Practice of the Lord's Supper used in Barwike-upon-Tweed by John Knoxe' (Lorimer, *John Knox and the Church of England*, pp. 290–2); and see McMillen, *The Worship of the Scottish Reformed Church*, pp. 25–26. For the Order of Geneva, see Maxwell, *John Knox's Genevan Service Book*.

of Common Prayer, but contained such changes as were required by the state of the English Church in Frankfort. In form the new order was far closer to the Book of Common Prayer than to Calvin's *La Forme* or to the 'Order of Geneva' which had been drawn up by Knox and his four supporters; but it excluded the responses, and contained no direction as to whether the communion was to be received kneeling or sitting. It was agreed that if any dispute arose as to the interpretation of the order of service, the dispute was to be referred to Calvin in Geneva, to Musculus in Basel, to Bullinger and Peter Martyr in Zürich, and to Viret in Lausanne. Every member of the congregation in Frankfort was to agree in writing to adhere to the agreement.

It was a great feat for Knox and Whittingham to have persuaded Lever to agree to this compromise, and it was due to the patience and skill that Knox had shown throughout the controversy. The agreement was accepted unanimously by the congregation at a meeting on 6 February, and was followed by a general reconciliation on all sides. 'This day was joyful', wrote Thomas Wood, 'thanks were given to God, brotherly reconciliation followed, great familiarity used, the former grudges seemed to be forgotten.'[1] The new unity lasted for little more than a month, and though the new Order of Service had been unanimously accepted until 30 April, long before this date arrived the whole edifice which Knox had built in Frankfort had been shattered; for on 13 March Richard Cox came to Frankfort with a number of English Protestant refugees.[2]

Cox was a man of a completely different type and background from any of the other refugees who had hitherto joined the congregation at Frankfort. Lever, Grindal, Whitehead, Bale, and Becon might prefer the English Prayer Book to Calvin's *La Forme* or the future 'Order of Geneva', and hold more conservative opinions on doctrine and the duty of Christian obedience; but they were all of them products of the Protestant movement in its

[1] *The Troubles at Frankfort*, pp. 37–38 (*Works*, iv. 30–32). Wood, not Whittingham, was probably the author of *The Troubles at Frankfort*; see P. Collinson, 'The authorship of *A Brieff Discours off the Troubles Begonne at Franckford*' (*Journal of Eccl. History*, ix. 188–208). For the text of the liturgy drawn up by Knox, Whittingham, Lever, and Parry, see Sprott, 'The Liturgy of Compromise' (in Wotherspoon, *The Second Prayer Book of King Edward VI*, pp. 231–56).

[2] For the events of 13–26 Mar., see *The Troubles at Frankfort*, pp. 38–45, and Knox's narrative (*Works*, iv. 32–49). See also Whittingham to a friend in England (1555) (in *The Troubles at Frankfort*, pp. 47–50); and Knox, *History*, i. 110–11.

Zwinglian and Edwardine phase, and had risen to prominence as preachers and pamphleteers. Cox was a product of officialdom and the ecclesiastical hierarchy in the days of Henrician despotism; his background and instincts were those of a government official and high ecclesiastic of the reign of Henry VIII. He first came into prominence when he was entrusted with the duty of bullying the leading doctors of Oxford University into expressing the opinion that Henry's marriage to Catherine of Aragon was invalid. He had played a leading part in compiling the conservative formulary, the King's Book, during the Catholic reaction of 1543; and he had frequently been employed in interrogating and persecuting Protestants during the last years of Henry's reign. Under Edward VI, as King's Almoner and Chancellor of the University of Oxford, he had distinguished himself by his drastic purge of superstitious books and images at Oxford, when he had ordered the destruction of large numbers of ancient manuscripts and rare books and paintings, so that it was said of him that he was the 'cancellor', not the Chancellor, of the University.[1] The other refugees who had joined the congregation at Frankfort, despite their passionate doctrinal arguments, were united by their determination to preserve the unity of the movement. Cox's aim was to destroy anything which savoured of sedition, disobedience to authority, and independence of thought.

The trouble started immediately after Cox's arrival. A day or so later, Cox and the refugees who had come with him attended the daily service of the English congregation. It was a day on which Lever was officiating, and Knox was present in the church as a member of the congregation. When Lever said the prayer, Cox and the other newcomers answered with the responses of the Book of Common Prayer. The elders of the congregation told them to be silent, but they continued to make the responses, and Lever made no attempt to stop them. Knox then remonstrated with them; but Cox replied that they would do as they had done in England, and that the church of the English congregation at Frankfort should have the face of an English church. To this Knox replied that he hoped that it would have the face of the Church of Christ. He raised the matter with Lever, and asked Lever to help him in suppressing Cox's practice, which was a breach of the agreement that had been made a month earlier by the

[1] Dixon, iii. 108–9.

congregation; but Lever said that he entirely supported Cox's attitude, and suggested that they should henceforth use the Litany of the Church of England, with the responses. Lever's attitude shocked Knox, for it was a flagrant violation of the compromise which had been reached, and he answered firmly that he would never agree to the responses being said. He accused Lever of being a promise-breaker, and of failing in his duty to the congregation that had elected him as their minister.

On the next Sunday, 17 March, Cox and his supporters again made the responses at the morning service when Lever was officiating. Knox was due to deliver the sermon at the afternoon service on that Sunday, and he struck back vigorously, attacking the imperfections of the Book of Common Prayer, and explaining the reasons that had led him to abandon the high opinions that he had originally held of the Book. He said that though his opponents claimed that the order of service which had been used in England was in no need of any improvement, the overthrow of religion in their country, and their exile from their homeland, was a punishment imposed by God for the sins that had prevailed in England under Edward VI. He referred to the imprisonment of Hooper at the time of the vestments controversy as proof of the imperfections of the services of the Book of Common Prayer; for if his opponents were continually referring to the steadfastness of Cranmer and Ridley to prove the merits of the Prayer Book which they had drafted, Knox could cite the case of Hooper, who had been burnt five weeks before, as proof that at least one martyr had been victimized as a result of the provisions of the Book of Common Prayer, even if it was not the same Book of Common Prayer as the Book for which the minority at Frankfort were contending. He also denounced the system of pluralities, which had been tolerated under Edward VI; it had been possible, he said, for one man to hold three, four, or five benefices 'to the slander of the Gospel and defraudation of Christ's flock of their lively food and sustenance'. This attack on pluralities was probably directed against Cox personally, for he had held many benefices at the same time under Henry VIII and Edward VI. Cox and his followers were infuriated by Knox's sermon, and when Knox left the pulpit, they accosted him and protested angrily against what he had said. Knox convened a meeting of the congregation for the same evening to discuss the breach of discipline and the repudiation of the compromise agreement by Lever and the minority, and after a heated discussion the meeting was adjourned till Tuesday.

On this Tuesday, 19 March 1555, in the Church of White Ladies at Frankfort, the first step was taken to split the English Protestant movement. This meeting began the sequence of events which caused the Protestant Churches of England and Scotland to take different paths, and led to the birth of English Puritanism. At the beginning of the meeting, Lever and his supporters asked that Cox and the brethren who had arrived in Frankfort six days before should be admitted to the congregation and allowed to vote. This put Knox in a great difficulty. If they were admitted, they would add their votes to those of Lever's faction, which would become the majority. If the congregation refused to admit them, it would end any possibility of uniting the groups at Strasbourg, Zürich, and Emden in one united Church, and would mean a split in the Protestant Church in exile.

The majority of the congregation at Frankfort objected to admitting Cox's group at this stage. They insisted that first the issue before the meeting, as to whether Lever had broken the terms of the compromise agreement of 6 February, should be decided without counting the votes of the new arrivals; and they also demanded that Cox's group should agree, before they were admitted, to accept the discipline of the congregation. They accused several members of Cox's group of having gone to mass and signed blasphemous articles in England, and said that before these individuals were admitted they ought to purge themselves and show true repentance for what they had done. Lever's supporters rejected these proposals with great indignation, and twice walked out of the meeting, but were persuaded to return. Knox then made one last effort in the cause of unity. He urged his supporters to admit Cox's group. He said that he knew that the motive of Lever and the minority in calling for their admission was to use their votes to carry a resolution exonerating Lever for his breach of the compromise agreement; but he was nevertheless prepared to admit them, because he believed that it was so obvious that Lever had broken the agreement that no one would be able to deny it. It is unlikely that Knox really believed that his opponents would feel morally incapable of voting against him; but he was prepared to risk the almost certain defeat of his resolution in order to prevent a split in the Church of England. He did not know the lengths to which his opponents would be prepared to go. Until now he had always succeeded, since he came to Frankfort, in persuading them to accept a compromise; he did not realize that Cox, unlike the opponents with whom he had hitherto had to deal, did not wish to see the growth and unity of the English congregation at Frankfort, but was determined to split and destroy a Church which was under the control of radical and subversive elements.

Knox's arguments persuaded a number of his supporters to vote in favour of admitting Cox's group, and though the majority of Knox's party voted against it, a sufficient number had come over to constitute a majority together with Lever's minority group. Cox and his followers were then invited to join the congregation and take part in the proceedings at the meeting, whereupon Cox immediately proposed that Knox should be dismissed from the office of minister to the congregation, and should be prohibited from preaching in the church, leaving Lever as the sole minister. The new members of the congregation and Lever's group together now formed the majority of the congregation, and Cox's resolution dismissing Knox was carried.

Knox had made every reasonable concession, but he was not prepared to submit to treatment of this kind. On the day after the meeting, on Wednesday, 20 March, Whittingham went to Glauburg and invoked his help. He told him that a group of Englishmen, who had arrived a week ago, were trying to prevent Knox, the properly elected minister of the congregation, from discharging his duties; they had forbidden Knox to preach at today's service, and were planning to introduce another, unauthorized, preacher in his place. Whittingham warned Glauburg that there was a danger of serious disturbances taking place in the Church of White Ladies. Glauburg sent an order to the English congregation, forbidding them to hold any service that day, and instructing them to elect a committee to draft yet another order of service for the English Church which would be acceptable to both parties. He directed that the committee was to consist of two delegates from each of the two contending factions, with Poullain in the chair. Knox, Whittingham, Lever, and Cox were chosen, and they met in Poullain's house on that same afternoon, together with Poullain, who took charge of the proceedings, laying down the points at issue which were to be discussed.

The committee met again next day, and after two days' discussion they had reached agreement on a number of points; but meanwhile an unpleasant and ominous incident occurred. During one of the breaks in the committee's discussions, Knox was visited in his lodgings by Edward Isaac. Isaac was a Protestant gentleman and justice of the peace in Kent, who had left England to avoid persecution, and had come to Frankfort the previous week with Cox.[1] He asked Knox, in a very friendly manner, to abandon his opposition to the Book of Common Prayer, and told him that if he did so, Cox's supporters would show him all possible friendship and favour. When Knox declined to do this, Isaac changed his tone; he threw out dark hints that if Knox persisted in his opposition to the Book of Common Prayer, he would find himself in serious danger. Knox was not the man to succumb to religious blackmail; he replied that he would be happy for his name to perish if this would ensure that God's Book and glory alone would be sought by their congregation.

On Friday, 22 March, Knox, Whittingham, Cox, Lever, and Poullain held their third meeting at Poullain's house, and they discussed the order of matins. Cox and Lever suggested that the service should begin with the words of the Book of Common Prayer, 'O Lord open Thou our lips', and 'We praise thee, O God'. Knox objected that the words were not to be found in Scripture, and said that they had been taken over by the Church of England from Papist services. Thereupon Cox and Lever refused to continue the meeting, and left the house. After two days of apparent progress, the discussions had suddenly broken down. Knox and Whittingham immediately convened a meeting of their supporters, and drew up a supplication to the city council of Frankfort, which was approved by the meeting and presented to Glauburg that same afternoon.

This supplication was a strong attack on Cox's faction and the Book of Common Prayer. News had just reached Frankfort that Hooper, whose German wife was living in Frankfort, had been burnt at Gloucester at the beginning of February, and the supplication described how Hooper had been thrown into prison in the reign of Edward VI by the supporters of the Book of Common Prayer because the Book required him to wear a rochet and a

[1] For Isaac, see Foxe, viii. 597–8; Cranmer to Henry VIII, 18 Feb. 1541 (Cranmer, *Works*, ii. 458); Strype, *Eccl. Mem.* iii [i]. 372.

bishop's robe, which Hooper, 'being well learned, and a long time nourished and brought up in Germany', had refused to do; if Cox's faction, supported by the authorities at Frankfort, were allowed to have their way, this harmful practice of wearing vestments would eventually be introduced into the Lutheran cities of Germany. The supplication therefore asked the city council to refer the whole matter to Calvin, Musculus, Bullinger, Peter Martyr, and Viret, and to ask these great theologians to draft an order of service for the use of the English congregation in Frankfort.[1]

On receiving this supplication, Glauburg went immediately to the Church of White Ladies, where the English congregation were assembled. He informed them that the city authorities were highly displeased at the conduct of the English refugees, and ordered them to adopt in future the identical service that Poullain's congregation were using; otherwise, or if there were any more arguments about their order of service, their permission to use the Church of White Ladies would be withdrawn. As soon as Glauburg had finished, Cox rose and constituted himself as spokesman for the whole congregation. He said that if this was the order of the magistrates, they would obey it without question, and expressed his deep regret that the conduct of their congregation had displeased the authorities. Next day, on the Saturday, the English congregation held their daily service in accordance with Poullain's order of service, which was almost identical with that which had been used in the first place by the English at Frankfort. Cox's supporters made no attempt to make responses or to depart in any way from the French order of service, and Knox prepared to preach in the church at the service on the Sunday.

But there were matters that touched the city authorities at Frankfort more closely than the Book of Common Prayer. On this Saturday, the day after Glauburg had given his final decision and Cox had agreed to accept the French service, Isaac and Parry visited one of the other city councillors and informed him that two years before, in the town of Amersham in England, Knox had preached a sermon in which he had said that the Emperor Charles V was worse than Nero, and had subsequently published this statement in a pamphlet which also contained treasonable and

[1] For the text of the Supplication, see *The Troubles at Frankfort*, pp. 40–43 (*Works*, iv. 35–37).

seditious statements about Philip and Mary, the King and Queen of England. They presented the councillor with a copy of Knox's *Admonition to England*, and indicated nine passages in the text which, in their opinion, were treasonable. Eight of them referred to Mary. These were Knox's statements that if Mary had been sent to Hell in the reign of Edward VI, her cruelty would not have been so manifest; that she had erected more gallows in London than Jezebel had erected in all Israel; that she had broken her promise to her people to maintain the Protestant religion and not to marry a foreigner; that she had betrayed her realm to Spain; that under an English name she had a Spaniard's heart; that God had suffered her, for our scourge, to come to authority; and two other occasions in the pamphlet where Knox had referred to Mary as a 'wicked woman'. The ninth passage was the reference to Charles V as being worse than Nero.[1]

It was this last statement that alarmed the councillor. The city of Frankfort could not afford to allow anyone to think that they were lax in punishing treason against the Emperor, when Charles might at any time be looking for an excuse to rescind his merciful decision of 1547 and destroy the freedom of the city. An extraordinary meeting of the city council was convened within a few hours. Whittingham was summoned to appear before the Consuls and councillors, and was ordered to give them, by 1 p.m., a Latin translation of the nine passages in Knox's *Admonition to England* to which Isaac and Parry had objected. Whittingham did as he was commanded, and the council, after discussing the case at another meeting in the afternoon, issued an order prohibiting Knox from preaching his Sunday sermon next day. Knox obeyed the order, but attended the service as an ordinary member of the congregation. As soon as he entered the church, Cox and all his supporters walked out, some of them protesting loudly that they would not remain in any place where Knox was present.

Next day, on the Monday, the city council met again, and decided to expel Knox from Frankfort. They summoned Whittingham, and told him that Isaac had approached them again, this time together with Jewel, and had asked what steps were being taken against Knox; and the councillors urged Whittingham to persuade Knox to leave Frankfort at once, because if anyone

[1] The nine passages in Knox's *Admonition to England* are in *Works*, iii. 294–6, 307–8.

denounced him to the Emperor or to his Council at Augsburg, the city council would be forced to accede to any request from Charles that Knox should be handed over to him. Knox decided to leave Frankfort next day. On that last evening, he called a private meeting of his supporters, and about fifty of them met at his house. Despite the order of the authorities forbidding him to preach, he made what Wood calls 'a most comfortable sermon'[1] on the joys which are prepared for God's elect who suffer persecution for His cause. Next day, on Tuesday, 26 March—less than a fortnight after Cox had arrived in Frankfort—Knox left Frankfort for Geneva. Some of his friends who had been at the meeting the night before gave an open demonstration of their support by escorting him for the first three or four miles of his journey.

Two days after Knox's departure, Cox persuaded the authorities at Frankfort to rescind Glauburg's order which directed that they should use Poullain's order of service, and to issue a new order requiring them to use the services of the Book of Common Prayer. Whittingham appealed to Glauburg, but Glauburg told him that in the circumstances he could do nothing, and urged Whittingham and his supporters to accept the position and put an end to the disputes among the English congregation. Cox then abolished the meetings of the congregation in the English Church, and arranged that all questions of discipline should be decided by himself as superintendent, subject to the orders of the city authorities. He appointed Whitehead to be pastor in Knox's place, and did away with the office of elders. Whittingham and his followers said that they would withdraw from Cox's congregation and form a congregation of their own; but Cox persuaded the Frankfort authorities to refuse to permit them the use of any church. Whittingham's party made a last attempt to preserve unity, and remained in Frankfort as members of Cox's congregation for five months; then, at the end of August, they received an invitation from Calvin to come to Geneva, and decided to leave Frankfort. Cox and Whitehead made an attempt to persuade them to remain, and accused them of causing a schism in the Church; but Whittingham replied that the responsibility for this rested with their opponents, whom they accused of many acts of oppression, chief among which was the denunciation of Knox. In September 1555 the Church of England in exile split, when

[1] *The Troubles at Frankfort*, p. 45 (*Works*, iv. 40).

Whittingham, Foxe, Gilby, Goodman, and Kethe left Frankfort with their followers. Foxe went to Basel, and the rest joined Knox in Geneva.[1]

On reaching Geneva, Knox wrote a short account of his experiences in Frankfort. It was restrained, simple, and unpretentious in tone, and had none of the savage sarcasm of his *History of the Reformation in Scotland* and the *Admonition to England*, or the emotional hyperbole of his letters to Mrs. Bowes. He stated that it was Cox, Bale, Turner, and Jewel who were responsible for denouncing him in Frankfort for treason to the Emperor, and that it was these four who persuaded Isaac and Parry to go to the city council; but he did not use any of the violent invective that he lavished on Papist bishops and rulers, and wrote that he forgave his enemies from the bottom of his heart. Knox did not wish to appear to be seeking revenge for private wrongs which had been committed against him personally, and despite the injury which they had done him, he was not prepared to deal with these Protestants, with whom he had not yet made any formal doctrinal or organizational split, as he would with the forces of Antichrist. His strongest censures were directed against Lever, whom he felt had betrayed him by supporting Cox's party and breaking the compromise agreement of 6 February. The venom of a man like Cox, who had never had anything in common with Knox except a formal Protestant unity, was easier to bear than the conduct of Lever, his fighting colleague of the Lenten sermons at Whitehall, when Knox believed that he had won him over by his tact and policy of compromise.[2]

But Knox's patience at Frankfort had not been altogether wasted. His opinions were slowly gaining ground among the refugees. In the course of the next year, Thomas Sampson, who supported Cox at Frankfort, and Lever himself left Frankfort for Geneva, where they joined Knox's congregation. When they returned to England in the reign of Elizabeth, both of them played an active part in the Puritan movement, and suffered persecution from Cox and his fellow bishops.

When Knox met Calvin, he informed him of all that had

[1] *The Troubles at Frankfort*, pp. 55–59; Whittingham to a friend in England (1555); Whittingham, Kethe, Gilby, etc. to Cox and the English at Frankfort, 27 Aug. 1555 (*The Troubles at Frankfort*, pp. 47–50, 54–55).

[2] Knox's narrative (*Works*, iv. 41–49).

happened at Frankfort. At the end of May 1555, Calvin wrote to Cox and his group at Frankfort, and not only criticized at length the imperfections of the Book of Common Prayer, but referred to the incident of Knox. 'Mr. Knox was, in my judgement, neither godly nor brotherly dealt with', he wrote, and he added that it would have been better if the English refugees had stayed in England rather than come, bringing with them into foreign countries the 'firebrand of cruelty' in order to set fire to those who resisted them.[1] On 20 September 1555, the English in Frankfort wrote at length to Calvin, and justified both the Book of Common Prayer and their conduct towards Knox. This letter is the only lengthy statement about the troubles at Frankfort written by Cox and his supporters. It was signed by Cox, Whitehead, Becon, Parry, Alvey, Cottisford and, more surprisingly, Bartholemew Traheron, who in the days of Edward VI had been a keen supporter of Hooper.

They wrote to Calvin that the more experienced members of their congregation at Frankfort had discovered that Knox had published a book which would give their enemies just ground for destroying the whole Church. 'For there were interspersed, throughout this work, dreadful and terrible invectives against the Queen of England, whom Knox sometimes called wicked Mary, and sometimes a monster. And he provoked King Philip with language which was almost as violent.' There is not, in fact, any reference to Philip personally in Knox's *Admonition to England*, though he refers to the domination of England by the Spaniards.

When these men, who are utterly devoted to religion and to our Church, had thoroughly studied this infamous pamphlet, they thought that it would be neither advantageous nor safe for us that Knox should be sheltered by our Church. One of them therefore approached Knox's intimate friends, and pointed out that it would be most advisable for Knox to leave the Church and go elsewhere; and this he earnestly advised him to do. He failed in this. Our friends, after considering more closely the danger which was undoubtedly impending, decided to take other action. The matter was at last denounced to the authorities, with no other object than that Knox should be ordered to leave the place. When the authorities were informed about the case, and had also discovered that the Emperor was branded in that pamphlet, they

[1] Calvin to the English at Frankfort, 31 May 1555 (*Calvini Op.* xv. 628–9, where the date is wrongly given as 12 June; *The Troubles at Frankfort*, pp. 51–53; *Works*, iv. 58–60).

realized that such a man might easily endanger not only our Church, but also their State, and ordered him to leave the city. . . . We can assure you, that that insane pamphlet of Knox's added much oil to the flame of persecution in England. For before that pamphlet was published, not one of our brethren had suffered death; and we are sure that you know how many excellent men perished in the flames as soon as it came out. We say nothing of how many other men of godly disposition have been exposed to the risk of losing all their property, and even their lives, merely because they had this book in their possession, or had read it.[1]

This last allegation against Knox has stuck, for historians have continued to repeat it even in the twentieth century, and to blame Knox's *Admonition to England* for the Marian persecution. The accusation is unjust, and almost ludicrous. Charles V, Henry II, and every Catholic ruler in Europe burned heretics, as Henry VIII had done; yet Cox and his friends believed that Mary, alone of them all, would not have burned heretics if Knox had not written a pamphlet. In fact, the reason for the delay in burning heretics in England was that the peers in the House of Lords had only been prepared to re-enact the heresy statute as part of a bargain by which the Pope confirmed them in possession of the monastic lands which they had purchased from Henry VIII.[2]

Cox's attack against Knox had succeeded in destroying the first attempt to establish a democratic form of government in the Church of England. After Knox had succeeded, by patience and skill, in conciliating and winning over all his critics, everything had been lost in the course of twelve turbulent days; for after Knox's expulsion from Frankfort, his opponents had carried the day on all points. His old comrades of earlier struggles—men like Lever, Grindal, and Sampson—had turned against him, and even Whittingham and his closest supporters had been stunned by the blow, and had temporarily abandoned the struggle in Frankfort.

It was Knox's *Admonition to England* that was responsible for the disaster. Six weeks before Knox's expulsion from Frankfort, the burnings in England, which had been awaited and dreaded for so long, had begun; but at the very moment when the English at

[1] The English at Frankfort to Calvin, 20 Sept. 1555 (*Calvini Op.* xv. 775–82; see cols. 779–81; *Works*, iv. 61–66, see pp. 63–65; *Orig. Letters*, pp. 755–63, see pp. 760–2).

[2] Renard to Charles V, 6 May and 21 Dec. 1554 (Weiss, iv. 346–7; *Span. Cal.* xii. 238; xiii. 131).

Frankfort heard the news that the fires of Smithfield were burning again, and that hardly a day passed on which one of their brethren was not slaughtered at Mary's orders, these Protestant refugees turned away in horror from their esteemed pastor when they learned that he had attacked Mary in a pamphlet. But Knox had no regrets, and no apologies to make about his attitude to Mary. In the account that he wrote of the events at Frankfort, he ended by stating that he did not retract one word that he had written in the *Admonition to England*, and hoped that he would one day have the time to write a longer book in which he would vindicate the doctrine which he had put forward there.[1] During the next three years, he explained and vindicated in writing his theory of resistance to authority. He soon had the opportunity to vindicate it in action.

[1] Knox's narrative (*Works*, iv. 49).

CHAPTER XII

Geneva and Scotland

WHEN Knox arrived in Geneva in April 1555, and for the second time attempted to settle down to a life of scholarship there, he took up his residence in a state that was governed on entirely different principles from any of the other countries in which he had taken refuge. Knox was deeply impressed by the régime in Geneva, and later tried, with limited success, to introduce a similar system of government into Scotland. In December 1556 he wrote that Geneva, 'I neither fear nor ashame to say, is the most perfect school of Christ that ever was in earth since the days of the Apostles. In other places, I confess Christ to be truly preached; but manners and religion so sincerely reformed, I have not yet seen in any other place.'[1]

By 1530 Geneva had thrown off the authority of the Duke of Savoy and had become an independent republic, consisting of the city of Geneva and a few villages outside its walls, a territory about 10 miles long and 10 miles wide, with a population of about 13,000. In 1535 the city became Protestant, thanks chiefly to the efforts of Farel; and next year Farel persuaded John Calvin, a 27-year-old Frenchman from Picardy who happened to be passing through Geneva, to remain there and assist him with his work. Calvin set out to enforce the rule of virtue in Geneva. A government of good men was to eradicate the vice and selfishness of the majority of the population by a combination of education and punishment.

Calvin encountered strong opposition in Geneva. His plan to establish moral government aroused the resistance of two main sections of the population—the rebellious elements among the people, and the influential upper-class families. The men with rebellious instincts and the youth resentful of authority, who had destroyed images and ridiculed the mass and the sacred relics of the old Church in the days of the Bishop of Geneva, continued to be a source of trouble to the new Protestant government. They

[1] Knox to Anne Locke, 9 Dec. 1556 (*Works*, iv. 240).

now mocked Calvin and the Church Consistory, and ridiculed the Psalms. Calvin had to deal with many more cases of blasphemy and mockery of religion than a ruler of a Catholic state that had never been disturbed by religious unrest; and as he could not rely on the traditional respect which was accorded to old-established conservative régimes, he was compelled to resort far more often to coercion and punishment. He also aroused the hatred of the upper classes. The principle that the State should punish vice was accepted in every Christian country; but it had come to be accepted that the upper classes had the privilege of contravening the morality laws. Gambling and card playing were prohibited in England at the time when Suffolk and Rutland won and lost large sums every night at cards; and in London and Paris adulterers were put in the pillory and driven through the town in a cart with a placard inscribed 'Adulterer' around their necks while Henry VIII and Francis I spent the tax-payer's money on gifts to their mistresses.

In Geneva, Calvin's Consistory enforced the morality laws against the most powerful families as strictly as against anyone else. Their love affairs and dances and gambling parties were pried into as eagerly, if not more eagerly, than those of any other class; and the Sumptuary Laws, which in other states were used to enforce class distinctions, were used in Geneva to suppress indecorous and provocative women's dress, which was popular among upper-class ladies. The upper classes and high officials of Geneva could not forgive the Consistory for attempting to deprive them of the pleasures in which people of their class and position could indulge in every other country in Christendom. But Calvin was supported by the middle class, the sober merchants who wished to see disrespect and rowdyism among the people suppressed, and had always been too industrious to indulge in the vices of the upper classes. Though Calvin was driven from Geneva by his opponents in 1538, his supporters were influential enough to recall him in 1541. For the next fourteen years, Geneva was a democratic two-party state, with the Calvinists and their opponents succeeding each other in office on the Little Council as they won or lost the annual elections. All the enemies of Calvin united into one party, and became known as the Libertines. The Libertine Party was led by Perrin, the Captain-General of Geneva, whose wife had been imprisoned for a few days by Calvin and the Consistory for having given a party at her house at which the guests danced all night. Madame Perrin had retaliated by attempting to ride down a pastor in the street.

The government of Calvin was less cruel, but more relentless, than the conservative governments of the old régimes. Servetus, who denied the doctrine of the Trinity, was the only man who was burnt for his opinions in Calvin's Geneva; in other cases, the death sentence for blasphemy—for the term 'heresy' was not used in Geneva—was carried out by beheading, not the fire, though Calvin failed to persuade the Libertine government to give Servetus the benefit of the more merciful death. Men who sang coarse songs to Psalm tunes, or who said that a braying ass was singing a Psalm, were punished by fine or banishment from the town for a short time, or occasionally, in the case of adolescents, by whipping; in Catholic states, men lost a tongue, a hand, or an ear for blaspheming the saints. Though adultery was punished by death in Geneva, the Consistory relied primarily on warnings, and public censure and humiliation, before proceeding to serious punishments. But the scale and thoroughness of the enforcement of the moral law far exceeded anything known elsewhere. In the great monarchical states, where hypocritical rulers themselves committed the sins which they publicly condemned, only a handful of men and women every year were punished for acts which the king and so many people were committing with impunity. In Geneva the sincere idealists of the Consistory every year summoned between 100 and 300 citizens, out of the small population, to appear before them on account of moral crimes.

The Consistory also dealt with conduct which was morally reprehensible, but which had never before, in other countries, been treated as a crime against the State. When the Consistory punished men who spoke disrespectfully of Calvin, they did no more than would have been done in any other state to those who spoke slightingly of their bishop and his officials; when a woman hairdresser was imprisoned for two days for giving a bride a too elaborate hair-style, this was not essentially different from the penalties inflicted in other countries for breaches of the Sumptuary Laws. But only in Calvin's Geneva was a youth whipped by the State for striking his mother with a stone, and a man punished for refusing to contribute to the upkeep of his starving parents, a wife for refusing to light a fire for her husband when he was ill, a husband for bullying behaviour towards his wife, a mother for negligently allowing her baby to fall into the fire and suffer injuries. Calvin was determined to compel the evil-minded majority to submit to the standards of decency imposed, and adhered to, by the upright few.

The opposition of the Libertine Party to Calvin reached a climax on the question of refugees. As the persecution of Protestants in France intensified after the accession of Henry II, Calvin insisted that Geneva should offer asylum to all French Protestants, and soon the city was full of French refugees. The scale of the immigration alarmed the Libertines, especially as Calvin wished to grant Genevan citizenship to the refugees. The Libertines knew that these Protestant zealots, who were ready to leave their homes and go into exile for their faith, would be resolute supporters of Calvin and the party which stood for a principled enforcement of the moral law; and their nationalist resentment at an influx of foreigners was combined with their fear that the arrival of additional refugees would mean an increase in strength for Calvin's party. The Libertines aroused hatred of the refugees among the population, and alleged that many of them were really French Catholics who had been sent to Geneva as spies of Henry II. But in 1554 the Calvinists were returned to office at the elections, and they put into force both a stricter enforcement of the moral laws and a more favourable policy towards the refugees. When Perrin proposed in the Little Council that no more refugees should be granted citizenship, the resolution was defeated, and resentment against the refugees increased. When Knox returned to Geneva in April 1555, the crisis was about to break.

In England, his first foreign land of refuge, Knox had enjoyed asylum for four years before being forced to flee from the country. In Frankfort, he had been expelled after four months. Now, when he came to Geneva for the third time as a refugee from Frankfort, he was nearly driven out after four weeks. On the evening of 16 May, a riot broke out in Geneva against the refugees. It began when revellers leaving the taverns started brawling and demonstrating in the streets against Calvin and the foreigners. The crowds grew, and the Captain-General, Perrin, riding up, put himself at the head of the rioters. The mob set fire to the house of a prominent French refugee; then, hearing that Calvin was entertaining some refugees at a party, they decided to march to Calvin's house. Loyal officers and guards blocked their way, and dispersed the mob, which put up no serious resistance; for at the critical moment Perrin lost his nerve and took no decisive action. Calvin seized his opportunity and crushed the Libertine Party, which he accused of attempting to overthrow the government by revolution. Several of the Libertine leaders were beheaded for high treason, and Perrin and many Libertines fled to Berne. At last, after nineteen years of struggle, Calvin's position in Geneva was unchallengeable. By 1560 the population of Geneva had risen to 20,000 by the admission of more than 6,000 refugees, including a few hundred English, Scottish, Italian, Spanish, and Dutch among this great mass of fugitives from France; and when nearly one in every three of the inhabitants of Geneva were refugees, Calvin's electoral majority and control of the city was permanently assured. He remained in complete control of Geneva until his death in 1564, when his government was continued, in a somewhat milder form, by his friend Theodore Beza.[1]

The ordinary citizen of Geneva might resent the discipline that Calvin imposed upon him; but to Knox, after the lawless violence of life in Scotland, the immorality and covetousness of the nobility in England, and the cowardly acquiescence of the merchants who ruled Frankfort, the austere but incorruptible régime in Geneva was an inspiration. At St. Andrews Castle, he had depended upon the support of men whose moral life disgraced the cause; in England, the success of the Protestant religion rested on the goodwill of time-serving and land-grabbing magnates; in Frankfort, he had been expelled by Protestants whose chief concern was to please a Catholic Emperor. But at last, in Geneva, Knox found a country ruled by men like himself, by Protestant idealists who enforced morality on the people and adhered strictly to the Word of God as expounded in Scripture, and who would defy the force of public opinion among their people rather than refuse asylum and assistance to their persecuted brothers in France and elsewhere. In Geneva, Knox definitely became a Calvinist, and conceived an admiration for Calvin which he had felt for no one since Wishart.

But again he was unable to settle down for long in Geneva. He

[1] For Calvin's régime in Geneva, and the riot of May 1555, see Choisy, *La Théocratie à Genève au temps de Calvin*; Gaberel, *Histoire de l'Église de Genève jusqu'en 1815*.

had only been there for four months when he decided to return to Scotland. A situation had developed in Scotland which offered great opportunities for the spread of Protestant doctrines. It had arisen as a result of the hostility between Mary of Lorraine, the Queen Dowager, and Arran. Mary of Lorraine had always resented the fact that Arran had assumed the regency, and as soon as the war with England had ended in 1550, she set about trying to build up a party against him, and to dismiss him from his office as Governor of Scotland. Arran, who had been created Duke of Châtelherault, with large estates in central France, was using his position to enrich himself and other members of the House of Hamilton. He refused to resign, and secured the support of many of the Scottish nobles against the Queen Dowager by pandering to anti-French sentiment.

For four years the internal and foreign policy of the Scottish government was affected by the feud between the Governor and the Queen Dowager, as Mary of Lorraine obtained the release of the prisoners of St. Andrews from the French galleys in order to spite Châtelherault, and Châtelherault conspired with Mary of Hungary in Brussels in order to defeat the intrigues of Mary of Lorraine. Mary of Lorraine had the backing of d'Oysel, the French ambassador, and the French army in Scotland, and could rely on the influence of her brothers, the Duke of Guise and the Cardinal of Lorraine, at the French Court; they were all disgusted with Châtelherault's incompetence and corruption, and wished to see Scotland governed by a Frenchwoman who could be relied upon to follow the advice of her eldest brother, the Duke, in all matters. At length the French decided to get rid of Châtelherault at all costs. Châtelherault and the Scottish Parliament were subjected to pressure and bribes, and in April 1554 Châtelherault resigned as Regent. Mary of Lorraine was appointed Regent by Act of the Scottish Parliament. She gave the highest offices in the State, including that of Keeper of the Great Seal, to Frenchmen. Her daughter Mary, the Queen of Scots, who was aged 11, remained at the French Court.[1]

[1] Knox, *History*, i. 111, 116–17, 129, 140; Mary of Lorraine to the Cardinal of Lorraine, 3 Oct. 1552; Mary of Lorraine to Henry II and d'Oysel, 6 Oct. 1552; Mary of Hungary to Charles V, 11 and 19 Nov. and 9 Dec. 1552; Mary of Hungary to Châtelherault (Nov. 1552); Mary of Hungary to Mary of Lorraine, 23 Dec. 1552 (*Span. Cal.* x. 585–9, 585–8 n., 595–604, 608–9); d'Oysel to Mary of Lorraine, 8 Aug. 1553 (*Foreign Correspondence with Marie de Lorraine 1548–1557*, ii. 304–5); d'Oysel to

Henry II was planning to marry Mary Queen of Scots to his son, the 10-year-old Dauphin Francis. He already occasionally referred to France and Scotland as 'my two kingdoms', and was eager to obtain the consent of the Scottish Parliament to the grant of the Crown Matrimonial to the Dauphin, which would give Francis the title and powers of King of Scotland. Mary of Lorraine was eager to win the goodwill of the Scottish nobility for this project, and she began to pursue a friendly policy towards the Protestant lords. She had taken into her service young William Maitland of Lethington, the son of old Sir Richard Maitland of Lethington. Sixty-five years later, William Maitland's son, James, in his *Narrative of the Principal Acts of the Regency during the Minority of Mary Queen of Scotland*, attributed the triumph of Protestantism in Scotland to the fact that Mary of Lorraine encouraged its growth in order to win the support of the Protestant nobility for the Queen's marriage to the Dauphin and the grant of the Crown Matrimonial to Francis, and only realized the danger when it was too late to crush the movement which she had fostered. This would explain the policy that the Queen Regent was pursuing at this time. Henry II and the Guises would have no objection; for they were already working in alliance with the German Lutheran princes and subsidizing the English Protestant refugees in France, while at the same time savagely persecuting the French Protestants.[1]

There had been no change in the law or religion of Scotland. The Scottish Church, under its Primate, John Hamilton, Archbishop of St. Andrews, the brother of the Duke of Châtelherault, was slowly reacting to the decrees of the Council of Trent by passing resolutions at meetings of Provincial Councils of the Church, condemning the immoral life of the clergy, and pluralities and non-residence; but though these decrees were sent to the bishops, and duly promulgated throughout the dioceses, neither Archbishop Hamilton nor the lower clergy dismissed their concubines. Protestantism was still heresy, and punishable by death at

Noailles, 21 Feb. 1553/4, and 4 and 15 Apr. 1554 (*Ambassades de Noailles*, iii. 80–81, 156–7); Pitscottie, ii. 112–15; Leslie, *History*, ii. 347–50, 352, 354; *Acts Parl. Scot.* ii. 600–2 (12 Apr. 1554); *Diurnal of Occurrents*, p. 266; Soranzo's report to the Venetian Senate (18 Aug. 1554) (*Ven. Cal.* v. 934).

[1] Henry II to d'Aramon, 27 Sept. 1550 (Charrière, *Négociations de la France dans le Levant*, ii. 121 n.); Henry II's order to officers of the Provinces, 31 Dec. 1549 (Teulet, i. 205–6); Maitland, *Narrative of the Principal Acts of the Regency*, pp. 19–25.

the stake; but since the execution of Adam Wallace in 1550, no heretic had been put to death. In October 1554 the Queen Regent quarrelled with a great Catholic nobleman, George Gordon, Earl of Huntly. The Gordons dominated all the north of Scotland outside the barbarous Highlands; their followers declared that whoever might be king of the south, Huntly would be king of the north. When Huntly became involved in a feud with one of his neighbours and disobeyed an order of the government, Mary of Lorraine imprisoned him in Edinburgh Castle.[1]

Having alienated both the Hamiltons and the Gordons, the Queen Regent became more than ever dependent upon the goodwill of nobles and lairds whose Protestant sympathies were well known. These included Lord James Stewart, the Prior of St. Andrews and the illegitimate son of James V; John Campbell, Earl of Argyll, and his son, the Lord of Lorne; Alexander Cunningham, Earl of Glencairn, one of the greatest magnates of the south-west; and Andrew Stewart, Lord Ochiltre, of Ochiltre in Ayrshire. Other lords were sympathetic, and in the next level of Scottish society beneath the nobility the Protestants were strong. It was in the class of lairds, or country gentlemen, who were excluded from Parliament and from political power, but were very influential in their localities, that the chief Protestant strength lay, apart from the support from the merchants of Dundee and the towns of the east coast. The Protestants were also supported by a number of important government officials, like James McGill of Nether Rankeillor the Clerk of Register, David Forrest the Master of the Mint, and, more cautiously, by William Maitland of Lethington, the Secretary of State.

By 1555 it was clear that Protestantism would be unofficially tolerated in Scotland for the time being. This gave the Protestants a great opportunity to expand and consolidate their power, and spread their propaganda among the people. It also aroused hopes that Mary of Lorraine might one day become a Protestant, as other Catholic rulers, like Henry VIII, Christian III of Denmark, and Gustavus Vasa of Sweden, had done, though in view of the Queen

[1] Statutes of Provincial Councils of 27 Nov. 1549, 26 Jan. 1551/2 and 10 Mar. 1558/9–10 Apr. 1559; Archbishop Hamilton to Archbishop Beaton, 31 Jan. 1558/9; Articles proponit to the Queen Regent (Mar.–Apr. 1559) (*Statutes of the Scottish Church*, pp. 84–190); Winning, 'Church Councils in Sixteenth Century Scotland' (*Essays on the Scottish Reformation*, pp. 332–58); Leslie, *History*, ii. 355–6; Lisle and Tunstall to Henry VIII, 9 Jan. 1542/3 (*State Pap.* v. 238).

Regent's ties with France, and French influence in Scotland, this was a very optimistic hope. But the Protestants were in need of preachers and pastors. Most of the Protestant clergy had fled abroad after 1547; but William Harlaw, who had gone to England as a refugee and had become chaplain to Edward VI, returned to Scotland after Mary came to the throne, when it became safer for a Protestant to live in Scotland than in England. Knox wrote in his *History* that Harlaw, though he did not excel in erudition, was worthy of praise for his zeal and diligent plainness in doctrine. Harlaw began preaching to Protestant congregations, and was joined by John Willock, who had originally been a Black Friar and had fled to England in 1539. At Mary's accession he went to Emden, where he entered the service of the Countess of East Friesland. In 1555 the Countess sent him to Scotland as her ambassador to negotiate a trade agreement with Mary of Lorraine, and here he combined his diplomatic duties with those of a Protestant propagandist. Soon afterwards Knox himself arrived in Scotland.[1]

Knox did not wish to leave Geneva and go to Scotland. During the last few years, he had been much more concerned with the affairs of the Church of England than with Scotland, and he had prepared himself for the task of organizing his radical English congregation in Geneva after the split at Frankfort. He had not spoken Scots for more than six years, and found it easier to speak and write in English or Latin than in his native tongue. He was also perhaps shrewd enough to realize that it might be very dangerous to go to Scotland. He would be in no immediate danger, but if Mary of Lorraine changed her policy again, and decided to stamp out heresy, a Protestant preacher who had attracted attention was likely to be arrested and burnt, while the Protestant nobles disengaged and bided their time in order to fight another day. But apart from knowing where his duty lay, Knox had received letters from Mrs. Bowes, and hoped that if he went to Scotland he would be able to see Marjory and her mother. He later wrote to Mrs. Bowes that it was only because of her that he had left Geneva and returned to Scotland; but it would in any case have been impossible for him to refuse to go to Scotland at a time when so many of the French preachers in Geneva were returning to face far greater risks on missions to their congregations in

[1] Knox, *History*, i. 118. Knox calls the Countess of East Friesland the 'Duchess of Emden'.

France. If Knox had hesitated for too long about going to Scotland, Calvin would have sent him there.[1]

Knox reached Edinburgh 'in the end of the harvest', which probably means that he arrived towards the end of September 1555, as the harvest officially ended at Michaelmas. He stayed first in the house of James Syme, a Protestant merchant, where he met David Forrest the Master of the Mint, and Sir James Erskine of Dun. Dun had fought well for the Scottish government during the last war against England, but he was now one of the most active and able leaders of the Protestant party. Knox also met James Barron, an Edinburgh merchant, and his wife, Elizabeth Anderson. Elizabeth was dying of a painful disease, and her courage and Protestant enthusiasm made a deep impression on Knox. He gave her spiritual consolation during her illness, and though she had never had any Protestant religious instruction and had learned all her doctrine from friars, she turned with relief to Knox and eagerly absorbed his teaching. When the end drew near, she asked her friends to sing a Psalm, and refused to receive the Catholic priests who visited her, denouncing their doctrine of the Real Presence, and crying: 'Depart from me, ye sergeants of Satan.' The priests left, saying that she was mad.[2]

It was probably in Edinburgh, in the autumn of 1555, soon after Knox's arrival, that he met Marjory and Mrs. Bowes for the first time since he left Northumberland for the Court of Edward VI nearly three years before.[3] We do not know where the reunion took place, but Mrs. Bowes and her daughter were with Knox in Scotland during his visit of 1555–6. It is usually assumed that Knox visited them at Norham on his way to Scotland, and took them with him to Edinburgh; but it is very unlikely that Knox ventured into England in 1555. Mrs. Bowes and Marjory had probably gone to Scotland some time before. It would be surprising if they remained at Norham until the autumn of 1555, for the lady of Norham and her daughter could hardly have avoided

[1] Knox to Mrs. Bowes, 4 Nov. 1555 (Knox, *Works*, iv. 217). For Knox's knowledge of Scots, see Marjorie Bald, 'The Pioneers of Anglicised Speech in Scotland' (*S.H.R.* xxiv. 182–4).

[2] Knox, *History*, i. 118–20. Knox states that the Psalm which was sung at Elizabeth Anderson's deathbed was the 103rd Psalm; but the words which he quotes from the Psalm come from John Hopkins's version (published in 1551) of the 146th Psalm. See McMillen, *The Worship of the Scottish Reformed Church*, pp. 16–17, and Croft Dickinson's note to Knox, *History*, i. 119 n.

[3] See *infra*, App. IV.

a show-down over the question of going to mass at an earlier date than this. There is no indication in any of Knox's letters or other writings of the repentance, the spiritual agony, or the intellectual shifts which we would have expected to find if Marjory and Mrs. Bowes had given way and even once gone to mass in England in Mary's reign; and as they could hardly have avoided punishment if they had refused to attend for nearly two years after the re-establishment of the mass in December 1553, they probably took refuge in Scotland, with its Papist but inefficient government, as early as 1554. It was a brave action for two women, who were used to the comforts of upper-class life in England, to cross the frontier secretly and illegally; but if they were prepared to face the risk and hardship, it was not difficult to cross the Border unobserved. To cross into Scotland was the easiest and safest way for a Protestant refugee to leave England, though it was not a course of action which would occur, or commend itself, to Protestants in the south of England, who risked the greater dangers of the sea voyage to reach Protestant territory in Germany and Switzerland. Mrs. Bowes's Scottish friends in Knox's old congregation at Berwick could have made all the necessary arrangements; and Richard Bowes may in the end have consented to their departure and facilitated their escape. It was the least embarrassing and unpleasant solution of the difficulty from his point of view.

It was probably in Edinburgh, soon after their reunion, that Knox married Marjory. Knox already considered Marjory as his wife by virtue of their precontract, and, as there were Protestant ministers in Edinburgh who were able to marry them, there seems no reason why they should have postponed the marriage any longer, though their first child was not born until May 1557.

As soon as he arrived in Edinburgh, Knox began reorganizing and stiffening the Protestant party. The first step was to stop the Protestants from going to mass; for during the previous years the Protestant lords and gentlemen who had been pardoned, and had made their peace with the Queen Regent, had been prepared, at least occasionally, to attend mass. Knox considered that it was unpardonable to bow down to idolatry, and he strongly urged the Scottish Protestants that they must never go to mass. The matter was thoroughly discussed one evening at a supper party given by Erskine of Dun in his house in the Canongate; for Dun, like many of the Scottish lords and some of the more prominent lairds, had a town house on the outskirts of Edinburgh. Dun invited Knox to meet Willock, Robert Lockhart, and two of their influential friends in the government, Forrest and William Maitland of Lethington. Knox argued 'that no-wise it was lawful to a Christian to present himself to that idol'. He was confronted with a Scriptural text to justify attendance at mass—the passage in the twenty-first chapter of the Acts, where Paul attends a religious service in the Jewish temple to show the Jews that Christians did not teach defection from the laws of Moses. Knox replied that Paul's attendance at a Jewish synagogue could not be compared to attendance at mass, because although the Jewish ceremonies had been superseded by Christian worship, they had originally been ordained by God, whereas the mass from the very beginning had always been idolatrous. In any case, as Paul was attacked by the Jews when he went to the temple, his attendance there had had unfortunate results, which showed that his decision to attend the Jewish service had not been inspired by the Holy Ghost. Knox's arguments won over his colleagues, and Lethington declared: 'I see perfectly, that our shifts will serve nothing before God, seeing that they stand us in so small stead before man.' If Mary of Lorraine had been as savage a persecutor as Mary Tudor, these worldly-wise politicians might not have agreed with Knox's interpretation of this passage from the Acts; but in Scotland the time was obviously ripe for a gesture of open resistance. No progress could be made at this stage unless the leading Protestants refused to attend mass.[1]

Edinburgh had never been a Protestant town. In 1543 the Protestants had had much less success there than in Dundee and Ayrshire; but Knox found encouraging signs in Edinburgh, though there was still no great Protestant enthusiasm. Soon after the supper party at Dun's house, Knox said goodbye to Marjory and Mrs. Bowes and travelled north with Dun to Dun Castle, near Montrose, which, like most of the trading towns of the east coast, was a Protestant stronghold. Knox stayed at Dun Castle for a month in October and November 1555. It was a remote and lonely little fortress, though the spires of Montrose could be seen in the distance across the flat, treeless country. In winter the wolves came in the night to eat the corpses in the churchyard outside the castle walls.[2]

[1] Knox, *History*, i. 120. [2] Ibid. 121.

Dun invited the local gentry and the merchants of Montrose to the castle to hear Knox preach, and nearly every day Knox was busily engaged in spreading Protestant doctrines. The surrounding country was in a far more Protestant mood than Edinburgh, and Knox, after the years of quarrels, intrigue, and defeat at the Court of Edward VI in England and the Church of White Ladies in Frankfort, was fired by the enthusiasm which he encountered among his congregations in Angus. His letter to Mrs. Bowes of 4 November, which was almost certainly written from Dun Castle, shows his mood of excitement and hope.

Albeit my journey toward Scotland, beloved mother, was most contrarious to my own judgement, before I did enterprise the same, yet this day I praise God for them who was the cause external of my resort to these quarters; that is, I praise God in you, and for you, whom He made the instrument to draw me from the den of my own ease (you alone did draw me from the rest of quiet study) to contemplate and behold the fervent thirst of our brethren, night and day sobbing and groaning for the bread of life. If I had not seen it with my eyes in my own country, I could not have believed it. I praised God when I was with you, perceiving that in the midst of Sodom God had more Lots than one, and more faithful daughters than two. But the fervency here doth far exceed all others that I have seen; and therefore ye shall patiently bear, although I spend here yet some days; for depart I cannot, unto such time as God quench their thirst a little. . . . Be assured that God stirs up more friends than we be ware of. . . . In great haste, the 4 of November 1555. Your son, John Knox.

The phrase 'in great haste' became a common form of ending for Knox in his letters during the next few years.[1]

After a month at Dun Castle, Knox returned to the south, and stayed with Sir James Sandilands of Calder in his house in the village which is now called Mid Calder in Midlothian, some 15 miles west of Edinburgh. Here he was visited by three powerful noblemen, Lord Erskine, who later became Earl of Mar; the Lord of Lorne, the son of the Earl of Argyll, who later became the fifth Earl; and Lord James Stewart, the Prior of St. Andrews. Two of these three visitors afterwards became regents of Scotland; they were already invaluable converts to the Protestant cause. They were so favourably impressed by Knox's doctrine that they said that he should preach it in public; but the Protestants were not

[1] Ibid. 121; Knox to Mrs. Bowes, 4 Nov. 1555 (*Works*, iv. 217–18).

yet strong enough to venture to hold services in churches or at great open-air rallies, and there was no attempt to break into parish churches as Wishart had done. The men who were organizing the Protestant party were experienced politicians who understood the art of winning political power, and were careful not to act prematurely. They held their prayer-meetings in the private houses of the gentry, and invited small congregations of influential local leaders rather than mass audiences; but they cautiously ventured to draw in wider circles as well. In December, Knox made frequent visits to Edinburgh, and preached there to many small congregations of merchants, but still only in private houses. He was beginning to make some progress in Edinburgh, though it lagged behind the most zealous Protestant strongholds.

After Christmas two gentlemen of Ayrshire, John Lockhart of Barr and Robert Campbell of Kinzeancleuch, came to Knox at Calder Hall and escorted him to the west, where he spent the rest of the winter preaching to the Protestants of Kyle and Carrick. He stayed in the houses of the Ayrshire gentlemen, in Barr's house at Barr in the deep valley at the foot of Polmaddie in the south, with Robert Campbell of Kinzeancleuch in the castle of the Kinzeancleuch above a gorge over the River Ayr near Mauchline, with Sir Hugh Wallace at Carnell near Kilmarnock, and with Sir James Chalmers at Gadgirth on the River Ayr. He stayed in the fishing port of Ayr, probably in a merchant's house. He also stayed at Ochiltre with Lord Ochiltre, and perhaps met for the first time Lord Ochiltre's daughter, Margaret Stewart of Ochiltre, who became his second wife, though at this time she was a child of 9 or 10. In one of his letters to Mrs. Bowes, which was probably written at this time from Ayrshire, he told her of the success of his work, using the metaphor of the blowing of the trumpet to describe his propaganda activities. 'The trumpet blew the old sound three days together', he wrote, 'till private houses of indifferent largeness could not contain the voice of it. . . . Oh sweet were the death that should follow such forty days in Edinburgh as here I have had three. Rejoice, mother, the time of our deliverance approacheth. . . . In haste, this Monday, your son John Knox.' Apart from preaching, Knox celebrated the communion in many of the houses where he stayed in Ayrshire.[1]

The authorities were now fully alive to what was happening,

[1] Knox, *History*, i. 121; Knox to Mrs. Bowes (1556) (*Works*, iv. 218).

but they were not sure of the identity of the preacher who was causing all the trouble in the west. According to the information that reached Knox, some of the officials at Court assumed that the preacher was an Englishman. This was doubtless because Knox used so many English words in his sermons, and preached in a language which was more like English than Scots. Knox referred to this two years later in his letter to Mary of Lorraine. 'When reasoning was before your Grace, what man it was that preached in Ayr, and divers men were of divers opinion, some affirming that it was an Englishman, and some supposing the contrary, a prelate, not of the least pride, said: "Nay, no Englishman, but it is Knox that knave." It was my Lord's pleasure so to baptize a poor man; the reason whereof, if it should be required, his rochet and mitre must stand for authority.'[1]

It was probably during Lent, while he was in the west, that Knox preached his sermon on the fourth chapter of Matthew, which he later put down in writing and circulated among his friends, though he never published it. When he returned to Geneva, he took the manuscript with him, and took the risk of sending it to his friend Mrs. Anne Locke in England. After Knox's death, Anne Locke lent the manuscript to the English Puritan, John Field. Field published it in London in 1583, without the consent of Anne Locke, who maintained that Knox had intended it to be read only by his personal friends. In this treatise, Knox argued that there was no scriptural authority for the practice of fasting in Lent. The story, in the fourth chapter of Matthew, of Christ's forty days' fast in the wilderness was always cited as the authority for Lent, but Knox argued that there was no justification for interpreting this passage as a commandment to us to follow Christ's example. If this was indeed the meaning of the passage, then we ought to eat nothing at all for forty days; but in fact Christ no more expected us to follow Him in this than in walking on the water. Knox's *Answers to some Questions concerning Baptism*, in which he criticized certain ceremonies adopted in baptism in the Catholic Church and the Church of England, may also have been written during his visit to Scotland. Knox said that Protestants must refuse to permit their children to be baptized by Catholic priests, but that those who had been polluted in their infancy with a Papist christening did not need to be

[1] Knox, *Letter to the Queen Regent* (1558 edn.) (*Works*, iv. 439).

baptized again by Protestant pastors, as the spirit of regeneration given by Christ 'hath purged us from that poison which we drank in the days of our blindness'. He took the opportunity to state that the people had no longer any obligation to pay tithes to the Church; for the proud prelates and filthy clergy neglected the poor, and spent the money which was paid to them on their own bellies. Knox's *Answers to some Questions concerning Baptism* was never published, but was doubtless circulated among his supporters.[1]

In March, Knox left Ayrshire and went to Finlayston in Renfrewshire, the residence of the Earl of Glencairn in the modern village of Longbank on the south side of the Clyde estuary. Glencairn was the most powerful and determined of all the Protestant supporters at this time; unlike most of the nobles who supported the Protestants, he was sincerely and passionately devoted to the cause, independently of any calculations of self-interest or politics. At Finlayston, Knox celebrated the communion and administered the sacrament to Glencairn and his family and several of his friends. He then returned to Calder, where he preached and administered the communion, not only to Sandilands and his household, but to people from the surrounding country. The sites of most of the houses which Knox visited in 1555–6 are now covered by large mansions erected in the eighteenth or late seventeenth centuries to replace or incorporate the smaller and simpler turrets in which Knox stayed; but the history of these houses is enriched by legends relating to Knox's visit, and nearly all these legends are connected with his celebration of communion—the room at Calder Hall, in which he is said to have celebrated the first public Protestant communion in Scotland; the silver chalice in the possession of the Cunningham family, which was stolen in the nineteenth century;[2] the great yew tree in the garden at Finlayston under which he celebrated the communion. It is quite impossible today to say whether these legends are true or false. Oral traditions may be accurate, or may have no basis at all in fact. The evidence

[1] Knox, *An Exposition upon the 4th of Matthew*; and see Field's Dedicatory Epistle to Anne Prouze (Anne Locke), 1 Jan. 1583; Knox, *Answers to some questions concerning Baptism* (*Works*, iv. 89–114, 119–28; see pp. 91, 99, 120). For Anne Locke, now Mrs. Anne Prouze of Exeter, see Collinson, 'The authorship of *A Brieff Discours of the Troubles Begonne at Franckford*' (*Journal of Eccl. History*, ix. 200).

[2] See John Knox, minister of Slamannon, to the Earl of Buchan, 28 Jan. 1779 (*H.M.C. 15th R.* 500–1); McMillen, *The Worship of the Scottish Reformed Church*, p. 28 n.

is quite insufficient to justify us in accepting them as true, but there is no reason why we should reject them as fictitious.

Whether true or false, these traditions illustrate the importance which was rightly attributed at the time, and since, to Knox's celebration of the communion. At first, when Knox celebrated the communion in the houses where he stayed in Kyle, only his host and his family and household were present; but at Calder, after Easter, the villagers of the surrounding country were invited to partake of communion in the house. In April, Knox paid a second visit to Dun Castle, and here the majority of the gentlemen of Angus attended his celebration of the communion. This new communion service, at which everyone sat together with the minister around a table, and which was so unlike the mass, was not only a symbol of unity among the congregation; it was the method by which Knox was forming the first national political party in modern history. When substantial numbers of people in Midlothian, and the majority of the gentlemen of Angus, went to the house of a local laird to receive the communion from Knox instead of going to mass in the parish church as the law prescribed, the safety of the State was being undermined.[1]

The Catholic Church thought that the time had come to act. They summoned Knox to appear before the Archbishop of St. Andrews and a special commission in the Church of the Black Friars in Edinburgh on 15 May 1556, to answer a charge of heresy. This was the moment of crisis for Knox and for the Protestant movement in Scotland. Scottish Protestants did not usually attend their trial when summoned on a charge of heresy; but Knox announced that he would comply with the summons, and Dun and other Protestant gentlemen prepared to escort him to Edinburgh and accompany him to the trial. When lairds came to Edinburgh to escort a friend or tenant to his trial, they did not come alone or unarmed, and the government faced the prospect of armed clashes in the streets and in the Black Friars' Church. Then on 9 May, six days before the date set for the hearing, the bishops quashed the order for the trial, and withdrew the summons against Knox. There was apparently some technical irregularity in the form of the summons, which was the official excuse for quashing the proceedings; but the real reason was that Mary of Lorraine intervened and ordered the bishops not to proceed against Knox.

[1] Knox, *History*, i. 121–2.

Someone had persuaded her to avoid the danger of violence in Edinburgh, and to continue her policy of winning the support of the Protestant nobles, by preventing the bishops from sending Knox to the stake.[1]

If the summons against Knox had not been withdrawn, it is unlikely that the Protestants would have put the matter to the test by attending his trial in force. In that case, from all that we know of Knox and the conduct of other Scottish Protestants when summoned on a charge of heresy, it is very unlikely that Knox would have appeared in the Black Friars' Church to face his trial. But as soon as they heard that the proceedings had been abandoned, the Protestants came to Edinburgh, encouraged by their opponents' weakness and determined to take advantage of the situation. On 15 May, the day on which Knox's trial was to have taken place, they moved into the palace of the Bishop of Dunkeld on the north side of the High Street, and Knox preached there to the largest congregation that he had ever addressed in Edinburgh. It was the first time since 1547 that the Protestants had ventured on an open demonstration of strength, and the interest and excitement which had been aroused by the prosecution of Knox and its ignominious conclusion was no doubt responsible for the size of the congregation. Encouraged by this success, Knox preached in the Bishop of Dunkeld's house at all hours every day for the next ten days. After this triumphant ten days' propaganda campaign, Protestantism for the first time really took root in Edinburgh. The Protestants never lost the ground that they gained there in May 1556.

One day during these ten days, Knox preached in Edinburgh, late on a summer evening, to a congregation which included the Earl Marischal, the hereditary Earl Marshal of Scotland. Glencairn had persuaded him to come to hear Knox preach. Marischal was favourably impressed by Knox's doctrine, and after the sermon he and Glencairn urged Knox to write a letter to the Queen Regent, inviting her to become a Protestant. The idea that Knox should write the letter probably emanated from Glencairn, and was an obvious step to take at this stage, when Mary of Lorraine was showing favour to the Protestants. The Protestant party was now gaining in influence so rapidly that Mary of Lorraine would eventually be obliged to take drastic action one way or the other, and either become a Protestant, or at least grant the Protestants

[1] Knox, *History*, i. 122; Knox, *Letter to the Queen Regent* (1556 edn.) (*Works*, iv. 77).

legal toleration and official recognition, or else suppress the movement by force. The Protestants' real object was perhaps to use Knox's letter for propaganda purposes, as the letter was soon afterwards printed as a pamphlet, together with the text of the sermon against the mass which Knox had delivered at Newcastle in April 1550.[1]

It was a recognition of the position which Knox had now attained in the Scottish Protestant movement that he was chosen to write, in his own name, this appeal to the Queen Regent from the Protestants. He, a man of humble birth, who had been a slave in the French galleys, and had held positions of honour only in England, had been chosen by a proud and ferocious nobility, who usually respected nothing except superior armed force, to be their spokesman in an approach to their ruler. He discharged the duty with considerable ability. A very different approach and style was required for such a letter than might have been expected from the author of the *Admonition to England*; but though Knox's style fell far short of the fulsome adulation with which English churchmen addressed a princess, he wrote to Mary of Lorraine in terms of proper respect.

He began by denying that he was a heretic, and thanking Mary of Lorraine for having intervened to save him from the bishops. 'I have looked rather for the sentence of death', he wrote, 'than to have written to your Grace in these last and manifest wicked days. . . . But blessed be God, the Father of our Lord Jesus Christ, who by the dew of His heavenly grace hath so quenched the fire of displeasure in your Grace's heart (which of late days I have understood) that Satan is frustrate of his enterprise and purpose.' He told her that she would be rewarded if she continued 'in like moderation and clemency towards others that most unjustly are and shall be accused, as that your Grace hath begun towards me and my most desperate matter'.

Knox then proceeded to utter a stern warning to the Queen Regent, though it was still couched in terms of deep respect.

Superfluous and foolish it shall appear to many that I, a man of base estate and condition, dare enterprise to admonish a princess so honourable,

[1] Knox, *History*, i. 122. The first edition of Knox's letter to the Queen Regent contains no date or place of publication. A slightly fuller version of the letter is contained in the manuscript volume of 1603 (see *infra*, App. IV). The letter is reprinted in *Works*, iv. 73–84.

endowed with wisdom and graces singularly. But when I consider the honour that God commandeth to be given to magistrates, which no doubt, if it be true honour, containeth in itself in lawful things obedience, and in all things love and reverence; when further I consider the troublesome estate of Christ Jesus' true religion, this day oppressed by blindness of men; and last, the multitude of flatterers, and the rare number of them that boldly and plainly dare speak the naked verity in presence of their princes, and principally in the cause of Christ Jesus. . . . I am compelled to say: Unless in your regiment and using of power your Grace be found different from the multitude of princes and head rulers, that this pre-eminence wherein ye are placed shall be your dejection to torment and pain everlasting. This proposition is sore; but alas, it is so true, that if I should conceal and hide it from your Grace, I committed no less treason against your Grace than I did if I saw you by imprudency take a cup which I knew to be poisoned or envenomed, and yet would not admonish you to abstain from drinking of the same. The religion which this day men defend by fire and sword is a cup envenomed, of which whosoever drinketh (except, by true repentance, he after drink of the water of life) drinketh therewith damnation and death.

Knox's letter to Mary of Lorraine shows the flexibility of his tactics, and his readiness to use all available means to obtain his religious objective. Two years before, he had shocked even his friends by his fearless attack on a princess and his renunciation of the doctrine of the duty of obedience to rulers; but he was nevertheless ready, if the opportunity presented itself, to urge another princess to use her royal authority to promulgate the Reformation against the wishes of her subjects, because, as he told her, 'ever from the beginning the multitude hath declined from God'. But Knox assured the Queen Regent that he understood the difficulties of her position, and stated that he would be satisfied if, as a first step, she granted religious toleration to the Protestants.

I am not ignorant how dangerous a thing it appeareth to the natural man to innovate anything in matters of religion. And partly, I consider that your Grace's power is not so free as a public reformation perchance would require. . . . Albeit suddenly ye may not do all things that ye would, yet shall ye not cease to do what ye may. Your Grace cannot hastily abolish all superstition, neither yet remove from offices unprofitable pastors which only feed themselves, the which to public reformation are requisite and necessary; but yet, if the zeal of God's glory be fervent in your Grace's heart, by wicked laws ye will not maintain manifest idolatry, neither yet will ye suffer the fury of bishops to murder and devour the poor members of Christ's body.[1]

The letter was handed to the Queen Regent personally by the Earl of Glencairn. A day or two later, Mary of Lorraine, having read it, gave it to James Beaton, the Archbishop of Glasgow, saying to him mockingly: 'Please you, my Lord, to read a pasquil' —a pasquil being the name given in Rome to lampoons and satires. Knox refers to the Queen Regent's remark, not only in his *History*, but in a second letter which he wrote to Mary of Lorraine herself in 1558; he was probably told about it by Lethington or Forrest, or some other courtier who was in touch with the Protestants. It was foolish of Mary of Lorraine to ridicule Knox. Knox was never a laughable figure, and Knox backed by Glencairn, Argyll, Lord James, and Ochiltre, and the Protestant lairds, deserved to be taken very seriously. But for the time being Mary of Lorraine had nothing to fear from Knox, for six weeks after he wrote his letter to her, he left Scotland and returned to Geneva.[2]

Knox's decision to leave Scotland in 1556, at a time when the Protestants, under his leadership, seemed to be advancing from one success to another, is not easy to explain, and appears at first sight to be less excusable than his flight from England in 1554. But the position was potentially very dangerous for Knox. The bishops would obviously revive the heresy proceedings against him as soon as the Queen Regent permitted them to do so; and Knox, with his usual political perspicacity, may have realized that it was inevitable that the Queen Regent would soon abandon her pro-Protestant policy. He probably thought that this change of policy was imminent, though here he made an error in his timing, as it did not occur for nearly two years. He evidently misjudged the political situation, and expected the reaction to set in sooner, and more drastically, than it did. But fear of death cannot have been the only reason for his departure. If Knox had merely been afraid of being burnt, the time to leave would have been two months earlier at the beginning of May, when he had been summoned to answer a charge of heresy.

Knox himself stated, in his *History*, that he left Scotland because his congregation in Geneva wrote to him and asked him to return

[1] Knox, *Letter to the Queen Regent* (1556 edn.) (*Works*, iv. 77–79, 82–83).

[2] Knox, *History*, i. 123; Knox, *Letter to the Queen Regent* (1558 edn.) (*Works*, iv. 457).

to them, and that he felt that it was his duty to obey their summons. He was no doubt tempted by the prospect of settling down at last to life with his wife in safety in Geneva, which he once called 'the den of my own ease'; but he had a duty, as well as a personal inclination, to return. The men who had supported him in Frankfort, and also some of his most prominent opponents there, had left Frankfort and travelled more than 300 miles to Geneva in order to demonstrate their support for him and join his congregation, only to find that he had left Geneva a few weeks before they arrived. If he stayed away too long, they might fall away from the congregation in Geneva, and adhere to other factions in Frankfort or Strasbourg. Knox was involved in the struggles of the English Church in exile, as well as with the Protestant Church in Scotland; and before we condemn him for deserting his post, we should remember that Knox was not only the father of the Scottish Reformation, but also one of the founders of English Puritanism.[1]

There was also, perhaps, another factor involved. In April 1558 Knox wrote a letter from Geneva to some women members of the Protestant party in Edinburgh in which he explained the reasons why he had hesitated to return to Scotland for a second time in the previous year.

> My God most justly hath permitted Satan to put in my mind such cogitations as did impede my journey toward you at this present, and they were these: I heard such troubles as appeared in that realm, I began to dispute with myself as followeth: Shall Christ, the author of peace, concord and quietness, be preached where war is proclaimed, sedition engendered, and tumults appear to rise? Shall not His Evangel be accused, as the cause of all calamity which is like to follow? What comfort canst thou have to see the one-half of the people rise up against the other; yea, to jeopard the one, to murder and destroy the other?[2]

This is perhaps the real explanation of Knox's reluctance to remain in Scotland and to return there; it explains his decision to return to Geneva in 1556, and his dilatoriness in setting out for Scotland in the summer of 1557 and November 1558. Geneva was not only the den of Knox's ease; it was also a place where Protestants engaged in quiet religious worship and theological discussion, and not, as in Scotland, in a ruthless struggle for power.

[1] Knox, *History*, i. 123; Knox to Mrs. Bowes, 4 Nov. 1555 (*Works*, iv. 217).
[2] Knox to the 'sisters in Edinburgh', 16 Apr. 1558 (*Works*, iv. 251).

Knox was attracted by the excitement of political struggle, but he was conscious of the consequences that might result. He did not mention this in his *History*, when he explained why he returned to Geneva; but the *History* was written long after Knox had suppressed all his former doubts about the probity of the Scottish Protestant movement. Did his powers of prophecy, in which he and his followers so firmly believed, enable Knox to foresee in 1556 the lies and trickery, the frame-ups and double-crossings, the murders and hangings that would be perpetrated in Scotland on behalf of Protestantism during the next seventeen years? If so, it was not one of the examples to which his followers chose to refer in order to prove that he was a prophet.

Knox sent Marjory and Mrs. Bowes to Dieppe, perhaps as early as the beginning of May, when the situation in Edinburgh seemed to be dangerous; but he did not go with them. Robert Campbell of Kinzeancleuch persuaded him to stay a little longer, and Knox left Edinburgh and went to Castle Campbell, the residence of the Earl of Argyll, high on the mountain side above Dollar in Clackmannanshire. He preached for several days at Castle Campbell, on one occasion, according to local tradition, standing on the sloping ground on the south side of the castle as he preached at an open-air prayer-meeting, looking out over the valley for thirty miles to the Pentland Hills. Then he left Scotland, although Colin Campbell of Glenorchy, who had heard him preach at Castle Campbell, tried to persuade him to stay; but he offered to return whenever he was summoned to come by the Protestant leaders.[1]

Before Knox left Scotland, he drew up detailed instructions as to how the Protestants' services and religious teaching should be carried on in his absence. These instructions, which are dated 7 July 1556, were printed, and published under the title *A Letter of Wholesome Counsel addressed to his Brethren in Scotland*.[2] This was intended to be a handbook of procedure for the guidance of

[1] Knox, *History*, i. 123–4. The local tradition at Castle Campbell is that Knox preached standing on the pulpit-shaped rock above the gorge on the south side of the castle, which is impossible, as it would mean that his audience must have stood in the gorge far below; but he may well have preached standing higher up, immediately beneath the south wall of the castle.

[2] It was first published, probably in 1556, together with Knox's *Exposition of the Sixth Psalm*, in a volume which contains no date or place of publication. It was reprinted, again in one volume with the *Exposition of the Sixth Psalm*, in London in 1580, and again reprinted in *Works*, iv. 133–40.

Protestant pastors and lairds as to how to ensure the thorough indoctrination of their servants, tenants, and supporters. Knox said that the Protestants ought to read some part of the Bible every day, and though he realized that even God's elect would sometimes get bored with the Bible if they read it every day, they should remember their brethren who lived in such bondage and thraldom that they were prohibited from reading the Bible at all. 'If such men', he wrote, 'as having liberty to read and exercise themselves in God's holy Scriptures, and yet begin to weary, because from time to time they read but one thing, I ask, why weary they not also every day to eat bread? Every day to drink wine? Every day to behold the brightness of the sun?'

But it was not enough for lairds and householders to read the Bible themselves. It was their duty to ensure that their families, servants and tenants did the same, for 'within your own houses, I say, in some cases, ye are bishops and kings; your wife, children, servants and family are your bishopric and charge'. They should assemble for common prayers at least once a day, and for Bible reading once a week; it was essential that they should meet as a united, organized group, and not as scattered individuals. He directed that these weekly Bible classes should begin with the members of the congregation making a public confession of their private sins to their brethren, and with a prayer invoking the help of Christ. Then they should read the Bible aloud, paying special attention to the Prophets and the Epistles, and reading one chapter from the Old Testament and one from the New, for 'it shall confirm you in these dangerous and perilous days to behold the face of Christ Jesus, His loving spouse and Church, from Abel to Himself, and from Himself to this day, in all ages to be one'. The proceedings were to end 'with thanksgiving and common prayers for princes, rulers and magistrates, for the liberty and free passage of Christ's Evangel, for the comfort and deliverance of our afflicted brethren in all places now persecuted, but most cruelly within the realm of France and England'.

The most important part of the proceedings, however, was to be the discussion which followed the reading aloud of the passage from Scripture. 'If any brother have exhortation, question or doubt, let him not fear to speak or move the same, so that he do it with moderation, either to edify or to be edified.' This would have two advantages: first, it would ensure that the whole of the

Bible was thoroughly understood; and secondly, it would enable the group to find out which of the brethren had the gifts of patience and modesty, and ability in public speaking; for

multiplication of words, prolixet interpretations and wilfulness in reasoning is to be avoided at all times and in all places, but chiefly in the congregation, where nothing ought to be respected except the glory of God, and comfort or edification of brethren. If anything occur within the text, or else arise in reasoning, which your judgement cannot resolve or capacities apprehend, let the same be noted and put in writing before ye dismiss the congregation, that when God shall offer unto you any interpreter, your doubts, being noted and known, may have the more expedite resolution.

If no one could resolve the difficulty, they should write to someone whose opinion they respected, and ask him to interpret the passage for them. Knox stated that he himself would prefer to spend fifteen hours in interpreting some passage of Scripture for any Bible-reading group who might write to him, rather than spend half an hour on anything else. Within a few years Knox and his colleagues in Geneva would provide the brethren with answers in advance to many of the questions—in the form of the extensive marginal notes in the Geneva Bible.[1]

Thirty years before, when Tyndale had first dreamed of translating the Bible into English, he had hoped that his translation would make every ploughboy as knowledgeable in Scripture as the most learned clerk. But Bible reading in Scotland, as organized by Knox, was leading to a result which would have appalled Tyndale. It was transforming the Protestant lords, lairds, merchants, artisans, and husbandmen into brethren of a revolutionary party. The servants and tenants still respected and obeyed their laird as they had always done; but after discussing Scripture with him once a week, they came to regard him also as the local leader of the brethren, who had put his power and armed strength at the service of God and the congregation. When Henry VIII permitted his subjects to read the Bible, he had emphasized that every man was to read it quietly to himself, and no one was permitted to read it aloud to others, or argue as to the meaning of the text, under threat of punishment. But Knox insisted that the Bible should be read aloud to the Protestants of the district assembled in a group;

[1] Knox, *Letter of Wholesome Counsel to his Brethren in Scotland* (*Works*, iv. 135–9).

and on this occasion he used no threats. 'If thus (or better) I shall hear that ye exercise yourselves, dear brethren, then will I praise God for your great obedience. . . . And because that I cannot suspect that ye will do the contrary at this present, I will use no threatenings, for my good hope is that ye shall walk as the sons of light in the midst of this wicked generation.'[1]

[1] Foxe, v. 117; Proclamation against arguing on Scripture (June 1539) (Strype, *Eccl. Mem.* i [ii]. 434–7); Knox, *Letter of Wholesome Counsel to his Brethren in Scotland* (*Works*, iv. 139).

CHAPTER XIII

The Letters from Dieppe

IN the middle of July 1556, Knox sailed from Scotland to Dieppe. Hardly had he left the country when the bishops again issued a summons for him to appear before them in Edinburgh on a charge of heresy. They made no attempt to serve the notice on him abroad, and as he did not come on the appointed day, they condemned him as a heretic in his absence. An effigy of Knox was thereupon publicly burned at the Cross of Edinburgh. Presumably Archbishop Hamilton and the bishops believed that by this procedure they could vindicate the authority of the canon law and the ecclesiastical courts without arousing the resistance of the Protestant lords and without being restrained by the Queen Regent. In fact, it only brought their authority into contempt. It gave Knox something of the halo of martyrdom without any of the disadvantages, and emphasized the impotence of the Church, which could do nothing against Knox as long as he was in Scotland, and could inflict punishment only on his effigy.[1]

At Dieppe, Knox rejoined Marjory and Mrs. Bowes. He stayed in Dieppe for a few weeks, and from here, on 8 August, he wrote a letter to a Protestant woman in Edinburgh. He warned her to resist temptation, above all the temptation to obey wicked magistrates in things unlawful, and urged her to remember that idolatry was even worse than adultery, because it was a transgression against the first of the Commandments. Knox signed this letter 'John Sinclair', and used this pseudonym in several letters that he wrote to Scotland after he left the country in 1556. According to the transcriber of Knox's letters in 1603, 'this was his mother's surname, which he wrote in time of trouble'. For some reason,

[1] Knox, *History*, i. 124; Knox, *Letter to the Queen Regent* (1558 edn.); Knox, *Appellation to the Nobility and Estates of Scotland* (*Works*, iv. 431, 468); see also Archibald Hamilton, *De Confusione Calvinianae sectae apud Scotos*, p. 61 n.; Davidson, 'Ane Breif Commendatioun of Uprichtnes', line 140 (in Rogers, 'Three Poets of the Scottish Reformation', *Trans. R.H.S.* iii. 250); Calderwood, i. 318.

although Knox used this false name in most of the letters that he wrote to Scotland after July 1556, he never used a pseudonym in any of the surviving letters that he wrote to his friends in England during Mary's reign, although the danger to Protestants was much greater, and conspiratorial methods were more necessary, in England than in Scotland; and it is not easy to see why he used a false name in some of his letters to Scotland, and not in others.[1]

From Dieppe, Knox went on to Geneva with Marjory and Mrs. Bowes. Here he found a thriving and united English congregation, which had been established there for nearly a year, having been granted in October 1555 the joint use, together with the Italian refugees, of the church of Notre-Dame-la-Neuve, which today is known as the Auditory. Since then the congregation had grown to over a hundred, and included many prominent leaders of the English refugees, though some of the more famous leaders did not stay long in Geneva, but came, and then went to other centres. Lever, who had come to Geneva from Frankfort, had already left for Wesel by the time that Knox returned from Scotland; but Whittingham, William Williams, Goodman, Gilby, Kethe, and Sampson were still there with their families; and Scory had come from Emden, and Pilkington from Basel. Both Scory and Sampson left Geneva after only a short stay. The congregation also included Thomas Cole, John Bodley and his 11-year-old son Thomas, who later founded the Bodleian Library at Oxford, Thomas Bertram, who had been a Protestant parson in Jersey, and old Harridaunce, who had been punished by Cranmer in the reign of Henry VIII for standing on a tub in his garden in Whitechapel and preaching without a licence to the passers-by in the street. There were a few Scottish refugees in Geneva, who were included in the English congregation, among them Sir John Borthwick, who had escaped from Scotland in 1540 when summoned to attend his trial for heresy before James V. Some of these men were able to maintain themselves, and assist their brethren, with money from the rents of their properties in England, which, despite the efforts of Mary's government to prevent it, were smuggled to them by sympathizers at home. Others took employment in Geneva as weavers, tailors, and tanners. By the end of

[1] Knox to a Protestant woman in Edinburgh, 8 Aug. 1556; Marginal note, by the transcriber of Knox's letters in 1603, to Letter XXXV (*Works*, iv. 223–4, 245).

1558, the number of people, including women and children, in the English congregation had risen to 184.[1]

When Knox reached Geneva, he was formally admitted as a member of the English congregation on 13 September 1556, together with his wife, his mother-in-law, his servant, James, and his pupil, Patrick, who had probably accompanied him from Scotland. It had always been intended, when the English Church was founded, that Knox should be one of their ministers as soon as he returned from Scotland, and when Goodman and Gilby were elected as the first ministers of the Church in November 1555, it was expressly provided that they had been chosen 'in the absence of John Knox'; but when Knox returned to Geneva, he did not take office until the annual elections in December. On 16 December 1556, Knox and Goodman were elected as ministers for the next twelve months, with Gilby, Williams, Whittingham, and William Fuller as seniors.[2]

This time Knox stayed in Geneva for a year, and was at last able to settle down to married life and study. In the summer his first child was born, a son, who was christened Nathaniel in the English church on 23 May 1557, with Whittingham as godfather. It was a quiet time, for there were no splits and doctrinal quarrels to disrupt the English congregation, and no arguments over the order of service. When the congregation was first formed in October 1555, they had agreed to adopt the order of service which had been drafted at Frankfort by Knox, Whittingham, Gilby, Foxe, and Cole, but which had been abandoned under the compromise reached with Lever, and never used in Frankfort. In February 1556 both the English text and a Latin translation were printed in Geneva by the printer Jean Crespin, under the title *The Form of Prayers and Ministration of the Sacraments, etc., used in the English Congregation at Geneva and approved by the Famous and Godly Learned Man John Calvin.* The book and the order of service were referred to among the English congregation as the Order of Geneva, although the native churches in Geneva used Calvin's *La Forme*, until after the Reformation in Scotland it became known as the Book of Common Order of the Church of Scotland.[3]

[1] *Livre des Anglois*; Martin, *Les Protestants Anglais réfugiés à Genève au temps de Calvin*, pp. 45, 47, 58–59, 65, 67–73.

[2] *Livre des Anglois*, p. 12.

[3] *Livre des Anglois*, p. 14. For the Order of Geneva, see Maxwell, *John Knox's Genevan Service Book*, where the history and significance of Calvin's *La Forme* is

The little republic of Geneva had become the haven of refuge for persecuted Protestants, and would soon become a centre from which missionaries would be sent out to foreign countries to foment ideological revolution. A modern historian has called Geneva a sixteenth-century Moscow;[1] but it was never one of the great powers of Europe, and could not rely on its own military strength for its defence. Its position was very precarious. The people of Geneva lived in constant fear of attack from the Duke of Savoy, who had not abandoned hope of recovering his authority over Geneva, and rumours of a united attempt by the Catholic sovereigns of Europe to crush the centre of Calvinism were always in the air. But as year after year went by, and the attack did not come—it took place, in a half-hearted manner, only in 1602—the Protestants became convinced that the hand of God alone had saved them from their enemies. This divine intervention took the form, as the Protestants themselves fully realized, of creating an irreconcilable split between the great Catholic powers. In the last resort, it was the protection of the Papist King of France that saved Geneva from invasion by the Emperor's ally, the Duke of Savoy. The conflict between France and the Empire, who had been almost continually at war for more than forty years, not only saved Geneva, but was responsible for the triumph of Protestantism in northern Europe. Cardinal Pole was very conscious of this, and considered that his most important task was the creation of a united front of the Catholic sovereigns against heresy. The Protestants, on the other hand, considered that Pole's efforts to secure peace in Christendom was the greatest menace which confronted them.[2]

After many months of patient negotiation, Pole succeeded in arranging a conference in May 1555 at Marcq, on neutral English territory near Calais, between representatives of France and the Emperor, with the English attending as neutrals in order to reconcile the belligerents. The most brilliant statesmen of Catholic

also examined. The text of the Order of Geneva is given in Knox, *Works*, iv. 157–214. The original edition printed by Crespin is dated 10 Feb. 1556. This is 1555/6, not 1556/7 as has been suggested, for in Geneva at this time the year began on 1 Jan.

[1] V. H. H. Green, *Renaissance and Reformation*, p. 176.

[2] Granvelle to Manrique de Lara, 24 Apr. 1554; Renard to Charles V, 9 July 1554; Pole to Charles V, 19 Jan. 1555; anonymous tract by an Italian Protestant (July 1555) (*Span. Cal.* xii. 226, 307–8; xiii. 143, 227); Pole to Paul IV (Mar. 1557); Surian to the Doge and Senate of Venice, 2 July 1557 (*Epistolarum Reginaldi Poli*, v. 22–25; *Ven. Cal.* v. 849, 952).

Europe were gathered together in the tent at Marcq—Cardinal Granvelle and his colleagues for the Emperor; the Cardinal of Lorraine and the Constable Montmorency for France; and Gardiner and Pole for England. But they were quite unable to achieve the unity which was so vital to all their interests. When the delegates met, Gardiner cynically declared that he could draft the first article of the peace treaty at once, a declaration that the Emperor and the King of France were united in their determination to resist the Turk and to crush heresy in Christendom, and that while he was doing this, the other delegates could get down to hard bargaining about Milan and the other articles of the treaty. After ten days the French broke off the negotiations, for they had heard that Cardinal Caraffa, their nominee, had been elected Pope. In the words of the Emperor's ambassador in Rome, the cardinals had continued in conclave until, from sheer exhaustion, they had elected a devil who would do no good to anyone.[1]

In February 1556, when both sides were short of money, a five-year truce was suddenly agreed between France and Philip II, who had succeeded his father Charles V as ruler of Spain and the Netherlands. It was a bad day for the Reformation. Henry II congratulated the English ambassador on the burning of Cranmer, and showed a willingness to extradite the English refugees in France; but war soon broke out again, with much greater bitterness and savagery than before, and by August, Philip's troops were marching on Rome and sacking the towns in the Papal States. The Pope began to excommunicate Philip and deprived Pole of his office of Legate in England; but Mary prohibited the Papal envoy from setting foot in her realm, and insisted that Pole should continue in his office. In the summer of 1557, England declared war on France, whereupon Scotland declared war on England. The situation, as Pole wrote to the Pope, was one from which only the heretics could derive any satisfaction.[2]

Meanwhile the persecution was raging in England. The English refugees in Geneva were in close touch with events in England,

[1] Lara to Charles V, 15 May 1555; Granvelle, etc. to Charles V, 23, 27, and 30 May, and 8 June 1555; King Philip to Joanna of Portugal, 29 May 1555 (*Span. Cal.* xiii. 188, 194, 200–2, 211).

[2] Truce of Vaucelles, 6 Feb. 1556; Lalaing to Philip II, 11 Apr. 1556 (*Span. Cal.* xiii. 260, 266); Noailles to Henry II, 7 May 1556 (*Ambassades de Noailles*, v. 353–4); Michiel to the Doge and Senate of Venice, 5 May 1556; Pole to Cardinal Morone, 21 Dec. 1556; Pole to (Archbishop Sauli), 25 May 1557 (*Ven. Cal.* vi. 477, 772, 900).

and heard with mounting anxiety the news of the burning of their friends and respected leaders. After Rogers, Saunders, and Hooper, and the first martyrs of February 1555, Ferrar the Bishop of St. Davids, and Bradford, had been burnt during the summer of 1555; Ridley and Latimer followed in the autumn, and Cranmer next spring. The scale of the persecution far surpassed anything which had been hitherto known in England, for over 280 Protestants were burnt between February 1555 and November 1558. At Basel, John Foxe was compiling his *Book of Martyrs* from the information which he received from England, and Knox was doing the same in Geneva, either from information obtained from Foxe, or from his own contacts in England.[1]

In December 1557 John Rough, Knox's colleague in St. Andrews Castle, fell a victim to the persecution. Rough had taken refuge in England when St. Andrews Castle fell, and at Mary's accession he fled to Emden, where he and his wife maintained themselves by knitting garments and engaging in the wool trade. In the autumn of 1557 he travelled to England, in connexion with his business, and, contacting the Protestants in London, accepted an invitation to preach at a secret prayer-meeting in the 'Saracen's Head' at Islington; but an informer told the authorities, who surrounded the inn and arrested Rough and all the congregation. Rough was burned at Smithfield. Even in exile the refugees were not safe from Mary. Sir John Cheke was arrested by Philip II's officers while travelling through the Netherlands, and extradited to England, where he only escaped the fire by making a humiliating public recantation which was a cause of shame to him and the English refugees abroad.[2]

Knox was particularly anxious about two of his old acquaintances in London, Mrs. Anne Locke and Mrs. Hickman. Anne Locke, who had been born Anne Vaughan, was the wife of Henry Locke, a London mercer who lived near Bow Church in Cheapside; and Mrs. Hickman was the wife of another London merchant. Knox had been very friendly with both women when he had lived in London, and they had heard many of his private

[1] See Knox's list of the names of the martyrs (*Works*, v. 523–36).

[2] Foxe, viii. 444–9. For the activities of Mary's agents among the English refugees abroad, see Mary I to Wotton, 29 May 1554; Wotton to Petre, 19 June and 13 July 1556 and 21 Jan. 1556/7 (*Cal. For. Pap. Mary*, Nos. 212, 509, 519, 571); Brett's report to Archbishop Heath (1556) in I. S. Leadam, 'A Narrative of the Pursuit of English Refugees in Germany under Queen Mary' (*Trans. R.H.S.* (N.S.), xi. 113–31).

confidences. He told them that they had treated him like a mother treats a son, though it is strange that Knox should have said this about his relationship with Mrs. Locke, as she cannot have been more than 25 in 1552, and was therefore nearly fifteen years younger than Knox. Anne Locke was a very gifted and enterprising woman, who translated into English Calvin's *Sermons upon the Song that Ezechias made after he had been sick and afflicted by the Hand of God*, and John Taffin's book *Of the Marks of the Children of God*.

In the autumn of 1556, Knox wrote to Mrs. Locke at least three times, sending the letters by merchants who were travelling to the market at Frankfort, to tell her of the anxiety that he felt for her safety. He advised Anne Locke and Mrs. Hickman to come to Geneva if they could. In a letter addressed to the two women jointly, he stated that he wished that all who unfeignedly loved God would come to Geneva, and strongly urged them both to leave England lest they be tempted to bow to idolatry. He did not attempt to hide from them the hardship of a life of exile, but, on the contrary, stressed it, thinking perhaps that this was the best way to persuade them that there was nothing shameful in fleeing from England.

In another letter, which was not addressed to Mrs. Hickman but was written to Anne Locke alone, he gave more personal reasons why he wished her to come to Geneva:

> Ye writ that your desire is earnest to see me. Dear sister, if I should express the thirst and languor which I have had for your presence, I should appear to pass measure. . . . Sometimes I sobbed, fearing what should become of you. . . . I weep and rejoice in remembrance of you; but that would evanish by the comfort of your presence, which I assure you is so dear to me, that if the charge of this little flock here, gathered together in Christ's name, did not impede me, my presence should prevent my letter.

Anne Locke followed Knox's advice, and travelled to Geneva with her children. Some modern writers have suggested that Mrs. Locke, like Mrs. Bowes, abandoned her husband in order to join Knox; but Henry Locke was a Protestant, and though he felt unable to leave England himself, he obviously had no objection to the departure of his wife and family. When Anne Locke returned to England after Elizabeth became Queen, she lived with her husband until his death, and Knox and Locke remained on friendly terms.[1]

Anne Locke arrived in Geneva in May 1557, with her infant son—who was the future poet, Henry Locke—her infant daughter, and her servant. Four days after she arrived, her daughter died. Knox did not choose to interpret this as a divine punishment inflicted upon Anne Locke for coming to Geneva. At least, there is no record that he ever asked her, as he asked Mary of Lorraine, to consider why God had taken her children from her.[2]

Anne Locke continued to correspond with Knox after they left Geneva in 1559, when he went to Scotland and she to England, though there is no record that they ever met again. After Locke died in 1571, Anne married Edward Dering, the brilliant young Cambridge divine, who must have been younger than Anne; and Anne may have been partly responsible for the fact that Dering, about this time, became a fearless Puritan critic of the established Church, and was involved in serious troubles with the authorities after he criticized the Queen in a sermon in her presence. After Dering's early death in 1576, Anne married the Exeter merchant Prouze, who served on three occasions as Mayor of Exeter. In 1590 Anne Prouze was still translating the books of foreign Protestant writers, and supplementing them with notes and dedicatory epistles that show traces of Knox's spirit.[3]

In May 1557 James Syme and James Barron arrived in Geneva, bringing Knox a letter from Glencairn, the Lord of Lorne, Erskine of Dun, and Lord James, inviting him to return to Scotland. They told him that the faithful whom he had left behind him would not only be glad to hear his doctrine, but would be ready, when the time arrived, to 'jeopard lives and goods in the forward-setting of the glory of God'. They wrote that although the Queen Regent was no more Protestant than she had been when Knox had left, she was showing hostility to the friars and was not persecuting Protestants.[4]

[1] Knox to Anne Locke and Mrs. Hickman (1556); Knox to Anne Locke, 19 Nov. and 9 Dec. 1556, and 4 Feb. 1559/60 (*Works*, iv. 219–22, 237–41; vi. 108).

[2] *Livre des Anglois*, p. 9; Knox, *Letter to the Queen Regent* (1558 edn.) (*Works*, iv. 453).

[3] See Collinson, 'The authorship of *A Brieff Discours of the Troubles Begonne at Franckford*' (*Journal of Eccl. History*, ix. 200); Anne Prouze's translation of John Taffin's *Of the markes of the children of God*, and her Dedicatory Epistle to the Countess of Warwick, in the 1st edn. of 1590 and the 2nd edn. of 1608.

[4] Glencairn, Lorne, Erskine of Dun, and Lord James to Knox, 10 Mar. 1556/7 (Knox, *History*, i. 132).

Knox was as usual reluctant to leave Geneva. He consulted his English congregation as to what he should do, and also discussed the matter with Calvin and other ministers; but they all agreed, as Knox puts it in his *History*, 'that he could not refuse that vocation, unless he would declare himself rebellious unto his God and unmerciful to his country'. Knox thereupon told Syme and Barron that he would visit Scotland 'with reasonable expedition' as soon as he had made the necessary arrangements for the care of his congregation in Geneva in his absence, and they returned to Scotland with his answer. Knox remained in Geneva for the whole of the summer, and did not leave for Scotland until more than four months later, at the end of September. Apart from the needs of his congregation in Geneva, he had other reasons for wishing to postpone his departure, though he does not mention this in his *History*. In April 1558, in his letter to the 'sisters in Edinburgh', he confessed that he delayed his departure because he did not wish to provide the occasion for the outbreak of civil war, until he realized that the same argument could have been used to deter the Apostles from preaching the doctrines of Christ. He may also have postponed his departure because of personal reasons, for his son Nathaniel had just been born when the letter from Scotland reached him.[1]

Knox reached Dieppe on 24 October, intending to take the first ship to Scotland. But here he found a letter waiting for him from a Protestant in Scotland, who informed him that new discussions were taking place among the Scottish Protestant leaders as to whether it was desirable that he should come to Scotland; the writer therefore urged him to wait at Dieppe for the time being until the Scottish Protestants had decided on their future course of action. Knox was also shown a second letter, which a Scottish Protestant gentleman had written to an acquaintance in Dieppe, asking him to tell Knox about the hesitations of the Protestants in Scotland and their unwillingness to take any action. The Queen Regent's negotiations for the marriage of the Queen of Scots to the Dauphin had reached a critical stage, and there were prospects of large bribes being available for any Scottish lord who supported the project; while the Duke of Châtelherault and the Hamiltons were doing all they could to thwart the marriage, as the Duke was

[1] Knox, *History*, i. 132–3; Knox to the 'sisters in Edinburgh' 16 Apr. 1558 (*Works*, iv. 251); *Livre des Anglois*, p. 14.

the heir to the throne of Scotland if the Queen of Scots died childless. The majority of the nobles, including those sympathetic to the Reformation, must have felt that the chances of making a successful bargain would be impaired if they were to arrange another preaching campaign for Knox at this time, and the more single-minded Protestants, like Glencairn and Erskine of Dun, thought it inadvisable to proceed without the goodwill of the nobility.

Knox was surprised and annoyed when he heard this news. On 27 October he wrote a letter of protest to Glencairn, Dun, the Lord of Lorne, and Lord James, who had sent him the invitation in the previous March. 'To some it may appear a small and light matter', he wrote, 'that I have cast off, and as it were abandoned, as well my particular care as my public office and charge, leaving my house and poor family destitute of all head, save God only, and committing that small (but to Christ dearly beloved) flock, over the which I was appointed one of the ministers, to the charge of another.' Knox's annoyance is understandable; for it was no light matter, in the sixteenth century, to travel the 800 miles from Geneva to Dieppe and back again for no valid reason, and there was always a risk that Knox would be arrested as a heretic whenever he travelled through France. But it was not because of his personal inconvenience, or any hardship to his family and congregation in Geneva, that he was most disturbed. He was primarily worried over the lack of resolution shown by the Scottish nobility.

In a few lines, at the end of a long letter, Knox put forward a political doctrine which had never before been expressly formulated, and which would have outraged Tyndale and all Protestant believers in the duty of Christian obedience. He stated that it was the duty of the nobility to compel the prince to introduce the Reformation. He did not clearly say by what means, whether physical or moral, this compulsion should be applied, but he compared it to the action that Moses had taken against Pharaoh.

> No less cause have ye to enter in your former enterprise, than Moses had to go to the presence of Pharaoh; for your subjects, yea, your brethren are oppressed, their bodies and souls held in bondage; and God speaketh to your consciences (unless ye be dead with the blind world) that you ought to hazard your own lives (be it against kings or emperors) for their deliverance. For only for that cause are ye called

princes of the people, and ye receive of your brethren honour, tribute, and homage at God's commandment; not by reason of your birth and progeny (as the most part of men falsely do suppose), but by reason of your office and duty, which is to vindicate and deliver your subjects and brethren from all violence and oppression, to the uttermost of your power. . . . The reformation of religion, and of public enormities, doth appertain to more than to the clergy, or chief rulers called kings.

The phrase 'chief rulers called kings' is significant. Instead of referring, with awe, to 'the prince', Knox compares 'chief rulers called kings' with other rulers, the nobility, whose duty it is to act when the chief ruler fails to do so.

In his letter Knox warned the nobles that, apart from the religious question, they were, by their inaction, permitting Scotland to be enslaved by the French. He particularly criticized them for supporting the war against England. In the war between the two Catholic power blocs, the Protestants were neutral, hoping that the war would be prolonged, and advocating defeatism in both England and Scotland. While Goodman, in his writings, was urging Englishmen to refuse to fight in a war at the behest of their Spanish masters, Knox urged the nobility of Scotland not to support a war against England in the interests of France. 'Ye have betrayed (in conscience I can except none that bear the name of nobility), and presently do fight to betray . . . your realm to the slavery of strangers. The war begun (although I acknowledge it to be the work of God) shall be your destruction, unless that, betime, remedy be provided.'[1]

As far as the war was concerned, the Scottish nobles provided the remedy. Before Knox's letter reached Scotland, Mary of Lorraine assembled an army, and sent it to Maxwellheugh, near Kelso, under the command of d'Oysel. When d'Oysel ordered them to cross the Border and attack Wark Castle, the lords mutinied and refused to march. Lethington's son states that when Lethington, as Secretary, informed the lords of the Queen Regent's order to cross the Border, they drew their daggers and would have killed him, had it not been for the fact that Lethington was personally known and liked by many of them.[2] Unlike his successor Riccio, Lethington had always been respectful and friendly towards the

[1] Knox to Glencairn, Lorne, Erskine of Dun, and Lord James, 27 Oct. 1557 (Knox, *History*, i. 133–6).

[2] Knox, *History*, i. 124–5; Leslie, *History*, ii. 371–2; Pitscottie, ii. 119–20; *Diurnal of Occurrents*, p. 267; Maitland, *Narrative of the Principal Acts of the Regency*, p. 11.

nobility. It was a wise precaution to adopt when dealing with lords whose first reaction, when given unwelcome orders from their sovereign, was to draw their daggers on the Secretary.

The Protestant lords then decided to take the final step in organizing themselves into a political party. They drew up a document, which was called the Common Band, or Covenant, and asked their supporters all over Scotland to sign it. The first to sign the covenant were Argyll, Glencairn, the Earl of Morton, the Lord of Lorne, and Erskine of Dun, who signed it in Edinburgh on 3 December 1557. Morton, who was the son of Sir George Douglas, had hitherto remained cautiously aloof from the Protestants, despite his family's association with the pro-English party in the days of Henry VIII. The signatories pledged themselves to defend the Evangel of Christ and His congregation from the rage of Satan and Antichrist with their whole power, substance, and very lives; to have faithful ministers purely and truly to minister Christ's Evangel and sacraments to His people; and to forsake and remove the congregation of Satan and all its superstitions, abominations, and idolatry. But no one in Scotland wrote to Knox in Dieppe to invite him to return; they did not even reply to his letter of 27 October.[1]

The Covenant was a formidable weapon in the hands of the Protestant lords for putting pressure on the Queen Regent; but they had no intention of rising in revolt against her, and wished to retain their liberty of manœuvre. It was easier to do this in Knox's absence. They were also perhaps offended by the tone of his letter, with its strictures on the nobles, and his assertion that they were not worthy of honour merely on the grounds of their birth and progeny; at any rate, they knew that a man who could write in this way might easily offend the other nobles if he came to Scotland. As for Knox's exhortation to them to undertake the reformation of public enormities if their sovereign did not do so, the Scottish nobles did not need Knox to tell them this; they had been exercising the right to coerce the king for over a hundred years, whenever Scotland had an infant king and was governed by a Regent.

[1] Knox, *Letter to his Brethren in Scotland*, 1 Dec. 1557 (*Works*, iv. 261). For the text of the Covenant, see Knox, *History*, i. 136–7; and see Hay Fleming, *The Reformation in Scotland*, pp. 278–80, for the date at which the various copies were signed. See also Donaldson, *Scotland: James V to James VII*, p. 89.

This thought must have occurred to Knox while he waited in vain in Dieppe for an answer from Scotland. As the news reached him in France of the mutiny at Maxwellheugh and the signing of the Covenant, he began to fear that the Protestant movement was being utilized by the lords for purely selfish ends. Four years before, Bullinger had warned him that when nobles rose against their king under the guise of defending the true religion, they might be using the religious issue in order to attract the support of honest men, although their real motives were worldly and evil. This warning had probably been reinforced more recently by Calvin; for Calvin strongly condemned any idea of furthering religion by revolt.

On 17 December 1557 Knox wrote from Dieppe to the Protestant lords in Scotland, and warned them that they would be committing a sin if, under the excuse of furthering religion, they rose in rebellion against their sovereign for reasons of ambition or for any secular motive. This letter must have come as a surprise to the lords after Knox's letter of 27 October, when he had condemned their vacillation and urged them to act to compel the Queen Regent to reform religion. Once again Knox was influenced, as he had been when he left Scotland and hesitated to return there, by the fear of civil war and his suspicions of the motives of the Protestant lords. Perhaps he was unconsciously affected by personal jealousy, and tried to hold the Scottish Protestant movement in check because it seemed as if it was going ahead without his participation and leaving him behind. But he was chiefly influenced by his fear that the Duke of Châtelherault was becoming associated with the movement, and that the congregation would be used as an instrument to further the dynastic ambitions of the Hamiltons, and Châtelherault's personal feud with Mary of Lorraine.

I will only advertise you [wrote Knox to the Protestant lords] of such bruit as I hear in these parts uncertainly noised, which is this, that contradiction and rebellion is made to the authority by some in that realm. In which point my conscience will not suffer me to keep back from you my counsel, yea, my judgement and commandment, which I communicate with you in God's fear and by the assurance of His truth; which is, that none of you that seek to promote the glory of Christ do suddenly disobey or displease the established authority in things lawful; neither yet, that ye assist or fortify such as for their own particular cause and worldly promotion would trouble the same. But in the bowels of Christ Jesus, I exhort you that with all simplicity and lawful obedience, joined with boldness in God and with open confession of your faith, ye seek the favours of the authority, that by it (if possible be) the cause in which ye labour may be promoted, or at the least not persecuted; which thing, after all humble request if ye cannot attain, then with open and solemn protestation of your obedience to be given to the authority in all things not plainly repugning to God, ye lawfully may attempt the extremity, which is, to provide, whether the authority will consent or no, that Christ's Evangel may be truly preached, and His holy sacraments rightly ministered unto you, and to your brethren, the subjects of that realm. And further, ye lawfully may, yea, and thereto is bound, to defend your brethren from persecution and tyranny, be it against princes or emperors, to the uttermost of your power, providing always, as I have said, that neither yourself deny lawful obedience, neither yet that ye assist nor promote those that seek authority and pre-eminence of worldly glory, yea, of the oppression and destruction of others; I mean of him who in the beginning of his authority and government began to profess Christ's truth, but suddenly sliding back, became a cruel persecutor of Christ's members, a manifest and open oppressor of all true subjects.

This was a reference to Châtelherault. Knox said that Châtelherault and his brother, the Archbishop of St. Andrews, would shortly be suppressed in God's last judgement for having shed the blood of Wishart, Adam Wallace, and other martyrs. He warned them to avoid all confederacy with Châtelherault.

Knox then hastened to assure the lords that nothing that he had written in this letter was intended to weaken their opposition to the war. 'That now I persuade you to give lawful obedience to the authority is nothing repugnant to that which I wrote before, touching the war begun; for a great difference there is betwixt lawful obedience and a fearful flattering of princes, or an unjust accomplishment of their desires in things which be required or devised for the destruction of a commonwealth.'[1]

This letter shows the hesitations and doubts which assailed Knox as he developed his revolutionary doctrines. Having reached, by 1554, the position that he put forward in his *Admonition to England*, he advanced a stage further with his letter to the lords of 27 October 1557. He then began to write his *First Blast of*

[1] Knox, 'To the Lords and others professing the truth in Scotland' (*Works*, iv. 276–86; the passages cited are on pp. 284–6).

the Trumpet against the Monstrous Regiment of Women, in which he openly called for revolution; but on 17 December came this second letter to the lords, reminding them that it was a sin to rise against the prince. After publishing the *First Blast of the Trumpet* in the following spring, he writes a few weeks later, on 16 April 1558, to the women in Edinburgh: 'Shall Christ, the author of peace, concord and quietness, be preached where war is proclaimed, sedition engendered, and tumults appear to rise?' But he rejects this argument when he remembers that if the Apostles had heeded it, they would never have propagated the Gospel. He followed this with his *Appellations to the Nobility and Commonalty of Scotland* in July, in which he finally reached the end of the road and called on the common people themselves to revolt.[1]

It is not surprising that Knox had doubts as he formulated his theory of the justification of revolution. The remarkable thing is that he continued to adhere to it, in view of the firmness with which Tyndale's doctrine was entrenched in the minds of his colleagues. He must have been under great pressure to abandon his position, not only from the leaders of the Church of England in exile, with whom he disagreed on many things, but from Calvin, whom he admired so deeply; but he never really retreated. Even in the letter to the lords of 17 December 1557, his hesitation is more apparent than real. His exhortation to the lords to obey their prince is so qualified by a permission to resist, not only for religion but also on the purely political issue of the war against England, that it seems to be little more than the payment of lip-service to the universally accepted principle of Christian obedience. There is a striking difference between the language of Knox's letter to the Scottish lords and Calvin's letter to Admiral Coligny. Calvin told Coligny that if the French Protestants resisted Henry II by force, this would be a sin that would bring disgrace on Protestantism. 'Better that we should all perish a hundred times than that we should cause the name of Christianity and the Gospel to be exposed to such shame.'[2] Knox took his ideas of Church organization and moral discipline from Calvin, but differed from him completely on the question of resistance to authority.

Knox wrote another letter from Dieppe to the Protestants in Scotland. In this letter, which is dated 1 December 1557, he

[1] *Works*, iii. 263–330; iv. 251, 365–420, 467–538.

[2] Calvin to Coligny (16 Apr. 1561) (*Calvini Op.* xviii. 426).

condemned the dissolute life that was led by certain Protestants. Not only had the Papists used this to discredit Protestantism, but, even more serious, it had caused some Protestants to split off from the Protestant congregations and form their own. Knox knew that the chief reason for the growth of Protestantism in Scotland and elsewhere had been the popular disgust with the corruptions and immorality of the Catholic Church, and it was alarming to find that some of the brethren, after abandoning Popery for this reason, were now likewise turning away from the Protestants on the same grounds. He blamed these people as perfectionists, who did not realize that there would inevitably be bad men in every organization, and he criticized them for applying a double standard to the Protestant congregations and other bodies. They made two mistakes. In the first place:

they do judge and pronounce of the doctrine and religion by the lives of the professors. Secondly, they require a greater purity and justice (denying any true Church to be where vices are known) than ever was found in any congregation since the beginning. Of which two errors must needs follow most horrible absurdities. . . . Amongst the Turks, the common multitude do live a more strait life in many things than God's Word does require; yea, and some of them, as concerning their external behaviour, may be judged irreprehensible. But what folly were it to prove and allow therefore their damnable doctrine and false religion; and on the other part, what age shall we find, from Abraham to Moses, from Moses to David, and from David to Christ, in which iniquity did not abound, yea, even in the household of God.

Knox argued that no one should separate himself from the true Church of Christ merely because some individual members of the Church did not lead a moral life. This was exactly the same argument that Scottish Catholics like Ninian Winzet and Quintin Kennedy, and reputable Catholic propagandists everywhere, were putting forward in order to persuade their members not to leave the Catholic Church and join the Protestants. Knox was well aware of this. 'But here do such as will join themselves to no congregation, except with that which is perfect in all things, object to us: But ye have left the assembly of Papists, and have gathered yourselves in companies apart.' The answer was that the Protestants had broken with the Catholic Church, not only because of the evil lives of the Catholics, but because its doctrines were blasphemous—because Christ's sacraments and ordinances were 'polluted and profaned by the vain inventions of men'. The only justification for leaving the Protestant Church would be if they could prove that the Protestants were also guilty of this, which they would never be able to do.

Knox followed with a strong attack on Arianism and Pelagianism and other Anabaptist heresies which asserted free will, justification by works and not by faith, or which denied the doctrine of the Trinity or the divinity of Christ. Like other revolutionary leaders, Knox, to use a modern phrase, was afraid of being 'outflanked on the Left', and he stated that these Anabaptists were more dangerous than Papists:

> For the venom and malice of Satan reigneth in all Papists (for the most part) is now more evident, even to infants, than that it can greatly hurt any, except such as willingly, and with appetite insatiable, do drink the poison of that harlot's cup, either for fear of corporal punishment or also for hope of worldly promotion. But in the other sort . . . the craft and malice of the Devil fighting against Christ is yet more covert, and therefore it is more dangerous and more to be feared; for under the colour and cloak of mortification of the flesh, of godly life, and of Christian justice, they are become privy blasphemers of Christ Jesus.

The brethren in Scotland must be on guard against them, and 'suffer no man without trial and examination to take upon him the office of a preacher, neither to travel amongst the simple sheep of Christ Jesus, assembling them in privy conventions'. Knox was determined that no Protestant preacher should be permitted to assemble the people in 'privy conventions' except the members of his own organization.[1]

While Knox was in Dieppe, he became involved in an agitation which had deeply stirred the French Protestant movement. It was the case of the martyrs of the Rue Saint-Jacques in Paris. In France the persecution of Protestants was spasmodic, but when it occurred it was more cruel than anywhere else in Europe. In Scotland and the Netherlands, the martyrs were often strangled at the stake before being burnt. In England, where they were burnt alive, they were usually permitted to hang a bag of gunpowder around their necks, which would explode when the flames touched it and end their torments. In France only heretics who recanted

[1] Knox, 'To his Brethren in Scotland', 1 Dec. 1557 (*Works*, iv. 261–75; the passages cited are on pp. 263–4, 267–71).

were granted the privilege of being merely burnt alive on an ordinary fire. Those who refused to recant were sentenced to be tortured first, and their tongues were cut out before they were taken to the stake to prevent them from addressing the spectators. Sometimes they were sentenced to be burnt suspended over a slow fire.

Fortunately for the Protestants, the persecution was carried out by three separate agencies who quarrelled with each other. The bishop's courts persecuted and sentenced heretics, as they did in all other Catholic countries; but the provincial *Parlements*, which were judicial bodies composed of laymen, mostly lawyers, also claimed the right to proceed against heretics; and Henry II had recently set up a centralized persecuting organization, the French Inquisition, or *Chambre Ardente*. These three bodies accused each other of trespassing on their jurisdictions, and were continually frustrating the activities of their fellow-persecutors. The Protestants in France were much less likely to be arrested and burnt than the Protestants in England, though they could never be sure when the authorities would strike.

In Paris there was the additional danger, which existed nowhere else in Europe, of the spontaneous action of the Catholic populace. The Parisians were fervently Catholic, and if the government was lax in persecuting Protestants in Paris, the people took the law into their own hands and lynched the heretics. But Protestantism was spreading in France. In the autumn of 1557 the Protestants for the first time became active in Dieppe, the preacher being supplied, as in most other towns in France, from the ranks of the French refugees in Geneva. At the end of August, little Jean Venable hobbled into Dieppe from Geneva, carrying a satchel strapped on his back. The satchel contained heretical books, which he secretly distributed among the people at Dieppe. His activities were directed by La Jonchée, the pastor at Rouen, who had also been sent from Geneva.[1]

The case of the martyrs of the Rue Saint-Jacques arose out of war hysteria, in the panic that followed the capture of Saint-Quentin by King Philip and his Spanish and English troops at the

[1] Daval, 'Mémoire . . . de ce qui s'est passé de plus mémorable pour le fait de la religion en l'Esglise de Dieppe' (*Histoire de la Réformation à Dieppe*, i. 7–8); Asseline, *Les Antiquitez et Chroniques de la Ville de Dieppe*, i. 272–3; Desmarquets, *Mémoires chronologiques pour servir à l'histoire de Dieppe*, i. 139.

end of August 1557. A few days after the news reached Paris, a congregation of some 400 Protestants assembled at night in an empty house in the Rue Saint-Jacques in Paris. When the news of the prayer-meeting spread among the Paris crowds, the mob attacked the house. Some of the Protestants were gentlemen, who carried arms, and were able to shoot and cut their way through the mob, and escape; but many were seized and hauled off to prison, including several aristocratic young ladies, who were spat at and manhandled by the mob. The story spread that the Protestants had used the house not for a prayer-meeting, but for a sexual orgy.

The prisoners were put on trial for heresy, and sentenced to be burnt; but the Protestants throughout France, and abroad, started an agitation for a reprieve. The government of Geneva and other Swiss cantons petitioned Henry II, without effect. On 27 September, two of the men were burnt, and Philippa de Luns, the beautiful young widow of the Seigneur de Graveron, was strangled at the stake after her face and feet had been scorched, the full sentence having been commuted by the King. Two more men were burnt on 3 October, one of whom was an inhabitant of Normandy who had attended the service in the Rue Saint-Jacques when he happened to be passing through Paris. Then Henry II reprieved the others, and commuted their sentences to imprisonment at the intercession of the Elector Palatine. Many of them recanted, and were released.[1]

The French Protestants wrote a pamphlet about the case, and while Knox was in Dieppe he decided to produce an English translation. One of his friends translated the pamphlet, and Knox himself wrote a preface and an epilogue, and made a few short additions to the original French text. For some reason, the English edition of the *Apology for the Protestants holden in Prison at Paris* was never published; perhaps it was considered inadvisable to do so after the death sentence on the survivors had been commuted.

Knox's manuscript, which is dated, from Dieppe, 7 December 1557, was written in a white-heat of indignation at the sufferings of his French brethren. He wrote that compared to the blind cruelty of princes today, the rage and tyranny of Nero himself had

[1] Des Gallars, *Histoire Ecclésiastique des Églises Réformées au Royaume de France*, pp. 139–57; Crespin, *Histoire des Martyrs*, pp. 872–80; and see Des Gallars to Calvin, 7 Sept. 1557 (*Calvini Op.* xvi. 602–3).

some face of justice and mercy; for Nero and his judges at least allowed Paul to speak in his own defence. But now

> the cause of innocents cannot be heard, but as sheep, without crime committed, they are led to the butcher; yea (which passeth all cruelty) the tongues of such as no man was ever able to convict of blasphemy against God or of injury spoken against their neighbours are commanded to be cut out, to the end that the people shall not hear them speak; the Devil and his servants in that declaring themselves more to fear the tongue of the sufferers than our brethren the sufferers do the torments and the fire. . . . Those slaves of Satan the doctors of Sorbonne and their adherents are so confounded by the wisdom of God, proceeding even from the mouths of women and children, that they dare not suffer their tongues to speak.

Knox indignantly repudiated the slander that the Protestants had assembled in the Rue Saint-Jacques to satisfy the lusts of the flesh. This rumour was not started 'by the rude and ignorant people, but a Cardinal (whose hypocrisy nevertheless is not able to cover his own filthiness) ashamed not openly at his table to affirm that most impudent and manifest lie'. This was a reference to the Cardinal of Lorraine, who, it was said, had tried to persuade the King to refuse to commute the death sentence on the prisoners. Knox also included a veiled reference to Diane de Poitiers, Duchess of Valentinois, the mistress of Henry II, who was the most powerful figure at the Court. 'But now, alas, in the Courts of those that will be called Most Christian Kings . . . who now are admitted to accuse most godly and most chaste ladies? Infamous women, yea, most horrible harlots; yea, some of them also being of the Privy Council.'

Knox took the opportunity, in his Preface, to refer to the problem that was now continually in his mind, the duty of obedience and resistance to princes. He stated that although for forty years the Protestants had been condemned as heretics, the true reason why rulers persecuted them was because they considered that Protestantism was a subversive and seditious movement. This was proved, he said, by the fact that Catholic rulers were prepared at times to tolerate heretics, and to make alliances with the Lutherans and the Turks. This truth is more clearly understood by modern historians than by most of Knox's contemporaries. Knox denied that Protestantism was seditious. Who had been the seditious trouble-makers at the house in the Rue Saint-Jacques—the

Protestants quietly worshipping in a private house, or the armed Catholic mob in the street who attacked the peaceful worshippers? The Protestants, he claimed, had always upheld the honour of princes, and had insisted that all men, including popes and cardinals, as well as the common people, must obey emperors, kings, and princes. Knox was much more reticent about the right and duty of subjects to resist idolatrous rulers than he had been in his *Admonition to England* and his letters to the Scottish Protestants; in fact, the opinions which he expressed in his *Apology for the Protestants holden in Prison at Paris* were on the whole well adapted to fit in with the French Protestants' line, that they were protecting the King from the evil advice and treason of the Cardinal of Lorraine. But Knox ventured to say that Protestants should resign from the service of Catholic kings. 'The regiment of princes is this day come to that heap of iniquity, that no godly man can brook office or authority under them; but in so doing, he shall be compelled not only against equity and justice to oppress the poor, but also expressedly to fight against God and His ordinance, either in maintaining of idolatry, or else in persecuting God's chosen children.'[1]

After staying in Dieppe for two months—two months that were very productive of ideas and literary output—Knox abandoned hope of receiving an invitation to visit Scotland; but before returning to Geneva, he visited La Rochelle. La Rochelle was the chief port, after Bordeaux, of south-western France, and did a busy trade carrying the red wine of the district to Scotland. It was also the chief port of departure for the longer and more adventurous journeys to the Canary Islands and America, and more and more ships sailed out into the Atlantic bound for Rio de Janeiro, where the French had established a small colony under the command of Villegaignon. Protestantism had begun to spread in La Rochelle, despite the attempts of the Bishop of Saintes to suppress it; and the fortitude of two of the burghers of the town who had been burnt for heresy had created a deep impression. In 1557 Richer, a Protestant pastor, returned from Rio de Janeiro, where Villegaignon was persecuting heretics, and began holding

[1] Knox, *An apology for the Protestants who are holden in Prison at Paris* (*Works*, iv. 297–347; the passages cited are on pp. 298–300, 323–5, 327, 340). No copy of the original French treatise is in existence, and Knox's translation exists only in the manuscript volume of 1603. For the French Protestants' line against the Cardinal of Lorraine, see *Epistre envoiee au Tigre de la France* (*Le Tigre de 1560*, pp. 37–38, 42).

secret prayer-meetings at night in private houses in La Rochelle. La Rochelle was under the authority of the King's Lieutenant in Guienne, Antoine de Bourbon, King of Navarre, whose wife, Jeanne d'Albret, Queen of Navarre, had always been a secret Protestant; but Antoine de Bourbon, who was a complete opportunist in religion, had not declared himself a Protestant, or done anything to check the activity of the Grand Vicar of the Bishop of Saintes in La Rochelle.[1]

We know nothing about Knox's visit to La Rochelle except a short passage in John Row's *History*. Row was the son of Knox's friend, John Row, who played an important part in Scotland immediately after the Reformation of 1560; and the younger John Row, writing his *History* in about 1640, recorded an incident that he had been told as a child by a man who was present in La Rochelle with Knox. The visit must have taken place at the end of January or beginning of February 1558. Knox was invited to preach at a service held in a private house in La Rochelle, at which he also baptized a child who had been carried many miles in order to be baptized by him. The father of the child was probably a Scottish resident in La Rochelle. One of the people who attended the service was the Scotsman who gave the information to John Row. He and a friend were invited to attend by a lady of noble rank, although they were both Catholics at the time. Knox said in his sermon that although he could now only preach in private, he hoped to preach the same doctrine publicly in St. Giles's Church in Edinburgh within two or three years. Row relates that although at the time these Scottish Catholics thought that Knox's prophecy was absurd, they were later converted to Protestantism when they encountered a terrible storm at sea on their way home to Scotland, and made a vow that if God preserved them safely they would become Protestants. They survived to hear Knox preach in St. Giles's after 1559.[2]

But Protestant doctrines were publicly preached in La Rochelle before they were publicly preached again in Edinburgh. Before Knox left La Rochelle, or very soon after his departure, the King and Queen of Navarre arrived in the town on their way from Nérac to the Court in Paris. They were accompanied by David and Boisnormant, two Protestant pastors who had returned to France

[1] Larousse, *Grand Dictionnaire Universel du XIXe Siècle*, x. 207.
[2] Row, *History of the Kirk of Scotland*, pp. 8–9.

from Geneva to join the King of Navarre's household and attempt to convert him. Antoine de Bourbon and Jeanne d'Albret attended mass while they were in La Rochelle, but they allowed David to preach in the great church of St. Bartholomew, where he delivered the first public Protestant sermon that had ever been preached in La Rochelle.[1] A few years later, during the civil war, the Bourbons converted La Rochelle into the greatest Protestant stronghold in France.

On his way back to Geneva, Knox passed through Lyons, which was also a flourishing trading town with a growing Protestant congregation. From Lyons, Knox wrote to his old friend in Edinburgh, Janet Adamson, the wife of Sir James McGill of Rankeillor Nether, the Clerk of Register, who was a Protestant and a friend of Knox. 'Your husband is dear to me,' Knox wrote to Janet, 'for that he is a man endued with some good gifts, but more dear for that he is your husband.' Janet had complained of McGill's marital coldness towards her, but Knox, though he had consulted Calvin about the case, could offer her no remedy but sympathy and prayers, and told her clearly that it was her duty to stay with her husband.

> Dear sister, the Prophets of God are oft impeded to pray for such as carnally they love unfeignedly. This I write, not that any such thing I find as yet within myself, but that I would advertise you that I dare promise nothing whereof the performance is not within my own power. If God will have you exercised under that kind of cross which is most bitter, to wit, to have your head appointed to you by God for your comfort, to be your enemy, with patience ye must abide His merciful deliverance, determining with yourself never to obey manifest iniquity for the pleasure of any mortal man.

Every Catholic priest and Protestant pastor would have agreed with Knox that it was the duty of Janet Adamson to continue living with an unkind husband; but at the same time that Knox was giving her this advice, he was giving shelter to Mrs. Bowes after she had left her husband. The fact that McGill was a Protestant and Richard Bowes a Catholic, and that Mrs. Bowes had left Norham for reasons of religion, made the two cases in no way comparable.[2]

[1] Barbot, *Histoire de La Rochelle depuis l'An 1199 jusques en 1575*, ii. 130–3.

[2] Knox to Janet Adamson (1557) (*Works*, iv. 245). Although McCrie, and several of Knox's recent biographers, have stated that Mrs. Bowes did not leave Norham

Knox returned to Geneva before the end of the winter, and remained there for nearly a year. During his absence, he and Goodman had been re-elected on 16 December 1557 as the ministers of the English congregation for the next year; but his pastoral duties left him time for writing. He wrote no less than six books and pamphlets in 1558. One of these created a greater uproar than anything that had been published in Europe since Luther's three great treatises.

and join Knox in Geneva until after her husband's death, there is no doubt that this is wrong; for Mrs. Bowes arrived in Geneva with Knox and Marjory on 13 Sept. 1556 (*Livre des Anglois*, p. 12); and Richard Bowes died between 11 Aug. and 13 Oct. 1558 (see Laing's Preface to *Works*, vi. lxi–lxii).

CHAPTER XIV

The First Blast of the Trumpet against the Monstrous Regiment of Women

THE *First Blast of the Trumpet against the Monstrous Regiment of Women*—or, to translate it into modern English, 'against the unnatural government of women'—was probably written while Knox was in Dieppe. It attracted far more attention than any of Knox's earlier works had done, and gained him a reputation among his contemporaries of being a revolutionary firebrand, and among future generations of being a woman-hater. He put forward the doctrine that it was against the law of God, as well as against the law of nature, for a woman to rule a kingdom; and here, for once, he had tradition and popular prejudice on his side. There had been several women sovereigns in Europe in recent times; but in France women were excluded altogether from the succession to the crown, and it was inconceivable that a woman could be elected as Holy Roman Emperor. Until Mary became Queen, no woman had reigned in England, except for Matilda in the twelfth century, who had been unable to defend her throne in the face of civil war. It was fear of the consequences of a woman ruler, and the necessity of producing a male heir, which had been the chief cause of Henry VIII's matrimonial adventures, of the divorce of Catherine of Aragon and the break with Rome, and the death of Anne Boleyn. Had it not been for the unfortunate coincidence that Jane Grey, the Protestants' candidate, was also a woman, it might have been possible to exclude Mary from the throne in 1553 on the grounds of her sex. This would certainly have been a far more convincing argument, in the people's eyes, than any of the reasons put forward in Edward VI's devise of the Crown.

The antagonism to a woman ruler was understandable, as it was still one of the chief functions of a sovereign to lead his armies into battle in person. When Mary declared war on France in the summer of 1557, and, in accordance with the usual form, sent a herald to Rheims to convey her challenge to the French King, Henry II burst out laughing, and commented: 'Consider how I stand when a woman sends to challenge me to war.' The idea of government by a woman regent was well established in the Netherlands, where Margaret of Austria and Mary of Hungary had ruled as regents for the emperors for nearly fifty years; but Mary of Hungary herself pointed out that in time of war it was impossible for a woman ruler to do her duty. She told Charles V that a woman, whatever her rank, was never feared or respected like a man, as the ineptitude of a woman, as compared to a man, was as obvious as the difference between white and black. Yet, despite this prejudice, in 1558 both England and Scotland were ruled by women.[1]

The inferiority and subjection of women to men was accepted both in theory and practice in all ranks of society. Medieval Christianity, though in one respect it exalted the position of women, had also passed adverse judgement on the whole sex, condemning women as the temptresses who ensnared men and distracted them from the paths of learning and piety. A religion which condemned sexual lust as mortal sin, and was conscious that this was the chief means by which women exercised power over men, naturally viewed the domination and influence of women with horror. This view, which had been inherited from the early Fathers of the Church, was held as firmly by Catholic as by Protestant theologians. The Scottish Augustinian monk, Robert Richardson, who later became a Protestant zealot, wrote a commentary on the regulations of St. Augustine for the governance of a monastery in 1530, before he had broken with the old Church, in which he quoted at length from Augustine's views on women, and added comments of his own. Men must beware of women, particularly of the charms of their hair; they must not look at a woman, for adultery begins with the eyes. If any man believed that he was strong enough to resist the temptation, he should ask himself: Am I more virtuous than David? Am I wiser than Solomon? Am I stronger than Samson?[2] These anti-feminist sentiments commended themselves to the Protestants, and as the

[1] Soranzo to the Doge and Senate of Venice, 9 June 1557 (*Ven. Cal.* vi. 927); Mary of Hungary to Charles V (Aug. 1555) (Weiss, iv. 473–4; *Span. Cal.* xiii. 242).

[2] Richardinus, *Commentary on the Rule of St. Augustine*, pp. 112–15; and see Vives, *De institutione foeminae Christianae* (1523); Agrippa, *De nobilitate et praecellentia foeminei sexus* (1529); Elyot, *The Defence of Good Women* (1540), etc. See also 1 Tim. ii. 9–14.

reading of the Bible spread, the Protestants placed as much emphasis on St. Paul's condemnation of women's vanities as the Catholics had done on the harsher strictures of Augustine and the early Fathers. The pro-feminist theories of intellectuals such as Vives, Cornelius Agrippa, and Elyot made no serious impact on wider circles; while the admiration for women that played so important a part in the life of royal Courts in the sixteenth century went hand in hand with sexual licence, and both were condemned together, by the preachers and merchants, as an example of the lust and moral degeneration of Catholic high society.

But although denunciations of the female sex were so common in the world in which Knox lived, there are very few to be found in the writings of Knox himself. There is no recorded instance before 1558 of Knox making any derogatory remarks about women. The questions which he submitted to Bullinger in March 1554 show that he was already considering the possibility of putting forward the theory that women could not lawfully rule; but neither this proposition, nor any general condemnations of feminine wickedness, are to be found in any of Knox's pamphlets or sermons, or in any of his private letters, before 1558. On the contrary, out of all Knox's letters that have survived, more than half were written to women, and many of them—like some of his other writings—show the high opinion which he had of the sisters in the congregation, though in accordance with the directive of Paul in Scripture he naturally excluded them from participation in the elections and weekly meetings. He obviously preferred the company and friendship of women to the company of men. He married twice, for the second time when he was an elderly man; he was on very intimate terms with Mrs. Bowes, Mrs. Locke, Mrs. Hickman, and Janet Adamson, while there is no record of his ever having felt strong personal affection for any man, except Goodman, for he regarded Calvin more as a revered teacher than as a close friend. In view of Knox's attitude towards women, there is every indication that he wrote *The First Blast of the Trumpet against the Monstrous Regiment of Women* because he decided, at Dieppe in the autumn of 1557, to pander to popular prejudices which he personally did not really share, though there were plenty of biblical texts with which he could justify his arguments to himself, as well as to his readers.

When Knox published *The First Blast of the Trumpet*, he was fully aware that it would lead him into serious trouble. He also knew that Calvin would not approve of it. Some time in 1557, before writing the book, he again consulted Calvin about the lawfulness of government by women, and had a long private talk with him. Calvin was no more encouraging now than he had been three years before. He told Knox that he believed that as government by women was a deviation from the original and proper order of nature, it must have been imposed, like slavery, as a punishment for the fall of man; but the example of Huldah and Deborah, and Isaiah's promise that queens should be the nursing mothers of the Church, proved that queens, by virtue of their royal prerogative, were in a different position from all other women. Calvin said that as it was well established, by custom and public consent, that in some countries women were entitled to succeed to the throne, it was undesirable to discuss the question at this time, as 'it would not be lawful to unsettle governments which are ordained by the peculiar providence of God'. So Knox went ahead without telling Calvin what he was doing. He managed to arrange for the book to be printed in Geneva without the knowledge of Calvin or the city authorities.[1] Unlike his previous works, it was published anonymously, and did not state the name of the printer or the place of publication. The title page of *The First Blast of the Trumpet* contained nothing in the nature of an imprint except the date 'MDLVIII'.

The First Blast of the Trumpet against the Monstrous Regiment of Women was written as an attack on Queen Mary of England, and despite the generality of the criticism implied in the title, the arguments about the evil of rule by women in general take up only a small proportion of the book. Most of it is simply an attack on the cruelties and tyranny of Mary, and an appeal to the English to overthrow her by revolution. Knox writes throughout as if he himself were an Englishman, or rather a native of the British Isles; for in the *First Blast* he shows clearly that he considers England and Scotland to be one island which ought to be united in one Protestant realm.

Knox laid his cards on the table with the opening words of the Preface.

Wonder it is, that amongst so many pregnant wits as the Isle of Great Britanny hath produced, so many godly and zealous preachers as

[1] Calvin to Cecil (1559) (*Calvini Op.* xvii. 490–1; *Zurich Letters*, i. 76–77).

England did some time nourish, and amongst so many learned, and men of grave judgement, as this day by Jezebel are exiled, none is found so stout of courage, so faithful to God, nor loving to their native country, that they dare admonish the inhabitants of that isle, how abominable before God is the empire or rule of a wicked woman, yea, of a traitress and bastard; and what may a people or nation, left destitute of a lawful head, do by the authority of God's Word in electing and appointing common rulers and magistrates.

Knox stated that he knew that his book would arouse criticism. 'The natural man, enemy to God, shall find, I know, many causes why no such doctrine ought to be published in these our dangerous days. First, for that it may tend to sedition. Secondarily, it shall be dangerous, not only to the writer or publisher, but also to all such as shall read the writings or favour this truth spoken. . . . I shall be called foolish, curious, despiteful, and a sower of sedition; and one day, perchance (although now be nameless) I may be attainted of treason.' He excused himself for publishing the pamphlet anonymously. 'My purpose is thrice to blow the trumpet in the same matter, if God so permit; twice I intend to do it without name; but at the last blast, to take the blame upon myself, that all others may be purged.'

Knox argued that the idea of a woman ruler was a violation of the law of nature, and an absurdity. If man was prepared to submit himself to the government of women, he would do what no other species of creation did, for no male animal was prepared to be ruled by his female. What would Aristotle have said if he had seen a woman sitting crowned in Parliament among the midst of men? If women were not permitted to have legal authority over their own children, how could they have authority over a whole nation? If women could not plead as barristers in the courts, how could a woman be the head of the whole judicial system, and be the ruler from whom the judges derived their authority? Here Knox exposed the illogical nature of a system which was to continue for 350 years after his time, under which women were ineligible for every public office except that of head of the State; and by doing this, he attacked the special position of the Crown and the whole mystique of monarchy. The theologians who taught that, though women must obey men in all other fields, men must obey a queen as they would obey a male sovereign, believed that the divinely ordained power of the prince was strong enough to prevail over the divinely ordained superiority of men over women. Knox's book, because it directly challenged this, was seditious.

Knox then indulged in strong denunciations of women as a sex, though some of the harshest language in his book is quotations from the early Fathers. 'Woman . . . ought at all times to have the punishment which was given to Eve sounding in her ears', is a quotation from St. John Chrysostom. 'Because that death did enter into the world by her, there is no boldness that ought to be permitted unto her, but she ought to be in humility', is St. Ambrose. 'Thou art the port and gate of the Devil. Thou art the first transgressor of God's law', is from Tertullian's book, *On Women's Apparel*.[1] This last quotation drew an approving comment from Knox:

> By these and many other grave sentences and quick interrogations did this godly writer labour to bring every woman in contemplation of herself, to the end that everyone, deeply weighing what sentence God had pronounced against the whole race and daughters of Eve, might not only learn daily to humble and subject themselves in the presence of God, but also that they should avoid and abhor whatsoever thing might exalt them or puff them up in pride, or that might be occasion that they should forget the curse and malediction of God. And what, I pray you, is more able to cause woman to forget her own condition, than if she be lifted up in authority above man?

We do not know how Marjory and Mrs. Bowes, and Mrs. Locke and the 'sisters in Edinburgh', reacted to these wholesale denunciations of their sex. They doubtless accepted them as happily as a modern Marxist of middle-class origin accepts denunciations of the 'bourgeoisie' as a class. Knox's women followers were probably the most enthusiastic defenders of his views on the government of women.

But Knox had taken the precaution of prefacing his denunciation of the sex with a statement that there were some exceptions to the rule. 'I except such as God, by singular privilege, and for certain causes known only to Himself, hath exempted from the common rank of woman, and do speak of women as nature and experience do this day declare them. Nature, I say, doth paint

[1] Chrysostom, 'In Cap. III Genes. Homil. XVII'; Ambrose, 'Commentaria in Epist. ad Timotheum Primam', c. 2; Tertullian, 'De Cultu Foeminarum' (Migne, *Patrologiae Cursus*, i. 1305; xvii. 468; [*Series Graeca*] liii. 146) (cited by Knox in *Works*, iv. 387, 385, 381–2).

them forth to be weak, frail, impatient, feeble and foolish; and experience hath declared them to be unconstant, variable, cruel and lacking the spirit of counsel and regiment.' Nor was Knox impressed by the example of Deborah in the Book of Judges, who was appointed by God to lead the people of Israel. After the accession of Elizabeth I, Deborah became the favourite biblical figure of the Protestant publicists; but now she was brushed aside, with the argument that an exceptional case does not establish a general rule. Neither the example of Deborah, nor 'the foolish consent of an ignorant multitude', could justify that which God had so plainly condemned.

The responsibility for this violation of the laws of God and nature rested with the English people.

> The insolent joy, the bonfires and banketting which were in London and elsewhere in England when that cursed Jezebel was proclaimed Queen, did witness to my heart that men were becomen more than enraged; for else how could they so have rejoiced at their own confusion and certain destruction? For what man was there of so base judgement (supposing that he had any light of God) who did not see the erecting of that monster to be the overthrow of true religion, and the accursed destruction of England and of the ancient liberties thereof? And yet, nevertheless, all men so triumphed as if God had delivered them from all calamity.

But God had most justly punished the horrible ingratitude of England and Scotland. When He offered them the opportunity of being joined together for ever in godly concord, England was proud and cruel, and Scotland was inconstant and fickle of promise. England again offended when, in the reign of Edward VI, she refused to listen to God's messengers who reprimanded her for her vices, but attributed every step in the reformation of religion not to God, but to the King. 'For what then was heard as concerning religion, but the King's proceedings, the King's proceedings must be obeyed.' England, which he called 'our country', was oppressed by Spain, and the nobility of England were fighting in a war in defence of their mortal enemy the Spaniard; and Scotland was oppressed by France. When referring to the persecution of Protestants in Spain and France, his choice of words showed that he realized that the Protestants had far more support in France than they had in Spain, for he blamed 'the odious nation of Spaniards', and 'the French King', for the persecutions.

Knox called on the English nobility and the House of Commons to remedy the situation. As they had been responsible for permitting Mary to succeed to the throne, they must repent, and to prove the sincerity of their repentance they must refuse to be her officers. They ought to act as the people of Judah did when they deposed Athaliah

killing at His commandment not only that cruel and mischievous woman, but also the people did destroy the temple of Baal, break his altars and images, and kill Mattan, Baal's high priest, before his altars. The same is the duty as well of the Estates as of the people that hath been blinded. First, they ought to remove from honour and authority that monster in nature; so call I a woman clad in the habit of man, yea, a woman against nature reigning above man. Secondarily, if any presume to defend that impiety, they ought not to fear first to pronounce, and then after to execute against them, the sentence of death.

Knox ended by warning the people of England that if God raised up any noble heart to overthrow Mary, anyone who fought in her defence would lift their hand against God. The cursed Jezebel of England boasted of her victory over Wyatt, but she had not prevailed against God: 'His throne is more high than that the length of their horns is able to reach.' But the fire of God's Word was already laid to those rotten props, which were burning already, although we could not see the flame. 'When they are consumed (as shortly they will be, for stubble and dry timber cannot long endure the fire) that rotten wall, the usurped and unjust empire of women, shall fall by itself in despite of all man, to the destruction of so many as shall labour to uphold it. And therefore let all man be advertised, for the trumpet hath once blown.'[1]

Christendom was appalled at *The First Blast of the Trumpet against the Monstrous Regiment of Women*; but Knox did not feel the full repercussions of the storm for several months. It took a little time for copies of the book to reach England, and for the English authorities to track and seize them and read the book, and inform the world of the poison that it contained. Meanwhile, in the summer of 1558, Knox published three tracts which put forward more clearly than ever before his theory of the lawfulness of revolution. These tracts took the form of an appeal against the sentence of the Scottish bishops who had condemned him, in his absence, as a

[1] Knox, *The First Blast of the Trumpet* (*Works*, iv. 363–420; see pp. 365, 367, 370–1, 373–4, 376–7, 382, 393–5, 402, 411–12, 415–20).

heretic. One was addressed to Mary of Lorraine, one to the nobility and Parliament, and the third, the most remarkable, to the common people of Scotland. His appeal to the Queen Regent was a new edition of the letter that he had written to her in 1556, with a new introduction and several additions to the text. In the introduction he informed Mary of Lorraine that he appealed from the unjust sentence of the bishops to 'a lawful and General Council', and was sending her an enlarged version of his letter of May 1556 in order to vindicate his doctrine, which the bishops had condemned. But the tone of the new passages in the new version of the letter was so much harsher than the first edition, that the nature of the two letters was entirely different.

After stating that martyrs had been cruelly murdered in Scotland, besides the many who had suffered in France, Italy, Spain, Flanders, and England, he reminded Mary of Lorraine how in 1540 her two small sons, aged 3 and 1, had both died of natural causes within six hours of each other, and that soon afterwards her husband James V had died, leaving only a daughter to succeed. He informed her that this was a divine punishment inflicted upon her, James V, and the realm for having upheld idolatry and shed the blood of the saints of God. Like all the Protestants and Catholics of his age, Knox believed that every misfortune which befell his enemies was a punishment for their sins, and every misfortune which befell his own supporters was a trial sent to test their patience, as Job had been tested. He then went so far as to make undisguised threats to Mary of Lorraine of the divine vengeance that would overtake her if she rebelled against God, and reminded her of the manner in which she had received his letter in May 1556.

> Whether ye did read it to the end or not, I am uncertain; one thing I know, that ye did deliver it to one of your prelates, saying, 'My Lord, will ye read a pasquil?' . . . My duty to God (who hath commanded me to flatter no prince in the earth) compelleth me to say, that if no more ye esteem the admonition of God nor the cardinals do the scoffing of pasquils, that then He shall shortly send you messengers with whom ye shall not be able on that manner to jest.

This prophecy was to be fulfilled within little more than twelve months.

In the *Admonition to England*, and more particularly in the *First Blast*, Knox had directly challenged the doctrine of Christian obedience by calling on the nobility to revolt against Queen Mary of England. In the second edition of his letter to the Queen Regent, he formulated his theory for the first time as a general moral and religious proposition. Men who supported an idolatrous prince, or who confirmed his action by their silence, 'give no true obedience; but as they are apostates from God, so are they traitor to their princes, whom by flattery they confirm in rebelling against God. Only they which to the death resist such wicked laws and decrees are acceptable to God and faithful to their princes.'[1]

He put this more clearly in the second tract, his appeal to the nobles and the Scottish Parliament against his condemnation as a heretic. This was addressed to the nobility and the Estates—that is to say, the Parliament of Scotland, which was composed of the three estates, the nobles, the clergy, and the commonalty, though the commonalty was represented only by delegates from the burgh councils of some fifty burghs, as the lairds were not represented in Parliament. In form Knox did not merely appeal to the nobility as a class, but to the Parliament of Scotland; and when he told them that God had given them the sword for the maintenance of the innocent and the punishment of malefactors, he was not, at least in theory, appealing to the nobility to take arbitrary measures, but to an established constitutional body.

Part of Knox's letter is taken up with legal argument; for he argued that the sentence against him was void because he was out of the jurisdiction when he was summoned, because the summons was not served upon him, and because the bishops were not impartial judges, as he had denounced them before the trial in his first letter to the Queen Regent. But most of the letter consisted of an appeal to the nobles and Parliament to exert their lawful authority over 'the whole rabble of your bishops'; and he offered 'to prove your bishops to be the very pestilence who have infected all Christianity'. He told them that it was their duty to prevent the bishops from persecuting Protestants, because they, the temporal rulers, were above the bishops, just as Moses was above Aaron the priest. They must ensure that their 'subjects' were rightly instructed in religion, and defended from oppression and tyranny, and that

[1] Knox, *Letter to the Queen Regent* (1558 edn.) (*Works*, iv. 429–60; see pp. 431, 441, 453–4, 457–8).

true teachers may be maintained, and such as blind and deceive the people, together also with all idle bellies which do rob and oppress the flock, may be removed and punished as God's law prescribeth. . . . For seeing that God only hath placed you in His chair, hath appointed you to be His lieutenants, and by His own seal hath marked you to be magistrates and to rule above your brethren, to whom nature nevertheless hath made you like in all points (for in conception, birth, life and death ye differ nothing from the common sort of men, but God only, as said is, hath promoted you, and of His especial favour hath given unto you this prerogative to be called gods); how horrible ingratitude were it then, that you should be found unfaithful to Him that thus hath honoured you.

At this point, after four years of progress, Knox took the final step in his renunciation of Tyndale's doctrines. He denounced the doctrine of Christian obedience as sinful.

Now the common song of all men is, 'We must obey our kings, be they good or be they bad; for God hath so commanded'. But horrible shall the vengeance be that shall be poured forth upon such blasphemers of God's holy name and ordinance. For it is no less blasphemy to say that God hath commanded kings to be obeyed when they command impiety, than to say that God by His precept is author and maintainer of all iniquity. True it is, God hath commanded kings to be obeyed, but like true it is, that in things which they commit against His glory, or when cruelly without cause they rage against their brethren, the members of Christ's body, He hath commanded no obedience, but rather He hath approved, yea, and greatly rewarded such as have opposed themselves to their ungodly commandments and blind rage.

If the nobles and the people obeyed and followed their kings in manifest iniquity, both the nobles and the people, but especially the nobles, would be punished, as Pharaoh's army was punished when they were all drowned. Why was every soldier in the army drowned? 'Because none was found so faithful to God, that he durst enterprise to resist nor againstand the manifest impiety of their princes. And therefore was God's wrath poured forth upon the one and the other.'

Knox did not ask the nobility and the Estates merely to protect the persecuted Protestants from the fury of the bishops; he did not expect them to adopt a passive and neutral role. He told them that they ought to put idolaters to death, as God had commanded;

and here he went further, and said that as Moses' commandment in Deuteronomy to slay the idolater was directed to the whole people, it was not only the nobles, but the population as a whole, who should put idolaters to death, in order to show their gratitude to God for all His favours bestowed upon them. He cited the collective punishments that Moses inflicted on cities where the whole population was exterminated, despite the fact that only a few of the inhabitants had committed idolatry, to show that the whole population must be held responsible if idolatry is not punished.

But Knox drew a distinction between the treatment which should be accorded to idolaters who had never known the truth, and those who had once known the true religion and had abandoned it in favour of idolatry. The Apostles did not put the non-Christian Gentiles to death, because they had never known the truth; but it was different with a country such as England, which had accepted the true religion under Edward VI and had then relapsed. In such cases, idolaters should be punished with death.

> And therefore I fear not to affirm that it had been the duty of the nobility, judges, rulers and people of England, not only to have resisted and againstanded Mary, that Jezebel, whom they call their Queen, but also to have punished her to the death, with all the sort of her idolatrous priests, together with all such as should have assisted her, what time that she and they openly began to suppress Christ's Evangel, to shed the blood of the saints of God, and to erect that most devilish idolatry . . . which once most justly by common oath was banished from that realm.

Knox did not call for an indiscriminate massacre of Catholics in Catholic states, but for a relentless application of the death penalty by a Protestant government against Catholic counter-revolutionaries.[1]

Along with his letter to the nobility and Estates, Knox published a letter addressed to the commonalty of Scotland, in which he enunciated some startling doctrines.

> Albeit God hath put and ordained distinction and difference betwixt the king and subjects, betwixt the rulers and the common people, in the regiment and administration of civil policies, yet in the hope of the

[1] Knox, *The Appellation from the sentence pronounced by the Bishops and Clergy to the Nobility and Estates of Scotland* (*Works*, iv. 465–520; the passages cited are at pp. 472, 480–2, 486, 496, 498, 507).

life to come He hath made all equal. For as in Christ Jesus the Jew hath no greater prerogative than hath the Gentile, the man than hath the woman, the learned than the unlearned, the lord than the servant, but all are one in Him . . . so constantly I affirm that to you it doth no less appertain than to your king or princes to provide that Christ Jesus be truly preached amongst you, seeing that without His true knowledge can neither of you both attain to salvation. And this is the point wherein, I say, all man is equal.

With his usual unflinching clarity, Knox laid down the duty of the common people in matters of religion.

Ye, although ye be but subjects, may lawfully require of your superiors, be it of your king, be it of your lords, rulers and powers, that they provide for you true preachers, and that they expel such as, under the name of pastors, devour and destroy the flock, not feeding the same as Christ Jesus hath commanded. And if in this point your superiors be negligent, or yet pretend to maintain tyrants in their tyranny, most justly ye may provide true teachers for yourselves, be it in your cities, towns or villages; them ye may maintain and defend against all that shall persecute them. . . . Ye may, moreover, withhold the fruits and profits which your false bishops and clergy most unjustly receive of you, unto such time as they be compelled faithfully to do their charge and duties.

This appeal to the common people to withhold their tithes from the Church was likely to be well received in Scotland.

Knox warned the people that it would be no excuse for them to say:

'We were but simple subjects, we could not redress the faults and crimes of our rulers, bishops and clergy; we called for reformation, and wished for the same; but lords' brethren were bishops, their sons were abbots, and the friends of great men had the possession of the Church, and so were we compelled to give obedience to all that they demanded.' These vain excuses, I say, will nothing avail you in the presence of God.

God would punish them, 'because ye assist and maintain your princes in their blind rage, and give no declaration that their tyranny displeaseth you'. When the original world perished by water, when Sodom and Gomorrah were burnt, and when Jerusalem was destroyed, the inhabitants were not all guilty; 'for some were young, and could not be oppressors, neither yet could defile themselves with unnatural and beastly lusts; some were pitiful and gentle of nature, and did not thirst for the blood of Christ nor of His Apostles'. Why, then, had they all been punished? It was because

in the original world none was found that either did resist tyranny and oppression, that universally was used, either yet that earnestly reprehended the same. In Sodom was none found that did againstand that furious and beastly multitude that did compass about and besiege the house of Lot; none would believe Lot, that the city should be destroyed. And finally in Jerusalem was none found that studied to repress the tyranny of the priests, who were conjured against Christ and His Evangel, but all fainted (I except ever such as gave witness with their blood or their flying that such impiety displeased them), all kept silence; by the which all approved iniquity, and joined hands with the tyrants, and so were all arrayed and set, as it had been in one battle, against the Omnipotent and against His Son Christ Jesus.[1]

Thus the texts of the Bible, which had so often been cited in support of the doctrine of Christian obedience, were used by Knox to justify revolution. Whereas almost every other sixteenth-century theologian taught the people that they must obey the king, not from fear of earthly punishment but from fear of God, Knox left them in no doubt that if they obeyed unjust commandments of wicked rulers they would receive a far more terrible punishment from God than any that could be inflicted upon them for the crime of high treason. Here Knox again put forward the argument which he had first used in the *Letter to the Faithful in London, Newcastle and Berwick*[2] in 1554—that when God inflicted collective punishments in the Old Testament, He wished to punish the people for their failure to overthrow wicked régimes by revolution. Knox's theology may seem out of date to twentieth-century theologians, but it is not so far removed from the modern politico-ethical arguments which, at least in war-time, hold a whole nation responsible for the crimes of its rulers if it makes no attempt to overthrow them.

The *Letter to the Commonalty of Scotland* was dated 14 July 1558. It was published together with the *Appellation to the Nobility and Estates of Scotland*. Unlike the *First Blast*, it was published in Knox's own name, and the title page stated that it was published

[1] Knox, *Letter to the Commonalty of Scotland* (*Works*, iv. 523–38; the passages cited are on pp. 527–8, 533–6).

[2] *Works*, iii. 189–90.

at Geneva, though the name of the printer was not given. The book also contained a tract by Gilby entitled *An Admonition to England and Scotland to call them to Repentance*, and a revolutionary poem by Kethe based on the ninety-fourth Psalm, with its challenge to the reader: 'Who now will up and rise with me against this wicked band?' As Gilby's name was not widely known, it was generally believed that his *Admonition* had been written by Knox, and that Knox had used the name 'Anthony Gilby' as a pseudonym. Gilby, in this tract, was the first of the English Protestants to attack the reputation of Henry VIII, for hitherto they had always attributed all the blame for Henry's persecution of Protestants to Gardiner. Gilby declared that 'that was no reformation, but a deformation, in the time of that tyrant and lecherous monster', but stated that Henry's policy towards Scotland had been 'most godly and praise-worthy', and that the responsibility for the sufferings which had been inflicted upon Edinburgh and the greater part of the realm rested on the Scots who had opposed the 'joining that isle together in perfect religion'.[1]

The last section of the book was a short note by Knox in which he admitted that he was the author of *The First Blast of the Trumpet*, and gave a short summary of the four propositions which he was going to put forward in *The Second Blast of the Trumpet.*

1. It is not birth only, nor propinquity of blood, that maketh a king lawfully to reign above a people professing Christ Jesus and His eternal verity, but in his election must the ordinance which God hath established in the election of inferior judges be observed.

2. No manifest idolater nor notorious transgressor of God's holy precepts ought to be promoted to any public regiment, honour or dignity in any realm, province or city that hath subjected the self to Christ Jesus and to His blessed Evangel.

3. Neither can oath nor promise bind any such people to obey and maintain tyrants against God and against His truth known.

4. But if either rashly they have promoted any manifest wicked person, or yet ignorantly have chosen such a one as after declareth himself unworthy of regiment above the people of God (and such be all idolaters and cruel persecutors) most justly may the same men depose and punish him that unadvisedly before they did nominate, appoint and elect.[2]

[1] Kethe, 'Psalme of David XCIIII'; Gilby, *An Admonition to England and Scotland* (*Works*, iv. 558–60, 563, 574).

[2] 'John Knox to the Reader' (*Works*, iv. 539–40).

The Appellation to the Nobility, Estates and Commonalty of Scotland was an even more revolutionary document than *The First Blast of the Trumpet*; but it caused much less of an uproar. The reason for this is clear: in the *Appellation*, Knox attacked Mary of Lorraine, and in the *First Blast* he attacked Mary Tudor. Mary Tudor, both as Queen of England and as the wife of King Philip, was a far more formidable opponent than Mary of Lorraine, and the efficient English government machine went into action to trace the author and denounce him in every country in Europe as an enemy of society. They would probably in any case have discovered before long that Knox had written the book, even if he had not admitted it in the Appendix to the *Appellation*, because there were not many printers in Europe who used the excellent Roman type with which the *First Blast* was printed; and now that the author was known, they had no difficulty in discovering the place of publication. Goodman had also written a book, *How Superior Powers ought to be Obeyed*, which is dated 'from Geneva', 1 January 1558, in which he argued, chiefly on the basis of biblical texts and the story of the Maccabees, that it was the duty of all classes of people to rise in armed revolt against an idolatrous sovereign, whether male or female. Goodman's book was published with a preface by Whittingham, while Kethe contributed a poem which called for revolution in England. *How Superior Powers ought to be Obeyed* and *The First Blast of the Trumpet* were bracketed together by the authorities, and soon the words 'Goodman and Knox' were arousing horror and fear in every country of Western Europe. In England a royal proclamation was issued in June 1558 against heretical and treasonable books imported from abroad. It ordered that anyone who obtained possession of such books must burn them at once, on pain of being summarily put to death under martial law.[1] It was the books of Knox and Goodman that were primarily aimed at.

Calvin and the government of Geneva were worried by the outcry, and were annoyed that the books had been published in Geneva. It was particularly embarrassing because on 24 June 1558, after both books had been published but before the storm really broke, both Knox and Goodman had been made citizens of Geneva. The English Protestant refugees at Strasbourg were naturally among the first to complain. Sir Anthony Cooke, who was one of the leaders of the Strasbourg refugees, wrote to Beza

[1] Strype, *Eccl. Mem.* iii [ii]. 130.

in Geneva to protest against the *First Blast*. Beza passed the letter to Calvin, who then read the book for the first time. Calvin wrote to the English group at Strasbourg, dissociating himself from Knox's opinions, and he and Beza took immediate steps to ban the sale of the *First Blast* and of Goodman's book in Geneva.[1]

Francis Hotman also condemned Knox. Hotman was the leading propagandist of the French Protestants and, as a refugee in Strasbourg, was sending pamphlets into France attacking the Catholics, and especially the Cardinal of Lorraine, whom he denounced, in his *Open Letter to the Tiger of France*, as a traitor to the King, who deserved death. But a direct attack on the monarchy shocked Hotman. On 12 December 1558 he wrote to Calvin to tell him how relieved the Protestants in Strasbourg had been to know that Calvin did not agree with Knox. Sixteen years later, Hotman himself wrote a book against government by women. In his *Franco-Gallia* he argued, on historical and constitutional grounds, that no woman could rule or hold any public office in France. His book was directed against Catherine de Medici; but, with an eye on Elizabeth in England, he stated that his arguments did not apply to any country except France.[2]

Knox's old friend John Foxe seems to have made some criticism of the *First Blast*, because on 18 May 1558 Knox wrote from Geneva to Foxe in Basel to defend his action in writing the book. 'My rude vehemency and inconsidered affirmations, which may appear rather to proceed from choler than of zeal and reason, I do not excuse; but to have used any other title more plausible, thereby to have allured the world by any art, as I never purposed, so do I not yet purpose; to me, it is enough to say that black is not white, and man's tyranny and foolishness is not God's perfect ordinance.'[3]

Elizabeth was indignant at *The First Blast of the Trumpet*. When she became Queen in November 1558, she was without a friend among the powers of Europe, and was opposed by all her bishops and some of her nobility. In view of the weakness of her position, she was far more embarrassed than Mary had been when the whole basis of her rule was undermined by the arguments of a

[1] *Livre des Anglois*, p. 5; Registre du Conseil (*Calvini Op.* xxi. 697); Calvin to Cecil (1559) (*Calvini Op.* xvii. 491; *Zurich Letters*, i. 77).

[2] Hotman to Calvin, 12 Dec. 1558 (*Calvini Op.* xvii. 396–7); Hotman, *Franco-Gallia*, p. 125. Hotman's authorship of *Letter to the Tiger of France* is doubtful.

[3] Knox to Foxe, 18 May 1558 (*Works*, v. 5).

prominent Protestant leader such as Knox. Her Secretary of State, Cecil, sent a protest to Calvin, who wrote and informed Cecil that Knox's book had been published without his consent. He assured Cecil that it was not merely in order to curry favour with Elizabeth that he had condemned the book; for he had, on the contrary, criticized it in his letter to the English refugees at Strasbourg while Queen Mary was still alive. The only reason why he had not condemned it publicly was because he did not wish to draw attention to the fact that it had been published in Geneva, for he was afraid that it might prejudice the position of all the refugees in Geneva. 'I think there would have been good reason to fear', he wrote to Cecil, 'that if the subject had been raised, then because of the thoughtless arrogance of one individual, the wretched crowd of exiles would have been expelled, not only from this city, but even from almost the whole world.' As late as 1566 Beza wrote to Bullinger that Elizabeth's hostility towards Calvinism was partly due to the fact that the *First Blast* had been published in Geneva.[1]

The English refugees at Strasbourg produced a reply to Knox. John Aylmer, who had been tutor to Jane Grey and later became Bishop of London, wrote a book which was published in Strasbourg in April 1559 under the title *A Harbour for Faithful and True Subjects against the late blown Blast concerning the Government of Women, wherein be confuted all such Reasons as a Stranger of late made in that Behalf, with a Brief Exhortation to Obedience*. Aylmer stated that he was writing a reply to the *First Blast* because Knox had 'almost cracked the duty of true obedience'; but the moderation of his language shows how far the English Protestants had advanced since 1555 in their attitude towards princes. They were now prepared to forgive Knox for criticizing Mary, though they still thought that it was wrong of him to do anything which was calculated to provoke a revolution against her. Aylmer wrote that Knox's error did not arise out of malice, but out of zeal, as his reason was blinded by the tears which Mary's cruelty had brought to his eyes; seeing the torments of the martyrs and the misgovernment of England, he had made the mistake of arguing from the particular to the general, and condemning the government of all women. Aylmer also made it clear that he resented the

[1] Calvin to Cecil (1559); Beza to Bullinger, 3 Sept. 1566 (*Calvini Op.* xvii. 490–2; Strype, *Annals of the Reformation*, i [ii]. 522; *Zurich Letters*, i. 77, 248).

fact that Knox, as an alien, should tell the English whom they ought to have as their sovereign. He argued that though it was obviously better for a nation to be ruled by a man than by a woman, if God gave a king no male heir, but only a daughter, it was clear that He intended the realm to be governed by a woman, and subjects must not resist or complain.[1]

Matthew Parker, who had remained in England, in hiding, throughout Mary's reign, and was about to become the Primate and most representative leader of the Protestant Church of England, considered that the *First Blast* and Goodman's book were subversive of the whole social order. In February 1559 he was shocked to find that the books were circulating in London, and wrote in alarm to his friend, Sir Nicholas Bacon, the Keeper of the Great Seal:

> If such principles be spread into men's heads, as now they be framed and referred to the judgement of the subject, of the tenant, and of the servant, to discuss what is tyranny, and to discern whether his prince, his landlord, his master, is a tyrant, by his own fancy and collection supposed, what Lord of the Council shall ride quietly minded in the streets among desperate beasts? What master shall be sure in his bed-chamber?[2]

Knox committed a grave political blunder in publishing *The First Blast of the Trumpet*. Elizabeth never forgave him for writing it, and as a result he found himself, at the crisis of his life and of the Scottish Reformation, in high disfavour with the Protestant Queen to whom the Protestants of Scotland and all Europe looked for help and leadership. By the time that Knox had finished writing the book, he had no doubt convinced himself that he passionately believed in the truth of the doctrine which he was advocating, and that, as he told Foxe, his conscience required him to proclaim to the world that government by women was sinful;[3] but in view of his political acumen, and his usual capacity for reconciling his principles with the immediate tactical interests of the Protestant cause, it is surprising that he committed the mistake of attacking the government of women in general, and not merely the government of Mary Tudor.

Knox ought to have realized, in the spring of 1558, the

1 Aylmer, *An Harborrowe for Faithfull and Trewe Subiectes*, sig. B–B3, R2.
2 Parker to Bacon, 1 Mar. 1558/9 (Parker, *Correspondence*, pp. 60–61).
3 Knox to Foxe, 18 May 1558 (*Works*, v. 5).

consequences that were likely to result from the publication of the *First Blast*. It is true that he did not know that Mary's health had begun to fail, and that she had barely six months to live, although he prophesied, in the *First Blast*, that she would reign for fewer years in the future than she had already reigned in the past; but everyone in England, and every statesman and diplomat in Europe, knew that Mary would not now have a child, and that when she died Elizabeth would succeed her. They also knew that though Elizabeth was going to mass and was pretending to be a Catholic, she was in fact a secret Protestant, who was supported by a majority of the members of Mary's Privy Council—the 'heretic elements' in the Council, as Renard, the Emperor's ambassador, called them—and was cheered by the people whenever she appeared in public. As for the Protestants in England, one of their poets described how, as they watched the burning of Cranmer and Ridley and all the humbler martyrs, and lived themselves under the shadow of the stake, 'we wished for our Elizabeth'. In the spring of 1558, at the very time when Knox was publishing the *First Blast*, Renard, whose diplomatic ability as well as his surname earned him the nickname of 'the fox', warned Philip II that Elizabeth's accession would mean the triumph of heresy, and the destruction of the Catholic Church in England, but that it would be impossible to prevent this disaster owing to her popularity and support among Englishmen of all classes.[1]

Only a refugee could have written *The First Blast of the Trumpet*. Knox and his friends in Geneva were in contact with the Protestants in England, but if they heard rumours about Elizabeth's secret Protestant sympathies, they did not believe them. In their eyes, Elizabeth was a Catholic; she had committed idolatry. They divided the English into three classes—martyrs, refugees, and collaborators. Yet if Knox had been able to feel the pulse of public opinion in England as well as he was able, in Dieppe, to learn what was happening in Scotland, he might not have made this error. He could have appealed to Elizabeth to repent and become a Protestant; he could have written to her as courteously as he wrote to Mary of Lorraine in the 1556 edition of his *Letter to the Queen Regent*.

[1] Knox, *The First Blast of the Trumpet* (*Works*, iv. 420); Renard to Charles V, 6 May 1554; Renard's notes for Philip II (Mar. 1558) (*Span. Cal.* xii. 238; xiii. 417); Thomas Bryce, 'The Register' (*Select Poetry of the reign of Queen Elizabeth*, i. 161–74).

But *The First Blast of the Trumpet* did not do much additional harm to Knox and to the Protestant cause. Even if Knox had never attacked the principle of government by women, he would have been no more popular with Elizabeth and the other governments of Christendom. Elizabeth detested Knox because he advocated revolution against princes, quite apart from anything that he wrote against women rulers, and was as indignant with Goodman as she was with Knox. On the other hand, Knox's writings in 1558 played their part in preparing the climate, and providing the ideological justification, for armed revolt in Scotland, and, through the example of Scotland, for the revolts in France and the Netherlands. These revolts were as necessary for the success of Protestantism in Europe, and for the security of Elizabeth's realm, as Elizabeth's assistance was for the victory of the Protestant revolutionaries.

CHAPTER XV

The Polemic against Anabaptism

THE people of the sixteenth century believed above all in the duty of obedience. The idea of freedom of thought and independent intellectual inquiry into matters of religion was utterly abhorrent to everyone except some detached intellectuals, a handful of theologians who were described as Anabaptists, and a few thinkers, like Sir Walter Raleigh, who were denounced as atheists. Anyone who resisted authority was considered to be guilty of pride, the worst of the seven deadly sins, the sin which Lucifer had committed when he rebelled against God. The duty of the Christian was to obey.

For the Catholics, this duty took the form of obedience to the Church and to the Pope. When the Protestants rejected obedience to the Church and Pope, they substituted obedience to the king. When Knox rejected obedience both to the Pope and to the king, he was compelled by his own conscience and by the general opinion of his contemporaries to find some other authority which could be unquestioningly obeyed. Knox therefore believed in the doctrine of unquestioning obedience to God. This, of course, led to the question as to what were the commandments of God; and Knox's answer was that they were to be found in the Bible, which was the Word of God, and nowhere else. This led to the further question as to who was to interpret the meaning of the text of the Bible. Mary Queen of Scots raised this problem with Knox in her first interview with him in 1561, when she said that the Catholic Church interpreted the Bible very differently from the way in which Knox interpreted it. Knox replied that it was not a question of how he interpreted it, or how the Catholic Church interpreted it, but of what the Word of God in fact said.[1] If Knox was to introduce a higher authority than Pope or prince, and rebut the accusation that he was claiming to interpret the will of God for

[1] Knox, *History*, ii. 18.

himself, he was compelled to resort, as far as possible, to a literal interpretation of every line in the Bible.

A passage in his *Appellation to the Nobility and Estates of Scotland* shows how Knox interpreted the duty of obedience to God. He reminded the lords of God's commandments when He gave the land of Canaan to the Israelites.

> First, He commanded the whole inhabitants of that country to be destroyed, and all monuments of their idolatry to be broken down; and thereafter he also straitly commandeth, that a city declining to idolatry should fall in the edge of the sword, and that the whole spoil of the same should be burnt, no portion of it reserved. To the carnal man this may appear a rigorous and severe judgement, yea, it may rather seem to be pronounced in a rage than in wisdom. For what city was ever yet in which, to man's judgement, were not to be found many innocent persons, as infants, children, and some simple and ignorant souls, who neither did nor could consent to such impiety? And yet we find no exception, but all are appointed to the cruel death. And as concerning the city, and the spoil of the same, man's reason cannot think but that it might have been better bestowed than to be consumed with fire, and so to profit no man. But in such cases will God that all creatures stoop, cover their faces, and desist from reasoning, when commandment is given to execute His judgement.[1]

Perhaps Knox, with his inquiring mind and his readiness to discard well-established and universally accepted doctrines, refers here to the apparent absurdity of the biblical text because he is beginning to doubt whether even the words of Scripture must always be regarded as infallible; but if so, the doubt, which would have been so dangerous for his personal safety and so damaging to his cause, is firmly suppressed, and he decides to cover his face and desist from reasoning any further.

Although Knox told Mary Queen of Scots that God 'plainly speaketh in His Word',[2] he and his colleagues believed, in practice, that there was a great deal to be said by way of interpreting the meaning of Scripture. When the leading members of his congregation in Geneva produced their new English translation of the Bible in 1560, they inserted marginal notes which ran to nearly 300,000 words, being approximately one-third of the length of the text of the Bible itself. The Geneva Bible became the most

[1] Knox, *Appellation to the Nobility and Estates of Scotland* (*Works*, iv. 502).
[2] Knox, *History*, ii. 18.

important instrument of propaganda of the radical Protestants in England and Scotland. Between 1560 and 1644, over 140 editions were published, and it was read in every Presbyterian and Puritan home in both realms. More than Foxe's *Book of Martyrs* or Knox's *History of the Reformation in Scotland*, it influenced the opinions of the English Puritans and the Scottish Covenanters.

We do not know whether Knox played any direct part in the translating—or, to speak more accurately, in the writing—of the Geneva Bible. It was published at Geneva in 1560, and the dedication to Elizabeth I from her 'humble subjects of the English Church at Geneva' is dated 10 April 1560. Much of the work was done after Knox left Geneva in January 1559, but as it took more than two years, and started very soon after Whittingham's translation of the New Testament was published in Geneva in 1557, Knox may have given some assistance with the Geneva Bible during his residence in Geneva in 1558. What is certain is that the marginal notes were very largely inspired by Knox's writings and political doctrines. The Geneva Bible was the work of the leaders of the English congregation at Geneva, and they put forward, in the notes, the political ideas of the two pastors of the congregation, Knox and Goodman. The notes in Whittingham's New Testament of 1557 are scanty and mild compared to the revolutionary doctrine contained in the enormously lengthy notes that are printed down the whole length of the margins and at the top and bottom of nearly every page of the Bible of 1560. This difference was chiefly due to the influence of the ideas which Knox had put forward in the books and pamphlets which he published in 1558, and to the effect of the revolutionary developments in France and Scotland during the three intervening years.[1]

The Geneva Bible taught the people of England and Scotland that they had a duty to resist wicked princes and to kill idolaters. It taught them that the established Church of the Jews at the time of Christ, like other established Churches in modern times, had condemned as innovators and seditious heretics the elect who

[1] For the authorship of the Geneva Bible, and the date at which it was written, see 'Epistle to the Reader' in the Geneva Bible, p. iiii, and the anonymous *The Life and Death of Mr. William Whittingham, Dean of Durham*, which was found among Anthony à Wood's manuscripts, and printed in Lorimer, *John Knox and the Church of England*, pp. 303–17 (see p. 306). See also *The Troubles at Frankfort*, pp. 191–2; Martin, *Les Protestants Anglais réfugiés à Genève*, p. 241; Hume Brown, *John Knox*, i. 205.

preached the true Word of God. It taught them to forgive injuries committed against private individuals, but not those committed against God and the Protestant party. It also taught the necessity of utilizing the help of evil men in politics; for God uses wicked men for His own purposes, and Jeremiah and the Jews in Babylon were saved in turn by Nebuchadnezzar and by Cyrus. The favourite texts of the supporters of the duty of Christian obedience to princes were interpreted anew by the authors of the Geneva Bible. Tyndale had repeatedly referred to the two incidents in the twenty-fourth and twenty-sixth chapters of the First Book of Samuel, when David, finding Saul at his mercy, did not slay him, for he would not lift his hand against his king, the Lord's anointed. David rejected Abishai's advice to kill the sleeping Saul, and said to Abishai: 'Destroy him not: for who can stretch forth his hand against the Lord's anointed and be guiltless?' The notes explained: 'To wit, in his own private cause: for Jehu slew two kings at God's appointment.' The killing of Jezebel was not passed by without comment. When Jezebel heard of Jehu's arrival, she painted her face, because, said the notes, 'being of an haughty and cruel nature, she would still retain her princely state and dignity'. When Jehu entered, Jezebel said: 'Had Zimri peace who slew his master?', which drew the comment: 'As though she would say, Can any traitor, or any that riseth against his superior, have good success?' But this argument no more impressed Jehu than it impressed John Knox. He ordered her to be thrown down, and her blood was sprinkled on the wall, and he trod her underfoot. 'This he did by the motion of the Spirit of God,' said the notes, 'that her blood should be shed, that had shed the blood of innocents, to be a spectacle and example of God's judgements to all tyrants.'[1]

The authors of the Geneva Bible did not urge their readers to adopt a literal reading of every passage, or to follow every directive, in the text. They explained that the use of certain Jewish ceremonies, which are described in such great detail, had been subsequently dispensed with in the New Testament; and sometimes they considered it necessary to explain that conduct was wrong, although it was not condemned in the Bible—for example,

[1] Tyndale, *Obedience of a Christian Man*; Tyndale, *Exposition upon the 5th, 6th, and 7th Chapters of Matthew* (Tyndale, *Works*, i. 176–7; ii. 65); Geneva Bible, notes to 1 Sam. xxvi. 9, and to 2 Kings ix. 30, 31, 33.

when Nebuchadnezzar worshipped Daniel. But no passage in the Pentateuch or in the Book of Kings that reported the killing of idolaters was given a modified interpretation; all were approved, from the executions carried out by Jehu to Moses' order that the lives of the women and children of Midian were not to be spared. Occasionally, the translators permitted themselves to criticize the conduct of an individual who receives nothing but praise in the biblical text. When King Asa, in the Book of Chronicles, removes his mother Maachah from being Queen, because she had made an idol in a grove, 'and Asa cut down her idol, and stamped it, and burned it at the brook Kidron', the notes commented: 'And herein he showed that he lacked zeal; for she ought to have died, both by the covenant and by the law of God; but he gave place to foolish pity.' The climax to the notes came at the end, in the Book of Revelation, where the notes in some chapters are longer than the actual biblical text itself, and call for an assault on the Church of Rome, which is the Antichrist referred to in the Book.[1]

While Knox was inspiring, and probably assisting, the authors of the Geneva Bible, he was engaged in writing, on his own account, a lengthy book on predestination, against Anabaptism. It was not printed until 1560, when it was published in Geneva by Crespin under the title *An Answer to a Great Number of Blasphemous Cavillations written by an Anabaptist and Adversary of God's Eternal Predestination. And Confuted by John Knox, Minister of God's Word in Scotland*; but Knox probably wrote it during the second half of 1558, and completed it before he left Geneva in January 1559, as he had very little time in which to do any writing during the next twelve months. The delay in publication was due to the storm which had been caused by *The First Blast of the Trumpet*. After this uproar, the authorities in Geneva hesitated to permit the publication of any book by Knox, even one which was devoted to the unobjectionable task of attacking Anabaptists, and the book was held up for some time until it passed the censorship. On 9 November 1559 the censor reported to the Little Council of Geneva that Knox's book was unobjectionable, and that at the request of the English congregation in Geneva, he recommended that permission should be given for it to be printed. Four days later, the Little Council authorized the publication on condition

[1] Geneva Bible, notes to Dan. ii. 46; to 2 Kings x. 6, 14, 23, 30; to Num. xxxi. 15, 17; to 2 Chron. xv. 16; and to Book of Revelation.

that it was not stated in the book that it was printed at Geneva, and that Whittingham and Barron undertook to make themselves responsible for the fact that the book contained nothing contrary to 'Catholic and orthodox' doctrine.[1] It was published under Crespin's imprint, but the place of publication was not given. It is an irony that the only book that Knox ever wrote against men more radical than himself, and that defended the Calvinist doctrine against Calvin's opponents and justified the actions of the government of Geneva against their critics, should have aroused more suspicions in Geneva than anything else that he published there.

The book on predestination is much longer than any of Knox's other books, being a volume of some 170,000 words.[2] Though the defence of the doctrine of predestination is the central theme, the book is more than this: it is an attack on all those opinions and sects which, in the religious and political jargon of the sixteenth century, were loosely referred to as Anabaptist, and which today could perhaps more appropriately be described as Anarchist. Knox manages in the book to attack nearly every variety of libertarianism—the Freewillers who opposed predestination, the supporters of religious toleration, the opponents of dogma, the Libertine Party in Geneva, and Münzer and the revolutionary peasants of the German revolt of 1525. He gives the impression that he is defending the doctrine of predestination because he regards it as a protection against all these evil consequences of libertarianism.

The book was a reply to a book written by an English Anabaptist, *The Confutation of the Errors of the Careless by Necessity*. The 'careless by necessity' was the author's designation for those who believed in predestination, who, he argued, were free of care with regard to their salvation because they believed that they must necessarily be saved, whatever they did. The identity of the author is unknown, and despite the most intensive modern research, no copy of his book has been traced, apart from the text which Knox reprinted in full in his own book. Knox states that *The Confutation of the Errors of the Careless by Necessity* was written in English, and that the author was a follower of Sebastian Castellio, the French Anabaptist who had formerly been a collaborator of Calvin, but

[1] Registres des Conseils de Genève, 9 and 13 Nov. 1559 (in *Works*, v. 16).

[2] It is reprinted, under the title of 'On Predestination', in *Works*, v 21–468. Knox's text alone runs to some 170,000 words, excluding the text of the Anabaptist's book, which is also published in the book.

had been driven from Geneva because he did not believe that the Song of Solomon was the Word of God. It has been suggested that the author was the English Anabaptist, Robert Cooke.[1]

In accordance with the well-recognized form of sixteenth-century doctrinal controversy, Knox reprinted the text of his opponent's book, and answered it paragraph by paragraph. This partly accounts for the length of Knox's reply, which is written in a repetitive and cumbersome style; but hidden among the verbiage, there are passages that show extreme lucidity of thought. There is also, as was usual in books of this kind, a good deal of personal abuse, Knox frequently addressing the Anabaptist as 'blasphemous mouth' and 'impudent liar'. In his theology, Knox adds nothing to Calvin, but his style and approach are very different. Calvin was more cool and subtle, Knox more passionate and direct. Knox is not as deep as Calvin, but he drives home the point to its brutal conclusion with a fearlessness and ruthlessness from which even Calvin flinched. Knox is less introspective, less concerned with the individual, than Calvin. After reading their books, we can understand why Calvin devoted himself to organizing a society which regulated the life of the individual, whereas Knox's life-work was the overthrow of a government and a Church.

Knox began by clearly formulating his proposition, that 'God in His eternal and immutable counsels hath once appointed and decreed whom He would take to salvation, and whom also He would leave in ruin and perdition.' He asserted that he would prove, by plain Scripture, that God had made this selection before the beginning of all time, though why God had chosen to do so could not be explained, but was most just, and would be revealed at the glorious coming of the Lord Jesus. Then, with merciless logic, he asserted the doctrine of predestination in its uncompromising severity, refusing to take advantage of any subterfuge, or to allow himself or his opponent any loop-hole through which to escape from its full implication. The Anabaptist author claimed that God loved all mankind, and a great part of Knox's book is taken up with repudiating this idea. 'You make the love of God

[1] Knox, *On Predestination* (*Works*, v. 24); Laing's notes to ibid. 16–14A; *Transactions of Baptist Historical Society*, iv. 90 (1914–15). For Castellio, see Bainton, *Concerning Heretics: an anonymous work attributed to Sebastian Castellio*; Bainton, *Studies on the Reformation*, pp. 139–84.

common to all men; and that do we constantly deny, and say that before all beginning God hath loved His elect in Christ Jesus, His Son, and that from the same eternity He hath reprobate others, whom for most just causes, in the time appointed to His judgement, He shall adjudge to torments and fire inextinguishable.'[1]

The Anabaptist asserted that God had not created any man with the intention of subjecting him to misery and pain. Knox will not have this.

God saith to the woman, In sorrow and dolour shalt thou bear thy children; to the man, In the sweat of thy face shalt thou eat thy bread; and also, Cursed is the earth for thy sake. Which (and many more places) plainly witness that God hath inflicted pain upon man whom He hath created. You answer, That did God for the sin of man. I confess; but yet is your foot fast in the snare. . . . If then God be subject to the law of nature . . . so that He is bound to do the selfsame thing to His births that nature moveth us to do to our children, I ask first, why did God suffer man created to His own image to fall into sin? Assuredly no natural father will wittingly and willingly suffer his children to fall into a pit or dungeon to destruction. And secondly I ask, why did not God (who is omnipotent, having all wisdom and goodness) provide another medicine for man than by death to overcome so many miseries? Thirdly, if God would that none should be born to misery, why did He not clearly purge the nature of Adam, why did He not stay that venom and corruption in our first father, why did He permit it to infect all his posterity? There is no shift that here can serve you. For if you say, God was provoked by the sins of the posterity, which He did foresee to be in them, so to do; I answer, that He foresaw nothing which His eternal and infinite power might not have removed and remedied, if so had pleased His godly wisdom. For then, as now, was He the God who alone may do whatsoever He will in Heaven and in earth.

God allowed men to sin so that He could pardon whom He would and harden whom He would. 'If these things do displease you, remember, first, that they are the voices of the Holy Ghost, and secondarily, call to your mind the condition of mankind.'[2]

When confronted with the text from Ezekiel, 'I will not the death of a sinner, but rather that he convert and live', Knox resorted to verbal quibbling:

The Prophet saith not 'I will the death of no creature', but saith 'I will not the death of a sinner'. Ye are not ignorant, I suppose, what

[1] *Works*, v. 42, 61, 112–13, 270–1, 309. [2] Ibid. 65, 83–84.

difference there is betwixt an universal negative, and an indefinite, or particular. Where ye say, God willeth the death of no creature, ye speak generally and universally, excepting none. But so doth not the Prophet, for he saith not 'I will the death of no creature', neither yet 'I will the death of no sinner', but simply saith 'I will not the death of a sinner'. I wonder that ye consider not that as there is difference betwixt creatures and creature, so that also there is difference betwixt sinners and sinner. Some creatures are appointed to death, for the use and sustentation of man. And dare you say that this is done against God's will? We be taught the contrary by His own mouth.[1]

On several occasions, Knox quotes the scriptural text which might be taken as the text of his whole book, and even as a text for the whole of Knox's life: 'Jacob have I loved, but Esau have I hated.' This hate for Esau could not be explained by the fact that Esau had committed some sinful act, for God had hated Esau when he was in his mother's womb.

I pray you, what light had Esau refused when God pronounced this sentence, The elder shall serve the younger? Upon the which, the Apostle, as before we have declared, doth conclude that ere the children had done either good or bad, the one was loved and the other was hated. That God doth nothing without a just cause, most willingly we confess; but that there is no justice in God to the ground whereof your blind reason doth not pierce, we constantly deny.[2]

The Anabaptist naturally made much of the argument that if men believe that they have been predestined to salvation by God's irrevocable election, they have no incentive to lead a moral life. In this respect, he argued, the supporters of predestination were no better than atheists. The same argument has been repeatedly used against both Calvinists and atheists during the last 400 years by those who believe that whether a man is rewarded or punished after death depends upon his actions during his life on earth. Knox used three arguments in reply. Firstly, he asserted that if one of God's elect should sin, he may be grievously punished in this world, as Adam and David were punished by God; but God still loved Adam and David after their sin, for 'that the elect cannot finally perish, neither yet that the reprobate can ever be saved, we constantly affirm'. Secondly, the doctrine of predestination did

[1] *Works*, v. 408–9. The text from Ezekiel is from Ezek. xviii. 23 in the Geneva Bible.

[2] Ibid. 146–57, 344; see Rom. ix. 13; Mal. i. 2, 3.

not assert that wicked men would be saved if God had chosen them as His elect, and that good men, who had been rejected as reprobates, would be condemned. 'Where ye burden us that we say "Let the reprobate do what they can, yet they must be damned", ye do most shamefully belie us. For we say and teach that whosoever declineth from evil, and constantly to the end doth good, shall most certainly be saved. But our doctrine is this, that because the reprobate have not the spirit of regeneration, therefore they cannot do those works that be acceptable before God.'[1]

But the strongest argument that Knox put forward was the argument of example. In the city where the doctrine of predestination was preached, a stricter moral discipline was enforced than any that had been seen since the days of the Apostles. If the Anabaptist was right, and belief in predestination led men to take the view that virtuous living was unnecessary, the Libertines would have been very content with the situation in Geneva, and would not have revolted against the discipline imposed; for Knox asserted that this, and not hatred of aliens, was the real cause of the disturbances of 1555. But why was Geneva so odious to the carnal men of this world? Was it not because

not only the licentious of the world, but even you dissembling hypocrites, cannot abide that the sword of God's vengeance shall strike the murderer, the blasphemer and such others as God by His Word commandeth to die? Not so by your judgements; he must live, he may repent. And those commonwealths do ye highly praise where men may live as they list, be subject to no law nor order. . . . But because in the streets of Geneva dare no notable malefactor more show his face (all praise and glory be unto God) than dare the owl in the bright sun, therefore is it hated, therefore it is called bloodthirsty, and thus blasphemously traduced.[2]

Then Knox, as if determined to bring in every issue most calculated to outrage the ideas of twentieth-century readers, refers to the case of Michael Servetus. Servetus, a Spanish Protestant refugee from the Spanish Inquisition, had expressed doubts, in his books, about the Trinity and other accepted dogmas. He was tried for these heresies in the court of the Catholic Bishop of Vienne in France, and sentenced to be burnt over a slow fire; but

[1] Ibid. 88, 232–6, 394. [2] Ibid. 209, 211–17.

he escaped from prison, and tried to make his way to Italy. While passing through Geneva, he was recognized, and at Calvin's insistence was charged and convicted of blasphemy, and burnt in 1553, though Calvin tried in vain to get the sentence changed to decapitation. The government and Church of every Protestant canton in Switzerland, and nearly everyone in Christendom, approved of the burning of Servetus; only Castellio and a few Anabaptist leaders protested against it.

Knox, in his book, justified the execution of Servetus, 'your dear brother for whose deliverance your champion Castalio solemnly did pray', and bitterly attacked the Anabaptist author for asserting that the burning of Cranmer, Ridley, and the English Protestant martyrs had been a just punishment inflicted upon them by God for their part in burning Joan Bocher, the English Anabaptist, in the reign of Edward VI. This interpretation of the deaths of 'those most constant martyrs of Christ Jesus' angered Knox so much that he said that he would not attempt to rebut this allegation with his pen, but would try to have his opponent arrested on a charge of blasphemy if he could apprehend him in any commonwealth where justice against blasphemers was administered. 'And hereof I give thee warning, lest that after thou shalt complain that under the cloak of friendship I deceived thee. Thy manifest defection from God, and this thy open blasphemy spoken against His eternal truth, and against such as most constantly did suffer for testimony of the same, have so broken and dissolved all familiarity which hath been betwixt us, that although thou were my natural brother I durst not conceal thy iniquity in this case.' This passage makes it clear that Knox believed that the Anabaptist author was a man with whom he was personally acquainted.[1]

The position appeared simple to Knox. 'Servetus was an abominable blasphemer against God, and you are justifiers of Servetus; therefore ye are blasphemers before God, like abominable as he was.' And if the Anabaptist claimed that the men who burned Servetus and the Anabaptists were wolves, rather than the sheep of Christ's flock, Knox asked him: 'I demand for answer whether Moses was a sheep or a wolf, and whether that fearful slaughter executed upon idolaters, without respect of persons, was not as great a persecution as the burning of Servetus and Joan of Kent.

[1] *Works*, v. 221–3.

To me, it appeareth greater.' For Moses had given them no opportunity to repent, but had ordered the brother to kill the brother, and the father not to spare the son. Nor had the position been altered by the coming of Jesus, for He had said that He did not come to break or destroy the law of His heavenly Father.[1]

Finally, Knox threw out a challenge to the Anabaptist.

But now of thee, O blasphemous mouth, I ask if thou be able to forge to thee and to thy pestilent faction another God than that God who most justly did drown and destroy by water all living creatures in earth, except so many as were preserved in the ark with Noah; who also did destroy by fire from Heaven Sodom and Gomorrah, with the cities adjacent, and the whole inhabitants of the same, Lot and his two daughters only reserved; who further, by the space of 4,000 years, did suffer all nations to walk in their own ways, revealing only His goodwill, and the light of His Word, to the seed of Abraham (to those that descended of Jacob, I mean).

Knox believed in this God and in His Son Christ Jesus, and would maintain His eternal verity 'not only against Jew, Turk and Papist, but also against you enraged Anabaptists, who can admit in God no justice which is not subject to the reach of your reason.'[2]

The doctrine of predestination, in the form in which Knox expounded it, may be repugnant to most modern readers, but it is easy to see why it attracted Knox. It was the antithesis of everything soft in religion. No one who accepted the doctrine of predestination would be likely to reject the moral discipline of Geneva, or to object to burning heretics. It was a guarantee against libertarianism and against religious toleration, which Knox denounced in the book as the sin of the city of Münster; for he stated that God had punished Münster with the rule of John of Leyden and the Anabaptists because the city had practised religious toleration. Intolerance of doctrinal dissent was an integral part of a disciplined revolutionary organization like that which Knox was creating, and predestination was the perfect doctrine for steeling the brethren of the congregation. Men who were fearless and ruthless enough to accept the doctrine of predestination had the fearlessness and ruthlessness which was required to destroy Popery in Scotland, France, and the Netherlands. When the supreme test arose at the outbreak of the civil

[1] Ibid. 224, 229. [2] Ibid. 392.

war in France, Castellio was useless to the Protestant movement; he condemned equally the atrocities committed by both the Catholics and the Protestants. But the Calvinists, who believed in predestination, were ready to die and kill for the cause.[1]

With the publication of his book on predestination, Knox ended his controversy with the Anabaptists. A few months later, he returned to Scotland to take part in a revolution against the Catholic Church, and in Scotland he did not have any trouble from Anabaptists. The Anabaptists did not come to Scotland till ninety years later, when they came in the ranks of Cromwell's army. By this time they could afford to be libertarians in religion, for they had substituted another discipline for the discipline of a religious organization. They vanquished Knox's Church, and forced it to turn for assistance to the descendant of Mary Queen of Scots, who broke the political power of the Protestant Church of Scotland. But Knox never had to face the problems of the seventeenth century.

[1] *Works*, v. 439; Castellio, *Conseil à la France désolée*, written in October 1562 (cited in Bainton, *Concerning Heretics: an anonymous work attributed to Sebastian Castellio*, pp. 259–60).

CHAPTER XVI

Dieppe

In December 1557 the Scottish Parliament passed a resolution in favour of the marriage of Mary Queen of Scots with Francis, the Dauphin of France. The Protestant lords voted in favour of the marriage, and Lord James Stewart and Erskine of Dun were appointed members of the delegation which was sent to France to negotiate the marriage treaty with Henry II. Mary of Lorraine had thus achieved her aim of winning the support of the Protestant lords for the marriage; but the bishops, and above all the Archbishop of St. Andrews, were dissatisfied. They were alarmed at the spread of heresy and at the absence of any measures to check it; and it was no consolation to the Archbishop to know that the Queen Regent, by this toleration of Protestantism, had won support for a marriage that lessened his brother's chances of succeeding to the Crown.

In April 1558 the bishops suddenly burned a Protestant martyr for the first time for eight years. Their action, though more savage, was in its way as contemptible as their process eighteen months earlier against Knox in his absence. Not daring to proceed against the great Protestant lords who had organized the signing of the Covenant, or the Protestants who had signed this heretical document and had organized themselves in the Congregation, they allowed two spiteful subordinates, one a parish priest and the other a gentleman in the household of the Archbishop of St. Andrews, to involve them in the burning of Walter Myln, an old priest who was more than 80 years old. Many years before, Myln had attracted the attention of Archbishop Hamilton as a result of his Protestant doctrine and his marriage as a priest, and he had moved to another district in order to escape arrest; but he was a simple old man, and in no sense a leader in the Protestant party. The parish priest of Dysart in Fife discovered that Myln was giving elementary instruction in the Bible to the children of a widow in a cottage in the parish. He arrested Myln, and sent him to Archbishop Hamilton, and accused him of heresy. As the bishop of the diocese, Hamilton could have dealt with the case himself in any way that he pleased; but he convened a commission of bishops and divines to sit in judgement on Myln, a course which normally was only adopted in very serious cases. Myln was condemned, and as he refused to recant he was sentenced to be burnt.

In accordance with the usual procedure, Hamilton issued an order to the Provost of St. Andrews, as the local officer of the civil power, to carry out the burning of Myln; but the Provost, who was sympathetic to the Protestants, or at least aware of their growing power in the country, refused to obey the order. He told the Archbishop that he would not arrange for the execution unless Myln was first tried by a civil Assize Court. Hamilton said that he was not eager to burn Myln, and suggested that the Provost should take Myln into his custody and arrange for his trial at the Assize, or do anything else with Myln that he thought fit; but at this point the Provost hesitated to take the responsibility on himself. Meanwhile one of the Archbishop's gentlemen decided to carry out the execution, and burn Myln in front of the priory of St. Andrews.

As the inhabitants of St. Andrews saw the pile for the bonfire being built up in the square, the rumour spread through the town that Myln was going to be burnt, and feelings ran high. At the last moment, the Archbishop's men ran into difficulties, for they could not find a suitable rope with which to bind Myln to the stake. They went to all the shops in the town, but they could not find any tradesman who was prepared to sell them a piece of rope for the burning of Myln. Eventually they found some rope, and thus were able to proceed with the execution. At the stake, Myln again refused to recant. 'I am four score years bygone,' he said, 'therefore by nature I have not long to live; but if I be burnt at this time, there shall a hundred rise in the ashes of my bones better nor I, and shall scatter the proud pack of you hypocrites that perturbs the servants of God. . . . I trust to God to His pleasure that I shall be the hindmost that shall suffer for this cause.' He was burnt, only three days after his trial, on 28 April 1558. When they saw the old man writhing in the flames, the crowd broke through the cordon of guards, and cut the rope that bound him, and Myln fell into the fire and died.

The people of St. Andrews erected a pile of stones in honour of Myln, to mark the place of his martyrdom. Whenever the priests and the Archbishop's servants demolished the memorial, the people rebuilt it, until the priests took the stones right away and used them to repair their houses.[1]

The Protestant lords and the Congregation had had no time to intervene to save Myln, but after the execution they made strong protests to the Queen Regent, and utilized to the full the indignation that had been aroused by his burning. In England the people watched in sullen resentment as another martyr was burnt every two or three days; but in Scotland the burning of this one old man, who was the first Protestant to be burnt since 1550 and only the fifteenth to be burnt in the last 150 years, brought the country to the verge of revolution. Mary of Lorraine informed the Protestant lords, who were now becoming known throughout Scotland as the 'Lords of the Congregation', that she had known nothing about the execution of Myln until after it had taken place, and deeply regretted it; but when they demanded that Archbishop Hamilton should be punished, she took no action. During the summer, the Protestant agitation spread and grew more violent. A new preacher suddenly appeared on the scene. This was Paul Methven, the son of a baker of Dundee, who preached to large congregations at open-air prayer-meetings, and roused Dundee, Angus, and Fife.

On 1 September, St. Giles's Day, a riot broke out in Edinburgh. The statue of St. Giles, the patron saint of Edinburgh, which in accordance with the annual custom was being carried in procession through the streets, was seized and smashed by Protestant demonstrators in the presence of Mary of Lorraine. In England or Flanders the men who desecrated the statue would have been burnt, or had their hands struck off; but the Scottish government took no action. On 8 November, Mary of Lorraine summoned Methven to appear before the Privy Council, and when he refused to come, he was put to the horn. The Protestants organized a band by which the signatories agreed to defend Methven from persecution, and presented it to the Queen Regent. The band was signed by nearly all the lairds in Angus, Fife, and Cunningham in Ayrshire, and by virtually the whole of the adult male population of Dundee. This was rebellion.[2]

[1] For Myln's case, see Pitscottie, ii. 130–6; Foxe, v. 644–7; Knox, *History*, i. 153–4.

[2] Knox, *History*, i. 127–9; Leslie, *History*, ii. 382–3; Pitscottie, ii. 136–40; Buchanan,

By this time, Glencairn, Lord James, Erskine of Dun, and other leaders of the Congregation had written to Knox and invited him to return to Scotland. The situation had now reached the point where they could ask an official government messenger to carry the letter, which was delivered to Knox in Geneva in November 1558 by John Gray, on his way to Rome, where he had been sent by the Queen Regent to obtain the Pope's bulls for the appointment of the new Bishop of Ross. They also wrote to Calvin to ask him to direct Knox to come, no doubt because they remembered the reluctance that Knox had shown on previous occasions at the prospect of leaving his congregation in Geneva and returning to Scotland.[1]

Once again, as on the two previous occasions on which he had been invited to return to Scotland, Knox was in no hurry to go. He did not reach Scotland until nearly six months after he received the invitation. The chief reason for his delay was almost certainly, as before, his distrust of the motives of the Scottish Protestant lords, and his fear of being used by them to start a civil war to further their own ambitions. There were also personal reasons for delaying his departure, for by a strange coincidence the invitation to return to Scotland, like the invitation that he had received in May 1557, arrived at a time when Marjory was on the point of giving birth to a child. His second son, Eleazer, was christened on 29 November 1558. Eleazer's godfather was the venerable Coverdale, who had translated the Bible into English before Henry VIII broke with Rome, and had been Bishop of Exeter under Edward VI. So, as the crisis rose in Scotland, Knox tarried in Geneva. On 16 December, after he had received the invitation to return to Scotland, he and Goodman were elected pastors of the English congregation in Geneva for the coming year, with Coverdale, Bodley, Williams, and Gilby as seniors.[2] Knox had probably not realized how far the situation had developed in Scotland; for, as so often during the previous ten years, his thoughts were on England rather than on Scotland.

History, ii. 242–4; Maitland, *Narrative of the Principal Acts of the Regency*, pp. 20–22; Spottiswood, i. 199; 'The Estate of Scotland' (*Wodrow Misc.* i. 53–55). See also *Accounts of the Lord High Treasurer of Scotland*, x. 364–5, 369–70, 402–3 (22 June, 7 July, and 7 Nov. 1558).

[1] Knox, *History*, i. 137. For Knox's reluctance to leave Geneva, see also Calvin to Arran, 1 Aug. 1558 (*Calvini Op.* xvii. 279).

[2] *Livre des Anglois*, pp. 13, 15.

On 10 November 1558 he wrote a pamphlet in the form of a letter to the people of England, and particularly to the members of his old congregations in Berwick and Newcastle, so many of whom had since become Catholics and gone to mass in obedience to Mary's laws. It was a long lamentation over the triumph of idolatry in England, and a denunciation of his readers for their 'horrible defection from God'. He denounced 'Jezebel' and the domination of the 'proud Spaniard', threatened the people with the divine vengeance, and urged them to take warning from the loss of Calais, which was sometimes called the sister town of Berwick, as both towns were English military bridgeheads on the frontier. The loss of Calais, which had been captured during the war by the French under the Duke of Guise, should 'move you to consider what is God's power'; for God's judgement would be 'poured forth in full perfection, not only upon the cruel murderers, but also upon such as by silence and flattery consent to their impiety'. He blamed himself for the apostasy of his old congregation in Northumberland, attributing it to his failure as a preacher there in the days of Edward VI; but he took comfort from the fact that Elijah and St. Paul had had similar experiences. 'In that behalf, have I the lot and sort common with the most part of God's true prophets.'

Knox added a postscript to his letter, explaining why he did not address his letter to any individual by name: 'The days are so wicked that I dare make special commendations to no man.'[1] He did not know, when he wrote the *Epistle unto the Inhabitants of Newcastle and Berwick*, that Mary was on her deathbed. The persecution was still raging unabated, and some zealous Catholic officials were hastening to burn their Protestant prisoners before Mary died; but a week after Knox wrote the letter, and long before it was received in England, Elizabeth was Queen. Her first action, like that of her brother and sister on their accessions in 1547 and 1553, was to issue a proclamation prohibiting anyone from making any unauthorized alterations in the religion established by law; but the persecution of Protestants stopped at once, all Protestants were released from prison, and within a few days the Queen was making gestures of hostility to the Catholic religion.

But though the English people and the Spanish ambassador,

[1] Knox, *Epistle unto the Inhabitants of Newcastle and Berwick* (*Works*, v. 473–94; see especially pp. 481, 485, 490, 492, 494).

Feria, knew that Elizabeth would make England Protestant once again, the refugees abroad did not immediately appreciate the situation. On 12 January 1559 Knox completed *A Brief Exhortation to England for the Speedy Embracing of Christ's Gospel, heretofore by the Tyranny of Mary Suppressed and Banished.* It was published, together with his *Epistle to the Inhabitants of Newcastle and Berwick*, at Geneva later in 1559. The theme of the *Brief Exhortation to England* was that the whole population of England had sinned by submitting to idolatry during Mary's reign, and by helping her to persecute Protestants, or at least not resisting her; and this collective guilt of the whole English nation could only be purged by reintroducing Protestantism in England, and putting the Catholics to death.

Elizabeth had decided to make England Protestant, but if she had read the *Brief Exhortation to England* it would only have made her more indignant with Knox. She believed that she was entitled, like Mary and every sovereign, to decide what religion should be established by law in England, and that all subjects must now obey her orders to make England Protestant, just as they had formerly obeyed Mary in making England Catholic. No one would be punished for having obeyed their sovereign in Mary's days and for having persecuted Protestants; but they would be punished if they now disobeyed the orders of Elizabeth. Knox's attitude that the English people had sinned in obeying Mary, and were morally obliged to atone by introducing the true religion, was anathema to Elizabeth, quite apart from the fact that he made it clear, in the *Brief Exhortation to England*, that this true religion was to be more Protestant in doctrine and ritual than Elizabeth intended.

Knox informed the English nation that they were all guilty.

> It is you all together who most cruelly have shed the blood of a number of your brethren and sisters, which from under the altar cry to be revenged. There is no person guiltless in God's presence who hath bowed their knees to idolatry (whatsoever excuse they list to pretend), but as all are idolaters, so are they and shall be reputed murderers before God, which do not wash away that infamy and innocent blood by unfeigned repentance.... The cause that I wrap you all in idolatry, all in murder and all in one and the same iniquity is that none of you hath done your duty, none hath remembered his office and charge, which was to have resisted to the uttermost of your powers that impiety in the beginning. But ye have all followed the wicked

commandment, all have consented to cruel murder, in so far as, in your eyes, your brethren have most unjustly suffered, and none opened his mouth to complain of that injury, cruelty and murder. I do ever except such as, either by their death, by abstaining from idolatry, or by avoiding the realm for the iniquity in the same committed, did give testimony that such an horrible falling from God did inwardly grieve them.

From Elizabeth's point of view, worse was to follow. 'Let not the King and his proceedings (whatsoever they be), not agreable to His Word, be a snare to thy conscience. O cursed were the hearts that first devised that phrase in matters of religion', which had led simple people to 'esteem every religion good and acceptable unto God which the King and Parliament did approve and command.' Knox demanded that God's commandments should 'be within thy limits and bounds so sure and established, that if prince, king or emperor would enterprise to change or disannul the same, that he be of thee reputed enemy to God; and therefore unworthy to reign above his people'; and he demanded that any man who attempted to destroy God's true religion after it had been established, and to erect idolatry, be sentenced to death, as God had commanded. He demanded the removal from office of all Catholics, and the abolition of plural benefices. 'In the name of the Lord Jesus I require of you that no dumb dog, no poisoned and pestilent Papist, none who before hath persecuted God's children, or obstinately maintained idolatry, be placed above the people of God.'

Knox urged the English clergy to enforce moral discipline throughout the country,

so that the ministers, albeit they lack the glorious titles of lords and the devilish pomp which before appeared in proud prelates, yet must they be so stout and so bold in God's cause that if the king himself would usurp any other authority in God's religion than becometh a member of Christ's body, that first he be admonished according to God's Word, and after, if he contemn the same, be subject to the yoke of discipline, to whom they shall boldly say, as Asarias the high priest said to Uzzias the King of Judah. . . . 'Pass out, therefore, for thou hast offended.'

He ended by making it clear that the English were to carry out his exhortations despite 'the lack of workmen to put things in such order as is requisite', even if this meant running the risk of revolution and a war of intervention from the Catholic powers.

As an appendix to the *Brief Exhortation to England*, Knox published a long list of the Protestant martyrs who had suffered under Mary up till the end of July 1558. It contained the names of the martyrs famous and humble, not only Rogers, Hooper, Ridley, and Cranmer, but the simple folk, from Thomas the blind boy at Gloucester to old Mother Tree at East Grinstead, from 'Michael's wife' at Ipswich to an unknown merchant's servant at Leicester. He stated that he had not yet sufficient evidence to compile another list—the list of the wicked accusers, false judges, and cruel tormentors of every one of these martyrs; but he hoped that one day he would be able to do so.[1]

Before he left Geneva, Knox made an attempt to reconcile the hostile factions in the Church of England, and extended the hand of friendship to his old opponents at Frankfort. Throughout the whole of the dispute at Frankfort, he had behaved with a moderation which was very different from his usual violent methods in controversy; and now he again showed how conciliatory he could be when he was dealing, not with the Papist enemy, but with Protestant factions whom he regarded as potential allies, despite all the injury that they had done him. When the news of Elizabeth's accession reached Geneva, the English congregation sent Kethe with a friendly letter to all the English congregations in exile, including the English at Frankfort. The letter, which was dated 15 December 1558, was signed by Knox, Goodman, Whittingham, and Gilby, as well as by Coverdale and Poullain and five others. After expressing their joy at the accession of 'the most virtuous and gracious Queen Elizabeth', they offered to forget all the quarrels of the past, and urged the need for friendship and unity; 'for what can the Papists wish more than that we should dissent one from another, and instead of preaching Jesus Christ and profitable doctrine, to contend one against another, either for superfluous ceremonies or other like trifles, from the which God of His mercy hath delivered us?'

The congregation at Frankfort replied on 3 January in an equally friendly letter. It was signed by eleven members of the congregation, including Isaac, who had denounced Knox to the authorities at Frankfort; but the writers stated that unfortunately most of the leading participants in the disputes of 1555 had already

[1] Knox, *A Brief Exhortation to England for the speedy embracing of Christ's Gospel* (*Works*, v. 501–36; see pp. 513–20, 529–31, 536).

returned to England, and so could not sign their letter. But beneath the friendly atmosphere, there were signs of trouble to come. The congregation at Geneva had expressed their conviction that the factions would be united in the future, as they had now acquired the knowledge of God's Word from 'the best reformed Churches' of Europe. The English at Frankfort replied that further controversy would be pointless, as all questions of order and ceremonies would henceforth be decided by neither party, but by Parliament and the authorities in England.[1]

On 28 January 1559 Knox left Geneva, leaving his wife and children and Mrs. Bowes behind, and arrived at Dieppe on 19 February. His first objective was not Scotland, but England, and he therefore wrote to the English government for permission to travel through England on his way to Scotland.[2] While he waited for an answer, he took a leading part in the stirring events that were taking place in Dieppe, where something like a mass conversion to Protestantism was in progress.

In the year 1558 the nature and prospects of French Protestantism changed. The small group of martyrs and idealists, who for thirty years had bravely endured the torments of the fire and the additional refinements of cruelty inflicted on heretics in France, were joined by great nobles and even Princes of the Blood, who were organizing their followers for civil war. At the head of the movement were Antoine de Bourbon, King of Navarre, and his brother, the Prince of Condé, and Gaspard de Coligny, Admiral of France, and his brother, Cardinal Châtillon. This Protestant cardinal was the brain behind the movement. Calvin estimated that there were now 300,000 Protestants in France. In May 1558, eight months after the martyrs of the Rue Saint-Jacques had been attacked at their peaceful prayer-meeting, the Rue Saint-Jacques was again the scene of Protestant activity. This time 10,000 Protestants, many of them carrying pistols, and including detachments of armed cavalry, marched down the Rue Saint-Jacques in military formation, singing Psalms and songs against the Pope. When the

[1] The English at Geneva to the English at Aarau, Basel, Strasbourg, Worms, Frankfort, etc., 15 Dec. 1558; the English at Frankfort to the English at Geneva, 3 Jan. 1559; and see the English at Aarau to the English at Geneva, 16 Jan. 1559 (*The Troubles at Frankfort*, pp. 186–92).

[2] Martin, *Les Protestants anglais réfugiés à Genève*, p. 141; Daval, *Histoire de la Réformation à Dieppe*, i. 10; Asseline, *Antiquitez et Chroniques de la Ville de Dieppe*, i. 284; Knox to Cecil, 10 Apr. 1559 (Knox, *History*, i. 284, 286).

leaders were arrested by the authorities in Paris, the King of Navarre sent armed retainers to release them.[1]

The movement spread rapidly into the provinces. Normandy, with its thriving clothing industry and trading ports, was particularly receptive to Protestant doctrines. In the great city of Rouen, many people became more or less openly Protestant, and from there 'the religion', as it was known in France, spread to Dieppe. Little Jean Venable, for all his courage, had proved to be incapable of organizing the congregation of Dieppe efficiently, and was replaced by another refugee from Geneva. In November 1558, Delaporte, the minister at Rouen, arrived in Dieppe, and began to preach in secret conventicles held in private houses at night. But soon afterwards, an exceptionally virulent outbreak of plague caused the Protestants to suspend their meetings, and other duties compelled Delaporte to leave Dieppe. The conversions in the town continued, but there was no Protestant minister available to officiate there.

When Knox arrived at Dieppe, and discovered the situation, he stepped into the breach. During the next six or seven weeks, he preached and officiated as minister at secret prayer-meetings in the town. Knox has often been accused of cowardice, but his conduct at Dieppe in the spring of 1559 is sufficient to rebut this accusation; for a minister who was present at secret Protestant services still ran a considerable risk of arrest, torture, and the fire. The Protestants were safe wherever they were protected by the armed servants of the Bourbons and the Châtillons; but anywhere else, at any time, the authorities might strike at random, surround a house, and seize a pastor and his congregation. The Protestants at Dieppe could not rely on the support of powerful protectors; for the King's Lieutenant in Normandy, the Duke of Bouillon, was an enthusiastic Catholic, as was the Archbishop of Rouen, Cardinal Louis de Bourbon, despite the fact that he was the brother of the King of Navarre and the Prince of Condé. Knox had already shown, and was soon to show again, how he reacted in the face of danger. As long as he was living in a place of safety, he was reluctant and slow to leave it and travel to the danger zone; when he found himself in the midst of danger,

[1] Calvin to Philip of Hesse, 24 Feb. 1558 (*Calvini Op.* xvii. 65); Michiel to the Doge and Senate of Venice, 22 and 29 May and 11 June 1558 (*Ven. Cal.* vi. 1235, 1239, 1240).

he did not hesitate, but threw himself into the struggle with passionate energy.

For some time, no attempt was made by the Duke of Bouillon, Cardinal Bourbon, or the *Chambre Ardente* to interfere with the secret meetings, in private houses at night, where Knox preached to larger and larger congregations, and after a few weeks the Protestants had grown so rapidly that a substantial proportion of the population of Dieppe had joined the movement. They then felt strong enough to hold their services openly in daylight, and Knox preached to ever larger congregations. According to Desmarquets, the eighteenth-century Catholic historian of Dieppe, Knox preached with great violence, and attacked Delaporte for the moderation which he had shown in his sermons in Dieppe; but Desmarquets was not only violently prejudiced against Knox, but was guilty of many inaccuracies in his book, and cannot be relied upon in this matter.

On 1 March 1559 the Protestants in Dieppe had their greatest success so far, when a number of prominent local magnates joined them, and were formally admitted to the congregation at a ceremony at which Knox officiated. They included the Sieur de Senarpont, who was the King's Lieutenant in Picardy and had behind him a distinguished career as an administrator and soldier, for as commander of the garrison at Boulogne he had had to deal with the English at Calais in peace and war before the French captured the English March. Senarpont's daughter, Madame de Monteraulier, and her husband, and the Sieur de Bracqueville and two of his daughters, were also admitted to the congregation by Knox on 1 March, along with a number of other ladies and gentlemen.[1]

Meanwhile Knox had received bad news from England. Elizabeth had refused him permission to visit England because of *The First Blast of the Trumpet*, and though he made a second application to the English government, this was likewise refused. On 6 April, Knox wrote to Anne Locke, who was returning to England, and had written to him from Geneva to ask whether it would be permissible for her to attend the services of the Book of

[1] For the situation at Dieppe, and Knox's activities there, see Daval, i. 10–11; the Protestants of Dieppe to Calvin, 12 Apr. 1559 (*Calvini Op.* xvii. 497); Asseline, i. 284–6 (where the ceremony of 1 Mar. is wrongly dated 30 Mar.); Desmarquets, *Mémoires chronologiques pour servir à l'histoire de Dieppe*, i. 141, 148. Desmarquets wrongly places Knox's sojourn in Dieppe in 1560.

Common Prayer. Knox told her that it was not permissible, and made a strong attack on the Book of Common Prayer and its 'diabolical inventions, viz., crossing in baptism, kneeling at the Lord's table, mummeling or singing of the Litany. . . . The whole order of your Book appeareth rather to be devised for upholding of massing priests than for any good instruction which the simple people can thereof receive.' Knox said that he knew that both Anne Locke and other people would say that his judgement was 'somewhat extreme', but the issue was whether God or man was to be obeyed in matters of religion. Many things that had happened in the four years since Knox had left Frankfort, including this last refusal of Elizabeth to let him come to England, had embittered him to the point where he could write in this way about the Book of Common Prayer. He now suggested that it was sinful to attend a service in the Church of England, in which he himself had formerly officiated as a minister under the same order of service.

> No man will I salute in commendation specially, although I bear goodwill to all that unfeignedly profess Christ Jesus; for to me it is written that my *First Blast* hath blown from me all my friends in England. . . . The *Second Blast*, I fear, shall sound somewhat more sharp, except men be more moderate than I hear they are . . . England hath refused me; but because, before, it did refuse Christ Jesus, the less do I regard the loss of that familiarity.[1]

On 10 April, Knox wrote to Cecil. He had known Cecil well when he was at the Court of Edward VI, in the days when Cecil was Secretary of State under Northumberland. Now Cecil once again held the same office under Elizabeth; but in the intervening years he had lived quietly in England, obtaining a pardon from Mary for his support of Jane Grey, going to mass, sitting as a Member of Parliament in the House of Commons, and holding minor appointments in the government service and in his town of Stamford. The letter which Cecil received from Knox was very different from the flattering and obsequious letters which he usually received since he had become the Secretary of State. Knox told Cecil that he had grievously sinned by committing idolatry and by consenting, through silence, to Mary's iniquities, but that God had spared him and had given him the opportunity to

[1] Knox to Cecil, 10 Apr. 1559 (Knox, *History*, i. 286); Knox to Anne Locke, 6 Apr. 1559 (*Works*, vi. 11–15).

redeem himself by rendering good service in the future to the Protestant cause.

To you, Sir, I say that as from God ye have received life, wisdom, honour and this present estate in the which now ye stand, so ought you wholly to employ the same to the advancement of His glory . . . which, alas, in times past ye have not done; but being overcome with common iniquity, ye have followed the world in the way of perdition. For to the suppressing of Christ's true Evangel, to the erecting of idolatry, and to the shedding of the blood of God's most dear children, have you, by silence, consented and subscribed. This your most horrible defection from the truth known, and once professed, hath God to this day mercifully spared; yea, to man's judgement, He hath utterly forgotten and pardoned the same.

God had preserved Cecil during Mary's reign, and 'although worthy of Hell, He hath promoted you to honours and dignity'.

Knox expressed surprise that he had been refused permission to pass through England on the way to his own country, and said that his request was so reasonable that he had almost come without troubling to ask for a licence; and yet he had heard that his request had been rejected with such vehemence

that the solicitors thereof did hardly escape imprisonment. And some of that flock, I hear, be so extremely handled that those that most cruelly have shed the blood of God's most dear children find this day amongst you greater favours than they do. . . . But I have, say you, written a treasonable [book] against the regiment and empire of women. If that be my offence, the poor flock is innocent (except such as this day do fastest cry treason); for, Sir, in God's presence I write, with none in that company did I consult before the finishing of the same; and therefore, in Christ's name, I require that the blame may lie upon me alone.

He denied that his book had been treasonable, and said that unless he was convinced by the arguments put forward in the reply to the *First Blast*, which he had heard was about to be published, he could not undertake to keep silence in the future on the question of the government of women.

Then, with almost breath-taking frankness, Knox proposed a bargain to the English government: if Elizabeth would admit that his theory about the government of women was correct as a general principle, he would proclaim that she was a Deborah and an exception to the rule.

If any think me either enemy to the person, or yet to the regiment, of her whom God hath now promoted, they are utterly deceived of me. For the miraculous work of God, comforting His afflicted by an infirm vessel, I do acknowledge, and the power of His most potent hand (raising up whom best pleaseth His mercy to suppress such as fight against His glory) I will obey, albeit that both nature and God's most perfect ordinance repugn to such regiment. More plainly to speak, if Queen Elizabeth shall confess that the extraordinary dispensation of God's great mercy maketh that lawful unto her, which both nature and God's law do deny to all women, then shall none in England be more willing to maintain her lawful authority than I shall be. But if (God's wondrous work set aside) she ground (as God forbid) the justness of her title upon consuetude, laws or ordinances of men; then I am assured that as such foolish presumption doth highly offend God's supreme Majesty, so do I greatly fear that her ingratitude shall not long lack punishment.[1]

Here Knox had hit the nail on the head in his summary of the difference between Elizabeth's attitude and his own. They were agreed on two points: they both believed that, in general, women should be under the subjection of men, and that Elizabeth herself was an exception to the rule. Where they differed was in the reason why Elizabeth was an exception. Elizabeth believed that she was an exception because she was a queen; Knox believed that she was an exception because she was a Protestant. Elizabeth intended to be a Protestant, but she believed that her subjects should obey her whatever she did; Knox believed that they should only obey her as long as she remained a Protestant, and the right kind of Protestant. This difference was deep, and quite irreconcilable.

Knox entrusted the letter to one of the messengers who regularly carried letters between Cecil and the English ambassador in Paris. When the messenger realized who Knox was, he at first refused to take the letter; but he finally agreed reluctantly to carry it to Cecil, after Knox had assured him that the letter contained nothing unmeet for Cecil to receive, unmeet for Knox to write, or unmeet for the messenger to carry. But Knox certainly made no attempt to flatter Cecil and Elizabeth in his letter. By informing Cecil that he deserved to be sent to Hell, by offering to recognize Elizabeth's authority on his own terms, even by his reference

[1] Knox to Cecil, 10 Apr. 1559 (Knox, *History*, i. 282–7; *Works*, vi. 15–21).

to the Queen's Majesty as 'Queen Elizabeth', although he knew well what was the proper way to refer to a queen in a letter to her Secretary, Knox had shown Cecil that he did not intend to try to win the favour of princes. Cecil did not reply to the letter. On 22 April, Knox sent him another copy of it, thinking no doubt that the letter of the 10th might have got lost; but no reply was received. Yet Cecil's reaction to the letter may not have been entirely unfavourable. Cecil was a mixture of unscrupulous careerist and sincere Protestant. He had betrayed Somerset and Northumberland in turn, and used every trick of flattery and deception to advance himself; but whenever he could, he used his position and his masterly grasp of Machiavellian statecraft to further the Protestant cause. Throughout Mary's reign he had used his influence in the House of Commons to protect the property of the Protestant refugees abroad; and when Elizabeth came to the throne, he had strongly urged her to declare herself a Protestant, after pointing out all the drawbacks and dangers which this course would entail. As Secretary of State, Cecil could not reply to Knox's letter; but Knox's appeal to him to atone for the sin which he had committed in collaborating under Mary may have touched a chord in him.[1]

In any case, Knox's letter did no harm to Protestantism. During the rest of Knox's lifetime, Elizabeth and Cecil repeatedly sent money and troops to support Knox's Church in Scotland, and assured its triumph, because they considered that it was essential for England's national security that no French or Spanish soldier should set foot in Scotland. They were not dissuaded from pursuing this course because Knox wrote a tactless letter; and if they had not considered that intervention in Scotland was necessary for English national interests, Knox could not have induced them to act, even if he had written with the heavy obsequiousness of Cranmer or the flattering subtleties of Lethington.

When Knox sent Cecil the second copy of his letter, on 22 April, he was still hoping to be granted permission to travel through England; but a few days later he changed his mind, and without waiting any longer he sailed to Scotland by the eastern road. On 29 April, Des Roches, the French Protestant pastor at Rouen,

[1] Throckmorton to Cecil, 14 May 1559 (Forbes, i. 90–91, where it is wrongly dated 15 May; *Cal. For. Pap. Eliz.* i. 683); Knox to Cecil, 22 Apr. 1559 (*Works*, vi. 20–21); Conyers Read, *Mr. Secretary Cecil and Queen Elizabeth*, pp. 111–12.

arrived at Dieppe and took charge of the congregation there. For another month the great public prayer-meetings continued at Dieppe; then the authorities struck. On 31 May, Adam Séquart, the Grand Vicar of the Archbishop of Rouen, arrived in Dieppe. He organized a procession with the Host through the streets, which led to violent clashes with the Protestants and Séquart began an intensive persecution. Des Roches was forced to flee from Dieppe, and returned to Rouen, while the Protestant movement in Dieppe was again driven underground. By this time Knox was busily engaged in another field of action. He arrived at Leith on 2 May 1559. His greatest hour had come.[1]

[1] Daval, i. 11–12; Asseline, i. 286; Desmarquets, i. 143; Knox, *History*, i. 161; 'The Estate of Scotland' (*Wodrow Misc.* i. 56).

CHAPTER XVII

The Revolution of 1559

KNOX sailed from Dieppe to Leith by the eastern road. Among the other passengers on the ship was a government messenger who was carrying a new cast of the Great Seal of Scotland which had been made in France. The arms of France, Scotland, and England were engraved on the seal. If Elizabeth was a bastard, as she was in the eyes of those who did not recognize the divorce of Henry VIII and Catherine of Aragon, Mary Queen of Scots was the lawful Queen of England, and by incorporating the English leopards with the lion of Scotland and the French fleur-de-lis on the arms of Francis and Mary, Henry II was asserting Mary's claim to the English throne. The existence of this new cast of the Great Seal containing the arms of England, and the fact that it was being sent to Scotland for use if the opportunity should arise, was a great State secret; but Knox indulged in a useful piece of espionage on the journey to Scotland. He entered into conversation with the government messenger, who showed him the Great Seal in the utmost secrecy. Knox was able, in due course, to pass on the information to the English government in order to exacerbate Elizabeth's suspicions of the designs of Mary Queen of Scots.[1]

Knox arrived in Scotland at a critical moment. In March 1559, Mary of Lorraine had turned firmly against the Protestants. She no longer needed the votes of the Protestant lords, who in November had joined with all the Estates in Parliament to vote in favour of the grant of the Crown Matrimonial to the Dauphin; and, encouraged by a subsidy of £40,000 granted to her by the bishops, she acceded to their demands that stern measures should be taken against heresy. She took steps to force the people to attend mass at Easter, and forbade anyone to celebrate the communion, except priests acting under the proper ecclesiastical

[1] Knox to Railton, 23 Oct. 1559; Sadler and Croft to Cecil, 27 Oct. 1559 (*Works*, vi. 86, 88–89).

authority. The Protestants defied the Queen Regent's order. At Easter, Methven administered the communion to large congregations in Dundee, where hardly anyone attended mass, and Willock did the same in Ayr.[1]

Mary of Lorraine summoned Methven, Willock, Harlaw, and John Christerson to appear before the Privy Council at Stirling on 10 May to answer to a charge of usurping the authority of the Church and preaching heresy and sedition. The Protestants rallied to the defence of their preachers, and again, as in May 1556 and November 1558, the Protestant lairds and the town of Dundee let it be known that they would come in strength to escort their preachers to their trial. They hoped that, as on the previous occasions, the summons would be withdrawn; but this time Mary of Lorraine stood firm.[2]

When Knox arrived in Edinburgh on 2 May, he walked right into the enemy's camp. The bishops had been holding a conference in the Black Friars' Church, and at their final meeting, on 3 May, when they were on the point of leaving the church, a man ran in to tell them the news that Knox had arrived from France and had been all night in the town. While Methven, Willock, and the other preachers were fifty miles away in Dundee, under the protection of their supporters, Knox, who had already been condemned as a heretic, was in Edinburgh at the mercy of the bishops. If they had moved quickly enough, they might have caught Knox; but the Queen Regent was in Glasgow, and as the bishops did not wish to act without her authority in so grave a matter, they immediately sent a messenger to Glasgow to inform her that Knox was in Edinburgh. As soon as Knox understood the situation, he decided to go to Dundee without delay, and join his fellow-preachers and supporters.[3]

On 3 May he wrote a hurried note 'in haste' to Anne Locke, telling her that he had arrived in Edinburgh,

[1] *Acts Parl. Scot.* ii. 503–20 (29 Nov. 1558); Knox, *History*, i. 141, 152, 158–60; Lord Herries, p. 37; *Accounts of Lord High Treasurer of Scotland*, x. 416 (9 Feb. 1558/9); Archbishop Hamilton to Archbishop Beaton, 31 Jan. 1558/9 (*Statutes of Scottish Church*, pp. 149–53); Sir James Melville's *Memoirs*, p. 27; Maitland, *Narrative of the Principal Acts of the Regency*, p. 24; Spottiswood, i. 266; Proceedings against Methven, Willock, etc., 10 May 1559 (Pitcairn, i [i]. 406–7); 'The Estate of Scotland' (*Wodrow Misc.* i. 56); Quintin Kennedy to Archbishop Beaton, 7 Apr. 1559 (*Wodrow Misc.* iv. 265–7).

[2] Pitcairn, i [i]. 406–7.

[3] 'The Estate of Scotland' (*Wodrow Misc.* i. 56–57), where the date of Knox's arrival is wrongly given as 30 Apr.).

uncertain as yet what God shall further work in this country, except that I see the battle shall be great, for Satan rageth even to the uttermost; and I am come (I praise my God) even in the brunt of the battle; for my fellow-preachers have a day appointed to answer before the Queen Regent, the 10th of this instant, where I intend (if God impede not) also to be present, be life, be death, or else be both, to glorify His godly name, who thus mercifully hath heard my long cries. Assist me, sister, with your prayers, that now I shrink not when the battle approacheth.

Next day he left Edinburgh, and arrived safely in Dundee, where he rejoined his colleagues, and announced that he would go with them to Stirling on 10 May to defend his doctrine before the Privy Council.[1]

But as the days went by, and the summonses were not withdrawn, it became clear that the Queen Regent had called the Protestants' bluff. If they carried out their threat to march in strength to Stirling, this would mean open rebellion, a step which they hesitated to take; so they decided to advance as far as Perth, where Protestantism had suddenly begun to spread rapidly, and send Erskine of Dun on to Stirling to ask the Queen Regent to withdraw the summonses. Mary of Lorraine treated Dun with great courtesy and charm, but gave him an evasive reply; and when Dun returned to Perth, the Protestants were more perplexed than ever as to what they should do next. Consequently, Knox and Methven and the other preachers spent the day of 10 May at Perth, and did not appear, either accompanied or unaccompanied, before the Privy Council. Next day the Protestants at Perth heard that the Queen Regent and the Privy Council had issued a proclamation under which Willock, Methven, Christerson, and Harlaw were put to the horn and declared to be rebels for non-appearance when summoned to answer charges of having unlawfully administered the Sacrament of the Altar, of spreading erroneous and seditious doctrines and heresies, and stirring up sedition and tumult against the authority of the King and Queen in the burgh of Perth and elsewhere. Their sponsors' bail was declared forfeited, and anyone who assisted the men at the horn were declared to be rebels.[2]

[1] Knox to Anne Locke, 3 May and 23 June 1559 (*Works*, vi. 21–22); Knox, *History*, i. 161.

[2] Knox, *History*, i. 160–1; Proceedings of 10 May 1559 (Pitcairn, i [i]. 406–7); Knox to Anne Locke, 23 June 1559 (*Works*, vi. 22–23).

On the day that this news arrived, Thursday, 11 May 1559, Knox preached in the Church of the Holy Cross of St. John the Baptist in Perth. St. John was the patron saint of Perth, which in the sixteenth century was usually called St. Johnston, and the Church of St. John was adorned with pictures and statues of the saints. Knox preached a vigorous sermon against idolatry. After he had finished his sermon, as most of the people of Perth were sitting down to their midday dinner, a Catholic priest appeared in the Church of St. John, and began to celebrate mass. One of Knox's younger supporters, an enthusiastic Protestant boy, cried out: 'This is intolerable, that when God by His Word hath plainly damned idolatry, we shall stand and see it used in despite.' The priest struck the boy a tremendous blow. During the next fourteen months, the repercussions of this blow were felt as far away as Amboise and Madrid. The boy threw a stone at the priest, which missed him and struck the box in which the Host was suspended, and the Congregation wrecked the church, destroying every idolatrous image and painting, except one recent painting contributed two years before by the glover's guild, which escaped and still survives today.[1]

The next objective was obvious—the friaries. Crossing the High Street, the Congregation attacked the houses of the Black Friars and the Grey Friars outside the walls of the town. As the news spread through Perth, the citizens left their dinner and joined in the attack, the zealous new Protestant converts being animated by revolutionary fervour to destroy evil, and the mob by desire for loot; for they had all heard stories of the wealth and luxuries which the hated friars, with their hypocritical vows of poverty, had accumulated in their friaries. In the house of the Franciscans they found what they were looking for; the Grey Friars had fine bed linen and large quantities of wine and ale, and the people were shocked at the amount of salted beef that was left over from the stocks of the previous winter, although there were only eight persons in the convent. 'The Grey Friars was a place so well provided', wrote Knox, 'that unless honest men had seen the same, we would have feared to have reported what provision they had.' There was much less to be found in the Dominican friary. Then the crowd broke into the Charterhouse, the great

[1] Knox, *History*, i. 162; see D. McRoberts, 'A Sixteenth Century picture of St. Bartholemew from Perth' (*Innes Rev*. x. 281–6).

Carthusian monastery founded by James I, where he had been buried after his murder in 1437 in a magnificent tomb.

The brethren of the Congregation showed restraint and discipline. They protected the lives of the friars, and tried to prevent looting, for they were acting to destroy idolatry, not to enrich themselves. They allowed the Prior of the Charterhouse to take away as much gold and silver as he could carry, and held the rest of the spoil in order to use it for the relief of the poor. This was considered to be simple justice, as the friars had purchased their wealth with the alms that had been paid to them to enable them to care for the poor. But not all the inhabitants of Perth were Protestant idealists, and a good deal of looting took place, for, as in every revolution, both noble and base elements were involved.[1]

Knox succinctly described the events of 11 May in a letter which he wrote six weeks later to Anne Locke, on 23 June.

> The Queen and her Council, nothing mindful of her and their promise, incontinent did call the preachers, and for lack of compearance did exile and put them and their assistants to the horn; which deceit being spied, the brethren sought the next remedy. At first, after complaint and appellation from such a deceitful sentence, they put their hands to reformation in St. Johnston, where the places of idolatry of Grey and Black Friars and of Charterhouse monks were made equal with the ground; all monuments of idolatry that could be apprehended, consumed with fire; and priests commanded, under pain of death, to desist from their blasphemous mass.

When he wrote his *History*, he found time to condemn the mob who came for loot. 'The whole multitude convened, not of the gentlemen, neither of them that were earnest professors, but of the rascal multitude. . . . The first invasion was upon the idolatry; and thereafter the common people began to seek some spoil.'[2]

The Queen Regent called on d'Oysel and his French soldiers to crush the rebels at Perth. The French garrison in Scotland consisted only of 1,500 Frenchmen, with another 500 Scots in French pay who served as regular soldiers in the French army in Scotland under d'Oysel's command;[3] but Mary of Lorraine relied also on

[1] Knox, *History*, i. 162–3.

[2] Knox to Anne Locke, 23 June 1559 (*Works*, vi. 23); Knox, *History*, i. 162.

[3] For the strength of Mary of Lorraine's French and Scottish forces, see 'The Estate of Scotland' (*Wodrow Misc.* i. 61, 67); Sadler and Croft to Cecil, 25 Nov. 1559 (Sadler, ii. 142); Knox, *History*, i. 179–80. Knox wrote to Anne Locke on 23 June

the help of the Scottish nobles, and turned both to Châtelherault and to the Protestant lords for assistance. No noble was supporting the rebels except Lord Ruthven, the Provost of Perth, who had found himself in the midst of the revolt and had given his full support to the Congregation; for the professors of the Gospel at Perth, who consisted of the brethren who had come from Dundee and the Protestants of Perth who had recently joined the movement, were under the leadership, not of any of the lords, but of Erskine of Dun and Knox. Lord James and the Lord of Lorne, who had become Earl of Argyll on his father's death, were at the Court at Stirling, and were embarrassed by the incidents of 11 May. They had hoped to use the Congregation to put pressure on the Queen Regent, but did not wish to launch a rebellion, and certainly did not approve of a revolutionary movement begun spontaneously by the common people. They declared their loyalty to the Queen Regent, and marched with d'Oysel and the army towards Perth. They reacted in the same way as the Lutheran princes of Germany had reacted to the iconoclasm of Carlstadt's followers and the Peasant War of 1525, and as the lords in every country of Europe reacted to mob violence, whatever its pretext.

If events in Scotland had followed the same course as in every other country, the Protestant lords would have united with the Queen Regent to crush the Congregation at Perth; but in Scotland there was a factor in the situation that was not present elsewhere. The rebels at Perth had a leader who, unlike Carlstadt and Münzer and the typical sixteenth-century agitator, was a shrewd political realist and a skilful diplomat, as well as a determined revolutionary. Knox was the only leader of a popular revolution in the sixteenth century who managed to persuade the nobles to join the revolutionary movement.

Mary of Lorraine sent all the French forces in Scotland to suppress the disturbances, placing the army under the joint command of d'Oysel and Châtelherault. While the army was assembling, the Congregation in Perth wrote appeals and political manifestoes addressed to their friends and enemies. These manifestoes were almost certainly written by Knox. One was addressed to the Queen Regent, and proclaimed the Congregation's loyalty to

1559 (*Works*, vi. 24) that the French had 8,000 troops in Scotland, whereas the Congregation had only 5,000 men; but this is almost certainly wrong.

Mary Queen of Scots, her husband, and to the Queen Regent herself, but stated that they were compelled to defend themselves against those who sought to attack them for reasons of religion. 'With most dolorous minds we are constrained, by unjust tyranny purposed against us, to declare unto your Grace, that except this cruelty be stayed by your wisdom, we will be compelled to take the sword of just defence against all that shall pursue us for the matter of religion, and for our conscience sake.' The letter was signed: 'Your Grace's obedient subjects in all things not repugnant to God, the faithful Congregation of Christ Jesus in Scotland.'[1]

They also wrote letters to d'Oysel and to every French captain in command of units stationed in Scotland, urging them not to let themselves be used by the priests to fight against the Scottish Protestants, and telling them that Henry II had not sent them any orders to do so. They stressed the friendship which had existed between the French and the Scots, and warned them that if they now attacked the Congregation, it would start a war of bitter revenge between the two countries. Another letter was addressed 'to the generation of Antichrist, the pestilent prelates and their shavelings within Scotland', and warned them that unless they dissociated themselves from their bands of bloody men of war, the Congregation would execute 'just vengeance and punishment' upon them. 'With the same measure that ye have measured against us, and yet intend to measure to others, it shall be measured unto you.... Yea, we shall begin that same war which God commanded Israel to execute against the Canaanites.'[2]

Knox makes it clear that these appeals were written for propaganda purposes, and were 'spread abroad in great abundance, to the end that some might come to the knowledge of men. ... These our letters were suppressed to the uttermost of their power, and yet they came to the knowledge of many.' The Congregation had their members and sympathizers everywhere. One of them put the letter to the Queen Regent on her cushion in the chapel royal at Stirling, where she saw it when she went to mass; and Protestant soldiers in the French army saw to it that their officers received the letters addressed to them.[3]

The Congregation in Perth wrote to their supporters in Angus, Fife, and Ayrshire, and appealed for help. 'Then repaired the

[1] The Congregation to Mary of Lorraine, 22 May 1559 (Knox, *History*, i. 164–5).
[2] Knox, *History*, i. 166, 171–2.
[3] Ibid. 166.

brethren from all quarters for our relief', wrote Knox. The lairds of Angus and Fife arrived with the citizens of Dundee, and took up their position a mile outside Perth, ready to fight the French soldiers, who had come within ten miles of the town. Lord Ruthven thought it was time to get out while the going was good, and deserted on 23 May to the Queen Regent's army; but although the loss, at this critical moment, of the only nobleman among their supporters deeply demoralized the Congregation, Knox and his colleagues stopped the rot, and within twelve hours morale was as high as ever.

D'Oysel and Châtelherault did not attack at once, but on 24 May sent Lord James and Argyll to persuade the Congregation to disperse. It was, perhaps, a fatal blunder, for an immediate assault might have crushed the Reformation. They may have wished to avoid bloodshed, and have been impressed by the courage and resolution of the men of Dundee and Fife who blocked their path; but the most important factor was the attitude of Argyll and Lord James, who at this juncture rendered a greater service to the Protestant cause in the Queen Regent's camp than they could have done in Perth. With so few forces at his disposal, d'Oysel could not disregard the desire of the Protestant lords to reach a compromise with their co-religionists. Argyll and Lord James spent two days in Perth negotiating with the rebels, and Knox succeeded in persuading them that this was not a popular rising which threatened the security of the State. He assured them that the Congregation were loyal to the Queen and the Queen Regent, and were only concerned with the defence of the true religion.

This delay of forty-eight hours saved the Congregation. When Knox's manifestoes reached the west, Glencairn and Campbell of Kinzeancleuch roused the brethren of Cunningham and Kyle. Kinzeancleuch rode through Ayrshire, contacting every Bible-reading class which Knox had planted there three years before, and Glencairn's authority and determination overcame the first hesitations. After the Earl had declared that he would, if necessary, go alone with a pike to join his brethren in St. Johnston, 2,500 men, including 1,200 horsemen, set out under his leadership for Perth, determined to settle the destinies of the 700,000 inhabitants of Scotland. In Glasgow they were met by Lyon Herald, who read a royal proclamation ordering them to disperse on pain of treason; but not one man turned back. D'Oysel sent soldiers to bar their passage at the ford across the Forth near Stirling; but west of Stirling they swung to the north, and made their way across the uplands by rough tracks and footpaths, and, avoiding the French soldiers, joined the Protestants in Perth.

D'Oysel and Châtelherault, knowing that Glencairn was on his way, had hastily offered terms to Erskine of Dun. Both the Queen Regent's army and the forces of the Congregation were to be disbanded, and the Congregation were to return to their homes; the town of Perth would submit to the Queen Regent's authority, and offer no resistance to the entry of the government officers, but no French soldiers were to enter the town; and a pardon was to be granted to all who had joined the Congregation. This was a stage that was reached in nearly every popular rising in Europe in the sixteenth century, for rulers and statesmen knew that it was the way to suppress a rebellion. Their small standing army could not easily defeat a large force of rebels, even though these were untrained and poorly armed; but by negotiating and pardoning the rebels, they could induce them to go home; and as the people could not conceive of deposing a king, and setting up their own government in his place, there was nothing else that they could do. Then in due course, under some pretext or other, the rebels could be rounded up in their villages, and hanged along the roadside in hundreds or in thousands. Only in Scotland in 1559 did matters turn out differently, because the skilful leadership of the Congregation, and their excellent organization, made it possible for them to call up the brethren at any time they chose. Unlike Münzer's peasants and Aske's Yorkshiremen, the Congregation could retreat and disengage, and yet preserve their organizational links and their revolutionary determination.

Knox and the other preachers persuaded their followers to accept the Queen Regent's terms. This was not an easy task, as the Congregation were eager to fight; but Knox knew that they had great reserves of strength which were not yet engaged. He told them that he knew that the Queen Regent would break the agreement, but that they should nevertheless agree to the terms in order to prove that they were not rebels, and to suffer hypocrisy to disclose itself. It was largely because of the attitude of Lord James and Argyll that Knox and Dun decided to accept the Queen Regent's terms; for Lord James and Argyll told Knox that if the terms were rejected, they would have to fight for the Queen

Regent, but that if an agreement were made, and later violated by the Queen Regent, they would fight on the side of the Congregation. The agreement was signed on 29 May, and next day the Congregation withdrew from Perth. Before they left, Knox preached a last sermon in the town. He thanked God that they had been preserved, and that no blood had been shed, but warned them that the Queen Regent and her Frenchmen would violate the terms of the agreement, and that the Congregation must be ready to come out again whenever they were called upon to protect a persecuted brother.

Both sides broke the agreement immediately. Under the terms of the truce, d'Oysel and Châtelherault had agreed that French soldiers should not enter Perth; but as soon as the Congregation had left Perth on 30 May, 400 Scottish soldiers who served in the French army marched in, aggressive and arrogant. As they passed the house of Patrick Murray, a prominent Protestant of Perth, they fired a few shots at a group of people who were standing on the stairs outside the house, and killed Murray's son, a boy of 10 or 12. Mary of Lorraine made light of the incident, but the murdered child was not forgotten by the Protestants, who exploited the murder to the full, especially the callousness of Mary of Lorraine. 'When children were slain', wrote Knox, substituting the plural for the singular, 'she did but smile, excusing the fact by the chance of fortune.'[1]

The Protestants accused the Queen Regent of breaking the agreement by sending French troops into Perth, arguing that Scottish soldiers who were paid by the King of France and served in the French forces were French soldiers within the meaning of the agreement. It was a good enough excuse to treat the truce as repudiated. The Congregation immediately sent word to Dun and the lairds of Fife, and to the Provost of Dundee, to call out the brethren to meet in St. Andrews on 11 June. Meanwhile Knox and his followers went to the fishing ports of Fife. He was warmly welcomed by the Protestants of Crail, where on Friday, 9 June, he preached a strong sermon, denouncing the Queen Regent for her violation of the truce terms. He said that there could be no

[1] For the events at Perth of 24–30 May, see Knox, *History*, i. 172–80; 'The Estate of Scotland' (*Wodrow Misc.* i. 58); Knox to Anne Locke, 23 June 1559 (*Works*, vi. 24); Buchanan, ii. 406; Spottiswood, i. 274; Keith, *History of Affairs of Church and State in Scotland*, i. 198–203.

quietness until one of the parties were masters. He called on them to expel the foreigners from the kingdom, and to prepare themselves either to die as men or to live victorious. After his sermon, the congregation destroyed all the altars and images in Crail. Next day, Knox preached at Anstruther, and here, too, the altars and images were destroyed.[1]

But the test was to come on Sunday, in St. Andrews. On the Saturday evening, Archbishop Hamilton moved into his archiepiscopal town, accompanied by 100 spears, with the intention of preventing Knox from preaching and causing trouble in St. Andrews. He sent word to Argyll and Lord James that if Knox tried to preach in his principal church, he would salute him with a round of shot fired from a dozen hagbuts, which would alight on Knox's nose. At this, Lord James and Argyll hesitated to force the issue. It is understandable that Lord James, as the Prior of St. Andrews, was reluctant to be involved in a violent clash with the Archbishop in the metropolitan seat; but Knox was determined to go ahead. He told the lords that it was in this church that he had preached his first sermon, and that when he was in the galleys he had confidently hoped that he would preach there once again before he died. He offered to preach in the parish church next day without any escort or protection, but preach he would. No doubt Knox and the Congregation, with their widespread contacts everywhere, knew that they had many supporters in St. Andrews, where the burning of Walter Myln had aroused so much opposition thirteen months before; for when Knox, with the full consent of Lord James and Argyll, presented himself at the parish church and preached on the ejection of the buyers and sellers from the temple of Jerusalem, there was no resistance from the Archbishop's men, and the people rose to Knox's exhortation to purge the Church of the profiteers who corrupted and defiled it. After his sermon, they went straight out of the church and destroyed the priory and all the monasteries in the town, with the full approval of the Provost and burgh council, as well as of the Prior, Lord James. 'And so that Sabbath and three days after', wrote Knox to Anne Locke, 'I did occupy the public place in the midst of the doctors, who to this day are dumb; even as dumb as their idols who were burnt in their presence.'[2]

[1] Knox, *History*, i. 181; Spottiswood, i. 275–6.

[2] Knox to Anne Locke, 23 June 1559 (*Works*, vi. 25); Knox, *History*, i. 181–2. For

Archbishop Hamilton had hurriedly left St. Andrews and gone to Falkland, eighteen miles away, where the Queen Regent was in residence with 800 French soldiers. When she heard of the destruction at St. Andrews, she ordered the French to attack the Congregation there, and the army set out under the leadership of d'Oysel and Châtelherault. But the call had already gone out to the Congregation to assemble again at Cupar in Fife, on the road from Falkland to St. Andrews, and on 13 June the two parties met in a thick mist on Cupar moor. Knox had arrived at Cupar with Lord James and Argyll on the previous evening, and during the night, and on the morning of the 13th, the Congregation arrived in strength.

When at night the Lords came to Cupar [wrote Knox], they were not a hundred horse, and a certain footmen, whom Lord James brought from the coast side; and yet before the next day at twelve hours (which was Tuesday the 13 of June) their number passed 3,000 men, which by God's providence came unto the Lords. From Lothian, the lairds of Ormiston, Calder, Halton, Restalrig and Colstoun. . . . The Lord Ruthven came from St. Johnston, with some horsemen with him. The Earl of Rothes, Sheriff of Fife, came with an honest company. The towns of Dundee and St. Andrews declared themselves both stout and faithful. Cupar, because it stood in greatest danger, assisted with the whole force. Finally, God did so multiply our number, that it appeared as if men had rained from the clouds.[1]

As the mist lifted, the 800 French soldiers found that they were facing 3,000 men armed with cannon, which the men of Dundee had obtained from the fort of Broughty Crag, and Châtelherault and d'Oysel were glad to negotiate. The Congregation, too, preferred to avoid a battle, partly perhaps because they hesitated to engage trained troops in the field, but probably chiefly because of the reluctance of Argyll and Lord James to enter into a direct clash with the Queen Regent's army. Châtelherault and d'Oysel offered to pardon all the members of the Congregation if they disbanded and agreed not to destroy any more abbeys. The Congregation refused these terms, but agreed to an armistice for six days, during which time they would not destroy any abbeys and would discuss a settlement with delegates whom the Queen Regent

a contemporary Catholic view of these events, see Grierson to the Dominican Prior of Paris, 6 Oct. 1559 (*Innes Rev.* ix. 216–17).

[1] Knox, *History*, i. 183.

was to send to St. Andrews for the purpose. But a few days later, apparently before the expiry of the truce, the Congregation burned the Dominican abbey of Lundores, for they interpreted the delay by the Queen Regent's delegates in arriving at St. Andrews as a repudiation of the truce by the Queen Regent. Knox wrote to Anne Locke, describing how the abbey 'was reformed, their altars overthrown, their idols, vestments of idolatry and mass books were burnt in their own presence, and they commanded to cast away their monkish habits'.[1]

The humiliation of the Queen Regent and the French at Cupar Muir had a serious effect on the morale of the Catholics. If the Congregation could rally sufficient forces to overawe the French garrisons in Scotland, it was obvious that no one else in the country could resist them, and many of the Catholics began to think of making terms with them. At Dundee and Perth, many of the monks and friars, after leaving their burnt-out houses, abandoned their habits. But Knox was under no illusion about the dangers that threatened. It was clear that Mary of Lorraine would ask Henry II for more troops to suppress the revolt, and that Henry's Catholic zeal and national interests would impel him to take whatever measures were necessary to save Scotland for the Catholic faith and the French Crown; and when Knox wrote to Anne Locke from St. Andrews on 23 June, he did not dare to hope that their success would be more than temporary:

> Now, forty days and more, hath my God used my tongue in my native country, to the manifestation of His glory. Whatsoever now shall follow, as touching my own carcass, His holy name be praised. The thirst of the poor people, as well as of the nobility here, is wondrous great, which putteth me in comfort that Christ Jesus shall triumph for a space here, in the north and extreme parts of the earth. We fear that the tyranny of France shall, under the cloak of religion, seek a plain conquest of us; but potent is God to confound their counsels and to break their force.[2]

Wherever the Congregation came, they took over the churches, after purging them of idolatry, and held their Protestant services in them. Here Knox again showed his usual political realism. The Order of Geneva was not generally known in Scotland, and very

[1] Knox to Anne Locke, 23 June 1559 (*Works*, vi. 26).

[2] Cecil to Throckmorton, 13 June 1559 (*Cal. For. Pap. Eliz.* i. 840); Knox to Anne Locke, 23 June 1559 (*Works*, vi. 26–27).

few copies, if any, were available for use by the Congregation; but for some years, the Scottish Protestants had been using the English Book of Common Prayer of 1552, because copies had been brought from England by the Scottish refugees when they returned to Scotland after Mary Tudor came to the throne. When the Congregation seized the churches in 1559, they continued to use the Second Book of Common Prayer. As far as we know, Knox did not make any objection to this; doctrinal purity could wait until after victory had been won. He himself, where he officiated, undoubtedly used the Order of Geneva, and other ministers, who used the English Prayer Book of 1552, probably introduced their own changes in certain matters, especially in sitting to receive communion, and in the singing of Psalms and songs by the congregation. This had been a feature of Scottish Protestant services for more than fifteen years, and the revolution of 1559 produced new versions of *The Good and Godly Ballads*. The Congregation now sang songs about 'the Pope, that pagan full of pride', the bishop who 'could not preach for playing with the lassies', 'the parish priest, that brutal beast', and the silly nuns who 'cast up their bums and heaved their hips on high'. Some modern writers have doubted whether songs such as this were actually sung in church during a religious service; but the Scottish Protestants were militant revolutionaries, who believed that they were serving God by ridiculing the false religion as well as by praising His name.[1]

The Congregation assembled before Perth on 24 June. The Queen Regent's 400 soldiers under Captain Cullen were still holding Perth, and the Congregation called on them to surrender, threatening that if they resisted and slew any of the Congregation, they would be treated as murderers and punished accordingly. Cullen replied that he would hold Perth until he received orders from the Queen Regent to surrender it; but after the Congregation had discharged two cannon shots into the town, and the garrison had made a brief resistance, a truce was concluded, under which it was agreed that the town would be surrendered if the Queen Regent did not send reinforcements to Cullen within twelve hours. Next day the garrison marched away with colours flying, and the

[1] Knox, *History*, i. 137; Grange to Percy, 1 July 1559 (*Works*, vi. 34); Cecil to Throckmorton, 9 July 1559 (Forbes, i. 155); *The Goude and Godlie Ballatis* (Saltire Society selections), pp. 60–62.

Congregation re-entered Perth. One of the brethren from Dundee had been killed, and two had been wounded, in the fighting; they were the first casualties in the revolution. Again the Congregation had avoided a major clash with the French army. 'We might have executed against them judgement without mercy,' wrote Knox, 'for that they had refused our former favours, and had slain one of our brethren, and hurt two in their resistance; and yet we suffered them freely to depart without any further molestation', because the Congregation thirsted for no man's blood.[1]

Two miles to the north of Perth stood the great abbey of Scone, where most of the kings of Scotland had been crowned in former times. The abbey was held as an additional perquisite by Patrick Hepburn, Bishop of Moray, who was particularly hated by the Congregation because of the part that he had played in the condemnation of Walter Myln. The Bishop, like his cousin, the young Earl of Bothwell, had hastened to support the Queen Regent, and had assembled his servants and tenants at Scone in order to help the garrison in Perth. After the capitulation of the garrison, the Lords of the Congregation in Perth wrote and informed him that unless he agreed to support the Congregation, the abbey of Scone, and his palace which adjoined it, would be destroyed. Hepburn immediately promised to support them, and to vote with the Protestant lords in Parliament against the clergy. But the men of Dundee were not satisfied. They were not prepared to leave the monuments of idolatry standing at Scone, and marched to the abbey, bent on destruction.

This put Knox and the leaders in a difficult position. It was one thing to write pamphlets in exile explaining how God had punished Saul for sparing Amalek, and to demand, in epistles to England from Geneva, that God's vengeance should be inflicted, through the medium of the Protestants, on the persecutors who had shed the blood of God's saints; but on the field of action, Knox realized that the Congregation's threats to destroy the houses of recalcitrant Catholics would be worthless if the houses of those who submitted were likewise burnt. The Protestant leaders sent Halyburton, the Provost of Dundee, to urge his townsmen to leave the abbey and the Bishop's palace alone; and when Knox heard that Halyburton was having great difficulty in restraining the men of Dundee, he himself hurried to Scone. But the poor of

[1] Knox, *History*, i. 189.

Perth had got there first, in search of loot; and when Knox reached Scone, he found that they were on the point of breaking into the Bishop's granary. He addressed the crowd, and eventually persuaded them not to enter the granary. Meanwhile Argyll and Lord James had arrived in response to the indignant protests of the Bishop, who had promised them his support only two hours before. At length the Congregation and the mob dispersed for the night, but next morning they came again. One of the brethren of Dundee looked in at the granary door, whereupon an illegitimate son of the Bishop, who, with the Bishop's household, was attempting to defend the abbey and palace, ran the man through with his rapier. This was too much for the men of Dundee, and the abbey of Scone and the Bishop's palace were looted and burnt to the ground.[1]

The destruction of the historic abbey of Scone, more than the burning of any other monastery, has been condemned by posterity. Many opponents of the Reformation, from Dr. Johnson downwards, have castigated Knox and his supporters for the wanton destruction of the historic buildings and art treasures of Scotland. At the time, the Catholics asserted that Knox had called for the systematic destruction of all monasteries, as a cool act of policy, in order to prevent the continuation of the monastic system. The Scottish Jesuit priests who reported to Pope Clement VIII on the state of Scotland in 1594, declared that Knox 'was always repeating to the mob his advice to pull the monasteries down to the ground, "for (said he) if you leave the nests standing the old birds are sure to come back to them".' This seems to be the earliest version of the words attributed to Knox in connexion with the destruction of the monasteries: 'Down with the nests, that the crows may not build again.'[2]

But the Congregation were responsible for only a small part of the destruction of the Scottish ecclesiastical buildings. The great abbeys of the Border Country had been destroyed fifteen years before by the armies of Henry VIII, though some of them were rebuilt, and destroyed again by the Congregation in 1559. The churches, none of which were destroyed by the Protestants, in many cases collapsed through disrepair under the Catholic régime

[1] Knox, *History*, i. 189–91.

[2] Boswell, *Life of Johnson*, i. 273; the Jesuits' report to Clement VIII (1594) (Stevenson-Nau, App. I, p. 110).

before 1559, because of neglect by the great monasteries and their lay priors who held the benefices of the parish churches, and in the Highlands churches were sometimes burnt in warfare between the clans. There are no recorded cases of wanton destruction of manuscripts by the Scottish Protestants, like the deliberate obliteration of Scottish historical records by Edward I, or, in the sixteenth century, the destruction of the manuscripts at Oxford by Cox in the reign of Edward VI. As far as the destruction of manuscripts is concerned, the cool policy decisions of kings and governments caused more damage than the passion of revolutionary mobs. The only casualties of the revolutionary fever of 1559 were the monastic buildings and the images in the churches. These could not be saved from religious zealots, who destroyed the emblems of a religion which they considered to be evil as ruthlessly as the Christian missionaries a thousand years earlier had destroyed the groves of the heathen deities in Germany and Britain, and as Spanish Anarchists, 400 years later, destroyed the sacred objects of the established Church.[1]

Knox showed his political genius at the burning of Scone. He exerted all his energies to save the abbey and the house of the hated persecutor of Walter Myln, because he realized that cowardly time-servers must be given an incentive to join the Congregation; but when the revolutionary enthusiasm of his followers got out of hand, he did not condemn it, but accepted it realistically. Similar incidents had taken place in Germany forty years earlier, and elsewhere in Europe. This was the moment at which Luther would have repudiated his followers, and publicly condemned the violence of the mob; but Knox understood and sympathized with the zeal which had inspired the destructions and indiscipline, though he condemned the act itself. The split between the lords and the people that occurred in Germany did not occur in Scotland. The Scottish Protestant movement did not divide into the lords and wealthy classes on the one side, obsessed

[1] For the controversy as to who destroyed the Scottish abbeys, see Hay Fleming, *The Reformation in Scotland*, pp. 315–58; Sir James Fergusson, *The White Hind and other Discoveries*, pp. 56–57; and, for the contrary view, McRoberts, 'Material Destruction caused by the Scottish Reformation' (*Essays on the Scottish Reformation*, pp. 415–62); Durkan, 'Paisley Abbey and Glasgow archives' (*Innes Rev*. xiv. 49). See also Croft to (Cecil), 3 July 1559 (*Sc. Cal.* i. 482); Archbishop Hamilton to the Dean of Christianity of the Merse, 9 Apr. 1556 (*Source Book of Scottish History*, ii. 143); *History of the Feuds and Conflicts among the Clans in the Northern Parts of Scotland*, pp. 20, 22 (in *Miscellanea Scotica*, vol. i).

above all by their fear of popular revolution, and the lower classes on the other, coming under extremist and Anabaptist influence, and turning a successful religious revolution into an unsuccessful social revolt. This was mainly due to the difference between social relationships in Germany and Scotland, and the free and easy social intercourse and friendship which had always existed between the Scottish lords and lairds and their tenants; but part of the credit is due to Knox. While Luther bitterly denounced the followers of Carlstadt and the revolutionary peasants in pamphlets, Knox confined himself to a few remarks about the 'rascal multitude' in his *History*, which he did not publish during his lifetime, and restrained the anger of Lord James and Argyll, just as he had tried to restrain the violence of the men of Dundee at Scone. He quotes with obvious approval the words of an old woman of Scone, who lived near the abbey, as she watched it go up in flames. She said to those who condemned the burning that no man is able to save where God wishes to punish.

> Since my remembrance [she said] this place hath been nothing else but a den of whoremongers. It is incredible to believe how many wives hath been adulterated, and virgins deflowered, by the filthy beasts which hath been fostered in this den; but especially by that wicked man who is called the Bishop. If all men knew as much as I, they would praise God; and no man would be offended.

Knox says that at these words 'were many pacified'.[1]

Within a day or so, the population at Stirling, hearing that Lord James and Argyll were on their way to the town, looted and destroyed the monasteries there, apparently from a desire for loot rather than from religious idealism. Meanwhile the Congregation at Perth set out for Edinburgh. On the way, they passed through Linlithgow, where Knox preached, and the monasteries were burnt and the images in the churches were destroyed. In Edinburgh, the burgh council, under Lord Seton as Provost, had been repeatedly declaring their loyalty to the Queen Regent ever since 11 May; but when they called out the citizens in the watch to guard the religious houses at night, one of the watch threw a stone at the windows of the monastery that he was supposed to be guarding. By the middle of June, the deans of the guilds were taking steps to protect their valuables, and as the Congregation

[1] Knox, *History*, i. 191.

marched from Perth, the burgh council decided, on 27 June, that the ornaments and silver eucharistic vessels should be removed from the churches and entrusted to the keeping of some of the baillies. But they had left it too late, and no one now waited for the burgh council's orders. On the 28th, the friars began to distribute their valuables to their friends to carry away with them, and the mob, hearing of what was happening at the religious houses, quickly went along to take the loot before it had all gone. The houses of the Black Friars and the Grey Friars were looted on 28 June.

Next day, the burgh council met in solemn session, and held 'long reasoning upon the coming of the Congregation to this burgh'. They decided to send seven of the baillies to meet the Congregation at Linlithgow, to welcome them and to ask them to ensure the safety of the buildings in Edinburgh; but while the burgh council were discussing the proposal, the Congregation were already approaching the West Port, and they marched in on the same day. Only 1,300 of the brethren had come to Edinburgh, with Knox, Argyll, and Lord James leading them; but this was more than enough against a demoralized enemy. Mary of Lorraine had shut herself up with the French garrison in the Castle of Dunbar, and the many Catholics in Edinburgh offered no resistance. The Congregation found nothing in the religious houses except the bare walls; even the doors and window-shutters had been removed by the looters. 'Wherethrough we were the less troubled in putting order to such places', wrote Knox.[1]

Knox went straight to St. Giles's Cathedral, and preached. It was exactly seven weeks since his first sermon at Perth, and in the last five days Perth had been recaptured, Scone destroyed, and Linlithgow purged of idolatry. But his sermon in St. Giles's was very moderate. As the looters had saved the Congregation the trouble of purging idolatry in Edinburgh, there was no purpose in inflaming the audience against the religious houses, and Knox emphasized that the Congregation were not rebels, but were loyal to their sovereigns and the Queen Regent, and wished only to reform religion. Mary of Lorraine, who next day sent a French

[1] Knox, *History*, i. 191–2; *Edinburgh Burgh Records*, iii. 36–37, 39–44 (14, 20, and 28 May, and 3, 14, 16, 27, and 29 June 1559); *Diurnal of Occurrents*, p. 53 (where the sack of the Edinburgh monasteries is said to be the work of the Lords of the Congregation, not the mob); 'The Estate of Scotland' (*Wodrow Misc.* i. 61).

gentleman to France to give Henry II news of the latest events, wrote that Knox had gone to great trouble in his sermon to protest that the Protestant leaders did not wish to seize the Crown, but only to further the Gospel. 'If it is only for the establishment of the said religion,' she wrote, 'the majority of the kingdom agrees with them in this.'[1]

Immediately after he had finished preaching, Knox found that a courier was on the point of leaving for London, and he therefore wrote a hurried letter to Anne Locke on the evening of 29 June. 'I could not but scribble these few words unto you, immediately after I was come from the very preaching place in St. Giles's Church in Edinburgh. . . . The professors are in Edinburgh. The Queen is retired into Dunbar. The fine [end] is known unto God. We mean no tumult, no alteration of authority, but only the reformation of religion and suppression of idolatry.' But in this moment of triumph, when the capital appeared to have surrendered to the Congregation, Knox was not carried away by a mood of unthinking optimism. He knew the dangers that confronted them, and faced them realistically. 'More trouble than ye see lieth upon me', he wrote in his letter to Anne Locke. He realized that the fate of the Scottish Reformation would be settled, not by the brethren of the Congregation, but by the great powers of Europe.[2]

[1] Mary of Lorraine's Instructions to Du Fresnoy (30 June 1559?) (Teulet, i. 335). Mary of Lorraine states that Knox's sermon was preached 'yesterday'. Teulet dates the document 'July 1559', and this is possible, in which case it refers, not to Knox's sermon of 29 June, but to some other sermon which he preached in the course of the next three weeks.

[2] Knox to Anne Locke, 29 June 1559 (*Works*, vi. 30, where it is wrongly dated 25 June).

CHAPTER XVIII

The Negotiations with England

By the middle of June 1559, Knox had realized that though the Congregation could bring men to Cupar Muir in such numbers that they seemed to rain from the clouds, a Protestant victory in Scotland could only be won by English troops. Within a few days of Cupar Muir, Knox wrote from St. Andrews to Cecil, asking for a licence to come to Newcastle or Durham, so that he could communicate to some English government official important information that he did not wish to set down in writing. Cecil did not reply, and in fact never received the letter.[1]

On the morning of 28 June, immediately before setting out from Perth for the march on Edinburgh, Knox wrote another letter to Cecil. After pointing out that this was the fourth time that he had written to him since he left Geneva, and that he had so far not received a reply, he again asked for a licence to visit England; for although he had heard that he had become so odious to Elizabeth and her Council that the mention of his name was unpleasing in their ears, there was no just cause for the Queen to think of him as her enemy. 'One thing I know, that England by me to this day hath received no hurt; yea, it hath received, by the power of God working in me, that benefit which yet to none in England is known, neither yet list I to boast of the same. Only this will I say, that when England and the usurped authority thereof was enemy to me, yet was I a friend to it, and the fruit of my friendship fanned the Borders in their greatest necessities.' This was probably a reference to the part which Knox's propaganda had played in persuading the Scottish lords to oppose the war against England in 1557, though Knox hesitated openly to claim credit for the mutiny at Maxwellheugh. 'My eye has long looked to a perpetual concord betwixt these two realms; the occasion whereof is now most present, if God shall move your

[1] Knox to Cecil, 28 June 1559 (*Works*, vi. 31); Cecil to Percy, 11 July 1559 (*Cal. For. Pap. Eliz.* i. 973).

hearts unfeignedly to seek the same.' Both England and Scotland 'stand in greater danger than many do espy'.

Knox wrote that Cecil had no doubt heard all sorts of rumours as to what was happening in Scotland.

> The truth is that many of the nobility, the most part of barons [lairds] and gentlemen, with many towns and one city, have put to their hands to remove idolatry and monuments of the same. The reformation is somewhat violent, because the adversaries be stubborn. None that professeth Christ Jesus with us usurpeth anything against the authority, neither yet intend to usurp, unless strangers be brought in to suborn, subdue and bring in bondage the liberties of this poor country. If any such thing be espied, I am uncertain what shall follow.[1]

The news of the events in Scotland had reached London before the end of May. At first the English government officials assumed that these disturbances that the preachers had stirred up would soon be 'pacified'; but when Cecil realized the seriousness of the movement, he saw the possibilities of using the religious revolt in Scotland to expel the French troops and convert Scotland from a French into an English satellite, thus removing the permanent threat of a war on two fronts which faced the English government whenever it went to war with France. This policy would bring great advantages for the security of Elizabeth's throne, for English national interests, and for the furtherance of the Protestant religion to which Cecil was sincerely devoted. He persuaded Elizabeth, with some hesitation, to adopt this policy; but they had to move with caution. The European war had ended in October 1558, and had been followed in April 1559 by the Treaty of Cateau-Cambrésis between England, France, and Spain, and in May by the Treaty of Upsettlington between England and Scotland. England was impoverished, and could not afford to put more than a few thousand men in the field; the state of the navy was precarious, as nearly half the ships were under repair; the loyalty of many of Elizabeth's Catholic subjects was doubtful; and Spain, antagonized by England's reconversion to Protestantism, could no longer be regarded as a reliable ally. Moreover, the French and Spanish governments had declared their intention, at Cateau-Cambrésis, of uniting to crush heresy, and were planning to cement this new friendship by a royal marriage.[2]

[1] Knox to Cecil, 28 June 1559 (*Works*, vi. 31–32; *Cal. For. Pap. Eliz.* i. 887).

[2] Croft to the Council, 19 May 1559; Cecil to Throckmorton, 26 May 1559;

On 8 July, Cecil, in a private letter, laid down his policy towards Scotland: the Congregation were to be helped 'first with promises, next with money, and last with arms'.[1] He was eager that, if possible, the Congregation should expel the French by their own efforts, without any open English aid being necessary; and he had no hope of persuading Elizabeth to help the Congregation unless she was convinced that they really meant business and deserved to be taken seriously. The Scottish lords, on the other hand, did not wish to commit themselves irrevocably to a course of open rebellion until they were sure that English aid could be relied upon, and that Elizabeth would not draw back at the last moment and abandon them to the vengeance of the French and the Queen Regent. During the next eight months, long negotiations were carried on between the English government and the Lords of the Congregation, with Cecil urging the Congregation to show more determination and do more for themselves, and the Congregation stressing their own weakness in order to convince Cecil that the French could only be defeated by English troops.

A further difficulty was the deep-rooted national hatred between English and Scots, which could not be easily removed even by ideological sympathies on grounds of religion. Sir Henry Percy, the Deputy Warden of the Eastern and Middle Marches, was convinced for a long time that the troubles in Scotland were a put-up job, and that Mary of Lorraine and the Congregation were really assembling their armies in order to make a joint attack on England. Even more serious was Elizabeth's hatred of rebellion, and the widely held belief throughout Christendom in the duty of obedience to rulers. Elizabeth's conscience, as well as her fear of the reactions of foreign kings, made her loath to appear to be supporting subjects who were rebelling against their Prince, particularly if the common people were taking a leading part in the revolt. The bishops of the Church of England were equally opposed to popular revolution, and their pleasure at seeing Popery overthrown in Scotland was qualified by their disgust at the methods by which this was being accomplished. In November

Northumberland to Cecil, 26 May and 5 and 18 June 1559; Croft to Parry, 14 June 1559 (*Cal. For. Pap. Eliz.* i. 710, 765, 861; *Sc. Cal.* i. 455, 460, 463, 465, 469); Pasquier to Fonsomme (1559); Pasquier to Serres, 1 Jan. 1595 (*Les Œuvres d'Estienne Pasquier*, cols. 77, 450).

[1] Cecil to Croft, 8 July 1559 (*Cal. For. Pap. Eliz.* i. 953; *Sc. Cal.* i. 486).

1559, Matthew Parker, the Archbishop-elect of Canterbury, wrote to Cecil: 'God keep us from such visitation as Knox have attempted in Scotland, the people to be orderers of things.'[1]

The cause of the Congregation, and of Knox in particular, was being ably assisted by Sir Nicholas Throckmorton, the English ambassador in Paris. It was men like Throckmorton who did so much to ensure the victory of Protestantism in Scotland and in Europe. Instead of bishops and priests, brought up in the old religion, who had formed the diplomatic corps in the days of Henry VIII and Edward VI, most of Elizabeth's ambassadors and political agents had spent their youth in the Protestant atmosphere of Edward's reign, and had seen their friends burnt and beheaded by Mary Tudor. Under Henry and Edward, the high government officials had restrained, as far as possible, the Protestant tendencies in the royal policy; but the younger generation who filled these positions under Elizabeth did all they could to commit the Queen to a more vigorous Protestant policy. Throckmorton, after being a refugee in France in Mary's reign, had been made ambassador there by Elizabeth. As early as June 1559, he was writing to Elizabeth and Cecil to stress the importance of the events in Scotland, and urging that, in view of Knox's abilities and his position in the Scottish Protestant movement, his regrettable book on the government of women should be overlooked.[2]

While Knox wrote to Cecil, Sir William Kirkcaldy of Grange wrote to Percy about the need for English aid. Percy sent the letter to Cecil, who decided to use Percy as his intermediary both with Grange and with Knox. On 11 July, Cecil wrote to Percy that Elizabeth's only objection to the policy of helping the Congregation was that no better persons than Knox and Grange had offered to come to England to contact the English government, for they were both private individuals. Cecil added that Knox, 'for his learning, as the matters now be, has no small credit, nevertheless his name here is not plausible'. Elizabeth and Cecil felt that it was essential that there should be some recognized body of persons in Scotland with whom they could negotiate, and this, in the sixteenth century, meant members of the nobility,

[1] Percy to Cecil, 4 July 1559 (*Cal. For. Pap. Eliz.* i. 936); Parker to Cecil, 6 Nov. 1559 (Parker, *Correspondence*, p. 105).

[2] Throckmorton to Cecil, 7 and 28 June and 19 July 1559; Throckmorton to Elizabeth I, 13 June 1559; Throckmorton to the Council, 21 June 1559 (Forbes, i. 118, 129–30, 145–8, 167).

or high officers of state.[1] Their minds, trained to think in terms of dynastic conflicts, turned to the Duke of Châtelherault. In view of Châtelherault's past record in changing sides, the fact that he was now the commander of the Queen Regent's forces was not unduly discouraging, and Cecil was convinced that he could win over Châtelherault by telling him that Mary of Lorraine and the Stewarts intended to exterminate the House of Hamilton. Here Cecil was assisted by a stroke of good fortune. Châtelherault's eldest son, who bore his father's old title of Earl of Arran, a young man of 22, was living on his father's estates at Châtelherault in France. He was caught up in the Protestant tide that was sweeping through the French nobility, and became a Protestant. In May 1559 he disappeared, and while Europe buzzed with rumours as to his whereabouts, Cecil and Throckmorton arranged for him to be smuggled by way of Geneva and Emden to London, where, after secret meetings with Elizabeth and Cecil, who denied all knowledge of him, he was conveyed to Berwick and across the Border into Scotland in September. Two years later, Arran went mad, and he has gone down in history as a ridiculous figure; but for one critical year in the history of Scotland and Europe, he was the hero of the Protestant cause, and performed this role with courage and ability.

In Edinburgh the Lords of the Congregation, and Knox in his sermons, were emphasizing their loyalty to the King and Queen and the Queen Regent, and that their only concern was to secure the reformation of religion. This line made it easier for Elizabeth and Cecil to help them; but at the same time, in their secret letters to the English government, Knox and Grange calmed the English fears that the Congregation would make a settlement with the French, and assured them that their aim was to expel the French from Scotland.[2] Knox also tried again to appease the indignation

[1] Grange to Percy, 25 June and 1 July 1559; Percy to Parry and Cecil, 28 June 1559; Cecil and Parry to Percy, 4 July 1559; Cecil to Percy, 4 and 11 July 1559; Percy to Cecil, 4 July 1559; Croft to Cecil, 14 July 1559 (*Works*, vi. 33–35, 37–40; *Cal. For. Pap. Eliz.* i. 880, 885, 907, 932, 934, 936, 973, 993; *Sc. Cal.* i. 474, 480, 483, 484, 491).

[2] The Lords of the Congregation to Mary of Lorraine, 2 July 1559 (Knox, *History*, i. 194–5); Grange to Cecil, 23 June and 17 July 1559; Balnavis to Cecil, 19 July 1559 (*Cal. For. Pap. Eliz.* i. 878, 1003, 1030; *Sc. Cal.* i. 471, 492, 495); Grange to Percy, 1 July 1559; Knox to Percy, 1 July 1559; the Lords of the Congregation to Cecil, 19 July 1559; the Lords of the Congregation to Elizabeth I, 19 July 1559 (these last two letters being written by Knox) (*Works*, vi. 33–36, 40–44).

which Elizabeth felt against him personally about *The First Blast of the Trumpet*. On 12 July he wrote to Cecil, and suggested, obscurely but unmistakably, that his doctrine about the government of women might again be useful one day. He was obviously thinking of Mary Queen of Scots, who, until Elizabeth married and had children, was the heir to the English throne. 'If the most part of women be such as willingly we would not they should reign over us; and if the most godly, and such as have rare gifts and graces, be yet mortal, we ought to take heed, lest that we, in establishing one judged godly and profitable to her country, make entrance and title to many; by whom not only shall the truth be impugned, but also shall the country be brought to bondage and slavery.'[1]

He enclosed with this letter a letter to Elizabeth, dated 20 July, which he asked Cecil to deliver to the Queen. He had already warned Cecil that his letter would be 'smelling nothing of flattery,'[2] and if Cecil showed the letter to Elizabeth, it must have lowered her opinion of Knox still further. Yet if Elizabeth had had any sympathy with Knox's point of view, his letter might have impressed her very favourably. It was respectful and sincere, and no more forthright than was considered proper, at least in theory, when a spiritual adviser addressed a sovereign. It was the content, not the style, of the letter which would have offended Elizabeth, for it expressed a view of monarchy which she could not accept. The letter shows the extent and the limits of Knox as a politician. He could manœuvre and deceive in order to further the cause, but he would not compromise in a statement of principle, and it was psychologically impossible for him to cringe even to help the Reformation in Scotland. He could trim to the extent of placing a cunningly favourable interpretation on his *First Blast*, but not when it came to telling Elizabeth what were her duties as a sovereign.

'Your Grace's displeasure against me', he began, 'most unjustly

[1] Knox to Cecil, 12 July 1559 (*Works*, vi. 45, where it is given in the form in which it is written in the original, in Knox's hand, in the Record Office). The version which Knox gives in his *History*, i. 290–1, is slightly different in parts, including the passage cited. There is a conflict of evidence as to the date when this letter was written; but it appears that Knox, after writing to Cecil on 12 July and mentioning in the letter that he was enclosing a letter to Elizabeth, did not in fact write this letter to the Queen until eight days later, and then sent both the letters together to Cecil.

[2] Knox to Cecil, 28 June 1559 (*Works*, vi. 31).

conceived, hath been, and is, to my wretched heart a burden grievous and almost intolerable'; but he could not understand why Elizabeth or anyone could be so offended with the *First Blast*, if they considered the time at which it was written. He had not harmed England by affirming 'that no woman may be exalted above any realm, to make the liberty of the same thrall to a strange, proud and cruel nation'.

'If I should flatter your Grace,' he wrote, 'I were no friend, but a deceivable traitor.' So he reminded her of her duty to atone for her submission to Mary by now furthering, to the utmost, the Protestant cause.

Forget your birth, and all title which thereupon doth hang; and consider deeply how, for fear of your life, ye did decline from God, and bow to idolatry. Let it not appear a small offence in your eyes that ye have declined from Christ Jesus in the day of His battle. Neither yet would I that ye should esteem that mercy to be vulgar and common which ye have received: to wit, that God hath covered your former offence, hath preserved you when ye were most unthankful; and in the end hath exalted and raised you up, not only from the dust, but also from the ports of death, to rule above His people, for the comfort of His Church. It appertaineth to you, therefore, to ground the justice of your authority, not upon that law which from year to year doth change, but upon the eternal providence of Him who, contrary to nature, and without your deserving, hath thus exalted your head. If thus, in God's presence, ye humble yourself, as in my heart I glorify God for that rest granted to His afflicted flock within England, under you, a weak instrument, so will I with tongue and pen justify your authority and regiment, as the Holy Ghost hath justified the same in Deborah, that blessed mother in Israel. But if the premises (as God forbid) neglected, ye shall begin to brag of your birth, and to build your authority and regiment upon your own law, flatter you whoso list, your felicity shall be short. Interpret my rude words in the best part, as written by him who is no enemy to your Grace.

This was a concept of kingship which Elizabeth could never accept.[1]

On 22 July, taking the Congregation completely by surprise, Mary of Lorraine and the French garrison issued forth from Dunbar and marched on Edinburgh. The lords prepared to resist, but as always when possession of Edinburgh was in question, a vital

[1] Knox to Elizabeth I, 20 July 1559 (*Works*, vi. 47–50; Knox, *History*, i. 291–4).

factor was the attitude of the castle. The Captain of the Castle controlled the fate of Edinburgh. From its height at the western end of the town, the cannon in the castle could bombard the whole length of the High Street, past the Church of St. Giles, the tolbooth and the markets, to the Nether Port, which divided Edinburgh from the burgh of Canongate. Lord Erskine, the Captain of the Castle, had hitherto remained neutral between the Queen Regent and the Congregation; but as the French advanced on Edinburgh, he told the Lords of the Congregation that he would support the Queen Regent with his cannon. The Congregation called out the town of Edinburgh and the lairds of Lothian to come to the rescue, but there was no time to send for aid to the brethren in Ayrshire or Dundee. They assembled on the crags outside Edinburgh, which today are called Calton Hill; but the Queen Regent's army marched to Leith, and once again a battle was avoided. Another agreement was signed on 24 July at the Links of Leith; for the Congregation were wary of Lord Erskine's guns in the castle, and the Queen Regent and d'Oysel were unwilling to antagonize Châtelherault and Huntly, who were in favour of compromise. The Congregation agreed to evacuate Edinburgh, and not to attack any priest or destroy any more of the religious houses until the Parliament assembled on 10 January 1560 to settle the religious question; and the Queen Regent agreed that the Catholic religion should not be restored in any place where it had been purged. Religious toleration was to be granted to both sides until 10 January. For some months the agreement was more or less observed. 'They are not able to prove that we broke the appointment in any jot,' wrote Knox in his *History*, 'except that a horned cap was taken off a proud priest's head, and cut in four quarters, because he said that he would wear it in despite of the Congregation.'[1]

After much argument it was agreed that the Congregation should retain the use of St. Giles's Church, though mass was being celebrated in the palace of Holyroodhouse for all who wished to attend. Knox had been elected as the minister by the congregation of Edinburgh, but the lords insisted that he should accompany

[1] Knox, *History*, i. 200–2, 214; 'The Estate of Scotland' (*Wodrow Misc.* i. 63–65); Agreement of the Links of Leith, 24 July 1559 (Knox, *History*, i. 202–4; Teulet, i. 327–8; *Cal. For. Pap. Eliz.* i. 1052; *Sc. Cal.* i. 500); Knox to Croft, 24 July 1559 (this letter is signed by Grange, but written in Knox's hand) (*Cal. For. Pap. Eliz.* i. 1056; *Sc. Cal.* i. 505, enclosure).

them when they withdrew from the town, and that Willock should remain to officiate in St. Giles's. In his *History*, Knox pays tribute to Willock's courage in remaining in Edinburgh; for though under the Agreement of the Links of Leith no French or Scottish soldiers were to be garrisoned in the town, they were free to enter it as individuals, and the Protestant preacher in St. Giles's might be in danger of assassination from a French soldier or Scottish Catholic. Knox does not explain why he himself did not stay in Edinburgh, but we know from another source that it was the lords who insisted that he should leave with them. Knox would have been in greater danger than Willock if he had remained in Edinburgh, for he was much more prominent and hated than Willock; and the lords needed him to advise them, and to carry on the negotiations with the English government. As for Willock, he encountered nothing worse than insults from the French soldiers in Edinburgh, who frequently created a disturbance when he preached in St. Giles's.[1]

Cecil had decided that, despite everything, he would have to negotiate with Knox. On 11 July he wrote to Percy that though he could not reply to Knox's letters, he was prepared to grant him a licence to enter England, and to meet him secretly, provided that Knox travelled under a false name, and in absolute secrecy, 'for otherwise the sequel will be fruitless, yea, very hurtful'. Knox was to come to Burghley, Cecil's house near Stamford; he must avoid the town of Stamford, and must enter Burghley through the back gate, where Cecil's servants would make him very welcome until Cecil himself arrived there on 25 July. Cecil told Percy to make it plain to Knox that it would be useless for him to come unless he was armed with credentials and guarantees from the principal Lords of the Congregation; for 'so many slights and finesses have been used before time by that nation, that were it not that in this common cause of religion there is no respect of nation, I would be loath to commit trust to any word or promise; and so may ye boldly, if ye think meet, write to them'.[2]

Knox did not keep this vitally important appointment with Cecil owing to a misunderstanding. Percy naturally did not tell him, openly in a letter, that Cecil himself wished to meet him at Stamford, but merely invited him to come secretly to Alnwick;

[1] Knox, *History*, i. 211, 213–14; 'The Estate of Scotland' (*Wodrow Misc.* i. 65).
[2] Cecil to Percy, 11 July 1559 (*Cal. For. Pap. Eliz.* i. 973).

and Knox, not realizing the importance of the visit, put off going to Alnwick when the Queen Regent's soldiers advanced on Edinburgh, for in the excitement of the events of 22–25 July the lords had no time to brief him for his mission to England. It was only on 30 July that the lords gave Knox his credentials and his instructions. On 1 August, Knox sailed from Pittenweem in Fife to Holy Island near Berwick, accompanied by Robert Hamilton, another minister of the Congregation, and in these unexpected circumstances again set foot in England. At Holy Island he was recognized, to the great annoyance of the English government officials, who blamed Knox for his lack of caution, though it would not have been easy for Knox, even after an absence of six years, to avoid recognition in the vicinity of Berwick. The English officials changed their plans, and instead of taking Knox to Alnwick to meet Percy, which was the original intention, he was taken in great secrecy, without anyone noticing, from Holy Island to the castle at Berwick, where he met Sir James Croft, the political adviser to the authorities in Northumberland. Though inferior in rank to Percy, Croft was much more influential with Elizabeth and Cecil, and a much abler diplomat. Knox had intended, while in England, to contact his brother-in-law, Sir Georges Bowes, who was Marshal of Berwick; but owing to the extreme secrecy of his visit he probably did not do so.[1]

Knox spent two nights at Berwick Castle, and had very full discussions with Croft. He asked Croft for English troops, and also for money, and told him that the Congregation had definitely decided to break the French alliance, and to make as close an alliance with England as Elizabeth required. He invited the English government to send political advisers to the Congregation, to ensure that the Congregation acted in accordance with English policy. Croft told Knox that the Queen could not negotiate with the Congregation unless they were represented by a properly constituted authority with which she could deal. Knox said that in that case they would elect a Council, composed of whomever Elizabeth might suggest. Knox suggested that Arran

[1] Percy to Cecil, 22 and 23 July and 4 Aug. 1559; Cecil to Knox, 28 July 1559; Cecil to Croft, 29 July 1559; Instructions of the Lords of the Congregation to Knox, 30 July 1559 (in Knox's hand); Knox to Croft (30 July 1559?); Knox to Percy, 2 Aug. 1559; Croft to Cecil, 3 Aug. 1559; Knox to Cecil, 15 Aug. 1559 (*Works*, vi. 55–62, 67; *Cal. For. Pap. Eliz.* i. 1045, 1051, 1087, 1096, 1097, 1119; *Sc. Cal.* i. 501, 508); Knox, *History*, i. 294–5.

should somehow be brought over from France to England, where the English government could find out whether he would be a suitable leader for the movement; if he proved to be unsatisfactory, Knox suggested that Lord James should be the leader. Croft could not tell Knox that Arran was already on his way, and probably did not yet know this himself. Knox also told Croft about the secret negotiations of Lord James and Argyll with Châtelherault, and how Châtelherault had promised to come over to the Congregation if French troops were not withdrawn from Scotland. Since he had become involved in active politics, Knox had overcome his scruples about collaborating with the persecutor of Wishart.[1]

Croft promised that the English government would send money secretly to the Congregation in the near future, but said that it was impossible for Elizabeth to support them openly. Knox returned to Scotland with this rather disappointing answer on 3 August, having agreed with Croft that it would be better if he did not go on to Stamford. Cecil had written a friendly letter to Knox, in which he expressed his regret that Knox had not come to Burghley on 25 July, signing himself 'Yours as a member of the same body in Christ, W. Cecil'; but he had given Percy and Croft authority to cancel Knox's visit to Burghley if they thought fit. They came to the conclusion that it was too risky for Knox to travel another 250 miles into England, in view of the fact that he had already been recognized, and that there were spies of the Scottish government in Northumberland; and Knox told them that he thought it would be best if a man of higher rank and greater eminence than himself, such as Balnavis, were to go to Cecil. He also said that he did not wish to be absent for so long from his flock in Scotland, who needed him as a preacher.[2]

On 3 August, Knox and Robert Hamilton left secretly by sea from Holy Island. Knox took with him a memorandum drawn up by Croft for him to show to the Lords of the Congregation, containing a statement of the extent to which the English government was prepared to assist the Congregation. As a precaution, Croft sent a second copy of this memorandum to the lords by Alexander Whitelaw, a Scottish Protestant who had been an

[1] Croft to Cecil, 3 Aug. 1559 (*Cal. For. Pap. Eliz.* i. 1119).

[2] Croft to Cecil, 3 and 4 Aug. 1559; Cecil to Knox, 28 July 1559 (*Works*, vi. 55–56, 61–62; *Cal. For. Pap. Eliz.* i. 1119; *Sc. Cal.* i. 511).

English agent for many years, and sent Whitelaw to Scotland overland. Knox arrived safely in Scotland by sea, and delivered the document to the lords at Stirling, where he found that Whitelaw had not yet arrived. Whitelaw had been detained by illness, but had then reached Prestonpans, where he contacted Knox's brother William, the merchant, who was again acting as a courier for the Congregation when he travelled on business. The Queen Regent's spies in Berwick had found out about Knox's visit, but not about his departure by sea, and, mistaking Whitelaw for Knox, reported that he was travelling by land. Lord Seton, who was watching out for Knox, came across Whitelaw and William Knox when they were leaving Prestonpans for Edinburgh, and chased them for three miles as far as Ormiston. When he realized that he was pursuing Knox's brother and another man, but not Knox himself, he let them go, without discovering the highly secret document that Whitelaw was carrying. Whitelaw eventually made contact with the Lords of the Congregation.[1]

Meanwhile the French government was taking steps to suppress the revolt in Scotland. On 10 July 1559, Henry II died from an eye-wound which he had accidentally received in a tournament; but under the new King, Francis II, the influence of the Guises was stronger than ever. Henry II's decision to send troops to Scotland was now pressed forward with greater vigour, and the Duke of Guise directed his brother, the young Marquis d'Elbœuf, to prepare a fleet to carry troops to their sister's rescue. Four ensigns of troops, 1,000 men in all, arrived at Leith at the end of August, bringing the total of French troops in Scotland to 2,500, and the total of the troops in the Queen Regent's forces to 3,000. Guise assured Mary of Lorraine that a much larger force was on the way; but the French government was nearly bankrupt after the war against Spain, and there was great economic distress in France. The Congregation could call up 14,000 men when necessary, but only about 1,000 of these had had military training, and at the moment they could not leave their fields because of the harvest. So the revolution marked time while the Guises tried to find money to send a large army and fleet to Scotland, while the Congregation collected the harvest, and while Elizabeth and Cecil

[1] Croft to Cecil, 3 and 4 Aug. 1559; Knox to Croft, 6 Aug. 1559; Argyll and Lord James to Cecil, 13 Aug. 1559 (*Works*, vi. 61, 63, 65–66; *Cal. For. Pap. Eliz.* i. 1119; *Sc. Cal.* i. 511); Knox, *History*, i. 214, 296.

waited to see how much they had to do to guarantee the victory of the Congregation.[1]

When Knox returned from Berwick, he found that the reluctance of the English government to give decisive aid was causing many of the Congregation to hesitate in resisting the Queen Regent and the French. Knox wrote a stream of letters to Cecil, Percy, and Croft, emphasizing the danger of the situation, and asking for English troops. On 6 August he wrote to Croft that unless the English government was 'more forward in this common action, ye will utterly discourage the hearts of all here. . . . They will not trifle; but if they cannot have present support of them, they will seek the next remedy (not that I mean that ever they intend to return to France) to preserve their own bodies, whatsoever become of the country, which our enemies may easily occupy; and when they have so done, make your account what may ensue towards yourself.'[2]

On 15 August he wrote to Cecil from St. Andrews to warn him that unless the English government changed its policy, it would be difficult for him and Grange and Balnavis to convince the lords that they could rely on England.

The case of these gentlemen stands thus: that unless without delay money be furnished to pay their soldiers (who in number are now but 500) for their service bypast, and to retain another 1000 footmen, with 300 horsemen for a time, they will be compelled, every man, to seek the next way for his own safety. I am assured (as flesh may be of flesh) that some of them will take a very hard life before that ever they compound, either with the Queen Regent, either yet with France. But this I dare not promise of all, unless in you they see greater forwardness to their support. To aid us so liberally as we require, to some of you will appear excessive, and to displease France, to many will appear dangerous. But, Sir, I hope that ye consider that our destruction were your greatest loss, and that when France shall be our full masters (which God avert), they will be but slender friends to you. . . . In this meantime, if ye lie as neutrals, what will be the end ye may easily conjecture. . . . How dangerous is in the drift of time, in such matters, ye are not ignorant.[3]

[1] Knox, *History*, i. 216; 'The Estate of Scotland' (*Wodrow Misc.* i. 67); Sadler and Croft to Cecil, 8 and 29 Sept., 12 and 24 Oct., and 5 and 25 Nov. 1559; Arran to Cecil, 17 Nov. 1559 (Sadler, i. 432; ii. 6, 40, 51–52, 82, 142; *Sc. Cal.* i. 549; *Cal. For. Pap. Eliz.* i. 1323; ii. 286). In addition to the 2,500 French soldiers, there were 500 Scots serving in the French army in Scotland; see Knox, *History*, i. 179–80; 'The Estate of Scotland' (*Wodrow Misc.* i. 61).

[2] Knox to Croft, 6 Aug. 1559 (*Works*, vi. 63).

[3] Knox to Cecil, 15 Aug. 1559 (*Works*, vi. 68–69).

The lords and lairds of the Congregation were especially disturbed that Elizabeth was not paying them pensions, as Henry VIII had done; and though Knox, Grange, and Balnavis pointed out that Elizabeth was in a weaker position at her accession than Henry had been at the height of his power when he was so greatly feared by his subjects, this argument, as Knox told Cecil, 'did satisfy some, but not all'. Knox realized that English gold would increase the Protestant zeal of his less idealistic supporters, but apart from this, some of the most sincere members of the Congregation, like Glencairn, Erskine of Dun, Ormiston, and Grange himself, could not continue indefinitely financing their servants and tenants while they engaged in the economically unproductive work of marching in support of the Congregation. But although Knox had been promised, when he was at Berwick at the beginning of August, that money would be sent, none at all had arrived by 21 September, when Knox wrote to Croft from St. Andrews, and again urged him to send financial help to Glencairn, Erskine of Dun, Ormiston, and Grange. 'Albeit that money, by the adversary party largely offered, could not corrupt them, yet should extreme poverty compel them to remain at home. . . . If any persuade you that they will or may serve without support, they do but deceive you . . . France seeketh all means to make them friends, and to diminish our number. Ye are not ignorant what poverty on the one part, and money largely offered upon the other part, is able to persuade.'[1]

In August, Knox fell ill, perhaps because the political tension had relaxed sufficiently for him to notice that his health was breaking down as a result of overwork. He was straining himself to the limit, often having only four hours' sleep a night, preaching and carrying on political and diplomatic negotiations, and occasionally finding time to think about non-political matters, and write a short letter to his old friends. On 28 August he wrote to Calvin, and asked him whether the bastard children of idolaters and excommunicated persons should be baptized before either their parents had been reconciled to the Church, or the children were old enough to ask for baptism themselves. He also asked whether the yearly revenues of the Church should be paid to Popish monks and priests who had recanted their old idolatry,

[1] Knox to Cecil, 15 Aug. 1559; Knox to Croft, 21 Sept. 1559 (*Works*, vi. 69, 80); Sadler and Croft to Cecil, 29 Sept. 1559 (Sadler, ii. 7).

but were found unfit to serve as ministers in the new Protestant Church. 'Because I say no to both questions, I am considered unjustly severe, not only by Papists but also by those who think themselves patrons of the truth. The fever which I have, the weight of labours pressing on me, and arrival of French artillery to attack us, prevent me from writing more. In haste, J. Knoxus.' Calvin replied on 8 November, and told Knox that he disagreed with him on both these points.[1]

On 2 September, Knox wrote to Anne Locke from St. Andrews, and told her that 'Christ Jesus is preached even in Edinburgh', and in all the other towns where the Congregation had established the ministry, which were St. Andrews, Dundee, Perth, Brechin, Montrose, Stirling, and Ayr. The Protestants had now begun to preach on the Borders, at Jedburgh and Kelso. 'Enemies we have many', he wrote, 'by reason of the Frenchmen who are lately arrived. . . . We do nothing but go about Jericho, blowing with trumpets, as God giveth strength, hoping victory by His power alone.' In his days in London, he had confided his most intimate secrets to Anne Locke; but he did not tell her now that he was relying on English troops as well as trumpets to assault the walls of Jericho. Nor did he tell her that the Book of Common Prayer, which he again condemned in the strongest terms in another letter to Anne Locke on 15 October, was being used, at least in its less objectionable form of 1552, in those towns in Scotland where Christ Jesus was preached.[2]

Knox was anxious to bring his wife and family to Scotland, and even more eager for Goodman to come. He felt that Goodman could be of great assistance to the cause in Scotland, and he wrote to Anne Locke that for Goodman's presence 'I more thirst than she that is my own flesh'. But Knox had quite lost contact with his congregation in Geneva, and with all his friends outside Scotland. On 17 March, in Dieppe, he had received a letter which Anne Locke had written to him from Geneva on 7 February; but after this, he heard nothing more from any of them until on 29 June, the day that the Congregation entered Edinburgh, he was handed a letter from Anne Locke written in London on 16 June.

[1] Knox to Calvin, 28 Aug. 1559; Knox to Anne Locke, 2 Sept. and 15 Oct. 1559; Knox to Railton, 23 Oct. 1559; Calvin to Knox, 8 Nov. 1559 (*Works*, vi. 75–78, 85, 88, 94–98; *Calvini Op.* xvii. 619–20, 665–8).

[2] Knox to Anne Locke, 2 Sept. and 15 Oct. 1559 (*Works*, vi. 78, 83–85).

She had written to him from Frankfort, on her journey to England, on 23 March; but Knox only received this letter in Dundee on 13 September. Meanwhile Marjory and Mrs. Bowes had set off from Geneva with the children to make their way to Scotland, accompanied by Goodman, who, though an Englishman himself, realized that he could be of more assistance to the cause by helping Knox in Scotland than by running into trouble with Elizabeth in England. When Lethington said to him that a foreigner should not interfere in another state, this international Calvinist replied that though he was a foreigner in Scotland, he was not a foreigner in the Church of God, and was as competent to serve it in Scotland as in his native England.[1]

Marjory and her mother and the children arrived in Paris with Goodman at the beginning of June 1559, and Throckmorton wrote to Elizabeth herself to ask her to grant them all a safe-conduct to travel through England to Scotland. Knox's position was very different from what it had been when he was in Dieppe in April, and Elizabeth granted a licence, not only to his family, but also to the hated Goodman, to pass through her realm. Goodman reached the Border before the end of August, and though he failed to meet his guide as arranged, he eventually crossed safely into Scotland. He was appointed as the pastor of the congregation in Ayr. Marjory stayed in England for another month, but rejoined Knox in St. Andrews on 20 September. Mrs. Bowes had not yet arrived in Scotland by the end of October, but not long afterwards she joined Knox and Marjory.[2]

In the middle of September, Knox was secretly approached by Robert Lockhart. Lockhart had approached the Queen Regent on his own initiative, and offered to try to arrange a compromise with the Congregation. Knox states in his *History* that Mary of Lorraine accepted Lockhart's offer because, 'knowing his simplicity, she was glad to employ him for her advantage', and insists that Lockhart was a loyal Protestant, though he says that he had no political understanding. Knox apparently did not know that a

[1] Knox to Anne Locke, 6 Apr., 23 and 29 June, and 15 Oct. 1559 (*Works*, vi. 11, 27, 30, 83, 85; the letter of 29 June is wrongly dated 25 June); Knox, *History*, ii. 100–1.

[2] Throckmorton to Elizabeth I, 13 June 1559 (Forbes, i. 129–30); Knox to Anne Locke, 2 Sept., 15 Oct., and 18 Nov. 1559; Knox to Croft, 21 Sept. 1559; Knox to Railton, 23 Oct. 1559 (*Works*, vi. 78, 80, 83, 88, 101); Goodman to Cecil, 26 Oct. 1559 (*Sc. Cal.* i. 554); Sadler and Croft to Cecil, 20 Oct. 1559 (Sadler, ii. 47).

few months later, the Queen Regent's government paid Lockhart a reward of £70. Lockhart contacted Glencairn, Ochiltre, Boyd, Erskine of Dun, and Knox and the other preachers, and assured them that the Queen Regent would dismiss her French advisers, and entrust all the high offices of state to Scotsmen. In the middle of September, Lockhart visited Knox in Dundee with a letter from the Queen Regent. Knox refused to accept the letter, as all the leaders of the Congregation had agreed not to enter into secret correspondence with her; but he had a long talk with Lockhart, emphasizing that he had no hatred for the Queen Regent, and wished only to advise her, as a 'very friend', to pursue a wiser course. His courtesy and moderate language led the inexperienced Lockhart to report to Mary of Lorraine that Knox might be induced to negotiate with her; and when Knox discovered this, at the end of October, he wrote to Mary of Lorraine and disillusioned her. In respectful and conventional language, he gently but firmly pointed out that he had not made any promise at all to Lockhart. The respectful style of his letter was very different from that of the second edition of his *Letter to the Queen Regent* in 1558; but Knox had no intention of publishing this document as a political propaganda pamphlet.[1]

Arran had now arrived at Hamilton with Thomas Randolph, the unofficial envoy of the English government to the Congregation, another of the younger Protestant officials who served Elizabeth. Arran and Randolph won over Châtelherault. Henceforth the Congregation's propaganda was on national, not religious, lines, and directed against the French instead of the bishops. This new policy had been thought out by Cecil with the object of winning over Châtelherault and appeasing the religious anxieties of Philip II, who was still nominally Elizabeth's ally. The Congregation were to make it clear that they were loyal to their sovereigns, but would not submit to being ruled by foreigners, as only 'the blood of Scotland' should govern Scotland under the King and Queen. Mary of Lorraine, who had betrayed the country to France, must be replaced by the Scottish-born Châtelherault. As the harvest was in, the Congregation, encouraged by promises of English money to pay their fighting men, and claiming

[1] Knox, *History*, i. 244–6; *Accounts of the Lord High Treasurer*, xi. 5, 12 (16 Jan. and 23 Feb. 1559/60); Knox to Mary of Lorraine, 26 Oct. 1559 (Knox, *History*, i. 245–6; *Works*, vi. 81–82, where it is wrongly dated 6 Oct.).

that Mary of Lorraine had broken the Agreement of the Links of Leith by bringing in fresh troops from France, called out the brethren to assemble at Stirling on 15 October, and three days later marched into Edinburgh. Mary of Lorraine withdrew from Holyroodhouse, and took refuge with the French garrison in Leith. The Congregation then decided to depose her formally from the regency. After sending her an ultimatum to demilitarize Leith, to which she replied by ordering the Congregation to leave Edinburgh on pain of treason, the Lords of the Congregation deposed Mary of Lorraine at a ceremony in the tolbooth of Edinburgh on 21 October, at which Knox and the preachers played their part.[1]

When the nobles, lairds, and representatives of the burghs had assembled, Lord Ruthven put the question to the preachers: 'Whether she that so contemptuously refused the most humble request of the born Councillors of the realm, being also but a Regent, whose pretences threatened the bondage of the whole commonwealth, ought to be suffered so tyrannously to empire above them?' Willock, as the acting minister of the congregation of Edinburgh, answered first. He said that though God 'appointed magistrates His lieutenants on earth, and has honoured them with His own title, calling them gods, that yet He did never so establish any but that, for just causes, they might have been deprived'. Then Knox was asked his opinion. He said that he agreed with Willock, but added three qualifications. Firstly, he said that the iniquity of the Queen Regent should not in any way weaken the obedience which they owed to their sovereigns; secondly, that even though the Queen Regent deserved to be deposed, God would punish them if they deposed her out of private malice, and not for the welfare of the commonwealth; and thirdly, that they should make it clear, in the sentence of deposition, that if she converted to the commonwealth, and submitted to the nobility, she should be reappointed as Regent. When Knox had finished,

[1] Knox, *History*, i. 232; Declarations of the Lords of the Congregation, 3 and 6 Oct. 1559 (Knox, *History*, i. 238–44; Burnet, vi. 418–24, where it is dated Aug. 1559; *Cal. For. Pap. Eliz.* ii. 20, 42, 45); Randolph to Sadler and Croft, 12 and 22 Oct. 1559 (*Cal. For. Pap. Eliz.* ii. 76, 116); the Lords of the Congregation to Mary of Lorraine, 19 Oct. 1559; Mary of Lorraine to the Lords of the Congregation, 21 Oct. 1559 (Knox, *History*, i. 247, 249; *Reg. P.C.S.* xiv. 168–70); Sadler and Croft to Cecil, 20 Oct. 1559 (Sadler, ii. 46–47); Buchanan, ii. 417–18; Spottiswood, i. 298–300; Calderwood, i. 537–9.

every person present in the tolbooth was asked to give his opinion, and everyone spoke in favour of deposition. They all signed a document in which, describing themselves as 'the nobility and commons of the Protestants of the Church of Scotland', they announced that they had unanimously decided, in the name of their Sovereign Lord and Lady, to suspend the commission granted by their sovereigns to the Queen Dowager, and deprived her of all authority. They then ordered that this Act of Suspension should be proclaimed at the market cross of Edinburgh.[1]

On this occasion Knox, who had done so much, by his theories and practice, to make the deposition possible, showed a restraint and a reluctance to proceed to extremes, as he had done when he wrote to the Protestant lords from Dieppe in December 1557. He was probably actuated by the same motive now as he had been two years before—his suspicion of Châtelherault. Whenever Châtelherault joined the Protestant movement, Knox feared, with good reason, that the cause was being polluted by improper motives, and suborned to serve the dynastic interests of the Hamiltons. His fears must have been confirmed by the hypocritical manifesto issued by the Lords of the Congregation on 3 October, which denounced the vices and treason of the Queen Regent and contrasted them with the virtues and patriotism of the Duke's Grace. Knox, who remembered the activities of Châtelherault at the time of Wishart's death, cannot have been impressed by the passage in the manifesto that related how Mary of Lorraine and d'Oysel had wished to promise a pardon to the defenders of St. Andrews Castle in 1546, in order to induce them to surrender, and then cut off their heads, but that their scheme had been thwarted by the upright conduct of Châtelherault.[2]

The month of October 1559 was a turning-point in Knox's position in the Scottish Protestant movement. From now on, the revolution was directed by Randolph in Scotland and by Cecil in London, and it was run along lines favoured by Elizabeth and not by Knox. Knox had been the prime mover in obtaining English intervention, and he knew how necessary it was; but both his letters at the time and his later *History* show that he was conscious how the movement was changing its nature and losing its idealism

[1] Knox, *History*, i. 249–55.

[2] Declaration of the Lords of the Congregation, 3 Oct. 1559 (Knox, *History*, i. 241; *Cal. For. Pap. Eliz.* ii. 20).

as the governments of Europe took over and made the Congregation and all Scotland a pawn in their international power politics.

Cecil gave a clear directive to his subordinates on 31 October, when he wrote to Croft and Sadler: 'Of all others, Knox's name is most odious here, if it be not Goodman's, and therefore I wish no mention of him.' Elizabeth and Cecil had no need of Knox now that they had Châtelherault. Their attitude quickly seeped through to Randolph and the Lords of the Congregation. After the deposition of the Queen Regent, a council of thirty notables, known as the Great Council of Scotland, was established to govern the realm during the absence of the King and Queen. It included Châtelherault and Huntly and Lord Erskine in Edinburgh Castle, as well as the leading Lords of the Congregation, along with eight lairds and the Provosts of Edinburgh, St. Andrews, and Dundee. Knox and the preachers were naturally not appointed to the Great Council. Nor were they included in the unofficial Council of the Congregation, which was set up in order to take the policy decisions for the Congregation. It consisted of Châtelherault, Arran, Argyll, Lord James, Glencairn, Ruthven, the Master of Maxwell, Dun, Pittarrow, Balnavis, Grange, and Halyburton, the Provost of Dundee, but not Knox. The Lords did, however, appoint another committee to advise them on religious affairs, and this consisted of Knox, Goodman, Willock, and Alexander Gordon, Bishop of Galloway, who had joined the Congregation and was hastily appointed to be the first member of the committee.[1]

Though Knox was excluded from the political direction, he was still watching the political developments with anxiety. On 23 October, at midnight, he wrote to Gregory Railton, an English Protestant who had been a refugee in Frankfort and was in touch with the English government officials in Northumberland: 'We are determined to assay the uttermost; but first we must have 3,000 more soldiers.'[2] Two days later, he wrote directly to Croft, and more insistently. 'Such is our estate, Right Worshipful, that unless present support be provided for us, you and we will both lament. . . . Proclamation is made by the drum for lifting of more

[1] Cecil to Sadler and Croft, 31 Oct. 1559 (Sadler, ii. 70); Randolph to Sadler and Croft (Oct. 1559); Randolph's memorandum (Oct. 1559) (*Sc. Cal.* i. 550, 551).

[2] Knox to Railton, 23 Oct. 1559 (*Works*, vi. 87). For Railton at Frankfort, see Frankfort Housing Lists, 15–16 Oct. 1556 (Mar.–Apr. 1557), and 10 June 1557 (Jung, *Die englische Flüchtlings-Gemeinde in Frankfurt-a-M.*, pp. 29, 34, 36).

men of war, but partly for lack of money, and partly because men have no will to hazard, we can make no number, and therefore as ye tender the weal and furtherance of this cause, provide that both men and money come unto us with all possible expedition.' Knox then suggested a way in which Croft could do this without England being involved in a war with France.

If ye fear to offend France, in heart it is already at defiance with you, and abideth only the opportunity and advantage. If you list to craft with them, the sending of a thousand or more men to us can break no league nor point of peace contracted betwixt you and France; for it is free for your subjects to serve in war any prince or nation for their wages. And if ye fear that such excuses shall not prevail, you may declare them rebels to your realm when ye shall be assured that they be in our company. Ye pay them wages where they lie presently, and yet they be idle; but here they would more profit us, if we might have them within six days, than 5,000 will do within forty days hereafter.

Knox told Croft that the Queen Dowager, as Knox called her since her deposition from the regency, was trying to win over the supporters of the Congregation. The Congregation had refused her offers, though 'more do judge us fools than do praise our constancy'. Mary of Lorraine was also putting rumours into circulation that England was preparing to do a secret deal with France, by which France would give back Calais in return for England abandoning the Congregation in Scotland. Knox raised this matter frankly with Croft in his letter of 25 October, because, as he told him, 'such rumours discourage many'.[1]

Croft firmly rejected Knox's suggestion that English soldiers should be sent unofficially to Scotland to help the Congregation, and then denounced as rebels by Elizabeth.

I cannot but marvel [he wrote on 27 October] that you, being a wise man, will require of us such present aid of men, money and ammunition as we cannot minister unto you without an open show and manifestation of ourselves to be as open enemies, whereas you know, by league and treaty we be bound to be friends. . . . And how I, being but a servant and minister here, may presume to do that you desire, tending to a plain breach of amity between so great princes whom it toucheth, I refer to your discretion; for as to your devises how to colour our doings in that part, you must think that the world is not so blind but that it will soon espy the same.

[1] Knox to Railton, 23 Oct. 1559; Knox to Croft, 25 Oct. 1559 (*Works*, vi. 87, 89–91).

Croft said that the Queen's honour would be touched if she broke the treaty with France in the underhand way which Knox had suggested. Elizabeth had no scruples about conducting secret negotiations with the Congregation while she assured Mary of Lorraine of her friendship and wished her success against her rebels, or in promising the French ambassador that if Arran came to England she would extradite him to France, within a week of having spoken with Arran at a secret interview; but she and her government, among its other deceitful practices, knew how to pretend that they were restrained by considerations of honour when they considered that dishonourable actions would be premature. Croft wrote that he could send money to the Congregation if he could rely on them to keep it secret; 'but, to be plain with you, ye are so open in your doings as you make men half afraid to deal with you'. But Croft did at least give Knox a categorical assurance that there would be no deal with France about Calais: 'for you may be sure that Calais cannot make us to neglect or refuse the establishment of this island in perpetual unity and concord.'[1]

Knox wrote a very restrained reply on 29 October. He said that he had received 'your reasonable answer to my unreasonable request', and fully appreciated that Croft could not exceed his instructions; but England should consider which was the greater risk, the danger of a break with France, or the destruction of the Scottish nobility. 'As touching the league and treaty, which now ye suppose to have with such as ye term your friends, I unfeignedly wish that it were so sure that you should never have occasion to break any point contracted. But whether it may stand with wisdom to have such respect to that which some do call honour, that in the meantime I shall see my friend perish, both till his destruction and mine, I refer to the judgement of the most honourable.' France had been at peace with England when it openly gave military assistance to Scotland in 1547–9, 'to both our displeasure; and yet I think that they neither would have confessed breach of treaty nor blemish of honour'.

In his letter to Croft, Knox warned him that unless speedy

[1] Croft to Knox, 27 Oct. 1559 (*Works*, vi. 91–92); Elizabeth I to Mary of Lorraine (7 Aug. 1559) (Teulet, i. 334–5; *Sc. Cal.* i. 518); Cecil to Throckmorton, 29 Aug. 1559; Throckmorton to Elizabeth I, 19 Sept. 1559 (*Cal. For. Pap. Eliz.* i. 1274, 1355); Quadra to Ferdinand I, 12 Sept. 1559 (*Span. Cal. Eliz.* i. 63).

order was taken, some members of the Congregation 'will repent that they saw Edinburgh at this voyage'.[1] His prophecy came true within two days. On 31 October, a black Hallowe'en for the Congregation, English money was sent to Scotland, £1,000—the first instalment of £3,000 wrung with great difficulty by Cecil from Elizabeth—only to be seized as it crossed the Border by a party of soldiers under the young Earl of Bothwell, who was fighting for Mary of Lorraine. This meant not only that the money was lost, but that Mary of Lorraine had evidence that Elizabeth was sending money to the Congregation, and she quickly informed the French and Spanish governments of the fact. As the news of Bothwell's exploit reached Edinburgh, Arran and Lord James and the horsemen of the Congregation left Edinburgh to attack Bothwell; but in their absence the French marched out of Leith and attacked the Congregation in Edinburgh. The men of Dundee fought well, but the hired mercenaries fled, and the French burned a bakehouse in the Canongate and killed ten soldiers of the Congregation, together with a number of random victims, including a Catholic, a drunken priest, and a woman and her baby.[2]

The next week was a bitter experience for Knox. He saw the morale of the movement collapse at the first check; the time-servers changed sides, the mercenaries deserted, the Catholics of Edinburgh came out into the open, and the leaders of the Congregation engaged in arguments and bickerings, and were unable to come to any firm decision as to their course of action.

> From that day back [Knox wrote in his *History*] the courage of many was dejected. With great difficulty could men be retained in the town; yea, some of the greatest estimation determined with themselves to leave the enterprise. Many fled away secretly, and those that did abide (a very few excepted) appeared destitute of counsel and manhood. . . . Thus we continued from the Wednesday, the last of October, till Monday the 5th of November, never two or three abiding firm in one opinion the space of twenty-four hours.

[1] Knox to Croft, 29 Oct. 1559 (*Works*, vi. 92–93).

[2] Knox, *History*, i. 258–61, 298; Elizabeth I to Sadler, 8 Aug. 1559 (*Works*, vi. 64–65); Sadler and Croft to Randolph, 31 Oct. and 5 Nov. 1559; Randolph to Sadler and Croft, 3 Nov. 1559; Sadler and Croft to Cecil, 5 Nov. 1559; Cecil to Sadler and Croft, 25 Nov. 1559 (Sadler, ii. 66, 74–75, 79–81, 138–9); Balnavis to Croft, 4 Nov. 1559; Châtelherault, Arran, and Lord James to Sadler, 6 Nov. 1559 (Keith, i. 383, 403–4); Balnavis to Sadler and Croft, 6 Nov. 1559 (*Cal. For. Pap. Eliz.* ii. 200); d'Oysel to Noailles, 12 Nov. 1559 (Teulet, i. 377–80).

On 6 November, the French attacked again, intercepting the food supplies that were being brought into Edinburgh for the Congregation. Arran and Lord James fought bravely, but again the mercenaries fled, and many refused to go into action at all. At midnight the leaders of the Congregation decided to evacuate Edinburgh, and they hastily retreated through the night to Stirling, abandoning most of their cannon to Lord Erskine in the castle, who had refused to intervene in the fighting on either side. The hardest blow to Knox was to see the joy of the people of Edinburgh at their defeat; for despite the sermons of Knox and Willock and the activities of the local Protestants, Edinburgh was still a predominantly Catholic town. 'The despiteful tongues of the wicked railed upon us, calling us traitors and heretics; everyone provoked other to cast stones at us.' One man cried out: 'Fie, give advertisement to the Frenchmen, that they may come, and we shall help them now to cut the throats of these heretics.' 'We would never have believed', wrote Knox, 'that our natural countrymen and women could have wished our destruction so unmercifully, and have so rejoiced in our adversity.'[1]

It was a moment when the Congregation needed a great leader, and Knox was there. On 8 November he preached to the Congregation at Stirling in the presence of Châtelherault and the Council of the Congregation. On the same day, in Edinburgh, Archbishop Hamilton was officiating at a ceremony in St. Giles's, purging it with holy water from the stain of heresy which had contaminated it in the last four months;[2] but at Stirling, Knox inspired the defeated brethren with his sermon. In his last sermons in St. Giles's, before the disaster, he had been preaching on the eightieth Psalm, and now at Stirling he continued with the same text as if nothing had intervened; but the text served as a rallying cry in the new situation. 'O Thou the Eternal, the God of Hosts, how long shalt Thou be angry against the prayer of Thy people? . . . O God of Hosts, turn us again; make Thy face to shine, and we shall be saved.'

Knox tried to revive the old spirit that had animated the Congregation in the summer, before the idealism and spontaneous

[1] Knox, *History*, i. 261–5; *Diurnal of Occurrents*, p. 54; News from Scotland, 10 Nov. 1559 (*Sc. Cal.* i. 566); Sadler and Croft to Cecil, 8 Nov. 1559; Randolph to Sadler and Croft, 11 Nov. 1559 (Sadler, ii. 91–92, 101–2); d'Oysel to Noailles, 12 Nov. 1559 (Teulet, i. 377–80).

[2] 'The Estate of Scotland' (*Wodrow Misc.* i. 73); Leslie, *History*, ii. 421.

revolutionary fervour had been replaced by the cold calculations of Cecil.

When we were a few number, in comparison of our enemies, when we had neither earl nor lord (a few excepted) to comfort us, we called upon God; we took Him for our protector, defence and only refuge. Amongst us was heard no bragging of multitude, of our strength, nor policy; we did only sob to God, to have respect to the equity of our cause, and to the cruel pursuit of the tyrantful enemy. But since that our number hath been thus multiplied, and chiefly since my Lord Duke's Grace with his friends have been joined with us, there was nothing heard but 'This lord will bring these many hundred spears; this man hath the credit to persuade this country; if this earl be ours, no man in such a bounds will trouble us.'

He said that it would be unfair to blame Châtelherault alone for this, as all of them were equally responsible; but he reminded them that at Perth, at Cupar Muir, and at Edinburgh Crags in July, Châtelherault had been on the side of their enemies, and had therefore not experienced the earlier set-backs and anxieties which they had undergone and survived. Châtelherault and his followers were therefore demoralized by this present defeat.

I am uncertain if my Lord's Grace hath unfeignedly repented of that his assistance to those murderers unjustly pursuing us. Yea, I am uncertain if he hath repented of that innocent blood of Christ's blessed martyrs, which was shed in his default. But let it be that so he hath done (as I hear that he hath confessed his offence before the lords and brethren of the Congregation); yet I am assured that neither he, neither yet his friends, did feel before this time the anguish and grief of hearts which we felt when, in their blind fury, they pursued us. And therefore hath God justly permitted both them and us to fall in this confusion at once; us, for that we put our trust and confidence in man; and them, because that they should feel in their own hearts how bitter was the cup which they made others to drink before them.

We know from several sources, apart from Knox's *History*, that this sermon was received with enthusiasm by the Congregation at Stirling, and many years afterwards his audience remembered how Knox, in the darkest hours, had revived their flagging morale.[1] But if the movement was to proceed along the lines devised by Cecil, the lords could not afford to antagonize Châtelherault in

[1] For Knox's sermon, see Knox, *History*, i. 265–70 (the passages cited are on pp. 265, 269–70); 'The Estate of Scotland' (*Wodrow Misc.* i. 72); Buchanan, ii. 422.

this way. After 8 November 1559, Knox never fully regained the confidence of the lords, and never again had a decisive influence on the policy of the Congregation. This soured his outlook, and brought him disappointment at the moment of victory. On 31 December 1559, he wrote to Anne Locke from St. Andrews: 'One day of troubles, since my last arrival in Scotland, hath more pierced my heart than all the torments of the galleys did the space of nineteen months; for that torment, for the most part, did touch the body, but this pierces the soul and inward affections. Then was I assuredly persuaded that I should not die till I had preached Christ Jesus even where I now am. And yet, having now my hearty desire, I am nothing satisfied, neither yet rejoice. My God, remove my unthankfulness.'[1]

[1] Knox to Anne Locke, 31 Dec. 1559 (*Works*, vi. 104).

CHAPTER XIX

The Victory of 1560

THE Congregation decided to make the most of their defeat. They sent Lethington, who had joined them a few days before the retreat from Edinburgh, to tell the English government that if the French were to be expelled from Scotland, it must be done by English troops. They had originally intended to send Knox, but Cecil had made it clear to Sadler and Croft, in his letter of 31 October, that Knox must not be sent to London, and Knox very willingly agreed that Lethington should replace him. Meanwhile the Lords decided to concentrate on holding Fife and the south-west. They divided into two, Châtelherault and Glencairn establishing themselves at Glasgow, and Arran and Lord James going to St. Andrews. The preachers also divided, Willock going to Glasgow, and Knox to St. Andrews with Lord James.[1]

In the decisive events of the next eight months, Knox was little more than an observer. He still wrote letters to the English government officials, but they were not taken seriously in London and Berwick. 'I like not Knox's audacity,' wrote Cecil to Croft and Sadler on 3 November, 'his writings do no good here, and therefore I do rather suppress them, and yet I mean not but that ye should continue in sending of them.' Randolph thought that Knox was capable of concocting a forgery in order to deceive the English government. In October 1559, Arran showed him a letter which Lord James was said to have received from France. In it the writer gave details of the French plans to send an army to Scotland, and urged the Scottish Protestants to seek help from England, as nothing else could save them. Randolph told Cecil that he thought that the letter did 'savour too much of Knox's

[1] Knox, *History*, i. 271, 298; Instructions of the Lords of the Congregation to Lethington (Nov. 1559); Cecil to Sadler and Croft, 31 Oct. 1559; Sadler and Croft to Cecil, 21 Nov. 1559 (Sadler, ii. 70, 129–30, 142–6); Balnavis to Cecil, 19 Nov. 1559 (*Cal. For. Pap. Eliz.* ii. 296; *Sc. Cal.* i. 584); Knox to Croft, 29 Oct. 1559 (*Works*, vi. 94).

style to come from France, though it will serve to good purpose'. But if Knox was prepared to forge a document to help the cause, his personal integrity was beyond question. On 4 November, the Lords of the Congregation decided that all the money contributed by their supporters, and all the rents that they had confiscated from churchmen who opposed them, should be entrusted to Knox's charge, as he at least could be relied upon to see that it was applied for the benefit of the movement, and not for any private use.[1]

On 18 November, Knox wrote to Cecil to urge him that if England intended to aid the Congregation, they should do so quickly, without further delay.

To drive time with France may appear to some profitable unto you, but, as before I have written, so yet I fear not again to affirm, that nothing hath been, is, nor shall be more hurtful to both, than that ye dissemble your favours towards us; for in the mean season the godly here are and shall be so oppressed, that after they cannot be able to serve, friends do faint and fall back from the enterprise. . . . The whole multitude here (a few number excepted) stand in such doubt that they cannot tell to whether party they shall incline. The French they favour not, and they see us so weak that very friends are afraid to join with us.[2]

On the same day Knox wrote to Anne Locke, and urged her to arrange for the Protestants in London to send money to the Congregation to enable them to pay their soldiers, for as the English government were still parsimonious, Knox hoped to eke out their financial help with voluntary contributions. He reminded Anne Locke that they had a common cause with the citizens of London. 'If we perish in this our enterprise,' he wrote, 'the limits of London will be straiter than they are now within few years.'[3]

In December, the French fleet under the Marquis d'Elbœuf sailed for Scotland with some 4,500 additional soldiers under the command of Sebastian of Luxemburg, Viscount of Martigues. Nine hundred of them landed at Leith, but the rest of the fleet, with fifteen ensigns of soldiers, were driven by storms on to the coasts of Flanders. Knox commented in his *History* that 'God fought for the defence of Scotland'; but at the time he was very anxious, and

[1] Randolph to Croft and Sadler, 12 Oct. 1559; Cecil to Croft and Sadler, 3 Nov. 1559 (Sadler, ii. 37, 73); Memorandum about means of raising money for the Congregation (4 Nov. 1559) (*Sc. Cal.* i. 559).

[2] Knox to Cecil, 18 Nov. 1559 (*Works*, vi. 99).

[3] Knox to Anne Locke, 18 Nov. 1559 (*Works*, vi. 101).

on 26 December he wrote to Croft that he feared that the French would capture either Stirling or St. Andrews. He suggested, however, that if the English sent a fleet to the Forth at once, they would be able to intercept d'Elbœuf's fleet and attack them when they arrived. He did not know that a fortnight before, Elizabeth had taken the daring decision to intervene in Scotland and send William Winter, one of her most experienced sea captains, with a fleet of fourteen ships to the Forth in midwinter. On the day after Knox wrote this letter, Winter sailed from Gillingham, with orders to 'annoy the French' by all possible means, but to claim, if challenged, that he was acting on his own responsibility without orders from his Queen. Six of his ships were lost in the gales, but he reached the Forth with the remaining eight on 22 January.[1]

During January and February, the French and the Congregation fought a guerrilla war in the snow in Fife and in the vicinity of Stirling. In his *History*, Knox relates many of the incidents of the campaign, the daring raids by Arran, Lord James, and Grange on the French line of march, the destruction of bridges and houses, and the cruelties that accompanied this war of a handful of determined partisans against the small foreign army of occupation. He tells of the poor craftsman near Glasgow who hid a chunk of bread under his shirt when the French were requisitioning food, and was stabbed by Martigues in person; of the Dutchman and the French Protestant boy who joined the Congregation, and were captured by the French and hanged from the church steeple at Kinghorn; of the old woman on the Whiteside hill near Bathgate in West Lothian, who, when a French soldier was searching her cottage and removing all her food, lifted up his heels and drowned him in a water tub. But only a brave minority took part in the resistance. The mass of the people of Fife showed no enthusiasm for the cause, and Lord James, Arran, and Grange, with less than 500 horsemen and 100 foot-soldiers, could not cause any real trouble to the French. The English officers were contemptuous of

[1] Knox, *History*, i. 275; Knox to Croft, 26 Dec. 1559 (*Works*, vi. 102); Killigrew and Jones to the Council, 18 Nov. 1559; Killigrew and Jones to Elizabeth I, 27 Dec. 1559 (Forbes, i. 263–5, 286–9); Edwards to Cecil, 26 Nov. and 12 Dec. 1559; Challoner to Cecil, 13 Jan. 1559/60 (*Cal. For. Pap. Eliz.* ii. 333, 408, 575); Cecil to Sadler and Croft, 13 and 16 Dec. 1559 (Sadler, ii. 173, 180); Elizabeth I's Instructions to Winter, 16 Dec. 1559 (Keith, i. 408–10); Winter's journal of the voyage, 27 Dec. 1559–20 Jan. 1559/60; Norfolk's Instructions to Winter (22 Jan. 1560); Croft to Winter, 21 Jan. 1559/60; Winter to Norfolk (25 Jan. 1560) (*Sc. Cal.* i. 620 (1), (3), and (4), 629; *Cal. For. Pap. Eliz.* ii. 623); *Diurnal of Occurrents*, p. 55.

the contribution of the Scottish Protestants towards their own religious and national liberation, though Randolph praised the valour and determination of Arran and Lord James. On 6 February, Knox wrote to Châtelherault and the Lords of the Congregation, reproaching them for their inaction and their failure to give any help to Winter and the English fleet. 'Your friends have lain in the Firth now fifteen days bypast (what was their former travail is not unknown); they have never received comfort of any man, him [Lord James] only excepted, more than if they had lain upon the coast of their mortal enemy.'[1]

According to Knox, when Mary of Lorraine heard of the French successes in Fife, she said: 'Where is now John Knox's God? My God is now stronger than his, yea, even in Fife.' But every French victory only drove Elizabeth to intervene more actively. On 27 February 1560 the Treaty of Berwick was concluded between Elizabeth and 'the noble and mighty Prince, James Duke of Châtelherault, second person of the realm of Scotland', with Lord James, Ruthven, the Master of Maxwell, Lethington, Wishart of Pittarrow, and Balnavis signing for Châtelherault. The treaty declared that Elizabeth, knowing that the Scottish nobility were loyal to their Queen, had agreed to protect them against the attempts of the French to conquer Scotland, suppress its liberties, and unite it to the Crown of France; in return, the Scottish lords agreed to fight against all the enemies of England. After many delays caused by Elizabeth's hesitations and the slowness of transport, an English force of some 9,000 soldiers, the largest number which they could immediately put in the field, marched into Scotland from Berwick on 29 March under the command of Lord Grey, and made contact with the forces of the Congregation at Prestonpans. The French withdrew to Leith, which was besieged by the English and the Congregation, while Mary of Lorraine took refuge in Edinburgh Castle with Lord Erskine, who still remained strictly neutral.[2]

[1] Knox, *History*, i. 277–82, 311; Randolph to Sadler and Croft, 21 Jan. and 4 Feb. 1559/60; Winter to Norfolk (25 Jan. 1560); Intelligence report sent by Norfolk to Cecil, 24 Feb. 1559/60; Percy to Cecil, 30 Apr. 1560; Grey to Elizabeth I (8 May 1560); Cecil to Montagu, 12 May 1560 (*Sc. Cal.* i. 616, 629, 642, 662, 781; *Cal. For. Pap. Eliz.* ii. 615, 687, 1098; iii. 55, 83); Knox to Châtelherault and the Lords at Glasgow, 6 Feb. 1559/60 (Knox, *History*, i. 299).

[2] Knox, *History*, i. 277; 'The Estate of Scotland' (*Wodrow Misc.* i. 82). For the articles of the Treaty of Berwick, 27 Feb. 1559/60, see Knox, *History*, i. 302–7. The estimates of the numbers of the English forces which marched from Berwick to

During the next three months, 3,500 French and Gascon soldiers and 500 Scots defended Leith against 11,000 English troops and 2,000 Scottish mercenaries hired by the Congregation with English money, while the fate of the Reformation in Scotland and the future destiny of the British Isles was decided in London, Amboise, and Madrid, and Knox watched impotently from St. Andrews. He sometimes preached, but there were no opportunities now to rally and inspire the forces of the Congregation. At the beginning of January 1560, during the fighting in Fife, he went to Cupar to preach to Arran and Lord James and their soldiers, who had just suffered a set-back in a clash with the French. Many of his audience approved of his sermon, but a reference that he made to Jehoshaphat, who always showed himself to the people, was resented by Arran. Arran, despite his great services to the cause, had offended many of the Congregation by his aloofness and his habit of keeping to his chamber; the young nobleman, though ready to risk his life bravely, and even recklessly, in the field, was not prepared to fraternize with the rank and file of the brethren. Knox's sermons might inspire most of the Congregation, but if at the same time he offended the Hamiltons, it was better if he did not preach at all, and he was asked not to preach for the time being.[1]

But although the influence of the Hamiltons had temporarily put him to silence, he was prepared to pay tribute where it was due. He praised the courage which Arran showed in the face of the enemy, though he considered that both he and Lord James had been guilty of foolish recklessness. On 29 January he wrote to Railton:

> I am judged amongst ourselves too extreme, and by reason thereof I have extracted myself from all public assemblies to my private study,

Leith vary considerably; cf. Stow, *Annals*, p. 641; 'The Estate of Scotland' (*Wodrow Misc.* i. 82); Knox, *History*, i. 311; *Two Missions of Jacques de la Brosse*, pp. 88–89. The official reports of the English commanders show that some 9,000 men marched from Berwick on 29 Mar., and that a further 2,000 reinforcements were later sent to Leith. On 25 May 1560, the total English force at Leith was 12,466, of whom only 7,600 were fit for service (Norfolk, Sadler, and Leek to the Council, 10 Apr. 1560 (*Sc. Cal.* i. 724); Valentine Brown's report, 25 May 1560 (Haynes, pp. 348–9); 'A note of all the Captains with the number of their bands which is going into Scotland at this journey' (1560); Percy to —, 27 Mar. 1560 (*H.M.C. Montagu*, pp. 7–9)). The French forces in Leith were estimated at 4,000 (Grey to Norfolk, 5 Apr. 1560; Norfolk, Sadler, and Leek to the Council, 10 Apr. 1560 (*Sc. Cal.* i. 711, 724)).

[1] Knox, *History*, i. 278; Knox to Railton, 29 Jan. 1559/60 (*Works*, vi. 105).

yet can I not cease to signify unto you that unless wisdom bridle the foolish boldness of some, all that favour the good success of this great and godly enterprise will one day mourn. If God's mighty hand had not defended these two young plants, they had both perished in this last danger, for what hazard took they when with fewer than 200 horsemen (I count our footmen as ciphers) they lay without fort or walled town within three miles of the enemy, having also the most part of that country unfriends. God is highly to be praised in the prudent boldness and painful diligence of the laird of Grange, who continually so did annoy the enemy that he cutted from them all victuals by land, except when they were compelled to move their whole camp. He hath been in great danger, and was once shot under the left breast, and yet God did preserve him.

The 'private study' to which Knox referred in this letter was probably the work of writing his *History of the Reformation in Scotland*, which he had begun before October 1559. When he found himself prevented from playing an active part in great historical events, he could at least write about them, and give expression to his passionate and aggressive instincts, which he was temporarily prevented from expressing in the pulpit.[1]

Writing was not the only activity in which Knox engaged in St. Andrews. During his five months' residence there, he began building a Calvinist society in the small area of Scotland which was under the control of the Congregation. He tackled three problems: the indoctrination of the people of St. Andrews with Protestant teaching; the treatment of the Catholics, particularly the Catholic clergy; and the suppression of vice among the people. The problem of the Catholic clergy was more serious in St. Andrews than elsewhere, because no town in Scotland had a greater number of priests and friars than St. Andrews, with its archiepiscopal officials, its priory and other monasteries, and its university teachers and scholars. Knox's view was that the Catholic clergy had all sinned, because they had worshipped the idol of the mass and had defended idolatry, even if they had not taken an active part in persecuting Protestant martyrs. He did not believe that they should be put to death, because this punishment should only be inflicted upon those who had once known the truth and had then relapsed into idolatry; but they should not be admitted as members of the Protestant congregations until they had confessed their errors and sincerely

[1] Knox to Railton, 23 Oct. 1559 and 29 Jan. 1559/60 (*Works*, vi. 87, 105–6).

repented of their sin. He was more reluctant to admit them into the Protestant Church as ministers. He did not exclude this in all cases, for he knew that nearly all the Protestant pastors, including he himself, had originally been ordained as Catholic priests; but he believed that they should be chosen as ministers only if they reached the required standard of learning, competence and moral integrity. The office of minister in the Protestant Church was not to be given automatically to every Catholic priest who was prepared to accept the new régime and climb on the bandwagon, as had happened in England.

This raised the question as to what was to happen to those Catholic priests who had never learned a trade, and suddenly found themselves ejected from their benefices in middle age or later in life. Some of the Protestants believed that they should be retired on pensions paid out of the yearly revenues of the Church; but Knox was against paying them pensions, and undoubtedly many of the Protestants took the attitude that these worthless and evil members of society, who had hitherto lived on the tithes that they extracted from the people, should be made to do an honest day's work for the first time in their lives. But the problem of depriving the Catholic clergy of their revenues was not dealt with so easily, or so satisfactorily from the Protestant point of view.[1]

During February and March 1560, a dozen or so priests appeared every Sunday at divine service in St. Andrews, and publicly recanted their old beliefs, on one occasion in the presence of Admiral Winter and his English naval officers. John Wilson, the vicar of Kinghorn, a former canon of the abbey of Holyroodhouse, promised that he would 'never consent nor agree that that lecherous swine the Bishop of Rome (who has rooted up the Lord's vineyard so far as in him was) shall practise, or exerce, or have any manner of authority, jurisdiction or power within Christ's Church here in this realm, or elsewhere'. He also renounced 'all manner of idolatry, superstition and hypocrisy, and especially the mass, as most abominable idolatry'. Fourteen other priests jointly confessed that they had long abstracted themselves and been slow in joining Christ's Congregation, for which they asked God's mercy and the forgiveness of this congregation. They renounced the Pope as Antichrist, and all his diabolical inventions. On 17 March, Friar Greson, the Prior Provincial-General of all

[1] Knox to Calvin, 29 Aug. 1559 (*Works*, vi. 76).

the Friars Preachers in Scotland, confessed that he had for over-long remained at the defence of divers kinds of superstition and idolatry, but was now ready, from the bottom of his heart, to conform his life to the Word and doctrine of the Eternal God, and promised to detest, abhor, and renounce for now and ever the Pope, the mass, the doctrine that priests might not marry, and all other ungodly opinions and inventions of men. Although it has been suggested that Knox drafted these confessions, this is very unlikely, because, though they are all identical in content, the wording is different in every case, and it seems that the Catholic clergy were invited to prove their sincerity by drafting a confession in their own words, and outdid each other in the virulence of their denunciation of the doctrines that they had so recently taught. Among the most eminent of the converts was John Winram, the Sub-Prior of St. Andrews, who had first encountered Knox in 1547, when he had summoned Knox and Rough to explain the sermons which they had preached in this same church in St. Andrews. The leading part that Winram had played at the trials of Wishart, Adam Wallace, and Walter Myln was forgiven, and he was very soon appointed to hold important offices in the Protestant Church.[1]

All the inhabitants were compelled to attend church every Sunday to hear Knox preach. Attendance at church was compulsory, in theory, in every country in Europe, but never before had it been so efficiently enforced. The Scottish Protestants worked out a system by which the elders, who had been elected by the congregation, visited each house during the week in the part of the town assigned to them, and delivered a ticket to the householder, which he was required to hand in when he attended church on Sunday. Absentees from church could thus be easily identified, and were punished in the Church courts along with adulterers, fornicators, and other moral deliquents.[2]

The Church courts did not inflict the cruel physical punishments which the State inflicted for civil crimes, but the mental punishments of public humiliation, the public confession in church, and the stool of repentance. The delinquent stood barefoot at the church door, clad in base and abject apparel, while the

[1] *St. Andrews Church Session Register*, i. 10–18 (Feb.–Mar. 1559/60).

[2] For the activities of the Church Sessions, and the enforcement of moral discipline, see the records of the Church Sessions in the various towns.

people entered the church, and was then brought in and placed on a high stool in the middle of the church, raised above the congregation for all to see him, while he confessed his sin, and the preacher reminded the congregation that every one of them was prone, on account of man's sinful nature, to commit similar, or greater, offences. After enduring this treatment for the prescribed number of Sundays, the guilty man or woman, if considered to be duly penitent, was forgiven, and all members of the congregation were ordered to forget the matter, and never to victimize the offender in future for his past offence.

The sanction behind the judgements of the Church courts was the threat of excommunication. Anyone who refused to submit to the punishments imposed was expelled from the Church by sentence of excommunication, and treated as a social outcast. The time-honoured Christian weapon of excommunication, which had been used since the earliest days of the Christian Church, and which we now call 'sending to Coventry', was very effective, except against those who were inspired by devotion to a cause to withstand the hatred and contempt of the majority. No one except the spouse and family was permitted to speak with an excommunicated person, except those appointed by the Church to convert him, and no one was to trade with him, or give him shelter or food, on pain of being excommunicated themselves, until the sinner made submission and was readmitted to the congregation.

One formidable weapon in bringing the excommunicated person to submission was the refusal of the Church to permit the baptism of his children. On this point, Knox's opinion had prevailed against Calvin's, and the Church decided that children of excommunicated persons should not be admitted to baptism until either the parent had repented, or the child was old enough to ask to be baptized himself, or his other parent, or a near relative, after showing that they abhorred the sin of the excommunicated person, brought the child to be baptized. 'If any think it severe', wrote Knox and his colleagues in the Book of Discipline, 'that the child should be punished for the iniquity of the father, let them understand that the sacraments appertain only to the faithful and to their seed; but such as stubbornly contemn all godly admonition, and obstinately remain in their iniquity, cannot be accounted amongst the faithful.' The threat of a refusal to baptize the children was particularly effective against the mothers of illegitimate children. Unmarried women who gave birth to a child were summoned before the court on a charge of fornication, and asked to reveal the name of the father, so that he too could be brought before the court. In many cases, the woman, after refusing to give the father's name, eventually did so when she realized that if she did not betray her lover, the child would not be baptized. Knox and the ministers of the Church believed that their refusal to baptize the child could not in any way affect God's eternal predestination of the child as elect or reprobate; but the ordinary man and woman in Scotland still believed that baptism was essential to the child's eternal salvation.[1]

The trials of offenders took place before the Church Session of the local congregation, which sat once a week for this purpose; and in St. Andrews in the spring of 1560, Knox sat every Thursday with the elders of the congregation, sometimes assisted by John Douglas, the Rector of the University, and Winram the Sub-Prior. Under the protection of the English fleet, this tribunal meted out Calvinist justice to the inhabitants of St. Andrews. Over eighty per cent. of the cases with which they dealt were charges of adultery or fornication. Knox and his colleagues did not wish to deal with cases of adultery, because they believed, in theory at least, that adultery should be punished with death, as the Bible directed, and should therefore be dealt with by the civil power; but as the civil power improperly allowed adulterers to live, they, too, had to be dealt with in the Church Session. Some months later, this was explained in the Book of Discipline, which was drafted by Knox and other leaders of the Church.

Blasphemy, adultery, murder, perjury and other crimes capital, worthy of death, ought not properly to fall under censure of the Church; because all such open transgressors of God's laws ought to be taken away by the civil sword. But drunkenness, excess (be it in apparel, or be it in eating and drinking), fornication, oppression of the poor by exactions, deceiving of them in buying or selling by wrong mete or measure, wanton words and licentious living tending to slander, do properly appertain to the Church of God, to punish the same as God's Word commandeth. But because this accursed Papistry hath brought in such confusion in the world, that neither was virtue rightly praised,

[1] Knox to Calvin, 28 Aug. 1559; Calvin to Knox, 8 Nov. 1559 (*Works*, vi. 76, 95–97; *Calvini Op.* xvii. 619, 666–7); *The Book of Discipline*, vii (Knox, *History*, ii. 308).

neither vice severely punished, the Church of God is compelled to draw the sword, which of God she hath received, against such open and manifest offenders, cursing and excommunicating all such, as well those whom the civil sword ought to punish as the others, from all participation with her in prayers and sacraments, till open repentance manifestly appear in them.[1]

The Church Session also dealt with offenders who spoke disrespectfully of Protestant doctrines and the Protestant ministers. At St. Andrews in April 1560, a woman was charged with saying that the spread of plague in the district was a punishment for the Protestant religious doctrine that had been taught in the burgh; and in May a man was brought before the Session for calling on the Devil to knock out John Knox's brains, and for saying that he would receive the sacrament after he had seen Knox hanged. By this time, Knox had left St. Andrews.[2]

The Church Sessions were very fair to accused persons, who were given every opportunity to provide for their defence. Cases were adjourned from week to week to comply with the defendants' requests for time to find evidence, and to suit their convenience. Refusals to appear in court, or unexplained absences, were leniently dealt with, and the defendant was given every opportunity to repent of his contempt and to attend and submit to the court. When men and women were found guilty of offences, a confession and repentance was nearly always accepted; the punishment of the stool of repentance was rarely imposed, and excommunication was almost never resorted to. Some sessions were naturally more lenient than others, and Knox's court at St. Andrews was more lenient than most. It was more lenient than it later became, when Goodman succeeded Knox as minister in St. Andrews, and considerably more lenient than John Brand's court in the Canongate at Edinburgh.[3]

In February and March 1560, Knox and the two elders, assisted by the Rector of the University and Winram, tried a divorce

[1] *The Book of Discipline*, vii (Knox, *History*, ii. 306).

[2] *St. Andrews Church Session Register*, i. 33, 36 (26 Apr. and 2 May 1560); and see i. 36, 41–42, 84 (2 and 9 May 1560 and 16 July 1561) for the cases of three other inhabitants of St. Andrews who were dealt with by the Church Session for criticizing Knox.

[3] Cf. *St. Andrews Church Session Register*, before and after April 1560; and *The Buik of the Kirk of the Canagait 1564–1567*. Cf. also the Register of the Church Sessions of other towns.

petition by a husband on the grounds of the wife's adultery. Unlike the old Church, the Protestants granted divorces for both adultery and desertion, but in the case of adultery followed it up with punitive measures against the divorced adulterer. The husband alleged that his wife had committed adultery, and relied on the evidence of two women who, standing on a stool outside the house at night, had peeped through cracks in boards, and had seen the wife's lover remove his hose in the wife's presence, and then blow out the candle in the room. The evidence would have been enough to satisfy most modern divorce-court judges that adultery had been committed; but Knox and his colleagues found the wife not guilty.[1]

In the middle of April, Knox returned to Edinburgh, being succeeded at St. Andrews by Goodman, who had come from Ayr. The English army had reached the neighbourhood of Edinburgh a fortnight earlier. Knox could preach again in St. Giles's to the people of Edinburgh, but the time was passed when his sermons could rouse the fighting men of the Congregation. Neither the English nor the Scottish soldiers who were deciding the destiny of Europe at Leith were likely to be inspired by Knox's sermons. The Scottish hired troops were cowardly and useless. Most of the English soldiers were untrained, and according to their commanders were as cowardly as the Scots. Their officer corps was not the disciplined and efficient body which had served in the armies of Henry VIII. Lord Grey, the commander at Leith, was at loggerheads with Croft, his political adviser, and with Sir Henry Percy, his second-in-command, and all of them were complaining of each other's conduct to the Duke of Norfolk, the commander-in-chief at Berwick. The captains exaggerated the numbers of the men in their companies in order to embezzle the extra sum paid to them by the government for the wages of these non-existent soldiers, and some of the soldiers, cheated of their pay, deserted.

At the end of April, Cecil, knowing that the French were equipping another large army to come to the relief of Leith, and that Elizabeth was hesitating to continue the campaign, ordered the English generals to capture Leith immediately by assault. The attack took place on 7 May, but it was not co-ordinated, as there was a misunderstanding between the English captains as to the

[1] See the case of Ranton *v.* Geddy, 1, 15, and 29 Feb., and 11, 14, 16, 21, and 24 Mar. 1559/60 (*St. Andrews Church Session Register*, i. 18–27).

time when it was to begin, and the scaling-ladders were too short to reach the top of the walls. The assault was ignominiously repulsed. The English commanders accused each other of treachery and rumours spread in Edinburgh that the English would withdraw from Scotland.[1]

Knox states in his *History* that the French stripped the bodies of the dead English soldiers and hung them in the sun over the walls of Leith, and that Mary of Lorraine, seeing them, said: 'Yonder are the fairest tapestry that ever I saw; I would that the whole fields that is betwix this place and yon were strewn with the same stuff.' As Mary of Lorraine was in Edinburgh Castle, it is difficult to believe that she could have seen the corpses on the walls of Leith, though Leith was clearly visible from the castle across the intervening fields; but Knox says that 'her words were heard of some, and misliked of many'. Preaching in St. Giles's, he denounced the conduct of the French and, by implication at least, the words of Mary of Lorraine. He declared that God would 'revenge that contumely done to His image, not only in the furious and godless soldiers, but even in such as rejoiced thereat'. Knox's friends in St. Andrews in 1546 had done precisely the same to the body of Cardinal Beaton after they had murdered him, to the subsequent warm approval of Knox; but Knox, in his *History*, states that his prophecy in this sermon proved true, as divine punishment soon overtook Mary of Lorraine. 'For within few days thereafter (yea, some say that same day), began her belly and loathsome legs to swell, and so continued, till that God did execute His judgements upon her.' In fact, Mary of Lorraine fell ill of dropsy at least ten days before Knox's sermon, and complained of the swelling of her legs on 29 April, before the attack on Leith had taken place. She died on 11 June.[2]

By this time, the French in Leith were being slowly starved into surrender, and Cecil and the Bishop of Valence, the French delegate, were on the Great North Road, travelling to Edinburgh to negotiate a peaceful settlement which left Scotland Protestant

[1] Knox, *History*, i. 318, 320; and see the reports of Lord Grey, Percy, Sadler, and Croft, and the English officers at Leith, to Norfolk, and Norfolk's reports to Elizabeth I and Cecil (Haynes, pp. 278, 299–301, 303–5, 312, 321, 346; *Cal. For. Pap. Eliz.* ii. 1015, 1088; iii. 44, 46, 48, 49, 55, 62, 75, 77, 78, 83, 164; *Sc. Cal.* i. 737, 777, 778[1] and [2], 779, 781, 784, 788, 790, 809).

[2] Knox, *History*, i. 319; Mary of Lorraine to d'Oysel and La Brosse, 29 Apr. 1560 (*Cal. For. Pap. Eliz.* ii. 1093).

and in the English orbit of influence. Guise's plans to send another fleet and army to Scotland had been thwarted by the desperate plight of the French treasury, and by the conspiracy of Amboise in March, when the French Protestants attempted a *coup d'état* to overthrow Guise and the Cardinal of Lorraine. The plot had been instigated with the intention of helping the Congregation in Scotland, and was planned in conjunction with Throckmorton. The conspiracy was discovered, Condé was arrested, and the Protestants who were directly implicated were executed, tortured, or sent to the galleys; but the plot, and the risk of an outbreak of civil war, deterred Guise from sending another expeditionary force to Scotland. Instead, invoking the Treaty of Cateau-Cambrésis, the French government asked Philip II for assistance in the suppression of sedition and heresy in Scotland.[1]

Knox, like the Jews in Babylon, was in the hands of God, and being unable to influence events, he waited for a pagan Cyrus to deliver him; for at the critical moment, the Scottish Reformation was saved by the Duke of Alva and Suleiman the Magnificent. If Philip II had responded to the French request for assistance in Scotland, Elizabeth would immediately have withdrawn her troops, and Knox's fear that Christ Jesus would be destroyed in His infancy in Scotland would have come to pass. But Philip was torn between his hatred of heresy and his traditional fear of France. His predicament had been clearly pointed out to him by his half-sister, Margaret of Parma, his Regent in the Netherlands, as early as 7 December 1559, a few days before Elizabeth decided to send Winter's fleet to Scotland. Margaret, like Philip's other advisers, knew that Elizabeth was seeking to destroy the Catholic Church in Scotland, and that this might soon lead to a Protestant revolt in France and elsewhere in Europe; but if the French triumphed in Scotland, this would be as great a disaster for Philip as the loss of Brussels. From Scotland, the French would overrun England; then, holding Dover as well as Calais, they would control the Straits, and could prevent the Spanish treasure fleet from the Indies from reaching the money market at Antwerp. Philip decided that the only way to prevent either of these evils was for him to intervene in Scotland himself and tell Elizabeth

[1] Arran and Lord James to Sadler and Croft, 19 Jan. 1559/60 (Sadler, ii. 229); Killigrew to Cecil, 7 Apr. 1560 (*Sc. Cal.* i. 717; *Cal. For. Pap. Eliz.* ii. 961); Francis II to Mary of Lorraine (Apr. 1560) (Forbes, i. 400–2).

that in order to protect her realm, to expel the French from Scotland and to suppress revolution, he was sending a Spanish army there.

If Philip had adhered to this policy, it would have put an end to the Protestant Church in Scotland, to Knox's sermons in St. Giles's, and to the power of the Church Sessions in Edinburgh and St. Andrews to regulate the lives of the Scottish people. Philip enrolled an army of 4,400 mercenaries, and embarked them in the ports of the Netherlands, whereupon Elizabeth immediately opened negotiations with France, which she had previously refused to do, and considered abandoning the Scottish enterprise. But in April, Philip asked Alva for his advice on the matter. Alva had been fighting the French for thirty-five years, and was delighted to see them in difficulties; he strongly advised Philip not to intervene, and to allow Elizabeth to expel the French from Scotland. Philip was still hesitating when he heard that the Turks had attacked the island of Djerba off North Africa and destroyed the Spanish fleet there. He ordered the fleet in the ports of the Netherlands to sail for Spain and Tripoli instead of Scotland, and told the French government, and Elizabeth, that he refused the French request for assistance.[1]

On 6 July, Cecil and the Bishop of Valence signed the Treaty of Edinburgh, by which the French agreed to withdraw all their troops from Scotland by a specified date, and all questions of religion were referred to the Scottish Parliament. Within four days, the Parliament had assembled. Knox officiated at a great thanksgiving service for the victory in St. Giles's, and preached there regularly throughout the time that Parliament was in session, taking his texts from the Book of Haggai.[2] During August, Parliament passed the necessary legislation to abolish the Catholic religion in Scotland and establish Protestantism as the State

[1] See the correspondence of Margaret of Parma, Quadra, Alva, and Glajon with Philip II, especially Alva's opinion on England and Scotland, 2 Aug. 1560 (wrongly dated 1562 in manuscript); the reports of Middleton, Gresham, Montagu, Chamberlain, and Throckmorton to Elizabeth I and Cecil; Cecil's letters and diary; and the reports of the Venetian Ambassadors (Teulet, ii. 462–509, 511–17, 527–36; *Span. Cal. Eliz.* i. 80, 95, 97, 99; *H.M.C., Cecil*, i. 585, 645; Haynes, pp. 258–9, 280–1, 289; Forbes, i. 1090; *Cal. For. Pap. Eliz.* ii. 1036, 1046, 1052, 1066, 1069; iii. 109, 817; *Ven. Cal.* vii. 132, 134, 153, 155, 163, 166, 173; Pollen, *Papal Negotiations with Mary Queen of Scots*, pp. 43–45, 456–8; Murdin, *A Collection of State Papers*, p. 750; *Sc. Cal.* i. 735, 804, 842, 869).

[2] See the Treaty of Edinburgh, and the Concessions to the Scottish Propositions, 6 July 1560 (Keith, i. 291–306; Knox, *History*, i. 323–31); Knox, *History*, i. 332–5.

religion. The Papal authority was abolished. The mass was made illegal, and anyone who celebrated or who attended mass was to be punished for the first offence by confiscation of all their property and imprisonment at the discretion of the judge, for the second offence by banishment from Scotland, and for the third offence by death. The Catholic bishops challenged the validity of the proceedings, as the Parliament had been convened by the authority of the revolutionary Great Council of Scotland which had replaced the Queen Regent in October 1559, and without any commission having been obtained from the King and Queen in France; but Archbishop Hamilton and his colleagues in Parliament did not venture to make any serious resistance to the proposed legislation.

Knox was not a member of Parliament, and took no part in the one-sided debates which preceded the enactment of the statutes which abolished the Catholic religion; but on 15 August he and the other ministers presented to Parliament the Confession of Faith, which stated the Protestant and Calvinist doctrine in a less controversial and dogmatic form than might have been expected. Knox and the ministers were invited to attend in Parliament—standing, not sitting as members—to defend the document from criticism; but neither the Archbishop of St. Andrews nor any of the other bishops present ventured to say anything against the Confession of Faith, and Parliament, in which the Catholic bishops sat and the Protestant pastors did not, accepted the Confession of Faith with only two dissentient votes, those of the Earl of Cassillis and the Earl of Caithness. On 24 August 1560 the legislation came into force, and Scotland became a Protestant state.[1]

The Confession of Faith had probably been modified in order to placate Elizabeth, for Lethington and Randolph were in communication with Cecil about it. The original draft was submitted to Lethington and Winram, who disliked the vehemence of the language, and especially the section dealing with the duty of

[1] Knox, *History*, i. 338–43; *Acts Parl. Scot.* ii. 525–35 (1–24 Aug. 1560); The Confession of Faith (Knox, *History*, ii. 255–72); Lethington to Cecil, 15 and 18 Aug. 1560; Randolph to Cecil, 15, 19, 25, and 27 Aug. and 7 Sept. 1560 (*Works*, vi. 110–21; *Sc. Cal.* i. 885, 886, 891, 893, 902; *Cal. For. Pap. Eliz.* iii. 431, 434, 454, 460, 501); and see C. G. Mortimer, 'The Scottish Hierarchy in 1560' (*Clergy Review*, xi. 442–50). Knox states, in his *History*, that the only temporal lords who voted against the Confession of Faith were Atholl, Somerville, and Borthwick; but this is almost certainly a slip, as Randolph, writing at the time, states that Cassillis and Caithness were the only dissentients.

obedience to rulers; for though the doctrine was theologically unobjectionable, they considered that it was politically inexpedient to include it at the present time. The Confession of Faith, in its final form, contained a section on obedience to the civil magistrate, in which the duty of obedience to emperors and princes was stated without qualification; but this was obviously not the original draft, because on 7 September, three weeks after the Confession of Faith had been accepted by Parliament, Randolph wrote to Cecil, and told him how glad he was that the section on obedience to the civil magistrates had been omitted. He was probably referring to a statement written by Knox, which laid down not only the duty of obedience to rulers, but the circumstances in which they could be disobeyed. But the disagreements among the Protestants about the Confession of Faith were carried on in secret; and Knox, with his usual realism, was obviously prepared to accept a compromise document that still caused Randolph some anxiety. On 13 September, Lethington wrote to Cecil, offering to modify the Confession of Faith by further legislation if Cecil was dissatisfied with it.[1]

There were more open disagreements in connexion with the Book of Discipline. On 29 April 1560, the Great Council of Scotland appointed Knox, Winram, Willock, John Douglas the Rector of St. Andrews University, John Spottiswood, and John Row to draft a document that would lay down the policy and discipline of the Church. They had completed the draft by 20 May, but did not present it to Parliament until January 1561.[2] The Book of Discipline provided for the enforcement of moral discipline through the Church Sessions, and for the organization of the Church. The local congregations were to elect their ministers from a list of candidates who had been approved by the Church leaders as being suitable in respect of their learning and moral life; this ensured that unsuitable ministers were not chosen by the congregation, now that the whole population was pressed into membership of the Church. The country was divided into ten dioceses, each diocese being under the jurisdiction of a superintendent, who would serve for three years. The first superintendents were to be appointed by the Great Council of Scotland, but thereafter the superintendents were to be elected every three

[1] Randolph to Cecil, 7 Sept. 1560; Lethington to Cecil, 13 Sept. 1560 (*Works*, vi. 120–1; *Sc. Cal.* i. 902, 903).

[2] Knox, *History*, i. 343, 345.

years by the congregation from a list of two or three candidates nominated by the ministers, elders, and deacons, and by the burgh councils of the diocese. The superintendents were required to travel continuously throughout their dioceses, to preach at least three times a week, and to supervise the behaviour of the ministers. 'These men', said the Book of Discipline, 'must not be suffered to live as your idle bishops have done heretofore.' Superintendents, like ministers, were to be removable at any time for misconduct.

The provisions of the Book of Discipline with regard to education have rightly become famous; for even allowing for the surprising importance already attached to education in Scotland, it is remarkable to find a group of men in the sixteenth century, in one of the poorest and most backward countries of Europe, who were prepared to draw up such a detailed and ambitious plan. Apart from providing that every child in Scotland was to go to school, they drafted a syllabus for the universities. In the place of the old university syllabus in which scholastic theology predominated, supplemented by a study of the classical Latin authors, with medicine taught only in Aberdeen, Knox and his colleagues included all the most modern subjects. One of the main purposes of the universities in their scheme was to educate men for the ministry, and the Book of Discipline stipulated that students for the ministry must study dialectics, mathematics, physics, ethics, economics, moral philosophy, and Hebrew. A syllabus was also laid down for students of law and medicine. The scheme was perhaps too ambitious to be practicable, for the shortage of teachers in some of the newer subjects might have been a difficulty; but the real impediment to the implementation of the scheme was the unwillingness of the wealthy classes to pay for it. Because of this, the scheme was not adopted in Knox's lifetime; but it was never quite forgotten, and it is largely due to Knox and the Protestant Reformation that universal education, which was not instituted in England till 1870, came in Scotland in 1696.

The Book of Discipline contained an important safeguard against any revival of Catholic worship, or against the development of any new Protestant or Anabaptist organization that might arise in opposition to Knox's Church. A provision in the Book forbade the administration of the communion by anyone except the ministers of the official Protestant Church, and particularly forbade the private mass and the administration of the communion in private houses. *The Book of Discipline* complained that 'where, not long ago, men stood in such admiration of that idol the mass that none durst presume to have said the mass but the foresworn shaven sort, the Beast's marked men, some dare now be so bold' as to minister the sacraments in open assemblies without authority; 'and some idiots, yet more wickedly and impudently', dared to minister it in their houses, 'without reverence, without word preached, and without minister, other than of companion to companion. . . . We fear not to affirm, that the one and the other deserve death; for if he who doth falsify the seal, subscription or coin of a king is adjudged worthy of death, what shall we think of him who plainly doth falsify the seals of Christ Jesus, Prince of the kings of the earth?' Knox and his colleagues had not forgotten the part which the administration of the communion in private houses had played in building up their own organization and destroying the authority of the State Church, and they were determined to prevent the Anabaptists or any other body from doing the same.[1]

On 27 January 1561, *The Book of Discipline* was approved by the Great Council, and was signed, at a ceremony in the tolbooth of Edinburgh, by nearly all the nobles, including Châtelherault, Arran, Lord James, Argyll, and the Bishop of Galloway: Only Lord Erskine refused to sign; 'and no wonder,' wrote Knox, 'for besides that he has a very Jezebel to his wife, if the poor, the schools, and the ministry of the Church had their own, his kitchen would lack two parts, and more, of that which he unjustly now possesses'. Erskine was the only noble who was honest enough to refuse to approve a project which none of them had any intention of putting into practice.[2]

Knox now settled down to his duties as minister of the congregation of Edinburgh. His colleagues wished to appoint him as one of the superintendents, but he refused to accept the office, perhaps on the grounds of his health; for though he was only 46, his health had begun to deteriorate after the exertions of the previous year. John Spottiswood was appointed as Superintendent of Lothian, and was formally admitted to his office at a ceremony in Edinburgh on 9 March 1561 at which Knox officiated.

[1] For the provisions of *The Book of Discipline*, see the text of the Book, in Knox, *History*, ii. 280–323; the passages cited are at pp. 292, 321–2.
[2] Knox, *History*, i. 344–5.

Winram was made Superintendent of Fife, Willock of Glasgow, while Erskine of Dun, though he had never been ordained as a priest or minister, was appointed Superintendent of Angus and the Mearns. But though officially Knox was merely the minister of Edinburgh, his position in the Church was unique, 'John Knox, minister of Edinburgh' being always appointed to serve with the superintendents on the committees and other bodies set up to act for the Church.[1]

As minister of the congregation of Edinburgh, Knox held an honoured position in the life of the burgh, and had many financial and other privileges. The salaries of the ministers were not high, for though the Book of Discipline stipulated that ministers should be paid more than the ordinary working man, so as to enable them to buy books, and travel, the poverty of the Church prevented adequate salaries from being paid. But the Church did not distribute its meagre funds equally. The superintendents were paid 500 marks a year—£333. 6*s.* 8*d.*—and were to receive further payments in kind of six chalders of bere, nine chalders of meal, and three chalders of oats, which in 1561 were worth at least £700, and rose in value in the next few years. The ministers were to be paid between 100 and 300 marks per year, exhorters were to receive 100 marks, and readers 40 marks. Knox was paid 300 marks, or £200, the highest salary payable to a minister, besides receiving additional casual payments from the Church at irregular intervals.[2]

Apart from the payments that he received from the Church, Knox also received payments and privileges from the burgh council of Edinburgh. When he first arrived in Edinburgh from St. Andrews in April 1560, he stayed in David Forrest's house; but within a fortnight he took up his residence in a house on the west side of Trunk Close, to the north of the High Street, which had formerly been occupied by the Abbot of Dunfermline, but was now let by the owner to a tailor. It is described in a contemporary document as a 'great mansion', with a garden and waste land attached. The tailor moved out in order to put the house at

[1] Randolph to Cecil, 5 Mar. 1560/1 (*Works*, vi. 122; *Sc. Cal.* i. 967); 'Form and Order of Election of Superintendents' (used at Edinburgh by Knox on 9 Mar. 1560/1) (Knox, *History*, ii. 273); Knox, *History*, i. 334.

[2] *The Book of Discipline* (5th Head) (Knox, *History*, ii. 289–90); Donaldson's Introduction to *Accounts of the Collectors of Thirds of Benefices*, p. xxi. For payments to Knox, see ibid., pp. 54, 61, 72, 128, 131, 141, 180, 191, 212, 297.

Knox's disposal. The burgh council paid Knox's rent to the landlord, and also paid for the furnishings of the house, and for a lock to the door; and they agreed to compensate the tailor for any inconvenience he had suffered through vacating the house in favour of Knox. In October 1560 the burgh council, besides paying Knox £120 for his own use, paid £20 for the cost of ironwork and fire work carried out at his house; and in November 1561 the burgh council ordered the Dean of Crafts to build a warm study for Knox at the house, 'with lights and windows thereto and all other necessaries'. Knox stayed in this house for at least four years, for we know that he was still there in November 1564; but by Michaelmas 1565 he had moved to another house. Here also the burgh council paid his rent. Knox was not one of those ministers who, as the Church so often complained during the next few years, lived in poverty, on the verge of destitution. He did not receive the great revenues which bishops of the old Church had received in Scotland and elsewhere, and which were being paid to the bishops of the Church of England; but his salary, with the payments in kind and his rent-free house, placed him well within the higher income group in Scotland, his income being the modern equivalent of some £7,000 a year free of tax.[1]

Knox's position as a respected member of the municipal establishment in Edinburgh to some extent alienated him from the poorer inhabitants, and from the craft guilds, who were always in conflict with the merchants who dominated the burgh council. Many of the craftsmen had been Catholics. Their holy days and worship of the patron saint of their craft tended to link them with the old religion;[2] and the Queen Regent had supported them in their efforts to win representation on the burgh council. The chief source of trouble, however, were the young apprentices to the craftsmen, who were known as the 'crafts children', and soon after Knox settled in Edinburgh, the crafts children became involved in a clash in connexion with the enforcement of moral discipline by the Church.

[1] *Edinburgh Burgh Records*, iii. 63–64, 76, 87, 97, 99, 104, 115, 128–9, 135–6, 154, 174, 177–8, 191, 210, 219, 245, 258, 260 (8 and 15 May, 30 Oct., and 20 Dec. 1560, 12 Feb. 1560/1, 5 Apr., 30 May, 5 Nov., and 31 Dec. 1561, 19 and 24 June and 11 Dec. 1562, 24 Apr., 3 May, and 29 Nov. 1564, 15 Nov. 1565, 25 Sept. 1566, 20 Feb. 1567/8, 19 Nov. 1568, 4 Mar. 1568/9).

[2] See R. Lamond, 'The Scottish Craft Guilds as a Religious Fraternity' (*S.H.R.* xvi. 191–211).

On 10 June 1560 the burgh council issued a decree under which adulterers, brothel-keepers, and whoremongers who had not sincerely repented of their misconduct were to be forced to stand in the irons at the market cross for six hours, and then hauled through the town in a cart for public execration[1]—a punishment that was freely used in England and other countries. For a second offence, the malefactors were to be branded on the cheek and banished from the town, and for the third offence they were to suffer death. A flesher named John Sanderson had obtained a decree of divorce from the old ecclesiastical courts of the Catholic Church, and had consequently put away his wife and cohabited with another woman; but Knox's Church Session did not recognize the validity of a decree of nullity pronounced by the Catholic Church courts on grounds that were not accepted by the Protestant Church as a reason for divorce. Sanderson was ordered to separate from his mistress, and when he did not comply, he was sentenced to stand at the cross and be carted.

On 22 November 1560 the deacon of the hammermen appeared before the burgh council, and demanded that the sentence on Sanderson be revoked, because 'they would not approve the same, nor no such extreme laws upon honest craftsmen'. The burgh council refused, pointing out that the craft guilds had approved of the statute against adulterers on 10 June, and the sentence was carried out; but when Sanderson was carted, the apprentices rioted, broke the cart, and set Sanderson free. The burgh council appealed to Châtelherault and the Great Council of Scotland for help in maintaining law and order in Edinburgh. The deacons of the crafts asked Knox to intercede with the authorities on behalf of the ringleaders of the riot. Knox agreed to do so, and though the burgh council ordered that some of the crafts children should be 'punished to the rigour, in example of others', there is no record that any punishment was inflicted.[2]

A more serious riot broke out in May 1561 in connexion with the Robin Hood festivities on May Day. In April the burgh council had issued a proclamation drawing the attention of the people of Edinburgh to the Act of Parliament which prohibited the election of a Robin Hood, or Abbot of Unreason, on May Day. This statute was not a Protestant measure against feast days, but

[1] *Edinburgh Burgh Records*, iii. 65 (10 June 1560).
[2] Ibid. 89–95 (22, 23, and 28 Nov. and 6 Dec. 1560); Knox, *History*, i. 355–6.

had been enacted by Mary of Lorraine's Parliament in 1555 to prevent disorder. The Robin Hood pageant appears to have been taken by the apprentices as an excuse for emulating Robin Hood in robbing the rich, and invariably led to violence. Despite the burgh council's proclamation, the apprentices assembled on May Day, and after electing one of their number as Robin Hood, they proceeded to take possession of the streets, stopping the passers-by and forcibly robbing them of their possessions. The ringleaders were arrested, and sentenced to death.

Knox was again visited by the deacons of the craft guilds, who asked him to intervene with the burgh council to ask for mercy for the condemned crafts children; but this time he refused. He told them that he had often interceded in their favour, but that his conscience told him that they exploited his intervention to further their iniquity. The deacons of the crafts then turned to threats, and said that if the men were not reprieved, both Knox and the baillies would regret it; but Knox answered that he would not hurt his conscience for fear of any man. When the apprentices, on 21 July, saw the gallows for the execution being erected at the market cross, they rioted and broke down the gallows, and attacked the tolbooth and freed the condemned men and all the other prisoners in the jail. The leaders of the riots of May Day and 21 July were put to the horn, and excommunicated by the Church. Eventually they expressed their repentance, were readmitted to the congregation, and were lifted from the horn; but they were never punished, and were pardoned by Mary when she returned from France. The apprentices had learned from the nobility that in Scotland self-help was the best remedy.[1]

Knox had scarcely settled down in his house in Trunk Close before he suffered a great personal loss in the death of his wife. After Marjory rejoined Knox in September 1559, she threw herself into the work of helping him with great energy, acting as his secretary, and sleeping as little as Knox himself. 'The rest of my wife hath been so unrestful since her arriving here,' wrote Knox to Anne Locke on 31 December 1559, 'that scarcely could she tell upon the morrow what she wrote at night.' Overwork should not have killed a young woman of 24, but we have no knowledge

[1] *Edinburgh Burgh Records*, iii. 107–8, 111–14, 116–18 (23 Apr., 10, 13, and 14 May, 11 and 16 June, and 11 July 1561); Pitcairn, i [i]. 409–10 (proceedings of 20 July and 8 Aug. 1561); Knox, *History*, i. 357–9, ii. 8.

of the cause of her death, which occurred in November or early December 1560. She left Knox with the two boys to care for; Nathaniel was aged 3½, and Eleazer 2. Mrs. Bowes went to England after her daughter's death; but in August 1562 Randolph, the English ambassador in Edinburgh, asked Cecil to grant a licence to Mrs. Bowes to return to Scotland, as Knox found it so difficult, with his other duties, to take care of the children. Mrs. Bowes probably lived with Knox from the autumn of 1562 until he remarried in 1564, and then again returned to England.[1]

Knox was deeply distressed at Marjory's death, but he had the consolation of religion, and he busied himself in his work. On 23 April, Calvin wrote to him to console with him on his loss. 'You found a wife', wrote Calvin, 'whose like is not found everywhere; but as you have rightly learned where to seek consolation in sorrow, I am sure that you are bearing this calamity with patience.' On the same day, Calvin wrote to Goodman: 'Although I am not a little grieved that our brother Knox has been deprived of the most delightful of wives, yet I rejoice that he has not been so afflicted by her death as to cease his active labours in the cause of Christ and the Church.'[2]

Knox mentions the death of Marjory in a passing reference in his *History*, and in a strange context. At the beginning of December 1560, Francis II suddenly fell ill, a month before his seventeenth birthday. Knox was the first person in Scotland to hear the news, for he had many contacts with the Protestants in France, and had a well-placed informant at the French Court. The Scottish Protestants knew that Francis's death would be greatly to their political advantage. It would sever the link which still bound Scotland to the French Crown, and would make it possible to oust French influence completely from Scotland without revolting against their prince. It would also transform the situation in France, where the power of the Guises depended on Mary Queen of Scots's influence over the King, and where the life of the Prince

[1] Knox to Anne Locke, 31 Dec. 1559; Randolph to Cecil, 4 Aug. 1562 (*Works*, vi. 104, 141–2; *Sc. Cal.* i. 1131). There is no further information about Mrs. Bowes, except that Knox wrote in July 1572 that she was dead (Knox, 'To the Faithful Reader', in *Answer to Tyrie*, in *Works*, vi. 563). The unreliable Surtees gives no authority for his statement (in his *History of Durham*, iv. 118) that Mrs. Bowes died in Edinburgh in 1568, and it is unlikely.

[2] Calvin to Knox, 23 Apr. 1561; Calvin to Goodman, 23 Apr. 1561 (*Calvini Op.* xviii. 434–6; *Works*, vi. 124–5).

of Condé, who was in prison awaiting death for his part in the conspiracy of Amboise, might be saved if Francis died in time.

As soon as Knox heard the news of the King's illness, he hastened to Châtelherault's town house—Hamilton House, in Kirk-o'-Field just outside Edinburgh—where he found Châtelherault and Lord James. He told them the good news, 'and willed them to be of good comfort'; for he assured them that his informant at the French Court was reliable, though he refused to tell them his name. 'While they were reasoning in divers purposes; and he upon the one part comforting them, and they upon the other part comforting him (for he was in no small heaviness by reason of the late death of his dear bedfellow, Marjory Bowes)', a messenger came from Lord Grey in Berwick with news of Francis's death. In his *History*, Knox does not hide his joy at the news. 'Unhappy Francis, husband to our sovereign, suddenly perisheth of a rotten ear. . . . The death of that child was not only the cause of joy to us in Scotland, but also by it were the faithful in France delivered, as it were, from the present death. . . . For as the said King sat at mass, he was suddenly stricken with an aposthume in that deaf ear that never would hear the truth of God.' Thus his personal grief at the death of his wife coincided with his political jubilation at the death of the 16-year-old boy. It is unfair to blame Knox for rejoicing at the death of Francis II unless we also remember the amount of suffering which the Protestants in France and Scotland were spared by the removal of the Guises' King; but it is ironic that the only mention in his writings of his private bereavement should be in connexion with the death of Francis.[1]

[1] Knox, *History*, i. 347–9, 351.

CHAPTER XX

The Struggle with Mary: 1561–1562

IN the autumn of 1560, the Great Council of Scotland invited Elizabeth to marry Arran, who was second in line of succession to the Scottish throne. They secretly suggested that Elizabeth should displace Mary, and reign with Arran as King and Queen of Scotland. Elizabeth refused. The offer of her hand in marriage was a great bargaining factor in international diplomacy, which she did not wish to relinquish at this stage; and she hesitated, for many reasons, to deprive Mary Queen of Scots of her throne. If she had accepted, it would have meant an end of Knox's activities, for Elizabeth or her representative in Holyroodhouse would soon have put him to silence if he had continued preaching under Elizabeth in the same style in which he preached during the next five years; and Knox, with his political sagacity, would certainly not have done so. Elizabeth's refusal gave the Great Council no real alternative but to accept Mary as their Queen. Mary was therefore invited to return to Scotland, and though she told her uncles that she would much prefer to retire to Touraine or Poitou, they persuaded her to go to Scotland. They later bitterly regretted that they had done so.[1]

The only card which the Catholics had to play in Scotland was the person of the 18-year-old Queen. Scotland had passed into the English zone of influence, and had become a Protestant state, and no foreign power was prepared to help Mary to reverse this. At the death of Francis II, the influence of the Guises at the French Court was destroyed, and the regency of the young King Charles IX passed to his mother, Catherine de Medici, who disliked the Guises and Mary Queen of Scots. Catherine de Medici had no

[1] The Lords of the Articles to Elizabeth I, 16 Aug. 1560; Memorandum of the Scottish Commissioners to the English Privy Council (Nov.–Dec. 1560); Elizabeth I to her Council, 8 Dec. 1560; Lethington to Cecil, 26 Feb. 1560/1; Burghley's memorandum for Shrewsbury, 1 Feb. 1571/2 (*Acts Parl. Scot.* ii. 605–6; Burnet, vi. 465–9; *Sc. Cal.* i. 885, 963; iv. 127; *Cal. For. Pap. Eliz.* iii. 431, 1033); Knox, *History*, i. 345–6, 350; Brantôme, *Recueil des Dames*, Discours III, Sur la Reyne d'Escosse (*Œuvres complètes de Brantôme*, vii. 413; *Book of the Ladies*, p. 96).

intention of helping Mary if she was involved in difficulties in Scotland, and Philip II, who still feared France more than England, was not willing to give her any practical assistance. Mary had nothing to hope for from any of the Catholic sovereigns of Europe, except pious ambiguities from Philip and unwise encouragement from the Pope. The Cardinal of Lorraine therefore advised her to pursue a friendly policy towards Elizabeth and the Protestant party in Scotland, being aware that in the course of time, if Elizabeth died childless, she would succeed to the throne of England. He even at one time advised her to become a Protestant;[1] but Mary's conscience prevented her from taking this step. When she finally compromised her Catholic principles, it was for love, not for power politics.

If Mary was going to reign in Scotland, it was essential for the Protestants that she should come under Protestant influence, and above all that she should marry a Protestant, and not a Catholic. Within a month of the death of Francis II in December 1560, Arran, who had just been rejected by Elizabeth, conceived the idea of marrying Mary, and began highly secret negotiations about this through an agent whom he sent from Scotland to the French Court. According to Randolph, the only person in Scotland to whom Arran confided his plan was Knox. Knox, despite all his distrust of the Hamiltons, may well have considered, with his political realism, that Mary would be least dangerous if she were married to the young Protestant noble who had played so important a part in the struggle against her mother; but Mary refused to marry Arran.[2]

Mary immediately came under the influence of her half-brother, Lord James. In the spring of 1561, Lord James went to France, and finding Mary near Joinville, the Guises' country residence in Champagne, persuaded her to return to Scotland, to pursue a pro-English policy, to do nothing to upset the Protestant religion that had been established in her kingdom, and to rely on him and Lethington as her chief advisers. A few weeks earlier, she had been visited by John Leslie, the Official of the diocese of Aberdeen, who later became Bishop of Ross and Mary's most reliable and wisest counsellor. He had been sent by Huntly and other

[1] Randolph to Cecil, 30 Jan. 1561/2 (*Sc. Cal.* i. 1071).

[2] Randolph to Cecil, 3 Jan. 1560/1; Lethington to Cecil, 26 Feb. 1560/1 (*Sc. Cal*, i. 945. 963).

Catholic nobles to persuade Mary to have Lord James arrested and detained in France, and sail to Aberdeen, where she could rely on Huntly and the Catholics to support her against her Protestant rebels.[1] But Mary, like her mother, was always suspicious of the Gordons, and was never eager to base her support on the Catholics in the north; she wished to reign in London, not in Aberdeen. She rejected Leslie's advice and turned to Lord James. Within a year of her return to Scotland, she allowed Lord James to provoke and crush a rebellion by Huntly, in the course of which Huntly was killed and one of his sons was executed, and the family attainted for treason, while the power of Châtelherault and the Hamiltons was weakened by a series of quiet but firm measures that were directed by Lord James.

The only price that Lord James paid for these advantages was that Mary was allowed to remain a Catholic and have mass celebrated in her chapel royal, and to set up a gay court in Scotland, comparable to the courts of any prince in Christendom. Lord James and the Protestant nobles had no great objection to Mary hearing mass in the chapel royal, provided that no one except the Queen and her household was allowed to be present; and they considered that a gay court was not only enjoyable, but increased the prestige of Mary and Scotland in the world. But Knox was outraged both by the mass and the gaiety. Before Lord James went to France to visit Mary, Knox had urged him not to agree that Mary should be permitted to have her mass if she returned to Scotland; and when Knox discovered that Lord James had given way on this point, he was deeply disturbed, and was convinced that Mary had tricked Lord James into complying with her deep-laid schemes to restore Popery in Scotland.[2]

Lord James, on his part, was anxious that Mary should be reassured that if she returned to Scotland, Knox would not incite a revolution against her. Mary had heard about Knox's *First Blast of the Trumpet*, and before Lord James left for France, he apparently asked Knox to give him some assurance in writing on this point. Knox knew that Mary's return was inevitable, and as he did not wish to appear to be calling for revolution against his prince, he gave Lord James the undertaking which he required. On 20 March 1561, Randolph wrote to Cecil: 'Mr. Knox in certain articles given unto my Lord James at this time hath

[1] Leslie, *History*, ii. 451–3. [2] Knox, *History*, i. 354–5.

mitigated somewhat the rigour of his book, referring much unto the time that the same was written.' But in July, Throckmorton reported to Elizabeth that Mary was convinced that Knox was the most dangerous man in her realm, and was determined that he should be banished from Scotland, or else she herself would not live there. Throckmorton told Elizabeth that Mary was sending her a copy of Knox's *First Blast* to prejudice her against Knox, and urged Elizabeth not to forget Knox's usefulness to England. 'Whatsoever she may insinuate against him,' he wrote, 'I take him to be as much for your purpose as any man of all that nation; and that his doing therein, and his zeal, sufficiently recompense his fault in writing that book, and therefore he is not to be driven out of that realm.'[1]

A few months later, Knox, hearing that Mary was trying to obtain a solemn repudiation of his doctrine about the government of women from learned men in many realms, wrote to Elizabeth, and warned her that Mary was trying to persuade her and her Privy Council to condemn him as a common enemy to women and their regiment. Although 'it were but foolishness to me to prescribe unto your Majesty what is to be done in anything', he thought it his duty to warn Elizabeth 'that neither doth our sovereign so greatly fear her own estate by reason of that book, neither yet doth she so unfeignedly favour the tranquility of your Majesty's reign and realm, that she would take so great and earnest pains, unless that her crafty counsel in so doing shot at a further mark'. This letter, with its reference to the 'crafty counsel' of his Queen, must have angered Elizabeth if she read the letter; but perhaps Cecil suppressed it. In any case, she and her ministers found Knox too useful as an agent to be prepared to dispense with his services, or to withdraw from him the unofficial protection which they accorded him against his own sovereign. Throckmorton advised Cecil that the more Mary sought to expel Knox from Scotland, so much the more ought Elizabeth to use all her friends and means to retain him there in credit and safety.[2]

Mary arrived at Leith by sea from France on 19 August 1561, and was enthusiastically welcomed by the people of Edinburgh.

[1] Randolph to Cecil, 20 Mar. 1560/1; Throckmorton to Elizabeth I, 13 July 1561 (*Cal. For. Pap. Eliz.* iv. 56, 304; *Sc. Cal.* i. 983).

[2] Knox to Elizabeth I, 6 Aug. 1561 (*Works*, vi. 126); Throckmorton to Cecil, 13 July 1561 (*Cal. For. Pap. Eliz.* iv. 306).

She was accompanied by three of her uncles, the Grand Prior, the Duke of Aumale, and the Marquis d'Elbœuf, the brothers of the Duke of Guise and the Cardinal of Lorraine. It was raining heavily, and there was a thick fog, and it was so dark that visibility was reduced to a few feet. The weather was phenomenal for the time of year, and Knox comments in his *History*: 'The very face of Heaven, the time of her arrival, did manifestly speak what comfort was brought unto this country with her, to wit, sorrow, dolour, darkness, and all impiety.'[1]

On the first Sunday after Mary's arrival, her Catholic chaplain, who had accompanied her from France, celebrated mass in the chapel royal at Holyroodhouse in the presence of Mary and her uncles and their escort. As the ceremony was about to begin, a band of Protestants, led by the Master of Lindsay and the lairds of Fife, tried to force their way into the chapel royal, crying out that 'the idolater priest should die the death'. They assaulted and wounded one of the servants, who was carrying the candle into the chapel, but then Lord James arrived, and drove them off. Meanwhile, in St. Giles's, Knox was preaching to an unusually large congregation, which included nearly all the nobility. He denounced the Queen in his sermon, thus providing the one discordant note in the universal chorus of welcome. The English ambassador, Randolph, was displeased, for the English government wished to give Mary every chance to co-operate with England under the guidance of Lord James and Lethington. He reported to Throckmorton that everyone in Scotland had been favourably impressed by Mary, 'saving John Knox, that thundereth out of the pulpit, that I fear nothing so much that one day he will mar all. He ruleth the roost, and of him all men stand in fear. Would God you knew how much I am amended myself; but now again in earnest', and he then referred to other matters. In Randolph's case, the fear that Knox inspired was tempered by ridicule.[2]

On the next Sunday, 31 August, Knox preached a more vehement sermon, 'inveighing against idolatry', as he himself phrased it, and denouncing Mary's mass at Holyroodhouse. He declared

[1] Knox, *History*, ii. 7. As to whether the visibility was reduced to 'a pair of boots' or 'a pair of butts', see Sir James Fergusson, 'A pair of Butts', and Croft Dickinson, 'A pair of Butts' (*S.H.R.* xxxiv. 21, 23, 188–9). See also Brantôme, *Recueil des Dames*, Disc. III (*Œuvres complètes de Brantôme*, vii. 418; *Book of the Ladies*, pp. 99–100).

[2] Knox, *History*, ii. 8; Randolph to Throckmorton, 26 Aug. 1561 (*Works*, vi. 128–9).

that he feared one mass more than if 10,000 armed enemies had landed in the realm to suppress the whole religion; for though God could disperse multitudes of enemies, He would abandon those who joined hands with idolatry. 'At these words', writes Knox, 'the guiders of the Court mocked', and said that Knox's admonition was very untimely. Knox had adopted a different attitude in 1559; he had not then feared one mass more than 10,000 French soldiers, for his repeated warnings to Cecil had been concerned with the danger of French reinforcements reaching Scotland, not with the fact that masses were still being said in many churches throughout the kingdom. But despite this hyperbole, Knox was being a profound realist in fearing the effect of a single mass. Such hard-headed politicians as Charles V and Elizabeth adopted the same attitude. Charles V had threatened to break off diplomatic relations with his ally Edward VI rather than permit the English ambassador in Brussels to hold a private Protestant service in his embassy, and Elizabeth acted similarly when she allowed her marriage negotiations with the Archduke Charles of Austria and with Henry, Duke of Anjou, to break down, rather than agree that her husband should be permitted to have his mass in private at her Court. Both Charles V and Elizabeth realized what would be the moral effect of permitting even a single exception to the uniformity enforced throughout the country, and how the mass, or Protestant service, of an ambassador or prince always turned, sooner or later, into a rally of the opposition forces; and Knox realized how the effect of the Act of Parliament that made attendance at mass an offence worthy of death would be weakened if the sovereign herself went regularly to mass in the chapel royal.[1]

Knox's position about the mass was more logical than Mary's; for the day after the tumult in the chapel royal, the Privy Council issued a proclamation in the Queen's name affirming that the Queen would uphold the Protestant religion, and that anyone who attempted to alter the state of religion in Scotland was to suffer death. The proclamation then added that no one must threaten to use violence against the Queen's servants, or the visitors from France, under any pretext whatever, also on pain of death. Arran

[1] Knox, *History*, ii. 12; Charles V to Scheyvfe, 7 Mar. 1551 (*Span. Cal.* x. 239); Wotton to the Council, 30 June and 11 Sept. 1551 (*Cal. For. Pap. Edw. VI*, Nos. 393, 436); Elizabeth I to Maximilian II (Apr. 1565?); Elizabeth I to Sussex, 10 Dec. 1567; Smith and Killigrew to Elizabeth I, 8 Jan. 1571/2; Smith to Burghley, 9 Jan. 1571/2 (*Cal. For. Pap. Eliz.* vii. 1805; viii. 1857; x. 20, 23).

protested against this proclamation, and stated, in a declaration which was perhaps drafted by Knox, that if any of the Queen's servants, or any Frenchman in Scotland, attended mass, they should be executed just as if they were to commit a murder, seeing that attendance at mass was much more hateful to God than murder; but no other nobleman supported Arran's protest, which was perhaps prompted by the fact that the Hamiltons were being excluded from all power at Court by Lord James.[1]

On Thursday, 4 September, Knox had his first meeting with Mary, who summoned him to Holyroodhouse. No one was present at the interview except Lord James, and two of the Maries, who withdrew to the far end of the gallery. We have only Knox's version, written five years later, of what took place at the audience, and some of the things that Mary is supposed to have said are almost certainly twisted and exaggerated; but most of the conversation is perfectly compatible with all that we know of the character of this high-spirited, outspoken, and rather silly girl who had been placed in a situation which would have baffled the wisest statesman. Mary asked Knox to explain why he had incited a revolt against her mother and herself, why he had written a book against the government of women, why he had caused sedition and violence in England, and whether it was true that he was a magician. Knox stated that in Scotland he had striven only to abolish Popery and defend the true religion; that the doctrine that he had put forward in the *First Blast* was true; that he had not fomented sedition and bloodshed in England, but had, on the contrary, been successful in appeasing the disorders among the garrison at Berwick; and that he was not a magician. Mary had obviously been told at the French Court that Knox was a magician, for during the next hundred years the Catholic propagandists often alleged that Knox practised magic. But some of Mary's questions were disarmingly to the point. She asked him whether, in view of his doctrines about the government of women, he challenged her authority to rule, a question which Knox evaded in a rambling answer, though he ended by saying that he was as content to live under her as Paul was to live under Nero, and pointed out that if he had wished to deny her authority to rule, he could have done so much more effectively before she returned from France. He virtually told her that whatever he might think in theory about

[1] Proclamation of 25 Aug. 1561 (*Reg. P.C.S.* i. 266–7); Knox, *History*, ii. 9–11.

the government of women, he would not refer to this question if she did not raise it, and had no intention of overthrowing her government.

Then Mary asked him how he could justify his doctrine that subjects were entitled to resist their rulers by force. Knox referred to Daniel and the three children who resisted Nebuchadnezzar, and said that although they had resisted by non-violent means, this was only because they did not have the opportunity to use force. He compared the action of subjects who rebel against an idolatrous prince to children who resist their father if he tries to slay them in a frenzy, and attempt to snatch the sword from his hand. Mary, taken aback, commented: 'Well then, I perceive that my subjects shall obey you and not me; and shall do what they list, and not what I command; and so must I be subject to them, and not they to me.' 'God forbid', answered Knox, 'that ever I take upon me to command any to obey me, or yet to set subjects at liberty to do what pleaseth them. But my travail is that both princes and subjects obey God.'[1]

After this first talk with Mary, some of Knox's friends asked him what he thought of the Queen. He replied: 'If there be not in her a proud mind, a crafty wit, and an indurate heart against God and His truth, my judgement faileth me.' His opinion of Mary was confirmed a month later, when Mary invalidated a proclamation of the Edinburgh burgh council which expelled all whoremongers and Papists from the town; she dismissed the Provost and baillies, and ordered that new officers be elected in their place, and that Edinburgh should be open to all the Queen's subjects. On 7 October, Knox wrote to Cecil and strongly condemned Mary's action in preventing the punishment of adulterers and idolaters. He said that all her actions showed that the Cardinal's lessons were so deeply imprinted in her heart that they could not be removed. 'I would be glad to be deceived, but I fear I shall not. In communication with her, I espied such craft as I have not found in such age. Since, hath the Court been dead to me, and I to it.' He told Cecil that everything that had been won was in danger, and that the whole blame lay on the necks of Lord James and Lethington.[2]

[1] Knox, *History*, ii. 13–20; see p. 17.

[2] Ibid. 20–23; *Edinburgh Burgh Records*, iii. 125–7 (2, 5, and 8 Oct. 1561); Knox to Cecil, 7 Oct. 1561 (*Works*, vi. 131–2).

It is difficult to accept Knox's estimate of Mary's character. A crafty woman would not have handled Knox as Mary did in this first interview, and would probably not have spoken with him at all, for she did not win over Knox or the Protestants by talking with him, and the Catholics in Scotland became demoralized when they heard that Mary had received Knox in audience. Knox's belief in Mary's craftiness was typical of a simplified, propagandist view, which sees every action of the enemy as a cunning manœuvre of diabolical ingenuity. Lethington was nearer the truth when he said, a few months later, that Mary lacked the maturity of judgement and ripeness of experience in high matters which Elizabeth possessed.[1]

But if Knox was wrong about Mary's character, he was right in his estimate of the potential danger of the situation. He feared that the presence of a Catholic Queen, and the mass in the chapel royal, would enable Popery to regain a foothold in Scotland; realizing that the revolutionary enthusiasm of 1559 was slowly evaporating, he feared that once one concession was accepted, more would follow. He noticed with dismay how men who had at first been indignant that mass was said in the chapel royal, soon came to accept it as a matter of course. 'The Queen's flattering words, upon the one part, ever still crying "Conscience, conscience; it is a sore thing to constrain the conscience"; and the subtle persuasions of her supposts [supporters] (we mean even of such as sometimes were judged most fervent with us) upon the other part, blinded all men.' When Lord James and the courtiers argued that Mary should be allowed liberty of worship, Knox replied that her liberty would be their thraldom before long.[2] He tried to warn his congregation in his sermons, and the English government in his private conversations with Randolph and his letters to Cecil; but his warnings were not heeded.

The acquiescence of the nobility in Mary's mass threw him into despair. On 2 October 1561 he wrote to Anne Locke, deploring 'the permission of that odious idol, the mass, by such as have professed themselves enemies to the same', and telling her that he longed for death. He explained that there was no hope of the preachers remedying the situation, for they had tried and failed,

[1] Randolph to Cecil, 7 Sept. 1561 and 15 Jan. 1561/2 (Keith, ii. 81; *Sc. Cal.* i. 1066); Knox, *History*, ii. 20.

[2] Knox, *History*, ii. 12, 24.

and the nobility did not care if Mary heard mass in her chapel, provided that she left them free to worship as they chose. 'Remedy there appeareth none, unless we would arm the hands of the people in whom abideth yet some sparks of God's fear.'[1]

The attacks of the preachers on the Queen became more vehement in November 1561, after Mary's mass on All Saints' Day had been celebrated with unusual ceremony. As a result, at the beginning of November a meeting was held in the house of McGill, the Clerk of Register, between some members of the government and the leading preachers. Lord James, the Earl of Morton, the Earl Marischal, Lethington, Sir John Bellenden the Justice Clerk, and McGill, argued that subjects might not lawfully forbid their Queen to have her mass; Knox, Row, George Hay, and Robert Hamilton argued that 'subjects might put their hand to suppress the idolatry of their prince'. Someone suggested that they should write to Calvin to ask his opinion, and Knox offered to write; but Lethington objected, and said that he would write the letter to Calvin himself, as he feared that Knox would frame the question in an unfair manner. Knox agreed with this, but in fact Lethington did not write, and Knox suspected that it was all a ruse to gain time. Knox did not disclose that about a fortnight earlier, he had written to Calvin on this very point.

> I am a continual trouble to you [he wrote to Calvin on 24 October], and I have no other to whom I can confide my anxieties. I frankly confess, my father, that I never before felt how weighty and difficult a matter it is to contend against hypocrisy under the guise of piety. I never so feared open enemies when in the midst of troubles I could hope for victory. But now this treacherous defection from Christ (which by them is styled merely an indulgence) so wounds me that my strength daily diminishes.

Knox probably realized that Calvin, with his belief in the duty of obedience to princes, would not give him a favourable reply, and for this reason did not tell Lethington and the others that he had already written to Calvin. Calvin's answer has not survived, but it was obviously not the answer that Knox desired; for when in June 1564, in another discussion about Mary's mass, Lethington again suggested consulting Calvin, Knox still did not reveal that he had already asked Calvin for his opinion.[2]

[1] Knox to Anne Locke, 2 Oct. 1561 (*Works*, vi. 129–30).

[2] Knox, *History*, ii. 23–24, 133–4; Knox to Calvin, 24 Oct. 1561 (*Works*, vi. 133–5).

Knox's attacks on Mary annoyed Lethington, for he felt that they weakened the Queen's authority, and that Knox, by exasperating Mary, made it more difficult for her advisers to persuade her to adopt a pro-English and Protestant policy. On 25 October 1561 he wrote to Cecil, praising Mary and criticizing Knox's conduct. 'You know the vehemence of Mr. Knox's spirit, which cannot be bridled; and that doth sometimes utter such sentences as cannot easily be digested by a weak stomach. I would wish he should deal with her more gently, being a young princess unpersuaded.' He added that he was sure that if Mary paid a state visit to Elizabeth, which he and Lord James were trying to arrange, Elizabeth would be able to do much with Mary in religion.[1]

Randolph's attitude towards Knox was more ambiguous. He considered him to be a slightly ridiculous figure, with his zest and lack of diplomatic evasiveness, and he had little patience with Knox's attacks on the gay life of the court; but he could not help admiring his sincerity and loyalty to the Protestant cause, and he knew that Knox, more than any other leader in Scottish politics, could be relied upon to pursue a pro-English policy, whatever criticisms he might have of the doctrines and liturgy of the Church of England, as long as Elizabeth continued to be the protector of international Protestantism. On 7 September 1561, after Knox's first sermon against Mary's mass, and his first interview with Mary, Randolph wrote to Cecil that 'the voice of one man is able, in one hour, to put more life in us than 500 trumpets continually blustering in our ears'. He told him that when Knox spoke to the Queen, 'he knocked so hastily upon her heart that he made her weep'. On 24 October, Randolph wrote to Cecil: 'Mr. Knox cannot be otherwise persuaded but many men are deceived in this woman. . . . His severity keepeth us in marvellous order; I commend better the success of his doings and preachings than the manner thereof, though I acknowledge his doctrine to be sound.'[2]

Later in the winter Randolph became more exasperated with Knox when rumours began to spread that Mary might become a Protestant and embrace the doctrines of the Church of England. This would have pleased Elizabeth and Randolph very much, but Knox realized that it would be a serious threat to the power of the

[1] Lethington to Cecil, 25 Oct. 1561 (*Works*, vi. 136–7).

[2] Randolph to Cecil, 7 Sept. and 24 Oct. 1561 (Keith, ii. 80–83, 94–102, where '500 trumpets' is wrongly printed as '600 trumpets)'.

Protestant Church in Scotland. If this had occurred, Christ Jesus might indeed have been destroyed in His infancy there; for the newly established Calvinist Church would have been in a much weaker position to withstand the attack of the Anglican governments of England and Scotland than it was seventy-five years later. The relations between Randolph and Knox became strained. On 30 January 1562, Randolph wrote to Cecil that he had discussed the position with Knox and other ministers, who were, 'to be plain with your Honour, as wilful as learned, which heartily I lament'. A fortnight later he wrote to Cecil that the preachers in Scotland were more vehement than discreet or learned. 'The little bruit that hath been here of late, that this Queen is advised by the Cardinal to embrace the religion of England, maketh them run almost wild, of the which they both say and preach that it is little better than when it was at the worst.' He added that on the previous Sunday, 8 February, Knox had attacked the use of the cross and the candle, which Elizabeth used in her chapel, though Knox did not mention this. Knox had given 'the cross and candle such a wipe, that as wise and learned as himself wished him to have held his peace. He recompensed the same with a marvellous, vehement and piercing prayer in the end of his sermon, for the continuance of amity and hearty love with England.'[1]

In the spring of 1562, the situation was transformed by the events in France. In March the Duke of Guise opened fire on a Protestant prayer-meeting at Vassy in Champagne, killing some forty Protestants; and in April civil war broke out. The French civil war reawakened Protestant zeal in Scotland. In Edinburgh young Protestants flocked to Randolph's house, asking him to arrange for their transport to France, where they wished to fight in Condé's army, and about a thousand Scottish volunteers joined the Prince's forces in France. Elizabeth abandoned her plan to meet Mary at Nottingham, and her relations with Mary cooled. Knox found that men were more ready to listen to his warnings of the menace of Popery, and Randolph warned the Scottish lords that if the Catholics triumphed in France, it would encourage Mary to pursue a more pro-Catholic policy. In August, Knox went to Stirling to meet some of the leading nobles and warn them of the danger; and on 16 August, Randolph wrote to Cecil:

[1] Randolph to Cecil, 30 Jan. and 12 Feb. 1561/2 (*Cal. For. Pap. Eliz.* iv. 855, 883; *Sc. Cal.* i. 1071, 1077).

'Where your Honour liketh none so well his earnestness, the self same is better approved of other than it was wont also to be.'[1]

But Mary continued to pursue a pro-Protestant policy. In the autumn she went to Aberdeenshire with Lord James, and suppressed Huntly's rebellion. The sight of Mary suppressing a revolt by the leading Catholic nobleman did not fit into Knox's picture of events, and in his *History* he evolved a far-fetched theory of a plot between Mary and Huntly to lure Lord James to the north, under the pretext of suppressing the revolt, so that Lord James could be seized and killed, though he admitted that he could not prove this, and that it was mere speculation on his part. But Mary's continued reliance on Lord James reassured Elizabeth, and by the end of 1562 her relations with Mary had once more become friendly. Negotiations were now in progress for the meeting between the Queens to take place at Nottingham in the following summer, and Randolph became more critical of Knox.

> I know his good zeal and affection that he beareth to our nation [wrote Randolph on 16 December 1562], I know also that his travail and care is great to unite the hearts of the princes and people of these two realms in perpetual love and hearty kindness. I know that he mistrusteth more in his own sovereign's part than he doth in ours, he hath no hope (to use his own terms) that she will ever come to God, or do good in the commonwealth. He is so full of mistrust in all her doings, words and sayings, as though he were either of God's privy counsel that know how He had determined of her from the beginning, or that he knew the secrets of her heart so well, that neither she did or could have for ever one good thought of God or of His true religion. Of these matters we commune oft; I yield as much as in conscience I may unto him, though we in some things differ in judgement; his fear is that new foreigners be brought into this realm.

Randolph was shocked that the ministers of the Protestant Church prayed that God should either make the Queen become a Protestant, or send her a short life[2]; but Knox continued to supply Randolph and Cecil with information and advice, whether

[1] Randolph to Cecil, 3 June and 16 Aug. 1562, and 31 Jan. and 10 Mar. 1562/3 (*Sc. Cal.* i. 1111, 1135, 1164, 1173); Elizabeth I's Instructions to Sir H. Sidney, 15 July 1562 (Haynes, pp. 391–3; Keith, ii. 148–51).

[2] Knox, *History*, ii. 53–54, 58, 62–63; Randolph to Cecil, 16 Dec. 1562 and 28 Feb. 1562/3 (*Works*, vi. 146; *Sc. Cal.* i. 1155, 1171). Knox's theory of Mary's connivance in Huntly's rebellion is confirmed by Huntly's grandson, Sir Robert Gordon of Gordonstoun, in his *Genealogical History of the Earldom of Sutherland*, pp. 140–2; but it is most unlikely to be true.

welcome or unwelcome. Sometimes he gave them military information, as he did in October 1563, after his return from preaching in Angus, when he wrote to Cecil that the garrison had been withdrawn from Inchkeith. More often his information was about the activities of Papist agents in England, which he had somehow discovered from his excellent private intelligence service. After his visit to Ayrshire in August 1562, he told Randolph that two Englishmen were residing with Quintin Kennedy, the Catholic Abbot of Crosraguel in Ayrshire. Randolph wrote to Cecil that although Knox had often sent him reports about the activities of Catholic agents in England, this was the first time that the information appeared to be definite. Knox also supplied Randolph with news from France and Flanders. Guzman de Silva, the Spanish ambassador in London, was convinced that Knox was in the pay of the English government.[1]

Knox suffered another serious set-back with the rejection of the Book of Discipline. At the meeting of the General Assembly of the Church in Edinburgh in December 1561, it was decided to ask the Queen and Privy Council to ratify and promulgate the Book of Discipline; but the attitude of the courtiers towards the General Assembly was disquieting. Knox's friend John Wood, Lord James's secretary, who had formerly been active in the affairs of the Church, announced that he would no longer attend the meetings of the General Assembly, and it became clear that the courtiers preferred to stay away—in Knox's words, 'to draw themselves apart from the society of their brethren'. When the Book of Discipline was presented to the Privy Council, it was rejected. Lethington ridiculed the idea of adopting it, and asked how many of those nobles who had so happily signed the resolution approving the Book at the meeting in the tolbooth of Edinburgh would be prepared in practice to be subjected to its provisions; he mockingly asked whether they believed that Châtelherault would do so. The rejection of the Book of Discipline not only meant that the educational projects of the Church were abandoned, but raised the question as to how the salaries of the ministers were to be paid.[2]

[1] Knox to Cecil, 6 Oct. 1563; Knox to Randolph, 3 (May) 1564; Randolph to Cecil, 31 Aug., 24 Sept., 18 Nov., and 16 Dec. 1562 (*Works*, vi. 144, 147, 529, 541–2; *Sc. Cal.* i. 1136, 1139, 1152, 1155; Stevenson, *Illustrations*, pp. 102–5; Keith, ii. 175–81); Guzman de Silva to Philip II, 21 Nov. 1564 (*Span. Cal. Eliz.* i. 275).

[2] Knox, *History*, ii. 25, 27.

The anomalous situation of a Catholic Queen in a Protestant country was paralleled by the anomaly of the two Churches in Scotland, a Protestant Church which operated everywhere and controlled the lives of the people, but had no property or income, and the old Church which was forbidden to celebrate the most fundamental and sacred of its rites on pain of imprisonment, banishment, and death, but which retained all its property. The reason for this was that the property of the Catholic Church was very largely in the hands of nobles, many of whom were leaders of the Protestant party. The property of the priory of St. Andrews would not be confiscated, because Lord James was the Prior; and as nearly every one of the Lords of the Congregation was similarly holding some monastery *in commendam*, the religious houses, which in England were suppressed before any doctrinal reformation had been carried through, were not suppressed in Scotland until nearly thirty years after the Reformation of 1560. The Catholic bishops and priests, though now forbidden by law to celebrate the mass or baptism, retained their rank and titles, and the bishops, along with the lay Protestant priors, continued to represent the Church in Parliament. A handful of the Catholic clergy remained faithful to their Church, and tried to work in increasingly difficult conditions. Some of them, including the Bishop of Orkney and the Bishop of Galloway, converted to Protestantism and became active in the Protestant Church. The majority did nothing, continued living on their tithes, and were happy to have a much better excuse than they had before the Reformation to neglect their pastoral duties.[1]

In December 1561 the Privy Council at last made provision for the Protestant ministers. The Archbishop of St. Andrews, on behalf of the Catholic Church, offered as a voluntary gift to surrender one-third of the Church revenues every year to the Queen for her use; and the Queen decided to use half of this money in paying the salaries of the Protestant preachers, and the remaining half in paying for her household expenditure. This should have meant that one-sixth of the money paid to the Church in tithes was spent on paying the salaries of the ministers of the only Church which was permitted to function in Scotland; but many of the more wealthy and influential holders of Church property, such as Lord James and others, were relieved by the Queen from

[1] Gouda to Laynez, 30 Sept. 1562 (Pollen, pp. 125–7, 137–8).

the obligation to pay over their third to the Crown, and were granted special permission to keep the whole of their ecclesiastical revenues for themselves. Knox was far from satisfied with the arrangement about the thirds, and attacked it in his sermons in St. Giles's. 'I see two parts freely given to the Devil,' he said, 'and the third must be divided betwix God and the Devil.' But Lethington merely commented that if the ministers were paid as much as they wanted out of the third paid to the Crown, the Queen would not be able to buy herself a new pair of shoes.[1]

The money raised by the half of the thirds was not enough to pay the salaries which the Church considered proper for its ministers, and some of them suffered considerable hardship; but despite the solicitude of the leaders of the Church for the welfare of the poor ministers, they did not attempt to divide their inadequate funds on an equal basis. The well-paid superintendents continued to receive their 500 marks per year, in money, and their large allotments of bere, meal, and oats, while the poorer ministers could not be paid the 100 marks to which they were entitled. Knox received the whole of his allotted salary of 300 marks per year, being paid £50 each quarter, as well as his ample payments in bere and oats, and his large, rent-free house and casual benefits from the burgh council of Edinburgh.[2]

In the spring of 1562, Knox was involved in a strange affair. He was approached by his old friend, James Barron, on behalf of the Earl of Bothwell, who wanted Knox to be the means of a reconciliation between him and Arran. The two young earls had been enemies since the days of the fighting of 1560, when Bothwell, who was one of the few noblemen who had supported Mary of Lorraine and the French, had denounced Arran as a traitor, and challenged him to fight in single combat. The political quarrel had turned into a quarrel about a woman in the autumn of 1561, when Bothwell and the Marquis d'Elbœuf, before the Marquis and his brothers returned to France, caused a riot in Edinburgh when they were pursuing a merchant's daughter who was Arran's mistress. This incident, which had delighted the lady and her family, had aroused the indignation of Knox and his colleagues. The

[1] *Reg. P.C.S.* i. 192 (22 Dec. 1561); Knox, *History*, ii. 29–30, 326–8.

[2] For the collection of the thirds, and their distribution amongst the ministers, see Donaldson's Introduction to *Accounts of the Collectors of Thirds of Benefices*, pp. x–xxvii, xxxiv–xxxv.

Protestant Church and the Edinburgh burgh council had petitioned the Queen to punish this outrageous action by d'Elbœuf and his French attendants; but they did not venture to summon Bothwell or Arran to appear before the Church Session on a charge of immorality, and when Bothwell asked Knox to make peace between him and Arran, Knox acted first and foremost as a politician. Bothwell might be a notorious libertine, but Knox appreciated the importance of winning over this brave and redoutable nobleman, who was a Protestant, to the side of the Congregation.

In March 1562, Knox met Bothwell at Barron's house. Bothwell told Knox that he repented of the immoral life which he had led, and of having supported the Queen Regent, and that he wished to end the feud which he was carrying on with Knox's old friend Cockburn of Ormiston; but his chief desire was for a reconciliation with Arran. Knox said that although this was the first time that they had met, he had always borne goodwill to Bothwell's house, as his father, grandfather, and great-grandfather had served Bothwell's ancestors, and some of them had died under the Hepburns' standard. Knox did not refer, when he was discussing the activities of Bothwell's ancestors, to the part that Bothwell's father had played in the martyrdom of Wishart; nor did he utter any real reproach to Bothwell about his immoral way of living, but stated that if Bothwell reconciled himself to God, there would be no difficulty about arranging reconciliations with men. Knox did not wish to make it hard for Bothwell to come over to the Protestant side. It has often been suggested that Knox acted in this way because of his family's hereditary loyalty to the Hepburns; but there is no reason to doubt Knox's own statement that his ties of kinship with Bothwell were not the main reason for his friendly attitude towards him.

Knox and Bothwell had a second meeting a few days later, at Knox's house, at which Knox promised to arrange a meeting between Bothwell and Arran. Within a few days, Bothwell had attacked Ormiston and his family when they were out hunting, and would have carried them off as prisoners if they had not been rescued by Ormiston's friends, who chased Bothwell to his castle of Dunbar. This unfortunate resumption by Bothwell of his old feud with Ormiston did not cause Knox to lose patience, and after reproaching Bothwell, who expressed his regret for the incident, Knox continued his efforts to arrange the meeting with Arran. On

23 March, Arran and Bothwell met and shook hands at Hamilton House in Kirk-o'-Field, in the presence of Knox and a few of their friends. Next day they appeared together in public when they attended the sermon in St. Giles's, and all Edinburgh was talking about the reconciliation of these two great enemies.

Four days after the handshaking at Hamilton House, on Good Friday, 27 March, Arran burst into Knox's house in a state of great indignation, and denounced Bothwell as a Judas who had betrayed him. He said that Bothwell had proposed to him, when they dined together on the previous day, that they should attack the royal palace at Falkland, where Mary was in residence, kill Lord James and Lethington, and kidnap Mary and carry her off to Dumbarton Castle, which was held by Châtelherault. There she was to be compelled to marry Arran, who, in addition to his former plans to marry Mary for dynastic reasons, had now fallen in love with her. Arran thought that Bothwell was a provocator, who intended to denounce him to the Privy Council as a party to the plot, or at least for failing to report it to the authorities.

Any English churchman in Knox's position would immediately have informed the Privy Council of what Arran had told him, both from a sense of duty and from fear of severe punishment if he did not do so; but Knox strongly advised Arran not to mention the matter. He told Arran that as he had had no treasonable intent, he could not be guilty of an offence, and should do nothing, but wait and see whether Bothwell denounced him. Arran then went to Châtelherault's house at Kinneill, where Châtelherault imprisoned him in his room; but Arran escaped, and revealed to Lord James the details of Bothwell's plot. He said that his relative, Gavin Hamilton, the lay Abbot of Kilwinning, was involved in the plot, and also alleged that his father had tried to murder him at Kinneill, though he later withdrew this accusation against Châtelherault.

When Knox heard of what Arran had done, he wrote to Lord James and told him that he believed that Arran was mad. The Queen and Lord James arrested Bothwell, Gavin Hamilton, and Arran, and imprisoned them all in Edinburgh Castle, where they were left to languish without any charge being brought against them; and although the Council assured Châtelherault that they were convinced of his innocence, they compelled him to hand over the custody of Dumbarton Castle to the Queen. At the end of

August, Bothwell escaped, and fled abroad. Arran, who complained of ill-treatment from his jailers, soon afterwards became a raving lunatic, with homicidal tendencies and sexual delusions concerning the Queen. He was kept in Edinburgh Castle for four years, and was then entrusted to the care of his mother, and after being confined in the houses of the Hamiltons for more than forty years, he died, still mad, an old man in 1609.[1]

In his *History*, Knox explains the whole story by saying that Arran was mad, and points out that he had warned Lord James of it before it was generally known; but there seems to have been a little more behind this incident than Knox reveals. Bothwell probably hoped to make an alliance with the Hamiltons against Lord James, whom he hated, and used Knox as a go-between because he knew that he was opposed to the Queen and the policy of Lord James. He also knew that Arran was in love with Mary, and with his usual lack of judgement he immediately suggested, at his first meeting with Arran, that Mary should be kidnapped and forced to marry Arran. Arran's mind was already unhinged, and fearing a double-cross from Bothwell, and hoping perhaps to win Mary's love by saving her from Bothwell's plot, he decided to reveal all to the Council. As for Knox, he was very disturbed at the drift of events and the policy of Lord James and Randolph, and, overcoming his scruples about collaborating with Châtelherault, he began to play with the idea of building up an opposition bloc of Bothwell and the Hamiltons. When Arran told him of his intention of denouncing Bothwell to the Council, Knox, like Châtelherault, tried to prevent him from doing so, as he realized that this would disrupt the new alliance between Bothwell and the Hamiltons, and would play into the hands of Lord James. Lord James took the opportunity to strike at both Bothwell and the Hamiltons. It was typical that of all the characters who were involved in the tentative attempt to build up an opposition party —Bothwell, Arran, Knox, Châtelherault, and Gavin Hamilton—

[1] For the affair of Arran and Bothwell, see Knox, *History*, ii. 33–42; Randolph to Cecil, 27 Dec. 1561, 31 Mar., 7, 9, and 25 Apr., 3 and 11 May, and 3 Dec. 1562, and 2 May 1566; Randolph to (Throckmorton), 7 Apr. 1562; Randolph to Elizabeth I, 9 Apr. 1562 (Keith, ii. 129–31; *Sc. Cal.* i. 1056, 1089, 1090, 1091, 1092, 1093, 1095, 1097, 1099; ii. 41, 378; *Cal. For. Pap. Eliz.* v. 141); Knox to Anne Locke, 6 May 1562 (*Works*, vi. 140–1); R. K. Hannay, 'The Earl of Arran and Queen Mary'; Marguerite Wood, 'The Imprisonment of the Earl of Arran' (*S.H.R.* xviii. 258–76; xxiv. 116–22).

only Knox, with his political acumen and his usual luck, emerged unscathed. A cook in Edinburgh told the passers-by in the High Street that 'Knox quarter is run', and that Knox had been scourged through the town in connexion with the affair of Arran and Bothwell; but it was the cook, not Knox, who in fact was scourged in the tolbooth, and put in the irons, by order of the burgh council, for his slanderous words against Knox.[1]

Knox continued his cautious friendship with the Hamiltons, and in November 1562, at Châtelherault's request, he arranged a meeting between Châtelherault and Randolph. He invited them both to supper at his house. Châtelherault promised Knox and Randolph that he would always remain a true Protestant and loyal to his Queen, and would always favour the English alliance. Randolph was sceptical of the Duke's promises. 'I will believe them all as I see them take effect,' he wrote to Cecil next day, 'but trust that it shall never lie in his word alone.'[2]

In the summer of 1562 a Papal Nuncio arrived in Scotland. He had been sent by the Pope to the Queen of Scots to invite her to send her bishops to the final session of the General Council of the Church at Trent. Never had an envoy from the Pope visited a Catholic sovereign under such extraordinary circumstances. The Papal Nuncio was not a cardinal travelling in state, but a devoted priest of the Society of Jesus, which Ignatius Loyola had founded twenty years before. The Jesuits were not, at least at this time, the subtle political intriguers that they later became in Protestant legend; they were a band of religious idealists, whose political *naïveté* exasperated the Cardinal of Lorraine beyond measure. When no one else was prepared to risk the journey to Scotland, Laynez, the General of the Jesuits, persuaded the Pope to give the official status of Nuncio to Nicholas of Gouda.[3] Gouda went to Paris, where he met the Scottish Jesuit, Edmund Hay, and together they travelled to Scotland in disguise. They had no experience of underground activity, and were identified by Scottish Protestants who were travelling on the same ship. As soon as the ship landed at Leith, these Protestants hastened to Edinburgh to tell Knox of the arrival of a secret envoy from the Pope to the

[1] *Edinburgh Burgh Records*, iii. 132 (8 Apr. 1562).

[2] Randolph to Cecil, 30 Nov. 1562 (Stevenson, *Illustrations*, p. 106).

[3] Pius IV to Mary Queen of Scots, 3 Dec. 1561; Gouda to Salmeron, 6 June 1562 (Pollen, pp. 72–75, 103–4); and see H. Chadwick, 'A memoir of Father Edmund Hay, S.I.' (*Archivum Historicum Societatis Iesu*, viii. 68).

Queen. Knox exposed the Papist plot in a sermon in St. Giles's; according to Gouda, he 'raged wonderfully in almost every sermon against the Pope as Antichrist', and declared that Gouda was an emissary of Satan and a Nuncio of Baal and Beelzebub. Gouda and Hay had to hide in the house of a Catholic in Leith.

It was, of course, out of the question for Mary to send any bishops to Trent; but she agreed to receive Hay and Gouda secretly, while Lord James and all the Council were attending the sermon in St. Giles's. She sent three horsemen to escort them secretly from Leith. They left the road, and made their way across the fields to Edinburgh, and on 24 July they visited Mary in Holyroodhouse. It was a hurried interview, for Mary was continually watching the time, for fear that the courtiers should return from the sermon before the Jesuits had left. Gouda gave her the Pope's letter, in which Pius urged her to follow the great example of Queen Mary of England; but she explained that the situation in Scotland was very different. 'To save a spark of the old faith', Gouda reported to Laynez, 'and the germs of future Catholicism, to wit, herself and the others who even now adhered to the orthodox religion, she had been obliged unwillingly and perforce to bear many things which she would not otherwise have borne.' She promised that she would never abandon the Catholic faith, but said that it would not be possible to send any of the bishops to Trent; and she forbade Gouda to try to deliver the Pope's letters to the bishops. 'She feared their delivery would be a sign for a revolution', wrote Gouda. After seeing the Queen, Gouda tried, in defiance of her instructions, to deliver the Pope's letters; but none of the bishops was prepared to meet him except the Bishop of Dunkeld, who received him in strict secrecy. The Protestant preachers continued to rouse the people against the Nuncio, and a French merchant who was mistaken for him was attacked and nearly killed by a band of Protestants; but Gouda and Hay got away safely on 13 September in a Flemish ship disguised as sailors.[1]

The Jesuits were deeply depressed by what they had seen in Scotland. The Catholics were terrified of being murdered and assaulted by the Protestants; priests were converting to Protestant-

[1] Gouda to Laynez, 30 Sept. 1562; Crichton's memoir, 6 May 1613 (Pollen, pp. 113–39, 144–8; see pp. 115–16, 131). See also Randolph to Cecil, 26 June and 1 Aug. 1562 (*Sc. Cal.* i. 1118, 1129).

ism; Catholics were victimized in the law courts, where litigants and witnesses were always asked whether they were members of the Congregation or Papists; the bishops led grossly immoral lives, making no attempt to fulfil their pastoral duties. Yet, for all the complaints of Nicholas of Gouda, the Catholics in Scotland were not proceeded against as heretics, and burnt by the authorities for their opinions, like the Protestants in Catholic countries. Though the people were compelled to attend the Protestant sermons on Sundays on pain of excommunication, any Catholic who was strong enough to resist the pressure of this weapon of social and economic boycott could contrive to absent himself from the sermon without fear of any further legal consequences; and against the higher Catholic clergy and the upper classes, with their own circle of friends and servants, excommunication was in practice a useless weapon. The law, however, placed two serious restrictions on the Catholics: the severe punishment for celebrating or attending mass, and the prohibition of any private baptism other than baptism in the Protestant churches. Gouda reported that the mass was celebrated in secret in many private houses; and though he complained that many children died unbaptized because the Protestant ministers only baptized children on Sundays, there were doubtless many cases of children being secretly baptized by Catholic priests.[1]

The worst ordeal to which the Catholics were subjected was mob violence, for the Scottish Protestants emulated, though they did not equal, the ferocity of the Catholic mobs in Paris and elsewhere in France. There were no cases of Catholics being actually killed by the mob in Scotland, as happened to so many Protestants in France; but there were cases of rough handling in the pillory and elsewhere. One priest who was caught celebrating mass at Easter 1565 is said to have had 10,000 eggs thrown at him as he stood bound in the pillory; and there were cases of priests being attacked by cut-throats in the streets at night, and at least two cases of murder—not by the mob, but by small bands of armed Protestants.[2]

As the Catholics were in no danger of being burnt for heresy,

[1] Gouda to Laynez, 30 Sept. 1562 (Pollen, pp. 123, 126–7, 135, 137).

[2] Alexander Clark to Randolph, 22(?) Apr. 1565 (*Sc. Cal.* ii. 171, enclosure); Knox's continuator, in Knox, *History*, ii. 141–2. Two Catholic religious men, Black and Ker, Abbot of Kelso, were murdered by Protestants on the night of Riccio's murder.

they could engage in disputations with the Protestants without facing the risk of being sent to the stake at the end of the disputation. The first of these disputations took place, at the initiative of the Protestants, soon after the meeting of the Reformation Parliament of August 1560. Knox and his colleagues, knowing that the town and university of Aberdeen was a hotbed of Popery, summoned several of the canons of Aberdeen to Edinburgh to explain their doctrines. The Catholics included Alexander Anderson, the Sub-Principal of Aberdeen University, and John Leslie. They took part in a disputation on the mass with Knox, Willock, and Goodman in a merchant's house in Edinburgh, the issue being whether the words of Christ were to be interpreted as instituting the mass as a sacrifice. In his *History*, Knox refers to this disputation in order to rebut the Papists' lie that the Protestants refused to dispute with them, and says that the Catholics were promised that they could speak their minds freely, and would be protected against ill-treatment and victimization; but the Protestants were obviously not eager to give their adversaries any opportunity for public propaganda, for the disputation did not take place in St. Giles's or in the tolbooth, but in a private house, and apparently without any audience being present.

There are two conflicting accounts of the disputation. Knox states that Anderson 'refused to dispute in his faith, abusing a place of Tertullian to cloak his ignorance', and that Leslie asserted: 'If our Master [Anderson] have nothing to say to it, I have nothing; for I know nothing but the canon law; and the greatest reason that ever I could find there is *nolumus* and *volumus* [we will not and we will].' Leslie himself writes that 'Alexander Anderson answered so cunningly, constantly and wholly, and of a godly manner, that the Catholics he much confirmed, the heretics he so fliet [terrified], and abased so far, that after that, of graver mysteries of the religion, or such kind of questions, with him or any other Catholic the heretics durst never enter'. At the end of the disputation, Knox and his colleagues ordered the Catholics to remain in Edinburgh and attend Knox's sermons in St. Giles's for their future education in the truth.[1]

Knox also took part in a disputation with Ninian Winzet, a Catholic priest who was master of the grammar school at Linlithgow, and who acted for a short while as confessor to Mary

[1] Knox, *History*, i. 352–4; Leslie, *History*, ii. 449–50.

Queen of Scots after her return from France. Knox himself says nothing about this disputation, but Leslie states that it was held at Linlithgow in the presence of the Lords of the Congregation, and that Winzet greatly distinguished himself, and embarrassed Knox with his arguments. In March 1562, Winzet again entered into controversy with Knox. He wrote him a letter in which he challenged him to show by what authority he acted in the Church. Winzet argued that no one was entitled to act as a minister of the Church unless he was either ordained by a man who had the power to ordain, or else was extraordinarily called by God Himself, like Elijah and the prophets of the Old Testament. But these prophets who had been extraordinarily called had all been given power to work miracles as a sign of their calling; so Winzet challenged Knox to show either that he had performed a miracle, or that he had been ordained by a lawful authority. Winzet knew that Knox had been ordained as a Catholic priest; but as any Catholic priest who wished to be admitted to the Congregation was required to confess that his activities as a priest had been idolatrous and sinful, it was obvious that Knox was not relying on his ordination by the Catholic Church as his authority for acting as a religious leader.

Knox did not reply directly to Winzet, but answered him in a sermon in St. Giles's on the following Sunday. He said that Winzet was wrong in asserting that all prophets who were extraordinarily called had been endowed with the power to work miracles, because neither John the Baptist nor Amos had worked any miracle. Winzet immediately wrote to Knox again, and stated that John the Baptist's extraordinary calling had been sufficiently proved by the signs and miracles which had occurred when he was in his mother's womb; as for Amos, he had been given the power to prophesy, and all his prophecies came true. Winzet's arguments, which had no doubt occurred to other people as well, explain why so much importance was attached to Knox's prophecies by his supporters, and by Knox himself. It probably also explains why Amos, the only prophet of the Old Testament who never performed a miracle, occupies a much more important place in sixteenth-century Protestant literature than in the text of the Bible.

Winzet was obviously at a disadvantage so long as he put his case in private letters to Knox, and Knox replied in public from the pulpit. He therefore challenged Knox to meet him in a public disputation. Knox ignored the challenge. The reason for this cannot have been that Knox was afraid that Winzet would worst him in a disputation, able though Winzet was in argument; his motive was obviously that of the eminent politician today, who refuses to meet a clever and rising young opponent in a public debate, so as not to give him a forum which he otherwise would not have. Holding all the advantages of propaganda facilities, Knox did not wish to provide Winzet with an equal opportunity. Knox similarly ignored a written challenge to take part in a disputation from René Benoît, one of Mary's French priests, who had come with her from France and remained in Scotland until August 1562. Benoît's challenge to Knox was answered by David Fergusson, the minister at Dunfermline, in his *Answer to an Epistle written by Renat Benedict*.

As Winzet was unable to induce Knox to dispute, he published a pamphlet, which was dated 31 July 1562 and entitled *The Last Blast of the Trumpet of God's Word against the Usurped Authority of John Knox and his Calvinian Brethren Intruded Preachers*. Winzet published his letters to Knox in this pamphlet, and developed his arguments further. His language was courteous and restrained. He admitted that the Catholic Church had been guilty of scandalous vices, for which Scotland had deservedly been punished by the scourge of heresy, but said that Knox and the other Protestants had been misguided in detaching themselves from Christ's Church. Winzet arranged for John Scot, an Edinburgh printer, to print the book; but when the Edinburgh burgh council heard of what was happening, they raided Scot's printing works, removed Scot to prison, and seized and destroyed all the copies of Winzet's book in the printing press. Winzet himself was on the premises at the time, but as the officers did not recognize him, he was allowed to go free. The Linlithgow burgh council then dismissed him from his post as headmaster of the grammar school, and banished him from the town. Knox announced that he intended to publish an answer to Winzet's book, but in fact he never did so. If he had done this, it would have meant that, in accordance with the usual practice, he would have had to publish the text of Winzet's tractate, and reply to each paragraph; and he obviously did not desire to give anyone the opportunity of reading the suppressed pamphlet of the ablest Catholic controversialist in Scotland.

Next year Winzet left Scotland, and lived the rest of his life abroad, becoming a doctor at the Sorbonne, and later Abbot of the Scottish Benedictine monastery at Ratisbon. As soon as he left Scotland, he published a book at Louvain in October 1563, *The Book of Four Score Three Questions touching Doctrine, Order and Manners proposed to the Preachers of the Protestants in Scotland.* He had sent a copy of the manuscript to Knox in February, before leaving Scotland. In this book, which was written in a much harsher style than his former work, he again challenged Knox to show whence he derived his authority as a religious leader, and attacked the validity of the Protestant doctrines. The Thirty-third Question was whether John Knox was a lawful minister.

If you, John Knox, we say, be called immediately by God, where are your marvels wrought by the Holy Spirit? For the marvels of woltring [overturning] of realms to ungodly sedition and discord we adnumber not to be of His gifts. But if ye be called by man, ye must show them to have had lawful power thereto. . . . Your lawful ordination by one of these two ways we desire you to show; since ye renounce and esteem that ordination null, or even wicked, by the which some time ye were called Sir John.

This reminder that he himself had once been one of the Pope's knights can hardly have been welcome to Knox.

Winzet's last shot was another open letter to Knox, dated from Louvain on 27 October 1563, which he published with *The Book of Four Score Three Questions*. In this he suggested that the reason why Knox had not replied to his tractate was because it was written in Scots, and Knox no longer understood the language which he had learned at his mother's knee. If this was the reason, he offered to translate his tractate into Latin for Knox's benefit, 'for I am not acquainted with your Southern'.[1]

It was more difficult for Knox to behave in a high-handed

[1] For the controversy between Winzet and Knox, see Winzet to Knox, 3, 10, and 12 Mar. 1561/2; Winzet, *The Last Blast of the Trumpet*; Winzet, *The Book of Four Score Three Questions* (Winzet, *Tractates*, i. 16–22, 39, 49–50, 56, 138); Leslie, *De Origine, Moribus et Rebus Gestis Scotorum*, pp. 582–4, and Dalrymple's manuscript translation 'The History of Scotland'; Conn, *De Duplici Statu Religionis apud Scotos*, p. 135; Knox, *The Reasoning which was betwix the Abbot of Crosraguel and John Knox* (*Works*, vi. 193); Report from Scotland to the Jesuits (Apr. 1562) (Pollen, pp. 97–99). See also Harrison's Preface to Winzet's *Tractates*, ii. xxvii–xxix. The date '20 February 1563', on which Winzet delivered the manuscript of his *Book of Four Score Three Questions* to Knox, is Feb. 1562/3, not 1563/4, for Winzet refers to this in his book, which is dated 13 Oct. 1563.

fashion towards Quintin Kennedy, the Abbot of Crosraguel. Quintin Kennedy, after fulfilling important diplomatic missions for Mary of Lorraine's government, had retired to his abbey near Maybole in Ayrshire, where he was safe in the territory of his nephew, the Earl of Cassillis. In August 1562, Knox went to Ayrshire, and in one of his sermons he attacked a sermon which Kennedy had preached a few days earlier. Kennedy wrote to Knox, who was at Ayr, and challenged him to dispute about the mass. A correspondence then took place between Knox and the Abbot, with both men adopting a coolly insulting tone, Knox being perhaps a little less discourteous than Kennedy. Knox agreed to take part in a disputation, but both he and Kennedy were conscious that they might be murdered by the other's supporters if they attended a disputation in the other's territory. Crosraguel was only ten miles from Ayr, but it was in Kennedy territory, whereas Ayr was a staunchly Protestant town.

The Abbot invited Knox to come to Crosraguel for the disputation, and stipulated that not more than twenty supporters of each side should be present, as there was a danger of a riot breaking out if larger numbers attended. He told Knox that the Earl of Cassillis, though he was opposed to the whole idea of holding a disputation lest it lead to violence, was prepared to give Knox a safe-conduct and ensure him protection, provided that he came to Crosraguel with no more than twenty supporters. Knox replied that it was pointless to dispute before only forty persons, of whom half would already be convinced of the truth, and the other half 'so addicted to your error that they will not be content that light be called light, and darkness darkness'; but he nevertheless agreed that no more than twenty persons on each side should be present, on condition that the disputation should take place at St. John's Church in Ayr. The Abbot refused to hold the disputation in Ayr. Eventually, it was agreed that it should be held in Maybole, in the house of the Provost, that each side should be accompanied by forty supporters, and that apart from these eighty supporters, as many members of the public should be admitted as could be accommodated in the Provost's house. Knox showed considerable courage in consenting to hold the disputation at Maybole, within two miles of Crosraguel Abbey, even with forty of his friends to escort him; for though Knox had recently slept in Maybole without coming to harm, it was a different matter to go there and arouse hostile passions at a disputation in Kennedy territory. But the disputation, which began on 28 September and lasted three days, passed off without violence from either side. The only question at issue was whether Melchizedek, in the Book of Genesis, had sacrificed bread and wine to God, as the Abbot maintained, or whether, as Knox claimed, he had only brought forth the bread and wine as provisions for Abraham's army. The Ayr burgh council paid the cost of sending food and drink to Maybole for the people attending the disputation, but as they had not sent enough for an adequate meal, the Provost of Maybole suggested, at the end of the disputation, that they should all go to Ayr for a banquet; but Quintin Kennedy absolutely refused to go to Ayr.[1]

In the following year Knox published a pamphlet containing the text of the disputation, which was printed in Edinburgh by the official government printer, Lekprevik, under the title *The Reasoning which was betwix the Abbot of Crosraguel and John Knox in Maybole concerning the Mass in the Year of God a Thousand Five Hundred Three Score and Two Years*. The preface of the pamphlet shows that Knox approached the issue of the mass more in the spirit of a political pamphleteer than of a doctor trained in the closely reasoned logic of the disputations of the schools. He claimed that the God of bread manufactured by the Papists in the mass was essentially the same as the Gods of wood and stone that the pagans of old had made, except that

the poor God of bread is most miserable of all other idols; for according to their matter, whereof they are made, they will remain without corruption many years. But within one year that God will putrify, and then he must be burnt; they can abide the vehemency of the wind, frost, rain or snow. But the wind will blow that God to the sea, the rain or the snow will make it dough again; yea, which is most of all to be feared, that God is a prey (if he be not well kept) to rats and mice; for they will desire no better dinner than round white Gods enough. But Oh then, what becometh of Christ's natural body? By miracle, it flies to the Heaven again, if the Papists teach truly; for how soon soever the mouse takes hold, so soon flieth Christ away, and letteth her gnaw the bread. A bold and puissant mouse, but a feeble and

[1] Quintin Kennedy to Knox, 6, 7, 24, and 25 Sept. 1562; Knox to Quintin Kennedy, 7 Sept. 1562 (*The Reasoning which was betwix the Abbot of Crosraguel and John Knox*, in *Works*, vi. 176–81, 183–4, 216; see p. 177. For the arguments in the disputation, see pp. 185–217); *Ayr Burgh Accounts 1534–1624*, p. 134.

miserable God; yet would I ask a question: whether hath the priest or the mouse greater power? By his words it is made a God; by her teeth it ceaseth to be a God; let them advise, and then answer. If any think that I ought not to mock that which the world so long hath holden, and great princes yet hold, in so great veneration, I answer, that not only I, but also all godly, ought not only to mock, but also to curse and detest, whatsoever is not God, and yet usurpeth the name, power and honour of God. . . . The idols of the Gentiles were more ancient than is the idol in the mass. . . . And yet feared not the prophet Isaias to mock and jest them.[1]

In his opening statement in his disputation with the Abbot of Crosraguel, Knox had proudly contrasted the moral integrity of the Protestant ministers with the flagrant vice of the priests of the old Church.

It pleaseth my Lord to term us wicked and deceitful preachers . . . I answer, that as by God's Word we accuse the whole mass of man's nature of corruption and wickedness, so do we not flatter ourselves, but willingly confess ourselves so subject to corruption and natural wickedness, that the good that we would do, we do it not, but the evil that we hate, that we do; yea, we do not deny but that in our lives and outward conversation there be many things both worthy of reformation and reprehension. But yet if our lives shall be compared with the lives of them that accuseth us, be it in general or be it in particular, we doubt not to be justified, both before God and man. For how many ministers this day within Scotland is my Lord Abbot (joining with him the whole rabble of the horned bishops) able to convict to be adulterers, fornicators, drunkards, bloodshedders, oppressors of the poor widow, fatherless or stranger; or yet that do idly live upon the sweat of other men's brows? And how many of them, from the highest to the lowest, are able to abide an assize of the forenamed crimes? And yet shall we be called by the wicked and deceitful preachers, even as if the strongest and most common harlot that ever was known in the bordell should slander and revile an honest and pudick matron.[2]

But before this statement was published in the verbatim report of the disputation, the case of Paul Methven had made a mockery of Knox's words.

Methven had been elected as the minister of Jedburgh after the victory of 1560. This was an important position, because the

[1] Knox, *The Reasoning which was betwix the Abbot of Crosraguel and John Knox* (*Works*, vi. 172–3).

[2] Ibid., 190.

Borders had not yet been converted, and Knox attached great importance, for political as well as religious reasons, to making the Border Protestant. Methven, who more than any other man could be said to have started the revolution of 1559 with his passionate sermons in Dundee, seemed an eminently suitable person for the post; but in the autumn of 1562 rumours began to circulate in Jedburgh that Methven was committing adultery with his young maidservant, while his elderly wife was absent from home. When the rumours reached the General Assembly at Edinburgh during its meeting in December, the Assembly directed Knox to investigate the charge, and to report to the Church Session of Edinburgh, and to Spottiswood, the Superintendent of Lothian.

Knox travelled to Jedburgh with some of the elders of the Church of Edinburgh, and on 3 January 1563 began the hearing of the case. He admits, in his *History*, that he and his colleagues were very eager to find Methven not guilty, and 'having a good opinion of the honesty and godliness of the man, travailed what they could (conscience not hurt) to purge him of the slander. But God, who would not that such villainy should be cloaked and concealed within His Church, otherwise had decreed.' When the evidence of eye-witnesses was becoming so strong that it could not be ignored, the maidservant's brother suddenly arrived in Jedburgh, though he lived in another district and did not know that Methven's case was being tried. This man disclosed that his sister had recently had an illegitimate baby in his house, and that he knew that Methven was the father. When Methven saw the brother appear as a witness, he immediately left Jedburgh, and disappeared; and Knox and the elders returned to Edinburgh to report that Methven was guilty. Spottiswood and the Edinburgh Church Session thereupon summoned Methven to appear to hear sentence passed against him, but he fled to England, and in his absence was deprived of his office as a minister, and excommunicated.

The action of Knox, in exposing the guilt of Methven, is a tribute to his integrity. He was very reluctant to condemn an esteemed colleague, but when the evidence was too strong to be questioned, he gave an honest judgement, although he must have realized the jubilation with which the Catholics and the enemies of the Church would greet the verdict. There is sadness, but no vindictiveness, in the manner in which Knox, in his *History*, tells the story of Methven's fall. In his account of the upsurge of 1558–9, he did not try to minimize Methven's part, describing how in 1558 'did God stir up his servant Paul Methven (his later fall ought not to deface the work of God in him)'. Knox used the case of Methven to contrast the determination of the Protestant Church to punish sin with the way in which the Catholic Church had tolerated the immorality of so many bishops and abbots, and pointed out that the adultery of David, the treason of Judas, and the abnegation of Peter had not vitiated the truth of the doctrine which they had previously taught.

In 1566 Methven returned to Scotland and asked the forgiveness of the Church. He was ordered to stand outside the church door and sit on the stool of repentance in Edinburgh, Jedburgh, and Dundee, after which he would be released from excommunication and readmitted as a member of the congregation. He declared that the penalty was very harsh, but it was decided that despite the sincerity of his repentance, he could not be treated more leniently because of the position which he had formerly held in the Church. He stood at the church door in Edinburgh, where he aroused great compassion among the congregation, and then did the same at Jedburgh; but he could not bring himself to do it in Dundee, where he had served the cause so well in 1558–9, and again fled to England. He became the vicar of a parish in Somerset, and later held two other benefices in the county, where he served for forty years until his death in 1606.[1]

Methven was not the only minister who failed to maintain the high standard of sexual morality which the Church enforced upon the people. Alexander Jarden, the minister of Kilspindie, near Perth, committed fornication with a virgin, and afterwards married her. In view of his repentance and subsequent marriage, he was forgiven by the Church Session, and after being suspended for a time from his office as minister by Winram, the Superintendent of Fife, he was readmitted next year by the General Assembly. Fornication was a much less serious offence than adultery. When Robert Richardson, the Lord High Treasurer of

[1] For Methven's case, see Knox, *History*, i. 148; ii. 66–67; *Booke of the Universall Kirk of Scotland*, i. 29, 31, 55–56, 79–81 (30 Dec. 1562, 25 June 1563, 27 Dec. 1564, and 26 June 1566); Knox's continuator (Knox, *History*, ii. 187–8); Randolph to Cecil, 22 Jan. 1562/3 (*Sc. Cal.* i. 1163); Weaver, *Somerset Incumbents*, pp. 115, 128, 474 (Kewstock, Locking, and Wells, v.).

Scotland, had an illegitimate child by an unmarried woman, he was forced to make public confession on the stool of repentance while Knox preached a sermon, in January 1564; but no further punishment was inflicted upon him.[1]

But even with regard to adultery, the practice of the Church was always less rigid than its theory. It was repeatedly demanding that the law of Scotland should be brought into conformity with the law of God by making adultery a capital offence, and Knox, in his *History*, protests against the mildness of the Act of Parliament of 1563, which imposed the death penalty for adultery only after a warning to desist from it had been given and ignored; but in no case was the death sentence for adultery carried out in Scotland, and when Methven wrote from England to the General Assembly, he was given an official assurance from the Church that if he returned to Scotland to submit to the punishment of the Church, he would be in no danger of being proceeded against under the statute of 1563.[2]

These cases of moral delinquency by ministers of the Church naturally encouraged the spread of rumours about other ministers. In June 1563 Euphamie Dundas, a widow of Edinburgh, speaking to a group of people in a public place, criticized the religious doctrines and sexual morals of the Protestant pastors in general, and then proceeded to state that a few days before, Knox had been caught and dragged out of a cave near the town, with a common whore, 'and that he had been a common harlot all his days'. The General Assembly thereupon wrote to the Edinburgh burgh council and requested them to summon Euphamie Dundas, and investigate whether the charge against Knox was true; and that if it was proved to be true, 'the said John Knox might be punished with all rigour, without favour; otherwise to take such order with her as might stand with the glory of God, and that slander might be taken from His Church'. On 25 June, Knox appeared before the burgh council, accompanied by his procurator John Chisholm, and began proceedings in an action of slander against Euphamie Dundas. There are no further records about the case.[3]

[1] *Booke of the Universall Kirk*, i. 45, 50 (31 Dec. 1563 and 29 June 1564); Randolph to Cecil, 31 Dec. 1563 (*Sc. Cal.* ii. 45).

[2] *Acts Parl. Scot.* ii. 539 (4 June 1563); Knox, *History*, ii. 79–80; *Booke of the Universall Kirk*, i. 55–56 (27 Dec. 1564).

[3] *Edinburgh Burgh Records*, iii. 162, 164 (18 and 25 June 1563).

CHAPTER XXI

The Struggle with Mary: 1563

As Knox, the Protestant watchdog, saw with alarm the gradual evaporation of anti-Catholic fervour in Scotland, he began to denounce the gay social life of Mary's court, attacking the Queen's dancing almost as vigorously as her mass. This seems to have been a new development in Knox's thinking; for there is no record of any criticism of dancing by Knox before 1562, although dances had been held at the court of Edward VI, Mary Tudor, and Elizabeth, and, above all, at the court of France, all the time that Knox was criticizing, in varying degrees, the governments of these dancing sovereigns. But the dancing at the court of Mary Queen of Scots became the symbol for Knox of royal and aristocratic frivolity and luxury, and his shrewd political intuition made him realize the corrupting effect that the gay life of the court would have on the revolutionary zeal of the Lords of the Congregation.

Knox first became seriously alarmed about this at the wedding of Lord James to Agnes Keith, the daughter of the Earl Marischal, in February 1562. They were married by Knox in the church of St. Giles's in the presence of the whole nobility of Scotland. Knox's sermon to the bridal pair was more concerned with politics than with the duties of matrimony; he told Lord James that he had hitherto rendered great services to God, but that if in future he pursued a different policy, men would say that it was because he was under the influence of his wife. Lord James and his bride and all the nobles went straight from St. Giles's to Holyroodhouse, where a great banquet and party was held at which the Queen was present. 'The greatness of the banquet, and the vanity used thereat, offended many godly,' wrote Knox in 1566, 'there began the masking which from year to year hath continued since.' This was untrue, for there had been masks at Holyroodhouse as early as the previous October, and Knox, in post-dating this reprehensible innovation, can only have intended, consciously or otherwise, to throw a part of the blame on Lord James, whom he was coming to regard as a traitor to the cause.[1]

In the autumn his hatred for Mary and her way of life was exacerbated by the news from France. A great royal army under Guise's command besieged the Protestant city of Rouen, and captured it by storm on 26 October. Both parties in France had committed acts of cruelty during the summer, and the Protestants throughout Europe were deeply moved by the reports that arrived of the Catholic atrocities at Rouen. The Scottish Protestant volunteers at Rouen, who had fought with great bravery, were refused quarter, and cut down; the few who were taken prisoner were immediately hanged, and the wounded were stabbed in cold blood as they lay on the ground. Of the total of 800, only seventeen survived; they were stripped of their hose, and forced to walk along the rampart amid the jeers of their captors before being sent as *forsairs* to the galleys. The fighting in France ended abruptly a few months later with the murder of Guise by a Protestant, and a compromise peace; but only a handful of the Scottish and English prisoners in the galleys were eventually set free, nearly five years later; they were the only survivors.[2]

About the time when the news reached Edinburgh, Mary held a ball at Holyroodhouse. This angered Knox. He had his informants in the palace, one of whom was apparently Alexander Cockburn, the son of the laird of Ormiston, who had been his pupil in the old days in Lothian and in the Castle of St. Andrews. They told him that Mary had danced excessively until after midnight to celebrate the fact that persecution had begun again in France. But Randolph was convinced that Mary was distressed at the outbreak of the French civil war. She feared that her Guise uncles would be defeated, and the fighting in France threatened

[1] Knox, *History*, ii. 32–33.

[2] Sir T. Smith's report to Cecil, 18–29 Oct. 1562; Vaughan to Cecil, 28 Oct. 1562; Throckmorton to Elizabeth I, 30 Oct. 1562; Young, Mayor of Rye, to Cecil, 31 Oct. and 2 Nov. 1562; Smith to Cecil, 7 Nov. 1562; Smith to Elizabeth I, 8 Nov. 1562; Killigrew to Challoner, 12 June 1563; the English prisoners to Smith, 31 Mar. (1564?) and 1 Apr. 1565; Smith to Morsilliers, 17 Mar. 1566; Smith to Charles IX, 17 Mar. 1566; Smith to d'Elbœuf, 24 Mar. 1566; Norris to Cecil, 2 Feb. 1566/7, 6 Apr. and 18 May 1567, and 12 Feb. 1568; the English prisoners to Norris, 25 Feb. 1566/7, and 12, 29, and 30 Apr. 1567; Norris to Throckmorton, 19 May 1567; the French government memorandum to Norris (June 1567); Charles IX to de la Garde, 18 Feb. 1568 (Forbes, ii. 165–9; *Cal. For. Pap. Eliz.* v. 920, 932, 950, 953, 969, 996, 998; vi. 871; viii. 227 [1], [2], and [3], 928, 972, 1068, 1084, 1145, 1148, 1218, 1223, 1374, 2004, 2019; *H.M.C. Cecil*, i. 977, 1050).

to wreck her growing friendship with Elizabeth for which Lord James and Lethington were working, and which Mary herself believed was essential if she was to maintain and strengthen her position in Scotland and succeed to the English throne. The story that reached Knox probably originated in flippant and indiscreet remarks by the Queen's Maries; for these gay and high-spirited young women preferred the Catholic gallants of the French Court to Knox's Protestants in Scotland, and made no secret as to where their sympathies lay in the French civil war.[1]

On Sunday, 13 December 1562, Knox attacked the Queen's dancing in his sermon in St. Giles's, denouncing the vanity of princes and their malice against those who loved virtue. He said that though dancing was nowhere commended in Scripture, he did not utterly condemn it, provided that two conditions were observed: the first was that the dancers did not neglect their business in order to dance, and the second, that they did not, like their fathers the Philistines, dance 'for the pleasure that they take in the displeasure [discomfiture] of God's people'. Two days later, he was summoned to an audience with Mary in Holyroodhouse. She received him in her bedchamber in the presence of Lord James, the Earl of Morton, Lethington, her Maries, and some common servants. Mary said that as Knox held different religious opinions from those of her uncles, she could not blame him for disapproving of them; but she had a request to make to Knox. If in future he heard that she had done anything of which he disapproved, he was to come to her and tell her, and she would listen to him.

Knox replied that he was convinced that Mary's uncles were enemies to God, who did not hesitate to spill the blood of many innocents, and that he knew that their enterprise would fail; but as far as Mary was concerned, he was eager to do all he could to please her, as long as he did not exceed the bounds of his vocation:

I am called, Madam, to a public function within the Church of God [he said] and am appointed by God to rebuke the sins and vices of all. I am not appointed to come to every man in particular to show him his offence; for that labour were infinite. If your Grace please to frequent the public sermons, then doubt I not but that ye shall fully understand both what I like and mislike, as well in your Majesty as in all others. Or

[1] Knox, *History*, ii. 42–43; Randolph to Cecil, 29 May and 12 Oct. 1562, 6 Feb. and 18 Mar. 1562/3, and 1 Apr. 1563 (*Sc. Cal.* i. 1107, 1144, 1166, 1174; ii. 2).

if your Grace will assign unto me a certain day and hour when it will please you to hear the form and substance of doctrine which is proponed in public to the churches of this realm, I will most gladly await upon your Grace's pleasure, time and place. But to wait upon your chamber door, or elsewhere, and then to have no further liberty but to whisper my mind in your Grace's ear, or to tell to you what others think and speak of you, neither will my conscience nor the vocation whereto God hath called me suffer it. For albeit at your Grace's commandment I am here now, yet cannot I tell what other men shall judge of me, that at this time of day am absent from my book and waiting upon the Court.

Mary commented: 'You will not always be at your book', and turned her back on him, and Knox left, having, in his own words, 'a reasonable merry countenance'. When some of the courtiers indignantly remarked that Knox showed no sign of fear, he answered: 'Why should the pleasing face of a gentlewoman effray me? I have looked in the faces of many angry men, and yet have not been afraid above measure.'[1]

Mary had every reason for her anger, and for her insult to Knox. Despite his specious arguments, his statement revealed his attitude towards Mary, and his conception of his functions. Both the Catholics and the Protestant followers of Tyndale held the traditional view that the most important duty that any priest could perform was to give private admonition to his sovereign, to censure him in private for his sins, while exhorting all his subjects, in public sermons, to observe the duty of obedience to the prince, and thus to ensure that the prince, guided by these spiritual directives, used his power in accordance with God's will. Knox had shown that he had an entirely different conception of his duties, and of the position of the prince. He did not intend to treat the prince any differently from any other member of his congregation. He would preach to both prince and subject, and denounce the sins of both in the same way with the same openness; he did not intend to waste time waiting on the Queen at court. Knox did not wish to admonish Mary in private, but to make propaganda against her in public. By all the accepted canons of sixteenth-century society, his attitude was scandalous; but if Mary did not have the power or the resolution to crush Knox, a pointless insult did not distress him in the least.

[1] Knox, *History*, ii. 43–46; Randolph to Cecil, 16 Dec. 1562 (*Works*, vi. 147; *Sc. Cal.* i. 1155).

Knox's denunciations of the dancing at court were not entirely ineffective; for though Mary and the courtiers paid no attention to him, he succeeded in reawakening the enthusiasm of his supporters. A fortnight after Knox's sermon, Randolph reported to Cecil that Mary had reduced the number of her balls and parties, but he thought that this was only because she was anxious about Guise's success in France. 'Mr. Knox is so hard on us that we have laid aside much of our dancing,' he wrote to Cecil on 30 December 1562, 'I doubt it more for heaviness of heart, that things proceed not well in France, than for fear of him.' But Randolph went on to tell Cecil how one of Mary's priests had been assaulted in the streets at night, and that Mary's musicians, the Frenchmen as well as the Scots, had refused to play at her mass on Christmas Day. This was undoubtedly because they feared violence. There were several cases of Mary's priests being attacked at night in the streets, and cut about the face and head. There is no reason to believe that Knox was a party to any of these acts of violence, and in view of the fact that people were beaten up and mutilated nearly every night in every town of Scotland, we cannot even be sure that all the attacks on the priests were inspired by religious motives; but Knox did not condemn these attacks, and he would not have shrunk from using any means in the fight against Mary and her mass. In October 1561 he had complained to Calvin that although Lord James was opposed to Mary's mass, 'he among others labours under this delusion, that he is afraid to overthrow that idol by violence'.[1]

At Easter, on 11 April 1563, a number of eminent Catholic leaders defied the law and celebrated mass in public. They included Archbishop Hamilton and the Prior of Whithorn, who was Lord Fleming's son and the brother of Mary Fleming of the Queen's Maries, and Winzet and ten others. As the government took no action against the offenders, the Protestant lairds of Ayrshire arrested some of the Catholic priests on their own initiative, and hauled them off to prison. They wrote to Quintin Kennedy and other leading Catholics in the west to warn them that if they celebrated mass, the lairds would not complain to the Queen or to the Council, but would themselves seize the offenders and put them to death as God's law required. When Mary heard of this,

[1] Randolph to Cecil, 30 Dec. 1562; Knox to Calvin, 24 Oct. 1561 (*Works*, vi. 135, 147–8; *Sc. Cal.* i. 1157).

she summoned Knox to visit her at Lochleven in Kinross, where she was in residence. Knox arrived in the afternoon at the castle on the island in the loch, and Mary spoke to him for two hours before her supper. She asked him to intervene with the Protestants of the west to persuade them not to punish any man for worshipping in the religion in which he believed. Knox replied that if the Queen would enforce the laws of her realm, he would promise that the Protestants would be quiet; but if she failed to do so, he feared that some would let the Papists understand that they would not be permitted to offend God's Majesty. He said that if princes did not do their duty and punish malefactors, the people were entitled to do so, as Samuel had slain the King of Amalek whom King Saul had saved. The people were also entitled to bridle kings who sought to strike innocent men in their rage. He advised Mary to 'let the Papists understand that their attemptates will not be suffered unpunished', and reminded her of the 'mutual contract' which existed between her and her people. 'They are bound to obey you, and that not but in God. Ye are bound to keep laws unto them. Ye crave of them service; they crave of you protection and defence against wicked doers. Now, Madam, if ye shall deny your duty unto them (which especially craves that ye punish malefactors), think ye to receive full obedience of them? I fear, Madam, ye shall not.' Knox says that Mary was 'somewhat offended' at this.

Knox slept at Lochleven Castle, intending to return to Edinburgh next morning. Many kings of Scotland would have had him murdered during the night, but Mary merely sent a messenger to him before sunrise, asking him to meet her on the mainland that day, when she went hawking in West Kinross. Knox did as he was directed, and spoke with her at the roadside. If Knox's account of their talk is correct, it was an extraordinary conversation. Mary began in an almost flippant vein, telling Knox that she was annoyed that Lord Ruthven had offered to give her a ring, because she thought that he was a magician, and criticizing Lethington for arranging for Ruthven to be a member of the Privy Council. Then she asked Knox to use his influence to prevent the election of Alexander Gordon, Bishop of Galloway, as Superintendent of Galloway, because she knew that he was using corrupt means to get himself elected. Since the Huntly rebellion of the previous autumn, Mary bore no goodwill to the Gordons;

and when Knox, on leaving Lochleven, went to Dumfries to supervise the election of the Superintendent of Galloway, he discovered that Mary's allegations against Gordon were true. Mary also asked Knox to approach the Earl of Argyll and urge him to show greater kindness to his wife, who was her half-sister, without telling Argyll that it was she who had asked him to write.

Mary ended the conversation by saying that she had decided, after their talk of the previous evening, to do as Knox wished, and enforce justice against all the Catholics who had celebrated mass. Lord James, who had seen Knox the night before and heard from him about his talk with Mary, had persuaded her to do this. Knox assured her that if she did so, she would enjoy rest and tranquillity within her realm. In his *History*, Knox wrote: 'This conference we have inserted to let the world see how deeply Mary Queen of Scotland can dissemble.' But Knox himself was being less than honest if he told Mary that she would have tranquillity in her realm provided that she enforced the law against the Catholics.[1]

Knox wrote to Argyll, as Mary had requested, and urged him, in firm language, to perform his matrimonial duties towards his wife; and in compliance with Mary's request, he did not reveal that the Queen had asked him to intervene in their matrimonial disputes. But at the end of the letter he inserted a passage that would have pleased Mary less. 'I most heartily pray your Lordship not to be absent from Edinburgh the 19 of this instant for such causes as I will not write. This much only I forewarn your Lordship, that it will not be profitable for the common quietness of this realm that the Papists brag, and that justice be mocked that day.' The event to which Knox was referring was the trial of Archbishop Hamilton, the Prior of Whithorn, and their complices on the charge of celebrating mass at Easter. The Archbishop did not know about this letter which Knox had written to Argyll, but he knew enough about Argyll's services to the Protestant cause to object to his sitting as one of the judges, and at the opening of the trial he protested against this on the grounds that Argyll would be biased; but his objection was overruled. The defendants were all sentenced to be imprisoned during the Queen's pleasure, and the Archbishop, who had been insulted and mocked by the spectators

[1] Knox, *History*, ii. 70–74.

at the trial, was imprisoned in Edinburgh Castle. Mary released him later in the summer.[1]

Meanwhile Knox had been involved in another clash with the Queen. In June, Mary opened Parliament in great state, and was loudly cheered by the people on her way to the tolbooth of Edinburgh. Knox was angered by the pomp, and alarmed by the popular applause for the Queen, and he preached a sermon against what he later termed, in his *History*, the 'stinking pride of women'. Then, towards the end of the Parliamentary session, he preached another sermon in the presence of most of the nobility, in which he referred to the Queen's marriage.

> I hear of the Queen's marriage: dukes, brethren to emperors, and kings, strive all for the best game. But this, my Lords, will I say (note the day, and bear witness after), whensoever the nobility of Scotland, professing the Lord Jesus, consents that an infidel (and all Papists are infidels) shall be head to your sovereign, ye do so far as in ye lieth to banish Christ Jesus from this realm; ye bring God's vengeance upon the country, a plague upon yourself, and perchance ye shall do small comfort to your sovereign.[2]

This sermon angered many of the lords, the Protestants as well as the Catholics. The question of Mary's marriage was the subject of complicated intrigues in every court in Europe; the Archduke Charles of Austria, Don Carlos of Spain, Eric XIV of Sweden, the Prince of Condé—for this Protestant leader was at one time the nominee of the Cardinal of Lorraine—and the Earl of Leicester, whom Elizabeth was urging her to marry, were all being considered as candidates for her hand. The marriage problem involved such considerations as the threat to English national security, the religious question, Mary's succession to the English crown, the relations between Philip II and the Emperor, and a possible alliance between the Guises and the Bourbons in France; and Lord James and Lethington were conducting elaborate and secret negotiations with most of the potential suitors. Knox's intervention exasperated them greatly. Events were soon to prove Knox right. As usual, while ignoring the diplomatic subtleties, Knox put his finger on the central political issue: the fate of the

[1] Knox to Argyll, 7 May 1563 (Knox, *History*, ii. 74–76); Randolph to Cecil, 1, 15, and 20 May, and 3 and 19 June 1563 (*Sc. Cal.* ii. 6, 7, 8, 9, 16); Proceedings of 19 May 1563 (Pitcairn, i [i]. 427–30); Knox, *History*, ii. 76–77, 84.

[2] Knox, *History*, ii. 77, 81.

Reformation in Scotland depended chiefly upon whether Mary married a Catholic or a Protestant.[1]

Mary summoned Knox to another interview. Lord Ochiltre and several of the Protestants escorted him as far as the courtyard of Holyroodhouse, but only Erskine of Dun was present at his talk with Mary. Mary burst into tears, and told Knox that she had patiently borne with all his criticism of herself and his abuse of her uncles; she had offered him the right of audience and private admonition, and had tried by all means to gain his friendship, yet he continued his hostility towards her. She swore to be revenged on him. We have only Knox's account of this interview, and of all his other talks with Mary; but there is plenty of evidence from other sources of Mary's habit of bursting into tears, and raging in a most undignified manner, in moments of crisis. Knox replied to the Queen that when it pleased God to deliver her from the bondage of error in which, for lack of true doctrine, she had been nourished, she would no longer find his utterances offensive. He said that he did not think that he caused offence to anyone, except when he was preaching; and when he was in the pulpit, he was not his own master, but was bound to speak as God directed, without flattering any flesh upon the face of the earth.

Then Mary asked him: 'What have ye to do with my marriage? Or what are ye within this commonwealth?' And Knox gave his famous reply: 'A subject born within the same, Madam. And albeit I neither be earl, lord nor baron within it, yet has God made me (how abject that ever I be in your eyes) a profitable member within the same; yea, Madam, to me it appertains no less to forewarn of such things as may hurt it, if I foresee them, than it does to any of the nobility; for both my vocation and conscience crave plainness of me.' A modern historian has made the comment: 'Modern democracy was born in that answer.' But it was not the democracy of universal suffrage, which, as Knox had pointed out in his *Letter to the Queen Regent* in 1558, would have meant that the sinners who were drowned in the Flood were right, because they could have outvoted Noah and the inmates of the Ark. Knox's democracy was much closer to a modern 'people's democracy', in which the State is ruled, not by a hereditary

[1] Randolph to Leicester, 7 Nov. 1564; Cecil's Instructions to Throckmorton, 24 Apr. 1565 (*Sc. Cal.* ii. 115, 170); Philip II to Quadra, 15 June 1563; Philip II to Guzman de Silva, 6 Aug. 1564 (*Span. Cal. Eliz.* i. 230, 259); Knox, *History*, ii. 81.

monarch or nobility, or by any social class, or by the mass of the people, but by a determined revolutionary minority, convinced of the righteousness of their cause and of the inevitability of their victory.[1]

Mary burst into tears once more, and Erskine of Dun, the chief organizer of the Congregation in 1557, comforted her by complimenting her on her beauty as gallantly as any Catholic courtier could have done. Nor was Knox ungenerous at this moment when his opponent, sacrificing her last traces of self-respect, sobbed out in impotence and defeat. He said that he never delighted in the weeping of any of God's creatures; he could scarcely bear the tears of his own sons when he beat them, and much less could he bear to see Mary weep. Mary ordered him to withdraw to the ante-room and wait there, and he waited for nearly an hour. He stood there, he says, 'as one whom men had never seen (so were all afraid), except that the Lord Ochiltre bore him company'. But Knox began teasing the ladies in what was apparently semi-good-humoured banter, and accepted as such by the ladies.

O fair ladies, how pleasing were this life of yours if it should ever abide, and then in the end that we might pass to Heaven with all this gay gear. But fie upon that knave Death, that will come whether we will or not! And when he has laid on his arrest, the foul worms will be busy with this flesh, be it never so fair and so tender; and the silly soul, I fear, shall be so feeble, that it can neither carry with it gold, garnishing, targetting [tasselling], pearl nor precious stones.

Then Erskine of Dun came out from the Queen, and ordered him to depart.[2]

At this time, Knox finally broke off his friendship with Lord James. Hearing that Lord James had been created Earl of Moray, he wrote him a courteous letter of congratulation, but stated that in view of their differences of opinion, he could no longer be of any assistance to him. Moray did not speak or write to Knox for more than eighteen months after this. But Knox continued his preaching as before, and stirred up fresh misgivings among many of his acquaintances by his prayer, which he used as a grace at his table after meals: 'Deliver us, O Lord, from the bondage of

[1] Knox, *History*, ii. 82–83; T. M. Lindsay, 'George Buchanan' (*George Buchanan Glasgow Quatercentenary Studies, 1906*, p. 29); Knox, *Letter to the Queen Regent* (1558 edn.) (*Works*, iv. 446).

[2] Knox, *History*, ii. 83–84.

idolatry. Preserve and keep us from the tyranny of strangers. Continue us in quietness and concord amongst ourselves, if thy good pleasure be, O Lord, for a season.' His friends asked him why he prayed that quietness should continue only for a season, and not permanently. Knox replied that he knew that quietness could not continue for long in a realm where idolatry had been suppressed and then was permitted to be erected again.[1]

On 8 August 1563, while Mary was in Stirling, the members of her household attended mass in the chapel of Holyroodhouse. Many of the Catholics in Edinburgh, who for the last few years had been reluctantly attending Knox's sermons in St. Giles's, decided on this occasion to go to mass at Holyroodhouse instead of attending in St. Giles's. As a result, next Sunday, 15 August, a band of brethren of the Congregation, armed with pistols, went to the chapel royal. Knox says that they merely engaged in peaceful picketing, taking a note of the names of all the people who came to mass; but he admits that a 'zealous brother' named Patrick Cranstoun broke into the chapel, and finding the priest preparing to celebrate mass, asked him how he dared to defy the law by celebrating mass when the Queen was not present. The Frenchwomen present were alarmed, and called the Queen's guard; and as a result, while twenty-two Catholics of Edinburgh were prosecuted by the Protestants for attending mass, the Queen on her return to Edinburgh ordered the prosecution of Cranstoun and Andrew Armstrong for forcible entry, violence, and riot in breaking into the chapel royal.

The trial of Cranstoun and Armstrong was fixed for 24 October. On 8 October, Knox wrote to the brethren all over Scotland, and reminded them how, in the past, they had rallied to the defence of any brother who was in danger, and how, 'since we have neglected, or at the least not frequented, our conventions and assemblies, the adversaries of Christ Jesus' holy Evangel have enterprised and boldened themselves publicly and secretly to do many things odious in God's presence'. He then told them how Cranstoun and Armstrong were to stand trial on 24 October for having 'in most quiet manner' taken the names of those attending the devilish ceremony of the mass at Holyroodhouse. Even on the evidence of Knox's *History* alone, this is a considerable under-statement of the activities of Cranstoun and Armstrong on

[1] Knox, *History*, ii. 78–79, 85.

15 August. 'These fearful summons are directed against them, to make (no doubt) preparation upon a few, that a door may be opened to execute cruelty upon a greater multitude.' Knox therefore called on the Congregation of the whole realm to assemble at Edinburgh on 24 October to protect their two dear brethren.

But the days of 1559 were passed, and the Congregation were not prepared to rise at the call of Knox alone, unsupported by Moray, Argyll, or Erskine of Dun, or any of the other leaders who had summoned them during the days of the revolution. Knox states in his *History* that the congregations in every quarter were preparing to send as many of the brothers as were necessary to Edinburgh, but that the project was betrayed to the Queen 'by the means of false brethren'. When Knox's letter was read to the congregation of Ayr, Robert Cunningham, the younger brother of the Earl of Glencairn, obtained possession of the letter and sent it to Henry Sinclair, Bishop of Ross, the President of the College of Justice. Though Knox complains of Robert Cunningham's betrayal, the Congregation had made no secret, in 1556, 1558, and 1559, of their preparations to attend the trials of their brethren, and relied on the knowledge of their intention preventing the trial from being held. Their failure to act in October 1563 was obviously due, not to any betrayal, but to their reluctance to follow Knox's directive. It is clear, though Knox does not mention this, that none of them in fact appeared at the trial of Cranstoun and Armstrong. The trial was nevertheless adjourned, and though the judicial records for the period are missing, it seems that no further criminal proceedings were taken either against the two Protestants charged with riotous assembly, or against the twenty-two Catholics charged with attending mass on the same occasion.[1] But the Queen and the Council took action against Knox.

Knox was summoned to appear before the Privy Council. In his *History* he gives a lengthy account of the proceedings, but it is unreliable, because it was probably not written until 1571, and is coloured by the prejudices which Knox held at that date. According to Knox's version, the Queen, Sinclair, and Lethington were determined to have Knox convicted and punished for high treason for having convened the Queen's subjects to assemble without

[1] For this incident, see Knox, *History*, ii. 87–90; Pitcairn, i [i]. 434–5 (Records of 1 and 24 Oct. and 13 Nov. 1563); Knox to the Brethren of the Congregation, 8 Oct. 1563 (Knox, *History*, ii. 88–89).

lawful authority, but the Lords of the Council, thanks chiefly to Lord Ruthven, refused to acquiesce in this plan, and after Knox had made a powerful speech in his defence, the Council unanimously decided that he was not guilty. It is more likely that Moray and Lethington, who still controlled the government, did not wish to antagonize the Protestant Church by prosecuting Knox, but preferred to keep him and the whole power of the Congregation in reserve, in case Mary should turn to other forces for assistance, and leave Moray and Lethington stranded and rejected by all sides. It is also possible that the influence of the English embassy was secretly exerted on Knox's behalf. Knox as usual had his informants at Court, this time John Spens of Condie, the Queen's Advocate, who visited Knox secretly before the hearing, and told him that he was in danger of being charged with high treason; but from Knox's account of the steps which the government took, it seems that they only intended to censure him and warn him to be more careful in future, and Spens may have been sent to Knox with the connivance of Moray and Lethington with this end in view.

Spens's visit to Knox was followed by attempts to subject him to moral pressure. The Master of Maxwell, who had played so gallant a part in the fighting in 1559–60, and had been a close friend of Knox, now told him that he would break off personal relations with him unless Knox asked pardon of the Queen for his offence. Knox replied that he had committed no offence, and that a few years ago greater things were not considered to be an offence. Maxwell said that times had changed, for in those days the Queen had been absent, and now she was here, and he warned Knox: 'Ye will find that men will not bear with you in times to come as they have done in times bypast.' Knox was next invited to meet Moray and Lethington in private at the house of McGill, the Clerk of Register; but they failed to persuade him to confess that he had been in the wrong and to ask the Queen's pardon. Four days later, on an evening in the middle of December 1563, Knox was summoned to appear before the Queen and Council. He was escorted to Holyroodhouse by the congregation of Edinburgh; in Edinburgh at least he could still persuade a considerable number to come out in his support. 'The brethren of the Church followed in such number that the inner close was full, and all the stairs, even to the chamber door where the Queen and Council sat.'

Knox was confronted with Mary, Châtelherault, Argyll, Moray, Glencairn, Marischal, Ruthven, Wishart of Pittarrow, Bellenden, old Richard Maitland of Lethington, as well as his son the Secretary of State, Sinclair, McGill, and Spens. Of the thirteen Councillors present, nine—or ten, if Châtelherault is included—had at one time been friends or collaborators of Knox; and though they deplored his action, they did not wish to punish him. Knox made no attempt to appease the Queen, but harangued the lords on the danger of Popery, warning them that if the Papists succeeded in murdering these two brothers, Cranstoun and Armstrong, they would begin to prepare their bloody enterprises against all the Protestants. One of the Councillors called him to order, saying: 'Ye forget yourself; ye are not now in the pulpit.' But they decided that he had not committed any criminal offence, and dismissed him, after Mary had commented that he was just an old fool. Knox obtained a vote of confidence from the General Assembly at their meeting a few days later. The Assembly confirmed that he had been entrusted in 1560 with the task of warning the Congregation if any brother was in danger, and instructed him to continue to fulfil this duty in the future.

Knox describes Mary's undignified behaviour on this occasion. He states that though she took her place at the Council table with great pomp, 'her pomp lacked one principal point, to wit, womanly gravity. For when she saw John Knox standing at the other end of the table bareheaded, she first smiled, and after gave a gawf [guffaw] of laughter.' Then she explained to the Councillors that she was laughing because Knox had once made her weep, and now she would see if she could make him weep. 'Wat ye whereat I laugh? Yon man gart me greit, and grat never tear himself; I will see if I can gar him greit.' If Knox had ever been capable of objectively reporting an utterance by Mary, he had lost this capacity by 1571, when he wrote this passage; but his account of Mary laughing and weeping in turn, with Lethington whispering in her ear and recalling her to her senses, may well be true, for Randolph reports her uncontrollable fits of weeping in the autumn of 1563. She was spending a great deal of her time in bed, complaining of a pain in her side, which Randolph thought was caused by psychological factors.[1]

[1] Knox, *History*, ii. 90–102; Randolph to Cecil, 1 May, 13 and 19 June, 13, 21, and 31 Dec. 1563, and 15 Jan. 1563/4 (*Sc. Cal.* ii. 6, 13, 16, 41, 42, 45, 46).

Knox soon gave Mary fresh cause for offence. On Palm Sunday, 25 March 1564, he married his second wife, Margaret Stewart of Ochiltre, the daughter of Lord Ochiltre. Knox was 50, and Margaret was 17. Marriages between elderly men and young girls were not at all uncommon in the sixteenth century, but Calvin had condemned them as undesirable, and had criticized Farel when, at the age of 69, he had married a girl who was under 16. Adverse comments were made on the discrepancies in the ages of Knox and Margaret, but much greater surprise and indignation was caused by the fact that Knox, a man of humble birth, had won the hand of a noble lady. Margaret was not only the daughter of one of the nobles of the realm, but was of royal blood. The connexion of the Stewarts of Ochiltre with the royal family was well known, for the family referred to their royal blood as a kind of title, being described as 'Stewart of Ochiltre of the royal race of Scots' in their leases and legal documents. Margaret Stewart was descended from James II, and her uncle, Lord Methven, had married Margaret Tudor, the Queen Dowager, the sister of Henry VIII and widow of James IV. Lord Ochiltre had for many years been a supporter of the Congregation, and Knox had been a frequent visitor to his house at Ochiltre in Ayrshire; but that he should have been prepared to marry his daughter to the son of a Haddington merchant, who had never held any official position in Scotland except minister of the congregation of Edinburgh, is a striking proof of how far the spirit of the Congregation had affected the attitude of the Scottish Protestant nobility. It is also evidence either of Lord Ochiltre's Protestant zeal, or of Margaret's affection for Knox, because in the spring of 1564, Knox's position was weaker than it had been for many years, not only with the Queen, but with most of the Protestant lords.

There had been rumours for more than a year that Knox was going to marry Margaret. On 22 January 1563, Randolph wrote to Cecil that 'Mr. Knox shall marry a very near kinswoman of the Duke's, a lord's daughter, a young lass not above 16 years of age', a piece of news that Randolph thought was incredible and laughable. This was almost certainly a reference to Margaret, for she was a great-granddaughter of Châtelherault's father, the first Earl of Arran, by his first marriage.[1]

[1] Randolph to Cecil, 22 Jan. 1562/3 (*Sc. Cal.* i. 1163). Randolph's statement appears to be the only surviving evidence as to Margaret's age. See also document of 6 Jan.

Randolph wrote to Cecil on 18 March 1564 that Mary 'stormeth wonderfully' at the forthcoming marriage of Knox with Margaret Stewart, 'for that she is of the blood and name'. Mary had promised to drive Knox out of Scotland, but Randolph thought that there would be much ado before Knox left the country. Randolph added that he personally was sorry that Knox was going to marry Margaret, but he gave no indication of the reason for his disapproval.[1] The only way in which the Catholics could explain the fact that Knox had been accepted by Lord Ochiltre and Margaret was that he had resorted to witchcraft.

The Catholic pamphleteer, Nicol Burne, in his *Disputation concerning the Controversed Heads of Religion*, which he published in Paris in 1581, states that before proposing to Margaret Stewart, Knox had asked for the hand of Barbara Hamilton, the daughter of the Duke of Châtelherault and the widow of Lord Fleming, who had been the leading lady in high society when Châtelherault was Regent ten years before. It is not impossible that in 1561 and 1562, when Knox was on fairly intimate terms with Arran and Châtelherault, he might have expressed a desire to marry Lady Fleming; but Nicol Burne is certainly wrong in stating that Knox's opposition to the Hamiltons was caused by his anger at being rejected as a suitor. For thirty years Knox opposed the Hamiltons whenever they were the mainstay of the Catholic party, but was prepared to support them when they turned against the Queen and assisted the Protestants.

Burne's book tells us more about the spirit of religious controversy in sixteenth-century Scotland than about the facts of Knox's wooing of Margaret. He tells how

> that renegade and perjured priest Sir John Knox . . . after the death of his first harlot, which he married incurring eternal damnation by breaking his vow and promise of chastity; when his age required rather that with tears and lamentation he should have chastised his flesh and bewailed the breaking of his vow, as also the horrible incest with his good-mother [step-mother] in a killogy of Haddington; yet . . . being kindled with an inquenchable lust and ambition, he durst be so bold to enterprise the suit of marriage with the most honourable lady, my Lady Fleming, my Lord Duke's eldest daughter, to the end that his seed,

1542/3 (*H.M.C. 6th R.* 635–6) for Ochiltre's designation. For Farel's case, see Calvin to Farel, 12 Sept. 1558; Calvin to the ministers of the Church of Neuchâtel, 26 Sept. 1558 (*Calvini Op.* xvii. 351–2).

[1] Randolph to Cecil, 18 Mar. 1563/4 (*Sc. Cal.* ii. 67).

being of the blood royal, and guided by their father's spirit, might have aspired to the Crown. And because he received a refusal, it is notoriously known how deadly he hated the whole house of the Hamiltons, albeit, being deceived by him, traitorously it was the chief upsetter and protector of his heresy. And this most honest refusal would neither stench his lust nor ambition; but a little after, he did pursue to have alliance with the honourable house of Ochiltre of the King's Majesty's own blood; riding there with a great court, on a trim gelding, not like a prophet or an old decrepit priest, as he was, but like as he had been one of the blood royal, with his bands of taffety fastened with golden rings and precious stones; and as is plainly reported in the country, by sorcery and witchcraft did so allure that poor gentlewoman, that she could not live without him; which appears of great probability, she being a damsel of noble blood, and he an old decrepit creature of most base degree of any that could be found in the country; so that such a noble house could not have degenerate so far, except John Knox had interposed the power of his master the Devil, who, as he transfigures himself sometimes in an angel of light, so he caused John Knox appear one of the most noble and lusty men that could be found in the world. But not to offend your ears longer with the filthy abominations of Sir John Knox.

Burne also describes how a young woman in Lord Ochiltre's house peeped through a hole in the door, and saw Knox talking to his master Satan in a black man's likeness, whereupon she fell down almost dead.[1]

By 1628, Alexander Baillie in Würzburg had improved on Burne's story. He related how Knox was so 'highly esteemed by lords and ladies and virgins (too lightly believing his flattering allurements and amorous tales)', that he proposed marriage to a young gentlewoman, 'being yet scarcely marriageable', who consented to marry him, 'to the everlasting loss of her honour and good name, and to the great dishonour and shame, yea, and sore heartbreak of that unfortunate lord her father'. Not long after the marriage, she awoke one night, 'she lying in her bed, and perceiving a black, ugly, ill-favoured man busily talking with him at the table in the same chamber, was so suddenly amazed, that she took sickness and died; as she revealed to two of her friends, being ladies come thither to visit her a little before her decease'.[2] In fact, Margaret Stewart survived Knox by about forty years.

[1] Nicol Burne, *The Disputation concerning the Controversit Headdis of Religion*, p. 143.
[2] Baillie, *A true information*, p. 40.

CHAPTER XXII

The Revolt of 1565 and the Murder of Riccio

AT the meeting of the General Assembly in June 1564, a disputation took place between the Protestant lords and courtiers and the leading superintendents and preachers. On the one side were Châtelherault, Argyll, Moray, Glencairn, Morton, Marischal, Rothes, the Master of Maxwell, Lethington, Bellenden, McGill, and Wishart of Pittarrow; on the other were Knox, Erskine of Dun, Spottiswood, Winram, John Craig, who was Knox's assistant minister in Edinburgh, Christison, David Lindsay, George Hay, and John Douglas, with Willock acting as Moderator. The superintendents wished the disputation to take place in public, but the courtiers insisted that it be held in private, and the superintendents agreed on condition that no final decision was reached without consulting the General Assembly. The disputation was in fact carried on almost exclusively between Knox and Lethington.

Lethington began by objecting to the fact that Knox, in his sermons, called Mary a slave of Satan, which stirred up the people against the Queen and her servants. Knox replied that Mary was a rebel against God, because she maintained that idol, the mass; and when Lethington said that Mary was sincerely convinced that her mass was good religion, Knox said that the men who had offered their children to Moloch, and the Turks, were also convinced that their religion was right, but in fact they were rebels against God. Lethington objected to Knox's prayer for the Queen, in which he asked God to 'illuminate her heart, if Thy good pleasure be', which appeared to throw doubt on whether she would convert to the true religion. Knox said that the Word of God taught him that prayers only profit the sons and daughters of God's election, and that he had good reason to doubt whether the Queen was one of the elect. Knox again evaded the suggestion which Lethington put forward, that he should visit Mary and privately admonish her when she did wrong; instead, he complained that she never attended his sermons in St. Giles's. Lethington said that this was not surprising, in view of the way in which Knox treated her. During this discussion, the Master of Maxwell interjected: 'If I were in the Queen's Majesty's place, I would not suffer such things as I hear.'

The disputation soon turned to the vital question of the duty of the subject to obey or resist a wicked prince. Lethington challenged Knox's doctrine that the people are punished for the sins of their rulers, and will only be saved if they resist their wicked princes. 'Then will ye make subjects to control their princes and rulers?' asked Lethington. 'And what harm', replied Knox, 'should the commonwealth receive, if that the corrupt affections of ignorant rulers were moderated, and so bridled by the wisdom and discretion of godly subjects, that they should do wrong nor violence to no man?' Lethington admitted that the Bible orders that the idolater shall die the death; but there was no commandment given to the people to punish their king if he was an idolater. 'I find no more privilege granted unto kings', said Knox, 'by God, more than unto the people, to offend God's Majesty.'

After quoting from the fifty-second Psalm to show that a subject sins if he obeys an order of his sovereign to kill an innocent man, Knox persuaded Lethington to admit that if the Queen were to order him to kill Knox, he could justifiably refuse; but he still maintained that he would not be entitled to resist the Queen by force if she tried to kill Knox. Knox said that if Lethington allowed the Queen to kill him when Lethington could have resisted, he would be guilty of his blood. Then they argued at length on all the examples from the Old Testament, and above all on Jehu, Lethington claiming that Jehu was already a king when he killed Jezebel, and Knox insisting that 'he was a mere subject, and no king when the prophet's servant came unto him; yea, and albeit that his fellow captains, hearing of the message, blew the trumpet and said "Jehu is king", yet I doubt not but Jezebel both thought and said he was a traitor; and so did many others that were in Israel and in Samaria.'

At the end of the disputation, Knox proposed that the matter should be discussed again before the General Assembly, where he would maintain five propositions—that it was lawful for subjects to refuse to obey the king's commands to kill innocent men, and to rescue innocent men from the king's hands; that subjects who obeyed the king's commands to kill innocent men were murderers; that God had sometimes ordered subjects to arm against their natural kings and to take vengeance upon them according to God's law; and 'that God's people have executed God's law against their king, having no further regard to him in that behalf than if he had been the most simple subject within this realm'. Despite Knox's protests, Lethington and the others refused to debate the matter in the General Assembly. 'Think ye it reasonable', said Lethington, 'that such a multitude as now are convened should reason and vote in these heads and matters that concern the Queen's Majesty's own person and affairs?' 'I think', said Knox, 'that whatsoever should bind, the multitude should hear.'

In this discussion in June 1564, the participants seem to stand on the threshold that separates the medieval from the modern world. The language is utterly alien to the twentieth-century mind, but the ideas that Knox put forward are almost commonplaces to us today. The clash between Knox and Lethington was a clash between old and new ideas, with the worldly young statesman standing for the old, and the ageing preacher standing for the new. When it came to citing the opinions of the leading thinkers of the age, Knox could not compete with Lethington; for Lethington cited Luther, Melanchthon, Bucer, Musculus, and Calvin in his support. Against them Knox could quote only the *Apology of Magdeburg*, which was issued by the Protestant ministers of the city when they rose to resist the Emperor Charles V in 1550, and which Knox summarized in one sentence: 'That to resist a tyrant is not to resist God, nor yet His ordinance.' But the future was on Knox's side.[1]

In the summer of 1564, a new and sinister element entered Scottish politics, which soon made all Knox's fears come true. Matthew Stewart, Earl of Lennox, returned from England after twenty years' absence, accompanied by his son, Henry Stewart, Lord Darnley. If Lennox could prove the invalidity of the divorce of Châtelherault's father from his former wife, Lennox, and not Châtelherault, was the next heir to the throne of Scotland if Mary died childless; and Lennox all his life had been engaged in a bitter feud with the Hamiltons. When Châtelherault, as Governor of

[1] Knox, *History*, ii. 107–34; the passages cited are on pp. 111, 120–1, 124, 129–30.

Scotland in 1543, pursued a pro-English policy, Lennox brought a force from France to invade Scotland; when Châtelherault changed, and led the national resistance to England, Lennox offered his services to Henry VIII, and married Henry's niece, Lady Margaret Douglas. After the peace of 1550, Lennox settled down at the English court, where he and his wife, having become Catholics, were in great favour during the reign of Mary Tudor; but at Elizabeth's accession they withdrew to their estates in Yorkshire, and were regarded as the leaders of the Catholic opposition to Elizabeth in the north.

In 1564 Elizabeth and Cecil made one of their rare diplomatic blunders. They had for several years been suspicious of Lady Lennox's plans for marrying Darnley to Mary Queen of Scots and thus uniting the English and Scottish Catholics; but now, alarmed at Lethington's negotiations with the Spanish ambassador in London for Mary's marriage to Don Carlos of Spain, they decided that if Mary was determined to marry a Catholic, it would be better if she married an English Catholic rather than a foreign Catholic prince. They therefore permitted Lennox and Darnley to go to Scotland in the hope that Darnley would marry Mary, though Knox had warned the English government, a few months previously, of the danger involved in granting a licence for Lennox and Darnley to come to Scotland. Mary immediately fell in love with this handsome youth of 18. But the Scottish Protestants were determined not to have a Catholic king. They were alarmed at the prospect of Mary's marriage to Darnley, and were not reassured by the fact that in February 1565 Darnley attended a sermon by Knox in St. Giles's. Randolph warned the English government that they would lose the support of the Scottish Protestants if the Darnley marriage took place, whereupon Elizabeth changed her policy and put the strongest diplomatic pressure on Mary not to marry Darnley, ultimately resorting to open threats of armed intervention. This angered Mary, who felt that she had been deceived by Elizabeth, and she married Darnley in July 1565. Moray, who realized that this meant the end of his influence at Court, was already assembling the Protestant lords and preparing for armed insurrection.[1]

[1] Knox to Randolph, 3 (May) 1564 (*Works*, vi. 541); Randolph to Cecil, 27 Feb. and 20 Mar. 1564/5, and 15 and 18 Apr. 1565; Cecil's Instructions to Throckmorton, 24 Apr. 1565; Throckmorton to Leicester and Cecil, 11 May 1565; Throckmorton to

The danger against which Knox had warned was now at hand; but when the moment for action arrived, he had no part to play. For two years he had not been on speaking terms with Moray, and Moray obviously considered that Knox would be more of a liability than an assistance in this struggle. Moray's chief ally in Scotland against Lennox and Darnley was naturally Châtelherault, while ultimately he relied on the intervention of English troops, or at least on English money to hire mercenaries. Neither Châtelherault nor Elizabeth would be more sympathetic to the cause if Knox was associated with it.

Mary and Darnley, who now bore the title of Henry, King of Scotland, though he had not been granted the Crown Matrimonial and the legal powers of king, were eager that their fight with Moray should not take the form of a religious war. They issued a proclamation in which they declared their intention of preserving the Protestant religion and the privileges of the Protestant Church, and reissued the proclamation that Mary had promulgated in August 1561, prohibiting anyone, on pain of death, from attempting to alter the state of religion that existed in Scotland at the time when the Queen returned from France. In accordance with this line of policy, Darnley attended the service in St. Giles's on Sunday, 19 August 1565. The Lords of the Congregation were already in open revolt. Moray and Grange and other Protestant leaders had been put to the horn, and proclamations had gone out for all citizens of Edinburgh between the ages of 60 and 16 to be ready, when called upon, to meet the King and Queen, 'boden in feir of war', with fifteen days' victuals.[1]

King Henry sat on a throne which had been specially erected for him in St. Giles's, and listened with increasing irritation to an unusually long sermon by Knox. Knox preached for an hour longer than usual, and the King had to miss his dinner, and go straight to the hawking after Knox had finished. The content of the sermon angered Darnley even more than the length. Knox afterwards published the sermon, in order to show that Darnley's objections were unjustified. The published text was written out by Knox from memory thirteen days after he delivered the sermon,

Elizabeth I, 21 May 1565; Elizabeth I to Randolph, 8 June 1565 (*Sc. Cal.* ii. 166, 168, 170, 176, 183, 195; *Cal. For. Pap. Eliz.* vii. 1159; Keith, ii. 268–75).

[1] *Diurnal of Occurrents*, p. 81; Proclamations of 16 July and 7 and 24 Aug. 1565 (*Sc. Cal.* ii. 209; *Accounts of Lord High Treasurer of Scotland*, xi. 395, 401).

and if he is correct in stating that, in the written text, he had not in any way modified the vehemence of his words, it was a milder sermon than many which Knox had preached. This is not surprising, for Knox had not lost his political caution, and realized that he was in enemy territory at a time when his old colleagues, including his father-in-law, Lord Ochiltre, were rising in revolt. He knew that he could no longer afford to take the risks that he had taken when Moray and the Protestant lords were in power. There were no denunciations of the Queen as a slave of Satan, or of the dancing at court; but a reference to Ahab and to women rulers was enough to anger Darnley.

Knox began by condemning those who believed that there should be no rulers.

> Whosoever would study to deface the order of regiment that God hath established, and by His holy Word allowed, and bring in such a confusion as no difference should be betwixt the upper powers and the subjects, doth nothing but evert and turn upside down the very throne of God, which He will to be fixed here upon earth. . . . For such is the furious rage of man's corrupt nature, that unless severe punishment were appointed, and put in execution, upon malefactors, better it were that man should live among brute and wild beasts than among men.

But the sword of God is not committed to the hand of rulers to use as it pleases them, but to punish vice and maintain virtue.

'Kings, then', said Knox, 'have not an absolute power in their regiment what pleaseth them; but this power is limited by God's Word; so that if they strike where God commandeth not, they are but murderers; and if they spare when God commandeth to strike, they and their throne are criminal and guilty of the wickedness that aboundeth upon the face of the earth for lack of punishment.' He made only one direct reference to Scotland, warning his congregation that if they disobeyed God, He would 'punish thee, Scotland, and thee, Edinburgh, in especial, that before punished the land of Judah and the city of Jerusalem'. He cited, without comment, the text from Isaiah: 'Children are extortioners of my people, and women have rule over them.' Then, after a passing reference to 'idolatry and Papistical abomination', he spoke about a succession of figures in the Old Testament—Abraham, Daniel, Shadrach, Meshach and Abednego, Darius, and Cyrus—and about the example of Christ. Only then did he refer to Ahab and his idolatry. God gave Ahab victory over Benhadad; 'but how did Ahab visit God again for His great benefit received? Did he remove his idolatry? Did he correct his idolatrous wife Jezebel? No, we find no such thing; but the one and the other we find to have continued and increased in former impiety. But what was the end hereof? The last visitation of God was, that dogs licked the blood of the one, and did eat the flesh of the other.'

Knox ended by saying that those who today fought for idolatry would be punished for all the blood of God's children that had been shed since the death of Abel. Since the days of Abel, the struggle had been waged between the two captains, Jesus Christ and Satan, and the members of Satan's army today would be held responsible for the crimes of their fellow-soldiers from the beginning. But he did not directly relate this struggle between Christ and Satan to the civil war that seemed about to begin in Scotland, nor did he mention the King or Queen by name.

Knox was summoned to appear before the Privy Council late at night. He had already gone to bed, but rose and went immediately to the Council, who reprimanded him for his sermon before the King, and ordered him not to preach again as long as the King and Queen were in Edinburgh. On 23 August the Edinburgh burgh council passed a resolution protesting against the order, declaring that they would never agree that Knox should be silenced, and that whenever Knox wished to preach, he was free to do so. They sent the Burgh Treasurer with some of the baillies to ask the King and Queen to rescind the order. But the ban on Knox's preaching only applied as long as the King and Queen remained in Edinburgh, and within a few days they left the town with their army, and marched against Moray and the lords at Glasgow.[2]

The lords evaded them, and their army of 1,000 cavalry, led by Châtelherault, Moray, Glencairn, Ochiltre, and Grange, marched on Edinburgh, which they entered at 5 p.m. on 31 August. They had fewer men than Mary, and unlike Mary they had no

[1] Knox, *A Sermon preached by Iohn Knox . . . upon Sonday, the 19 of August 1565* (*Works*, vi. 227–73; see pp. 236–9, 242, 256, 270); Knox's continuator, in Knox, *History*, ii. 159; and see Isaiah iii. 12.

[2] Knox's Preface to *A Sermon preached by Iohn Knox* (*Works*, vi. 230); *Diurnal of Occurrents*, p. 81; *Edinburgh Burgh Records*, iii. 200 (23 Aug. 1565); Manifesto of the Lords of the Congregation, 19 Sept. 1565 (*Sc. Cal.* ii. 274, enclosure); Knox's continuator, in Knox, *History*, ii. 159–60.

hagbutters, whose harquebuses played so decisive a part in sixteenth-century warfare. They were reluctant to fight against their sovereigns without definite pledges of support from England, and were handicapped by the defensive spirit which obsessed them. The citizens of Edinburgh did not resist the lords, but none of them joined their army, or showed any enthusiasm for their cause. 'In this town', wrote Randolph to Cecil, 'they find neither help nor comfort of any kind.'[1]

Next day, on 1 September, Lord Erskine, who had recently been created Earl of Mar, sent an ultimatum from the castle to the lords. He demanded that they leave Edinburgh with their army within two hours, or he would open fire upon them with the cannon of the castle. As the lords disregarded the ultimatum, Mar bombarded the town all through the afternoon and evening and throughout the night, and at three o'clock in the morning the lords' army withdrew from Edinburgh after holding the town for thirty-four hours. Knox had spent the day writing out the text of the sermon that he had preached before the King, and he ended with these words: 'Lord, in Thy hands I commend my spirit; for the terrible roaring of guns and the noise of armour do so pierce my heart that my soul thirsteth to depart. The last of August 1565, at 4 at afternoon.' He added a marginal note of explanation in the published text: 'The Castle of Edinburgh was shooting against the exiled for Christ Jesus' sake.' Not for the first time, Knox made an error as to the date, for it was in fact on 1 September, not 31 August.[2]

Next day Mary and Darnley entered Edinburgh, and issued a proclamation rebuking the citizens for failing to resist the rebels, and warning them that anyone who resisted the royal authority would be hanged. They then set off in pursuit of the lords, who retreated before them, with the royal army chasing them around in circles all over the south of Scotland. This campaign became known as the Chase-about-Raid; it ended when the lords, after retiring to Dumfries, crossed the frontier into England. Elizabeth repudiated them, and in an interview with Moray, which the Spanish ambassador was invited to witness, severely admonished

[1] Randolph to Cecil, 31 Aug. and 1 and 2 Sept. 1565 (*Sc. Cal.* ii. 239, 241, 245); Bedford to Cecil, 2 Sept. 1565 (*Cal. For. Pap. Eliz.* vii. 1450).

[2] Randolph to Cecil, 2 Sept. 1565 (*Sc. Cal.* ii. 245); *Diurnal of Occurrents*, p. 82; Guzman de Silva to Philip II, 10 Sept. 1565 (*Span. Cal. Eliz.* i. 319); Knox, *A sermon preached by Iohn Knox* (*Works*, vi. 273).

him for having dared to resist his Queen; but she refused to extradite the rebels to Scotland. Châtelherault made his own private approach to Mary, and was pardoned on condition that he went to France, and he withdrew to his estates at Châtelherault; Moray and the others remained at Newcastle.[1]

Although the Catholic King and Queen had triumphed in Scotland, the position of the Protestant Church was not immediately affected. Many of the Protestant lords, such as Morton, Ruthven, and Lindsay, had supported Mary and Darnley against the rebels, and the King and Queen were eager not to introduce the religious issue, or to appear to be persecuting Protestants. The Church was therefore free to criticize Ahab and Jezebel with impunity, and did so at the General Assembly of December 1565. In the previous June, the General Assembly had sent a petition to Mary, asking her to abandon the mass and to surrender her half of the thirds of the benefices for the maintenance of the ministers of the Protestant Church. Mary refused both requests.[2]

This was a serious blow to the hopes of the ministers. Many of them were suffering economic hardship, which had become acute after the winters of 1563–4 and 1564–5, when for two years in succession Scotland experienced the coldest weather within living memory, which led to widespread starvation throughout the realm. The General Assembly instructed Knox to write a letter of encouragement to all the ministers, and he wrote to them on 28 December, urging them not to give up their vocation as pastors, but to continue, at great sacrifices to themselves, to serve their flock; for though it was justifiable to flee from one city into another to escape persecution, it was never justifiable for a preacher to give up his vocation. Knox also wrote a letter to all the brethren of the Congregation, explaining the position about the ministers' salaries, and asking them to support their ministers by voluntary contributions. He reminded them of how Obadiah, the servant of Ahab and Jezebel, hid a hundred prophets of the Lord in caves, and fed them with bread and water, at a time 'when by them (but Jezebel chiefly) the prophets of the Lord were destroyed', and when 'both the King and the Queen sought the

[1] *Edinburgh Burgh Records*, iii. 204–5 (3 Sept. 1565); the Council to (Sir T. Smith), 23 Oct. 1565 (*Sc. Cal.* ii. 287); Guzman de Silva to Philip II, 5 Nov. 1565 (*Span. Cal. Eliz.* i. 330).

[2] Petition of the General Assembly to Mary Queen of Scots; Mary Queen of Scots' answer (*Booke of the Universall Kirk*, i. 58–60, 67–68 (26 June and 25 Dec. 1565)).

subversion of true religion'; and he called on the Congregation to feed their pastors today.[1]

The General Assembly also decided to order a General Fast on the last Sunday in February and the first Sunday in March in 1566, and published a document, which was written by Knox, explaining to the brethren the reason for holding the fast, and the order that was to be adopted on the fast days. It would have nothing in common with the vain Papistical fasts—'for what fasting is it, to abstain from flesh, and to fill the belly with fish, wine, spice and other delicates?' These fast days would follow the practice adopted by David and other biblical figures. Nothing at all was to be eaten on the two fast days from 8 p.m. on the Saturday until after 5 p.m. on the Sunday, and then only bread and drink was to be taken. Those who felt unable to fast on grounds of health were not obliged to do so, but 'we exhort them to use their liberty (if any they take) in secret, lest that others either follow their evil example, or else judge them to be despisers of so necessary an exercise'. No games of any kind were to be played on the fast days. The two sermons on the Sunday were to be longer than usual, but not so long that they became tedious; the whole service in church should not exceed three hours in the morning, and two hours in the afternoon. The whole week between the two fast days was to be a period of humiliation, during which no one was to wear any gorgeous apparel. The last Sunday in February and the first Sunday in March had been chosen, not because there was anything special about these days, but because they happened to be the last two Sundays before the forthcoming meeting of Parliament; and in fact the fast days were later postponed, and held on the first two Sundays in March.

Knox explained that there were two kinds of fast: the private fast, in which any brother could engage for private reasons whenever he thought fit, on any day he chose, and which should be done secretly, without boasting as the Papists did; and the public fast, which was proclaimed by the Church for special reasons of public importance. This General Fast was being proclaimed because the brethren had allowed the realm, which God had once

[1] *Booke of the Universall Kirk*, i. 73 (28 Dec. 1565); the General Assembly to the ministers (28 Dec. 1565); the General Assembly to 'all faithful', 28 Dec. 1565 (*Works*, vi. 423–6, 431–6; see p. 435). For the weather, see Randolph to Cecil, 15 Jan. and 21 Feb. 1563/4, 23–24 Dec. 1564, and 15 Jan., 5 and 19 Feb., and 1–3 Mar. 1564/5 (*Sc. Cal.* ii. 46, 60, 128, 135, 143, 147, 153).

purged, to be polluted again with the mass; and some of those whom God had once made instruments to suppress that impiety had been chiefly responsible for conveying that idol throughout all the quarters of the realm. Moreover, the Queen's Majesty 'hath given answer in plain words that that religion in which she hath been nourished (and that is mere abomination), she will maintain and defend'. But it was not only events in Scotland that required these days of humiliation; there were the international plans of the Catholics in Europe, which had been formulated by the Council of Trent, to exterminate all Lutherans and Calvinists, under which King Philip of Spain was to attack the Huguenots in France, and the Dukes of Savoy and Ferrara were to attack Geneva, and 'not leave it till that they have put it to sack, saving in it no living creature'. Then Knox, after a brief review of the slaughter of 100,000 Protestants in France, of the deaths from plague in England and the war between Denmark and Sweden, turned again to the situation at home, and appealed to the nobility and wealthier classes to cease their oppression of the poor. This is one of the few passages in Knox's surviving works in which, turning aside from the immediate religious and political conflict, he deals in broad terms with social obligations.

Knox warned all classes that it was not enough to obey the civil laws; for

> the eyes of our God pierceth deeper than man's law can stretch. The law of men cannot convict the earl, the lord, the baron [laird] or gentleman for oppressing of the poor labourers of the ground; for his defence is ready, I may do with my own as best pleaseth me. The merchant is just enough in his own conceit, if before men he cannot be convict of theft and deceit. The artificer and craftsman thinketh himself free before God, albeit that he neither work sufficient stuff, nor yet sell for reasonable price; the world is evil, (saith he), and how can men live if they do not as other do? And thus doth every man lean upon the iniquity of another, and thinketh himself sufficiently excused when that he meeteth craft with craft, and repulseth back violence either with deceit or else with open injury.

He reminded them that Christ had said: 'Whatsoever that ye would men should do unto you, do ye the like unto them', and called on the nobility and gentry

> to try their own consciences, whether that they would be content that they should be entreated (if God had made them husbandmen and

labourers of the ground) as they have entreated, and presently doth entreat, such as sometimes had a moderate and reasonable life under their predecessors; whether, we say, that they would be content that their steadings and malinges should be raised from male to ferme, from one ferme to two, and so going upward, till that for poverty the ancient labourers are compelled to leave the ground in the hands of the lord.[1]

At the end of February, Mary expelled Randolph from Scotland, as she had discovered that he had given money to Moray and the rebels in 1565. On 7 March she opened Parliament in state, and declared her will that Parliament should pass an Act attainting as traitors all the rebels who had fled to England, and confiscating all their property. But Parliament transacted no further business. On the evening of 9 March 1566, a band of some twenty men broke into the Queen's room in Holyroodhouse and murdered her secretary David Riccio, dragging him from the room where he was having supper with Mary, the Countess of Argyll, and a few gentlemen, and stabbing him to death in the ante-room. The murderers included Ruthven, Morton and Lindsay, Cockburn of Ormiston, Sandilands of Calder, and Ker of Faldonside, and were led by the King himself. After killing Riccio, the murderers held Mary prisoner in the palace. As the rumours of what had happened spread through Edinburgh, the town bell began to toll, and the Provost and many of the other citizens marched to Holyroodhouse to rescue the Queen; but they found their passage blocked by a band of 500 men who guarded the courtyard, among whom was the 'zealous brother'[2] Patrick Cranstoun, and Andrew Armstrong and other members of the Congregation, who persuaded the Provost and his followers to disperse and go home. On the same night, John Black, one of Mary's Catholic friars, who was apparently a man of very immoral life, was murdered in his bed. A few weeks earlier, he had been badly wounded in the street by Andrew Armstrong and three other Protestants.

Next day, a proclamation was issued in the King's name proroguing Parliament, and ordering all those who had come to Edinburgh to attend Parliament to leave the town within three hours, on pain of death; and in the evening Moray, Grange, and Ochiltre, and the leaders of the revolt of 1565, returned from

[1] *The Order of the General Fast* (*Works*, vi. 391–422; see pp. 401–2, 410, 412–14, 416–17); and see *Booke of the Universall Kirk*, i. 76 (28 Dec. 1565).

[2] Knox, *History*, ii. 87.

England to Edinburgh. The object of the plot was to reverse the recent anti-English trends in Mary's policy, to bring Mary again under the control of Moray and the Protestant lords, and to prevent the attainder and forfeiture of the rebel lords in Parliament. The men who murdered Riccio had supported Mary against the rebels of 1565; but Moray and the refugees in England were parties to the plot, and arrived in Edinburgh within twenty-four hours of Riccio's death.

The only mystery is why Riccio was killed. This Italian musician had become Mary's private secretary in 1564, and wrote the letters which she occasionally sent to the Pope and Philip II and other Catholic sovereigns; but there is no real reason to believe the story that he was an important Papal secret agent, or the master mind in the background who directed the moves in the Catholic revival in Scotland and the marriage with Darnley. It is very unlikely that he was Mary's lover; but Mary treated him with a casual informality in public which greatly annoyed the nobles, who resented his arrogance. Darnley became madly jealous of him, and agreed with Ruthven and Morton and the other murderers to kill Riccio, being convinced that he was an adulterer who had seduced his wife. Darnley was also encouraged by a promise by Ruthven and Morton, to which Moray and Ochiltre in England were also party, that they would persuade Parliament to grant him the Crown Matrimonial, with the powers as well as the title of king, which Mary had refused to do. The original intention was to hang Riccio after some form of summary trial; but in the excitement, the King stabbed him with his dagger, and all the others then followed suit.[1]

[1] For contemporary accounts of Riccio, his murder, and the ensuing events, see the reports of Randolph, Bedford, de Foix, and Guzman de Silva; the Band between Darnley and the Lords; the account of the murder by Ruthven; Mary Queen of Scots' letter to Archbishop Beaton, 2 Apr. 1566; and the declarations by Huntly and Argyll, and Moray's reply, in Jan. 1568/9 (*Sc. Cal.* ii. 124, 153, 174, 191, 284, 346, 351, 364, 947; *Cal. For. Pap. Eliz.* vii. 1510; viii. 56; Teulet, ii. 50, 76, 93, 118–20; *Maitland Misc.* iii. 188–91; Stevenson, *Illustrations*, pp. 119–20; Keith, ii. 330–5, 411–23; iii. 260–78; Wright, *Queen Elizabeth and her times*, pp. 226–35; *S.H.R.* xxxiv. 135–9; *Span. Cal. Eliz.* i. 343–4, 347–50); Pitcairn, i [i]. 478–86 (Proceedings of 1 Apr.–31 July 1566); *Diurnal of Occurrents*, pp. 89–98; Nau, pp. 3–13, 215–24; Sir James Melville's *Memoirs*, pp. 60–61; Buchanan, *History*, ii. 299–301, 306–13; and see Moray to Cecil, 8 Mar. 1565/6 (*Sc. Cal.* ii. 355). For Black and his murder, see Randolph to Cecil, 3 June 1563 and 13 Mar. 1565/6; Bedford to Cecil, 13 Mar. 1565/6 (*Sc. Cal.* ii. 9, 358–9); Pitcairn, i [i]. 475–6 (proceedings of 12 Feb. 1565/6); *Edinburgh Burgh Records*, iii. 131 (8 Apr. 1562); Guzman de Silva to Philip II, 23 Mar.

The murder of Riccio was one of the most cynical and unscrupulous actions of the sixteenth century. The Protestant leaders who planned the *coup d'état* knew that Riccio was neither Mary's lover nor a Catholic agent of any importance; but by inflaming Darnley's jealousy to the point where he murdered Riccio in Mary's presence, they succeeded in creating an irreconcilable antagonism between the King and Queen, thus splitting the unity of the Catholic party in Scotland. The fact that this involved the death of Riccio did not deter them in the least, as they greatly disliked him; and the circumstances in which the crime was committed—the dragging of the screaming Riccio from Mary's presence and the physical force used to restrain the Queen—which made it in sixteenth-century eyes a far more terrible outrage than the murder of Friar Black in his bed, was actually an advantage, as it made it more difficult for Mary to forgive what her husband had done and to reunite the Catholic party.

Knox was a party to the conspiracy. This has been strongly denied by many historians, but all the evidence indicates that he knew of the plans for the *coup d'état* in advance, and fully supported them, though he was not one of the organizers of the plot. If Cranstoun and Armstrong and other stalwarts of the Congregation were approached and invited to assist by guarding the courtyard of the palace, it is almost certain that Knox, with his private intelligence service and his informants at Court, knew about it. It is more than likely that some of the lesser conspirators, if not the leading ones, asked Knox's advice as to whether they should take part, and were encouraged by him to do so. Knox approved whole-heartedly of the murder of Riccio, and warmly praises the murderers in his *History*.[1]

A document has been found among Cecil's papers, an unsigned and undated memorandum not addressed to anyone, with no title or heading, and written in an unidentifiable sixteenth-century hand. It reads as follows:

The Earl Morton; the Lord Ruthven; the Lord Lindsay; the Secretary [Lethington]; the Master of Ruthven. Lords: Ormiston; Brunstane; Haughton; Lochlinnie; Elphinstone; Patrick Murray; Patrick Ballentine;

1566 (*Span. Cal. Eliz.* i. 344); Parkhurst to Bullinger, 21 Aug. 1566 (Burnet, vi. 538; *Zurich Letters*, i. 241). For a defence of Black's moral character, see Durkan, in *Innes Rev.* i. 159–60.

[1] Knox, *History*, i. 44, 112.

George Douglas; Andrew Ker of Faldonside. All these were at the death of Davy and privy thereunto, and are now in displeasure with the Queen, and their houses taken and spoiled. John Knox, John Craig, preachers.

On the back of the document, it is endorsed in the handwriting of Cecil's clerk: '*Martij* 1565. Names of such as were consenting to the death of David.' The date '*Martij* 1565' on the endorsement shows that the document had been received in London by 24 March 1566, when, by the calendar then in force in England and Scotland, the year 1565 ended; and it was attached to a letter written to Cecil from Randolph in Berwick on 21 March. Some historians have rejected the evidence on the grounds that Knox was certainly not present at the killing in Holyroodhouse, and that as the document states that 'all these were at the death of Davy and privy thereunto', and includes Knox's name in the list, it is obviously unreliable. In fact, however, the writer of the memorandum does not suggest that Knox and Craig were present at the murder, or that their houses were taken and spoiled; for this reference to houses, which means castles or peels, is quite inapplicable to the two preachers. Their names are added on a lower line, without further comment from the writer, but included in the endorsement by Cecil's clerk: 'Names of such as were consenting to the death of David.' The document is not absolutely reliable, for it is wrong in stating that Lethington was present, though he too was a party to the plot; but it confirms all the other indications that Knox knew about the murder in advance and approved of it, even though he did not actively participate in person.[1]

On the evening of 11 March, two days after Riccio's death, Mary persuaded Darnley, who was passionately in love with her, to desert his confederates and help her to escape to Dunbar. When the lords in Edinburgh discovered, on the morning of the 12th, that Mary had escaped, they were greatly disturbed, but did not despair of success; and as the news arrived that Mary had raised

[1] For the document, see Randolph to Cecil, 21 Mar. 1565/6 (*Sc. Cal.* ii. 363, where it is printed in full); but see Information sent to Bedford (1567) (Stevenson, *Illustrations*, pp. 169–70). For the controversy as to Knox's complicity in Riccio's murder, see Tytler, *History of Scotland*, ii. 390, 445–8; iii. 359–64, with Eadie's comments; Hume Brown, *John Knox*, ii. 304–10; Hay Fleming, *Mary Queen of Scots*, pp. 395–6.

an army in Dunbar, they prepared to hold Edinburgh against her. But on 15 March, a herald ventured to read out a proclamation at the market cross of Edinburgh, calling on all lieges between 60 and 16 to meet the King and Queen at Musselburgh on the 17th to march against the rebels; and this demoralized the lords. Next day, they decided to retreat. At seven o'clock on the morning of the 17th, all the leaders of the *coup d'état* left Edinburgh and went to Linlithgow; and at two o'clock in the afternoon of the same day, Knox also left the town. A contemporary diarist in Edinburgh recorded that Knox's departure caused 'a great mourning of the godly of religion'.[1]

Next day, the King and Queen and their army entered Edinburgh, and some of the men who had kept watch in the courtyard of Holyroodhouse on the night of Riccio's death were summoned to appear on a charge of high treason, and put to the horn for non-compearance. Three of them were caught and sentenced to death; one of these, Thomas Scott, the Deputy-Sheriff of Perth, was hanged in Edinburgh on 2 April. The leaders who had carried out the killing fled to England. Moray and the rebels of 1565 were now pardoned by Mary, but Morton, Ruthven, Lindsay, and the other murderers, whose crime had made it possible for Moray and the rest to return, had taken their place as refugees in Northumberland. Elizabeth, after publicly ordering them to leave her realm at once, secretly allowed them to remain in hiding in Newcastle.[2]

Knox was not put to the horn. He had remained on the fringe of the plot, with knowledge of it and approving of it, but never really involved. He was not in the inner counsels of the conspirators, and was able to dissociate himself from them. When they retreated to Linlithgow, he did not go with them, but left Edinburgh separately a few hours later, and went to Ayrshire.[3] He had not left Edinburgh after the collapse of the revolt of 1565, although he had always had far closer ties with the leaders of that revolt, one of whom was his father-in-law, than with Morton and Ruthven and the Riccio murderers; but with his usual inside information and political intuition, he realized that Mary was in a

1 *Diurnal of Occurrents*, pp. 93–94.

2 Morton to Cecil, 16 May 1566; Elizabeth I to Mary Queen of Scots, 13 June 1566; Leicester to Cecil, 11 July 1566 (*Sc. Cal.* ii. 382, 394, 412); Forster to Cecil, 16 May 1566 (*Cal. For. Pap. Eliz.* viii. 385).

3 Knox's continuator, in Knox, *History*, ii. 183.

much sterner mood in March 1566 than she had been in the autumn of 1565.

A few days before leaving Edinburgh, Knox composed a prayer for use in his private meditation. He first published it in 1572 in his *Answer to Tyrie*, stating that it was 'pronounced by my half-dead tongue before I was compelled to leave my flock of Edinburgh'. It is dated from Edinburgh on 12 March 1566, which was the day on which Mary's escape from Holyroodhouse was discovered. If this date is correct, it shows that Knox had already decided to flee from Edinburgh when the murderers of Riccio were still intending to resist the Queen and defend the town; but Knox so often made mistakes about dates that we cannot be sure that it was written before the 15th. The prayer asked God to put an end, at His pleasure, to Knox's miserable life, 'for justice and truth are not to be found amongst the sons of men'. He prayed to God to forgive his manifold sins, 'and chiefly those whereof the world is not able to accuse me', and gave thanks that he had been given the power of prophecy. He stated that he had no doubt that he had been elected to eternal salvation, and would rise again in glory, 'howsoever it be that the wicked for a time shall trod me and others Thy servants under their feet. . . . Let Thy merciful providence look upon my desolate bedfellow, the fruit of her bosom, and my two dear children Nathaniel and Eleazer. Now, Lord, put end to my misery.'[1] These last words make it clear that Margaret remained behind in Edinburgh, and that her eldest daughter, Martha, was about to be born.

Whatever the degree of Knox's involvement in the murder of Riccio, his attitude towards it shows a sorry decline from the principled attitude which he had adopted in the galleys in 1548, when he had advised Grange and his colleagues in Mont-Saint-Michel that they were only justified in trying to escape if they could do so without taking the life of any of their jailers. Morally, the murder of Riccio was far more reprehensible than the murder of Beaton or Guise. Riccio was not killed because he was a persecutor on whom the Protestants inflicted retribution, or even because he was a formidable enemy whose removal was essential for the success of the cause, but because of the beneficial consequences which would indirectly result from the fact that Darnley killed him. The moral justification for the murder was

[1] Knox, Preface to *Answer to Tyrie* (*Works*, vi. 483–4).

that as Riccio was an adulterer, his killers were carrying out the divine commandment that adulterers should be put to death; but no one seriously believed that this was the motive for the events of 9 March. Knox hardly troubled to mention it when he wrote about the slaughter of David in his *History* two months later,[1] and—most significantly of all—does not even consider the moral aspect of the affair. Randolph and Elizabeth's diplomats still hesitated to be involved in murder, and could never quite disregard the ethical question when discussing plans for the assassination of political opponents; but Knox had no qualms about doing anything that benefited the cause. The stabbing of Riccio, the brutal assault on Black by Knox's protégé, Andrew Armstrong, and his Protestant murder-gang, the subsequent killing of the wounded friar in bed, the adaptation to the religious struggle of the traditional slaughtering and mutilating practices of Scottish life, were all accepted by Knox without demur or afterthoughts. He had ceased to regard murder from the point of view of a moral philosopher, but considered it only in the spirit of a secret service operative.

[1] Knox, *History*, i. 44, 112; ii. 5.

CHAPTER XXIII

The Revolution of 1567

THE defeat of the Riccio conspirators put Mary in a stronger position than she had been in since she returned to Scotland. Her relations with Elizabeth became almost friendly, and both the Pope and Philip II agreed to send her a secret subsidy to enable her to take the first slow and careful steps to re-establish the Catholic religion in Scotland. In the place of the lords who had murdered Riccio, she appointed men of lesser rank to her Privy Council, among them James Balfour, Parson of Flisk, who had been at Knox's side when he was rowing and dying in the galleys, but had now, to Knox's great indignation, gone over to Mary. Meanwhile, Knox was living secretly somewhere in Kyle. The exact place of residence was a well-kept secret, but it was almost certainly in Kinzeancleuch Castle with Robert Campbell of Kinzeancleuch.[1]

Here he resumed his work on his *History of the Reformation within the Realm of Scotland*. He had first begun to write the book in the summer of 1559 as a contemporary record of the events that were then taking place, and by September 1560 he had written what eventually became Part II of the book, an account of the revolutionary upheaval from the beginning, in 1558, to the retreat of the Congregation from Edinburgh, and his sermon at Stirling, in November 1559. On 23 September 1560, Randolph, at Knox's request, sent the manuscript to Cecil, and told him that Knox would continue the work if Cecil liked it. In 1563 Knox was writing the third part, dealing with events from November 1559

[1] Philip II to Guzman de Silva, 24 Oct. 1565; Guzman de Silva to Philip II, 20 July 1566 (*Span. Cal. Eliz.* i. 329, 369); Pius V to Mary Queen of Scots, 12 May 1566 (Pollen, pp. 236–8); News letter from Rome, 18 May and 22 June 1566; Castagna to Bonelli, 7 June 1566 (*Papal Cal.* i. 369, 381, 386); Knox's continuator, in Knox, *History*, ii. 183; Davidson, *A Memorial of Two Worthye Christians, Robert Campbel of the Kinyeancleugh and his Wife Elizabeth Campbel*, ll. 463–8 (in Rogers, 'Three Poets of the Scottish Reformation,' *Trans. R.H.S.* iii. 263–94); Parkhurst to Bullinger, 21 Aug. 1566; Grindal to Bullinger, 27 Aug. 1566 (Burnet, vi. 539, 541; *Zurich Letters*, i. 242, 244).

to July 1561, and soon afterwards he wrote the first part, in which he dealt with the development of the Protestant movement before 1558, from the first martyrdom at Glasgow in 1422—he did not mention the burning of Resby in 1407—to the signing of the first Covenant by the Congregation in December 1557. Now in Kyle, during the summer of 1566, he revised the whole of these three parts, and wrote a fourth, dealing with events from Mary's arrival in Scotland in August 1561 to October 1563, when he summoned the Congregation to assemble to prevent the trial of Cranstoun and Armstrong. It was not until 1571 and 1572 that he continued the book with the account of his examination before the Queen and the Privy Council in December 1563, ending with his disputation with Lethington at the meeting of the General Assembly in June 1564. The fifth part, covering the period from June 1564 to August 1567, was not written by Knox. It may have been written by Knox's secretary, Richard Bannatyne, from notes collected by Knox during his lifetime; but it was first published by David Buchanan in 1644, and was perhaps written by David Buchanan himself.[1]

The *History of the Reformation in Scotland* has always been the most widely read of Knox's works, and Hume Brown has suggested that Knox's great posthumous fame is largely due to the fact that he wrote the *History*. He himself is the central figure of the book, but it is a chronicle of a movement, not a personal autobiography, and the most striking thing about the book is the way in which he identifies himself with his party. Like Caesar and Trotsky, he refers to himself in the third person as 'John Knox'; but the Congregation is always referred to as 'we'. No one could accuse Knox of underestimating his own importance, but there are many occasions in the book when he describes some praiseworthy action by a person whom he refuses to name, when the person in fact was himself, whereas every other brother who made a contribution, however modest, to the success of the cause is identified by name. This does not give the impression of being mock modesty, any more than does the use of such quaint phrases as 'John Knox had forewarned us, by his letters from Geneva, of all dangers that he foresaw to ensue on our enterprise', and

[1] For the dates at which the various parts of the *History* were written, see Knox to Railton, 23 Oct. 1559; Randolph to Cecil, 23 Sept. 1560 (*Works*, vi. 87, 121; *Sc. Cal.* i. 906; *Cal. For. Pap. Eliz.* iii. 550); and see Croft Dickinson's Introduction to Knox, *History*, i. lxxxviii–cix.

'the said John took his leave from us . . . and exhorted us to prayers'.[1]

Like all Knox's writings, the style is vivid, the humour is lively and caustic, and the spirit is aggressive and often savage; but there is a difference between the parts which he wrote in 1559–60 and 1563, and the passages which he added in 1566 and 1571. It is possible to deduce the dates at which the various parts of the book were written, and at which the corrections and additions were made, from the dates inserted in some of the marginal notes, and from the handwriting in the manuscript, because Knox dictated the book to different secretaries in the different years. We do not know the identity of the secretary who helped Knox when he was hiding in Ayrshire;[2] but the passages in this man's hand show the bitterness of Knox's mood in the summer of 1566. The fourth part which he now wrote, and the additions and marginal notes that he inserted into the parts that he had written in earlier years, are marked by vitriolic outbursts of hatred which he did not show before. Knox had never been mild and tolerant, but now, along with the passionate denunciations of a revolutionary leader, there was the petty malice of a spiteful old man. The chief target of his hate is Mary Queen of Scots, though Mary of Lorraine, Cardinal Beaton, Balfour, and the Cardinal of Lorraine are also slandered and abused, and waverers like Moray and Lethington are harshly dealt with. Mary Queen of Scots is 'our Jezebel mistress' who 'now does ring [reign] for a plague to this realm'; and he throws doubt on Mary's legitimacy, without a shred of evidence, by referring to 'King James V, whose daughter she is called'. But 'let men patiently abide', he wrote, 'and turn unto their God, and then shall He either destroy that whore in her whoredom, or else He shall put it in the hearts of a multitude to take the same vengeance upon her that has been taken of Jezebel and Athaliah. . . . For greater abomination was never in the nature of any woman than is in her.'[3]

Again and again, he snipes at Mary's dancing. Knox was not alone among sixteenth-century religious leaders in condemning dancing, which had been denounced by Archbishop Hamilton,

[1] Hume Brown, *John Knox*, ii. 211; Knox, *History*, i. 123, 282.

[2] But see the suggestion of J. P. Finlayson that part of the section of the manuscript which was written in 1566 is in the hand of Knox's nephew, Paul Knox (Finlayson, 'A volume associated with John Knox' (*S.H.R.* xxxviii. 171)).

[3] Knox, *History*, i. 39, 59, 103, 322.

the Primate of Mary's own Church, as a sin and a provocation to commit adultery. In theory, Knox only disapproved of dancing if it interfered with work, or if the dances were held to celebrate a Catholic victory in the French civil war; but he went beyond this rational attitude in his constant references to dancing in his bitter mood of 1566. He refers to 'avarice, oppression of the poor, excess, riotous cheer, banqueting, immoderate dancing, and whoredom, that thereof ensues'. He states that though Mary could 'play the hypocrite in full perfection', and kept herself very grave in the Council, 'how soon that ever her French fillocks [fillies], fiddlers, and others of that band got the house alone, there might be seen skipping not very comely for honest women. Her common talk was, in secret, she saw nothing in Scotland but gravity, which repugned altogether to her nature, for she was brought up in joyousity; so termed she her dancing and other things thereto belonging.' But Sir James Melville, who spent much time at both the Scottish and English Courts, states that Mary did not dance 'so high and disposedly' as Elizabeth. Where skipping with fiddlers was concerned, the Jezebel of Holyroodhouse showed more restraint than the Deborah in Whitehall.[1]

Knox made dancing responsible for the affair of Châtelard. Châtelard was a young French poet who accompanied Mary from France, and fell in love with her. One evening he was discovered hiding under her bed. His offence was overlooked, but a few days later he forced his way into her presence in order to implore her forgiveness, whereupon he was arrested, at Mary's insistence, and beheaded within a week for attempted rape of the Queen. None of the contemporary accounts of the Châtelard case gives a satisfactory explanation of what really occurred; but Knox's version is the only one which introduces dancing. 'Amongst the minions of the Court there was one named Monsieur Chattelet, a Frenchman, that at that time passed all others in credit with the Queen. In dancing of the Purpose (so term they that dance in the which man and woman talk secretly—wise men would judge such fashions more like to the bordell than to the comeliness of honest women), in this dance the Queen chose Chattelet, and Chattelet took the Queen.' And after describing the execution of 'poor Chattelet', he comments: 'So received Chattelet the reward of his

[1] *The Catechism of John Hamilton, Archbishop of St. Andrews*, p. 91; Knox, *History*, ii. 25, 64; Sir James Melville, *Memoirs*, p. 125.

dancing; for he lacked his head that his tongue should not utter the secrets of our Queen.'[1]

Dancing is also connected with a wholly unfounded allegation against the morals of Mary Livingstone, one of the Maries. Knox refers to 'whores and whoredom' at the Court, and states that

it was well known that shame hastened marriage betwix John Sempill, called the Dancer, and Mary Livingstone, surnamed the Lusty. What bruit the Maries and the rest of the dancers of the Court had, the ballads of that age did witness, which we for modesty's sake omit. But this was the common complaint of the godly and wise men, that if they thought that such a Court should long continue, and if they looked for no other life to come, they would have wished their sons and daughters rather to have been brought up with fiddlers and dancers, and to have been exercised in flinging upon a floor, and in the rest that thereof follows, than to have been nourished in the company of the godly, and exercised in virtue.

Knox also made a vague innuendo against Annabella Murray, Lady Erskine, whom he described as 'a sweet morsel for the Devil's mouth'. His chief denunciation, however, was directed against Mary Queen of Scots. 'We call her not a whore (albeit her dame heard more than we will write), but she was brought up in the company of the wildest whoremongers (yea, of such as no more regard incest than honest men regard the company of their lawful wives); in the company of such men, we say, was our Queen brought up. What she was, and is, herself best knows, and God, we doubt not, will further declare.' It was only next year, after her abdication and imprisonment, that he added against the words 'God, we doubt not, will further declare', a marginal note: 'God has now done it, 1567.'[2]

Knox sometimes broke into his description of past events to insert a passage in his *History* referring to the situation in 1566. In several places, he makes an approving reference to the murder of Riccio. In dealing with the events of 1543, he speaks of 'Lord Ruthven, father to him that prudently gave counsel to take just

[1] Knox, *History*, ii. 68–69. For the other contemporary accounts of the Châtelard case, see the reports of Randolph, Quadra, and others (*Sc. Cal.* i. 1170, 1171; *Cal. For. Pap. Eliz.* vi. 350, 743; *Ven. Cal.* vii. 322, 324; *Span. Cal. Eliz.* i. 216; Baluze, *Miscellanea*, iv. 306; *Papal Cal.* i. 227; Döllinger, *Concil von Trient*, ii. 115; Pollen, pp. 164–6; Teulet, iii. 3–5); and see Brantôme, *Recueil des Dames*, Disc. III (*Œuvres complètes de Brantôme*, vii. 449–53; *Book of the Ladies*, pp. 117–20).

[2] Knox, *History*, ii. 36, 77, 102.

punishment upon that knave Davie, for that he abused the unhappy King Harry in more cases than one'; and he breaks into his account of the release of the prisoners of St. Andrews Castle from the galleys in 1550 to refer to 'that great abuser of this commonwealth, that poltroon and vile knave Davie', who

was justly punished, the 9th of March in the year of God 1565, for abusing of the commonwealth, and for his other villainy, which we list not to express, by the counsel and hands of James Douglas Earl of Morton, Patrick Lord Lindsay, and the Lord Ruthven, with other assisters in their company, who all, for their just act, and most worthy of all praise, are now unworthily left of their brethren, and suffer the bitterness of banishment and exile.

But God would restore to Scotland these men, now unjustly pursued, and would punish the head and tail that troubled the just, and maintained impiety. He explained what he meant by the head and the tail. 'The head is known; the tail has two branches: the temporal lords that maintain her abominations, and her flattering Councillors', such as 'blasphemous Balfour', the Bishop of Brechin John Sinclair, 'blind of one eye in the body, but of both in his soul', and John Leslie, 'priest's gett [bastard]'.[1]

Although Knox spoke so admiringly of Morton and Ruthven, who only a few months previously had fought for Mary against the rebels of 1565, he made many strictures on Moray, who had changed places with the murderers of Riccio and was again in favour at Court. In the preface to Part IV of the *History*, he attacked Moray, holding him responsible for the

miserable dispersion of God's people within this realm, this day, anno 1566, in May. . . . While that Papists were so confounded that none within the realm durst more avow the hearing or saying of mass than the thieves of Liddisdale durst avow the stowth [theft] in presence of an upright judge, there were Protestants found that ashamed not at tables, and other open places, to ask: 'Why may not the Queen have her own mass, and the form of her religion? What can that hurt us or our religion?' And from these two, 'Why' and 'What', at length sprang out this affirmative: 'The Queen's mass and her priests will we maintain; this hand and this rapier shall fight in their defence, etc.'

The inconvenients were shown, both by tongue and pen; but the advertisers were judged to be men of unquiet spirits. Their credit was

[1] Knox, *History*, i. 44, 112–13.

defaced at the hands of such as before were not ashamed to have used their counsel in matters of greater importance than to have resisted the mass. But then, my Lord, my master, may not be thus used; he has that honour to be the Queen's brother; and therefore we will that all men shall understand that he must tender her as his sister; and whosoever will counsel him to displease her, or the least that appertains unto her, shall not find him their friend; yea, they are worthy to be hanged that would so counsel him.[1]

Knox was expecting the worst when he wrote this preface in May 1566. He thought that Catholic worship would spread in Scotland, and that the murderers of Riccio would be hounded to death. 'Although masses be multiplied in all quarters of the realm,' he wrote, 'who can stop the Queen's subjects to live of the Queen's religion? . . . The Queen has lost her trusty servant Davie; he was dear unto her; and therefore, for her honour's sake, she must show rigour to revenge his death.' But here he was assuming that his enemy had his own determination and ruthlessness. In fact, Mary did not strike down her opponents, as Knox expected, though the Papal Nuncio in Paris, Laureo, Bishop of Mondovi, advised her to do so. Instead, she allowed herself to be persuaded by Sir James Melville and Bothwell, against her better judgement, to pardon Morton and the murderers of Riccio, who returned to Scotland in December and were restored to their lands and estates. Melville's advice was well meant, if foolish; he hoped that if Mary pardoned the nobility, there would be peace in Scotland. Bothwell, who was already Mary's lover, hoped that Morton and his friends would help him to murder Darnley; for he knew that they hated Darnley because he had betrayed them to Mary after Riccio's death. The members of the Congregation who were at the horn for guarding the courtyard of the palace on 9 March also escaped scot-free in the traditional manner; for after their trials had been repeatedly adjourned in their absence, they were eventually relaxed from the horn. Thomas Scott was the only man to be executed for the murder of Riccio and the unsuccessful *coup d'état*.[2]

[1] Knox, *History*, ii. 4–5.

[2] Ibid., 5–6; Laureo to Bonelli, 21 Aug. and 12 Nov. 1566; Thomson, *Quo tempore Scotia Religionem Christianum suscepit;* Tritonio, *Vita Vincentii Laurei Cardinalis* (Pollen, pp. 270–2, 277–8, 312, 314, 406, 408–9; Stevenson-Nau, pp. 122–3); Sir James Melville, *Memoirs*, pp. 82–84; Pitcairn, i [i]. 478–86 (1 Apr.–31 July 1566).

It was now quite safe for Knox to return to Edinburgh, but he apparently did not do so. He seems to have been in a bad state of health and nerves, with his physical ailments made worse by his mental depression, and he remained in Kyle. In June, Craig asked the General Assembly to appoint another minister to assist him in Edinburgh, as he could not manage alone; but Knox remained officially the minister of the congregation of Edinburgh, and in this capacity signed a letter, along with forty other signatories, which the Church wrote to Beza in Geneva on 4 September 1566. It was in reply to a letter that Beza had written to Knox when he sent him a copy of the new Confession of Faith that had been jointly issued by the Calvinists at Geneva and all the Protestant Churches of Switzerland. The Church of Scotland agreed with all the points in the Second Swiss Confession, except that the Scots could not agree to celebrate Christmas, Circumcision, Passion, Easter, Ascension, and Whitsun, as there was no commandment in the Bible to do so.[1]

During the summer, Knox heard from the wife of the owner of the house in Edinburgh into which he had moved about a year before. She told him that his rent for the previous Michaelmas quarter had not been paid, and threatened to sue him for it. Knox wrote to his lawyer in Edinburgh, who on 25 September told the burgh council that if they did not pay the rent at once, Knox would have to pay it himself; but the Burgh Treasurer was immediately instructed to pay the money due to Knox's landlord.[2]

Knox may have returned to Edinburgh for the meeting of the General Assembly at the end of December; but if so, he did not stay there long, for immediately after the General Assembly had ended, he went to England. For many years he had been yearning to return to Northumberland, and he now had another reason to go, for his two sons were being educated there. They later went to the university in Cambridge, but at this time the boys, who were aged 9 and 8, were probably at Dalden, or at Streatlam near Barnard Castle, or elsewhere on the Bowes estates in Northumberland or Durham, in the charge of their grandmother, Mrs. Bowes, and their uncles, Sir George and Robert Bowes. It is not clear why Knox sent his sons to be educated in England when he

[1] *Booke of the Universall Kirk*, i. 81 (26 June 1566); the General Assembly to Beza, 4 Sept. 1566 (*Works*, vi. 544–8).

[2] *Edinburgh Burgh Records*, iii. 219 (25 Sept. 1566).

disapproved so strongly of the English Prayer Book and of so much of the religious policy of Elizabeth, of whom he wrote, in his *History*, that she was 'neither good Protestant not yet resolute Papist; let the world judge which is the third'.[1] Perhaps personal relationships in his family after his marriage to Margaret Stewart had something to do with the decision.

Knox obtained a licence from the English government to visit England, and in December 1566 the General Assembly granted him leave of absence until 25 June next, in order that he might go to England to visit his children and for other business. This other business concerned the difficulties which the English Puritans were encountering about vestments. Several English clergymen who, like Hooper in the days of Edward VI, refused to wear the vestments prescribed by law, were summoned before the bishops' courts and imprisoned and dismissed from their benefices, among them Thomas Sampson, Knox's old opponent at Frankfort. The Scottish Church intervened on behalf of the Puritans, and the General Assembly instructed Knox to write to the leaders of the Church of England, and intercede on their behalf. Knox's letter, which was written from the superintendents and ministers of the Church of Scotland to 'their brethren the bishops and pastors of England, who have renounced the Roman Antichrist and does profess with them the Lord Jesus in sincerity', was friendly in tone. It appealed to them to show Christian charity to those of the English clergy whose conscience did not permit them to wear vestments, those 'Romish rags', and urged them not to do unto others what they would not others to do unto them. This letter was dated from Edinburgh on 27 December 1566, and signed by ten superintendents and ministers, but not by Knox, who obviously realized that if his name was associated with the request, it would do more harm than good, as well as perhaps leading the English government to revoke their licence to him to visit England. The English bishops paid no attention to this letter.[2]

It must have been about this time that Knox intervened once more in the religious struggles in France. The civil war had ended in 1563 with a compromise peace, under which some measure of toleration had been granted to the Protestants. In Dieppe, as in many other towns, they had been permitted to worship

[1] Knox, *History*, i. 369.
[2] *Booke of the Universall Kirk*, i. 84–88 (27 Dec. 1566) (*Works*, vi. 437–40).

publicly in one of the churches in the town, but had agreed to surrender several other churches that they had occupied, for use as places of Catholic worship. Knox wrote from Scotland to his old friends in Dieppe, and criticized them for accepting the position. We know about his letters only from the eighteenth-century Catholic author, Desmarquets, who is a biased and unreliable authority; but there is nothing improbable in his assertion that Knox upbraided the Protestants of Dieppe for tolerating idolatry, and warned them that Dieppe would not escape the divine punishment if they permitted the blasphemous mass to be celebrated there. Desmarquets states that some of Knox's letters were intercepted by Sigongne, the Catholic Governor of Dieppe, who thereupon took measures to forestall any Protestant rising; and when the second civil war broke out all over France in October 1567, an attempted revolt of the Protestants in Dieppe was immediately crushed because of Sigongne's preparations to meet it. The interception of Knox's letters may have helped to put Sigongne on his guard; but there is no reason to believe that it had a decisive effect on the outcome of the revolt in Dieppe.[1]

We know almost nothing about Knox's activities during his six months in England in 1567. On 11 March, the Earl of Bedford, the Lord Warden of the Eastern Marches, wrote from Berwick to Cecil, enclosing a letter from Knox and urging Cecil to grant Knox's suit.[2] Knox's letter has been lost, but it was probably in favour of the English Puritans in connexion with the vestments controversy; and Bedford, who was strongly anti-Catholic and radical on religious issues, would have been sympathetic to it. But Knox's stay in England was probably chiefly a holiday, spent in the company of Mrs. Bowes and his sons in Durham or Northumberland, and contacting his old friends in Berwick and Newcastle.

The disgust of the English Puritans with the vestments and other superstitious practices of the Church of England led many of them to sever themselves completely from the Church. Although the leaders of the movement opposed a break with the Church, the younger and more extreme Puritans in London refused to attend their parish church, and held secret and illegal

[1] Desmarquets, i. 210–11. Desmarquets, who is often wrong about dates, gives the date of Knox's letter as 1565, and of the unsuccessful rising in Dieppe as October 1566; but in fact the rising occurred in October 1567.

[2] Bedford to Cecil, 11 Mar. 1566/7 (*Cal. For. Pap. Eliz.* viii 1006).

prayer-meetings, as they had done during the reign of Mary. Nearly a hundred of them were arrested at a prayer-meeting in Plumbers' Hall in June 1567. Next winter, after Knox had returned to Scotland, he received a letter from some of the imprisoned Puritans; and one of their colleagues, who was at liberty, travelled to Scotland to see Knox. The Church of Scotland was the model and the inspiration of these English Puritans; they wrote to Knox: 'We desire no other order than you hold.' But Knox gave them no encouragement, and threw the whole weight of his authority behind the moderate leaders who condemned the separatist movement. This was duly reported to Grindal, the Bishop of London, who was dealing with the case, and who used the name of Knox to demoralize the separatists.

Knox wrote to the separatists that he could not support those who obstinately refused to hear the message of salvation at the mouths of men who did not please them in all things. He reminded them that when Paul disagreed with Peter and Barnabas, he did not prohibit the Christians from attending their sermons; and Paul had submitted to the Jewish ceremony of purification in order to conciliate the Jews. He criticized the separatists for condemning the public ministry of England: 'God forbid', he wrote, 'that we should damn all for false prophets and heretics that agree not with us in our apparel and other opinions, that teacheth the substance of doctrine and salvation in Christ Jesus.'

Knox's arguments did not convince the separatists. They pointed out that Peter and Barnabas did not teach false doctrine, and that the ceremony of purification was not sinful; but they had reckoned without Knox's political acumen if they expected him to encourage a hopeless revolt against Elizabeth's Church at such a time. In 1559, when Knox was waiting in vain at Dieppe for a passport to travel through England, and was being denounced by Elizabeth's propagandists as the author of the *First Blast*, he had told Anne Locke that it was sinful to attend a service conducted under the provisions of the Book of Common Prayer; but it was different now, when Elizabeth was the mainstay of the Protestants of Europe, and when her ambassador in Edinburgh was Knox's chief protector. So, while he urged the Protestants of Dieppe to reject toleration and to upset the compromise peace, he told the English Puritans to overlook the imperfections of the Church of England, and to conform to Elizabeth's laws, as fifteen years earlier he had ordered his congregation at Berwick to submit to the government of Edward VI.[1]

While Knox was in England, Darnley was murdered. It is impossible to be sure who murdered him, but the evidence indicates that in December 1566 Mary, Bothwell, and Lethington decided that it would be advisable to have him killed, as his irresponsible conduct was endangering the safety of the throne. Mary and Bothwell also had their own personal reasons for wishing to remove him, as they were lovers and wished to marry. Bothwell invited Morton and various other enemies of the King to collaborate in murdering him; but they preferred to sit back and let Bothwell kill their enemy without their assistance.

On the night of 9 February 1567, the house at Kirk-o'-Field just outside Edinburgh, where Darnley lodged, was blown up by gunpowder, probably by Bothwell and his men, with Mary's connivance, and next morning the King was found strangled in the garden. His father, Lennox, accused Bothwell of the murder, and Bothwell was put on trial; but he arrived at the trial accompanied by 300 hagbutters, and Lennox, hearing this, refused to attend. Bothwell was therefore acquitted. No one except Lennox was particularly distressed at the King's death, and though a few anonymous leaflets were circulated accusing Bothwell of the murder, Mary would almost certainly have weathered the storm if she had not married Bothwell in May 1567. The Scottish nobility would not accept Bothwell as Mary's husband. Mary's marriage to Bothwell, who was a Protestant, was performed in accordance with the Protestant marriage service by the Protestant Bishop of Orkney, after Craig had refused to read the banns in St. Giles's; and Mary granted a larger share of the thirds to the Protestant Church. These measures failed to win over the Church, and only succeeded in completely alienating the sympathies of the Catholics. The Pope and Philip II considered that Mary had betrayed the Catholic Church, and washed their hands of her.[2]

The whole Scottish nobility united against Mary and Bothwell, though the revolt did not have any active popular support except

[1] Letter to Knox (May 1568) (Lorimer, *John Knox and the Church of England*, pp. 298–300). See Collinson, *The Elizabethan Puritan Movement*, pp. 87–89; and see Knox to Anne Locke, 6 Apr. 1559 (*Works*, vi. 11–15).

[2] For the Papal policy, see Laureo to Bonelli, 26 Mar. and 1 July 1567; Bonelli to Laureo, 2 July 1567; and see Bottoni to Alphonso, Duke of Ferrara, 30 May 1567 (Pollen, pp. cxxix–cxxx, 373–4, 376, 392–4, 396–7).

in Edinburgh. The leaders of the revolution were Morton, Lindsay, and Grange, with Ochiltre also playing a leading part. Moray had gone abroad in April on a visit to France and Geneva, and Châtelherault was still living in France; but all the other lords, except Huntly, either joined the movement, or, like the Hamiltons, adopted an attitude of friendly neutrality. On 15 June, Mary surrendered to the lords at Carberry Hill. Bothwell fled to the north, and then to Orkney, where he was pursued by a fleet commanded by Grange, and ultimately escaped to Norway. Mary was brought back to Edinburgh amid a howling mob who demanded her death, and next day was taken to Lochleven and imprisoned in the castle on the island. The government of Scotland was in the hands of a Council of lords, which was dominated by Morton and Lethington. Lethington, almost alone of the leading figures in Scotland, had at first adhered to Bothwell and Mary; but he joined the lords after Carberry Hill, and placed his diplomatic experience at the disposal of the new régime.

The capture of Mary coincided with the end of Knox's holiday, and by 25 June, when his leave of absence expired, he had returned to Edinburgh, like a jackal moving in for the kill. He arrived in time for the usual half-yearly meeting of the General Assembly at the end of June. Knox and his colleagues realized that Mary's downfall was the Church's opportunity, and decided to hold an extraordinary meeting of the General Assembly on 20 July, at which they could press their demands on the Council of the lords. On 26 June, they wrote a letter to all the nobles, which was signed by Knox, Erskine of Dun, Row, Spottiswood, Craig, and John Douglas, reminding them of the dangers that threatened the Church, of 'the lamed and impotent members of Christ lying in the street as dung, perishing for hunger and cold, yea, and the whole flock of Jesus Christ within this realm continually threatened with the execution of that most cruel decreit of the last Council of Trent, wherein was determined and decreed to make a sacrifice of the whole professors within all Europe, by the tyranny of that Roman Antichrist.'[1] They pointed out that this threat was already being carried out in France and Flanders. Meanwhile, Knox resumed his preaching in St. Giles's. The overthrow of Mary had revived his energies and his spirits and gave him a splendid opportunity to give vent to his hatred of the Queen. His

[1] *Booke of the Universall Kirk*, i. 94 (26 June 1567).

defenceless opponent was at last at his mercy, and without a trace of pity or magnanimity he struck remorselessly at the helpless Mary.

In every sermon, Knox demanded that Mary be put to death. On the evening of 15 June, when Mary came with her captors from Carberry Hill, the Edinburgh mob had greeted her with cries of 'Burn the whore', and Knox was determined to whip up their hatred to such a pitch that it would be impossible for the lords to resist the popular demand that she should be put on trial and executed for murder and adultery. Craig and the other preachers followed Knox's lead, and called for Mary's execution, insisting that she was as much subject as anyone else to the law of God, which prescribed that murder and adultery were to be punished by death. The women of Edinburgh were particularly vehement against the Queen, asking why she alone should be allowed to sin with impunity. There was a certain justice in this demand, for Mary had always been in favour of stern enforcement of the moral law. She had insisted on the execution of Châtelard for his attempted rape upon her, and of her French apothecary and French lady's maid who were hanged in Edinburgh in 1563 for performing an abortion of their illegitimate child. In the previous autumn, when she was repeatedly committing adultery with Bothwell, she had sent an order to the Edinburgh burgh council to punish adulterers 'without any exception of persons'.[1]

But this demand that the Queen should not be above the law was hypocritical. While Knox was preaching these sermons, the General Assembly on 28 June dealt with the case of John Spottiswood, a former elder of the church of Mauchline in Ayrshire, who had been excommunicated for committing adultery on several occasions when he was an elder, but was nevertheless being given shelter by Sir William Hamilton of Sanquhar. The General Assembly wrote to Sanquhar, and ordered him to turn Spottiswood out of his house, under threat of proceedings in the Church Session,

[1] Drury to Cecil, 20 June 1567 (*Cal. For. Pap. Eliz.* viii. 1324); Throckmorton to Elizabeth I, 14 and 18 July 1567 (Stevenson, *Illustrations*, pp. 207–8, 222; *Works*, vi. 552); Maitland, *The Apology for William Maitland of Lethington*, p. 221; Brantôme, *Recueil des Dames*, Disc. III (*Œuvres complètes de Brantôme*, vii. 452–3; *Book of the Ladies*, p. 120); Randolph to Cecil, 15 Feb. 1562/3 and 21 and 31 Dec. 1563 (*Sc. Cal.* i. 1170; ii. 42, 45); Buchanan, *Ane Detectioun of the doingis of Marie Quene of Scottis*; Diary relating to Mary Queen of Scots (Anderson, *Collections*, ii. 7–8, 269); *Edinburgh Burgh Records*, iii. 217 (13 Sept. 1566).

so that Spottiswood, being abhorred by the faithful, might by God's grace repent his impiety and return to the company of the faithful; but there was no suggestion that the erring elder should be put to death. As for Morton, the leader of the rising against the adulterous Queen, he had several illegitimate sons, who were officially described as such, a few years later, in the records of the Privy Seal, when Morton, as Regent of Scotland, presented them with grants of ecclesiastical property and the forfeited lands of criminals.[1] It was almost as hypocritical to demand that Mary should be executed for murder as for adultery. Murder cases in Scotland were more often settled by a compensation agreement with the family of the victim than by the execution of the murderer; and the lords who had led the revolution, and now governed Scotland, had not only been involved in several murders, but some of them were as much a party to the murder of Darnley as Mary herself.

The crowning hypocrisy was the posthumous idolization of Darnley by the Protestant revolutionaries. 'The right noble and excellent Prince, King Henry Stewart', as the lords described him in the band which they signed demanding the punishment of Bothwell for his shameful and treasonable murder, had been not only an adulterer and a murderer, but was also the champion of the Catholic cause in Scotland, who had been responsible for luring Mary away from her pro-English policy and her dependence on Moray and the Protestant lords. Darnley had regularly attended the idolatrous mass, and had shown no signs of repentance before his death. If Knox had reason to doubt whether Mary had been chosen as one of the elect in God's eternal predestination, he had just as much reason to doubt it in the case of Darnley; but no suggestion that Darnley was a reprobate appeared in the official propaganda line in July 1567. The Protestants also tried to have things both ways as far as Darnley's position as a king was concerned; for while Knox and the people of Edinburgh were insisting that a queen was as much subject to the law as anyone else, the lords in their propaganda emphasized that Darnley was a king, and that his murderers were guilty of treason.[2]

[1] *Booke of the Universall Kirk*, i. 98–99 (28 June 1567); *Reg. of Privy Seal of Scotland*, vii. 730, 812, 813, 849, 1039, 1267, 1313, 1347, 1373 (16 Oct. and 26 Dec. 1576, 17 Jan. 1576/7, 22 May, 14 Nov., and 7 and 19 Dec. 1577, and 1 Jan. 1577/8).

[2] *Edinburgh Burgh Records*, iii. 234 (2 July 1567); Throckmorton to Elizabeth I, 18 July 1567 (Stevenson, *Illustrations*, p. 222); *Reg. P.C.S.* i. 544–5 (10 Aug. 1567);

We have no record of the text of Knox's sermons in July 1567, and there is no reason to believe that he himself was guilty of this hypocrisy. In view of his fundamental honesty in matters of principle, it is unlikely that he indulged in praise of Darnley, or demanded the death penalty for Mary on the grounds that her crime was regicide; but the Knox of 1557, who had warned the Scottish Protestants that they would commit a sin if they rose in revolt to further the ambitions of Châtelherault instead of the cause of religion, would have detected the hypocrisy in the propaganda of the lords. He would have been suspicious of the motives of Morton, the leader of this revolution, who had refused to give any aid to the Congregation in 1559 and 1560, and even as recently as 1565 had helped Mary to suppress the revolt of Moray and the Lords of the Congregation. But Knox preferred to close his eyes to this aspect, and think only about punishing Mary. In striking Mary, he could feel that he was the instrument of the divine vengeance against all the Catholic sovereigns of Europe who had burned and tortured his brethren, and his personal friends, in Scotland, England, France, and the Netherlands. If Mary Tudor, Henry II, and Philip II were beyond his reach, Mary Stewart was in his clutches, and could be made to suffer retribution for all the crimes of her fellow soldiers in the army of Satan since the days of Abel, even though she herself had never persecuted anyone, and would never have been a prisoner in Protestant hands if she had not fallen in love with a Protestant. If Mary had followed the advice of the Papal Nuncio, and had put the whole of the Protestant nobility to death instead of murdering her Catholic husband, Knox would probably have been hiding in Ayrshire or in England instead of calling for Mary's death in the pulpit of St. Giles's.

The Scottish revolution of 1567 stands in time almost equidistant from the deposition and murder of Edward II in England and the execution of Louis XVI in France. It was partly a revolt of a medieval feudal nobility against a weak and pleasure-loving sovereign, and partly the first modern revolution of a people against the principle of the divine right of kings. Morton, stabbing Riccio with his own hand, and challenging Bothwell at Carberry Hill to settle the issue in single combat with two-handed swords,

Diurnal of Occurrents, pp. 105, 113, 116; Buchanan (?), 'Exhortation to the Lords of the King's Council against the Hamiltons' (17 Feb. 1569/70) (*Sc. Cal.* iii. 123).

is in some ways more primitive than the English barons of the early fourteenth century; but Knox, inciting the people to judge and execute their Queen because the punishment of wicked princes appertains to the subjects, is a predecessor of Marat. It was this element in the situation that alarmed Elizabeth. She condemned Mary's refusal to prosecute the murderers of Darnley, and, above all, her marriage to Bothwell; but she was shocked that subjects should take it upon themselves to judge their prince. She therefore sent Throckmorton to Edinburgh at the beginning of July with instructions to see Mary, to urge her to repudiate Bothwell and agree to proceed against him for the murder of the King, and to insist that the lords treat Mary with the respect due to her as their sovereign. Cecil, on the other hand, was reluctant to alienate the pro-English sympathies of the Scottish Protestant lords, and tried to restrain Elizabeth's indignation at the affront to monarchy. Throckmorton, the man on the spot, was personally sympathetic to Mary, but resolutely determined to further the cause of international Protestantism, and by his reports to his Queen, and his handling of the situation in Edinburgh, he was largely responsible for preventing Elizabeth from taking any decisive action to help Mary.

The lords' negotiations with Throckmorton were conducted largely by Lethington. They refused to permit Throckmorton to visit Mary at Lochleven, and argued that it was impossible to release her from restraint as long as she was still infatuated with Bothwell. They pointed out to Throckmorton that they were under strong pressure from Knox and the people to put Mary on trial and punish her with death, and while assuring Throckmorton that they were doing their utmost to protect Mary from the people's wrath, they warned him that if Elizabeth made any move in favour of Mary, this would so inflame the people that they would be unable to save her life. They also tried to play off the French against the English. Moray visited the French Court on his way home from Geneva. Catherine de Medici, who as usual was quite unprincipled, was more interested in deriving some temporary advantage from the situation than in assisting Elizabeth to maintain the rights of princes. While she tried to persuade all other governments that Elizabeth had instigated the revolt of the Scottish lords against Mary, the French ambassador in Scotland, du Croc, made it clear to the lords that the King of France was not interested in Mary's fate, and would be very ready to renew the Old Alliance with the new Scottish government.[1]

Throckmorton's chief anxiety was the effect on the situation of the inflammatory sermons of the preachers, and he was alarmed at what would happen at the meeting of the General Assembly on 20 July. When he first arrived in Edinburgh on 12 July, Knox was in the west. Archbishop Spottiswood and later writers have stated that Knox went to the west to deliver to the Hamiltons the Church's letter to the nobility of 26 June; but this appears to be based on a misinterpretation of the records of the General Assembly.[2] Knox probably went to Ayrshire to impress upon the brethren there the great opportunity which the developments presented to the Church, and the importance of their attending the meeting of the General Assembly on 20 July. As soon as Knox returned to Edinburgh on 17 July, Throckmorton got in touch with him, and spoke with him and Craig, and with other ministers; but he was quite unable to persuade Knox and Craig to change their attitude. 'I find them both very austere in this conference', he wrote to Elizabeth on 18 July, 'they are furnished with many arguments, some forth of the Scriptures, some forth of histories, some grounded (as they say) upon the laws of this realm, some upon practices used in this realm, and some upon the conditions and oath made by their prince at her coronation.'[3]

Next day, Throckmorton attended Knox's sermon in St. Giles's. Knox preached on a text from the Book of Kings, and Throckmorton told Elizabeth that he 'did weigh vehemently against the Queen, and persuaded extremity towards her, by application of

[1] For the policy of Elizabeth I, and of the Scottish lords, see Throckmorton's reports to Elizabeth I and Cecil, and the instructions from Elizabeth I and Cecil to Throckmorton, 30 June–1 Sept. 1567 (Stevenson, *Illustrations*, pp. 195–9, 202–9, 214–25, 227–41, 245–64, 267–78, 281–3, 289–92, 297–301; Keith, ii. 677, 699, 702, 734–49, 757–63; *Sc. Cal.* ii. 540, 542, 557–60, 562–71, 573–7, 580–2, 584–6, 588–90, 592–7, 599–601, 605–10, 616); and see Guzman de Silva to Philip II, 21 July and 9 Aug. 1567 and 2 Feb. 1568 (*Span. Cal. Eliz.* i. 432, 435; ii. 5). For French policy, see Instructions to Villeroy (June (?) 1567), and the reports of Correr, Guzman de Silva, Throckmorton, and Norris (Teulet, ii. 182–5; *Ven. Cal.* vii. 393–6, 398, 420, 423; *Span. Cal. Eliz.* i. 430, 435, 439, 444; Stevenson, *Illustrations*, pp. 197–9, 218–19, 268–71; Keith, ii. 746; *Cal. For. Pap. Eliz.* viii. 1264, 1502; *H.M.C., Pepys*, pp. 119–20).

[2] Knox's continuator, in Knox, *History*, ii. 213–14; Spottiswood, ii. 63. Cf. *Booke of the Universall Kirk*, i. 93–96 (26 June 1567), where it is stated that the Church's letter was to be distributed to the nobility as directed by the superintendents and quarters of countries, not by Knox and the other signatories of the letter.

[3] Throckmorton to Elizabeth I, 18 July 1567 (Stevenson, *Illustrations*, pp. 219–23).

his text'. After the sermon, Throckmorton spoke to all the lords who were present in St. Giles's, and urged them to persuade the Council to restrain the preachers from preaching about Mary until they had decided what to do with her. He warned the lords that if the ministers continued to inflame the people, as they did every day in their sermons, it would no longer be possible for the Council to adopt a lenient attitude towards Mary, even if they wished to do so. He wrote to Elizabeth that Mary was in great peril of her life, for the people who were coming to the meeting of the General Assembly were vehemently intent on her destruction. 'It is public speech of all estates (saving the Councillors) that she had no more privilege to commit murder nor adultery than any other private person.'[1]

Lethington and the lords of the Council had obviously not taken Knox into their confidence about their diplomatic negotiations with Throckmorton and du Croc; for in his sermons, Knox not only denounced Mary, but warned against the dangers of a French alliance, and stressed the necessity of preserving friendship with England. On 21 July, Throckmorton wrote to Elizabeth:

> Master Knox doth in his sermons daily pray for the continuation of amity betwixt England and Scotland, and doth likewise admonish his auditory to eschew their old alliance with France, as they would fly from the pots of Egypt, which brought them nothing but sugared poison; notwithstanding, he doth continue his severe exhortations as well against the Queen as against Bothwell, threatening the great plague of God to this whole country if she be spared from her condign punishment.

Next day, Bedford, in Berwick, wrote to Cecil: 'Our unruly neighbours ride as fast as they did, and cease not. Mr. Knox, in his preachings, thundereth out cannon shot against the alliance with France, using all persuasions to lean to the amity of England. He utters also very sharp words against that Queen.' Knox did not realize that his anti-French sermons conflicted with the policy of Lethington, who was trying hard to persuade Throckmorton to take seriously his threat that the lords would renew the Old Alliance with France if Elizabeth attempted to help Mary. But if Knox did not assist the diplomatic manœuvres of Lethington, he as usual understood the more fundamental realities of the situation. The estrangement with England was only a temporary

[1] Throckmorton to Elizabeth I, 19 July 1567 (Keith, ii. 684–94).

phenomenon, and the events of the next few years showed more clearly than ever that the success of the Protestant Reformation in Scotland depended on English money, English pikemen, and English hagbutters, and ultimately on English cannon.[1]

On 23 July, Bedford wrote to Cecil that Knox was very eager to come to Berwick in eight days' time, and asked Cecil for instructions as to whether he ought to grant Knox a licence to come; he assured Cecil that Knox would not be permitted to preach in Berwick. As usual, Knox looked towards England, and wished to go to England. He probably hoped to persuade Bedford and the authorities in Northumberland to adopt a more favourable policy towards the lords in Scotland; but in the circumstances he was naturally refused permission to visit England.[2]

On 24 July, the lords went to Lochleven Castle, and forced Mary to abdicate in favour of her 13-months-old son. She eventually signed the deed of abdication after Lord Lindsay had laid forcible hands on her person, and after she had been threatened with death if she refused to sign. Throckmorton, who had managed to smuggle a letter to Mary, assured her that if she abdicated under duress when she was in prison, her abdication would have no legal effect. In the document, she appointed Moray, who was still in France, to be Regent for the infant King, and a Council of Regency, consisting of the leading lords, was to act until Moray's return.[3]

On 29 July, James VI was crowned King in the parish church at Stirling. Throckmorton, on instructions from London, refused to attend the coronation. The Hamiltons also boycotted the ceremony, though Châtelherault's kinsman, Arthur Hamilton, attended in order to make a declaration that nothing in the proceedings could affect the rights of the Duke of Châtelherault to the Crown of Scotland if James VI died without heirs. The King was crowned by the Bishop of Orkney, who was recognized as a bishop by the Catholics and as a minister of the Church by the

[1] Throckmorton to Elizabeth I, 21 July 1567 (Stevenson, *Illustrations*, p. 240); Bedford to Cecil, 22 July 1567 (*Cal. For. Pap. Eliz.* viii. 1490).

[2] Bedford to Cecil, 23 July 1567 (*Cal. For. Pap. Eliz.* viii. 1499).

[3] Mary Queen of Scots' abdication, and accompanying declarations, 24 July 1567 (Keith, ii. 706–12); Mary Queen of Scots' Instructions to her Commissioners at York, 29 Sept. 1568 (Labanoff, *Lettres, Instructions et Mémoires de Marie Stuart*, ii. 204–5); Mary Queen of Scots' Commissioners' reply to Moray, etc., at York, 16 Oct. 1568 (*Sc. Cal.* ii. 859).

Protestants; and though some of the usual Catholic ceremonies were dispensed with, the rite of anointing was retained, though Knox and the preachers are said to have objected to it. Knox preached the sermon at the coronation on a text from the Book of Kings relating to the accession of the infant Jehoash, and performed an unprecedented duty in the concluding phase of the ceremony. The coronation of a Scottish king ended with representatives of the estates of the realm 'asking instruments', by which they proclaimed that the world should take notice of the solemn act which had taken place, and that no one could plead ignorance of it. Sir John Bellenden, the Justice Clerk, on behalf of the Estates, along with Knox and Campbell of Kinzeancleuch, 'asked acts, instruments and documents' at the coronation of James VI. The fact that Knox, who is described in the official records simply as 'John Knox, minister', was selected to ask instruments, was official recognition of the position of the Protestant Church in the government of Scotland, though it was not represented in Parliament. The nobles and lairds were probably very pleased to leave the honour of asking instruments to Knox and Kinzeancleuch, for if Mary ever returned to the throne, the men who had asked instruments at the illegal coronation would find it more difficult than many of the other rebels to avoid being selected as the scapegoats in trials for treason.[1]

On 27 July, Elizabeth, against the advice of Cecil, sent instructions to Throckmorton to tell the lords in Edinburgh that if Mary were put to death, she would send an army to invade Scotland and punish the traitors who had dared to slay their prince. Lethington replied that they did not intend to execute Mary, but that if English troops crossed the frontier, she would be executed at once. He added that English armies had often invaded Scotland, but could do nothing worse than burn the houses of the Scots, which would be rebuilt as soon as the English had left; and if England pursued an unfriendly policy, the lords would make an alliance with France. Throckmorton then left Edinburgh, refusing to recognize James VI as King; but in due course, Elizabeth was compelled to recognize the new King when the English and Scottish representatives met in their regular days of

[1] *Reg. P.C.S.* i. 537–42 (29 July 1567); Throckmorton to Elizabeth I, 26 and 31 July 1567 (Stevenson, *Illustrations*, pp. 247–52, 255–60); Elizabeth I to Throckmorton, 27 July 1567 (Keith, ii. 702–6).

truce to settle the local disputes on the Border. Mary remained in prison at Lochleven.[1]

The overthrow of the Catholic Queen did not assuage Knox's hatred and anger. In the autumn of 1567, his nephew Paul, the son of William Knox the merchant, came to live with him in his new house in Edinburgh. Paul was about 14 years of age, and was preparing to go to St. Andrews University and to study for the ministry; in his uncle's house he could find great opportunities for study and religious guidance. While he was staying with Knox, he read aloud to him the *Annals of Bavaria* by the German historian, Aventinus (Johann Turmair), which was a history of southern Germany from the days of the Roman Caesars to the middle of the fifteenth century. It had been written nearly fifty years before, and the Latin edition had been posthumously published in Ingolstadt in 1554 in a censored version from which many strictures on the Catholic Church had been omitted. A copy was apparently given to Knox by his friend, George Hay. As Paul Knox read, he underlined certain passages and marked others in the margin, and sometimes wrote short comments in Latin in the margin; but the markings and notes were clearly not the original contributions of the 14-year-old Paul himself, but inserted by him at the direction of his uncle 'John Knox, minister of the Word', to whom, as Paul noted in the volume, he read the book between 10 September 1567 and 15 January 1568.

Only comparatively few passages are marked in all the 835 large pages of Aventinus's book, and there are very few marginal comments; but the passages selected for marking, and the wording of the comments, give a revealing glimpse of the mind of the embittered old Knox of 1567. Apart from some passages dealing with the numerical strength of armies and other military affairs, which seem always to have interested Knox, the sections marked deal almost exclusively with strange portents of God's anger, such as comets, monstrous births, and swarms of locusts; with tortures, massacres, and other tales of cruelty; and with the pride of

[1] Leicester to Throckmorton, 22 July 1567; Elizabeth I to Throckmorton, 27 July and 11 Aug. 1567; Throckmorton to Leicester, 31 July 1567; Throckmorton to Elizabeth I, 9 and 22 Aug. 1567; Cecil to Throckmorton, 11 Aug. 1567; Bedford to Elizabeth I, 1 Sept. 1567; Elizabeth I to Bedford, 8 Sept. 1567; Drury to Cecil, 28 Oct. 1567; Elizabeth I to the Lord Wardens (Nov. 1567) (*Cal. For. Pap. Eliz.* viii. 1500, 1657, 1674, 1790, 1798; *Sc. Cal.* ii. 577, 580, 584, 588, 592, 593; Keith, ii. 702–6, 741–7).

women. The cruel punishments of the Roman law, the practice of the wives of the North German tribesmen of disembowelling their enemies, the pogroms of Jews in Germany in the Middle Ages—as well as Aventinus's denunciations of the Jews for the ritual murder of Christian children—are all marked without comment; but any account of a woman showing strength and exercising power brings forth marginal fulminations about the arrogance of women.

Far more than *The First Blast of the Trumpet*, these marginal notes show a deep-rooted hatred of women. In the *First Blast*, like the *Admonition to England* and all the other pamphlets that he wrote in Dieppe and Geneva, Knox resorted to vitriolic denunciation in order to advocate a political policy; in the notes to Aventinus's *Annals of Bavaria*, as in the later additions to the *History of the Reformation in Scotland*, there is only petty spite for no ulterior motive. Knox not only makes two references to 'unhappy Mary', the Queen of Scots, but castigates every woman —from Zenobia, Queen of Palmyra, in the third century to Kunigunda, the wife of King Otakar of Bohemia, in the thirteenth century—for acts of bravery and self-assertion that he would have praised as valour in a man; and the account of the execution of the aged Brunhilda, Queen of Austrasia, in 613, who was torn to pieces by wild horses after she had been ultimately defeated in a long and savage civil war, wins Knox's warm approval with the comment: 'The cruel punishment was just.'[1]

If the *First Blast* was written largely as political propaganda, Knox had now come to believe his own propaganda. Margaret Stewart had a far less balanced, and a far more thwarted, husband than Marjory Bowes.

1 'Iustum supplicium'. See Aventinus, *Annalium Boiorum* (copy in Edinburgh University Library), title-page, and notes on pp. 48, 138, 181, 219, 278, 398, 712, 717, 776, 835; and see J. P. Finlayson, 'A volume associated with John Knox' (*S.H.R.* xxxviii. 170–2).

CHAPTER XXIV

The Murder of Moray and the Civil War

THE Parliament of December 1567 marked the triumph of Knox and the Church. An unprecedented number of statutes were passed, no less than ninety-two being enacted during the fortnight that Parliament was in session. Nineteen of these concerned religion, and established the Protestant religion and Church more firmly than before. Before Parliament met, the Privy Council, in accordance with the usual practice, appointed a number of Lords of the Articles, whose duty was to recommend bills to Parliament for enactment in the forthcoming session. Contrary to all precedent, four ministers of the Church—Spottiswood, Knox, Craig, and Lindsay—were chosen to sit with the fourteen Lords of the Articles when legislation affecting the Church was being considered.

The statutes concerning religion, which had been approved by Knox and his colleagues and the Lords of the Articles on 3 December, twelve days before Parliament met, re-enacted the legislation of the Parliament of 1560. The legal doubt that had existed as to the validity of these statutes, which had never been ratified by Mary, was now removed; their legality could not be challenged by anyone who accepted James VI as the lawful King. Other statutes enacted that the existing Protestant Church of Scotland was 'the only true and holy Church of Jesus Christ within this realm', and that the Confession of Faith of 1560 was to be the official religious doctrine of the nation. It was enacted that, in future, kings were to swear at their coronation that they would govern Scotland according to the Word of God revealed in the New and Old Testaments. No one was henceforth to hold any public office in the State unless he professed the religion as now established, and no one was permitted to instruct the young in schools unless he had been approved by the Church. For the first time, fornication was made a criminal offence to be punished in the criminal courts, as well as by the censures of the Church

Sessions. It was henceforth to be punished by fine, or by imprisonment and the pillory for those who could not afford to pay the fine. For the third offence the fornicators were to be punished by a fine of £100, or by imprisonment for twenty-four days on bread and water, ducking in the deepest and foulest pond, and banishment from the town.

Most important of all, satisfactory provision was made at last for the financial support of the Protestant Church. A statute enacted that the whole of the thirds of ecclesiastical benefices, which now in nearly every case meant lands held by lay nobles and lairds, were to be available for the Church, instead of half of it going to the Crown: only after the needs of the Church had been satisfied was the balance to be paid to the Crown. It was also decided, for the first time, that the collection of the thirds should be administered by collectors appointed by the Church, instead of by government officials who were ready to help the more powerful landowners to evade their share of the burden of paying the thirds.

Apart from the legislation affecting the Church, the other enactments, with which Knox and the ministers had not been concerned, included Acts that ratified the abdication of Mary and the coronation of James VI, the appointment of Moray as Regent, and all other acts done by the lords since Darnley's murder. Mary was officially accused, for the first time, of complicity in the murder of Darnley, the Act for 'the retention of our Sovereign Lord's mother's person' declaring that some private letters written by her to Bothwell showed that she was an accessory to the murder of the King, her lawful husband, 'and therefore justly deserves whatsoever has been done to her in any time bygone, or that shall be used towards her, for the said cause in time coming, which shall be used by advice of the nobility'. Mary bitterly resented the fact that Parliament should have condemned her without permitting her to speak or write one word in her defence; but the unlimited powers to punish Mary, which had been given to the lords in advance, were likely to remain a dead letter in practice as long as Elizabeth resolutely continued to support her. A bill providing that women were ineligible to hold the public authority in the realm was approved by the Lords of the Articles, but was not proceeded with in Parliament.[1]

[1] For the legislation of the Parliament of 3–29 Dec. 1567, see *Acts Parl. Scot.* iii. 3–44. For a Catholic comment on it, see the report to Archbishop Beaton, sent to

The revolution of 1567 completed the victory of the Reformation; but the enthusiasm of 1559 and 1560 had gone. In those days the whole country had been seized with moral fervour; men and women of all classes had publicly confessed their sins before the congregation, promising eagerly to reform their way of life.[1] Now the Calvinist discipline was quietly and sullenly accepted without resistance or enthusiasm, as the Church Sessions sat, week after week, to punish sexual offences, immodesty in dress, and trading on Sundays. The Church courts succeeded, with the resolute support of the merchants on the burgh councils, in enforcing obedience, in introducing a drab uniformity, and in suppressing whatever colour and gaiety existed in Scottish life. Many of the people perhaps yearned for the old days, when a handful of idealists were burnt, and the ordinary man and woman were left in peace by the Church authorities, rather than this new régime that had been imposed upon Scotland in the interests of the foreign policy of the great powers. But under the efficient and determined Protestant Church, which had replaced the rotten Catholic edifice, no one could escape the systematic religious indoctrination and the rigid control of every aspect of life, except by joining the lawless elements of the population. This was now a more risky operation than previously, for Moray as Regent enforced law and order far more ruthlessly than any government had done for many years in Scotland; but though he hanged thieves wholesale in the Border regions, all over Scotland crime continued largely unchecked.

Even the most eminent leaders of the Protestant Church seem to have been less enthusiastic in practice than in theory about the new society that they had established in Scotland in imitation of Geneva, the most perfect school of Christ; for many of them showed a marked preference for life in England. In 1565 Goodman left Scotland and returned to England, and lived there for the rest of his life, as a vicar and archdeacon of the Church of England, although he was obliged to recant some of his extreme Protestant opinions, and his doctrine of revolution, before Archbishop Parker and Cox, and was forbidden to preach. In 1566 Willock went to England, and overstayed his leave for so long

di Borgia, the Provincial-General of the Jesuits in Rome (probably in Dec. 1567), in Stevenson-Nau, pp. 147–54. For the thirds, see Donaldson's Introduction to *Accounts of the Collectors of Thirds of Benefices*, pp. xxix-xxxiii. See also Mary Queen of Scots' memorandum to all Christian Princes (June 1568) (Labanoff, vii. 321–2).

[1] Randolph to Killigrew, 20 June 1560 (*Sc. Cal.* i. 826).

that in January 1568 Knox, on the instructions of the General Assembly, wrote to Willock, ordering him to return to Scotland and resume his pastoral duties at once.[1] Willock complied with the summons, but soon afterwards left Scotland again, and ended his days as Rector of Loughborough, a benefice which he had been granted in the days of Edward VI. Knox himself sent both his sons to be educated in England, and used his influence to enable them to be naturalized as English denizens; and he was filled with a longing to return to England and live there with the survivors of his old congregation of Geneva. On 14 February 1568, he wrote to his friend, John Wood, who had been sent by Moray on a diplomatic mission to England.

> God comfort that dispersed little flock, amongst whom I once lived with quietness of conscience and contentment of heart; and amongst whom I would be content to end my days, if so it might stand with God's good pleasure. For seeing it hath pleased His majesty, above all men's expectation, to prosper that work for the performing whereof I left that company, I would even as gladly return to them, if they stood in need of my labours, as ever I was glad to be delivered from the rage of mine enemies. I can give you no reason that I should so desire, other than that my heart so thirsteth.

But despite his satisfaction with his achievement in Scotland, he was anxious about the future. He feared the outcome of the civil war in France, which had again broken out, and of the real or imagined directives of the Council of Trent to suppress Protestantism everywhere in Europe; and he wrote to Wood: 'In my opinion, England and Scotland have both no less cause to fear than the faithful in France.'[2]

His fears were confirmed when, on 2 May 1568, Mary escaped from Lochleven and took refuge with the Hamiltons. She was joined by the greater part of the Scottish nobility—nine earls, nine bishops, and eighteen lords—and within a few days had raised an army of 6,000 men. Though she offered to pardon all her rebels who submitted to her, she drafted a proclamation, in which she denounced nineteen of her leading enemies in very bitter language

[1] The General Assembly to Willock (2 Jan. 1567/8); Knox to John Wood, 14 Feb. 1567/8 and 10 Sept. 1568 (*Booke of the Universall Kirk*, i. 120–2; *Works*, vi. 445–6, 559–60); see also Willock to Cecil, 29 May 1562; Randolph to Cecil, 30 May 1562 (*Sc. Cal.* i. 1108, 1109).

[2] Knox to John Wood, 14 Feb. 1567/8 (*Works*, vi. 558).

for their treason and personal ingratitude. Beginning with Morton and Moray, 'that beastly traitor', a 'bastard gotten in shameful adultery', she proceeded to castigate 'the mischeant unworthy traitor' Lethington, and 'the ingrate traitor' James Balfour, who had been promoted from being a galley slave to the office of Clerk of Register; John Hay; the Bishop of Orkney; the 'hellhounds' Cesford and Andrew Ker of Faldonside; the 'shameless butcher' George Douglas; and 'those crafty, perjured foxes and open traitors . . . of the progeny of cruel Cain', Wishart of Pittarrow, Balnavis, McGill, Haliburton, Robert Richardson, John Wood, and 'the rest of that pestiferous faction'. In this lengthy catalogue of 'godless traitors, common murderers and throat-cutters', whom no prince could pardon, there is no mention of Knox, or of any of the other ministers of the Church. Mary could not have overlooked the existence of the preacher who had been demanding her death in the pulpit of St. Giles's during the previous summer; but again, as in her conflict with the rebel lords of 1565, she was anxious not to fight on the religious issue. She therefore contented herself with a passing reference to 'mischievous ministers' whose painted sermons, coloured with holiness and hypocrisy, sought not only to seduce the people, but to delude God Himself; for she hoped to rally many Protestants, especially the Hamiltons, to her support. Mary now relied, against Moray, on the help of the great family which she had treated with such disfavour when she was in power, and the leader of the revolt of 1565 was referred to, in the proclamation, as 'our dearest father adoptive, the good Duke of Châtelherault'.[1]

Mary's army was defeated at Langside, near Glasgow, by an inferior force under Moray, Morton, and Grange. On 17 May, Mary fled into England without applying for a safe-conduct, but relying on the friendship which Elizabeth had shown to her during the previous summer. In England she was treated with the respect due to her rank, but was held in honourable custody for nineteen years, until she ended her life in a manner that was inconceivable in 1568. As soon as she arrived in England, Mary asked Elizabeth to restore her to her throne by force, or, if she was not prepared to do this, to permit her to leave England to visit some other prince who would help her. Elizabeth announced that she would

[1] Mary Queen of Scots' Proclamation (May 1568) (Fraser, *The Lennox*, ii. 437–47, see especially pp. 439–42; and see Hay Fleming, *Mary Queen of Scots*, pp. 487–9).

restore Mary as soon as she was convinced that Mary was innocent of Darnley's murder, and provided that a suitable agreement could be reached which would safeguard the lives and interests of the Scottish Protestant lords who had deposed Mary.

In August 1568, the Queen's lords assembled an army in the north and west, and prepared to overthrow Moray's government in Edinburgh and re-establish Mary as Queen; but Elizabeth persuaded Mary to order them to agree to a truce while Elizabeth negotiated a peaceful settlement.[1] By agreeing to the truce in order to retain Elizabeth's goodwill, Mary made her greatest mistake, for never again did her followers in Scotland have victory within their grasp; and her hopes that Elizabeth would restore her to her throne were finally shattered after three years of disappointments. Mary, who was in no position to bargain, agreed to all Elizabeth's conditions for her restoration; but Cecil was determined, in the last resort, not to allow the Scottish Protestants to be destroyed, and while Mary was encouraged with false hopes, at every crisis England intervened decisively on the side of the King's lords. The King's lords, appreciating the situation, were continually raising their price in their negotiations with Elizabeth, though they knew that they depended on her for support, and from time to time were filled with fear that she would conclude a bargain with Mary at their expense.

Knox shared the fears of the King's lords, and watched the development of the political negotiations with great apprehension. He was still physically active, though at the age of 54 he was no longer in good health. He preached regularly in St. Giles's, three times during the week as well as twice on Sundays, and continued to play a leading part in the affairs of the Church. Although he held no official position except minister of the congregation of Edinburgh, he acted as a kind of extraordinary superintendent in several dioceses, travelling through Ayrshire and Fife on the instructions of the General Assembly in order to supervise and discipline the ministers of whom adverse reports had been received, as well as preaching all over the south of Scotland. His enemies regarded his activities with dread. When James Beaton, the Archbishop of Glasgow, who was in France representing Mary as her ambassador at the French Court, was sued for £1,000 in a property dispute in the law courts in Glasgow, his Chamberlain,

[1] Mary Queen of Scots to Elizabeth I, 6 Aug. 1568 (*Sc. Cal.* ii. 754).

Thomas Archibald, wrote to the Archbishop in October 1569 that he would have no chance to win the case, because 'John Knox is against your Lordship extremely', and Knox had great influence over the court. Knox was now fully satisfied with the government. He had quite forgiven Moray for his former collaboration with Mary, and warmly praised his strong rule as Regent.[1]

In his spare time, not surprisingly perhaps, Knox quarrelled with his landlord about who was liable to carry out the repairs of his house. When he returned to Edinburgh from England in 1567, he moved into a new house which was situated, like the house where he had lived for several years after 1560, in Trunk Close. As the landlord refused to do the repairs, the burgh council withheld Knox's rent, and repeatedly directed the landlord to carry out the repairs. Eventually, the burgh council carried out the repairs themselves, and paid the rent due from Knox to the landlord after deducting the cost of the repairs.[2]

Knox was as usual very well informed about political events and diplomatic negotiations, and expressed his anxieties and uttered his warnings in letters to his old friends. On 10 September 1568, he wrote to John Wood in England and warned him about the activities of Châtelherault, who was intriguing at the French court. 'We look daily for the arrival of the Duke and his Frenchmen, sent to restore Satan to his kingdom in the person of his dearest lieutenant, sent, I say, to repress religion, not from the King of France, but from the Cardinal of Lorraine in favour of his dearest niece. Let England take heed, for assuredly their neighbours' houses are on fire.' He urged Wood to persuade the English to help Moray's government, especially with money; for without English aid they would be unable to resist their Scottish enemies, 'unless God work miraculously', and much less could they withstand 'the puissance of France, the substance of the Pope, and the malice of the House of Guise'. He said that the aim of the enemy was to murder the Regent, who had already had one very narrow escape, and to cut the throat of the innocent King.[3]

[1] *Edinburgh Burgh Records*, iii. 129, 131, 183–4 (31 Dec. 1561, 8 Apr. 1562, 18 Aug. 1564); *Booke of the Universall Kirk*, i. 37, 57, 73, 123, 130 (28 June 1563, 25 June 1564, 28 Dec. 1565, and 1 and 9 July 1568); Archibald to Archbishop Beaton, 30 Oct. 1569 (*Papers illustrative of the reigns of Queen Mary and James VI*, p. 37).

[2] *Edinburgh Burgh Records*, iii. 258, 260 (19 Nov. 1568 and 4 Mar. 1568/9); see also Hume Brown, *John Knox*, ii. 317.

[3] Knox to Wood, 10 Sept. 1568 (*Works*, vi. 561).

In Scotland itself, the situation for the King's lords improved during the next twelve months. Moray succeeded in re-establishing his authority in Scotland by firmness and trickery. Huntly submitted to him, and Châtelherault and Lord Herries—the former Master of Maxwell—after being invited to Edinburgh under a promise of safe conduct in order to discuss a peaceful settlement, were imprisoned in Edinburgh Castle. The danger to the King's party came from England, where Leslie, Mary's ambassador, made good progress in his negotiations with Elizabeth and Cecil, and it began to appear as if Elizabeth had finally decided to restore Mary to the throne. Meanwhile, Moray and Lethington were secretly planning to marry Mary to the Duke of Norfolk. By the summer of 1569 it was widely believed in Scotland that Mary was about to return as Queen, and Knox's hatred of Mary rose higher than ever. He could do nothing to influence the dangerous negotiations that were taking place at the English court, and his political impotence and his declining health increased his bitterness. On 19 August 1569, he wrote to a friend in England in a state of great depression, and told him that he had been expecting death from day to day for the last seven years. 'I see England become more foolish than foolish Scotland,' he wrote, 'for foolish Scotland would not obey the mouth of God, when He had delivered that vile adulteress and cruel murderer of her own husband in their own hands, to have suffered as her iniquity deserved; and therefore now sob they for the foolish pity.' But England had been equally foolish, because the 'uniting of the two realms by marriage of that wicked woman upon the man to whom I wish a better luck, is here divulged; which, being refused upon our part, we are boasted with fire and sword, and that wicked woman shall be placed in authority again'.[1]

In November 1569 the whole situation was changed by the outbreak of a formidable insurrection against Elizabeth in the north of England. The rebels, led by the Catholic Earls of Northumberland and Westmorland, declared that they were fighting to suppress heresy. They captured Durham, where they celebrated

[1] Moray to Forster, 15 Mar. 1568/9; Hunsdon to Cecil, 18 Apr. and 9 Aug. 1569; Herries to Elizabeth I, 5 July 1569; Herries to Moray (24 July 1569); John Douglas to Cecil, 15 Aug. 1569; Moray to Elizabeth I, 29 Oct. 1569; Duke of Norfolk's confession, 10 Nov. 1571 (*Cal. For. Pap. Eliz.* ix. 170, 374; *Sc. Cal.* ii. 1090, 1105, 1120, 1188; iv. 43; Haynes, pp. 514–15); Knox to a friend in England, 19 Aug. 1569 (*Works*, vi. 566–7).

mass in the cathedral and burned the Book of Common Prayer and the English Bible; but within a month they had fled before an army sent against them under the command of the Earl of Sussex. Large units of them crossed the frontier into Scotland, and sheltered with the Scottish Borderers. Elizabeth demanded that the rebels be rounded up and extradited by Moray's government; but the Borderers refused to hand them over to Moray, as it was a well-established tradition that the English and Scottish Borderers gave each other shelter and refuge across the Border when they were pursued by their own governments. Moray succeeded in capturing the Earl of Northumberland, but refused to hand him over to Elizabeth, retaining him instead as a prisoner in Lochleven Castle in order to use his surrender as a bargaining factor with Elizabeth. Northumberland was kept at Lochleven for more than two years, while Lord Lindsay and Douglas of Lochleven received payments for his keep from the Countess of Northumberland, who was in Flanders; but the English government's purse was deeper than Lady Northumberland's, and in May 1572 Northumberland was sold to the English authorities at Berwick for £10,000. He was beheaded in York. The other English rebels remained at large in the south of Scotland, and joined forces with Mary's supporters.

The rising in the north of England prompted Knox to write to Cecil on 2 January 1570. 'If ye strike not at the roots,' he wrote, 'the branches that appear to be broken will bud again (and that more quickly than men can believe) with greater force than we would wish.' This was perhaps a reference to Mary Queen of Scots, and a hint that Elizabeth should put her to death; but Knox's short letter is far from clear, perhaps because he was in a bad state of health. He signed himself 'John Knox with his one foot in the grave'. Later in the year he had a stroke, a kind of apoplexy, which deprived him of the power of speech. The rumour spread through Scotland and England that he had been struck dumb by the divine vengeance; but to the joy of his followers, he confounded his critics by making a complete recovery, and within a short time he was preaching regularly every Sunday, though at first he confined himself to this weekly sermon and did not preach on the weekdays.[1]

On Saturday, 21 January 1570, Moray was assassinated. He was

[1] Knox to Cecil, 2 Jan. 1569/70 (*Works*, vi. 568); Bannatyne, p. 62.

shot as he rode through the streets of Linlithgow, while returning from Dumbarton to Edinburgh, by James Hamilton of Bothwellhaugh, a nephew of the Archbishop of St. Andrews. Bothwellhaugh escaped through the garden of the Archbishop's house in Linlithgow, and mounted a horse which was waiting, saddled, for him there, and after spending the night in Châtelherault's castle at Hamilton, made his way to France. He was rewarded with a pension from Mary. According to Knox's servant, Richard Bannatyne, Knox had suspected that the Regent would be killed on his journey. He warned Moray that the Master of Graham was luring him to Dumbarton in order that he should be murdered. When Moray was at Stirling, on his way home from Dumbarton, Knox twice sent Bannatyne to the Countess of Moray to urge her to persuade her husband not to come through Linlithgow when he returned to Edinburgh. Bannatyne does not claim this as an example of Knox's prophetic powers, and it may be that the informants who so often supplied Knox with secret intelligence had told him details of the murder plot in advance. He often gave warnings about real and imaginary conspiracies to the English authorities.[1]

The King's supporters made great lamentation and propaganda over the death of the 'good Regent'. Moray died shortly before midnight in the house at Linlithgow to which he had been carried, and the news of the murder had reached Edinburgh before Knox preached his usual sermon on Sunday morning in St. Giles's. The only report of this sermon is that which was compiled by Calderwood eighty years later. According to Calderwood, Knox praised Moray warmly, and said that his only fault was that, out of foolish pity, he had not put Mary to death. He prayed that the two treasonable and cruel murders of Darnley and Moray might be punished, denounced Mary as the murderer of her own husband, and implored God to forgive Scotland and England for having spared 'the life of that most wicked woman'.[2]

Archbishop Spottiswood, who was the son of Knox's colleague, John Spottiswood, and became an Episcopalian Archbishop of St. Andrews in the reign of Charles I, tells another story

[1] Bothwellhaugh to Raulet, 18 Aug. (1570) (*H.M.C.*, *Cecil*, i. 1514); Mary Queen of Scots to Archbishop Beaton, 28 Aug. 1571 (Labanoff, iii. 354); Bannatyne, pp. 289–90; Hunsdon to Cecil, 26 Jan. 1569/70 (*Cal. For. Pap. Eliz.* ix. 640). See also Randolph to Cecil, 31 Aug. 1562 (*Sc. Cal.* i. 1136).

[2] Calderwood's manuscript (*Works*, vi. 568–70).

in connexion with this sermon of 22 January. He says that when Knox went into the pulpit to preach, he found a piece of paper there. He glanced at it as he began to preach, thinking that it was a request from some person that he should remember him in his prayers; but in fact it was an anonymous note containing the words: 'Take up the man whom you accounted another God, and consider the end whereto his ambition hath brought him.' The comment was mild compared with what Knox was in the habit of saying when his political opponents died; but Knox was shocked by the words. After reading the note, he put it down without any sign of emotion, and preached as if nothing had happened; but at the end of his sermon he said that although all men should lament the murder of Moray, 'there be some that rejoice in this wicked fact, making it the subject of their mirth; amongst whom there is one that hath caused a writing to be cast in this place, insulting upon that which is all good men's sorrow. This wicked man, whosoever he be, shall not go unpunished, and shall die where none shall be to lament him.'

The note had been written by Lethington's younger brother, Thomas Maitland. Thomas Maitland was in St. Giles's to hear the sermon, and when he returned home, he told his sister, Lady Trabrowne, what had transpired, and ridiculed Knox's prophecy; but she, who had previously tried to dissuade Thomas Maitland from writing the note to Knox, was most distressed and alarmed when she heard what Knox had said in his sermon. 'None of this man's denunciations', she said, 'are wont to prove idle, but have their own effect.' Two years later, Thomas Maitland, who was travelling in Europe as a student, died in Italy of a disease at the age of 22 without any of his acquaintances being near him, thus proving the truth of Knox's prophecy. Calderwood tells the story a little differently; but Spottiswood states that he heard his version from Lady Trabrowne herself. As she was sympathetic to Knox and the King's lords, and disapproved of her brother's action, it would not be at all surprising if in later years she slightly enlarged upon Knox's words, so as to turn his general words of condemnation into a specific prophecy of Thomas Maitland's death in Italy.[1]

A few days after Moray's death, Thomas Maitland wrote a longer and more formidable attack on Moray and Knox. He published an account of an imaginary conversation between Moray,

[1] Spottiswood, ii. 121–2; Calderwood, ii. 525.

Lord Lindsay, Wishart of Pittarrow, John Wood, McGill, Haliburton, and Knox. Maitland's tract was anonymous, and claimed to be written by a man who had overheard the conversation while he was lying on a bed in the same room, unknown to the Regent and his companions. The pamphlet, which contains brilliant imitations of the style of speaking of all the participants in the conversation, and especially of Knox, could be interpreted either as a satire or as a verbatim report of a conversation that had actually taken place, according to the degree of sophistication of the reader. It described how Knox and his colleagues urged Moray to murder the infant James VI and make himself King. Knox points out that there was nothing to hope for from the King, as he was born of such wicked parents, and that kings should not succeed to the throne by the right of hereditary succession. Knox then declares that, having shown in his book *The First Blast of the Trumpet* that women have no right to rule, he has just completed another book, which is about to be printed, in which he proves that bastards can inherit the Crown.

The pamphlet was privately circulated among the Queen's lords and their friends, who greatly enjoyed the satire; but a copy came into the hands of Alice Sandilands, the wife of the laird of Ormiston, who was an admirer of Knox. She brought the pamphlet to Knox, and asked him if the allegations were true. Knox replied: 'Ye shall know my answer afterwards', and next day, when he preached, he said that whoever was the writer of the pamphlet, it was the Devil, the father of lies, who had inspired it; and he declared: 'The things by them affirmed, and by others believed, are as false as God is true.'[1]

The murder of Moray embittered Scottish politics, and was exploited by all the King's supporters who favoured a ruthless policy towards the Hamiltons and the other supporters of the Queen. After the victory at Langside, Moray had released most of his prisoners and pardoned them. One of these pardoned prisoners was Bothwellhaugh, who according to Calderwood was released, with some other prisoners, after Knox had interceded with the Regent on their behalf. But any gratitude that Bothwellhaugh might have felt towards Moray disappeared when one of the King's supporters took his castle, which Moray had declared to be forfeited, and according to one story turned Bothwellhaugh's

[1] Bannatyne, pp. 5–14.

wife out into the fields in her nightshift in the middle of a winter's night;[1] but though this personal injury, for which Bothwellhaugh considered Moray to be responsible, was one of the motives for the murder, the King's men cited the case of Bothwellhaugh as a proof of the folly of pursuing a merciful policy towards their opponents. As soon as Moray died, the King's men burned Archbishop Hamilton's house in Linlithgow from which Bothwellhaugh had fired his hagbut, as a reprisal for the crime.[2]

A few days before the murder of Moray, Knox had been approached by Gavin Hamilton, the lay Abbot of Kilwinning, and other members of his family. They asked Knox to intervene with Moray in favour of Châtelherault, who was still in prison in Edinburgh Castle, and to use his good offices on behalf of other Hamiltons. Knox replied that he would have nothing to do with the Archbishop of St. Andrews as long as he continued to be a Papist, but was prepared to do all he could to help any other Hamilton who acknowledged James VI as King. A week or so later, a few days after the assassination of Moray, Gavin Hamilton again approached Knox; but this time, Knox refused to speak with him, and sent him a message, telling him: 'I have not the Regent to make suit unto for the Hamiltons.'[3]

On Tuesday, 14 February, Moray's funeral took place in St. Giles's. The Scottish Protestants, following the Calvinist practice in Geneva, condemned excessive pomp and mourning at funerals. The Book of Discipline had prohibited funeral sermons, on the grounds that it would lead to the glorification of the deceased at the funerals of the wealthy, and to invidious distinctions between the funerals of the rich and the poor; and it also directed that no one was to be buried in the church itself, but only in the churchyard. But these rules were suspended for this great propaganda demonstration against the Hamiltons. Moray's corpse was brought from Holyroodhouse to St. Giles's, being carried by eight nobles, including Morton, Glencairn, Lindsay, and Ochiltre, while Grange walked in front of the coffin carrying Moray's banner.

[1] *Historie of King James the Sext*, pp. 45–46. This story, in its traditional form, is untrue; see Laing, 'Notice respecting the Monument of the Regent Earl of Moray' (*Proceedings of the Society of Antiquaries of Scotland*, vi. 55). But Laing hardly succeeds in disproving the whole story.

[2] Gate and Drury to Hunsdon, 26 Jan. 1569/70; Proclamation of the Scottish Privy Council (17 Feb. 1570) (*Sc. Cal.* iii. 94, 124); Buchanan, *History*, ii. 363; Pitscottie, ii. 225.

[3] Bannatyne, pp. 14–15.

Moray was buried within the church, in the presence of all the nobility who supported the King, and a congregation of 3,000 people; and Knox preached a sermon. His text was: 'Blessed are they that die in the Lord', and he moved the congregation to tears.[1]

The propaganda continued after the funeral. Ballads were circulated praising Moray and denouncing the Hamiltons; and Knox received letters from his friends in England which encouraged him to exacerbate the hatred. Willock, who had found some excuse to return to England at the first opportunity, wrote to Knox early in March, expressing his horror of the crime of 'these bloody beasts' the Hamiltons; and Goodman wrote to him, urging the Scottish lords to revenge the foul, devilish murder on the whole tribe of Hamiltons, as the wrong committed against the wife of the Levite was avenged against the Benjamites. Moray's half-brother, Douglas of Lochleven, demanded that the Hamiltons should be punished for the murder, and the King's lords called a conference in Edinburgh on 4 March to discuss what measures could be taken against them. All over the country, men by the name of Hamilton were attacked by those neighbours with whom they had a boundary dispute, who killed or mutilated them, and burned their houses, ostensibly to revenge the death of the good Regent. The Hamiltons decided to take action to forestall their enemies. Three days after Moray's funeral, they assembled their forces at Linlithgow. It was the beginning of three years of civil war between the King's lords and the Queen's lords.[2]

[1] The Book of Discipline, ix [4] (Knox, *History*, ii. 319–20); Randolph to Cecil, 22 Feb. 1569/70 (*Sc. Cal.* iii. 130; *Works*, vi. 570–1); Calderwood, ii. 525–6; *Diurnal of Occurrents*, p. 158. See also Contract for the erection of Moray's tomb, 20 Feb. 1569/70, and for Grange's mourning, 26 Jan. 1569/70 (*H.M.C. 6th R.* 646, and *Proceedings of the Society of Antiquaries*, vi. 52–53).

[2] Willock to Knox (Feb. 1570); Goodman to Knox (Feb. 1570) (Bannatyne, pp. 21–22); Gate and Drury to Hunsdon, 26 Jan. 1569/70; Memorandum to the Lords of the Convention (14 Feb. 1569/70); Buchanan (?), 'Exhortation to the Lords of the King's Council against the Hamiltons' (17 Feb. 1569/70); Proclamation of Scottish Privy Council (17 Feb. 1569/70); Randolph to Cecil, 1 Mar. 1569/70; William Douglas and Moray's kin to Scottish Privy Council (Mar. 1570); Proclamation of Scottish Privy Council, 8 May 1570 (*Sc. Cal.* iii. 94, 120, 123, 124, 142, 151, 221); List of Hamiltons who have been killed or forfeited (*c.* 1570) (*Registrum Honoris de Morton*, i. 65–68); Bannatyne, pp. 15–16. For the ballads, see, e.g., 'Ye mountains mourn, ye valleys weep'; 'The Regent's tragedy'; 'The deploration of the cruel murder of James, Earl of Moray'; 'The King's Complaint'; 'The poisoned shot'; 'The wholesome admonition', and others. Some of these are printed in *Satirical Poems of the time of the Reformation*.

In April 1570 the Queen's forces marched into Edinburgh. Then Elizabeth intervened. Her ambassador in Scotland and her officials in Berwick reported that the King's lords would collapse within a few weeks unless they were supported by English troops; and in the middle of April, the Earl of Sussex crossed the Border with 4,000 men, with orders to punish the English rebels and all the Scots who had supported them, and to support the King's lords. Sussex obeyed his instructions to spare the lands of the King's supporters, although his grandfather had warned him never to trust any Scotsman; but he devastated the Border districts. He boasted that every Scottish child would remember this lesson for the rest of his life, and Lethington complained that Sussex's armies had wrought more destruction in Scotland than any English army had done for a hundred years. After devastating the south, Sussex chased the Queen's lords from Edinburgh to the west, and burned Hamilton. The Hamiltons and the Queen's men made no attempt to resist.[1]

The King's lords welcomed Sussex as an ally who had come to help them suppress a revolt. They raised a force of 4,000 soldiers to march at the side of the English army; but the devastations roused the anger of many Scots. The Queen's lords denounced the King's lords as traitors who had helped the old enemies to invade Scotland. In the wake of the English army came Lennox. Lennox, who had returned to England after Darnley's death, was chosen by the King's lords and a Parliament of their supporters to be the new Regent. The King's lords had secretly informed Elizabeth that they would elect as Regent anyone whom she chose to nominate; and Elizabeth chose the former leader of the English and Scottish Catholics. Lady Lennox remained at the English court to intrigue on her husband's behalf, and to act as a kind of hostage.[2]

[1] Sussex to Elizabeth I, 4 Feb. 1568/9, and 23 Apr. and 1 and 4 May 1570; Sussex to Cecil, 10 Apr. 1570; Lethington to Sussex, 2 June 1570; Randolph to Sussex, 26 June 1570 (*Cal. For. Pap. Eliz.* ix. 96; *Sc. Cal.* iii. 190, 209, 213, 300 [1], 317).

[2] The King's Lords' Instructions to Pitcairn, 1 May 1570; the King's Lords' Instructions to Colville (5 May 1570); Morton to Elizabeth I, 5 May 1570; Lennox to Cecil, 11 May and 20 July 1570; Sussex to Cecil, 28 May and 16 June 1570; Morton to Pitcairn, 30 May 1570; Proclamation of the Queen's Lords, 13 June 1570; Report from Scotland, 19 June 1570; Lennox to Elizabeth I, 20 July 1570; Lennox to Lady Lennox, 16 Sept. 1570 (*Sc. Cal.* iii. 208, 214–15, 230, 262, 264, 288, 295, 302, 368–9, 469).

The appointment of Lennox as Regent caused more resentment in Scotland; for though the King's lords claimed that Lennox, as the King's grandfather, was the most suitable choice, the people remembered that Lennox had lived for twenty years at the English court, had taken the oath of allegiance as an English subject, and had formerly been attainted as a traitor by the Scottish Parliament. Lennox, as Regent, issued a proclamation denying that he was a sworn subject of Elizabeth, and ordered that anyone who said so was to be punished with death.[1]

The Queen's men, who proclaimed their allegiance to Mary as their Queen, included the Gordons in the north and the Hamiltons in the west, and most of the Scottish nobility, including Lord Home, Lord Herries, and the Earl of Argyll, who had played so prominent a part in the revolution of 1559. The robber lairds of the Border also supported Mary. Morton and the Douglases, and most of the lairds of central Scotland, supported Lennox. In the towns the burgh councils and the merchants supported Lennox, while many of the craft guilds and poorer classes sympathized with Mary's followers. The Queen's lords were organized and directed by Lethington. Like the Hamiltons, Lethington acted, not out of devotion to the Catholic religion or to Mary, or even out of a desire for personal power or gain, but simply out of an instinct of self-preservation. Shortly before Moray's death, Lethington had been accused in the Privy Council of having been an accessory to the murder of Darnley, and was imprisoned in Edinburgh Castle to await his trial. The post of Captain of the Castle had been entrusted to Grange. Grange had a personal loyalty to Moray; as late as March 1571, Moray's widow was writing to Grange, and addressing him as 'truest friend'. But after Moray's murder he was won over by Lethington, who persuaded him to release Châtelherault and Lord Herries, as well as Lethington himself, from imprisonment in the castle, and to adopt an attitude of neutrality between the King's lords and the Queen's lords. From this position, Grange soon passed to active support for the Queen's lords.[2]

[1] Proclamation of the Scottish Privy Council (10 Aug. 1570 (?)) (*Reg. P.C.S.* xiv. 69–71); Huntly to Hay, 31 July 1570; Proclamation of James VI, 5 Aug. 1570; Drury to the Council, 23 May 1571; Drury to Burghley, 5 and 30 Sept. 1571 (*Sc. Cal.* iii. 397, 402 [1], 758, 959; *Cal. For. Pap. Eliz.* ix. 1994).

[2] Lady Moray to Grange, 7 Mar. 1570/1 (*H.M.C. 6th R.* 651–2); Grange to Randolph, 26 Apr. 1570 (*Sc. Cal.* iii. 193).

The fighting between King's men and Queen's men, which contemporaries honoured with the name of a civil war, consisted largely of more or less organized raids, murders, and robberies committed by the supporters of the one side against the other. They attacked the houses of their opponents, destroyed their crops, and seized their rents. Many men, like Knox's brother-in-law, the Master of Ochiltre, were shot at in their houses through the window by hagbutters in the street.[1] Occasionally, the two sides met in battle, but there were never more than two or three hundred men engaged on either side. The King's forces consisted of hagbutters and men of war hired with English money; the Queen's, of hagbutters and men of war hired with French money, and supplemented by bands of Border robbers, and the English northern rebels who had fled to Scotland. The King's lords treated their opponents as traitors and rebels, and usually hanged their prisoners without trial; the Queen's lords, most of whom had at one time sworn allegiance to James VI and were really only fighting for a compromise peace that would safeguard their own lives and property, did not retaliate. They and their Borderers engaged in robbery and spasmodic murders rather than in the systematic executions carried out by Lennox and Morton.

Meanwhile, in England, Elizabeth was still negotiating with Mary, largely in order to please the French government, with whom she was negotiating an alliance against Spain. These negotiations with Mary, which so alarmed the King's lords, in fact assisted them; for Mary was continually restraining her supporters in Scotland in order not to antagonize Elizabeth. Elizabeth repeatedly arranged truces in the fighting in Scotland, usually when the Queen's men were on the point of gaining some advantage. Both sides violated the truces. The violations by the King's lords brought protests from Elizabeth; the violations by the Queen's lords brought threats of immediate English military intervention.[2]

The civil war divided the Protestant Church of Scotland, for there were Protestants as well as Catholics among the Queen's party. Huntly and the Gordons, who ruled everything north of

[1] Randolph to Sussex, 9 Aug. 1570 (*Sc. Cal.* iii. 406).

[2] For violations of the truce, see the complaints of the Queen's lords, and the reply and complaints of the King's lords (Dec. 1570 and Jan. 1570/1) (*Sc. Cal.* iii. 594–5, 608).

Angus in Mary's name, were Catholics; but Châtelherault and all the Hamiltons except the Archbishop of St. Andrews were Protestants, as were Lethington and Grange, and most of the rest of the Queen's men. Lethington wrote to Mary that he had hopes of winning over several Protestant ministers, though he thought that Knox would be 'inflexible'. But while the Queen's lords continually assured Elizabeth of their friendship towards England and their gratitude to her for her assistance in overthrowing Popery in Scotland, they were in secret communication both with the French government and with Alva in Brussels. Here the possession of Dumbarton Castle, which was held by Lord Fleming and Archbishop Hamilton for the Queen, was of vital importance. This potential foreign bridgehead in the British Isles was a menace to Protestantism in both Scotland and England.[1]

The General Assembly in June 1570 came out strongly in support of the King's lords, ordering all ministers to pray for the King on pain of excommunication.[2] Knox was one of the keenest supporters of this policy; but the Church was not united on the issue. The Protestants in the Queen's party claimed that the Church must pray for Mary as Queen, praying that her sins should be forgiven and that she should see the error of her ways and convert to Protestantism. Only a handful of the Protestant clergy adopted this attitude; but a larger and continually increasing number of ministers wished to be neutral between the two factions, and to devote themselves to religious teaching and the enforcement of the moral law without taking sides in the political struggle. Knox denounced this attitude; he argued that the primary duty of the ministers was to expose the sin of those who supported Mary and the traitors who resisted the King's authority. With his usual ruthlessness and political clear-sightedness, he saw only the fundamental reality of the situation. The struggle between King's men and Queen's men was a struggle between Elizabeth and Philip II, between Protestantism and Catholicism. Any Protestant who

[1] Lethington to Mary Queen of Scots, 20 Sept. 1569; Proclamation of the Queen's lords (Apr. 1570); John Gordon to Elizabeth I, 18 Apr. 1570; Châtelherault to Alva, (10) Aug. 1570; Randolph to (Hunsdon), (25) Aug. 1570 (wrongly dated 5 Aug.); Lennox to Cecil, 7 Sept. 1570; Examination of Leslie, 13 May 1571 (*Sc. Cal.* ii. 1142; iii. 181, 184, 408, 432, 444, 740). For the Spanish view of the importance of the struggle in Scotland, see Guerau de Spes to Philip II, 21 Dec. 1571 (*Span. Cal. Eliz.* ii. 296).

[2] *Booke of the Universall Kirk*, i. 177–8 (July 1570).

deserted the good cause and supported the Hamiltons and the Castilians in Edinburgh, whether he acted from family loyalty, from Scottish patriotism, from hatred of the former Catholic, Lennox, or from disgust at the cruelties and moral degeneration of the King's lords, was in Knox's eyes a traitor who deserved to be hanged.

In Edinburgh Castle, Grange watched the actions of the King's lords with increasing anxiety. He seems to have been largely influenced by his suspicion of Lennox and of English domination over Scotland, though his opponents claimed that Lethington won him over by a promise that he would be appointed Prior of St. Andrews if the Queen's men won. Grange became further incensed in August 1570, when Lennox, in a sudden raid, captured Brechin, which was held by a garrison of mercenaries engaged by Huntly, and hanged thirty-four members of the garrison after their surrender, though he spared one man who bought his pardon from him with a payment of £1,000. But it was not until Christmas that Grange irrevocably joined the Queen's side in connexion with an incident that involved him in a clash with Knox.[1]

Grange's cousin, John Kirkcaldy, was set upon in Dunfermline by the servants of some lairds who disliked him, and was beaten in the face and on the head with batons. Soon afterwards, Grange heard that one of the assailants was in Leith, and he sent six soldiers from the castle to attack the man and beat him likewise with batons. The soldiers came upon their victim on the shore at Leith, and duly beat him up; but one of them exceeded his instructions, and struck the man with the anchor of one of the ships moored on the shore, and slew him. The watch then arrived, and the soldiers fled back to the castle; but one of them was

1 For Grange's attitude, see Grange to Randolph, 16 and 26 Apr. 1570; Randolph to Cecil, 17 Apr. and 2 May 1570; Morton to Randolph, 25 Apr. 1570; Sussex to Grange, 26 Apr. and 1 May 1570; Grange to Sussex, 29 Apr. and 3 May 1570; Randolph to Grange, 1 May 1570; Sussex to Grange and Lethington, 4 May 1570; Sussex to Cecil, 6 Aug. 1570; Elizabeth I to Drury, 20 May 1571 (*Sc. Cal.* iii. 183 and enclosure, 192, 193, 210, 211, 213 (enclosures (3), (4), (5), (6), and (10)), 399, 753); Grange to Lady Moray, 20 May 1570 (*H.M.C. 6th R.* 650). For the King's lords' propagandists' view of Grange and Lethington, see Robert Sempill's poem 'The Crooked Leads the Blind'. For the raid of Brechin, see Randolph to Sussex, 7, 12, 14, 16, and 17 Aug. 1570; Lethington to Leslie, 15 Aug. 1570; Sussex to Cecil, 16 Aug. 1570; Lennox to Cecil, 20 Aug. 1570; Leslie's memorandum, 1 Sept. 1570 (*Sc. Cal.* iii. 404 [3], 410, 415, 417, 419, 419 [1], 422, 426, 437).

captured, and imprisoned in the tolbooth of Edinburgh. Grange decided to set him free. On the evening of 21 December 1570, he marched down from the castle with a band of men, and in a carefully planned operation broke open the gate of the tolbooth and freed his soldier and all the other prisoners, whom he enlisted in the garrison of the castle. This caused a commotion in the town, and Grange, for good measure, fired nine rounds of the castle cannon into Edinburgh.

Next Sunday, on 24 December, Knox denounced Grange's action in the pulpit in St. Giles's. He said that he had never seen such a tyrannous act. If the committer had been a man without God, a throat-cutter, he would have been no more moved than by the many other riots which he had seen; 'but to see stars fall from Heaven, and a man of knowledge to commit so manifest treason, what godly heart cannot but lament, tremble and fear? ... Within these few years men would have looked for other fruits of that man than now buddeth forth.' Grange drafted a protest against Knox's sermon, and asked Craig to read it out in the pulpit; but Craig refused to intervene. Grange then made a formal complaint to the Church Session of Edinburgh that Knox had called him a murderer and a throat-cutter.

Knox attacked Grange in a number of other sermons, in which he pointed out that he had not said that Grange was a murderer and a throat-cutter, but asserted that Grange had committed murder in the eyes of God when he sent his soldiers to beat up the man at Leith with batons. Grange eventually stated that he was satisfied that Knox had not called him a murderer and cut-throat; but Knox continued to criticize Grange's conduct.

The English government and the King's lords made great play with the incident of 21 December. Within less than a month, Cecil had written a protest to Grange, and Grange's conduct was denounced by the King's men all over Scotland, as well as by the English government's propagandists. Glencairn and Ochiltre and other notables in the west wrote to Grange, stating that they had heard that he intended to kill Knox, and asking him to give an undertaking that Knox would come to no harm. The outcry that was aroused by Grange's action, as compared with the utter indifference with which Knox and his colleagues treated similar or more outrageous crimes committed by the King's supporters, shows that the incident was deliberately used for propaganda purposes. In view of Knox's habitual contacts with the English government, it is significant that the campaign of denunciation against Grange began with a sermon by Knox, and it would be interesting to know whether Knox had been in touch with the English embassy before he preached his sermon of 24 December.[1]

Despite the apprehensions of Ochiltre and his colleagues for his safety, Knox was in no danger from Grange. The last thing that Grange and Lethington wanted was to harm Knox, for nothing could have been more calculated to convince the world that the Queen's lords were fighting to restore Popery in Scotland. If any preacher had spoken against Lennox and Morton in a town where the King's lords had a garrison of soldiers, as Knox spoke against Mary and Grange under the eyes of the garrison of Edinburgh Castle, he would immediately have been arrested, and worse might have befallen him; but Knox was in no danger in Edinburgh. The garrison regarded him merely as a minor nuisance. They named one of their loudest cannons 'Knox'. Soon afterwards the cannon exploded, killing some of the gunners. This was quite a frequent occurrence in sixteenth-century warfare; but Knox's admirers were certain that it was a divine punishment inflicted on the soldiers who had mocked the man of God.[2]

In March 1571 a meeting of the General Assembly was held in Edinburgh. It coincided with some manœuvres carried out by Grange, who staged a mock attack on the castle in order to test the defences. The attackers pretended to be the Queen of England's army, and were decisively repulsed. The manœuvres, which were conducted in the evening with great noise of gunfire and shouting, annoyed the King's supporters in Edinburgh; but Knox told the guests whom he was entertaining to supper that before destruction goes pride, as Solomon had said. 'I saw as great bravery in the Castle of St. Andrews', said Knox, 'and yet few days brought a miserable desolation.' Knox had not forgotten any of the lessons that he had learned in 1547.[3]

[1] For this incident, see Bannatyne, pp. 70–81; Grange to Cecil, 25 Dec. 1570 and 29 Jan. 1570/1; Grange's complaint against Knox, 28 Dec. 1570; Knox's reply and Grange's reply (Dec. 1570–Jan. 1571); Glencairn, Ochiltre, etc. to Grange, 3 Jan. 1570/1; Cecil to Grange, 10 Jan. 1570/1; Drury to Cecil, 14 Jan. 1570/1; Leslie, Alexander Gordon, and Livingstone to Grange, 20 Jan. 1570/1 (*Sc. Cal.* iii. 585, 606, 616; *Cal. For. Pap. Eliz.* ix. 1505; Bannatyne, pp. 73–75, 77–82); *Diurnal of Occurrents*, p. 197.

[2] Bannatyne, p. 175.

[3] Ibid., p. 91.

While the General Assembly was in session, a number of anonymous denunciations of Knox were thrown into the meetings of the Assembly, or fixed to the door of St. Giles's. Some of the bills were brought to Knox as he was dressing on the morning of 10 March by the bellman who found them. One of the bills complained that Knox did not pray for the Queen, but had, on the contrary, 'openly in this church of Edinburgh most seditiously detracted, railed and inveighed against our Sovereign Lady, the nobility and other subjects of this realm professing Her Grace's obedience, naming her an idolatress and murderer, and an adulteress'. When Knox saw the bill, he wrote in the margin: 'No Sovereign Lady is she to me, nor yet to this realm, and so ye are traitors.' Knox's servant, Bannatyne, without consulting him, went to the General Assembly and asked them to pass a vote of confidence in Knox and express their support of his attacks on the Queen; but the Assembly refused to do this. The members were by no means unanimous in support of Knox, and most of them were not eager to enter into controversy in his defence, or on the merits of praying for the King or the Queen. They also tried to discourage Knox from replying to the bills, and urged him to ignore them; but he insisted on writing a reply. 'That I have called her an obstinate idolatress, one that consented to the murder of her own husband, and one that has committed whoredom and villainous adultery, I gladly grant', he wrote; but he denied that he had said that 'their Sovereign (mine she is not)' could never repent. The Queen's men obviously succeeded in misrepresenting Knox's attitude on this question; for an inhabitant of Edinburgh noted in his diary that Knox refused to pray for the Queen, although it was the duty of a minister to pray for all those who had fallen, and that the majority of the people of Edinburgh resented Knox's attitude. The diarist evidently did not appreciate that the issue was whether Knox should recognize Mary as Queen.[1]

Within ten days, another anonymous bill was fixed to the church door. It referred to Knox's book *The First Blast of the Trumpet*. It claimed that if Knox's doctrine was false, he should be condemned as a seditious man and false doctor; but if it was true, why did Knox support the government of the Queen of England, not only in praying for the maintenance of her estate in the pulpit, 'but also

[1] Ibid., pp. 91–100; the passages cited are on pp. 92, 97–98; *Diurnal of Occurrents*, p. 201; Drury to Burghley, 11 Mar. 1570/1 (*Cal. For. Pap. Eliz.* ix. 1604).

in suiting and procuring, by himself and others of his alluring, by all means possible her aid and support against his own native country and liberty thereof?' Knox replied to this at some length in a written statement which showed that he appreciated the strength of the public feeling against Elizabeth and England. He said that the fact that he prayed for a commonwealth did not mean that he supported everything that was done in that commonwealth, for Jeremiah had called on the Jews to pray for Nebuchadnezzar, though he did not approve of his cruelty against Jerusalem; 'neither yet does the seeking of help (even from the wicked) prove that the godly justifies the wicked'. He also stated that he would give anyone 'a lie in his throat that either dare or will say that ever I sought support against my native country. What I have been to my country, albeit this unthankful age will not know, yet the ages to come will be compelled to bear witness to the truth.'[1]

On 2 April 1571 a small band of the King's men, under Captain Crawfurd, marched silently on a misty night to Dumbarton, and, by a prodigious feat of courage, skill, and physical endurance, scaled the 250-foot rock on which the castle stood, and entered it at the highest point, which was unguarded because the defenders thought that it was inaccessible. After a short skirmish, the garrison, which was taken completely by surprise, surrendered. Captain Crawfurd wrote to Knox, and give him a detailed account of the operation.[2] Archbishop Hamilton was captured when the castle was taken, and a few days later he was hanged at Stirling in his Archbishop's vestments, after a summary trial, on a charge of having been involved in the murders of Darnley and Moray. The Queen's lords were indignant at the hanging of the Archbishop; but Elizabeth was too happy about the capture of Dumbarton to make even a formal protest against the execution; for the fall of the castle had freed her from the fear that a French or Spanish army could land at the main port in the west of Scotland.[3] Mary

[1] Bannatyne, pp. 100–3.

[2] Drury to the Council, 9 Apr. 1571 (wrongly dated 1570) (*Cal. For. Pap. Eliz.* ix. 1644); Crawfurd to Knox (14 Jan. 1572?) (Bannatyne, pp. 106–7, where the letter is dated '14 January', no year being given). The date may be an error, though it is not impossible that Crawfurd, who wrote to Knox at the request of Robert Fairlie of Braid, did not do so until more than nine months after the capture of the castle.

[3] Randolph to Lennox, 10 Apr. 1571; Elizabeth I to Lennox, 22 Apr. 1571 (*Sc. Cal.* iii. 691, 713); Herries to Scrope, 10 Apr. 1571 (*Cal. For. Pap. Eliz.* ix. 1647); Mary Queen of Scots to Alva, 18 Apr. 1571 (Labanoff, iii. 269–71).

had meanwhile entered into communication with Ridolfi, an Italian adventurer, who planned to assassinate Elizabeth and bring a Spanish army from Flanders to England to put Mary on the English throne. In October 1571, Cecil discovered the plot, and Mary was lost. There was henceforth no danger that Elizabeth would restore her to the throne of Scotland, and the English Parliament declared that she should be put to death.

The Queen's lords retaliated for the fall of Dumbarton by occupying Edinburgh—Lethington, Huntly, and the Hamiltons joining Grange in the castle. But this did not deter Knox from continuing to preach strongly in favour of the King's side; and when he heard that Grange was receiving the Hamiltons in the castle, he issued a formal protest.

> The Captain of the Castle has declared [he wrote] by his letter to a gentleman of honest fame, that he will receive the Duke and his sons, and will accompany them. He has this hour, upon Friday the 20 of April 1571, Claud Hamilton in the Castle of Edinburgh, Arthur of Meriton, Robert of Inchmachan, and a sort of the strongest throat-cutters of the Hamiltons going plainly upon Edinburgh causeway [High Street]. However that he be blinded, whosoever fears God sees his hands defiled with his master's blood, in that he joins with the maintainers of the murder. . . . John Knox, trusting end of travails.[1]

The Hamiltons were in an ugly mood after the hanging of the Archbishop, and Knox's followers feared for his safety. On the night of 20 April, the day that the Hamiltons arrived in the town, some of the brethren watched all night in Knox's house to protect him from harm. But Grange was anxious that Knox should not be harmed, either because of their old personal friendship, or because he realized the use which Lennox, Morton, and Cecil could make of Knox as a martyr. He offered to send Captain Melville, who was an old Protestant, with a guard to protect Knox. Knox apparently refused to accept this offer of protection, for Bannatyne commented that Grange 'would give the wolf the wether to keep'. According to David Buchanan and Calderwood, someone fired a shot through Knox's window one night, which would have killed him if he had been sitting in his usual chair, at the head of the table with his back to the window; but on this occasion he happened to be sitting at the side of the table, and

[1] Bannatyne, p. 109.

the shot hit the bottom of the chandelier. David Buchanan and Calderwood wrote that the hole in the chandelier was still to be seen in their time. If this incident occurred, it was probably at the time of the occupation of Edinburgh by the Queen's lords; but in this case it is strange that Bannatyne, who was living with Knox, does not mention it in his *Memorials*.[1]

Grange decided to compel Knox and all active supporters of the King's lords to leave Edinburgh. On 27 April, Captain Melville, though an officer in the Queen's forces, wrote to Robert Fairlie of Braid, who was fighting on the King's side, and asked him to persuade Knox to leave Edinburgh. Braid warned Melville that he could not urge Knox to leave his vocation, and that if the Queen's men harmed Knox, God would revenge the wrong; but on 30 April Grange issued a proclamation ordering all supporters of Lennox, as he termed the King's men, to leave Edinburgh within six hours. Many of the members of the congregation of Edinburgh came to Craig, and asked him to persuade Knox to leave. Knox at first refused to go, but eventually agreed, after Craig and his colleagues had told him that if he stayed he would be risking the lives of those brethren who would insist on protecting him against the Hamiltons. On 5 May, Knox left Edinburgh, and, crossing the water, went to Abbotshall in Fife. On the previous day Grange's soldiers had begun demolishing part of St. Giles's in order to prevent it being used as cover from the castle cannon by any of the King's soldiers who might enter the town.[2]

[1] Bannatyne, p. 111; Life of Knox, in Knox's *History*, 1644 Edinburgh edn., unpag.; Calderwood, iii. 242. For the anger of the Queen's lords at the execution of Archbishop Hamilton, see Herries to Scrope, 10 Apr. 1571 (*Cal. For. Pap. Eliz.* ix. 1647).

[2] Bannatyne, pp. 113–19; Robert Melville to Braid (27 Apr. 1571); Braid to Robert Melville (Apr.–May 1571); Grange's Proclamation (30 Apr. 1571) (Bannatyne, pp. 114–16); *Diurnal of Occurrents*, p. 211; Drury to the Council, 13 May 1571 (*Cal. For. Pap. Eliz.* ix. 1698). Knox did not attend a meeting with Lethington in the castle before leaving Edinburgh; see App. VI.

CHAPTER XXV

St. Andrews and Edinburgh

IN July 1571, Knox went to St. Andrews, where he stayed for thirteen months. As in the winter of 1559–60, he watched as a passive spectator in St. Andrews while the future of Scotland was being decided by hagbutters and the great powers of Europe. In Edinburgh the Bishop of Galloway preached in Knox's pulpit, proclaiming his devotion to the Protestant religion, and telling the congregation that though Mary had sinned, she was as much their lawful Queen as David was a lawful king after he had committed adultery. The Edinburgh burgh council ceased to function, but life continued in the town, though Morton's soldiers from Leith occupied the Canongate, and dug trenches there, and Grange bombarded them with the cannon which he had placed on the roof of St. Giles's and other buildings in Edinburgh, destroying houses and causing many casualties among the civilian population. Grange pulled down many of the houses in the town in order to facilitate military operations. The King's soldiers tried to starve the castle into surrender by hanging every farmer who sent supplies to the Castilians; but Grange sent parties of soldiers to requisition foodstuffs from the farms, and accumulated enough stocks to feed the garrison for more than a year. Sometimes Grange's soldiers would encounter Morton's men, and sharp clashes took place on the Burgh Moor. The King's lords hanged many of their prisoners, including Captain Cullen, one of the most famous Scottish commanders of the age. At last Grange retaliated, and hanged one of the King's mercenaries whom he had captured, and the hanging of prisoners was then stopped.[1]

[1] Text of Alexander Gordon's sermon of 17 June 1571; Drury to the Council, 15, 17, 20, and 23 May 1571; Report from Scotland, 3 June 1571; Drury to Burghley, 9 June, 24 July, and 9 Oct. 1571; Leslie to Mary Queen of Scots (Aug. 1571); Report from Scotland, 26 Feb. 1572; Drury and Randolph to Hunsdon, 26 Feb. and 10 Apr. 1572; Memorandum of Lord Seton's negotiations with Alva, 18 Apr. 1572; Hunsdon to Burghley, 18 Apr., 9 May, and 16 June 1572; Errington to Hunsdon, 27 Apr. 1572; Lethington and Grange to Hunsdon and Drury, 8 May 1572; Drury to

In September, Grange sent a band of 400 soldiers to attack Stirling in the middle of the night and capture Lennox and Morton. The operation was nearly successful, but failed owing to the indiscipline of the Borderers in Grange's force, who began looting in Stirling, and allowed the King's lords to assemble their men. Lennox was taken prisoner, but was shot when the Queen's men were compelled to make a hasty retreat. His death was treated as murder by the King's lords, and the captain who killed him, who was captured, was tortured and broken on the wheel. This method of execution, by which the condemned man had his bones broken with iron bars, and was left on the wheel 'to live in pain and repentance . . . as long as it pleases God to give him life', was not a normal mode of punishment in Scotland, but was taken over by the Scottish Protestants from the French Catholics, and used on this special occasion. The King's lords chose Erskine, the Earl of Mar, to succeed Lennox as Regent.[1]

At St. Andrews, Knox lodged in the old priory, near St. Leonard's College. He was old and ill, but he went every day to the church to preach. James Melville, who later became minister of Kilrenny in Fife, was at this time a 15-year-old student at St. Leonard's College. He saw Knox walking to the church every day. Knox was well wrapped up with furs around his neck, and walked slowly, leaning on a staff which he carried in his right hand, while Bannatyne held him under the left armpit and helped him along. When he reached the church, he had to be helped into the pulpit by Bannatyne and other people; but once he began to preach, he was transformed. During the year that he was in St. Andrews, he preached on the Book of Daniel. For the first half-hour, he spoke about the text in general terms, in a quiet voice; but when he

Hunsdon, 7 and 14 June and 12 July 1572; News from Scotland, 3 July 1572 (*Sc. Cal.* iii. 758, 779, 790, 805, 840, 877; iv. 7, 132, 250 [2], 345[1], 363 enclosure, 379, 388; *Cal. For. Pap. Eliz.* ix. 1707, 1710, 1714; x. 143, 144, 232, 255, 257, 299, 347, 348, 403, 421, 458, 469); *Historie of King James the Sext*, pp. 68–69, 75, 102–3; *Diurnal of Occurrents*, pp. 233, 262–3, 265, 291–6, 299.

[1] Report from the King's lords, 4 Sept. 1571; letter to Drury, 5 Sept. 1571; letter to Burghley, 5 Sept. 1571; Lethington to Mary Queen of Scots, 5 Sept. 1571; Grange and Lethington to Drury, 6 Sept. 1571; Morton to Drumlanrig, 8 Sept. 1571; Mar to Drury, 13 Sept. 1571; Drury to Burghley, 13 Sept. 1571; 1st examination of Capt. Bell, 5 Sept. 1571; Capt. Bell's 2nd deposition, 6 Sept. 1571; Capt. Calder's deposition, 6 Sept. 1571 (*Sc. Cal.* iii. 912–14, 917, 921, 938, 940, 941 [4], [5], and [6]; *Cal. For. Pap. Eliz.* ix. 2014). The reports of the King's lords give the number of the Queen's men engaged in the raid of Stirling as somewhat less than that given by Grange and Lethington.

began to apply the text to current events, denouncing Grange, the Hamiltons, and Mary, his oratory became so forceful that young Melville, who was trying to take notes of what he was saying, was overcome by emotion and terror, and could no longer hold his pen. He says that Knox was so vigorous that it seemed as if he would shatter the pulpit and fly away out of it. On one occasion he preached against a witch who had been convicted and sentenced to death. She was brought into the church and fastened to a pillar facing the pulpit, while Knox denounced her and her witchcraft. After the sermon, she was executed.[1]

Knox's violent attacks on the Hamiltons and the Queen's party aroused opposition in St. Andrews, and involved him in an inter-college dispute. The minister in St. Andrews was Robert Hamilton, who had succeeded Goodman. Twelve years earlier, he had gone with Knox to Berwick to negotiate with the English government during the crisis of 1559, and since then he had occupied important positions, having been Moderator of the General Assembly in March 1571. He was one of the governing body of St. Mary's College in St. Andrews, of which he became Principal a few years later. Robert Hamilton had adopted an attitude of neutrality in the civil war, for which he had been publicly criticized by the undergraduates of St. Leonard's College. St. Leonard's had always been more progressive academically than the other colleges, and its students and regents supported the King's side. St. Mary's and St. Salvator's Colleges sympathized with the Queen's lords as openly as they dared. James Melville says that, unlike his fellow students at St. Leonard's, they 'hated Mr. Knox and the good cause'.[2]

According to Melville, Robert Hamilton objected to Knox's attacks on Grange, and his statements that the Castle of Edinburgh would run like a sandglass and spew out the Captain with shame, not at the gate but down over the wall. Robert Hamilton also objected to Knox's wholesale attacks on his namesakes. The religious struggle in Scotland was rapidly degenerating into a tribal war of Douglases against Hamiltons. The people in Edinburgh were calling the civil war 'the Douglas wars'; and George Buchanan and the other propagandists for the King's lords were denouncing the Hamiltons as a clan, and making the position of

[1] Melville, *Diary*, pp. 26, 33, 58; Bannatyne, p. 255.
[2] Melville, *Diary*, p. 26.

Protestant Hamiltons increasingly difficult. Knox, in his sermons, repeatedly declared that 'Hamiltons are murderers'.[1]

In November 1571, Bannatyne was told by Robert Hamilton's friend, James Hamilton, that Robert Hamilton was spreading a rumour that Knox was as great a murderer as any Hamilton in Scotland, because he and Moray had once planned to murder Darnley in Perth. Knox threatened to bring proceedings for slander against Robert Hamilton before the Church Session; but Robert Hamilton denied that he had ever said such a thing. After this, James Hamilton was hated by the other members of St. Mary's College, who would not forgive him for having told Bannatyne what Robert Hamilton had said. Whenever he appeared, he was greeted with cries of 'Knox's bird'. He could not bear this treatment, and left the college because of it.[2]

But the students of St. Leonard's College greatly admired Knox. James Melville wrote in his memoirs, thirty years later, that the greatest benefit that he derived from his residence at the University was seeing and hearing 'that extraordinary man of God, Mr. John Knox', the 'prophet and apostle of our nation'. He describes how 'Mr. Knox would sometimes come in, and repose him in our college yard, and call us scholars unto him, and bless us, and exhort us to know God and His work in our country, and stand by the good cause, to use our time well, and learn the good instruction, and follow the good example of our masters.' Knox became very friendly with John Davidson, the future minister of Prestonpans, who at that time was one of the regents of St. Leonard's. Davidson was a poet and prose writer. In July 1571, Knox attended a performance of a play that Davidson had written to celebrate the wedding of John Colville, a minister of the Church who later played an important part in Scottish politics. The Church had not yet condemned the theatre as sinful. The play was about the storming and capture of the Castle of Edinburgh. The final scene showed Grange and two of his colleagues being hanged in effigy, 'according to Mr. Knox's doctrine'. Melville states that Knox, in his sermons, had been prophesying that Grange would be hanged in the face of the sun.[3]

[1] Melville, *Diary*, p. 33; *Diurnal of Occurrents*, p. 294; *Historie of King James the Sext*, p. 103; Buchanan (?), 'Exhortation to the Lords of the King's Council against the Hamiltons' (17 Feb. 1569/70) (*Sc. Cal.* iii. 123); Bannatyne, p. 262.

[2] Bannatyne, pp. 258–62.

[3] Melville, *Diary*, pp. 26–27, 31, 34.

While Knox was in St. Andrews, he became involved in the beginning of a struggle which, after his death, was to have a profound effect on the Church of Scotland. It concerned the appointment of new bishops. As the Catholic bishops of the old Church died, new bishops were appointed to take their place. These bishops were Protestants, but had no place in the structure of the Protestant Church, with its ministers and superintendents. They were supposed to be a kind of additional superintendent, but in fact they merely enjoyed the tithes, two-thirds of which were still payable to them as the successors of the Catholic bishops. The remaining third was now divided between the Protestant Church and the government on a basis less favourable to the Church than that which they had been able to obtain immediately after the overthrow of Mary in 1567.

The question of bishops was temporarily settled by a compromise agreement which was reached between the Church and the Privy Council of the King's lords at Leith in January 1572. The Church agreed to accept the bishops on condition that the lords who held the right of presenting them agreed to appoint only Protestant ministers who were acceptable to the Church. The lords were free to make whatever private arrangement they liked with their nominees, and usually agreed with the new bishop that, as a condition of his appointment, he would assign the greater part of the revenues to the lord who appointed him.[1]

These bishops appointed by the lords became known as 'tulchan bishops', the tulchan being a calf-skin stuffed with straw which farmers placed under their cows to make the cow give her milk. The preacher, Patrick Constantine, declared that whereas formerly, under Popery, they had had 'my Lord Bishop', now they had 'my Lord's Bishop', but he hoped that soon they would have only 'the Lord's Bishop'—the superintendents.[2]

The archiepiscopal see of St. Andrews had been vacant since the execution of Archbishop Hamilton. Mar and the Privy Council granted Morton the right to nominate the new Archbishop, and Morton appointed John Douglas, the Rector of St. Andrews University, after Douglas had agreed to assign all his share of the

[1] See Moray to the General Assembly, 30 June 1569; the Agreement of Leith, 16 Jan. 1571/2 (*Booke of the Universall Kirk*, i. 139, 151–2, 154, 168–9, 208–35 (8 Mar. 1568/9, 9 July 1569, (Mar. 1569/70), and 16 and 23 Jan. 1571/2)); Donaldson's Introduction to *Accounts of the Collectors of Thirds of Benefices*, pp. xxxii–xxxiii.

[2] Melville, *Diary*, pp. 31–32.

tithes to Morton. As soon as the Agreement of Leith had been reached with the Church, Morton came to St. Andrews for the ceremony of the election and installation of the Archbishop. On 6 February 1572, Douglas 'gave specimen doctrine' in a sermon in St. Andrews in order to show his suitability for the office, and two days later he was elected Archbishop by the congregation, though several people spoke and voted against him. Knox was asked to inaugurate Douglas as Archbishop at the service on Sunday, 10 February; but he refused, despite his personal affection for Douglas. Knox preached the sermon as usual in the church, before a congregation that included Morton, but apparently made no reference to the inauguration of Douglas. As soon as Knox had finished, Winram, the Superintendent of Fife, took his place in the pulpit and conducted the inauguration service.[1]

John Rutherford, the Dean of Faculty and head of St. Salvator's College, resented Knox's refusal to inaugurate his university colleague, and said that Knox had objected to the appointment of Douglas only because Knox wished to be Archbishop himself. When Knox heard this, he commented that many years ago he could have had a wealthier bishopric than St. Andrews if he had wanted it.[2]

Knox's attitude in the controversy about the tulchan bishops is often referred to today, particularly by those who wish to prove that he did not object to episcopacy as such, but only to the disgraceful transactions that took place in connexion with the appointment of Archbishop Douglas and the tulchan bishops. The developments in Scotland prevented the issue of episcopacy from ever being discussed purely on its merits; for bishops during the regency and the early years of the reign of James VI meant tulchan bishops, and the doctrinal objections to bishops could not be separated from the resentment that was felt at the fraudulent operations of Morton and the other lords. On the question of tulchan bishops, there is no doubt as to where Knox's sympathies lay in 1571 and 1572; but he did not put up a serious fight against them, either before or after the Agreement of Leith. His political realism made him reluctant to split the unity of the King's side. He did not attempt to fight the corruption of Morton as he had fought, at least to some extent, the corruption of Northumberland and the Protestant lords in England; he was now much older,

[1] Bannatyne, pp. 222–3; Melville, *Diary*, p. 31.

[2] Bannatyne, p. 256.

much more tired and ill, and much more cynical than he had been twenty years before. His only interest was to crush the Queen's men, and especially Grange and the Castilians in Edinburgh.

> God reveals to me [Knox wrote to Sir James Douglas of Drumlanrig on 26 May 1572] that the action that is defended against these traitors and murderers of the Castle of Edinburgh is just, and in the end shall prevail against Satan and all them that maintains that wicked society. . . . I see that the traffic with that Babylon, the Castle of Edinburgh, shall once bring Scotland in that misery that we and our posterity shall mourn for a time.

Knox knew as well as Cecil and Elizabeth that as long as Edinburgh Castle was held in Mary's name, there was always a danger that Alva's troops might land in Scotland. If Alva came and won, this would mean the re-establishment of Popery, in England as well as in Scotland, and a decisive defeat for the Protestant cause in Europe, though the butcher of the Dutch Protestants had promised the Queen's lords that he would grant full religious toleration when his armies occupied Scotland.[1]

In private, Knox was prepared to be more outspoken about the faults of the King's lords. On 19 July 1572, he wrote to Wishart of Pittarrow:

> Both the parties stand, as it were, fighting against God Himself in justification of their wickedness; the murderers assembled in the Castle of Edinburgh and their assisters, justifying all that they have done to be well and rightly done; and the contrary party as little respecting the troubling and oppressing of the poor Church of God as ever they did. For if they can have the Church lands to be annexed to their houses, they appear to take no more care of the instruction of the ignorant and of the feeding of the flock of Jesus Christ than ever did the Papists, whom we have condemned, and yet are worse ourselves in that behalf. For they, according to their blind zeal, spared nothing that might either have maintained or holden up that which they took for God's service; but we, alas, in the midst of the light forget the Heaven and draw to the earth.

[1] Knox to Drumlanrig, 26 May 1572 (*Works*, vi. 615–16); Memorandum of Seton's negotiations with Alva, 18 Apr. 1572 (*Sc. Cal.* iv. 250 [2]; *Cal. For. Pap. Eliz.* x. 257); and see Guerau de Spes to Philip II, 8 Jan. 1569 (*Span. Cal. Eliz.* ii. 70). For the Catholic plans for a Spanish invasion of Scotland, see also Ridolfi to Philip II (1571) (*Papal Cal.* i. 782); Mary Queen of Scots' Instructions to Ridolfi (Mar. 1571); Mary Queen of Scots to Alva, 18 Apr. 1571 (Labanoff, iii. 269–71).

But Knox was too astute a politician to say this publicly in the pulpit.[1]

Though Knox did not publicly denounce the system of the tulchan bishops, he was quick to react to any attempt by the new Primate to interfere with the functioning of the Church. Archibald Hamilton, a young undergraduate from the Western Isles, refused to attend Knox's sermons, because Knox had stated repeatedly that 'Hamiltons are murderers'. When the Church Session asked him to explain his failure to attend the services, Archibald Hamilton appealed to Archbishop Douglas, who was still the Rector of the University; and on 18 July 1572, Douglas, along with the Bishop of Caithness, Winram, and Wilkie and Rutherford, the heads of St. Leonard's and St. Salvator's Colleges, came with Archibald Hamilton to Knox's lodgings in the abbey to discuss the matter. Knox immediately protested that this assembly of private persons had no right to judge the Church of God.

> I protest that neither the pulpit of St. Andrews, neither yet of any congregation within the realm, be subject to the censure of the schools, University or faculty within the same; but only that it be reserved to God, the Judge of all, and to the General Assembly gathered within the same realm, lawfully. The reason of this my protestation is that I look for no better regiment in times to come than has been in ages passing before us; in the which, it is evident that universities, orders well established, and men raised up to defend the Church of God, have oppressed it.

Archibald Hamilton replied with his own protestation, in which he denied that he wished to subject the Church to the interference of the universities, but said that as a member of the University he was free from the discipline of Knox.[2] A few years later, Archibald Hamilton became a Catholic and emigrated to France. He was the source of most of the hostile stories about Knox's private life that were published by him and his fellow-Catholic writers.

A fortnight later, Knox wrote to the General Assembly, which

[1] Knox to Pittarrow, 19 July (1572) (*Works*, vi. 617). Calderwood, iii. 113–14, wrongly gives the date of this letter as 1571.

[2] Knox's protestation, 18 July 1572; Archibald Hamilton's protestation (July 1572) (Bannatyne, pp. 262–3).

was meeting in Perth, on the question of the relationship of the Church and the universities.

Albeit I have taken my leave not only of you, dear brethren, but also of the whole world and all worldly affairs; yet, remaining in the flesh, I could not nor cannot cease to admonish you of things which I know to be most prejudicial to the Church of Christ Jesus within this realm. Above all things, preserve the Church from the bondage of the universities. Persuade them to rule themselves peaceably, and order their schools in Christ; but subject never the pulpit to their judgement, neither yet exempt them from your jurisdiction.

He added that he was in full agreement with the articles which Winram and Robert Pont were presenting to the General Assembly. These articles, amongst other things, asked the General Assembly to clarify the position as to the respective authority of the bishops and the superintendents, and to consider whether it was proper that the bishop of a great diocese should at the same time be the rector of a university.[1]

In July 1572, Knox published his last pamphlet, *An Answer to a Letter of a Jesuit named Tyrie*. It was published by Lekprevik, the government printer, who, like Knox, had come to St. Andrews when the King's supporters were expelled from Edinburgh. Most of the pamphlet had been written in 1566 in reply to a letter that Tyrie had written to his brother from his refuge in France; for the brother, who was a Protestant laird, had sent the letter to Knox and had asked him to reply to it. At that time, Knox had decided not to publish his reply; but now he changed his mind, because Tyrie was publishing a number of Catholic propaganda pamphlets in France. Knox, replying paragraph by paragraph to Tyrie's tractate, rebutted Tyrie's claim that the Church of Rome was the Holy Catholic Church, outside of which, as Knox admitted, there could be no salvation. Knox said that the term 'Catholic Church' meant 'Universal Church', and nothing more; but the Church of Rome could not be the Holy Catholic Church unless it was holy, 'and this we think shall be very hard to Mr. Tyrie and all the Jesuits in Europe to prove'. Drawing largely on his study of Aventinus's *History of Bavaria*, he dealt with the private vices and political crimes of the Popes during the early Middle Ages.

Tyrie, like so many other Catholic pamphleteers, had placed

[1] Knox to the General Assembly, 5 Aug. 1572, and the articles presented to the General Assembly (*Booke of the Universall Kirk*, i. 247–9; *Works*, vi. 619–21).

great emphasis on the contrast between the unity of the Catholic Church and the repeated splits and doctrinal quarrels among the Protestants. Knox replied that the disagreements among the Apostles and the early Christian sects did not prove that their teaching was wrong; and he pointed out that whatever might be the position among the Protestants in other countries, there were no splits among the Protestants in Scotland. At the end of the pamphlet, he published a letter that he had written to Mrs. Bowes from Dieppe in 1554, because, as he wrote to Wishart of Pittarrow, if the letter 'serve not for this estate of Scotland, yet it will serve a troubled conscience, so long as the Church of God remaineth in either realm'. It was the only one of Knox's letters to Mrs. Bowes to be published in his lifetime.[1]

On 31 July 1572, the King's lords and the Queen's lords agreed to a truce which had been virtually forced upon them by the joint action of the English and French governments. This made it possible for the King's supporters to return to Edinburgh, though Grange and Lethington remained in control of the castle. Knox was invited to return by some of the members of the congregation in Edinburgh, who were dissatisfied with the neutral attitude in the civil war that Craig had adopted in his sermons in St. Giles's during the previous year. Knox had not been forgotten in Edinburgh during his absence, and rumours about his activities in St. Andrews had been circulating there. Lady Home, in Edinburgh Castle, had said that she had heard that Knox had been banished from St. Andrews because he had raised up the Devil in St. Leonard's yards, and that when Bannatyne saw the Devil, complete with horns, he ran wild, and died of shock.[2]

Knox was now very ill. On 19 July he wrote to Wishart of Pittarrow that he was working on his *Answer to Tyrie* in bed, and got up only once a week; and at about the same time he wrote a warm letter of farewell to Goodman in England, and told him that he had no hope that they would meet again in this life, as he

[1] Knox, *Answer to Tyrie*; Knox to Pittarrow, 19 July 1572 (*Works*, vi. 479–520, 617–18; and see pp. 489, 510). See also Tyrie's *Refutation of ane answer made by Sir Iohn Knox to a letter sent by Iames Tyrie to his umquhile brother*, published in Paris in 1573 (in *Catholic Tractates*, pp. 1–29).

[2] Elizabeth I to Montmorency and Foix, 28 June 1572; Elizabeth I to Mar, 4 July 1572; Du Croc's proposals for a truce, 14 July 1572; the truce terms, 30 July 1572 (*Cal. For. Pap. Eliz.* x. 448, 459, 473, 505; *Sc. Cal.* iv. 381, 399)); Bannatyne, pp. 216, 253; the Church of Edinburgh to Knox, 5 Aug. 1572 (Bannatyne, p. 254).

was too ill to be carried from country to country. But Knox managed to undertake the journey from St. Andrews to Edinburgh. He left St. Andrews, 'with the grief and tears of the godly, but to the great joy of the wicked', and landed at Leith on 23 August. There he rested for some days, and then proceeded to Edinburgh. The burgh council found him lodgings in a house near the Nether Port. It was not very close to St. Giles's, but many of the houses at the western end of the town had been destroyed during the recent fighting. The house had belonged to James Mosman, the goldsmith, who was a prominent supporter of the Queen's lords and was in the castle with Grange. It is known today as 'John Knox's house'.[1]

On Sunday, 31 August, Knox preached in St. Giles's for the first time for sixteen months; but his voice was so weak that he could not be heard by a large part of the congregation. The acoustics in St. Giles's were bad; Knox had never succeeded in making himself heard throughout the whole church, and now his weak voice was a serious impediment to his preaching there. He therefore arranged for services to be held in the tolbooth of Edinburgh, and he continued to officiate and preach in this smaller room for another two months. He preached there every Sunday, and Killigrew, the English ambassador, stated that though his voice could hardly be heard, he preached with as much vehemence and zeal as ever.[2]

On 7 September, Knox wrote to James Lawson at the University of Aberdeen, and invited Lawson to visit him. Knox had decided that he would have to resign his office as minister of Edinburgh, and wished that Lawson should succeed him, for Craig, apart from his unpopularity and neutral attitude in the civil war, had left Edinburgh. The General Assembly at Perth referred

[1] Knox to Pittarrow, 19 July 1572; Knox to Goodman (July 1572); Smeton's account of Knox's death (*Works*, vi. 617–18, 652); Bannatyne, pp. 255, 263. For the dispute as to whether Knox ever lived at 'John Knox's house', see Peter Miller, 'John Knox and his manse', and 'Supplementary Notes on John Knox's House'; Sir D. Wilson, 'John Knox's House, Netherbow, Edinburgh'; Guthrie, 'Is "John Knox's House" entitled to the name?' and 'The Traditional Belief in John Knox's house at the Netherbow vindicated'; and Robert Miller, 'Where did John Knox live in Edinburgh?' (*Proceedings of the Society of Antiquaries of Scotland*, xxv. 138–62, 333–48; xxviii. 406–11; xxxiii. 80–115, 249–73 (Feb. and Mar. 1891, May 1893, and Jan. and Mar. 1899); Hume Brown, *John Knox*, ii. 317–19.

[2] Bannatyne, p. 263; Killigrew to Burghley and Leicester (6 Oct. 1572) (*Sc. Cal.* iv. 452; *Works*, vi. 633).

the question of Knox's successor to the Superintendent of Lothian and to Knox, and to the congregation of Edinburgh, who invited Lawson to come to Edinburgh, so that they could see if he was a suitable preacher. Knox added a postscript to the letter: 'Make haste, my brother, otherwise you will come too late'.[1]

On 24 August 1572, the Massacre of St. Bartholomew took place in Paris, when the Huguenots who had come to Paris for the wedding of the young King Henry of Navarre to Marguerite de Valois, the sister of Charles IX, were murdered on the orders of the government by the Catholic gentlemen and the people of Paris. Grange's brother, James Kirkcaldy, who had gone to Paris to ask the French government for aid, was nearly killed in the massacre, and was shocked at what he saw. Many murders and massacres had been perpetrated by both Catholics and Protestants in France during the previous ten years; but the Massacre of St. Bartholomew not only far exceeded the others in the number of the victims, but was a heavy set-back for English foreign policy and for the prospects of international Protestantism. During the previous year, the influence of Coligny and the French Protestants at Court had led Charles IX and Catherine de Medici to make a treaty of friendship with England, and preparations were ready for France to declare war on Spain and invade the Netherlands in support of William the Silent and the Protestants; but the Massacre of St. Bartholomew completely altered the whole international balance of power in favour of the Catholics. The massacre was probably an unpremeditated action induced by panic, with the intention of forestalling an imaginary Protestant plan to massacre the Catholics in Paris in reprisal for the attempted assassination of Coligny by a hagbutter of the Guises two days before; but the Protestants saw it as a proof that the Catholics were carrying out the project of the Council of Trent to exterminate Protestants everywhere. Elizabeth was cautious in her comments, and continued her policy of friendship with France; but in Scotland the King's lords had no reason for reticence. The Privy Council issued a statement which, though not directly referring to France, condemned the cruel massacres that had recently occurred in many countries in pursuance of the decisions of the Council of Trent, and called on the people of Scotland to rally to resist the plans of

[1] Knox to Lawson, 7 Sept. 1572 (Bannatyne, p. 264; *Works*, vi. 632); *Booke of the Universall Kirk*, i. 245 (Aug. 1572).

the Papists in Scotland. The ministers in the pulpit directly denounced the massacre.[1]

Knox was the most vigorous of all the preachers in his condemnation of the events in Paris. He denounced Charles IX as a traitor and murderer of his people, and said that unless he repented, no son of his loins would rule France in peace and quiet. The French ambassador, du Croc, protested to Mar and the Council about the sermons of the ministers, and particularly about Knox's sermon; but the Council said that they had no power to restrict the preachers from saying what they wished in the pulpit, and du Croc left Scotland.[2]

In the middle of September, Killigrew arrived in Scotland as the English ambassador. He made it his business to visit Knox soon after his arrival. Knox asked Killigrew to give his last commendations to Cecil, who was now Lord Burghley. 'He thanked God', wrote Killigrew to Burghley, 'he had obtained at His hands that the Gospel of Jesus Christ is truly and simply preached throughout Scotland, which doth so comfort him, as he now desireth to be out of this miserable life. He said further, that it was not long of your Lordship that he was not a great bishop in England; but that effect grown in Scotland, he being an instrument, doth much more satisfy him.' Knox then warned Killigrew not to trust Grange and Lethington. Killigrew had been sent to Scotland to make a last attempt to induce them to come to terms with the King's lords; but Knox assured Killigrew that the Castilians were working for the ruin of Elizabeth.[3]

Killigrew had also been entrusted with another and more secret mission—so secret that it had not been included in his written instructions, but only told to him verbally by Elizabeth herself. With the English Parliament clamouring for Mary's execution for her part in the Ridolfi plot, Elizabeth and Cecil were considering the possibility of handing Mary over to the King's lords to be put on trial and punished in Scotland; and Killigrew was ordered to discover the reactions of the King's lords to this proposal. As the English government was well aware

[1] Kincaid to Burghley, 5 Jan. (1572); James Kirkcaldy to Lethington, 22–25 Aug. 1572; Report to Burghley (Sept. 1572) (*Cal. For. Pap. Eliz.* x. 9, 584, p. 185; *Sc. Cal.* iv. 424); James VI's proclamation, 3 Oct. 1572 (Bannatyne, pp. 271–3); *Booke of the Universall Kirk*, i. 250–1 (3 Oct. 1572).

[2] Bannatyne, pp. 273–4.

[3] Killigrew to Burghley and Leicester (6 Oct. 1572) (*Sc. Cal.* iv. 452; *Works*, vi. 633).

of the eagerness with which Knox, in 1567, had demanded that Mary should be brought to trial, it would have been natural for them to enlist his support for the proposal now that they themselves were in favour of it; but in view of the extreme secrecy involved, it is not surprising that the only evidence that Killigrew discussed the matter with Knox is a cryptic passage which may perhaps refer to something completely different. 'The postscript to your Lordship's letter I answer thus', wrote Killigrew to Burghley on 6 October, 'I trust to satisfy Morton, and for John Knox, that that thing ye may see by my despatch to Master Secretary is done, and doing daily; the people in general well bent to England, abhorring the fact in France, and fearing their tyranny. John Knox is now so feeble as scarce can he stand alone, or speak to be heard of any audience....' The 'great matter', as the proposal for Mary's extradition was called in the English diplomatic correspondence, was under consideration for a long time; but the King's lords were only prepared to agree to it if English troops were sent to keep order during Mary's trial, and the proposal came to nothing.[1]

At the end of October the weather turned unusually cold for the time of year, with great gales sweeping the country. On 29 October, Mar died; he was the only one of the four Regents of James VI to die from natural causes. Knox's life was also drawing to its close during the darkest weeks of the year, and at the darkest time in the history of Scotland. Never before had crime and lawlessness been so rife. The fabric of government, which had managed to survive the English invasions of the forties and the revolution of 1559–60, had now broken down completely; for the day-to-day work of government, along with the idealism and religious fervour of the Reformation, had disappeared in the sordid violence of the Douglas wars. But Knox was happy, for he knew that the good cause had triumphed, now that Elizabeth had irrevocably turned against Mary after the discovery of the Ridolfi plot. He had nothing more to live for. He had only one more duty to perform, to see that Lawson was installed as his successor as the minister to the congregation of Edinburgh. After

[1] Killigrew to Burghley and Leicester (6 Oct. 1572) (*Sc. Cal.* iv. 452; *Works*, vi. 633). For the plan to surrender Mary to the King's lords for trial, see Killigrew to Burghley and Leicester, 19 Oct. 1572; Pitcairn's notes for Killigrew, 28 Oct. 1572; Killigrew to Walsingham, 25 June 1574 (*Sc. Cal.* iv. 461, 469, 788; *Cal. For. Pap. Eliz.* x. 613, 621, 1474).

Lawson had preached a number of sermons, the congregation were fully satisfied with him, and elected him as their minister. He was inaugurated on Sunday, 9 November. Knox preached as usual in the tolbooth, and then went with the rest to St. Giles's for the inauguration ceremony. He was helped up into the pulpit, and from there preached to Lawson on his duties as minister; but only very few people could hear what he said. Afterwards he walked slowly back to his house, leaning on his staff and escorted by the whole congregation. He never went out again.[1]

Next day he had a bad attack of coughing, and took to his bed. His friends urged him to send for his physician, and he willingly agreed, 'saying that he was unwilling either to despise or neglect ordinary means, although he knew that the Lord would soon put an end to his warfare'. He quickly grew weaker, and by Thursday, 13 November, he was too ill to read. As he could no longer read the Psalms and other parts of Scripture which he usually read every day, his wife and Bannatyne read aloud to him the seventeenth chapter of St. John, the fifty-third chapter of Isaiah, a chapter from the Epistle to the Ephesians, and some sermons of Calvin in French; he had asked them to read these passages to him if he ever became too ill to read himself. On Friday the 14th, his household were shocked to find him trying to get out of bed, because he thought that it was Sunday and he had to go to church to preach. Next day he was much better. Before he became so ill, he had invited some friends to supper on that Saturday, and he would not cancel the invitation; and he was well enough to rise and sit with them at the supper table. He ordered a new hogshead of wine to be pierced, and urged his guests to drink it as freely as they wished, as he himself would not live long enough to finish the wine in that cask. Next day, on the Sunday, he refused to eat because he thought that it was the first Sunday of the fast proclaimed by the Church, until it was pointed out to him that the fast was to begin a week later, on Sunday the 23rd.

During the next week, he was visited by many friends who came to say a last farewell, including some of the greatest nobles in Scotland. On Monday the 17th, the leading members of the Church of Edinburgh came at his request. A few days earlier, Lethington had written to the Church Session of Edinburgh,

[1] Bannatyne, pp. 279–81; Stow, *Annals*, p. 674; Smeton's account of Knox's death (*Works*, vi. 653–4).

complaining that Knox had called him an atheist. Knox was too ill to make a formal reply, but he told the ministers who visited him that though he had never accused Lethington of being an atheist, the godlessness of Lethington was proved by the ruins of the houses in Edinburgh that had been destroyed or demolished by the Castilians during the military operations before the truce. Knox also reminded the ministers of their responsibility for ensuring that James VI obeyed the will of God when he was old enough to rule himself.[1]

On Wednesday, 19 November, Morton, Lord Boyd, and Douglas of Drumlanrig came. Knox spoke with each of them alone. 'What purpose was among them', wrote Bannatyne, 'none but themselves knew.' But what was said between him and Morton became known nine years later, when Morton revealed it on the morning of the day on which he was executed. Knox knew, as did every other well-informed person, that Morton would be chosen as the new Regent by the lords in a few days' time. As soon as they were alone, Knox asked Morton whether he had known anything about the murder of Darnley. Morton assured him that he had known nothing of it. Knox then said that God had granted Morton many riches and other benefits that He had not given to other men, and was now about to give him the office of Regent; and he urged Morton to use these benefits better in time to come than he had done in the past. Knox's question to Morton about Darnley's death is remarkable. All the time that Knox was demanding that Mary should be put to death for Darnley's murder, he had suspected in his heart that his champion, Morton, the leader of the Protestant cause in Scotland, was also guilty.[2]

On 21 November, Knox ordered Bannatyne to prepare his coffin. About this time, he was visited by a gentlewoman whom he knew. When she began to praise him, he reprimanded her: 'Tongue, tongue, lady; flesh of itself is over proud, and needs no means to esteem the self.' He urged her to 'cast away stinking pride', and reminded her of what a poor woman had said to her long ago: 'Lady, lady, the black ox has never tramped yet upon your foot.' According to Thomas Smeton, who seven years later published an account of Knox's death, he was visited on the 22nd by the leading members of the congregation of Edinburgh. He

[1] Woddmyngton to Walsingham, 15 May 1582 (*Cal. of Border Pap.* i. 122).
[2] Morton's confession, 2 June 1581 (Bannatyne, pp. 326–7).

spoke to them at some length, despite the great difficulty which he now had in speaking, exhorting them to religious constancy. The others then withdrew, and he spoke alone to Lawson and David Lindsay about Grange.

You have formerly been witnesses [he said] of the courage and constancy of Grange in the cause of the Lord; but now, alas, into what a gulf has he precipitated himself. I entreat you not to refuse the request which I now make to you. Go, and tell him in my name that unless he is yet brought to repentance, he shall die miserably; for neither the craggy rock in which he miserably trusts, nor the carnal prudence of that man [Lethington] whom he looks upon as a demi-god, nor the assistance of foreigners, as he falsely flatters himself, shall deliver them; but he shall be disgracefully dragged from his nest to punishment, and hung on a gallows in the face of the sun, unless he speedily amend his life, and flee to the mercy of God. The man's soul is dear to me, and I would not have it perish if I could save it.

Lawson and Lindsay did as they were asked, but Grange refused to change his course of action.

On the morning of Monday, 24 November 1572, Knox insisted on getting up and putting on his hose and doublet. He sat in a chair for half an hour, and then went back to bed. He was visited by Robert Campbell of Kinzeancleuch, whom he asked to take care of his wife and children. By the afternoon it was clear that death would come at any minute, but he still lingered on. He was in no pain, except when he tried to speak. At about midday, he asked his wife to read aloud the fifteenth chapter of the First Epistle to the Corinthians, and said that he commended his soul, spirit, and body to God, ticking off his soul, spirit, and body on three of his fingers. At about 5 p.m. he said to Margaret: 'Go read where I cast my first anchor'; and she read to him the seventeenth chapter of John's Gospel. From time to time he sipped a little weak ale. At seven o'clock he fell asleep, but at ten o'clock he seemed to stir, and the ordinary evening prayers were said in his room. His physician asked him if he heard the prayers. Knox replied: 'I would to God that ye and all men heard them as I have heard them; and I praise God of that Heavenly sound.' He died at about 11 p.m., peacefully, in no pain. Bannatyne and Kinzeancleuch sat beside him as he died.[1]

[1] For the account of Knox's last illness and death, see Bannatyne, pp. 281–9; Smeton's account (*Works*, vi. 634–44, 654–60). See also Melville, *Diary*, pp. 34–35.

He was buried two days later, on 26 November. Morton, who had been chosen as Regent on the day of Knox's death, attended the funeral with all the King's lords who were in Edinburgh. Morton declared, at the funeral, that Knox 'neither feared nor flattered any flesh'.[1] This was a tribute from a man whom Knox had never ventured seriously to oppose, and who, in his turn, had taken care to avoid a conflict with Knox. Morton and Knox had a healthy respect for each other.

By his will, Knox disposed of assets amounting to a total of £1,526, including £830 owing to him in debts. £80 of this was owed to him by Lord Ochiltre. We do not know for how long Ochiltre had been indebted to Knox; but if Knox often lent money to his father-in-law, it is surprising that Nicol Burne and his colleagues did not mention it as an explanation of why Knox succeeded in winning the hand of a noble lady. Knox owed no debts himself. In modern money, the equivalent of some £25,000 was owing to him, and his total assets were worth about £45,000. He bequeathed many silver cups and spoons.

The will, which Knox had made at St. Andrews on 13 May 1572, was a lengthy document. It was addressed 'first unto the Papists and to the unthankful world', whom he informed that although his life had been odious to them, and that they had often sought his destruction, yet his death would be the greatest calamity which would befall them. 'A dead man have I been almost these two years last bypast, and yet I would that they should ripely consider in what better estate they and their matters stand in, than it has done before. . . . But because they will not admit me for an admonisher, I give them over to the judgement of Him who knows the hearts of all.' He then proceeded to address the Congregation, and to assure them that he had never exceeded the bounds of God's Scriptures, before passing to the operative parts of the will. He left £500 to Marjory's brother, Robert Bowes, in trust for his two sons in England, and also left them £30 worth of his books, and two silver drinking cups 'marked with J.K.M. on the one side, and on the other side with E.B.N'. He left £100 to pay for the education of his nephew Paul Knox. He left the rest of his property to Margaret Stewart and his three daughters.[2]

[1] Melville, *Diary*, p. 60.

[2] Knox's Will, 13 May 1572 (*Works*, vi. liii–lviii; the passages cited are on pp. lv, lvii).

In February 1573, Morton entered into secret negotiations with Huntly and the Hamiltons separately, as a result of which they acknowledged James VI as King and Morton as Regent, and were pardoned and restored to their lands. Only Edinburgh Castle held out for Mary. In April, Elizabeth at last sent English troops with cannon to batter the castle into surrender. After mining operations had failed, the English guns knocked down David's Tower, which blocked the castle well, and as the Castilians could not hold out without water, they surrendered on 28 May. By the terms of surrender, the English general, Sir William Drury, allowed all the defenders to go free except the leaders, who were handed over to Morton. Morton referred the question of their fate to Elizabeth, but pointed out to her that the ministers, in their sermons, were demanding that Grange and the others should be put to death; and Elizabeth told Morton that he could do with them as he thought fit. On 3 August, Grange and his brother James and two of his colleagues, one of whom was Mosman the goldsmith, were hanged. Lethington had died suddenly soon after the surrender of the castle; he probably committed suicide.[1]

Thus two of Knox's prophecies were apparently fulfilled. All the chronicles state that when Grange met Drury in front of the castle walls to discuss the terms of surrender, he was unable to come out through the castle gate because it was blocked by the stones that had fallen after the English bombardment. He was therefore let down over the wall by a rope, or ladder. Knox had prophesied that Grange would be spewed out of the castle, not at the gate but over the wall. When Grange was hanged at the market cross of Edinburgh on a sunny afternoon, he was hanged facing towards the east; but before he died, his body swung round to face the west, so he was hanged, as Knox had foretold, in the face of the sun. There are several eye-witnesses to these events, but they were all of them ardent followers of Knox, and wrote after the prophecies had been fulfilled. Drury, who wrote a detailed report to Burghley of his negotiations with Grange for

[1] Drury to Burghley, 23 May and 18 June 1573; Terms of surrender of Edinburgh Castle, 29 May 1573; Report on the siege of Edinburgh Castle (Aug. 1573(?) wrongly dated May 1573 in *Sc. Cal.* iv. 666 and *Cal. For. Pap. Eliz.* x. 1009); Elizabeth I to Morton, 9 June and 19 July 1573; Morton to Burghley, 26 June 1573; Morton's memorandum for Killigrew (26 June 1573); Morton to Killigrew, 5 Aug. 1573 (*Cal. For. Pap. Eliz.* x. 978, 987, 1009, 1024, 1044, 1055, 1056, 1117, 1118; *Sc. Cal.* iv. 659, 665, 666, 686, 695, 701, 702, 708, 712, and enclosure).

the surrender of the castle, does not mention that Grange came down over the wall to meet him, though within a few years the story was being told by the ballad-mongers, and by Holinshed in his chronicle. Thomas Smeton, who in 1579 told the story of Knox's dying prophecies about Grange in his book *An Orthodox Answer to the Poisonous Dialogue of Archibald Hamilton the Apostate*, was not even in Scotland at the time of Knox's death, though he may have obtained his information from Lawson; and like Smeton, James Melville, describing Grange's execution and Knox's prophecy about it, had the advantage of hindsight when he wrote his memoirs in 1600. Bannatyne's account of Knox's last years, which was written early in 1573 before the fall of Edinburgh Castle, contains no mention of any prophecies that Grange would come down over the wall, or be hanged in the face of the sun.[1]

The fall of Edinburgh Castle put an end to the civil war, and left Morton in control. He adopted a far firmer attitude towards the Protestant Church than any of his predecessors, or Mary, had done. When the ministers protested against his tulchan bishops, he threatened to have them hanged. In 1581 he was overthrown by a conspiracy directed by Esmé Stuart d'Aubigny—an agent of the Guises—James Balfour, and Knox's brother-in-law, James Stewart of Ochiltre. The English ambassador, who was Knox's other brother-in-law, Sir Robert Bowes, intervened in Morton's favour, but Elizabeth ultimately decided to leave him to his fate. He was put on trial for the murder of Darnley, and was sentenced to be beheaded. On the morning of his execution, he was visited by two ministers of the Church, and confessed to them that he had known beforehand about Darnley's death, because Bothwell had asked him to take part in the murder, but that he had refused to do this. Morton then told the ministers about his last talk with Knox on 19 November 1572.[2]

Knox's two sons both died young. Eight days after Knox's death, both Nathaniel and Eleazer were admitted as students at Cambridge University. Nathaniel took part in amateur theatricals

[1] Cf. Killigrew to Burghley and Leicester, 27 May 1573; Drury to the Council, 28 May 1573 (*Cal. For. Pap. Eliz.* x. 984, 986; *Sc. Cal.* iv. 662, 664); Smeton (in *Works*, vi. 657); Melville, *Diary*, pp. 33–36; Holinshed, *Chronicles of England, Scotland and Ireland*, v. 671.

[2] Melville, *Diary*, pp. 67–68; Morton's confession, 2 June 1581 (Bannatyne, pp. 326–7). For the overthrow of Morton, see Maurice Lee Jr., 'The fall of the Regent Morton: a problem in satellite diplomacy' (*Journal of Modern History*, xxviii. 111–29).

at Cambridge, playing the part of Lord Hastings in Dr. Legg's play about Richard III at a performance at St. John's College in 1579. He died of disease in 1580, when he was just 23. Eleazer, after a distinguished university career, was ordained in the Church of England, and was appointed Vicar of Clacton Magna in Essex; but he died in 1591, at the age of 32.

Knox had three daughters by Margaret Stewart, who were aged about 6, 4, and 2 when he died. The eldest daughter, Martha, like her mother, married a much older man, becoming the wife of Knox's friend, Robert Fairlie of Braid, and dying at the age of 26 in 1592, leaving three sons and a daughter. The second daughter, Margaret Knox, married Zachary Pont, the printer, who later became a minister in the far north and Archdean of Caithness. Pont and Margaret Knox had at least two sons. Knox's third daughter, Elizabeth, married John Welsh, who was active as a minister in the Church in opposition to the policy of James VI after his accession to the English throne, and was banished to France. Elizabeth Knox returned to Scotland after her husband's death, and died at Ayr in 1625.[1]

Margaret Stewart, who was only 25 when Knox died in 1572, was apparently attracted by men of violent temperament, for after Knox she chose as her second husband Andrew Ker of Faldonside, the most brutal of the murderers of Riccio, who had pressed his pistol to the womb of the pregnant Queen during the struggle in the little room in Holyroodhouse. He died in 1598. We have a glimpse of Margaret a few years after this, visiting Knox's old admirer, John Davidson, the minister of Prestonpans, with her son John Ker, who had just returned from a visit to Paris. Young Ker was dressed in the fine costumes that were worn by Parisian students, but Davidson pointed out to him the folly of wearing such clothes, which so affected Ker that he reformed his way of life, and soon after entered the Church as a minister. Margaret had evidently been more tolerant of her son's modish style of dress. She died about 1612.[2]

[1] Laing's Introduction to *Works*, vi. lxiii–lxv, lxix–lxxiii.

[2] Row, *History of the Kirk of Scotland*, p. 462; Laing's Preface to *Works*, vi. lxviii.

CHAPTER XXVI

Conclusion

KNOX was right when he wrote in his will that his death would not help the Papists. It had no effect at all on the struggle in Scotland. His funeral in Edinburgh was attended by all the notables; but the foreign politicians and diplomats, on whom the fate of Scotland depended, hardly noticed Knox's death, or at least did not refer to it in any of their letters that survive. Mary Queen of Scots did not mention it in her letters; in fact, though nearly 750 of Mary's letters have survived, they contain only two brief references to Knox. One is in a letter written in September 1571, recommending John Gordon to the Archbishop of Glasgow in France, in which she mentions that Gordon had written against Knox and had maintained that she was the lawful Queen of Scotland. The other is in a letter to La Mothe Fénelon, the French ambassador in London, in June 1572, when she denounces Knox for his theory about the government of women. There was also one occasion after Knox's death when Mary referred to him in conversation. In April 1584, she told Cecil's agent Waad—inaccurately, and perhaps facetiously—that if Elizabeth could complain of having been excommunicated and deposed by the Pope, she herself was worse off, for she had been excommunicated and deposed by Knox, a simple minister. Mary's French secretary, Claude Nau, who wrote a history of Mary's reign while he was with her during her imprisonment in England, did not mention Knox at all in any of the surviving passages of his manuscript. In the code that Mary used in her letters from her prisons in England, she had a cipher to represent the name of all the people to whom she was likely to refer in her correspondence. There was a cipher for nearly every Scottish lord and politician of prominence; but she had no cipher for Knox.[1]

[1] Bannatyne, p. 290; Mary Queen of Scots to Archbishop Beaton, 18 Sept. 1571 (Labanoff, iii. 374–5); Mary Queen of Scots to Fénelon, 10 June 1572 (*E.H.R.* lii.

By 1570, Knox, as an individual, had ceased to count as a factor in politics. But among certain sections of the Church of Scotland, his influence was great. There were many Scottish Protestants who hated Knox, who considered that he had 'the most part of the wite [blame] of all the cummers [troubles] in Scotland since the slaughter of umquhile [deceased] the Cardinal'; but there were many who loved and revered him, and saw him, in Bannatyne's words, as the 'light of Scotland'. It was because of this that Grange and Lethington and the Queen's men, though they arrested Knox's servant, and singled out for attack a soldier in the King's forces whom they knew bore the name of Knox, did not dare to touch Knox himself. No one could harm Knox without arousing the indignation of large sections of the Congregation, and no one could afford to disregard the Congregation. Knox's strength had always lain in his group and party. A powerful individualist by temperament, his influence lay in the organization that he built up and dominated. Mary had no cipher for 'Knox' in her code, but she had a cipher for 'the Congregation'.[1]

The rulers and politicians feared Knox's ideas more than his actions. Long after they had ceased to care about his influence in Scotland, they denounced *The First Blast of the Trumpet*. Replies to the book were published before Knox's death, not only by Aylmer, but by several Catholic writers. Harding referred to the *First Blast* in his polemic with Jewel, who, as he had shown in Frankfort, had no love for Knox, and hastened to dissociate himself and the Protestant cause from Knox's attack on women rulers. Peter Frarin at Louvain attacked the *First Blast* in his *Oration against the Unlawful Insurrections of the Protestants of our Time*, which was published in 1566. Frarin, who was under the impression that Goodman was the author of the *First Blast*, denounced 'the impudent, vile and shameless villain traitor', and mockingly contrasted his hatred of women rulers with the 'fond and filthy' affection shown to women by most Protestant preachers, who liked women so much that they thought that no one could live celibate for a single day.[2]

82–83); Waad's report on his talk with Mary Queen of Scots on 24 Apr. 1584 (*Sc. Cal.* vii. 72, p. 83); Nau's manuscript (written *c.* 1575), in Stevenson-Nau; Mary Queen of Scots' cipher (*H.M.C. 6th R.* 638).

[1] *Diurnal of Occurrents*, p. 320; Bannatyne pp. 124, 229, 289; Mary Queen of Scots' cipher (*H.M.C. 6th R.* 638).

[2] Harding, *A confutation of a booke intituled an Apologie of the Church of England*,

A more formidable reply to the *First Blast* was written by John Leslie, the Bishop of Ross, in his *Defence of the Regiment of Women*, which he published under the name of Morgan Phillips at Liège in 1571. As Mary's ambassador at Elizabeth's Court, Leslie was deeply involved in the Ridolfi plot, and was arrested, and confined as a prisoner in the house of Cox, who was now Bishop of Ely. Whatever their other differences, the prisoner and his keeper could agree on the subject of Knox. Leslie noted in his diary that on 21 August 1571 he discussed the government of commonwealths with Cox, who 'despites John Knox and Goodman with the band, for the writing against the regiment of women, and others their singular opinions, and holds them Puritans'.[1]

Richard Bertie, the husband of the Duchess of Suffolk, also wrote a reply to the *First Blast*, though he never published it. Bertie was almost a Puritan himself, but as a loyal subject of Elizabeth he could not tolerate Knox's doctrines about the government of women.[2]

Knox's *History of the Reformation in Scotland* angered the sovereigns and their supporters as much as the *First Blast*, chiefly because it contained the report of Knox's disputation with Lethington, when he had asserted that subjects were entitled to resist tyrants by armed force. Knox did not publish the *History* during his lifetime, perhaps partly because so many of his comments, particularly his strictures on individuals such as Moray, became inappropriate as the political situation changed. When the *History* was first published by the English Puritans in London in 1587, it was immediately suppressed by Elizabeth's government. By this time, Whitgift was Archbishop of Canterbury, and the drive against Puritanism in England had begun in earnest. In February 1589, Bancroft, who later succeeded Whitgift as Archbishop, preached his famous sermon against Puritanism at Paul's Cross in

p. 173; Jewel, *The Defence of the Apology of the Church of England* (Jewel, *Works*, iv. 665); Frarin, *Oration against the Unlawfull Insurrections of the Protestantes of our time*, sig. E5. See also Phillips, 'The Background of Spenser's Attitude Toward Women Rulers' (*Huntingdon Library Quarterly*, v. 5–32).

[1] Morgan Phillips, 'Defence of the Regiment of Women' (published in the 2nd edn. of Leslie's *Defence of the Honour of the right high, mighty and noble Princess Mary, Queen of Scotland and Dowager of France*); see also Leslie, op. cit., pp. 48–49 (in Anderson, *Collections*, vol. i.), and Leslie, *De Titulo et iure Serenissimae Principis Mariae Reginae*, p. 9 (published at Rheims in 1580); Leslie's Diary, 21 Aug. 1571 (*Bannatyne Misc.* iii. 143).

[2] B.M. Add. MSS. 48043, fols. 1–9.

London, in the course of which he attacked Knox and the doctrines of the Church of Scotland with such vigour that the General Assembly wrote to Elizabeth to protest; but Bancroft justified his sermon to Burghley by stating that the writings of Knox and Buchanan were 'trumpets of rebellion'.[1]

When James VI grew to manhood, and began his struggle to maintain the principles of kingship against the Church of Scotland, he conceived a great hatred of the man who had preached and 'asked instruments' at his coronation when he was 13 months old. Andrew Melville and the preachers were repeatedly admonishing James for the contempt with which he spoke of the man of God. In his *Basilicon Doron*, James denounced the 'infamous invectives' in Knox's *History* and in Buchanan's books, and advised his son, Prince Henry, to whom he addressed the book: 'If any of these infamous libels remain in your days, use the law upon the keepers thereof, for in that point I would have you a Pythagorist, to think that the spirits of those archibellisis of rebellion are flitted into them that hoard their books or maintain their opinions, punishing them even as if it were their authors risen again.' Eighty years later, Knox was still considered to be a danger to the established order. His doctrine that subjects might lawfully resist and kill wicked kings was included among the opinions condemned by the University authorities at Oxford during the Tory reaction of the last years of Charles II's reign. Knox's writings were publicly burnt, and members of the University were forbidden to read them.[2]

But the Church of Scotland, or, to speak more accurately, a part of the Church of Scotland, has for 400 years regarded Knox with a veneration that is only accorded to a very small number of historical figures. Like Joan of Arc and George Washington, Knox is almost above criticism in the eyes of his supporters. This veneration began immediately after his death. In 1573 John Davidson published his poem *A Brief Commendation of Uprightness*, in

[1] Hume Brown, *John Knox*, ii. 214 and n. For Bancroft's sermon, see 'A sermon preached at Paules Crosse the 9 of Februarie . . . Anno 1588' [1588/9]; the General Assembly to Elizabeth I (undated) (*Wodrow Misc.* i. 477–96); and see Donaldson, 'The Attitude of Whitgift and Bancroft to the Scottish Church' (*Trans. R.H.S.* 4th Ser. xxiv. 109–12).

[2] Fontenay to Mary Queen of Scots (Jan. 1583) (*Sc. Cal.* vi. 298); 'The Conference and reasoning between the King and James Gibson, minister of Pencatland, 21 Dec. 1585 at Linlithgow before Secret Council' (*H.M.C. 7th R.* 430); James VI, *Basilicon Doron*, p. 149; Proclamation of Oxford University, 21 July 1683 (Wilkins, iv. 610–12).

which he attributed Knox's escape from danger in the galleys, in England under Mary Tudor, and in Scotland when confronting Mary Queen of Scots and the Privy Council in December 1563 and the anger of the Queen's men in 1571, to the direct intervention of God on behalf of His prophet. The Protestants could make effective propaganda, not only out of the constancy of the martyrs, but also out of Knox's flair for avoiding martyrdom. Although Davidson had met Knox at St. Andrews, and wrote within a few months of his death, his statements cannot be considered reliable. His story of how Knox was preserved by divine providence in the galleys, when the crew had been bribed by the Papists to throw him overboard, and survived, although nearly all his companions lost their lives, is in complete contradiction to Knox's own account in his *History* of his experiences in the galleys.[1]

The stories about Knox's prophetic powers, showing how his prophecies came true, were also circulated within a very few years of his death by Smeton, and were later repeated and elaborated by James Melville and many other Scottish Protestant writers. In 1812 Knox's biographer, McCrie, stated that he believed that God gave the power to foretell the future as a special gift to men of outstanding virtue, and that Knox may have possessed this gift. As recently as 1937 a Scottish historian wrote that he agreed with McCrie on this point.[2]

In death, as in life, Knox has belonged to the Church of Scotland. But it is difficult to imagine Knox as a member of this Church in any of the four centuries during which it has acclaimed him as the Great Reformer. He had little in common with the fanatical Covenanters of the seventeenth century. It is hard to believe that Knox would have supported Charles II against Cromwell, would have refused to let his generals fight a battle on a Sunday, or would have associated himself with the impracticable politics of the Cameronians. He is even further removed from the Presbyterian minister of the nineteenth century, although today in England he is usually regarded as a ridiculous Victorian figure, staid and respectable, a butt for humourists whose wit seems mild and insipid compared with Knox's own.

[1] Davidson, 'Ane Breif Commendatioun of Uprichtnes', ll. 129–92 (in Rogers, 'Three Poets of the Scottish Reformation', in *Trans. R.H.S.* iii. 250–1).

[2] Smeton's account of Knox's death (*Works*, vi. 657); Melville, *Diary*, pp. 33–36; McCrie, *Life of John Knox*, pp. 367–8; Moffat Gillon, *John Davidson of Prestonpans*, pp. 246–7. See also Calderwood, iii. 237–8.

Knox is one of the most ruthless and successful revolutionary leaders in history. He was more ruthless, at least in theory, than any revolutionary of more recent times. Dictators ancient and modern have killed their opponents whenever they considered that this was expedient. Revolutionary mobs have killed oppressors out of a desire for vengeance and justice. But Knox and his Puritans are the only modern revolutionaries who proclaimed that it was sinful not to kill their enemies. The sin of Saul was his decision to spare Amalek. No Jacobin or Bolshevik spoke so often of 'foolish pity' as did Knox. Yet McCrie rightly claims that Knox never used his power to destroy a personal, as opposed to a political, enemy;[1] and in the small but vital sector of the European struggle in which he was engaged, there was very little loss of life.

There can be no doubt as to his success. Revolutionary régimes do not usually last for 400 years; but the new order that Knox established by revolutionary violence in 1560 survived all dangers, until it ceased to be a matter of political controversy. In the course of time it lost many of the features which Knox considered essential. Its role as a political power controlling the State did not survive the repression of Charles II and James II and the settlement of 1688; and it was not entirely successful in enforcing its morality on the people. Even modern totalitarian régimes have not interfered more drastically with the private life of its citizens than did Knox's Church Sessions, with their incessant investigations into the activities of fornicators; but before the death of James VI and I, English travellers were reporting that sexual immorality was widespread in Scotland, and far more flagrant than in England;[2] and today no Scotsman walks in fear of the stool of repentance or of excommunication. But the purely religious side of Knox's work has survived. The Church of Scotland still worships today, in all essentials, as it did in Knox's time. In every town and village of Scotland, the Church service is based on the Order of Geneva, and the communion is received sitting. This is John Knox's achievement. He was, after all, a religious

[1] McCrie, p. 361.

[2] Sir Anthony Weldon (?), *A Perfect Description of the People and Country of Scotland*; John Taylor, *The Pennyless Pilgrimage, or the Moneyless Perambulation of John Taylor, alias the King's Majesty's Water Poet* (in Hume Brown, *Early Travellers in Scotland*, pp. 97–103, 107–30; see pp. 101, 125). Weldon visited Scotland in 1617, and Taylor in 1618.

man and a religious leader, and though all his life he was absorbed in political struggle, and would never have accepted the idea of a non-political Church, the daily and weekly religious service was the central thing in his life. This still remains.

The establishment of Calvinism and the Church of Scotland was due to Knox. Knox's biographer, Hume Brown, has pointed out that it was more important for the success of the Reformation in Scotland that Lord James Stewart and the Earl of Argyll became Protestants than that Knox did.[1] In fact, the overthrow of Catholicism in Scotland was due much more to Elizabeth and Cecil than to either Knox or Lord James; but it was because of Knox that the Church of Rome was replaced by Calvinism and not by Anglicanism. The obvious thing would have been for the English armies and diplomatic agents to have brought Anglicanism with them when they came to Scotland and overthrew Popery, and for Lord James and all the lords and lairds to have accepted the doctrines of the Church of England when they accepted English money. It was thanks to Knox, and the organization that he moulded, that Presbyterianism was established in Scotland. Presbyterianism, in its full sense, did not develop until the fight against the tulchan bishops began a year or two after Knox's death; but though Andrew Melville, not Knox, was the leader in this struggle, Melville was Knox's heir. Knox was prepared to shelve the issue of bishops until after the Queen's lords had been defeated; but his spirit animated Melville and Davidson. It is sometimes suggested that Knox was not opposed to bishops, because he not only accepted the Agreement of Leith, but had found a place for superintendents in his system; but the author of The Book of Discipline, with its elected ministers and superintendents, would never have supported bishops as they existed in the Church of James VI and Charles I.

Knox is one of the important theorists of modern times. His importance has been overlooked because of the language in which he expressed his ideas; but when Knox wrote about the punishments inflicted on Pharaoh's soldiers for their docile compliance with orders, and the zeal of Jehu in killing wicked kings, he was putting forward ideas that were far more important for the future than the politico-legal theories of government of Bodin and Sir Thomas Smith and the intellectuals of his age. Only Buchanan can

[1] Hume Brown, *John Knox*, ii. 3.

equal Knox in importance. It is often suggested that Knox's doctrine of resistance to rulers was basically the same as Calvin's; but Calvin, who adopted the theory of the justification of armed resistance to Papist rulers so belatedly and so reluctantly, never reached the position which Knox attained as early as 1558. Calvin not only condemned the conspiracy of Amboise in 1560, and denounced tyrannicide as a sin, but told the French Huguenots that their resistance could only be justified if it was led by a Prince of the Blood. Knox's theory was no more derived from Calvin than from his old teacher at St. Andrews University, John Major, who advocated the advantages of limited monarchy, but never wrote a book that was banned by the authorities on pain of death, or instigated a revolution.

The difference between the position of Knox and Calvin is particularly striking, because Calvin's doctrine of the authority of the lesser magistrates was as suitable for application in Scotland as it was in France. The theory that the nobility and the lesser magistrates, like the ephors in ancient Sparta, had the power and the duty to act against the chief magistrate if he was an idolater, was developed, with many qualifications, by Calvin, and more resolutely by Beza and the French Calvinists after Calvin's death. This theory was sufficient to justify all the actions of the Lords of the Congregation; but though it was adopted by many of the Scottish Protestants, and was vigorously expounded by Knox himself in his *Appellation to the Nobility and Estates of Scotland*, it played a comparatively unimportant part in Knox's justification of revolution. In his *Appellation to the Commonalty of Scotland*, and in his later utterances, he placed far more emphasis on the duty of the individual, whatever his rank, to resist evil rulers by all means at his disposal, including armed force, because all subjects who obeyed their evil rulers would be punished as Pharaoh's soldiers were punished.

It was this aspect of Knox's doctrine which was quoted by Milton in the regicide tracts. The revolutionary political philosophy of the English Puritans was derived from Knox, though the Puritans of the seventeenth century who put these theories into practice in England were in some respects closer to the Anabaptists whom Knox denounced so violently than they were to Knox's Presbyterians. Through Milton, Knox influenced, by example if not by doctrine, the men of 1776 and 1789, whose outlook has shaped all subsequent political thought and action. As Aylmer said, Knox almost cracked the duty of obedience;[1] and under his successors, the crack grew until it shattered the doctrine that had enabled the kings of the sixteenth century, without the technical resources of a modern totalitarian state at their disposal, to maintain an equally tyrannical régime. Because of this, Knox, despite his intolerance, his dogmatic adherence to every word of Scripture, and the tyranny of his Church Sessions, was a great contributor to the struggle for human freedom. He taught the people that they had a duty to fight for the right, irrespective of national allegiance and the orders of their governments. Modern democracy is grounded upon this principle which Knox deduced from the texts of Exodus and the Book of Kings.

The personality of Knox, magnificent and terrible, has fascinated and appalled posterity. The aristocratic eighteenth century condemned him; the puritanical and radical nineteenth century admired him. The twentieth century, which is anti-puritanical and conscious of the menace of determined revolutionary minorities, cannot accept the nineteenth-century view of Knox; but while giving thanks that we do not have to live under the kind of régime that he established, we can appreciate the tribute that was paid to him, ten years after his death, by his English Puritan follower, John Field: 'What a heroical and bold spirit he was!'[2]

[1] Aylmer, *An Harborrowe for Faithfull and Trewe Subiectes*, sig. B; see also Milton, *The Tenure of Kings and Magistrates*; Milton, *Observations upon the Articles of Peace with the Irish Rebels* (*Complete Prose Works of John Milton*, iii. 223–5, 248, 329).

[2] Field's Epistle Dedicatory to Anne Prouze [Anne Locke], 1 Jan. 1583, in Knox's *Exposition upon the 4th of Matthew* (*Works*, iv. 91).

APPENDIX I

The Date of Knox's Birth

THE statement that Knox was born in 1505 was first published in the Life of Knox in David Buchanan's edition of Knox's *History of the Reformation in Scotland* in 1644. It was never challenged until 27 May 1904, when, on the eve of the quatercentenary celebrations of Knox's birth, *The Scotsman* published a letter from Hay Fleming, who combined extreme Protestant prejudice with great historical erudition. Hay Fleming pointed out that there were strong grounds for believing that Knox was born some ten years after 1505. This did not prevent the quatercentenary celebrations from being held in 1905, and the conservatism of historians is so strong that it has taken nearly fifty years for it to be generally accepted that Knox was born, not in 1505, but in 1514 or 1515, though all the evidence supports Hay Fleming's opinion.

In 1579, seven years after Knox's death, Beza was writing his book *Icones*, in which he published short biographies of eminent European Protestants. Beza wrote to Scotland, asking for information about Knox. He received a reply from Sir Peter Young, who was the tutor of the young King James VI. Young mentioned, amongst other things, that Knox, who died on 24 November 1572, was in his fifty-ninth year at the time of his death. When Beza published his *Icones* in 1580, he stated that Knox died at the age of 57. There must have been many people still living in Geneva in 1580 who had known Knox when he resided there twenty-two years before, and some of them may have known Knox's age at the time, and told Beza that he was in fact two years younger than Sir Peter Young had said. Young's statement may have been corrected by James Lawson, Knox's successor as minister at St. Giles's, who, according to Young's letter, was intending to write to Beza to give him more information about Knox. But it is more likely that the statement in *Icones* was a printer's error, for there is at least one other obvious misprint in the section on Knox in the book.[1] The best available evidence therefore indicates that Knox was in his fifty-ninth year, or aged 58, on 24 November 1572, and was born in 1514.

No writer until David Buchanan in 1644—if Buchanan was in fact the author of the biography that was published in his edition of Knox's

[1] Young to Beza, 13 Nov. 1579 (Hume Brown, *John Knox*, ii. 322–4); Beza, *Icones*, sig. Ee3. In *Icones*, the date of Knox's death is wrongly given as 24 Dec. 1572.

History—suggested that Knox was born in 1505; until then, all historians followed Beza's statement in *Icones* that he died at the age of 57.[1] There is apparent confirmation of Buchanan's date in Archbishop Spottiswood's *History of the Church of Scotland*, where it is stated that Knox died in his sixty-seventh year; but Hay Fleming has shown that this, far from confirming Buchanan's statement, explains the reason for his error. Spottiswood's book was first published in 1655, but had been written at some time before Spottiswood's death in 1639. Hay Fleming discovered that Spottiswood, in his original manuscript, had written that Knox died in his fifty-seventh year; and he also found evidence which suggests that David Buchanan had read Spottiswood's manuscript before he published Knox's *History* in 1644. As Spottiswood wrote his '5' in such a way that it looks very like a '6', Hay Fleming deduced that David Buchanan, like Spottiswood's printer, misread '57th' as '67th', and that it was because of this error that Buchanan gave 1505 as the date of Knox's birth.[2]

Despite the fact that Hay Fleming developed his arguments fully and irrefutably in an article in *The Bookman* in September 1905, the historians clung obstinately to the belief that Knox was born in 1505, though A. T. Innes, in his article on Knox in the 1910 edition of the *Encyclopaedia Britannica*, and Andrew Lang, were almost prepared to accept Hay Fleming's date. Edwin Muir, in his entertaining but unsound biography of Knox in 1929, states that one letter from Young to Beza is not sufficient to outweigh the tradition that Knox was born in 1505; but for more than seventy years after Knox's death there was an unchallenged tradition that he was 57 when he died—though this, too, is probably a year out—and the later tradition can be traced to David Buchanan's error in 1644 as clearly as the older tradition can be traced to Beza's book in 1580. Another argument put forward by Muir and other writers is the fact that Knox, at the end of his life, is described by all his contemporaries, and by himself, as being feeble and decrepit, and this picture of a dying old man is much more compatible with Knox's being in his sixties rather than in his fifties. But apart from the well-known fact that in the sixteenth century men aged much earlier than they do now, there are in fact very few references by contemporaries to Knox's being old, except in connexion with his marriage to a

[1] The short life of Knox, in the 1644 edn. of Knox's *History*, is unsigned; unlike other parts of the Introduction, it is not signed with the initials 'D. B.' (David Buchanan). The life of Knox published in the London edition of 1644 is a much abbreviated version of the life in the 1644 Edinburgh edition. The statement that Knox was born in 1505 is in both editions. Beza's statement in *Icones* was followed by Verheiden in his *Effigies* in 1602, and by Melchior Adam in his *Vitae Theologicae* in 1618.

[2] Hay Fleming, 'The date of Knox's birth', in *The Bookman*, xxviii. 193–6; Spottiswood, ii. 184. Spottiswood wrongly gives the date of Knox's death as 27 Nov.

girl of 17. The contemporaries tell us that he was ill, not old. From Young's letter to Beza, it appears that Knox's hair never turned white, and even at the time of his death was only flecked with grey. It was through illness, not age, that Knox had to be helped along the street and into the pulpit, and had, in his own words, 'one foot in the grave' when he was 55.[1]

Hay Fleming's conclusions have recently been confirmed by the researches of his religious adversaries. David Buchanan, in his Life of Knox, states that Knox was ordained in the Church 'before the time ordinarily allowed by the canons'. The canon law prohibited anyone from being ordained a priest before reaching the age of 24, unless a dispensation had been obtained. In 1955 the historians of the *Innes Review* discovered, among the papers of William Murdoch, a note that John Knox was ordained a priest on Easter Eve, 18 April 1536, which is obviously an incorrect transcription of 15 April, which was Easter Eve in 1536. Murdoch was a Jesuit missionary who was sent secretly to Scotland to carry on illegal propaganda activity at the beginning of the seventeenth century; and this note about Knox's ordination was found among his papers when he was arrested in 1607. There is reason for believing that it was written by Murdoch's Jesuit colleague, McQuhirrie, and that it is an extract from the register of the Bishop of Dunblane. The question of Knox's ordination would have been of interest to the Jesuits, as it had been raised in controversy, and as the discovery of this proof of his ordination would have been unwelcome to the Jesuits rather than the reverse, there is no reason to doubt the truth of the information that they recorded. If Knox was under the canonical age when he was ordained, he must have been born after 15 April 1512.[2]

There is another possible indication of the date of Knox's birth, though a far less certain one. Knox records in his *History* that during his talk with Bothwell in 1562, he said to Bothwell: 'My lord, my grandfather, goodsire and father have served your Lordship's predecessors, and some of them have died under their standards.'[3] 'Grandfather, goodsire and father' mean, in modern language, great-grandfather, grandfather, and father. As the Earls of Bothwell were the local territorial magnate in the neighbourhood of Haddington, it was natural that Knox's ancestors, if they had answered the call for all men between

[1] Knox to Cecil, 2 Jan. 1569/70 (*Works*, vi. 568); Andrew Lang, *John Knox and the Reformation*, pp. 4–6; Muir, *John Knox: portrait of a Calvinist*, pp. 310–11.

[2] Life of Knox, in 1644 edn. of Knox's *History* (Edinburgh edn., unpag., London edn., sig. a); Peter J. Shearman, 'Father Alexander McQuhirrie, S.J.'; Rev. W. J. Anderson, in 'The Ordination of John Knox: a symposium' (*Innes Rev*. vi. 42–45, 103–4).

[3] Knox, *History*, ii. 38.

the ages of 60 and 16 to go against the 'ancient enemies of England', would have marched in the contingent led by the Earl of Bothwell. Knox's phrase 'died under their standards' is hardly applicable to dying fighting for the Hepburns in a family feud or in some minor expedition against the Border robbers, and suggests that his ancestor fell when fighting under the leadership of an Earl of Bothwell in a Scottish army royal. If this is so, it was probably at Flodden, because in the fifty years before Knox's birth the Scots had not fought any other major battle, and had suffered very few losses in their minor campaigns against England; but at Flodden, their losses were very heavy, and many families in the land lost a relative at Flodden. Both Knox's father and grandfather could have been between the ages of 16 and 60 in September 1513, and might therefore have died at Flodden. If Knox's father died there, Knox, even if he was a posthumous child, cannot have been born later than the spring of 1514.

APPENDIX II

Knox's University

BEZA says that Knox studied under John Major at St. Andrews University. St. Andrews was the university to which a citizen of Haddington would normally go, as Haddington was in the diocese of St. Andrews; but there is no record in the surviving registers of St. Andrews that Knox was incorporated in the University, and there is an entry in the register of Glasgow University that a student named John Knox was incorporated there in 1522. John Major was teaching at Glasgow in 1522, before proceeding to St. Andrews in 1523; and it was therefore believed all through the nineteenth century that Beza was mistaken, and that it was at Glasgow, not St. Andrews, that Knox studied under Major. This opinion was based on the assumption that Knox was born in 1505; as he was in fact nine years younger, he could not have gone to Glasgow University in 1522. This student incorporated at Glasgow was undoubtedly another John Knox—probably one of those distant cousins of Knox who lived in the west of Scotland. Knox himself almost certainly went to the University of St. Andrews, as Beza stated.[1]

There has been some argument as to what subject Knox was studying when he studied 'at the feet of John Major', as Beza expresses it. Major first taught at St. Andrews when he left Glasgow University in 1523. During his first period at St. Andrews in 1523–6, he may have lectured in Arts at the Paedagogium. From 1526 to 1531, Major was teaching at the Sorbonne in Paris. He returned to St. Andrews in 1531, and stayed there until his death in 1550. During this period after 1531, he was certainly teaching theology at St. Salvator's College. As Knox was born in or about 1514, and not in 1505, he could not have been studying at St. Andrews by 1526; so it is clear that it was theology, and not Arts, that he studied under Major.[2]

[1] Beza, *Icones*, sig. Ee3; *Munimenta Alme Universitatis Glasguensis*, ii. 147 (25 Oct. 1522); Life of Knox, in 1644 edn. of Knox's *History* (Edinburgh edn., unpag., London edn. sig. a).

[2] J. M. Anderson's Introduction to *Early Records of the University of St. Andrews*, pp. xxxviii–xli.

APPENDIX III

Knox's Examination before the English Privy Council in 1553

THERE is no contemporary authority for the fact that Knox was summoned before the English Privy Council and examined about his refusal to accept the benefice in Bread Street in London and his objection to kneeling to receive communion. The only account is in David Buchanan's Life of Knox in the 1644 edition of Knox's *History*, and in Calderwood's *History of the Kirk of Scotland*,[1] which was written shortly before Calderwood's death in 1650, and published posthumously. David Buchanan states that he obtained his information from a letter written in Knox's own hand. Calderwood, as is his frequent habit, follows David Buchanan almost verbatim; but he gives the date of Knox's appearance before the Privy Council as 14 April 1553, whereas from David Buchanan's account it appears that this was the date of Knox's letter in which the incident was described. There is no mention of it in the Acts of the Privy Council, but there is nothing surprising in this, as the Acts are in the nature of minutes, and usually only decisions that called for some action to be taken were recorded in them. There are several other cases in which a discussion or examination, which is known to have taken place in the Privy Council, is not recorded.

It is more difficult to explain the contradiction between the list of Councillors present, as given by David Buchanan and Calderwood, and the list of attendances in the Acts of the Privy Council. David Buchanan and Calderwood state that those present included Cranmer, Goodrich, Paulet, Bedford, Northampton, Shrewsbury, 'the Chamberlain'—by which Lord Darcy, the Lord Chamberlain of the Household, is presumably meant, and not the Lord Great Chamberlain, Northampton, or the Vice-Chamberlain, Sir John Gates—the two Secretaries (Petre and Cecil) and 'others'. Presumably Northumberland was not present; for if he had been, his name would obviously have been specifically mentioned. The Acts of the Privy Council record that at the meeting of the Council on 14 April, which was held at Greenwich, there were present Paulet, Northumberland, Northampton, Shrewsbury, Pembroke, Darcy,

[1] The passage appears only in the Edinburgh edition (unpaginated) of Knox's *History*, and is omitted in the London edition. See Calderwood, i. 280.

Gates, and Cecil. There is no meeting of the Council at which all the Councillors listed by David Buchanan and Calderwood were present, between 2 February 1553, when Knox refused the benefice in Bread Street, and 16 June 1553.[1] After this, the Council records are lost for the remaining three weeks of Edward VI's reign; but the meeting in question obviously took place before 2 June, when, as the Acts of the Privy Council record, Knox was sent to Buckinghamshire. Perhaps Knox was not summoned to a full meeting of the Council, but was interviewed by a Council committee, or at a less formal meeting of some of the Councillors.

David Buchanan and Calderwood give the impression that at this time, Knox and his congregation were still sitting to receive communion. They say that at the meeting of the Privy Council, Knox was asked: 'Thirdly, why he kneeled not at the Lord's Supper.' On this point, 'there was great contention betwixt the whole table and him', but eventually Knox 'was dismissed with some gentle speeches, and willed to advise with himself if he could communicate according to that order. But he ever abhorred it.' But Knox's letter to his congregation in Berwick,[2] in which he instructed them to submit and to receive the communion on their knees, though it is undated, must have been written several months earlier, probably between 27 October 1552, when the Council decided to issue the black rubric, and 1 November, when the Second Book of Common Prayer came into force. If the meeting took place on or just before 14 April 1553, any discussion about Knox's refusal to kneel to receive communion must have concerned his trouble-making in the past, not his present disobedience. Knox might have written a letter on 14 April 1553 in which he described a confrontation with the Privy Council that had taken place some six months earlier, in the autumn of 1552, just before he instructed his congregation in Berwick to submit; but at that time he had not refused to accept any benefice.

[1] See *A.P.C.* 2 Feb. 1552/3–16 June 1553.

[2] Printed in Lorimer, *John Knox and the Church of England*, pp. 251–65.

APPENDIX IV

The Date of Knox's Letters to Mrs. Bowes

KNOX's letters to Mrs. Bowes are contained, along with other letters and some of Knox's other writings, in a manuscript book which, after having been in turn in the hands of Wodrow, McCrie, and David Laing, is now in Edinburgh University Library. As the original copies of all the letters to Mrs. Bowes have been lost, this manuscript is the earliest record of the letters. McCrie published some of them in the Appendix to his Life of Knox in 1812, and all of them were published by Laing in Knox's Collected Works, for the Wodrow Society, in 1854.

It is clear from statements in the manuscript that the letters were copied in 1603. McCrie believed that the transcriber was Knox's son-in-law, John Welsh, but Laing pointed out that they are not written in his hand.[1] The manuscript is inscribed with the statement, which was apparently written in 1683, that the book formerly belonged to Margaret Stewart, Knox's widow. The manuscript may have been in her possession at one time, but it is more likely that it was the original letters, not the copy in the manuscript book, which were in Margaret's possession, and that in 1603 some relative or acquaintance of Margaret copied into the book the original letters which had been in Margaret's possession for more than thirty years.

There is no doubt that the dates given in the manuscript of 1603 (and in the text printed from this manuscript by McCrie and David Laing) are wrong in the case of at least two of the letters, and there are strong reasons to believe that the dates of several of the other letters are also wrong. This has led to some serious misapprehensions as to Knox's movements and activities in 1553. The text of the letters indicates the following conclusions as to the dates of the letters, which are here numbered in the order in which they are numbered by the transcriber of 1603 and by Laing in Volume III of Knox's *Works*.[2]

Letter I is dated from London, 23 June 1553. It is headed by the transcriber of 1603: 'The first letter to his mother-in-law Elizabeth Bowes'; but the transcriber evidently did not intend to indicate that it

[1] Laing, in *Works*, iii. 335.

[2] In the manuscript, the letters are numbered in Arabic numerals, and two of the letters (those immediately following No. 9 and No. 18) are unnumbered. In *Works*, Laing used Roman numerals, and numbered the two unnumbered letters 'IX. 2' and 'XVIII. 2'.

was the first letter which Knox wrote to Mrs. Bowes, but was merely numbering it as the first letter in his manuscript book; because the second letter in the book, which is headed: 'The 2 to his mother', is dated from Dieppe, 20 July 1554, which, even if the dates that the transcriber gives for the other letters were correct, would make it one of the later letters which Knox wrote to her. Thereafter the transcriber simply numbered the letters 'No. 3', 'No. 4', etc. The date of this first letter, 23 June 1553, is obviously correct, as Knox states in the letter that he received Mrs. Bowes's letter on 21 June; and the year is correct, as 1553 was almost certainly the only year in Knox's life (except perhaps 1549) when he was in London on 23 June. In this letter, as in several of his other letters to her, Knox addresses Mrs. Bowes as 'mother'. We know from Knox's own statement that he called her mother because he was betrothed to Marjory. In some of his letters to Mrs. Bowes, he addresses her as 'sister', the mode of address that he normally used when writing to women members of his congregation. Obviously the letters in which he called Mrs. Bowes 'sister' were written before his precontract with Marjory, and those in which he called her 'mother' were written after the precontract.

Letter II is dated from Dieppe, 20 July 1554. This is obviously correct, because Knox gave the same date when he published the letter in his *Answer to Tyrie*.

Letter III is dated from Newcastle, 26 February 1553. Knox, before his visit to the Continent, would certainly not have used the new-style calendar under which the year begins on 1 January, but would have used the calendar in force throughout his lifetime in England and Scotland, under which the year began on 25 March. If Knox had dated the original letter '26 February 1553', he would have meant 26 February 1553/4, when Knox was in Switzerland (see Appendix V), and not in Newcastle. The date 1553 must therefore have been inserted by the transcriber in 1603 to indicate that it was written on 26 February 1552/3; the practice of beginning the year on 1 January had been introduced in Scotland in 1600. Laing, who pointed out that it could not have been written in 1553/4, did not realize that 1552/3 must also be wrong if Letter XVIII (ii) is correctly dated, and that in any case it was certainly not written in that year. We do not know the date when Knox returned from Newcastle to London after his sermon in Newcastle at Christmas 1552, but it was certainly before 26 February 1553. He was offered the benefice in London on 2 February, and was one of the Lenten preachers to the King; and in 1553 Ash Wednesday was on 15 February. He wrote to Mrs. Bowes from London on 1 March 1553 (Letter XVIII (ii)), and could hardly have been in Newcastle three days before. This letter of 26 February was written before his precontract to Marjory, because Mrs. Bowes is addressed as 'sister'. It was probably written on 26 February 1551/2, or possibly 1550/1.

Letters IV, V, VII, XIII, and XIV are all dated 'Newcastle, 1553'. Obviously, Knox would not have given the year, but no day or month, when he dated the letter, and the year '1553' must be an insertion of the transcriber. Laing suggested that Knox himself may have made a note of the year on the letter, at some later date. This is not impossible, as we know that Knox sometimes made mistakes about dates. All these letters were probably written in 1551 or 1552, before Knox's precontract to Marjory, as Mrs. Bowes is addressed as 'sister' in all of them.

Letter VI is dated 'at Newcastle, this Tuesday, 22nd December 1553'. It is strange that neither McCrie, Laing, nor Hume Brown and other biographers have pointed out that 22 December was not a Tuesday in 1553. But the day of the week must be correct, for in the letter Knox refers to Saturday, 19 December. The letter was therefore certainly written on Tuesday, 22 December 1551. In the letter, Mrs. Bowes is addressed as 'sister'. Knox writes in the letter: 'I may not answer the places of Scripture, nor yet write the Exposition of the Sixth Psalm, for every day of this week must I preach, if the wicked carcass will permit.' These last words refer to the fact that Knox was suffering from illness. As Knox finished writing the first part of his *Exposition of the Sixth Psalm* on 6 January 1554, it is understandable that the transcriber thought that the year of this letter was 1553; but the day of the week shows that this is impossible. This mistake has led most of Knox's biographers to commit the much more serious error of stating that Knox was publicly preaching in Northumberland in December 1553—five months after Mary's accession, and a few days after the mass was restored.

Letter VIII is dated, like Letters IV, V, VII, XIII, and XIV, from Newcastle '1553', with no day or month. The reference to the Earl of Westmorland having summoned Knox to appear before him at his peril suggests that it may have been written soon after Knox's sermon at Christmas 1552. If so, it is interesting to note that Mrs. Bowes is still addressed as 'sister', and places the date of the precontract as immediately before Knox's return to London in January 1553, very soon after this letter was written.

Letter IX is dated from Carlisle, 26 July 1553. While it is not an absolute impossibility that Knox was in Carlisle on this date, it is very unlikely, as he was in London on 19 July 1553, and in Kent early in

September. In any case, Mrs. Bowes is addressed as 'sister' in the letter. The year is almost certainly 1552, when Knox was accompanying Northumberland as his preacher when the Duke travelled along the Borders. Northumberland was in Carlisle on 27 July 1552.[1] But 1551, 1550, or even 1549, are possible.

Letter IX (ii) is dated '1553', and no place is given. In it, Knox writes: 'My brother William Knox is presently with me.' It was probably written after September 1552, when the Privy Council granted a licence to William Knox, permitting him to trade with any English port in a vessel of 100 tons.[2] It was probably written from Newcastle during Knox's visit there in December 1552 and January 1553. Mrs. Bowes is addressed as 'sister'.

Letter X is dated only '1553', and no place is given. Mrs. Bowes is addressed as 'sister', but there is no other indication of the date. It is evidently before the precontract of January 1553.

Letter XI is dated from Newcastle, 23 March 1553. If Knox had written this date, it would have meant 23 March 1553/4, when Knox was in Switzerland. On 23 March 1552/3, he was in London. Mrs. Bowes is addressed as 'sister'. The date is probably 23 March 1551/2, but possibly 1550/1 or 1549/50.

Letter XII is dated 'from Carlisle, this Friday after sermon, 1553'. Obviously '1553' was added by the transcriber. Mrs. Bowes is addressed as 'sister'. The letter was almost certainly written on Friday, 29 July 1552, when Knox was in Carlisle with Northumberland.

Letter XV is dated '1553', and no place is given. It was certainly written in October or November 1553, and almost certainly from Newcastle. It is written to Mrs. Bowes and Marjory jointly, who are addressed as 'dear mother and spouse'.

Letter XVI is dated '1553', and no place given. The year must be right, for Mrs. Bowes is addressed as 'mother'. There is no other indication as to the date.

Letter XVII is dated 20 September 1553, and no place is given. The date is almost certainly correct, and it was probably written in London. Mrs. Bowes is addressed as 'mother'.

Letter XVIII is undated, and no place is given. It contains the account of Knox's interview with Sir Robert Bowes on '6 November'.

1 See Northumberland to Cecil, 27 July 1552 (*Cal. St. Pap. Dom., Edw. VI, etc.* i. 42).

2 Strype, *Eccl. Mem.* ii [i]. 525.

It was almost certainly written in November 1553, soon after 6 November, from Newcastle or somewhere else in Northumberland. Mrs. Bowes is addressed as 'mother'.

Letter XVIII (ii) is dated from London, 1 March 1553. It was not written on 1 March 1553/4, when Knox was in Switzerland, but undoubtedly on 1 March 1552/3, and shows conclusively that Letter III, from Newcastle, was not written on 26 February 1552/3. Mrs. Bowes is addressed as 'mother', and Marjory is referred to as 'my dearest spouse'. It is therefore further evidence that Knox's precontract with Marjory took place during his visit to Northumberland in December 1552–January 1553.

Letter XIX is dated 'London, 1553'. The year is correct, as Mrs. Bowes is addressed as 'mother'. As Knox tells Mrs. Bowes, in the letter, that he hopes to be with her shortly, it is most likely to have been written just before Knox left London for Northumberland in late September or early October 1553. But as there are no references to any of the difficulties and dangers that faced them at this time, it may have been written earlier in 1553, before the death of Edward VI, and may refer to an intended visit by Knox to Northumberland that never took place.

Letter XX is from Newcastle, and is undated ('this Saturday, at Newcastle'). As Mrs. Bowes is addressed as 'mother', it was probably written very soon after the precontract, and immediately before Knox returned to London in January 1553. It is less likely to have been written while Knox was at Newcastle after Mary's accession in the autumn of 1553.

Letter XXI is undated, and the place of writing is not given. It was written in 1553, as Mrs. Bowes is addressed as 'mother'. There is no other indication of the date.

Letter XXII is undated, and no place is given. Mrs. Bowes is addressed as 'sister' in the opening words, and as 'mother' in the last line. This suggests that it was written very soon after the precontract, before Knox had acquired the habit of addressing Mrs. Bowes as 'mother'—probably in January 1553.

Letter XXIII is dated '1554', and no place is given. It was almost certainly written from somewhere on the Continent, probably Dieppe, after January 1554. Mrs. Bowes is addressed as 'mother'.

Letter XXIV is undated, and no place is given; it is a letter, not to Mrs. Bowes, but to Marjory, who is addressed as 'sister'. Knox states, in the letter, that it was the first letter which he had written to her. The date is probably 1551 or the first half of 1552, and it was probably written from Newcastle; but it may have been written in 1550, or in the second half of 1552 from London.

Letters XXV and XXVI are undated, and no place is given. There is no definite indication that they were written to Mrs. Bowes, but they probably were. If so, they were written before January 1553, as Mrs. Bowes is addressed as 'sister'. There is no other indication of the date.

The rest of the letters in the manuscript book of 1603 cover the period between November 1555 and 1558; they are printed by Laing in Volume IV of Knox's *Works*. There is no reason to question the accuracy of the dates of any of these letters. The only one that raises any difficulty is the letter that Knox wrote from Geneva to Mrs. Guthrie (Janet Henderson) in Scotland (Letter XXXVI in Knox's *Works*). It is dated 16 March 1557, which Laing interpreted as meaning 1557/8. In Geneva the year began on 1 January, and 16 March 1557 in Geneva was 16 March 1556 in Scotland. There is no indication in the text as to whether Knox, in writing from Geneva, was using the new-style calendar of Geneva, or the old-style calendar of his correspondent in Scotland. The letter may therefore have been written on either 16 March 1557 or 16 March 1558. Knox was almost certainly in Geneva on both dates; but the earlier date is the more likely, for in general the English refugees in Geneva, and other towns where the new-style calendar was in force, used the new-style calendar in their letters during their years of exile. Laing, in his notes in Knox's *Works*, states that it was in 1557/8, because Knox wrote in the letter that he would return to Scotland 'whenever a greater number among you shall call upon me than now hath bound me to serve them'.[1] Laing interprets this as a reference to the invitation which Knox had received in the summer of 1557 from the Lords of the Congregation; but in March 1558, Knox's worry was not about the small number of Scots who had invited him to return, but about the fact that the Lords of the Congregation had withdrawn their invitation and had told him not to come. The meaning of this passage seems rather to be that Knox will return to Scotland when the number of Scots inviting him exceeds the numbers in the English congregation that Knox is serving in Geneva. When Knox left Scotland in 1556, he gave as his reason that the English in Geneva had asked him to be their pastor; and in view of this, the passage in this letter to Janet Henderson seems more likely to have been written in March 1557 than in March 1558.

There is no doubt as to the date of Knox's letter to Mrs. Bowes of 4 November 1555 (Letter XVII in the manuscript of 1603 and in

[1] *Works*, iv. 247–8.

Knox's *Works*; for the relevant passages, see *supra*, p. 227); but a problem of some importance arises in regard to the place where it was written. This letter is the only evidence for the common belief that Knox returned to England in the reign of Mary Tudor, and visited Mrs. Bowes and Marjory at Norham on his way to Scotland in 1555. It has generally been assumed that Knox wrote this letter from Scotland to Mrs. Bowes at Norham; but it is more likely that he wrote it from Dun Castle to Mrs. Bowes in Edinburgh, and that the constancy in the midst of Sodom, which Knox had noticed when he was with Mrs. Bowes, referred, not to the constancy of the Protestants in England, but to the situation in Edinburgh, which was still largely Catholic in 1555.

APPENDIX V

The Date of Knox's Departure from England and Visit to Switzerland in January–March 1554

As stated in Chapter X, there are very strong grounds for believing that Knox was the Scot who visited Calvin and Bullinger in February and March 1554, and submitted questions to Bullinger on the lawfulness of resistance to idolatrous princes. It was certainly not Goodman, the Englishman, who was still in England at the time. But if Knox left England for Dieppe, and Dieppe for Switzerland, on the usually accepted dates, he cannot have been the Scot who submitted the questions to Bullinger.

Bullinger's letter to Calvin, containing the Scot's questions and his own answers, is dated from Zürich, 26 March 1554. Calvin's letter to Viret, informing him that he has seen the Scot who seeks the opinion of Zürich and who is travelling to Zürich via Lausanne, is dated '7 Calendas Martii 1554' in Calvin's original letter, which still exists—i.e., 23 February 1554. In the English Philadelphia translation, Calvin's letter is dated 9 March 1554, because the editor believed that Calvin made a slip of the pen, intending to write '7 Idus Martii', not '7 Calendas Martii'. The editor of the *Corpus Reformatorum* cannot explain why the American editor believed that the letter was written on 9 March; but it may have been in order to make it possible for Knox to have been the Scot to whom Calvin referred; for it is generally believed that Knox was in Dieppe on 28 February 1554. However, it does not help much to suggest that Calvin misdated his letter, for even if it was written on 9 March, it is very unlikely that he could already have met Knox if Knox had only left Dieppe on 28 February, as this would mean that Knox, who had no particular reason to hurry over his journey, had travelled 420 miles, in winter, in eight days at the most. According to Beza, the shortest time for the journey from Dieppe to Geneva was eleven days.[1]

The second part of Knox's *Exposition of the Sixth Psalm* is dated 'upon the very point of my journey, the last of February 1553'. There is no indication in the text of the *Exposition of the Sixth Psalm* as to the place where Knox was writing. McCrie and Laing assumed that it was

[1] Calvin to Viret, 23 Feb. 1554; Bullinger to Calvin, 26 Mar. 1554 (*Calvini Op*. xv. 38–39, 90–91).

Dieppe. Knox's *Letter to the Faithful in London, Newcastle and Berwick* contains the statement that it was written 'upon my departure from Dieppe, 1553, whither God knoweth'; and as Knox had suggested, in the first part of the *Exposition of the Sixth Psalm*, on 6 January 1554, that the second part would be sent to Mrs. Bowes, not from the south, but by some other means, he might well have finished it at Dieppe, along with the *Letter to the Faithful in London, Newcastle and Berwick*, when he was on the point of leaving Dieppe for Switzerland on 28 February 1554. Hume Brown assumed, with equally little justification, that the second part of the *Exposition of the Sixth Psalm* was written in England, and on the strength of this assumption alone, states that McCrie was wrong in stating that Knox reached Dieppe on 28 January, because as he was still in England on 28 February, he could not have reached Dieppe before the beginning of March. In this, as in so many other things, Hume Brown has been followed by most modern biographers of Knox. At the same time, Hume Brown, completely ignoring Calvin's letter to Viret, states that Knox was the Scot whom Calvin sent to Bullinger and who submitted the questions to Bullinger. This would be quite impossible if Knox was in England on 28 February.[1]

The first edition of the *Exposition of the Sixth Psalm*, though it does not state the printer's name, the place of publication, or the date, was evidently published in 1556. A second edition was published in London in 1580. In both of these editions, the last two paragraphs of the first part, and the last sentence of the second part, are omitted. These are the passages that contain the two dates, 6 January and 28 February 1554.[2] There is thus no indication of the date in the first printed edition. The dates are supplied from different sources. The last two paragraphs of the first part are contained in a manuscript which belonged to John Foxe, and which contains the whole of Knox's original draft of the first part. In this manuscript, the date 'this 6th of January' (no year is added) is written in Knox's hand. But Knox's original manuscript of the second part has not survived. The last sentence of this part is contained only in the manuscript volume of Knox's letters to Mrs. Bowes, which were copied out by the transcriber in 1603, which also contains the text of the *Exposition of the Sixth Psalm*. This transcriber, of whose unreliability as to dates we have so many examples (see Appendix IV), is therefore the only authority for the fact that the second part of the *Exposition of the Sixth Psalm* was finished on 28 February.

On 10 May 1554, Knox wrote 'from Dieppe' his *Comfortable Epistle to his Afflicted Brethren in England*. Here again, the only authority for the

[1] See *Works*, iii. 113, 156, 215; McCrie, pp. 78, 81 n.; Hume Brown, *John Knox*, i. 147–8 and n.

[2] See Laing, in *Works*, iii. 114. The omitted passages are in *Works*, iii. 132–3, 156.

date is the manuscript of 1603, but this time there is no reason to doubt its accuracy. In it, Knox wrote: 'Since 28 January, I have travelled through all the congregations of Helvetia, and have reasoned with all the pastors and many other excellently learned men upon such matters as now I cannot commit to writing.' McCrie, who believed that Knox left Dieppe for Switzerland on 28 February, states that Knox inserted the date 28 January 'counting from the time he came to France', although earlier McCrie stated, with no authority, that Knox landed at Dieppe on 20 January. Other biographers have suggested that 28 January was the day on which Knox left England for Dieppe, which was why he dated the beginning of his travels through Switzerland from that day; and others, that the date 28 January is a slip, and that 28 February was indicated. Hume Brown, who believed that Knox was still in England on 28 February, solved the problem by omitting the reference to 28 January from this quotation from the *Comfortable Epistle to his Afflicted Brethren in England*.[1]

In view of the fact that it is almost certain that Knox was the Scot who visited Calvin and Bullinger, the simplest, as well as the most satisfactory, explanation is that Knox, after finishing the first part of the *Exposition of the Sixth Psalm* (probably in London) on 6 January, went to Dieppe, where he completed his *Letter to the Faithful in London, Newcastle and Berwick*, and wrote the second part of the *Exposition of the Sixth Psalm*, 'upon the very point of my journey' on 28 January 1553/4; and that through an error in transcription, this was changed to '28 February', and then reproduced as 'the last of February 1553' by the transcriber of 1603. After leaving Dieppe on 28 January, Knox travelled at a reasonable speed to Geneva, and had spoken with Calvin before Calvin wrote his letter to Viret, which he dated, quite correctly, '7 Calendas Martii', i.e. 23 February. Knox then went on to Lausanne and Zürich, and had submitted his questions to Bullinger before Bullinger wrote to Calvin on 26 March. In his *Comfortable Epistle to his Afflicted Brethren in England*, Knox, writing in Dieppe, naturally dated the beginning of his travels in Switzerland from 28 January, the day he left Dieppe.

It is interesting to note that this means that Knox had left England before the outbreak of the Wyatt Rebellion. If he had stayed until the beginning of March, he would have been in England, probably in London, during the rising. In this case, he would probably have made more allusions to the Wyatt Rebellion in his books, inserting passing references to it, and recounting little anecdotes about the things that he had seen.

[1] *Works*, iii. 235–6; McCrie, pp. 73, 81 n.; Hume Brown, *John Knox*, i. 154.

APPENDIX VI

The Conference with Lethington in Edinburgh Castle

Bannatyne inserted in his *Memorials* a short document, written by an author whom he does not identify, which describes how the author, and other leaders of the Protestant Church, visited Edinburgh Castle during the civil war of 1571–2, and held a conference there with Lethington, Grange, James Balfour, and Châtelherault. The author states that he was addressed as 'Master John'. This, together with the fact that the document came into Bannatyne's possession, naturally suggests that 'Master John' was Knox; and a description of this famous meeting, with Lethington playing with a little dog, appears in nearly all the recent biographies of Knox. Hume Brown stated that there was no doubt that Knox was 'Master John'.

In fact, however, Knox cannot have been the author of this document, and could not have been present at the conference. Bannatyne inserts the document in a section of his *Memorials* which is preceded, a few pages earlier, by the heading 'A Memorial of such things as was done in this town of Edinburgh since the departure of John Knox, minister, out of the same sore against his will'. Hume Brown answers this by stating that the document was inserted in the wrong place in Bannatyne's *Memorials*. But Châtelherault, who was present at the meeting, arrived in Edinburgh on 4 May 1571, and Knox left Edinburgh next day, proceeding in due course to St. Andrews, where he stayed until he returned to Edinburgh in August 1572. It is therefore suggested that the conference took place immediately before Knox left Edinburgh, on 4 or 5 May 1571; but in fact it must have been soon after the middle of January 1572. 'Master John's' document begins with the heading: 'Certain Commissioners sent to the Castle, by the General Church convened in Leith, to pacify the troubles of this country.' The General Assembly, after meeting in Edinburgh in March 1571 and in Stirling in August 1571, met in Leith from 12 to 23 January 1572.

All Knox's biographers have expressed their surprise at the friendly manner in which Lethington and 'Master John' discussed their differences of opinion, and have usually attributed it to the fact that Knox was old and tired. But Knox's bitterness towards the 'murderers assembled in the Castle of Edinburgh' rose to the highest pitch during the last year of his life. 'Master John' was conciliatory because he was not Knox, but a member of the influential party in the Church that Knox denounced for its readiness to seek a compromise with the Queen's lords. 'Master John' cannot have been John Craig or John Winram, because he refers to both of them in his document; but he is much more likely to have been John Spottiswood, the Superintendent of Lothian, John Row, or even John Douglas, rather than John Knox. It would be surprising if the Church had selected Knox as one of the Commissioners sent to visit the Castilians on a mission designed to 'pacify the troubles of this country', or if Knox had spoken in the way in which 'Master John' spoke at the meeting. Nor is 'Master John's' style of writing reminiscent of Knox's style.[1]

[1] Bannatyne, pp. 117–18, 125-32; *Diurnal of Occurrents*, p. 211; *Booke of the Universall Kirk*, pp. 203, 232; Hume Brown, *John Knox*, ii. 263–5; Andrew Lang, *John Knox and the Reformation*, p. 266; Lord Eustace Percy, *John Knox*, p. 413. Lethington, Grange, Châtelherault and Balfour were in Edinburgh Castle in February 1572; see 'The lords of either party now present in Leith and Edinburgh,' 23 Feb. 1571/2 (Sc. Cal. iv. 145, 146).

ABBREVIATIONS

(For the full title of book referred to, see the Bibliography.)

A.P.C.: *Acts of the Privy Council of England* (ed. Dasent).

Cal. For. Pap. Edw. VI: *Calendar of State Papers (Foreign Series) of the reign of Edward VI.*

Cal. For. Pap. Eliz.: *Calendar of State Papers (Foreign Series) of the reign of Elizabeth.*

Cal. For. Pap. Mary: *Calendar of State Papers (Foreign Series) of the reign of Mary.*

Cal. Pat. Rolls, Edw. VI: *Calendar of the Patent Rolls, Edward VI.*

Cal. Pat. Rolls, Ph. & Mary: *Calendar of the Patent Rolls, Philip and Mary.*

Cal. St. Pap. Dom., Edw. VI etc., vol. i: *Calendar of State Papers (Domestic Series) of the reigns of Edward VI, Mary, Elizabeth, 1547–1580* (ed. Lemon).

Cal. St. Pap. Dom., Edw. VI etc., vol. vi: *Calendar of State Papers (Domestic Series) of the reign of Elizabeth 1601–1603, with Addenda 1547–1565* (ed. H. A. F. Green).

E. H. R.: *English Historical Review.*

H.M.C., 3rd R.: *Third Report of the Royal Commission on Historical Manuscripts.*

H.M.C., 5th R.: *Fifth Report of the Royal Commission on Historical Manuscripts.*

H.M.C., 6th R.: *Sixth Report of the Royal Commission on Historical Manuscripts.*

H.M.C., 7th R.: *Seventh Report of the Royal Commission on Historical Manuscripts.*

H.M.C., 12th R. iv: *Twelfth Report of the Royal Commission on Historical Manuscripts, Part iv.*

H.M.C., 15th R.: *Fifteenth Report of the Royal Commission on Historical Manuscripts.*

H.M.C., Cecil: *Historical Manuscripts Commission—Calendar of the Manuscripts of the Marquis of Salisbury.*

H.M.C., Montagu: *Historical Manuscripts Commission—Report on the Manuscripts of Lord Montagu of Beaulieu.*

H.M.C., Pepys: *Historical Manuscripts Commission—Report on the Pepys Manuscripts.*

H.M.C., Rutland: *Historical Manuscripts Commission—The Manuscripts of the Duke of Rutland.*

Knox, *History*: *John Knox's History of the Reformation in Scotland* (Croft Dickinson's 1949 ed.).

Knox's *History*, 1644 Edinburgh ed.: Knox, *The Historie of the reformation of the Church of Scotland* (Edinburgh, 1644 ed.).

Knox's *History*, 1644 London ed.: Knox, *The Historie of the reformation of the Church of Scotland* (London, 1644 ed.).

Labanoff: *Lettres, Instructions et Mémoires de Marie Stuart, Reine d'Écosse* (ed. Labanoff).

L.P.: *Letters and Papers of the Reign of King Henry VIII.*

Melville, *Diary*: *The Autobiography and Diary of Mr. James Melville, Minister of Kilrenny in Fife and Professor of Theology in the University of St. Andrews.*

Melville, *Memoirs*: *The Memoirs of his Own Life, by Sir James Melville of Halhill.*

Papal. Cal.: *Calendar of State Papers relating to English affairs preserved principally at Rome.*

Reg. P.C.S.: *Register of the Privy Council of Scotland.*

Sc. Cal.: *Calendar of Scottish State Papers relating to Mary Queen of Scots 1547–1603* (ed. Bain).

S.H.R.: *Scottish Historical Review.*

S.H.S. Misc.: *Miscellany of the Scottish History Society.*

Span. Cal.: *Calendar of Letters, Documents and State Papers relating to the Negotiations between England and Spain in Simancas and elsewhere* (1485–1558).

Span. Cal. Eliz.: *Calendar of Letters and State Papers relating to English Affairs preserved principally in the Archives of Simancas* (1558–1603).

State Pap.: *State Papers during the reign of Henry VIII.*

Stevenson-Nau: *The History of Mary Stewart. By Claude Nau, her Secretary. With illustrative papers from the Secret Archives of the Vatican* (ed. Stevenson).

Trans. R.H.S.: *Transactions of the Royal Historical Society.*

Ven. Cal.: *Calendar of State Papers and Manuscripts relating to English Affairs in the Archives of Venice and other Libraries in Northern Italy.*

Works: *The Works of John Knox* (ed. D. Laing).

BIBLIOGRAPHY

Abbotsford Club. *Miscellany of the Abbotsford Club*, vol. i (Edinburgh, 1837).

Accounts of Collectors of Thirds of Benefices 1561–1572 (ed. G. Donaldson) (Edinburgh, 1949).

Accounts of the Lord High Treasurer of Scotland (ed. Sir J. Balfour Paul) (Edinburgh, 1908–16).

Acta Facultatis Artium Universitatis Sanctiandree 1413–1588 (ed. Annie I. Dunlop) (Edinburgh, 1964).

Acts of the Lords of Council in Public Affairs 1501–1554 (ed. R. K. Hannay) (Edinburgh, 1932).

Acts of the Parliament of Scotland (Edinburgh, 1814).

Acts of the Privy Council of England (New Series) (ed. J. R. Dasent) (London, 1890–1907) (cited as *A.P.C.*)

ADAM, MELCHIOR. *Decades duae Continentes Vitas Theologorum Exterorum Principum* (*Vitae Theologicae*) (Frankfort-on-Main, 1618).

AENEAS SILVIUS. See PIUS II.

AGRIPPA VON NETTESHEIM, HENRY CORNELIUS. *De nobilitate et praecellentia foeminei sexus* (Cologne, 1532).

AITKEN, J. M. *The Trial of George Buchanan before the Lisbon Inquisition* (Edinburgh, 1939).

A LASCO, J. *Forma ac ratio Ecclesiastici Ministerii, in peregrinorum . . . instituta Londini in Anglia* (first published in 1555). See A LASCO, *Opera*.

—— *Joannis a Lasco Opera* (ed. A. Kuyper) (Amsterdam, 1866).

ALESS, A. *Of the auctorite of the word of god agaynst the bisshop of london* (Leipzig (?), 1540).

ALLEN, J. W. *A History of Political Thought in the Sixteenth Century* (London, 1928).

Ambassades de Noailles. See NOAILLES.

AMBROSE, SAINT. *Commentaria in Epist. ad Timotheum Primam*. See MIGNE.

ANDERSON, J. *Collections relating to the history of Mary Queen of Scotland* (Edinburgh, 1727).

ANDERSON, W. J. 'John Knox as Registrar' (*Innes Review*, vol. vii) (Glasgow, Spring 1956).

—— 'Narratives of the Scottish Reformation: 1. Report of Father Robert Abercrombie, S.J., in the year 1580; 2. Thomas Innes on Catholicism in Scotland 1560–1653' (ibid., vol. vii) (Glasgow, Spring and Autumn 1956).

—— 'Presbyteries' Trial' (ibid., vol. viii) (Glasgow, Autumn 1957).

ASSELINE, D. *Les Antiquitez et Chroniques de la Ville de Dieppe* (Dieppe, 1874) (written probably between 1682 and 1703).

AVENTINUS (JOHANN TURMAIR). *Annalium Boiorum* (Ingolstadt, 1554) (see the copy in Edinburgh University Library).

AYLMER, J. *An Harborrowe for Faithfull & Trewe Subiectes agaynst the late blowne Blaste concerninge the Gouvernmēt of Women, wherein be confuted all such reasons as a straunger of late made in that behalfe* (Strasbourg, 1559).

Ayr Burgh Accounts 1534–1624 (ed. G. S. Pryde) (Edinburgh, 1937).

BAILLIE, A. *A true information of the Vnhallowed offspring, progresse & impoisoned fruits of our Scottish Caluinian gospel, & gospellers* (Würzburg, 1628).

BAINTON, R. H. *Concerning Heretics: an anonymous work attributed to Sebastian Castellio* (New York, 1935).

—— *Studies on the Reformation* (London, 1964).

BALD, MARJORIE. 'The Pioneers of Anglicised Speech in Scotland' (*Scottish Historical Review*, vol. xxiv) (Edinburgh, April 1927).

—— 'Vernacular Books imported into Scotland: 1500 to 1625' (ibid., vol. xxiii) (Edinburgh, July 1926).

BALE, J. *Kynge Johan: a play* (London, 1838).

—— *Select Works of John Bale* (Cambridge, 1849).

—— *The Examinations of Anne Askew*. See BALE, *Works*.

—— *The Vocacyon of John Bale to the Bishopperycke of Ossorie*. See *Harleian Miscellany*.

BALUZE, E. *Miscellanea novo ordine digesta* (Lucca, 1761–4) (first published in Paris, 1678–83).

BANCROFT, R. *A sermon preached at Paules Crosse the 9 of Februarie . . . Anno 1588* [1588/9]. See *Wodrow Miscellany*. vol. i.

BANNATYNE, G. *Short Epigrams against Women*. See *Bannatyne Manuscript*.

—— *The Bannatyne Manuscript. Writtin in tyme of pest, 1568* (ed. W. Tod Ritchie) (Edinburgh and London, 1930).

Bannatyne Miscellany, vols. ii and iii (Edinburgh, 1836, 1855).

BANNATYNE, R. *Memorials of Transactions in Scotland 1569–1573* (Edinburgh, 1836) (written in 1573).

BARBÉ, L. *Kirkcaldy of Grange* (Edinburgh, 1897).

—— *The Story of John Knox* (Glasgow, 1921).

BARBOT, A. *Histoire de La Rochelle depuis l'An 1199 jusques en 1575* (vols. xvi–xvii of *Archives Historiques de la Saintonge et de l'Auris*) (Paris and Saintes, 1889) (written between 1613 and 1625).

BARBOUR, R. W. *The Evangelical Succession* (Edinburgh, 1883).

BARCLAY, G. 'Account of the Parish of Haddington' (*Archaeologica Scotica*, vol. i) (Edinburgh, 1792).

BARRY, J. C. 'William Hay of Aberdeen: a Sixteenth Century Scottish Theologian and Canonist' (*Innes Review*, vol. ii) (Glasgow, December 1951).

BARWICK, G. F. 'A sidelight on the Mystery of Mary Stuart: Pietro Bizoni's Contemporary Account of the Murders of Riccio and Darnley' (*Scottish Historical Review*, vol. xxi) (Edinburgh, January 1924).

BEAUGUÉ, J. DE. *Histoire de la Guerre d'Écosse* (Edinburgh, 1830) (first published, Paris, 1556).

BECON, T. Jewel of Joy. See BECON, *Works*.

—— *The Catechism with other pieces* (Cambridge, 1844) (cited as Becon, *Works*, vol. ii).

BELLESHEIM, A. *History of the Catholic Church of Scotland* (Edinburgh and London, 1887).

BENOÎT, R. *Epistola Renati Benedicti . . . ad Johannem Knox atque alios in Scotia ministros*, 1561. See FERGUSSON, *Tracts*.

BEZA, T. *Icones* (Geneva, 1580).

Beza, T. *Les Vrais pourtraits des hommes illustres* (Geneva, 1581) (French translation of *Icones*).

Bible. See *Geneva Bible*: and Whittingham.

Blackwood, A. *Martyre de Marie Stuart* (Paris, 1587). See Jebb.

Boece, H. *The Chronicles of Scotland compiled by Hector Boece. Translated in Scots by John Bellenden, 1531* (ed. Edith C. Batho and H. Winifred Husbands) (Edinburgh and London, 1941).

Book of Discipline. See Knox, *History of the Reformation in Scotland* (1949 ed.)

Booke of the Universall Kirk of Scotland. Acts and Proceedings of the Genera Assemblies of the Kirk of Scotland. Part First, 1560–1587 (Edinburgh, 1839).

Borgeaud, C. 'Le "Vrai Portrait" de John Knox' (*Bulletin de la Société de l'Histoire du Protestantisme français*, vol. lxxxiv) (Paris, 1935) (lecture at Berne University, 2 June 1934).

Boswell, J. *Boswell's Life of Johnson* (ed. G. B. Hill and L. F. Powell) (Oxford, 1964) (first published, London, 1791).

Bowen, Marjorie (Preedy, G.). *Life of John Knox* (1st ed., sub. nom. George Preedy, London, 1940; 2nd ed., sub. nom. Marjorie Bowen, London, 1949).

Bower, W. *Scotichronon* (written in 1447). See Rankin.

Brantôme, P. de Bourdeille, Seigneur de. *Book of the Ladies* (London, 1899) (English translation of *Recueil des Dames*).

—— *Œuvres complètes de Pierre de Bourdeille, Seigneur de Brantôme* (Paris, 1864–82).

—— *Recueil des Dames* (written *c.* 1600). See Brantôme, *Œuvres*.

Brief View of the State of Scotland in the Sixteenth Century. See Pinkerton.

Briegerus, J. *Flores Calvinistici Decerpti ex vita Roberti Dudlei Comitis Lecestriae . . . Ioannis Calvini, Thomae Cranmeri, Ioannis Knoxij* (Naples, 1585).

Brill, E. V. K. 'A Sixteenth Century complaint against the Scots' (*Scottish Historical Review*, vol. xxvii) (Edinburgh, October 1948).

Brown, P. Hume. *Early Travellers in Scotland* (Edinburgh, 1891).

—— *John Knox: a biography* (London, 1895).

—— *Scotland before 1700 from contemporary documents* (Edinburgh, 1893).

—— *Scotland in the time of Queen Mary* (London, 1904).

Bryce, Moir. 'Mary Stuart's voyage to France in 1548' (*English Historical Review*, vol. xxii) (London, January 1907).

Bryce, T. *A Compendious Register in Metre conteigning the names and pacient suffryngs of the membres of Jesus Christ* (London, 1559). See *Select Poetry of the reign of Queen Elizabeth*.

Bucer, M. *Censura*. See Bucer, *Scripta Anglicana*.

—— *Scripta Anglicana* (Basel, 1577).

Buchanan, D. (?) *Life of Knox*. See Knox, *History of the Reformation in Scotland* (1644 eds.)

Buchanan, G. *An Appendix to the History of Scotland, containing: I. A Detection of the Actions of Mary Queen of Scots; II. De Jure Regni apud Scotos* (London, 1721).

—— *Ane Detectioun of the doingis of Marie Quene of Scottis*. See Anderson, *Collections*.

—— *De Jure Regni apud Scotos* (Austin, Texas, 1949).

—— *History of Scotland* (Edinburgh, 1751).

The Buik of the Kirk of the Canagait 1564–1567 (ed. Alma B. Calderwood) (Edinburgh, 1961).

BUNGENER, F. *Calvin: his life, his labours and his writings* (Edinburgh, 1863) (translated from the original French).

BURLEIGH, J. H. S. *A Church History of Scotland* (Oxford, 1960).

BURNE, N. *The Disputation concerning the Controversit Headdis of Religion, haldin in the Realme of Scotland* (Paris, 1581).

BURNET, G. *History of the Reformation of the Church of England* (ed. N. Pocock) (Oxford, 1865) (first published 1679–1715).

BURNS, J. H. 'Knox and Bullinger' (*Scottish Historical Review*, vol. xxxiv) (Edinburgh, April 1955).

—— 'The Political Ideas of the Scottish Reformation' (*Aberdeen University Review*, vol. xxxvi) (Aberdeen, Spring 1956).

—— 'The Scotland of John Major' (*Innes Review*, vol. ii) (Glasgow, December 1951).

—— 'Three Scottish Catholic critics of George Buchanan' (ibid., vol. i) (Glasgow, December 1950).

CALDERWOOD, D. *The History of the Kirk of Scotland* (Edinburgh, 1842) (written *c.* 1650).

Calendar of Letters and Papers relating to the affairs of the Borders of England and Scotland (ed. J. Bain) (Edinburgh, 1894–6) (cited as *Cal. of Border Papers*).

Calendar of Letters and State Papers relating to English Affairs preserved principally in the Archives of Simancas (1558–1603) (ed. M. A. S. Hume, etc.) (London, 1892–9) (cited as *Span. Cal. Eliz.*)

Calendar of Letters, Documents and State Papers relating to the Negotiations between England and Spain in Simancas and elsewhere (1485–1558) (ed. P. de Goyangos, G. Mattingly, R. Tyler, etc.) (London, 1862–1954) (cited as *Span. Cal.*)

Calendar of Scottish State Papers relating to Mary Queen of Scots 1547–1603 (ed. J. Bain, W. K. Boyd, etc.) (Edinburgh, 1898–1952) (cited as *Sc. Cal.*)

Calendar of State Papers and Manuscripts relating to English Affairs in the Archives of Venice (ed. Rawdon Brown, Cavendish Bentinck, etc.) (London, 1864–1940) (cited as *Ven. Cal.*).

Calendar of State Papers (Domestic Series) of the reigns of Edward VI, Mary, Elizabeth, 1547–1580 (ed. R. Lemon) (London, 1856) (cited as *Cal. St. Pap. Dom., Edw. VI etc.*, vol. i).

Calendar of State Papers (Domestic Series) of the reign of Elizabeth 1601–1603, with Addenda 1547–1565 (ed. H. A. F. Green) (London, 1870) (cited as *Cal. St. Pap. Dom., Edw. VI etc.*, vol. vi).

Calendar of State Papers (Foreign Series) of the reign of Edward VI 1547–1553 (ed. W. B. Turnbull) (London, 1861) (cited as *Cal. For. Pap. Edw. VI*).

Calendar of State Papers (Foreign Series) of the reign of Elizabeth, 1558–1589) (ed. J. Stevenson, etc.) (London, 1863–1950) (cited as *Cal. For. Pap. Eliz.*).

Calendar of State Papers (Foreign Series) of the reign of Mary 1553–1558 (ed. W. B. Turnbull) (London, 1861) (cited as *Cal. For. Pap. Mary*).

Calendar of State Papers relating to English affairs preserved principally at Rome (ed. J. M. Rigg) (London, 1916–26) (cited as *Papal Cal.*).

Calendar of the Patent Rolls, Edward VI, 1547–1553 (London, 1924–7) (cited as *Cal. Pat. Rolls, Edw. VI*).

Calendar of the Patent Rolls, Philip and Mary, 1553–1558 (London, 1936–9) (cited as *Cal. Pat. Rolls, Ph. & Mary*).
CALVIN, J. *Calvini Opera* (vols. xxix–lxxxvii of *Corpus Reformatorum*, ed. C. G. Bretschneider and H. F. Bindseil) (Brunswick and Berlin, 1863–1900).
—— *Sermons of John Calvin upon the Songe that Ezechias made after he had bene sicke, and afflicted by the hand of God* (translated by Anne Locke) (London, 1560).
—— *The Institutes of the Christian Religion* (Philadelphia, 1935).
Camden Miscellany, vol. xii (ed. C. L. Kingsford) (London, 1910).
CARDWELL, E. *The Reformation of the Ecclesiastical Laws* (Oxford, 1850).
CARLYLE, T. *On Heroes, Hero-Worship and the Heroic in History* (London, 1901 ed.) (first published, London, 1841).
CASTELLIO, S. *De Haereticis, an sint persequendi* (Basel, 1554). See BAINTON, *Concerning Heretics*.
—— *Conseil à la France désolée* (Paris(?), 1562). See BAINTON, *Concerning Heretics*.
The Catechism of John Hamilton, Archbishop of St. Andrews, 1552 (ed. T. G. Law) (Oxford, 1884).
Catholic Tractates of the Sixteenth Century (ed. T. G. Law) (Edinburgh and London, 1901).
CAUSSIN, N. 'L'Histoire de l'incomparable Reyne Marie Stvart' (first published in *La Cour Sainte*, Paris, 1645). See JEBB.
CAUT, R. G. *The College of St. Salvator* (Edinburgh, 1950).
CHADWICK, H. 'A Memoir of Father Edmund Hay, S. I.' (*Archivum Historicum Societatis Iesu*, vol. viii) (Rome, 1939).
CHAMBERS, D. *Discovrs de la Legitime Svccession des Femmes* (Paris, 1579). See JEBB.
CHAMBERS, R. *Domestic Annals of Scotland* (Edinburgh, 1858–61).
CHARRIÈRE, E. *Négociations de la France dans le Levant* (Paris, 1848–60).
Charters and other documents relating to the City of Edinburgh A.D. 1143–1540 (Edinburgh, 1871).
Charters and Writs concerning the Royal Burgh of Haddington 1318–1543 (ed. J. G. Wallace-James) (Haddington, 1895).
CHENEVIÈRE, M–E. *La pensée politique de Calvin* (Geneva and Paris, 1937).
CHOISY, E. *La Théocratie à Genève au temps de Calvin* (Geneva, 1897).
CHRISTOPHERSON, J. *An exhortation to all menne to take hede and beware of rebellion* (London, 1554).
Chronicle of Perth . . . from the year 1210 to 1668 (Edinburgh, 1831).
Chronicle of Queen Jane and of Two Years of Queen Mary (ed. J. G. Nichols) (London, 1850).
CHRYSOSTOM, SAINT JOHN. *In Cap. III Genes. Homil. XVII.* See MIGNE.
COLLINSON, P. 'The authorship of *A Brieff Discours off the Troubles Begonne at Franckford*' (*Journal of Ecclesiastical History*, vol. ix) (London, 1958).
—— *The Elizabethan Puritan Movement* (London, 1967).
Common Errors in Scottish History (ed. G. Donaldson) (Historical Association pamphlet) (London, 1956).
Common Prayer, First Book of. See *Liturgies of Edward VI*.
Common Prayer, Second Book of. See *Liturgies of Edward VI*.
Common Prayer. *The Boke of common prayer and administracion of the Sacramentes, and other rites and ceremonies in the Churche of England* (London, 1552). (See

copies in British Museum, B.M. Cat. c. 21. d. 14; c. 36. f. 18; c. 36. l. 16; G. 12099.)

The Complaynt of Scotland, with ane Exortatione to the Thre Estaits to be vigilante in the Deffens of their Public veil, 1549 (ed. J. A. H. Murray) (London, 1872).

Confession of the Faith of the Switzerlands (translated by George Wishart) (London, 1548 (?)). See *Wodrow Miscellany*, vol. i.

CONN, G. *De Duplici Statu Religionis apud Scotos* (Rome, 1628).

—— *Vita Mariae Stuartae* (Rome, 1624).

COOPER, J. 'The Principals of the University of Glasgow before the Reformation' (*Scottish Historical Review*, vol. xi) (Edinburgh, April 1914).

Correspondance politique de Odet de Selve. See SELVE.

COULTON, C. G. *Scottish Abbeys and Social Life* (Cambridge, 1933).

COWAN, H. *The Influence of the Scottish Church in Christendom* (London, 1896).

CRANMER, T. *The Remains of Thomas Cranmer.* See JENKYNS.

—— *The Works of Thomas Cranmer* (ed. J. E. Cox) (Cambridge, 1844–6).

CRESPIN, J. Histoire des Martyrs. *Actes de Martyrs . . . depuis le temps de Vviclef et de Hus iusques à present* (Geneva, 1564).

DALYELL, SIR J. G. *Fragments of Scottish History* (Edinburgh, 1798).

DAVAL, G. and J. *Histoire de la Réformation à Dieppe 1557–1657 par Guillaume et Jean Daval dits les Policiens Religionnaires* (ed. E. Lessens) (Rouen, 1878) (written *c.* 1600–60).

DAVIDSON, J. *A Memorial of Two Worthye Christians, Robert Campbel of the Kinyeancleugh and his Wife Elizabeth Campbel* (Edinburgh, 1595). See ROGERS, 'Three Poets of the Scottish Reformation'.

—— *Ane Breif Commendatioun of Uprichtnes* (St. Andrews, 1573). See ROGERS, 'Three Poets of the Scottish Reformation'.

—— *Ane Schort Discurs of the Estaitis quha hes caus to deploir the Deith of this Excellent Servand of God* (St. Andrews, 1573). See ROGERS, 'Three Poets of the Scottish Reformation'.

DES GALLARS. See GALLARS.

DESMARQUETS, J. A. S. *Mémoires chronologiques pour servir à l'histoire de Dieppe* (Paris, 1785).

DICKINSON, GLADYS. 'Instructions to the French Ambassador, 30 March 1550' (*Scottish Historical Review*, vol. xxvi) (Edinburgh, October 1947).

—— *Mission de Beccarie de Pavie, Baron de Fourquevaux, en Écosse, 1549* (Oxford, 1948).

—— 'Some Notes on the Scottish Army in the first half of the Sixteenth Century' (*Scottish Historical Review*, vol. xxviii) (Edinburgh, October 1949).

DICKINSON, W. CROFT. 'A pair of Butts' (ibid., vol. xxxiv) (Edinburgh, October 1955).

—— *Scotland from the earliest times to 1603* (London and Edinburgh, 1961).

Diurnal of Remarkable Occurrents (Edinburgh, 1833) (written in 1575).

DIXON, R. W. *History of the Church of England from the Abolition of the Roman Jurisdiction* (London, 1878–1902).

Documentos Inéditos. *Colección de Documentos Inéditos para la Historia de España* (ed. M. Fernandez de Navarrete) (Madrid, 1842–95).

DÖLLINGER, J. J. I. VON. *Sammlung von Urkunden zur Geschichte des Concils von Trient* (Nordlingen, 1876).

DONALDSON, G. '"Flitting Fri", the Beggars' Summons and Knox's sermon at Perth' (*Scottish Historical Review*, vol. xxxix) (Edinburgh, October, 1960).

—— *Scotland: Church and Nation through sixteen centuries* (London, 1960).

—— *Scotland: James V to James VII* (Edinburgh, 1965).

—— 'Sources for the study of Scottish Ecclesiastical Organization and Personnel 1560–1600' (*Bulletin of the Institute of Historical Research*, vol. xix) (London, 1942–3).

—— 'The attitude of Whitgift and Bancroft to the Scottish Church' (*Transactions of the Royal Historical Society*, 4th series, vol. xxiv) (London, 1942).

—— 'The "example of Denmark" in the Scottish Reformation' (*Scottish Historical Review*, vol. xxvii) (Edinburgh, April 1948).

—— 'The Scottish Episcopate at the Reformation' (*English Historical Review*, vol. lx) (London, September 1945).

DORMAN, T. *A proofe of certayne Articles in religion denied by M. Ivell* (Antwerp, 1564).

DUNLOP, ANNIE I. 'Scottish Student Life in the Fifteenth Century' (*Scottish Historical Review*, vol. xxvi) (Edinburgh, April 1947).

DUPONT, E. 'Les Prisonniers Écossais du Mont Saint Michel (en Normandie) au XVIe Siècle' (ibid., vol. iii) (Edinburgh, July 1906).

DURKAN, J. 'Education in the Century of the Reformation'. See *Essays on the Scottish Reformation.*

—— 'George Wishart: his early life' (*Scottish Historical Review*, vol. xxxii) (Edinburgh, April 1953).

—— 'Paisley Abbey and Glasgow Archives' (*Innes Review*, vol. xiv) (Glasgow, Spring 1963).

Early Records of the University of St. Andrews (ed. J. M. Anderson) (Edinburgh, 1926).

EASSON, D. E. 'The Reformation and the Monasteries in Scotland and England: some comparisons' (*Transactions of the Scottish Ecclesiological Society,* vol. xv (i) (Aberdeen, 1957).

Edinburgh Burgh Records. *Extracts from the Records of the Burgh of Edinburgh 1403–1589* (Edinburgh, 1869–82).

EDWARDS, J. 'A Scottish Bond of Friendship betwixt Lord Lovat and the Captain of Clanranald, 1572' (*Scottish Historical Review*, vol. xxix) (Edinburgh, April 1927).

ELYOT, SIR T. *The Defence of Good Women* (London, 1545).

ENGLAND, SYLVIA L. 'Some unpublished letters of Mary Queen of Scots' (*English Historical Review*, vol. lii) (London, January 1937).

Epistre envoiee au Tigre de la France. See *Tigre de 1560.*

An Epitome of the title that the Kynges Maiestie of Englande hath to the soueraigntie of Scotland (London, 1548). See *Complaynt of Scotland.*

Essays on the Scottish Reformation 1513–1625 (ed. D. McRoberts) (Glasgow, 1962).

Estate of Scotland. *A Historie of the Estate of Scotland from July 1558 to April 1560* (written probably in the sixteenth century). See *Wodrow Miscellany*, vol. i.

Exchequer Rolls of Scotland (ed. J. Stuart, G. P. M'Neill, etc.) (Edinburgh, 1878–1908).

Extracts from the Council Register of the Burgh of Aberdeen 1398–1570 (Aberdeen, 1844).

FERGUSSON, D. *Ane Answer to ane Epistle written by Renat Benedict . . . to John Knox and the rest of his brethren* (Edinburgh, 1563). See FERGUSSON, *Tracts*.

—— *Ane Sermon preichit befoir the Regent and Nobilitie . . . in the Church of Leith . . . on Sonday the 13 of Ianuarie. Anno Do. 1571* [1571/2] (St. Andrews, 1572). See FERGUSSON, *Tracts*.

—— *Tracts by David Fergusson, minister of Dunfermline 1563–1572* (ed. D. Laing) (Edinburgh, 1860).

FERGUSSON OF KILKERRAN, SIR J. 'A pair of Butts' (*Scottish Historical Review*, vol. xxxiv) (Edinburgh, April 1955).

—— *The White Hind and other Discoveries* (London, 1963).

FIELD, J. 'Epistle Dedicatory to Anne Prouze' in Knox's *Exposition upon the 4th of Matthew*. See KNOX, *Works*, vol. iv.

FIGGIS, J. N. 'On some political theories of the early Jesuits' (*Transactions of the Royal Historical Society*, New Series, vol. xi) (London, 1897).

FINLAYSON, J. P. 'A volume associated with John Knox' (*Scottish Historical Review*, vol. xxxviii) (Edinburgh, October 1959).

FIRTH, SIR C. H. 'The portraits of historians in the National Portrait Gallery' (*Transactions of the Royal Historical Society*, 4th series, vol. vi) (London, 1923).

FISCHER, T. A. *The Scots in Eastern and Western Prussia* (Edinburgh, 1903).

FLEMING, D. HAY. *Mary Queen of Scots* (London, 1898).

—— 'The date of Knox's birth' (*The Bookman*, vol. xxviii) (London, September 1905).

—— 'The Influence of Knox' (*Scottish Historical Review*, vol. ii) (Edinburgh, January 1905).

—— 'The Influence of the Reformation on Social and Cultural Life in Scotland' (ibid., vol. xv) (October 1917).

—— *The Reformation in Scotland* (Edinburgh, 1910).

Flodden Papers: diplomatic correspondence between the Courts of France and Scotland 1507–1517 (ed. Marguerite Wood) (Edinburgh, 1933).

FORBES, P. *A full view of the Public Transactions in the reign of Queen Elizabeth* (London, 1740–1).

FORBES-LEITH, W. *Narratives of Scottish Catholics under Mary Stuart and James VI* (Edinburgh, 1885).

Foreign Correspondence with Marie de Lorraine, Queen of Scotland, 1548–1557 (ed. Marguerite Wood) (Edinburgh, 1925).

FOWLER, W. *An Answer to the Calumnious Letter and erroneous propositiouns of an apostat named M. Jo. Hamiltoun* (Edinburgh, 1581). See FOWLER, *Works*.

—— *The Works of William Fowler, secretary to Queen Anne, wife of James VI* (ed. H. W. Meikle) (Edinburgh, 1936).

FOXE, J. The Book of Martyrs. *The Acts and Monuments of John Foxe* (ed. J. Pratt) (London, 1877) (cited as 'Foxe').

—— *Rerum in Ecclesia gestarum* (Basel, 1559) (2nd Latin ed.) (cited as 'Foxe, Latin ed'.).

FRANCISQUE-MICHEL. *Les Écossais en France: les Français en Écosse* (London, 1862).

FRARIN, P. *Oration against the Unlawfull Insurrections of the Protestantes of our time* (Antwerp, 1566).

FRASER, J. *Chronicle of the Frasers.* (*The Wardlaw MS.*, written 1666–1700, ed. W. Mackay) (Edinburgh, 1905).

FRASER, SIR W. *The Lennox* (Edinburgh, 1874).

FROUDE, J. A. *The History of England from the fall of Wolsey to the defeat of the Spanish Armada* (London, 1893 ed.) (first published 1856–70).

—— 'The Influence of the Reformation on the Scottish Character' (lecture in November 1865). See FROUDE, *Short Studies on Great Subjects.*

—— *Short Studies on Great Subjects* (Oxford, 1924 ed.).

FUESSLI, J. C. *Epistolae ad ecclesiae Helveticae Reformatoribus vel ad eos scriptae* (Zürich, 1742).

FULKE, W. *Stapleton's Fortress Overthrown*, etc. (ed. R. Gibbings) (Cambridge, 1843) (cited as FULKE, *Works*, vol. ii).

—— *T. Stapleton and Martiall (two Popish Heretikes) confuted and of their particular heresies detected* (London, 1580). See FULKE, *Works*, vol. ii.

GABEREL, J. *Histoire de l'Église de Genève depuis le commencement de la Réformation jusqu'en 1815* (Geneva, 1853–62).

GACHARD, L. P. *Collection des Voyages des Souverains des Pays-Bas* (Brussels, 1876–82).

GAIRDNER, J. *Lollardy and the Reformation in England* (London, 1908–13).

GALLARS, N. DES. *Histoire Ecclésiastique des Églises Réformées au Royaume de France* (ed. G. Baum and E. Cunitz) (Paris, 1883) (first published, Antwerp, 1580).

GARRETT, CHRISTINA. *The Marian Exiles* (Cambridge, 1938).

GATHERER, W. A. 'Queen Mary's Journey from Aberdeen to Inverness, 1562' (*Scottish Historical Review*, vol. xxxiii) (Edinburgh, April 1954).

Geneva Bible. *The Bible and Holy Scriptvres conteyned in the Olde and Newe Testament . . . With moste profitable annotations vpon all the hard places, and other things of great importance* (1st ed., Geneva, 1560).

George Buchanan Glasgow Quatercentenary Studies 1906 (ed. T. M. Lindsay) (Glasgow, 1907).

GILBY, A. *An Admonition to England and Scotland to bring them to repentance* (first published, Geneva, 1558). See KNOX, *Works.*

GILLON, M. *John Davidson of Prestonpans* (London, 1937).

GONZALEZ DE MENDOZA, P. 'Memoria de lo Sucedido en el Concilio de Trento' (written in 1562). See DÖLLINGER.

Good and Godly Ballads. *The Gude and Godly Ballatis, reprinted from the edition of 1567* (ed. A. F. Mitchell) (Scottish Text Society ed.) (Edinburgh, 1897).

The Gude and Godlie Ballatis (selected and edited by Iain Ross) (Saltire Society ed.) (Edinburgh, 1940).

GOODMAN, C. *How Superior Powers ought to be obeyed* (New York, 1931 ed.) (facsimile of 1st ed., Geneva, 1558).

GORDON OF GORDONSTOUN, SIR R. *Genealogical History of the Earldom of Sutherland* (Edinburgh, 1813) (written about 1630).

GRAHAM, S. *The Anatomie of Humours and the Passionate Sparke of a relenting minde* (Edinburgh, 1830 ed.) (first published, Edinburgh 1609).

GRANT, I. F. *The Social and Economic Development of Scotland before 1603* (Edinburgh, 1930).

GRANT, J. *History of the Burgh Schools of Scotland* (London, 1876).

GRAY, J. R. 'The Political Theory of John Knox' (*Church History*, vol. viii) (New York, June 1939).

GREEN, V. H. H. *Renaissance and Reformation* (London, 1952).

Greyfriars Chronicle. *Chronicle of the Greyfriars of London* (ed. J. G. Nichols) (London, 1852) (written *c.* 1556).

GRIEVE, HILDA. 'The Deprived Married Clergy in Essex 1553–1561' (*Transactions of the Royal Historical Society*, 4th series, vol. xxii) (London, 1940).

GROSS, C. *The Gild Merchant* (Oxford, 1927 ed.)

GUTHRIE, C. J. 'Is "John Knox's House" entitled to the name?' (*Proceedings of the Society of Antiquaries of Scotland*, vol. xxv) (Edinburgh, March 1891).

—— 'The Traditional Belief in John Knox's house at the Netherbow vindicated' (*Proceedings of the Society of Antiquaries of Scotland*, vol. xxxiii) (Edinburgh, March 1899).

HAMILTON, A. *Calvinianae Confusionis demonstratio* (Paris, 1581).

—— *De Confusione Calvinianae sectae apud Scotos* (Paris, 1577).

HAMILTON, J. *A facile traictise, contenand, first, ane infallible reul to discern trew from fals religion* (Louvain, 1600).

Hamilton Papers (ed. J. Bain) (Edinburgh, 1890–2).

HANNAY, R. K. 'Letters of the Papal Legate in Scotland, 1543' (*Scottish Historical Review*, vol. xi) (Edinburgh, October 1913).

—— 'On the Church Lands at the Reformation' (ibid., vol. xvi) (Edinburgh, October 1918).

—— 'The Earl of Arran and Queen Mary' (ibid., vol. xviii) (Edinburgh, July 1921).

HARDING, T. *A Confutation of a booke intitvled an Apologie of the Chvrch of England* (Antwerp, 1565).

HARDWICK, C. *A History of the Articles of Religion* (London, 1884).

The Harleian Miscellany (London, 1808–13).

HARRYSON, J. *An Exhortacion to the Scottes to conforme themselves to the honourable, Expedient and godly Union betweene the two realmes of Englande and Scotland* (London, 1547). See *Complaynt of Scotland.*

HART, A. B. 'Knox as a man of the world' (*American Historical Review*, vol. xiii) (New York, January 1908).

HARVEY, C. C. 'A Sixteenth Century Rental of Haddington' (*Scottish Historical Review*, vol. x) (Edinburgh, July 1913).

HAY, ALEXANDER. 'The Scottish Nobility in An. Dom. 1577' (written on 28 December 1577). See ROGERS, 'An Estimate of the Scottish Nobility'.

HAY, ARCHIBALD. *Ad D. Davidem Betoun Card. Panegyricus.* See FLEMING, D. HAY, *The Reformation in Scotland.*

HAYNES, S. *A Collection of State Papers . . . left by William Cecill Lord Burghley* (London, 1740).

HAYWARD, SIR J. *Annals of the first four years of the reign of Queen Elizabeth* (London, 1840) (written *c.* 1590).

HENDERSON, L. O. 'The Old Tweed Border Bridge' (*Scottish Historical Review*, vol. xxxiii) (Edinburgh, April 1954).

HENDERSON, T. F. *Mary Queen of Scots* (London, 1905).

HERRIES, LORD. *Historical Memoirs of the Reign of Mary Queen of Scots and a portion of the Reign of King James VI* (Edinburgh, 1836) (written *c.* 1650).

HILL, G. 'The Sermons of John Watson, Canon of Aberdeen' (*Innes Review*, vol. xv) (Glasgow, Spring 1964).

Historical Manuscripts, Reports of the Royal Commission on, Third Report (London, 1872).

—— *Fifth Report* (London, 1876).

—— *Sixth Report* (London, 1877–8).

—— *Seventh Report* (London, 1879).

—— *Twelfth Report, Part iv—The Manuscripts of The Duke of Rutland*, vol. i (London, 1888) (cited as *H.M.C., 12th R.*, iv).

—— *Fifteenth Report* (London, 1896–9).

—— *Calendar of the Manuscripts of The Marquis of Salisbury*, vols. i and ii (London, 1883–5) (cited as *H.M.C., Cecil*).

—— *Report on the Manuscripts of Lord Montagu of Beaulieu* (London, 1900) (cited as *H.M.C., Montagu*).

—— *Report on the Pepys Manuscripts* (London, 1911) (cited as *H.M.C., Pepys*).

—— *The Manuscripts of The Duke of Rutland*, vol. iv (London, 1905) (cited as *H.M.C., Rutland*).

The Historie and Life of King James the Sext (Edinburgh, 1825) (written *c.* 1596).

History of Northumberland (Northumberland County Committee) (Newcastle, 1893–1940).

History of the Feuds and Conflicts among the Clans in the Northern Parts of Scotland and in the Western Isles (Glasgow, 1818) (written *c.* 1600).

HOLDSWORTH, W. *History of English Law* (London, 1903–9).

HOLINSHED, R. *Chronicles of England, Scotland and Ireland* (London, 1807–8 ed.) (first published, London, 1578).

HOOPER, J. *An apologye made by . . . John Hooper* (London, 1562). See HOOPER, *Later Writings*.

—— *Later Writings of Bishop Hooper* (Cambridge, 1852) (cited as Hooper, *Works*, vol. ii).

—— *The Works of John Hooper* (Cambridge, 1843) (cited as Hooper, *Works*, vol. i).

HOSACK, J. *Mary Queen of Scots and her accusers* (Edinburgh, 1870–4).

HOTMAN, F. *Franco-Gallia* (London, 1711) (written in 1574).

House of Lords Journal, vol. i (1509–78).

HUDSON, W. S. *John Ponet: Advocate of Limited Monarchy* (Chicago, 1942).

HUGGARDE, M. *The Displaying of the Protestantes* (London (?), 1556).

HURAULT, E. *John Knox et ses relations avec les Églises réformées du continent* (Cahors, 1902).

HUTCHINSON, W. *The History and Antiquities of the County Palatine of Durham* (Carlisle, 1794).

JAL, A. *Archéologie Navale* (Paris, 1840).

JAMES IV. *The Letters of James IV 1505–1513* (calendared by R. K. Hannay; ed. R. L. Mackie and Anne Spilman) (Edinburgh, 1953).

JAMES, V. *Letters of James V* (calendared by R. K. Hannay, ed. D. Hay) (Edinburgh, 1954).

JAMES VI. *The Basilicon Doron of James VI* (ed. J. Craigie) (Edinburgh and London, 1944) (first published, Edinburgh, 1599).

JEAN DE MEUN. *Le Roman de la Rose* (written *c.* 1280). See BROWN, *Early Travellers in Scotland.*

JEBB, S. *De Vita & Rebus Gestis Serenissimae Principis Mariae Scotorum Reginae* (London, 1725).

JENKYNS, H. *The Remains of Thomas Cranmer* (Oxford, 1833).

JEWEL, J. *A defence of the Apologie of the Churche of Englande* (London, 1567). See JEWEL, *Works.*

—— *The Works of John Jewel* (Cambridge, 1845–50).

JOHNSTON, R. *Historia Rerum Britannicarum . . . ab Anno 1572 ad Annum 1628* (Amsterdam, 1655).

JOHNSTON OF WARRISTOUN, SIR A. *Diary*, vol. ii, 1650–1654 (ed. D. Hay Fleming) (Edinburgh, 1919).

JUNG, R. *Die englische Flüchtlings-Gemeinde in Frankfurt-a-M. 1554–1559* (Frankfort-on-Main, 1910).

JUVENAL DES URSINS. *Histoire de Charles VI, Roy de France* (ed. D. Godefroy) (Paris, 1614) (written *c.* 1422).

KAULEK, J. *Correspondance politique de M.M. de Castillon et de Marillac 1537–1542* (Paris, 1885).

KEITH, R. *History of the Affairs of Church and State in Scotland* (Edinburgh, 1844–50) (first published, Edinburgh, 1734).

KETHE, W. 'Psalme of David XCIIII'. See KNOX, *Works*, vol. iv.

King Edward's Journal. See BURNET.

KNOX, J. *A confession & declaratiō of praiers . . . vpon the death of that most vertuous and moste famous king Edward the VI* (London (?), 1554). See KNOX, *Works*, vol. iii.

—— *A godly letter sent to the fayethfull in London, Newcastell, Barwyke, and to all other within the realme off Englande, that love the cominge of our Lorde Jesus* (London (?), 1554). See KNOX, *Works*, vol. iii.

—— *A Faythfull admonition . . . unto the professours of Gods iruthe in England* (London (?), 1554). See KNOX, *Works*, vol. iii.

—— *The Copie of a letter, sent to the ladye Mary dowagire, Regent of Scotland, by J. Knox in the yeare 1556. Here is also a notable sermon, made by the sayde J. Knox, wherein is euydentlye proued that the masse is and alwayes hath bene abhominable before God and Idolatrye* (Geneva (?), 1556). See KNOX, *Works*, vols. iii and iv.

—— *The first Blast of the Trumpet against the Monstrous Regiment of women* (Geneva, 1558). See KNOX, *Works*, vol. iv.

—— *The Appellation of John Knox from the cruell . . . sentence pronounced against him by the false bishoppes and clergey of Scotland: with his supplication and exhortation to the nobilitie, estates and cōmunaltie of the same realme* (Geneva, 1558). See KNOX, *Works*, vol. iv.

—— *The Copie of an epistle sent by John Knox . . . vnto the inhabitants of Newcastle & Barwike. In the ende whereof is added a briefe exhortation to England for the spedie imbrasing of Christes Gospel heretofore suppressed & banished* (Geneva, 1559). See KNOX, *Works*, vol. v.

KNOX, J. *An Answer to a great number of blasphemous cavillations written by an Anabaptist and adversarie to Gods eternal Predestination* (Geneva, 1560). See KNOX, *Works*, vol. v.

—— *A sermon preached by Iohn Knox in the Publique audience of the Church of Edenbrough . . . the 19 of August 1565* (Edinburgh, 1566). See KNOX, *Works*, vol. vi.

—— *An Answer to a letter of a Iesuit named Tyrie* (St. Andrews, 1572). See KNOX, *Works*, vol. vi.

—— *The first booke of the History of the Reformation of religioun within the realme of Scotland* (London, 1587).

—— *The Historie of the reformation of the Church of Scotland* (Edinburgh, 1644) (cited as Knox's History, 1644 Edinburgh ed.).

—— *The Historie of the reformation of the Church of Scotland* (London, 1644) (cited as Knox's History, 1644 London ed.).

—— *John Knox's History of the Reformation in Scotland* (ed. W. Croft Dickinson) (Edinburgh and London, 1949) (cited as Knox, *History*).

—— *The Works of John Knox* (ed. D. Laing) (Edinburgh, 1846–64) (cited as *Works*).

KRIEGK, G. L. *Deutsches Bürgerthum in Mittelalter . . . mit besonderer Beziehung auf Frankfurt-a-M.* (Frankfort-on-Main, 1868).

KUIPERS, C. H. *Quintin Kennedy (1520–1564): Two Eucharistic Tracts* (Nijmegen, no date) (lecture at Nijmegen University, 15 June 1964).

LABANOFF, PRINCE A. See MARY QUEEN OF SCOTS.

LAING, D. 'Documents connected with Knox as a notary' (*Proceedings of the Society of Antiquaries of Scotland*, vol. iii) (Edinburgh, January 1858).

—— 'Notice respecting the Monument of the Regent Earl of Moray' (ibid., vol. vi) (Edinburgh, January 1865).

LAING, J. *De Vita et Moribus atque Rebus Gestis Haereticorum nostri temporis* (Paris, 1581).

LAMOND, R. 'The Scottish Craft Guild as a Religious Fraternity' (*Scottish Historical Review*, vol. xvi) (Edinburgh, April 1919).

LANG, A. *Historical Mysteries* (London, 1904).

—— *John Knox and the Reformation* (London, 1905).

—— 'Knox as Historian' (*Scottish Historical Review*, vol. ii) (Edinburgh, January 1905).

—— 'Portraits and Jewels of Mary Stuart' (ibid., vol. iii) (Edinburgh, January 1906).

—— 'The Mystery of the Kirks'. See LANG, *Historical Mysteries*.

LAROUSSE, P. *Grand Dictionnaire Universel du XIXe. Siècle* (Paris, 1866–76).

LEADAM, I. S. 'A Narrative of the Pursuit of English Refugees in Germany under Queen Mary' (*Transactions of the Royal Historical Society*, New Series, vol. xi) (London, 1897).

LEE, M. *James Stewart Earl of Moray* (New York, 1953).

—— 'John Knox and his History' (*Scottish Historical Review*, vol. xlv) (Edinburgh, April 1966).

—— 'The Fall of the Regent Morton: a Problem in Satellite Diplomacy' (*Journal of Modern History*, vol. xxviii) (Chicago, June 1956).

LEISHMAN, J. F. *A Son of Knox and other Studies Antiquarian and Biographical* (Glasgow, 1909).

LESLIE, J. *A perfect Accompt given to . . . Marie Queene of Scots . . . Of his whole Charge and Proceedings during the Time of his Ambassage . . . in England.* See ANDERSON, *Collections.*
—— *A Treatise concerning the Defence of the Honour of . . . Marie Queene of Scotlande. . . . With a declaration . . . that the Regiment of Women is conformable to the Lawe of God and Nature. Made by Morgan Philippes* (Liège, 1571).
—— *Defence of the Honour of . . . Mary, Queen of Scotland* (first published, London, 1569; 2nd ed., Liège, 1571). See ANDERSON, *Collections.*
—— *De Illustrium Foeminarum in Repub. Administranda.* See LESLIE, *De Titulo . . . Mariae Reginae.*
—— *De Origine, Moribus et Rebus Gestis Scotorum.* See LESLIE, *The Historie of Scotland.*
—— *De Titulo et iure Serenissimae Principis Mariae Reginae* (Rheims, 1580).
—— *Diary.* See *Bannatyne Miscellany*, vol. iii.
—— *The Historie of Scotland* (Father James Dalrymple's translation of 1596) (ed. E. G. Cody and W. Murison) (Edinburgh and London, 1888–95).
Letters and Papers (Foreign and Domestic) of the Reign of King Henry VIII (ed. J. Brewer and J. Gairdner) (London, 1862–1910) (cited as *L.P.*).
Letters of James IV. See JAMES IV.
Letters of James V. See JAMES V.
The Life and Death of Mr. William Whittingham, Dean of Durham (written probably *c.* 1600). See LORIMER, *John Knox and the Church of England.*
LINDSAY OF THE MOUNT, SIR D. *Kitteis Confessioun.* See LINDSAY, *Works.*
—— *The Works of Sir David Lindsay of the Mount* (ed. D. Harner) (Edinburgh and London, 1931–6).
LINDSAY, T. M. 'George Buchanan.' See *George Buchanan Glasgow Quatercentenary Studies.*
Liturgies of Edward VI (ed. J. Ketley) (Cambridge, 1844).
Livre des Anglois, à Genève (ed. J. S. Burn) (London, 1831) (written in 1555–60).
LLOYD, C. *Formularies of Faith put forth by authority during the reign of Henry VIII* (Oxford, 1856 ed.) (first published, Oxford, 1825).
'London Chronicle 1523–1555.' See 'Two London Chronicles'.
LORIMER, P. *John Knox and the Church of England* (London, 1875).
—— *Precursors of Knox: Patrick Hamilton* (Edinburgh, 1857).
LYNCH, J. 'Philip II and the Papacy' (*Transactions of the Royal Historica Society*, 5th series, vol. xi) (London, 1961).
MCCRIE, T. *Life of John Knox* (Edinburgh and London, 1839 ed.) (first published, Edinburgh, 1812).
MACDONALD, C. M. 'John Major and Humanism' (*Scottish Historical Review*, vol. xiii) (Edinburgh, January 1916).
MCEWEN, J. S. *The Faith of John Knox* (London, 1961).
MCGILL, J. and BELLENDEN, J. *Discours Particulier d'Escosse* (ed. T. Thomson) (Edinburgh, 1824) (written on 11 January 1558/9).
MACGREGOR, G. *The Thundering Scot* (London, 1958).
MCHARDY, J. 'The Priesthood of Knox' (*Innes Review*, vol. vii) (Glasgow, Spring 1956).
MACHYN, H. *The Diary of Henry Machyn, Citizen and Merchant-Taylor of London, from A.D. 1500 to A.D. 1563* (ed. J. G. Nichols) (London, 1848).

McKay, D. 'Parish Life in Scotland 1500–1560.' See *Essays on the Scottish Reformation.*

Mackenzie, Agnes Muir. *The Scotland of Queen Mary and the Religious Wars 1513–1638* (Edinburgh, 1936, reprinted 1957).

Mackenzie, W. Mackay. *The Secret of Flodden* (Edinburgh, 1931).

Mackie, J. D. 'Henry VIII and Scotland' (*Transactions of the Royal Historical Society*, 4th series, vol. xxix) (London, 1947).

—— *John Knox* (Historical Association pamphlet) (London, 1951).

—— 'Scotland and the Renaissance' (*Proceedings of the Royal Philosophical Society of Glasgow*, vol. lxi.) (Glasgow, 1934).

Mackie, R. L. *King James IV of Scotland* (Edinburgh, 1958).

McMillen, M. *The Worship of the Scottish Reformed Church 1550–1638* (London, 1931).

McRoberts, D. 'A Sixteenth Century Picture of St. Bartholemew from Perth' (*Innes Review*, vol. x) (Glasgow, Autumn 1959).

—— 'Material Destruction caused by the Scottish Reformation.' See *Essays on the Scottish Reformation.*

Maitland Club Miscellany. *Miscellany of the Maitland Club*, vols. i, iii (Edinburgh, 1834, 1843).

Maitland Folio M.S., containing Poems by Sir Richard Maitland, Dunbar, Douglas, Henryson and others, vol. i (ed. W. A. Craigie) (Edinburgh and London, 1919).

Maitland, J. 'The Apology for William Maitland of Lethington 1610' (ed. A. Lang) (*Ane Apology for William Maitland of Lidington . . . written by his only son, James Maitland*). See *Miscellany of the Scottish History Society.*

—— *Maitland's Narrative of the Principal Acts of the Regency, during the Minority . . . of Mary, Queen of Scotland* (ed. W. S. Fitch) (Ipswich, 1842 (?)).

Maitland of Lethington, Sir R. Poems. See *Maitland Folio M.S.*

Major, J. *Historia Majoris Britanniae tam Angliae quam Scotiae* (Paris, 1521). See Major, *History of Greater Britain.*

—— *History of Greater Britain* (ed. A. Constable) (Edinburgh, 1892).

Marioreybanks, G. *Annals of Scotland from the yeir 1514 to the yeir 1591* (ed. J. G. Dalyell) (Edinburgh, 1814) (written *c.* 1591).

Marteilhe, J. *Memoirs of a Protestant condemned to the Galleys of France for his Religion* (translated by Oliver Goldsmith) (London, 1895 ed.) (first published, London, 1758).

Martin, C. *Les Protestants Anglais réfugiés à Genève au temps de Calvin 1555–1560* (Geneva, 1915).

Mary of Lorraine. See *Foreign Correspondence with Marie de Lorraine*; and see *Scottish Correspondence of Mary of Lorraine.*

Mary, Queen of Scots. *A Letter from Mary Queen of Scots to the Duke of Guise, January 1562* (ed. J. H. Pollen) (Edinburgh, 1904).

—— *Lettres, Instructions et Mémoires de Marie Stuart, Reine d'Écosse* (ed. Prince A. Labanoff) (London, 1844) (cited as Labanoff).

Mathieson, W. Law. *Politics and Religion: a study of Scottish History from the Reformation to the Revolution* (Glasgow, 1902).

Maxwell, Sir H. 'A Son of Thunder'. See Maxwell, *Inter Alia.*

—— *Inter Alia* (Glasgow, 1924).

MAXWELL, W. D. *John Knox's Genevan Service Book* (Edinburgh, 1931).

MELVILLE, J. *The Autobiography and Diary of Mr. James Melville, Minister of Kilrenny in Fife and Professor of Theology in the University of St. Andrews* (ed. R. Pitcairn) (Edinburgh, 1842) (written in 1600) (cited as Melville, *Diary*).

MELVILLE OF HALHILL, SIR J. *The Memoirs of his Own Life, by Sir James Melville of Halhill* (London, 1922 ed.) (written *c.* 1605; first published, London, 1683) (cited as Melville, *Memoirs*).

MEUN, J. DE. See JEAN DE MEUN.

MEZGER, A. *John Knox et ses rapports avec Calvin* (Montauban, 1905).

MIGNE, J. P. *Patrologiae Cursus Completus* (Paris, 1844–66).

MILL, ANNA JEAN. *Medieval Plays in Scotland* (Edinburgh, 1927).

MILLER, P. 'John Knox and his Manse' (*Proceedings of the Society of Antiquaries of Scotland*, vol. xxv) (Edinburgh, February 1891).

—— 'Supplementary Notes on John Knox's House' (ibid., vol. xxvii) (Edinburgh, May 1893).

MILLER, R. 'Where did John Knox live in Edinburgh?' (ibid., vol. xxxiii) (Edinburgh, January 1899).

MILTON, J. *Complete Prose Works of John Milton* (New Haven and London, 1953–66).

—— *Articles of Peace made . . . with the Irish Rebels and Papists, by James Earle of Ormond* (London, 1649). See MILTON, *Complete Prose Works.*

—— *The Tenure of Kings and Magistrates* (London, 1649). See MILTON, *Complete Prose Works.*

Miscellaneous Papers Principally Illustrative of Events in the Reigns of Queen Mary and King James VI (ed. W. J. Duncan) (Glasgow, 1834).

Miscellany. For Miscellanies of the Abbotsford Club, the Bannatyne Club, the Camden Society, the Harleian Miscellany, the Maitland Club, the Scottish History Society, the Spalding Club, the Spottiswood Society, and the Wodrow Society, see Abbotsford; Bannatyne; Camden; Harleian; Maitland; Scottish History Society; Spalding; Spottiswood; and Wodrow.

MONTGOMERIE, A. *The Poems of Alexander Montgomerie* (ed. J. Cranstoun) (Edinburgh and London, 1887) (written *c.* 1600).

MORICE, R. 'A declaration concernyng . . . that most Reverent Father in God, Thomas Cranmer, late archebisshopp of Canterbury' (written *c.* 1565). See *Narratives of the Days of the Reformation.*

MORTIMER, C. G. 'The Scottish Hierarchy in 1560' (*Clergy Review*, vol. xii) (London, 1936).

MORYSON, F. *An Itinerary written by Fynes Moryson, Gent.* (London, 1617). See BROWN, *Early Travellers in Scotland.*

MUIR, E. *John Knox: portrait of a Calvinist* (London, 1929).

MULLER, J. A. *The Letters of Stephen Gardiner* (Cambridge, 1933).

Munimenta Alme Universitatis Glasguensis (Glasgow, 1854).

MURDIN, W. *A Collection of State Papers . . . left by W. Cecill Lord Burghley* (London, 1759).

MURRAY, D. *Legal Practice in Ayr and the West of Scotland in the Fifteenth and Sixteenth Centuries* (Glasgow, 1910).

Narratives of the Days of the Reformation (ed. J. G. Nichols) (London, 1859).

NAU, C. *The History of Mary Stewart, from the Murder of Riccio until her Flight into England. By Claude Nau, her Secretary . . . With illustrative papers from the Secret Archives of the Vatican* (ed. J. Stevenson) (Edinburgh, 1883) (cited as Stevenson-Nau).

NOAILLES, A. DE. *Ambassades de M.M. de Noailles en Angleterre* (ed. A. de Vertot) (Leyden, 1763).

'The Ordination of John Knox: a symposium' (*Innes Review*, vol. vi) (Glasgow, Autumn 1955).

Original Letters relative to the English Reformation (ed. H. Robinson) (Cambridge, 1846–7).

PANTERO-PANTERA. *L'Armata Navale* (Rome, 1614). See JAL.

PARK, W. 'Letter of Thomas Randolph to the Earl of Leicester, 14th February 1566' (*Scottish Historical Review*, vol. xxxiv) (Edinburgh, October 1955).

PARKER, M. *Correspondence of Matthew Parker* (Cambridge, 1853).

—— *De Antiquitate Britannicae Ecclesiae & Priuilegiis Ecclesiae Cantuariensis, cum Archiepiscopis eiusdem 70* (London, 1572).

PASQUIER, E. *Les Œuvres d'Estienne Pasquier* (Amsterdam, 1723).

PATON, H. M. 'Old Edinburgh' (*Scottish Historical Review*, vol. xxxii) (Edinburgh, April 1953).

PATRICK, M. *Four Centuries of Scottish Psalmody* (Oxford, 1949).

PAUL, SIR J. B. 'Clerical Life in Scotland in the Sixteenth Century' (*Scottish Historical Review*, vol. xvii) (Edinburgh, April 1920).

—— 'Edinburgh in 1544 and Hertford's Invasion' (ibid., vol. viii) (Edinburgh, January 1911).

—— 'Social Life in Scotland in the Sixteenth Century' (ibid., vol. xvii) (Edinburgh, July 1920).

PERCY, LORD E. *John Knox* (London, 1937).

PHILIPPSON, M. *Histoire du Règne de Marie Stuart* (Paris, 1892).

PHILLIPS, J. E. 'The Background of Spenser's Attitude toward Women Rulers' (*Huntingdon Library Quarterly*, vol. v) (San Marino, California, 1941).

PHILLIPS, M. See LESLIE, *A Treatise concerning the Defence of the Honour of . . . Marie Queene of Scotland.*

PINKERTON, J. *The History of Scotland from the Accession of the House of Stuart to that of Mary* (London, 1797).

PITCAIRN, R. *Criminal Trials in Scotland from A.D. 1488 to A.D. 1624* (Edinburgh, 1833).

PITSCOTTIE, R. LINDSAY OF. *The Historie and Cronicles of Scotland* (ed. Æ. J. G. Mackay) (Edinburgh and London, 1899) (written *c.* 1575).

PIUS II, POPE (AENEAS SILVIUS). *Aeneas Silvius in Europam* (Memmingen, 1490).

—— *Commentarii Rerum Memorabilium* (Rome, 1584).

POCOCK, N. 'The Condition of Morals and Religious Belief in the Reign of Edward VI' (*English Historical Review*, vol. x) (London, July 1895).

POLE, R. *Epistolarum Reginaldi Poli* (ed. A. M. Quirini) (Brixen, 1744–57).

POLLARD, A. F. 'The Protector Somerset and Scotland' (*English Historical Review*, vol. xiii) (London, July 1898).

POLLEN, J. H. *Papal Negotiations with Mary Queen of Scots* (Edinburgh, 1901).

—— 'The Dispensation for the Marriage of Mary Stuart with Darnley, and its date' (*Scottish Historical Review*, vol. iv) (Edinburgh, April 1907).

PONET, J. *A shorte treatise of politike power and of the true Obedience which subjects owe to Kings and other civile Governours* (Strasbourg (?), 1556). See HUDSON.

PREEDY, G. See BOWEN, MARJORIE.

Protocol Book of Mark Carruthers 1531–1561 (ed. R. C. Reid) (Edinburgh, 1956).

Protocol Book of Sir Alexander Gaw 1540–1558 (ed. J. Anderson and W. Angus) (Edinburgh, 1910).

Protocol Book of Sir John Cristisone 1518–1551 (ed. R. H. Lindsay) (Edinburgh, 1930).

Protocol Book of Sir Robert Rollok 1534–1552 (ed. W. Angus) (Edinburgh, 1931).

Protocol Books of Dominus Thomas Johnsoun 1528–1578 (ed. J. Beveridge and J. Russell) (Edinburgh, 1920).

RAINALD, W. *Calvino-Turcismus* (Antwerp, 1597).

RANKIN, E. B. 'Whitekirk and the Burnt Candlemas' (*Scottish Historical Review*, vol. xiii) (Edinburgh, January 1916).

READ, CONYERS. *Mr. Secretary Cecil and Queen Elizabeth* (London, 1955).

READ, EVELYN. *Catherine, Duchess of Suffolk* (London, 1962).

Reformatio Legum Ecclesiasticarum. See CARDWELL.

Register of Ministers, Exhorters and Readers and of their Stipends after the Period of the Reformation (Edinburgh, 1830).

Register of the Consultations of the Ministers of Edinburgh, 1652–1657 (ed. W. Stephen) (Edinburgh, 1921).

Register of the Privy Council of Scotland (ed. D. Masson) (Edinburgh, 1877–98).

Register of the Privy Seal of Scotland (ed. D. Hay Fleming, J. Beveridge, G. Donaldson) (Edinburgh, 1936–66).

Registrum Episcopatus Glasguensis (Edinburgh, 1843).

Registrum Honoris de Morton (Edinburgh, 1853).

REID, W. STAMFORD. 'Clerical Taxation: the Scottish Alternative to Dissolution of the Monasteries 1530–1560' (*Catholic Historical Review*, vol. xxxv) (Washington, D.C., July 1948).

—— 'The Middle Class Factor in the Scottish Reformation' (*Church History*, vol. xvi) (New York, September 1947).

—— 'The Scottish Counter-Reformation before 1560' (ibid., vol. xiv) (New York, June 1945).

Rentale Sancti Andree, being the Chamberlain and Gravitor Accounts of the Archbishopric in the time of Cardinal Betoun 1538–1546 (ed. R. K. Hannay) (Edinburgh, 1913).

RENWICK, A. M. *The story of the Scottish Reformation* (London, 1960).

'Report of the Jesuits to Pope Clement VIII in 1594.' See NAU.

RIBIER, G. *Lettres et Memoires d'Estat . . . sous les Regnes de François premier, Henry II et François II* (Paris, 1677) (first published, Blois, 1666).

RICART, R., etc. *The Maire of Bristowe is kalendar* (ed. Lucy Toulmin Smith) (London, 1872) (written in 1479–1698).

RICHARDINUS, R. See RICHARDSON, R.

RICHARDSON, J. 'On the present state of the question "Where was John Knox born?"' (*Proceedings of the Society of Antiquaries of Scotland*, vol. iii) (Edinburgh, January 1858).

RICHARDSON, R. *Commentary on the Rule of St. Augustine* (Edinburgh, 1935) (first published, Paris, 1530).

Richmondshire Wills. *Wills and Inventories from the registry of the Archdeaconry of Richmond* (ed. J. Raine) (Durham, 1853).

RIDLEY, J. *Nicholas Ridley* (London, 1957).

—— *Thomas Cranmer* (Oxford, 1962).

RIDLEY, N. *A Piteous Lamentation of the Miserable Estate of the Churche of Christ in England* (written in 1555; first published, London, 1566). See RIDLEY, *Works.*

—— *The Works of Nicholas Ridley* (Cambridge, 1841).

ROGERS, C. 'An Estimate of the Scottish Nobility during the Minority of James VI and subsequently' (*Transactions of the Royal Historical Society*, vol. ii) (London, 1875).

—— *Genealogical Memoirs of John Knox and of the family of Knox* (London, 1879).

—— 'Memoir of George Wishart, the Scottish Martyr' (*Transactions of the Royal Historical Society*, vol. iv) (London, 1876).

—— 'The Staggering State of Scottish Statesmen. From 1550 to 1650. By Sir John Scott of Scotstarveit' (ibid., vol. i) (London, 1875).

—— 'Three Poets of the Scottish Reformation' (ibid., vol. iii) (London, 1876)

ROGERS, T. *History of Agriculture and Prices* (Oxford, 1872).

ROLLAND, J. *The sevin Seages: translatit out of prois in Scottis meter be Johne Rolland in Dalkeith* (ed. G. F. Black) (Edinburgh, 1932) (first published, Edinburgh, 1578).

ROSS, A. 'More about the Archbishop of Athens' (*Innes Review*, vol. xiv) (Glasgow, Spring 1963).

—— 'Some Scottish Catholic Historians' (ibid., vol. i) (Glasgow, June 1950).

ROW, J. *History of the Kirk of Scotland* (Edinburgh, 1842) (written *c.* 1634–50).

RUSSELL, E. *Maitland of Lethington* (London, 1912).

Sadler Papers. *The State Papers and Letters of Sir Ralph Sadler* (ed. A. Clifford) (Edinburgh, 1809).

St. Andrews Church Register. *Register of the Ministers, Elders and Deacons of the Christian Congregation of St. Andrews 1559–1600* (ed. D. Hay Fleming) (Edinburgh, 1889).

Satirical Poems of the time of the Reformation (ed. J. Cranstoun) (Edinburgh and London, 1891).

SCOT, W. *An Apologetical Narration of the State and Government of the Kirk of Scotland since the Reformation* (Edinburgh, 1846) (written by William Scot, minister of Cupar, 1558–1642).

Scotia Redeviva (Edinburgh, 1826).

SCOTT, A. 'Ane Ballat maid to the Derisioun and Scorne of wantoun wemen.' See SCOTT, *Poems.*

—— *The Poems of Alexander Scott* (ed. J. Cranstoun) (Edinburgh and London, 1896) (written probably between 1545 and 1568).

SCOTT OF SCOTSTARVEIT, SIR J. *The Staggering State of the Scots Statesmen for one hundred years, viz., from 1550 to 1650* (Edinburgh, 1754). See ROGERS, C.

Scottish Antiquary, vol. xiii (Edinburgh, January and April 1899).

Scottish Correspondence of Mary of Lorraine (ed. Annie I. Cameron) (Edinburgh, 1927).

Scottish History Society. *Miscellany of the Scottish History Society*, vol. ii (Edinburgh, 1904).

'A Scottish Journie, being an Account in verse of a tour from Edinburgh to Glasgow in 1641. By P. J.' (ed. C. H. Firth). See *Miscellany of the Scottish History Society*.

Select Poetry Chiefly Devotional of the Reign of Queen Elizabeth (ed. E. Farr) (Cambridge, 1845).

Selections from the Records of the Church Session, Presbytery and Synod of Aberdeen (Aberdeen, 1846).

Selections from the Records of the Regality of Melrose and from the MSS. of the Earl of Haddington (ed. C. S. Romanes) (vol. iii, 1547–1706) (Edinburgh, 1917).

SELVE, O. DE. *Correspondance politique de Odet de Selve* (ed. G. Lefèvre-Pontalis) (Paris, 1888).

SHAW, D. *The General Assemblies of the Church of Scotland 1560–1600* (Edinburgh, 1964).

SHEARMAN, P. J. 'Father Alexander McQuhirrie, S.J.' (*Innes Review*, vol. vi) (Glasgow, Spring 1955).

SINCLAIR, G. A. 'The Scots at Solway Moss' (*Scottish Historical Review*, vol. ii) (Edinburgh, April 1905).

—— 'The Scottish Trader in Sweden' (ibid., vol. xxv) (Edinburgh, July 1928).

SMETON, T. *Ad Virulentum Archibaldi Hamiltoni Apostatae Dialogum, De Confusione Calvinianae Sectae apud Scotos, impiè conscriptum orthodoxa responsio* (Edinburgh, 1579). See KNOX, *Works*, vol. vi.

SMITH, D. B. 'Le Testament du Gentil Cossoys' (*Scottish Historical Review*, vol. xvii) (Edinburgh, April 1920).

Source Book of Scottish History (ed. W. Croft Dickinson, G. Donaldson and Isabel Milne) (London and Edinburgh, 1952).

Spalding Club. *Miscellany of the Spalding Club,* vol. ii (Aberdeen, 1842).

SPOTTISWOOD, J. *The History of the Church of Scotland* (Bannatyne Club ed.) (Edinburgh, 1850) (first published, London, 1655).

Spottiswood Miscellany, vol. ii (Edinburgh, 1845).

SPROTT, G. W. 'The Liturgy of Compromise used in the English Congregation at Frankfort from an unpublished M.S.' See WOTHERSPOON.

STAPLETON, T. *A Fortresse of the Faith* (Antwerp, 1565).

State Papers during the Reign of Henry VIII (London, 1831–2).

Statutes of the Realm (London, 1810–24).

Statutes of the Scottish Church 1225–1559 (*Concilia Scotiae*) (ed. D. Patrick) (Edinburgh, 1907).

STEVENSON, J. *Selections from unpublished Manuscripts . . . illustrating the Reign of Mary Queen of Scotland* (Glasgow, 1837). (cited as Stevenson, *Illustrations*).

—— Stevenson–Nau. See NAU.

STEVENSON, ROBERT LOUIS. *Familiar Studies of Men and Books* (London, 1925 ed.) (first published, London, 1882).

—— 'John Knox and his Relations with Women.' See STEVENSON, R. L., *Familiar Studies of Men and Books*.

Stirling Burgh Records. *Extracts from the Records of the Royal Burgh of Stirling* (ed. R. Renwick) (Glasgow, 1887–9).

STOW, J. *Annales, or A Generall Chronicle of England* (London, 1631) (first published, London, 1580).

STRICKLAND, AGNES. *Lives of the Queens of England* (London, 1851–2 ed.).

STRONG, J. *A History of Secondary Education in Scotland* (Oxford, 1909).

STRYPE, J. *Annals of the Reformation* (Oxford, 1824 ed.) (first published, London, 1709).

—— *Ecclesiastical Memorials* (Oxford, 1822 ed.) (first published, London, 1721).

—— *The History of the Life and Acts of . . . Edmund Grindal* (Oxford, 1821 ed.) (first published, London, 1710).

SURTEES, R. *The History and Antiquities of the County Palatine of Durham* (London, 1816–40).

SWAVE, P. Diary (1535). See *Letters and Papers of the Reign of King Henry VIII.*

TAFFIN, J. *Of the markes of the children of God . . . To the faithfull of the Low Countrie. By Iohn Taffin. Translated out of French by Anne Prouse* (London, 1590; 2nd ed., 1608, 3rd ed., 1634).

TAYLOR, J. *The Pennyles Pilgrimage, or the Money-lesse Perambulation of Iohn Taylor, alias the King's Majesties Water-Poet* (London, 1618). See BROWN, *Early Travellers in Scotland.*

TERTULLIAN. *De Cultu Foeminarum.* See MIGNE.

TEULET, A. *Papiers d'État, Pièces et Documents relatifs à l'Histoire de l'Écosse au XVIe siècle* (Paris, 1851–60).

The late expedicioun in Scotlande made by the Kynges Hyhnes Armye (London, 1544). See DALYELL.

The Troubles at Frankfort. *A Brieff Discours off the Troubles begonne at Franckford in Germany Anno Domini 1554* (Heidelberg, 1575).

THEINER, A. *Vetera monumenta Hibernorum et Scotorum historiam illustrantia 1216–1547* (Rome, 1864).

THOMSON, G. *De Antiquitate Christianae religionis apud Scotos* (Rome and Douai, 1594). See *Miscellany of the Scottish History Society.*

—— 'Quo tempore Scotia Religionem Christianum susceperit ac quibus gradibus in haeresim sit delapsa.' See 'Report of the Jesuits to Pope Clement VIII in 1594'.

THOMSON, T. 'Notices of the Kers of Samuelston, etc.' (*Proceedings of the Society of Antiquaries of Scotland*, vol. iii) (Edinburgh, January 1858).

Le Tigre de 1560 (ed. C. Read) (Paris, 1875).

Transactions of the Baptist Historical Society, vol. iv (London, 1914–15).

TRITONIO, R. *Vita Vincentii Laurei Cardinalis* (Bologna, 1599).

A True Representation of the Rise, Progress and State of the present division in the Church of Scotland (1657). See *Register of the Consultations of Ministers.*

TUNSTALL, C. *De veritate Corporis et Sanguinis Domini Nostri Iesu Christi in Eucharistia* (Paris, 1554).

'Two London Chronicles from the Collections of John Stow'. See *Camden Miscellany.*

Two Missions of Jacques de la Brosse: an account of the affairs of Scotland in the year 1543, and The Journal of the Siege of Leith 1560 (ed. Gladys Dickinson) (Edinburgh, 1942).

TYNDALE, W. *Exposition upon the 5th, 6th and 7th Chapters of Matthew*. See TYNDALE, *Works*, vol. ii.
—— *The Obedience of a Christian Man*. See TYNDALE, *Works*, vol. i.
—— Works: *Doctrinal Treatises and Introductions to different portions of the Holy Scriptures* (Cambridge, 1848) (cited as Tyndale, *Works*, vol. i).
—— Ibid., *Expositions and Notes on sundry portions of Holy Scripture, together with the Practice of Prelates* (Cambridge, 1849) (cited as Tyndale, *Works*, vol. ii).
TYRIE, J. *The Refutation of ane Answer made by Schir Iohn Knox to ane letter sent by Iames Tyrie to his umquhile brother* (Paris, 1573). See *Catholic Tractates*.
TYTLER, P. F. *England under the Reigns of Edward VI and Mary* (London, 1839).
—— *History of Scotland* (Eadie ed.) (London and Glasgow, 1873–7).
URSINS. See JUVENAL DES URSINS.
VERHEIDEN, J. *Praestantium aliquot Theologorum qui Rom. Antichristum praecipue oppugnarunt, Effigies* (The Hague, 1602).
VIVES, J. L. *De institutione foeminae Christianae* (Antwerp, 1524).
WALLACE, HELEN M. 'Berwick in the Reign of Queen Elizabeth' (*English Historical Review*, vol. xlvi) (London, January 1931).
WALZER, M. *The Revolution of the Saints: a study in the origin of radical politics* (London, 1966).
WARRACK, J. *Domestic Life in Scotland 1488–1688* (London, 1920).
Warrender Papers (ed. Annie I. Cameron, introd. R. Reit) (Edinburgh, 1931).
WATT, H. *John Knox in Controversy* (Edinburgh, 1950).
WEAVER, F. W. *Somerset Incumbents* (Bristol, 1889).
WEISS, C. H. *Papiers d'État du Cardinal de Granvelle* (Paris, 1841–52).
WELDON, SIR A. (?) *A Perfect Description of the People and Country of Scotland. By James Howel, Gent.* (London, 1649). See BROWN, *Early Travellers in Scotland*.
WHITLEY, ELIZABETH. *Plain Mr. Knox* (London, 1960).
WHITTINGHAM, W. *The Newe Testament of our Lord Iesus Christ conferred diligently with the Greke and best approued translations* (Geneva, 1557).
WILKINS, D. *Concilia Magnae Britanniae et Hiberniae* (London, 1737).
WILSON, SIR D. 'Supplementary Notes on John Knox's House, Netherbow, Edinburgh' (*Proceedings of the Society of Antiquaries of Scotland*, vol. xxv) (Edinburgh, February 1891).
WINNING, T. 'Church Councils in Sixteenth Century Scotland.' See *Essays on the Scottish Reformation*.
WINZET, N. *Certain Tractates together with the Book of Four Score Three Questions and a translation of Vincentius Lirinensis* (ed. J. Harrison) (Edinburgh and London, 1888).
—— *Certane Tractatis for Reformatioun of Doctryne & manneris* (Edinburgh, 1562). See WINZET, *Certain Tractates*.
—— *The Buke of Four Scoir Thre Questions* (Antwerp, 1563). See WINZET, *Certain Tractates*.
—— *The last blast of the Trompet of Godis worde aganis the usurpit auctoritie of Johne Knox and his Calviniane brether intrudit Precherouris* (Edinburgh, 1562). See WINZET, *Certain Tractates*.

Wodrow Miscellany. *Miscellany of the Wodrow Society*, vol. i (ed. D. Laing) (Edinburgh, 1844).

WODROW, R. *Collections upon the lives of the Reformers and most eminent ministers of the Church of Scotland* (Glasgow, 1834) (written 1707–22).

WOOD, MARGUERITE. 'The Imprisonment of the Earl of Arran' (*Scottish Historical Review*, vol. xxiv) (Edinburgh, October 1926).

WOTHERSPOON, H. J. *The Second Prayer Book of King Edward VI* (Edinburgh and London, 1905).

WRIGHT, T. *Queen Elizabeth and her times* (London, 1838).

WRIOTHESLEY, C. *A Chronicle of England from A.D. 1485 to 1559* (ed. W. D. Hamilton) (London, 1875–7) (written 1530–59).

Zürich Letters (Cambridge, 1852–5.)

INDEX